Las Derechas

The Extreme Right in Argentina, Brazil, and Chile, 1890–1939

LAS DERECHAS

The Extreme Right in Argentina, Brazil, and Chile, 1890–1939

SANDRA MCGEE DEUTSCH

STANFORD UNIVERSITY PRESS

Stanford, California

Stanford University Press
Stanford, California

© 1999 by the Board of Trustees of the
Leland Stanford Junior University

Printed in the United States of America
CIP data appear at the end of the book

To my parents

CONTENTS

ACKNOWLEDGMENTS

Researching and writing comparative history is a collaborative and complicated effort. Most historians specialize in one country, and therefore to write knowledgeably about three, I turned to experts on other regions to locate sources, pinpoint useful lines of inquiry, and avoid grievous errors. I also relied on colleagues with broad vision to read the entire manuscript and ensure that it made sense. The need to consult archives and libraries in several nations meant heavy travel expenses. Thus, I incurred many debts of gratitude, more than would have been the case had I confined myself to one country.

Various sources provided the funding necessary to conduct the research and write the book. I thank the Center for Inter-American and Border Studies, University Research Institute, and the vice president for academic affairs at the University of Texas at El Paso. I also wish to thank the American Philosophical Society, the American Historical Association Beveridge Award committee, the National Endowment for the Humanities, the Council for International Educational Exchange Fulbright Program, and the American Council of Learned Societies for their generous support.

Many colleagues contributed their time, insights, and materials. I want to express my deep appreciation to David Bushnell, Charles Bergquist, Richard Walter, and Ronald Newton for reading and commenting on the entire manuscript. My heartfelt thanks go to Jeff Lesser for acquainting me with many details of life and research in Brazil and reading large chunks of the manuscript, and to Jeffrey Needell, for his painstaking critique of an equally large portion. I also am extremely grateful to Carlos Maldonado for his hospitality, assistance with sources, and comments on the Chilean subchapters. June Hahner was very generous in sharing her Brazilian contacts and expertise, and Lolita Bruington and Selma Simonstein helped make my stays in Brazil and Chile pleasant and rewarding. I thank Ronald Dolkart, Paul Drake, and Joel Horowitz for reading the sections on their respective countries of specialization. I also am indebted to Anita Weinstein, Paul Drake, and Michael Hall for facilitating my research in Argentina, Chile, and Brazil, respectively. Howard Campbell, Max Kele, Paul Lewis, Margaret Power, Raanan Rein, Margaret Schellenberg, Rose Spalding, and Kathleen Staudt offered useful suggestions on various chapters, as did Asunción Lavrin, who also gave me some sources, and Cheryl Martin, whose encouragement has sustained me throughout this project. The following scholars supplied materials, provided ideas, and helped me attain access to sources: in Argentina, Dora Barrancos, Edgardo Bilsky, Federico Finchelstein, Floreal Forni, Noemí Girbal de Blacha, Raúl García Heras, José María Ghío, Adela Harispuru, Julio Irazusta, Fortunato Mallimaci, Carlos Mayo, Gershon Rabin, Eduardo Saguier, and Leo Senkman; in Brazil, José Murilo de Carvalho, Rony Cytrynowicz, Nachman Falbel, René Gertz, Edgar Magalhães, Marcos Chor Maio, Nancy Naro, Lúcia Lippi de Oliveira, and Hélgio Trindade; in Chile, Sofía Correa, Alicia Frohman, Joaquín Fermandois, Enrique Hermosilla, Tomás Moulián, Carlos Ruiz, René Salinas Meza, Verónica Valdivia, María Elena Valenzuela, and Manfred Wilhelmy; in the United States, Jonathan Ablard, María Piedad Alliende Edwards, Charles Ambler, Dain Borges, Lila Caimari, Thomas Cohen, Michael Conniff, Margaret Crahan, Alex De Grand, Georgette Dorn, Elisa Fernández, Edward Gibson, David Hackett, Charles Hale, Ana María Kapelucz-Poppi, Charles Kenney, Joseph Love, Larry Lauerhass, Eul-Soo Pang, Karin Rosemblatt, William Sater, William Smith, Judith Sweeney, Steven Volk, and Barbara Weinstein; and in Canada, David Sheinin. I value this project not only for what it has taught me but for how it has created and strengthened friendships across national boundaries.

I am also indebted to archivists and librarians at many institutions. In Argentina, the personnel at the Archivo de *La Prensa*, Archivo General de la Nación, Archivo Gráfico de la Nación, Biblioteca Nacional, Biblioteca Juan B. Justo, Biblioteca del Consejo Deliberante, Biblioteca del Instituto di Tella, Biblioteca Tornquist, Centro de Documentación e Información sobre Judaísmo Argentino "Marc Turkow," Delegación de Asociaciones Israelitas Argentinas Archivo de Prensa, libraries of the Colegio de Escribanos and

Jockey Club, and YIVO archive have been very helpful and attentive over the years. In Brazil, I appreciated the knowledgeable personal attention offered at the Arquivo da Cúria de São Paulo, Arquivo do Estado de São Paulo, Arquivo Histórico Judaico Brasileiro, Arquivo Leuenroth and Biblioteca Hélio Vianna of the Instituto de Filosofia e Ciências Humanas of the Universidade Estadual de Campinas, Arquivo Nacional, Arquivo Público e Histórico do Município de Rio Claro, Biblioteca da Federação Israelita do Estado de São Paulo, Biblioteca Municipal Mário de Andrade de São Paulo, Biblioteca Nacional, Casa Rui Barbosa, Centro de Pesquisa e Documentação de História Contemporânea do Brasil and library of the Fundação Getúlio Vargas, library of the Faculdade de Direito de São Paulo, Instituto de Filosofia e Ciências Humanas of the Universidade Nacional de Rio Grande do Sul, Instituto Histórico e Geográfico Brasileiro, Instituto Histórico e Geográfico de São Paulo, library of IUPERJ, and Museu Histórico Nacional. I thank the staffs at the Archivo Nacional, Biblioteca Nacional, Biblioteca del Congreso, library of FLACSO, and Departamento de Fotografía of the Museo Histórico Nacional in Chile for their friendly assistance. Finally, I am grateful to the personnel at the following institutions in the United States: the Library of Congress, National Archives, Oliveira Lima Library of Catholic University, and the libraries at UCLA, University of New Mexico, University of Texas at El Paso, and University of Texas at Austin.

I wish to thank the editors at Stanford University Press for helping to bring this project to fruition. I particularly appreciate Norris Pope's encouragement and his confidence in my work. Peter Kahn kindly answered my many queries and relieved my concerns on several occasions.

I am grateful to several publishers and the editors of various journals for permission to reuse material in the current book. Short portions of Chapters 1 and 9 appeared in David Sheinin and Lois Baer Barr, eds., *The Jewish Diaspora in Latin America: New Studies on History and Literature* (New York: Garland, 1996); other passages in Part 3 appeared in *Estudios Interdisciplinarios de América Latina y el Caribe* 8 (July–Dec. 1997). Parts of Chapter 6 are a revised version of material appearing in the *Hispanic American Historical Review* 64 (May 1984). Finally, small portions of Chapters 2 and 10 previously appeared in different form in my book *Counterrevolution in Argentina, 1900–1932: The Argentine Patriotic League* (Lincoln: University of Nebraska Press, 1986), and much of the Argentine section of Chapter 6 represents a condensed and substantially revised version of information from that book.

Last but not least, I would like to thank those who are closest to me. Matis and Rita Finkel, Nina Finkel, Dean Conis, and Ann and Herschel Ankowski have nourished me with their love and support. Bill Durrer has solved my computer problems, coped with an author's anxieties, and encouraged me to pursue my intellectual dreams. He is a genuine soul mate.

S. M. D.

ABBREVIATIONS

ABC	Argentina, Brazil, and Chile
NSDAP	National Socialist German Workers Party (Nazis)
TFP	Tradición, Familia, y Propiedad or Tradição, Família, e Propiedad

ARGENTINA

AGN	Archivo General de la Nación
AJN	Alianza de la Juventud Nacionalista
ANA/ADUNA	Acción Nacionalista Argentina/Afirmación de una Nueva Argentina
ANT	Asociación Nacional del Trabajo
CGT	Confederación General del Trabajo
CPACC	Comisión Popular Argentina Contra el Comunismo
FONA	Federación Obrera Nacionalista Argentina
FORA	Federación Obrera Regional Argentina
FORJA	Fuerza de Orientación Radical de la Joven Argentina
LCA	Legión Cívica Argentina
LNR	*La Nueva República*
LPA	Liga Patriótica Argentina
LR	Liga Republicana
MODIN	Movimiento para la Dignidad y la Independencia
PAN	Partido Autonomista Nacional
PDN	Partido Demócrata Nacional

PDP	Partido Demócrata Progresista
PFA	Partido Fascista Argentino
UCEDE	Unión del Centro Democrático
UCR	Unión Cívica Radical
UNES	Unión Nacionalista de Estudiantes Secundarios
UNF	Unión Nacional Fascista

BRAZIL

AIB	Ação Integralista Brasileira
AN	Arquivo Nacional
ANL	Aliança Nacional Libertadora
AO	*A Offensiva*
APHMRC	Arquivo Público e Histórico do Município de Rio Claro
ARENA	Aliança Renovadora Nacional
ASB	Ação Social Brasileira
ASN	Ação Social Nacionalista
Caju	Centro Acadêmico de Estudos Jurídicos
CM	*Correio da Manhã*
CPDOC/FGV	Centro de Pesquisa e Documentação de História Contemporânea do Brasil da Fundação Getúlio Vargas
DSB	Defesa Social Brasileira
ESG	Escola Superior de Guerra
FBPF	Federação Brasileira pelo Progresso Feminino
GB	*Gil Blas*
IHGB	Instituto Histórico e Geográfico Brasileiro
IHGSP	Instituto Histórico e Geográfico de São Paulo
IPES	Instituto de Pesquisas e Estudos Sociais
ISEB	Instituto Superior de Estudos Brasileiros
LCT	Legião Cearense do Trabalho
LDN	Liga da Defesa Nacional
LEC	Liga Eleitoral Católica
LMB	Legião da Mulher Brasileira
LN	Liga Nacionalista
MDB	Movimento Democrático Brasileiro
MHN	Museu Histórico Nacional
OESP	*O Estado de São Paulo*
PN	Propaganda Nativista
PRONA	Partido da Reedificação da Ordem Nacional
PRP	Partido Republicano Paulista

PRP	Partido de Representação Popular
PSP	Partido Social Progresista
PTB	Partido Trabalhista Brasileiro
SEP	Sociedade de Estudos Políticos
UDN	União Democrática Nacional

CHILE

AChA	Acción Chilena Anticomunista
ADT	Asociación del Trabajo
AJCF	Asociación de la Juventud Católica Femenina
ANC	Archivo Nacional
ANEC	Asociación Nacional de Estudiantes Católicos
AOAN	Asamblea Obrera de Alimentación Nacional
AR	Acción Republicana
BIMR	*Boletín Informativo de la Milicia Republicana*
FECH	Federación de Estudiantes de Chile
FOCh	Federación Obrera de Chile
FOM	Federación Obrera de Magallanes
GNU	Grupo Nacista Universitario
IWW	International Workers of the World
LPM	Liga Patriótica Militar y Círculo de Oficiales Retirados
MN	Movimiento Nacionalista de Chile
MNS	Movimiento Nacional Socialista
MRNS	Movimiento Revolucionario Nacional Sindicalista
PAL	Partido Agrario Laborista
PNF	Partido Nacional Fascista
RN	Renovación Nacional
TEA	Tenacidad Entusiasmo Abnegación
TNA	Tropas Nacistas de Asalto
UDI	Unión Democrática Independiente
VPS	Vanguardia Popular Socialista

GREAT BRITAIN

PRO	Public Records Office

Las Derechas

The Extreme Right in
Argentina, Brazil, and Chile,
1890–1939

Introduction

The nonspecialist who scans the titles of scholarly works on twentieth-century Latin America would almost certainly conclude that leftism and revolutionary change characterize the region's recent past. Yet the right has ruled Latin America more frequently than the left, and even when out of power, profoundly conservative and antirevolutionary groups have greatly influenced the area. As José Luis Romero pointed out, the persistence of antiquated socioeconomic structures and the manner in which dependent capitalist development has reinforced these structures have given particular weight to right-wing movements and political thought in the region.[1]

Nevertheless, revolutions hold more appeal for researchers than the groups that oppose them. Since the early 1960s and the Cuban revolution, Latin Americanists—many of whom would consider themselves progressives or liberals (in the United States context)—have preferred to examine leftist movements. Some have simply dismissed the right as Neanderthal or as the lunatic fringe. Even when they recognize its importance, however, most scholars have chosen not to examine a viewpoint they find repugnant or depressing.

Thus, despite its significance, the twentieth-century Latin American right has received relatively little scholarly attention. Some researchers have examined individual movements and leaders, and three academic studies covering the entire trajectory of the Argentine right have also appeared.[2] These works have yielded valuable information on right-wing ideology and practice, but they focus on single countries.[3] Only Romero has attempted to

1

trace the evolution of the right in several nations. Because it antedated most of the secondary works on the right, however, and because Romero chose to survey all of Latin America from colonial times to the 1950s, his discussion, while suggestive, remained sketchy. In short, no one has explicitly compared the rightist organizations, ideas, and actions that have emerged in different national settings. Nor has anyone posed the following questions in a comparative context: How have the class and gender composition, motives, and programs of the right varied over time and between countries? How successfully have rightist groups incorporated local concerns, rather than simple European dogma, into their agendas? How have their activities affected labor mobilization? How would one describe the relationships among rightist groups, and between them and the military, the Catholic Church, the government, and political parties? Finally, what has been the lasting legacy of the right?

The following study of Argentine, Brazilian, and Chilean—or ABC—rightist groups, which considers the period from 1890 to 1939, will address these questions. The ABC powers are excellent subjects for comparative analysis for several reasons, not the least because they are among the most important nations of Latin America. Scholars have tended to see Argentina and Chile as polar opposites;[4] Brazil fits between them in certain respects and differs markedly from both in others. Argentina (from 1976 to 1983), Brazil (1964 to 1985), and Chile (1973 to 1990) recently experienced rightist military rule,[5] and the groups that sustained these regimes retain strength. All three had significant rightist movements in the period under study that heralded some aspects of these dictatorships. Furthermore, the extent of rightist influence has varied from nation to nation. To explain this crucial divergence is one of the aims of this study.[6]

Several interrelated factors dictate the choice of this particular era. The years from 1890 to 1939 witnessed the development of modern extreme right-wing doctrine and the height of the power of such groups in these countries. This was precisely the time when European fascism developed and flourished; given that Latin Americans were very much aware of the international context, this overlap was not coincidental. Although I refer occasionally to the international context and European influences, I do not focus on them.[7] Since I concentrate on the domestic roots of the right, the narrative ends around the time of World War II. By 1939 the movements had become intertwined with European events, and some of them had declined.

In this book I seek to dispel commonly held myths about the right in Latin America. According to one myth, rightists have uniformly opposed the struggle of the impoverished for economic improvement. But although they fear social upheaval, not all have favored a completely static order. According to another myth, the right consists of moneyed interests who have upheld free-market principles and frequently collaborated with foreign imperialism. This may be the case for some members of the right,[8] yet with their dislike of international capitalism, others have appeared "progressive" on economic issues. Nor has the right consisted solely of men, as older secondary works sometimes suggest. Rightists' distrust of autonomous mass mobilization has not kept them from attempting to organize broad movements of men and women under their own direction. While some scholars have claimed that Latin America did not provide the proper socioeconomic setting for fascism, certain of these movements indeed fit in that category. And, despite their suspicions about immigrants and Jews, not all rightists have been racists.

What, then, is the right? To define it is no simple task, for it is a more nebulous construct than the left, which usually organizes itself on the basis of explicit principles. In contrast, Roger Eatwell described the right as simply "a variety of responses to the left." I would modify his statement to say that the right consolidates in reaction to the egalitarian and liberating political tendencies of the moment—whatever these may be—and other factors it believes are undermining the socioeconomic order. It fears that leveling impulses and universal revolutionary ideals will weaken respect for authority, private property, cherished traditions,[9] and the particularities of family, locality, and nation. Thus, to define it one must relate the right to the immediate setting, more so than for other political tendencies.[10]

As underlying conditions evolve, so does the right. Eugen Weber, Stanley Payne, and other European specialists, as well as Carlos Waisman for Argentina, noted changes within the right since the early 1800s. Several researchers described an old and a new right. The old right at the turn of the century accepted representative government and other liberal trappings to varying degrees. This demonstrated its desire to blunt and co-opt the liberal challenge to its ideas, as well as its willingness to tinker with the status quo in order to maintain it as far as possible. More authoritarian and antiliberal than its predecessor, the new right, which consolidated after World War I in Latin America and somewhat earlier in Europe, disparaged electoral politics. Albert O. Hirschman discerned three waves of reaction: the first against the French Revolution's view of civil rights, the second against universal suffrage, and the third against the welfare state. Eatwell found five rightist styles of thought. The reactionary and moderate right emerged as responses to classical liberalism, the radical and extreme right reacted against socialism in the dawning age of mass politics, and the post-1945 new right has opposed socialist and welfare states.[11]

Moreover, the right has never been monolithic. Weber and Arno Mayer identified three types of rightist factions in Europe in the late nineteenth and early twentieth century. They included conservatives, or moderate opponents of change; reactionaries, who wished to restore the past; and fascists or counterrevolutionaries, who shared the reactionaries' hatred of the present but differed from them in their violence, opportunism, and radicalism.[12]

However useful for Europe, these neat distinctions do not always apply to Latin America, but they provide a point of departure. The right in the ABC countries has also changed over time and contained moderate and extreme tendencies.[13] *Las derechas*, a term commonly used in Chile, is far more accurate than the singular *la derecha*, and partly for this reason I use it as the title for this book. As there is no comparable term in English, at times I will use the word *right* rather than the more awkward *rightists*. This word choice, however, does not imply that the right was a single, undifferentiated whole, for the reality was quite the opposite.

I focus on what I call the extreme, radical, or far right. These were the rightists who most resolutely opposed egalitarianism, leftism, and other threatening changes, often through measures outside the electoral realm. Of varying social composition, the extreme right contained many voices that I attempt to bring to life, for one cannot understand political movements by looking at only one or two leaders. The intellectuals prominent in the organizations addressed primarily members of the elite, but other thinkers interpreted their ideas to a larger audience. To understand the variety within the far right, it is critical to examine its lowbrow and highbrow figures, its few female and many male exponents, and its mass-circulation periodicals and its more erudite tomes. Only in this manner can one grasp the complexity of thought and fluidity of positions. Furthermore, one must examine the actions that put the ideology into practice—or sometimes contradicted it.[14] Its rallies, demonstrations, and brutal clashes with opponents reveal the flavor of the radical right and the rich texture of its history.

Extreme right-wing movements defined themselves as masculine, which they saw as synonymous with strength. In doing so, they distinguished themselves from women, whom they regarded as inherently weak. Yet some groups cultivated women as part of a strategy to attract a broad constituency and to defeat the left. Inevitably, tension and ambiguity surrounded this recruitment of women. Even in the absence of such appeals, gender infused their rhetoric. This concern was not unique to the far right, but it was an important characteristic of this political persuasion.[15]

The extreme right contrasted with the moderate right, or the conservatives, whose main constituency was the elite. Sometimes joined by the church and the military, the moderate right defended the existing system in order to maximize its control, although its ideas and tactics varied. At times the extreme right's methods of opposing revolutionary change alienated moderates within the right. During periods of crisis, however, moderate rightists cultivated the extremists and adopted features of their ideology and practice. As scholars have noted for Europe, at these moments the theoretical distinctions among rightist groups faded.[16] Thus the extreme right provides a window for viewing the entire rightist spectrum.

The book title, *Las Derechas*, underlines the differences between the moderate and extreme right as well as those within each sector. It also calls attention to the differences among the ABC countries. The most intriguing question is why the extreme right attained a deeper, more persistent influence in Argentina than it did in Brazil or especially Chile. Some might dispute this assertion by noting that Brazil claimed the largest single group of the 1890–1939 period in terms of numbers, the Integralistas. They might also point out that of the three countries, Chile experienced the longest rightwing dictatorship under one leader, that of Augusto Pinochet (1973–90). Yet only in Argentina did the far right leave a profound imprint on governments in every decade between 1930 and the 1980s. Only there has it appropriated the term *nationalism* for itself, for it is commonly known by that name. No such appropriation has occurred in either Brazil or Chile, where at different times leftists have claimed the nationalist mantle or various political movements have contested it.[17]

Two authors have attempted to account for the divergent paths of nationalism in Argentina and Chile. Emphasizing the impact of immigration, Carl Solberg found that Argentine nationalism arose as an upper-class ideology directed against the predominantly immigrant working class, whereas the Chilean middle class became the mouthpiece of a nationalism that attacked foreign capitalism, in the shape of competing European interests, instead of foreign workers. Addressing a similar question, Charles Bergquist focused on export structures and the struggles of workers in the export sectors. The relative prosperity of, and extent of local control over, the export economy in Argentina as compared with Chile, he noted, weakened economic nationalism in the former and reinforced it in the latter. Moreover, the cohesiveness of Chilean nitrate workers, in contrast to the fragmented labor force in the Argentine livestock and cereal sectors, enabled Chilean laborers to make their combined critique of capitalism and foreign imperialism attractive to other social groups.[18]

As I examined the history of the right and added Brazil to these considerations, I tested these variables and found others. Export structures were vital parts of the background, and immigration helped explain the rise of radical right-wing movements but diminished in importance over time. The strength of the left and organized labor as a whole, not just of workers in export sectors, influenced the character and vigor of the extreme right. The Catholic Church's and the military's perceptions of their status and of society at large affected their willingness to collaborate with—and fortify— the extreme right. The unity and influence of conservative forces and of the political system were especially critical in determining the space available for groups further to the right. These factors account for the relative prominence of the Argentine extreme right as compared with the Brazilian and Chilean variants.

If there are crucial differences among the ABC countries, there also are similarities. One important similarity, which may also hold true for other parts of Latin America, is that there were three distinct periods of rightist activity in the years under study. The book is organized into broad sections corresponding to these periods. This typology emphasizes change over time, diversity within the right, and the variables of labor and the left, the military, the church, conservatism and the political system, and, at least early on, immigration.

The first period covers the antecedents of the modern extreme right, between roughly 1890 and World War I. At that time, all three ABC economies rested on exports: Chile on nitrates, Brazil on coffee, and Argentina on grains and animal products. This period, which represented the height of export-led prosperity, witnessed criticism of this path of economic development, and of the liberalism that justified it, for promoting class conflict, foreign domination, a rapacious elite, and national disunity and weakness. A few rightists voiced suspicions of the electoral system, and some officers put forth the military as a reformist institution blessedly above partisan fray. Attaining greater national control of wealth preoccupied several authors, while Social Catholic men and women proposed welfare measures to alleviate poverty and weaken the left's appeal. Immigrants and, in Chile, Peruvians and Bolivians in the north symbolized the various threats discerned by the right.[19] The most visible precursors of the extreme right, therefore, were the nativist Chilean Ligas Patrióticas, the Brazilian Jacobinos, and the

Argentine vigilantes. Moderate rightist ruling groups acknowledged some of the extremists' ideas but often rejected their violence and radicalism. Yet the distinction between moderates and extremists was not firm.

During the second period, from World War I to the mid-1920s, militant labor began to replace the foreign presence as the main catalyst of rightist action. Usually tied to the military, bourgeois rightist groups proclaimed their "nationalism" in the face of war and revolution abroad and, in particular, workers' mobilizations at home. In Chile, extreme rightists also used the border conflict with Peru and Bolivia to assert their nationalist credentials. The perceived leftist threat pushed moderate rightists into embracing such extremist organizations as the Liga Patriótica Argentina and Ligas Patrióticas of Chile, but they had reservations about a similar organization, Ação Social Nacionalista of Brazil. Always active in the church, women began to move into secular rightist groups. Fluctuating world demand for these nations' exports produced crises that lent further impetus to the growing radical rightist critique of economic and political liberalism. So, too, did the Cursos de Cultura Católica in Argentina and the Centro Dom Vital in Brazil, which trained a generation of intellectuals in Catholic corporatist thought.

The third period spanned the late 1920s to 1939, when the Great Depression fostered widespread disillusionment with liberal economics and existing political systems. These years witnessed a proliferation of groups influenced by Catholicism and European fascism, which opposed liberalism, democracy, labor, progressive feminism, and Jews. Their main characteristic, however, was their attempt to offer a radical alternative to the left, drawing upon ideas developed earlier by Social Catholics as well as a military style of masculinity. By emphasizing the need for drastic, albeit non-Marxist change along nationalistic lines, Argentine Nacionalismo, Ação Integralista Brasileira, and Movimiento Nacional Socialista of Chile attracted a broad following of men and women. They also found allies in the church, the military, and ruling circles, particularly in Argentina. Relations among rightist factions were not always harmonious, but they set their disagreements aside when it was expedient. Moreover, moderate rightists took on some extremist trappings. By 1939, radical rightist forces in Brazil and Chile were in disarray, yet the Argentine movement retained its corporate identity and influence.

Knowledge of events before 1939 is vital to an understanding of this persistent difference. As I show in the last chapter, the past continues to influence the present. While the movements in all three countries left a significant legacy, Argentina's tumultuous history since the 1930s suggests that this inheritance has been particularly weighty there.

PART 1

Antecedents, 1890–1914

Around the turn of the century, some Argentines, Brazilians, and Chileans started to question aspects of the reigning liberal and cosmopolitan mindset. Part of their critique harkened back to the Catholic and Iberian past, but much was new. Lurking beneath their words was the perception of national decline or stagnation. So, too, was the fear of what they frequently termed "dissolution," signifying the unraveling not only of local custom but of authority, property, and gender relations. Thus these intellectuals, statesmen, Catholic activists, and military officers limited their criticism of the status quo, suggesting alternative policies that would protect national interests, neutralize workers' demands for change, and leave the fundamentals of the system intact. As epitomized by the Chilean Ligas Patrióticas, Argentine vigilante groups, and Brazilian Jacobinos, nativism brought many of these strands together. In the process of formation, factions within the right were still amorphous.

Differences were also apparent among the countries. Radical rightist sentiments were emerging mostly in the elite in Argentina but had a more diverse base in Brazil and Chile. Antisemitism found greater resonance among Argentines than Chileans and Brazilians, who were preoccupied with other foreign groups and with racial questions. Reacting to labor militancy, Catholic men and women in Argentina and Chile were addressing the social question more vigorously than in Brazil. The weakness of the moderate right in Argentina and Brazil would leave a larger space for radical rightist activity than in Chile.

CHAPTER 1

Chile: The Decline of a Manly People

Most of the ingredients of extreme right-wing ideology and practice were present in Chile by 1914. The inadequacy of the export economy was apparent to many observers, as was the need for a sweeping nationalist program that would give priority to Chilean needs, conditions, and ideas rather than foreign ones. Military officers, Catholics, and other groups began to identify the growing labor movement as a threat to national unity and social harmony. Related to these views were attitudes critical of parliamentary government, secularism, perceived national weakness, and especially foreign residents.

Nationalism, Antiliberalism, and Race

At the turn of the century, Chileans of diverse ideological backgrounds, usually tied to the provincial elites or middle sectors, detected serious flaws in the nation's development.[1] The gravest problems were economic. The nitrate export sector had spurred the expansion of cities, railroads, industry, and agriculture in the south, and nitrate revenues had financed education and public works. The British firms that dominated this sector by the late nineteenth century, however, remitted much of the profits. Moreover, the demand for nitrate was unstable, and when it declined, the impact on employment and the rest of the economy was severe. The government's inflationary policies also hurt workers' salaries. Wealth differences between rich and poor, and between urban and rural dwellers, were marked.[2] The terrible poverty that afflicted the majority of Chileans, the extreme dependence on nitrate, and foreign control of this industry concerned local observers.

Many contemporaries sensed a moral crisis in society. A formerly austere and honorable upper class had become greedy and ostentatious, flaunting its wealth before the impoverished masses. Enamored of European goods and ideas, it appeared to be handing the country's resources over to foreigners.

Governmental structures also invited criticism. Since 1891 Congress had dominated the political scene. The Conservatives, Liberals, Radicals, and Democrats were among the many parties; the first two spoke for the elite, and their power rested upon a rural base. The Conservative alliance with the Catholic Church distinguished this party from the anticlerical Liberals and Radicals. Favoring reform were the middle-class Radicals and pro-labor Democrats. Frequent splintering and shifting alliances made it difficult to pass significant legislation. Moreover, the upper class used voting restrictions and electoral fraud to reinforce its control. Corrupt, elitist, and divided, the parliamentary regime seemed incapable of handling the nation's mounting problems.

Some individuals doubted the ability of the old political bodies to address these critical issues. The traditional parties' indifference to pressing economic and social matters disillusioned Conservative economist Guillermo Subercaseaux, who decided that particularly those of the moderate right—the Conservatives and various Liberal factions—no longer had reason to exist. Once Latin American liberals had achieved their goals, he charged, they had become conservative, and at least those conservatives who wanted to maintain the status quo rather than return to old dogmas had become liberal. Not surprisingly, he abandoned the Conservatives and founded the Nationalist Union in 1913, which he converted into a full-fledged party in 1915—the first self-styled nationalist party in Spanish America. The Nationalists managed to elect only one deputy, Subercaseaux, and disintegrated in 1920. Still, they attracted attention in provincial cities, the press, and intellectual circles.[3]

Liberalism was also under attack. Two influential writers, the historian Francisco A. Encina and the fiery journalist Tancredo Pinochet Le-Brun, called for studying Chile as it was and devising policies that fit its actual situation, rather than ones corresponding to abstract theories. In this regard, Encina criticized the local adoption of a denationalizing European model of classical education. He endorsed a mid-nineteenth-century visiting French economist who advised Chileans to lay the foundations of an industrial economy by establishing vocational education and postponing the development of humanistic learning. Encina regretted that these sensible ideas did not appeal to a generation "dazzled by the sonorous emptiness of liberty, equality, progress, law and democratic representative government" because they were too reminiscent of Diego Portales, the authoritarian leader of the 1830s. Revealing similar sentiments, Tancredo Pinochet, whose father had won and lost a mining fortune, ridiculed the tendency to sacrifice patriotism to universalistic notions of humanity. These passages manifested both authors' distaste for liberalism and utopianism. Of higher-class background than Pinochet, Encina, a landed aristocrat from Talca and future Nationalist Party member, also showed his authoritarian bent and provided an early revindication of Portalian rule.[4]

Many Chilean critics of liberalism accepted positivism. Like Encina, Pinochet, and Subercaseaux, positivists spurned theories and abstractions, which they saw as promoting disorder and revolution, in favor of facts derived from observation of reality.[5] Although racism and social Darwinism did not, strictly speaking, form part of positivistic doctrine, the three currents came together in Chile and the rest of Latin America.

Several Chilean writers interpreted history as a struggle for survival among races and among nations. They mainly wanted to improve internal conditions in order to strengthen the Chilean ability to compete in this test of fortitude. Encina lamented the fact that foreigners had outstripped locals in exploiting Chilean resources, supplying the Chilean market, and shaping Chilean minds. He dedicated his famous book *Nuestra inferioridad económica* (1912) to the task of teaching his fellow citizens how to improve their competitive position. The "doctrine of social solidarity," in his view, would only weaken the sense of nationalism; so, too, would socialism, although he admitted that it was not yet prominent in his country. Characterizing Chile as a "manly, restless, valiant and generous boy," Pinochet attributed its abdication of wealth to foreigners and hence its poor showing in the struggle for survival to a misplaced sense of international fraternity, a "chivalrous" generosity that only hurt its practitioners.[6] These remarks revealed not only their authors' social Darwinism but also their opposition to benevolent and cosmopolitan liberal doctrine. Pinochet's gendered metaphor served a similar purpose; he hoped that his likable youth would mature into a strong, selfish, but no less manly adult.

Relatively unimportant in Pinochet's work, racism pervaded Encina's. While he concluded that the Chilean race was the strongest and most capable in Latin America, Encina blamed foreign economic control largely on its genetic flaws. To this inevitably inferior product of race mixing, the Spanish and Araucanians had contributed their worst traits, which the positive effects of Basque immigration and the rigorous environment were insufficient to overcome. Another problem was the inherent tendency of a mestizo people to be overly susceptible to outside influences—in this case, foreign ideas imparted through classical education that weakened the local sense of initiative. Once the supply of good land had run out by 1865 and diminished the possibilities for agricultural expansion, these racial factors inhibited Chilean mobility into new fields of enterprise, enabling Europeans to usurp them.[7] Encina continued to uphold racist (and authoritarian) beliefs throughout his long career as writer and historian.

Racism was even more evident in a book that Encina admired, Nicolás Palacios's widely read *Raza chilena* (1904). The son of poor farmers, a veteran of the War of the Pacific (1879–83), and a doctor who had practiced among nitrate workers in the north, Palacio devised his own social Darwinist and gendered explanation of Chilean ills. Unlike Encina, he emphasized the positive aspects of the *raza*, which in his view represented the fusion of Araucanians and Spaniards of northern European, Gothic descent. While he agreed with Encina that race mixture usually resulted in degeneration, he regarded this particular union as felicitous. The Chilean race had inherited a "manly or patriarchal psychology" and, on balance, a positive mix of features from the two warrior peoples. Virile and imperious, the Goths easily subdued the Araucanian women, accustomed as they were to domination and polygamy at the hands of their own men. It was natural for the stern yet compassionate northern Europeans to take care of the meek, long-suffering Indian females in this manner. The Araucanians' honesty, chastity, faithfulness, and humility, so characteristic of women of patriarchal races, affected the Chilean race. After the original miscegenation, the difficult circumstances of colonial life selected the hardiest, most adaptable individuals. The result was the Chilean mestizos—manly, warlike, incorruptible, sturdy, and open to new ideas.[8]

If the race was strong, what had led to the decline of the nationality and growth of foreign control? Palacios faulted the elite's low estimation of Chilean capabilities and the Latin influence. Preferring European customs, ideas, and persons to the native, the upper class hoped to replace Chilean peasants with immigrants. To accomplish this goal, the government resorted to the extreme of forcing Chileans off their land and handing it over to foreign colonists. Yet the diseases, criminal tendencies, and harmful customs the immigrants brought to the country ironically proved that they were racially inferior to the Chileans. Palacios attributed these poor qualities to the Latin origins of most of the new arrivals. Smooth, superficial, and untrustworthy, they were all too well suited to the low art of commerce, which they monopolized in Chile. Worst of all, the Latin "race" was matriarchal, and Latin immigrants and ideas had alarmingly feminized a once patriarchal Chile. The matriarchal fear of war had led to the decline of the military and to growing calls for world peace. Incapable of objective analysis, matriarchal races failed to discern differences among races, which prompted them to view all humans as equal and deny the need for struggle. Indeed, Palacios associated female-dominated races with an exaggerated emphasis on beneficence, which in turn he tied to socialism, moral decay, and social dissolution.[9] Palacios's and Pinochet's preoccupation with manliness indicated their desire to strengthen Chile against internal and particularly external threats.

Like Encina and Pinochet, Palacios was ambivalent about democracy. He admitted that socialism and democracy resembled each other to some extent, but he insisted that only the first negated progress. He also saw socialism as a foreign import, implying that democracy was suitably native in origin. The main distinction between the two, however, was that socialism, by advocating the equality of all, represented "the politics of the feminine soul," whereas the type of democracy he favored, that of equality of opportunity, stood for "the politics of the man."[10] Even so limited a definition of socialism repelled this social Darwinist. His race and gender hierarchies, as well as his elevation of tough "male" struggle and individual effort over soft "female" policies of peace and mutual assistance, indicated his hostility to the equality and social solidarity that normally characterize democratic systems.

Similarly, his social Darwinism seemed to belie his economic nationalism. He implied that with its genetically honed talents, the Chilean race was well suited to the task of building an industrial society. Free-trade policies, which did not correspond to a world of national rivalry, had impeded Chilean industrial development. Palacios advocated protectionism and government sponsorship of vocational education, and he called for an end to official favoritism toward foreigners in commerce and industry.[11] Yet considering Palacios's other views, one would think that such policies would constitute a dangerous feminine form of beneficence that would weaken the male sense of initiative and the vigor of the race. He seemed to consider it legitimate to help the nation in its struggle for survival, but not individuals caught in the same trap.

One may criticize Palacios on other grounds. For example, he based his racial theories, which even some contemporaries viewed as extreme, on erroneous assumptions about the Spanish and the Indians. The conquerors were not pure "Goths," the native-American women were not necessarily chaste and submissive, nor were all the Indians patriarchally organized.[12] One might also question his statistics on the Latin character of nineteenth-century immigration. As of 1907, only 30.9 percent of the foreigners on Chilean soil were "Latin," that is, of French, Italian, and Spanish descent. Whatever their "race," the tiny proportion of immigrants in the populace—2.9 percent in 1895 and 4.1 percent in 1907—could hardly have influenced Chilean culture to the extent Palacios claimed.[13] Moreover, he praised German settlers who, from his standpoint, held positive "Gothic" traits, but they also had displaced Chilean rural dwellers.[14] Despite these faults, *Raza chilena*, with its exaltation of the nationality, its dread of leftist utopianism, and its concern over European dominance, appealed to many, particularly members of the middle sectors who feared foreign competition.

Encina's economic nationalism was more internally consistent than that of Palacios. Disagreeing with liberal economic as well as political doctrine, Encina extolled the ideas of the German economist Georg Friedrich List on the differing development of nations and the struggle among them for international domination. European economic penetration meant the repatriation of profits, the stimulation of consumption rather than local production, and the decay of nationalism. Free trade had also promoted the servile imitation of foreign customs and an unhealthy craving for foreign goods, which Encina saw as contradicting the native soul, "so virile and so Chilean" in other respects. In its present role as an exporter of raw materials and importer of finished goods, Chile would never become a great power; to achieve this status the nation would have to industrialize on its own. To do so it was necessary to train the people vocationally, so that they could move into the roles that they had allowed foreigners to monopolize. It would take time for educators to lift the people, with their racial deficiencies, to the European level. Nevertheless, such reforms, as well as a stable economic policy based on Chilean conditions rather than abstract theory, could help end the country's subordination.[15]

Pinochet also decried the loss of control over national wealth and guiding ideas; all was slipping through Chilean hands ("Todo se nos va"). Particularly shameful was the government's preference for foreign products, enterprises, and personnel, when it should have encouraged local initiative and helped native-born citizens. The government should set the welfare of its own people as a priority and offer Chileans obligatory and nationalistic

schooling, decent housing, employment, sanitation, and alcoholism preven-
tion programs. The authorities could also promote economic nationalism
by establishing protective tariffs and savings banks where Chileans could
accumulate their own capital for industrialization. Pinochet favored "nationalizing" industry, which he defined as state aid to Chilean entrepreneurs, and the "Chileanizing" of immigrants.[16] The object of these and of
Encina's policies was to create a strong nation that could compete with others in the struggle for survival.

Subercaseaux's ideas on increasing Chilean economic autonomy reflected some of Pinochet's and Encina's positions. The Nationalist spokesman favored protecting industries that had a good chance of prospering in
Chile or served national defense. To enlarge the market for Chilean manu-
factures, he urged the country to move toward an economic union with its
neighbors. Banks, insurance companies, and the merchant marine should
be in the hands of Chileans or foreign residents. However, he admitted the
need for foreign capital and technology in large-scale enterprises and for a
flexible tariff policy favoring imports for industrial use. He urged the government to stimulate development by promoting new industry, improving
infrastructure, and stabilizing fiscal policies. It should also eradicate poverty
through obligatory primary education and social legislation. Economic advancement required modifying the state; a powerful executive branch
would provide more stability and unity of decision making than the parliamentary regime, dominated by partisan opportunism. This strong state
would not be a socialist one, which Subercaseaux and his party opposed.[17]
The authoritarian implications of Subercaseaux's views would become evident in later years.

Nativism

As is evident, the immigrant presence elicited hostile responses from writers in this period. Although they frequently singled out the Germans for
praise, they also criticized them and other groups for their unwillingness to
assimilate. Foreigners were typically accused of parasitism, unscrupulous
business practices, favoritism toward their own nationality, and even criminal tendencies. Reluctant to blame capitalism and particularly native-born
entrepreneurs for exploiting workers, many authors, like Palacios, attributed
leftism to "agitators" from overseas. Of all immigrants, Syrians, Lebanese,
Chinese, and especially Jews received the heaviest denunciations.[18]

Antisemitism preceded the arrival of Jews. Although few Jews had come to Chile, various spokesmen in the early 1880s opposed further entries, claiming that they would foment unrest, spread their religion, and isolate themselves from Christians. Moreover, some writers insisted that Jews were responsible for paper money and other harmful financial policies, as well as loans to Chile's enemy, Peru. Despite the presence of only about 100 Jews in the early 1900s, criticism of supposed Jewish business abuses was widespread. When people burned Judas in effigy during Holy Week, they commonly identified this figure with hated businessmen, and the popular press seized upon this conflation of Judaism and capitalism.[19]

The foremost example of antisemitism in print was Palacios's *Raza chilena*. In his opinion, the Jews constituted a "closed race, perfectly homogeneous and of a particular and uniform psychology." They lacked soul, a basic prerequisite for nationalism, and for this reason the wealthy Jews' plans to create a Jewish nation had failed. If they had ever possessed a sense of *patria*, centuries of homelessness had taken it away from them, he thought, although the same data could have led him to the opposite conclusion. Thus, such Jewish writers as Karl Marx despised nationalism and, supposedly "out of love for humanity," advocated socialism, although Palacios hinted that their actual motive was their "race's" welfare. Persecution had sharpened the Jewish survival skills of race pride, financial prowess, greed, and dissimulation. Anti-Jewish repression had diminished in the advanced societies, and the author admitted that some Jews had served and identified with those societies. Still, he believed that Jews ultimately sought to destroy those countries.[20]

Palacios reserved his greatest ire for Marx, suggesting that the desire to avenge Jewish martyrs and demolish nations had impelled this "Mephistophelean being" to give a scientific veneer to socialism and anarchism. He doubted that this intelligent man believed in his own malicious and fanciful notions, including racial equality. In matriarchal European countries, socialist propaganda had achieved success; in Chile, the flawed upper class fueled its growth. The victory of this dissolvent doctrine would promote the violence of the rabble and the greed of the Jews.

Writing before Chile contained a noticeable Jewish community, Palacios criticized imaginary Jews, representing modern forces he despised, rather than real ones. The contradictions in *Raza chilena* evinced its author's radical antisemitism.[21] How Jewish avarice could support a movement that sought to abolish profit was not made clear. The idea that Jews would benefit by demolishing nations to which they had given their allegiance also was difficult to comprehend.

The victims of the gravest displays of nativist feeling in this and the next period were not Jews but Peruvian residents. As a result of the War of the Pacific, Chile had acquired Antofagasta from Bolivia and Tarapacá from Peru, and it also occupied the former Peruvian provinces of Tacna and Arica. Between 1883 and 1929, when Peru reabsorbed Tacna and abandoned its claim to Arica, the government asserted its sovereignty over the north by "Chileanizing" it. It faced a challenging task, particularly in Tarapacá, where in 1907 almost 40 percent of the inhabitants were foreign, with 23,574 Peruvians and 12,528 Bolivians out of a total population of 110,036. Most businessmen and property owners were foreign-born, and the numerous Peruvians maintained their cultural institutions and loyalties.[22]

Tensions rose in May 1911. After the government violently suppressed the nitrate workers' strike of 1907, the British nitrate companies of Tarapacá attempted to replace Chilean laborers with Peruvians, Bolivians, and Asians, whom they regarded as docile, low-wage workers. The firms also played off these groups against Chileans by making Peruvians foremen and recruiting Peruvians and Bolivians for their private police forces. Angered by such policies, as well as what they viewed as Peruvian separateness and predominance in commerce and white-collar employment, working- and middle-class Chileans agitated to reduce this group's presence in the mines and other areas of the economy. Criticism of Chilean heroes in local Peruvian papers also roused anger, as did a campaign of false rumors that Peruvians had attacked the Chilean consulate in Callao and were sending troops to the border.[23]

Some Chileans in Iquique took matters into their own hands. Masked men attacked the printing press of *La Voz del Perú*, one of the offending newspapers, on May 26. The next evening others assembled in the Sociedad Protectora de Trabajadores to plan a patriotic meeting for May 28. This organization was affiliated with the Liberal Democrats, the party of the overthrown nationalistic president, José Manuel Balmaceda (1886–91), which had campaigned against exploitation of workers, economic imperialism, and Peruvian and Bolivian residents. When the meeting ended, some headed to the Plaza Prat, where a few members of the crowd shouted, "Down with the *cholos*," a derogatory term reserved for Chile's dark-skinned neighbors, and denounced the Peruvian press. A mob ran through the streets, attacking Peruvian institutions and businesses and the Peruvian consulate. These assaults continued the following night, forcing the Peruvian consul to seek refuge in the U.S. consulate.[24]

The rally of May 28 inaugurated the Liga Patriótica Nacional de Tarapacá. The Liga favored closing all Peruvian newspapers and schools in the province, repatriating the Peruvian consul stationed in Iquique, limiting or prohibiting Peruvian immigration, and excluding Peruvians from teaching positions, public posts, the merchant marine, and maritime unions. It thought that these measures, as well as the proposed requirement that 80 percent of all nitrate employees and workers be Chilean, would reduce Peruvian influence in the economy and government. (In fact, 72 percent of nitrate personnel were Chilean.) Forcing all men born in the north to do military service, forbidding Peruvians to raise their flags on Peruvian holidays, and strengthening military defenses near the border would further "de-Peruvianize." After this initial meeting, citizens congregated in other northern towns to create Liga chapters. Members of civic groups and worker associations attended these events, indicating the broad appeal of nativism.[25]

Military authorities and government officials also attended, including Intendant Máximo Lira of Tacna and prominent Liberal Democrat Anselmo Blanlot Holley. Their participation, as well as the inability of the Iquique police to control the lawlessness, suggested local government complicity. At the same time, national authorities officially apologized to Peru for the Iquique incidents and conducted an investigation whose results were critical of northern citizens.[26]

The Liga campaign spread throughout Chile. Citizens held rallies and threatened Peruvians in localities as far south as Valparaíso. There the Liga Patriótica hosted a demonstration on June 18 that attracted 20,000 onlookers, including many combatants of the War of the Pacific. With this event, the Círculo de Jefes y Oficiales Retirados and the Liga Patriótica Militar, two allied veterans' associations centered in Santiago, aligned themselves with the Liga Patriótica.[27]

Another violent episode hurt the Ligas. Members of labor, veteran, and civic groups from Arica attended a Liga Patriótica rally in Tacna on July 18. On the return trip only half of the 800 participants fit in the train. Some of those left behind rioted and destroyed two Peruvian printing presses and the Club Peruano, and the disorders spread to Arica. Again, the national government investigated and condemned the incident.[28]

Perhaps because of government pressure, the Ligas were largely inactive until late November, when they held a flurry of peaceful demonstrations until January 1912. Organized by the Liga Patriótica Militar, the most important rally took place in December in the Teatro Municipal in Santiago. Retired officers, members of the elite, and prominent politicians attended, including Jorge Balmaceda, nephew of the deposed president, and future president Arturo Alessandri. The domestication of what had been a violent movement did not, however, suffice to save it. Anxious to strengthen Chile's image abroad and attract foreign capital, the government may have ordered its dissolution.[29]

Opposition to Labor

The Ligas may have signified more than a reaction against Peruvians. *El Grito Popular* of Iquique, a labor organ founded by the famous radical Luis Emilio Recabarren, claimed that the Liberal Democrats had created the Liga to attract a worker base. The participation of Balmacedistas and the location of the Liga's first meeting supported Recabarren's theory. He saw Liga appeals to workers as an attempt to divert them from their struggles and divide their forces. Perhaps Recabarren meant this was an effort to undermine the Socialist Worker Party, which he was organizing in Iquique. Not devoid of chauvinism, the newspaper nevertheless opposed vigilante "patriotism." To truly Chileanize the north, it favored Democratic congressman Malaquías Concha's proposal that property be given to Chileans who worked in the region. Another paper founded by Recabarren, *El Despertar de los Trabajadores* of Iquique, suggested that Liga nationalism masked a desire for partisan political gain and wartime profits.[30]

Significantly, on at least one occasion nativists threatened workers. Angered by its opposition to the anti-Peruvian campaign, a mob destroyed the printing press of *El Comunista* in Antofagasta in July 1911. Some sources, however, suggested that the perpetrators were police and soldiers in civilian clothes.[31]

Antiworker vigilantes were not new to Chile. On October 22, 1905, workers held a giant protest march in Santiago against the tariff on Argentine beef, which contributed to the high cost of living. When the demonstration turned into a riot, policemen and firemen, unable to contain the destruction, organized and armed civilian auxiliaries. They were joined by brigades of social club members, municipal employees, and upper-class youths, bearing weapons from the War Ministry. The official forces and the armed civilians ended the disorders by October 27, amid accusations of unwarranted brutality. When army troops arrived, they simply assumed control over existing patrols.[32]

While the military played little role in the events of October 1905, it participated in other repressive episodes, such as the massacre of hundreds of strikers in Iquique on December 21, 1907. Even when they were not actively coercing workers, some sectors within the armed forces professed antilabor sentiments. Military spokesmen noted leftists' opposition to the draft and the armed forces, perceiving their internationalism, secularism, and class consciousness as undermining national traditions and unity. Nevertheless, military officers themselves were beginning to criticize oligarchical rule. They denounced the parliamentary regime's corruption, partisanship, and interference in internal military affairs. Observing the malnourishment and illiteracy of many conscripts, officers also blamed the elite for neglecting the masses and thereby increasing the risk of revolution. Their German training led them to admire that nation's combination of autocratic rule, a strong military, and social legislation. These concerns surfaced in the Liga Militar (1907) and the Liga Naval (1910 or 1911), which planned a revolt in 1912. The coup attempt fizzled and the organizations faded, but the feelings remained.[33]

Antileftist themes also infused the discourse of civilian elites. Encina, Palacios, and Subercaseaux explicitly opposed socialism; Pinochet did so implicitly by ridiculing benevolent internationalism. The Darwinists in this group regarded social solidarity as illusory and misguided. All viewed trickle-down, nationalistic policies as the best means of eradicating poverty, and all favored change controlled from above. Such notions as welfare programs and socialism, in Palacios's opinion, were Latin in origin, products of a mentality foreign to Chile.

Others concluded that leftism and labor militancy were also foreign imports. They insisted that jobs and land were available for all in Chile who wished to work, permitting upward mobility to a degree unknown in Europe. Thus immigrant-led agitation was responsible for class conflict. After a port strike in Valparaíso in 1912, Guillermo Subercaseaux introduced a residence law refusing entry to foreign radicals and facilitating their deportation. Yet the native origin of the overwhelming majority of laborers weakened the anti-immigrant argument. For this reason, as well as devotion to liberal economic theory and legal tradition, Congress did not pass an immigration restriction law until after the Russian Revolution.[34]

Some who did not blame immigrants still considered labor organizing unjustified. They favored strengthening the forces of order to repress workers, and some Conservatives even implied that eliminating mass education (which hardly existed) and liberal freedoms would result in social peace. A growing number of observers, however, joined Pinochet in admitting that extreme wealth differences and severe labor exploitation spurred lower-class discontent. Reformers associated with the Radicals, Democrats, and some Liberal factions—groups that would form the Liberal Alliance in 1920—began to propose social legislation. Prominent Radicals and Liberals recommended that the state recognize workers' rights to organize, bargain collectively, and receive a free education. Malaquías Concha went considerably further in proposing a labor code and social security system. Even the landowners' association, the Sociedad Nacional de Agricultura, advocated building housing for workers and setting up savings funds. A belief in the inferiority of the poor—and in the need to control them to avert revolution—however, characterized the Radical, Liberal, and Sociedad plans.[35]

Conservatives, the Church, and Women

Conservatives and the Catholic Church also were interested in social reform, a concern that fit within the context of their struggle against the liberal state. Not completely clerical or antiliberal in its early years, the Conservative Party increasingly allied with the church when Liberals and Radicals began to pass religious tolerance and secularization laws in the 1860s. While the attempt to shield the church from liberal reform failed, the clergy regarded Conservatives as its only reliable allies and openly campaigned for this party's candidates, despite disapproval by some members of the hierarchy.[36]

The struggle of Conservatives and the church against laicism did not turn them against or marginalize them from the political system, however, nor did it signify a complete rejection of liberalism. Although their power in an increasingly urban Chile was diminishing, Conservatives, and through them the church, still commanded a strong political presence. Both accepted the constitutional republican form of government and the core of free-market economics, while criticizing liberal materialism and secularism. Some church intellectuals even found the scientific character of positivism and Darwinism appealing. Thus the Conservative and Catholic challenge to liberalism was limited.[37]

Yet a new orientation that would question some liberal economic assumptions, called Social Catholicism, was emerging. This was the church's attempt in Europe to win workers away from religious indifference, liberalism, and socialism by proposing reforms that would not endanger the class hierarchy. Building upon these ideas and long ties to charity, Catholics founded the first "workers' circle" in Santiago in 1878 and the Sociedad de Obreros de San José in 1883 to Christianize, educate, and moralize laborers. The first *patronato*, or center of Catholic training for young workers, arose in 1890. Priests and aristocrats, among them many Conservatives, directed these labor groups.[38]

By the 1890s labor activities had begun to preoccupy the Chilean elite, and the church reflected this concern as well as the continuing desire to strengthen itself against liberal secularization efforts. Archbishop Mariano Casanova of Santiago described Pope Leo XIII's *Rerum Novarum* in five pastorals in 1891, emphasizing the pope's disapproval of socialism and strikes. The dissemination of *Rerum Novarum* stimulated discussion of the social question at Catholic congresses in 1905 and 1910 and other forums. While participants approved of change, they placed it within the context of social harmony and elite control over church-sponsored labor groups.[39]

The Conservative Party declared its allegiance to social Christian principles, although it did not suggest means of putting them into practice. Still, party members were instrumental in securing the limited social legislation of the period. These included regulations on the sale of alcohol (1902), the construction and inspection of workers' housing (1906), and Sunday rest for workers (1907). Indicating the new attention paid to worker conflict, the executive established a labor office in the ministry of industry and public works (1907). Congressmen presented and debated more far-reaching bills, but did not approve them.[40] Continuing allegiance to liberal economics, as well as the much-criticized focus of the parliamentary regime on immediate political ends, impeded further change.

Women also participated in Social Catholicism. Expected to concern themselves with pious social works, upper-class women had been involved in diverse religious charities in the nineteenth century. Adding to this heritage, nuns of the Sacred Heart order, who arrived in Chile in the mid-1800s, organized the graduates of their prestigious girls' school into the Hijas de María, who attempted to unite the social classes through philanthropy. Many of these charitable works focused on preparing working-class women for Christian marriage and motherhood. The concern shifted somewhat with women's growing involvement in union activities, as they took part in a quarter of the strikes between 1902 and 1908. This militancy and perceptions of immorality in the media sparked a new national organization under the church's authority. Founded by the aristocratic Amalia Errázuriz de Subercaseaux in 1912, the Liga de Damas Chilenas monitored cultural activities and began to direct its attention toward the female poor.[41]

Social Catholics in 1910 could pride themselves on the growth of their institutions. In that year 15,000 laborers belonged to sixty-four workers' circles around the country, and the Sociedad de Obreros de San José had

20,000 members in Santiago. Yet the movement faced severe dilemmas. Militant workers spurned its belief in hierarchy, worker submissiveness, and medieval-style labor associations; those who were devout proclaimed the "Socialist Christ," which the church found abhorrent. Social Catholic ties with the Conservative Party weakened its potential. Finally, only a minority of Catholics, Conservatives, and priests genuinely followed Social Catholicism. Of those who did, many saw no contradiction between such views and economic liberalism, revealing the superficiality of their vision.[42]

Conclusion

The weak Social Catholic movement was but one of the antecedents of the modern radical right. The literature of crisis school questioned the liberal path of economic development and asserted nationalistic, racist, and sometimes authoritarian solutions to Chile's problems. Several writers affirmed the nation's manly character against foreign domination and the threat of internal dissolution. The precursors' hostility toward Jews, immigrants, and particularly Peruvian residents indicated their ethnic chauvinism; the paucity of the first two groups, however, limited these prejudices. Despite the Ligas Patrióticas' popular base, which included workers, antilabor sentiments were an important feature of the incipient far right. Women's circumscribed role in the political sphere and male pronouncements on gender made this right largely masculine in character. While Catholic and secular rightists criticized the liberal oligarchy, neither proposed to replace it with a more egalitarian society. The division between these two sectors was noteworthy, as was the lack of communication between them. The strength of the church and of moderate rightist Conservatives and Liberals was considerable, which would limit the space for the extreme right in the future.

CHAPTER 2

A Polluted Argentina

In Argentina as well as Chile, criticism of liberalism on political and philosophical grounds was common. Here, too, the military, the elite, and Social Catholics feared the growing labor movement and sought to repress or control it. Yet the differences between the two countries were striking. To a much greater extent than in Chile, the emerging extreme right was tied to the upper class and the Catholic Church, and it opposed Jews and immigrants. Argentines also tended to view the export economy and their country's future more positively than their Chilean counterparts.

In some respects the Argentine elite was stronger than its Chilean cousin. Centered in the pampas, its agricultural enterprises produced a large percentage of the nation's exports. Although foreigners dominated transportation, meatpacking plants, and trade links to Europe, the elite's ownership of land gave it much control over the meat and grain export sector, whose vitality accounted for the extraordinary performance of the Argentine economy. Economic success had awarded hegemony to upper-class liberalism and legitimized the Argentine oligarchy's authority, expressed through the National Autonomist Party, or PAN. An alliance of provincial political forces, PAN also perpetuated itself in office through electoral fraud.[1]

There was some dissatisfaction with the export economy, but such sentiments were not pervasive. Starting in the 1870s, Vicente Fidel López, Carlos Pellegrini, and other statesmen disapproved of the mounting foreign debt and British control of resources, advocating protectionism and local ownership of enterprises. At the turn of the century, the left-leaning poet

Leopoldo Lugones began to speak out in favor of raising tariffs, as did former foreign minister and deputy Estanislao Zeballos. Socialist Party leader Juan B. Justo warned of the evils of foreign dominance and profit remittances as early as 1896, yet he and his party generally favored economic liberalism. Argentina was the South American showcase of export-led growth, and relatively few of its inhabitants, even on the left, perceived the flaws of this model, compared with their Chilean contemporaries.[2]

Nativism

Unwilling to disparage the economic system, most critics focused on indirect effects of economic liberalism that they disliked, such as immigration. Regarding the local Creole population as dark-skinned, ignorant, and backward, Argentine liberals relied on immigrants to form a reliable labor force and a stable republic. The expanding economy attracted about 2.2 million permanent settlers from abroad between 1870 and 1910, dwarfing the comparable figures for Chile. By 1914 immigrants composed almost a third of the population and an even higher percentage of the inhabitants in the capital city and littoral provinces, the nation's economic heartland. Most of the newcomers, however, were southern and eastern Europeans, not the northerners that liberals had preferred, and their origins sparked unfavorable comments even from those who supported immigration. More important, their presence transformed the social structure and culture in ways that the original proponents of immigration had not foreseen. Not content with remaining landless peons or tenant farmers, foreigners composed 86 percent of the lower and 66 percent of the middle classes in the city of Buenos Aires by the early 1900s. As these two classes began their struggles to secure a more equitable distribution of wealth and power, the elite reacted against them by flaunting its "nationalism" against their foreign identity.[3]

The depression of 1890, which temporarily dampened Argentine economic optimism, prompted an important critique of immigration. In *La bolsa*, Julián Martel blamed Jewish international capital and its credulous Argentine tools for the feverish speculation that led to the stock market crash of that year. Rather than analyzing the hardships endured by the lower and middle classes, he focused on the losses suffered by the oligarchy and overlooked the foreign debt it had contracted. That the British were the main foreign interest in Argentina, and that they and the Argentine elite were the primary beneficiaries of the financial manipulations, also escaped his attention.[4]

Influenced by French antisemitism, Martel accused the 2,400 Jews in Argentina of using gold, the white slave trade, and hypocrisy, cruelty, and greed to undermine Christians. As had Nicolás Palacios, he connected Jewish capitalism to socialism. The author implied that Jewish men dominated Argentina, just as the Jewish prostitution ring, the Zwi Migdal, dominated its women. In his view, Jews had polluted the country; so, too, had the entire wave of immigrants, whose materialism, artificial foreign customs, and lack of civic concern infected the nation. He decried the promiscuity he saw in the chaotic mix of classes and "races" and the commercialization of society. With her sensuality, supposed foreign origins, and paid sexual services, the prostitute symbolized the threat to Argentina. Martel thought that racial decadence resulted from intermarriage between foreigners and locals; "the variety of types into which dominating cosmopolitanism has decomposed the Argentine woman" repelled him.[5] Here, women symbolized all Creoles, demographically overwhelmed by the immigrant tide and disintegrating culturally in its wake. As for the Chilean writers, womanhood—whether Argentine or immigrant—denoted weakness and decay.

Some authors have described Martel as a representative of the Creole middle class. To support this view they have cited his native-born, humble beginnings, his dark skin, and his difficulty in earning a living as a journalist, as well as his enmity toward immigrant businessmen. His reluctance to attack the elite and the economic structure, and his preoccupation with dissolvent cosmopolitanism, however, mark him as a spokesman for the upper class. Or perhaps his views indicated the precarious status of the Argentine middle sectors, tied to the fate of the export economy and its aristocratic local managers.[6]

Ricardo Rojas picked similar targets. As the son of the governor of Santiago del Estero province and a member of an old political family, Rojas had lived in the capital since adolescence. His provincial upbringing made it difficult for him to accept the cosmopolitanism and "mercantilism of the port." In *La restauración nacionalista* (1909), Rojas denounced the domination of British capital and Italian immigrants over local businesses and the labor force, respectively. British, Jewish, and even Italian interests regarded Argentina as their colony, and a foreign association of Jewish bankers virtually ruled the country, he claimed. Buenos Aires was but an intermediary between the impoverished interior and the foreign metropolis. Yet Rojas situated these tidbits of economic nationalism within a context of complaints against immigration, imported ideas, and especially schools serving foreign communities, which he saw as vehicles of "national dissolution." Of these, the Jewish schools particularly threatened the Argentine nationality: they reinforced a sense of separatism in a group that differed significantly from the majority. The pupils of these institutions might choose to be Jews rather than full-fledged Argentines, and this decision could incite prejudice where none had previously existed. To correct these problems and build a mature sense of nationalism, Rojas advocated educational and cultural renewal, drawing primarily upon local inspiration.[7]

Rojas insisted that he did not favor xenophobia, a rejection of all European thought, an end to immigration, or a return to outmoded socioeconomic structures. Disavowing the French counterrevolutionary version, he advocated a secular, democratic, and pacifist nationalism. Nevertheless, both he and the French radical right attributed the splintering of the nation to liberalism. The destructive individualism of Buenos Aires had impeded nationalism, and the "excessive" and overly theoretical liberalism of the constitution had permitted the antipatriotic abuses of the private schools. In the local context, freedom of education meant subjecting a heterogeneous new nation to "the commerce of adventurers without a fatherland, to the greed of international sects, or to the invasion of imperialist powers." One could not allow this abstract principle to endanger the nation.[8]

Rojas's belief in democracy and his relatively mild tone distinguished his thought from that of the future radical right. Still, his book influenced that political persuasion. His apparent moderation did not completely disguise Rojas's opposition to Jews, liberalism, and labor or his overlap with Martel, whose work he praised. He ignored the fact that Jewish and other colonies had founded schools because few public ones existed, and the Jewish institutions received non-Jewish students and government support. Moreover, he disregarded evidence of antisemitism before the mass arrivals of Jews in the 1890s; his own statements blaming prejudice on the Jews themselves revealed such feelings. Finally, his remarks coupling Italian workers with British capital suggested that he viewed them as equivalent dangers, attributing to laborers a power they did not possess.[9]

Opposition to Labor

The Argentine labor movement was the largest in Latin America. Its foreign composition, however, played into the right's hands. Congress identified immigrants with antinationalism when, on the occasion of an anarchist-led general strike, it passed a residence law in 1902. Workers nevertheless continued their organizational efforts, which reached a peak in 1909–10. In November 1909, a Russian Jewish worker, Simón Radowitzky, killed the police chief of the capital, Ramón L. Falcón, in retaliation for a police massacre the previous May Day. Radowitzky's background further aroused upper-class hostility against Jews and immigrants.[10]

The youth section of the ruling PAN loudly protested foreign "dissolution." At Falcón's funeral, Ricardo Rojas's brother Julio, a distinguished lawyer and PAN member, denounced the assassin as one who lacked a name, a fatherland, and a God. The "improvised cosmopolitanism" of the law had permitted foreigners to besiege the nationality, he warned, adding that native-born Argentines would have to defend themselves. Indeed, the night before the funeral, a group—perhaps of the same Autonomist Youth—had already defended the nationality by attacking *La Protesta*, the anarchist newspaper. Manuel Carlés, future president of the Liga Patriótica Argentina, a radical rightist movement of the postwar years, also delivered a fiery eulogy.[11]

Policemen, Catholics, and prominent citizens continued to target labor organizations and *La Protesta*. For their part workers carried out demonstrations and strikes directed largely against the residence law, culminating during the centennial of Argentine independence in May 1910. Embarrassed by the timing of these actions, upper-class citizens responded with demonstrations of their own. "Like a dozing lion, [the people] stood up, noble and enraged, upon sensing the steps of strangers in their domains," declared Father Miguel de Andrea, a Social Catholic. Thousands of "virile" hands, as De Andrea put it, carried the flag through the streets, claiming the city for nationalism.[12] Fights broke out between the young standard-bearers and workers who, they thought, excluded themselves from the nation. Women also shared in this symbolic display of "imagined community."[13] Aristocratic members of the Hijas de María, the Liga de Damas Católicas, and other prestigious female Catholic organizations, as well as of the Sociedad de Beneficencia, the female upper-class charitable foundation, sponsored a mass celebrating independence on May 21. De Andrea addressed the women at the mass, and together they paraded from the church to the tomb of José de San Martín, the father of Argentine independence, defiantly singing the national anthem.

Other citizens forcibly suppressed workers.[14] General Luis Dellepiane, Falcón's successor as police chief, recruited upper-class youth for the Policía Civil Auxiliar to help keep order during the centennial festivities. This group may have participated in attacks, joined by police, on three worker newspapers and the headquarters of the Socialist Party and several labor organizations the evening of May 14. Marauders also entered a Jewish neighborhood, Barrio Once, where they assaulted a grocery store and a Jewish socialist center. By raping several women, they asserted their dominance over foreigners. The riot indicated the manner in which upper-class Argentines linked leftism with the Jewish community, a connection reinforced by Martel and Radowitzky.

The rapid growth of the Jewish collectivity to more than 100,000 between 1890 and 1914 alarmed nativists. No foreign group suffered more at the hands of upper-class nationalists, despite the fact that Italians and Spaniards, representing the two largest immigrant communities, outnumbered Jews among leftists. As in Chile, many criticized Jews not only for radicalism but for alleged business practices. Officials and writers predicted that Jews would isolate themselves in urban enclaves. The existence of Jewish agricultural colonies did not force them to retract their views; that most of these failed, like other immigrant settlements, only confirmed their suspicions. Jewish involvement in organized prostitution also inspired revulsion, but antisemites ignored the many Jewish opponents of this practice.[15]

The riot of May 14 sparked further conflict. On June 26 a bomb blast injured fourteen people in the Teatro Colón. As a result of this bombing, which police blamed on anarchists, Congress passed the Social Defense Law, which harshly repressed labor activists and excluded foreign radicals from Argentina.

Cultural Nationalism

The nationalism that the elite used to distinguish itself from immigrants partly consisted of renewed pride in the long denigrated Hispanic past. Around the turn of the century, some writers began to dissent from the prevailing liberal view of Argentine history, which had identified the Hispanic interior with barbarism and the cosmopolitan littoral region with civilization. The city no longer seemed the image of progress; instead, it presented the spectacle of class conflict and immorality, conditions that upper-class intellectuals blamed on foreigners. Nor did strongmen such as Juan Manuel de Rosas, the authoritarian governor of Buenos Aires province (1829–32, 1835–52), seem as worthy of condemnation as before. Influenced by a positivist stress on evolution, race, and psychology, historians such as Ernesto Quesada and Francisco Ramos Mejía viewed Rosas and other caudillos as logical outgrowths of their chaotic time. Ricardo Rojas found such figures more genuinely national and willing to defend the country against foreigners than many prominent liberals. The revisionist writers considered Rosas's methods appropriate for a period in which the masses were unprepared for political participation—conditions that no longer prevailed. Nevertheless, these aristocratic authors supplied arguments that other members of their class used to denigrate cosmopolitan Buenos Aires and the lower- and middle-class struggles for economic and political change.[16]

A new admiration for the gauchos and Creoles of the interior accompanied the rehabilitation of the caudillos they had followed. Once seen as ignorant and barbaric, the disappearing gaucho now emerged as the epitome of *argentinidad.* In a lecture series in 1913, the poet Leopoldo Lugones extolled this rural figure for his virility, generosity, individualism, and spiritualism, qualities contrasting with the foreign-born urban worker's material values and monotonous chores. The gaucho's characteristics continued to influence the Argentine character, Lugones claimed, even as his inferior Indian ancestry faded in the population. Significantly, the poet combined these racial remarks with a diatribe against democracy; he also ignored the landowners' exploitation of rural workers and ascribed to the latter the upper-class qualities he esteemed. Other admirers praised rural inhabitants for their loyalty to their employers and lack of ambition. Whether they described native-born Argentines as aristocratic or subservient, these writers rejected the upward mobility and social change sought by immigrants in favor of hierarchy and an idealized version of the past.[17]

Lugones's background helped account for his views. The descendant of an old yet downwardly mobile family of Córdoba, the poet made his living in government jobs acquired through political connections. The advent of democracy appeared to threaten his livelihood as well as the elite to which he tenuously belonged, and his declining economic status may have reinforced his aesthetic and antimaterialistic bent. Despite his initial flirtations with socialism and then anarchism, by 1906 he advocated government by a talented minority and military dominance in civilian affairs.[18]

Lugones, Rojas, and another writer, Manuel Gálvez, were the major exponents of what scholars have termed cultural nationalism; indeed, compared with the Chilean literature of crisis, the overwhelmingly cultural character of Argentine nationalism and its lack of economic content were striking. Gálvez also belonged to an old provincial family, but unlike Lugones's it had retained its wealth. Economic change and immigration, however, had resulted in the formation of new political groups in his native Santa Fe that vied with his family and his class for control. Nevertheless, it would be inaccurate to describe the three authors as representatives of a declining class, for during this period the allies of their families still ruled Santa Fe, Santiago del Estero, and Córdoba.[19]

Gálvez harshly criticized cosmopolitanism and emphasized the Hispanic component of the Argentine nationality. The arrival of Italians, Jews, and anarchists, as well as foreign culture and ideas, distressed him. He traced this excessive love of Europe back to the early-nineteenth-century liberals, whom he compared unfavorably with Rosas's inward-looking followers, rooted to Argentine soil. Rejecting cosmopolitanism, Gálvez embraced the Spanish-inspired affirmation of rural life, idealism, heroism, and, particularly, spiritualism, qualities that he found conspicuously lacking in Buenos Aires. His journeys to the interior and to Spain, a religious conversion, and his reading of French and Spanish conservatives inspired these values.[20]

Gálvez, along with Rojas and Lugones, formed part of the reaction against positivism which, in contrast to Chile, became widespread among Argentine intellectuals. Influenced by European idealism and the Uruguayan writer José Enrique Rodó, antipositivists favored what they saw as the warm philosophical Spanish heritage over the cold utilitarianism of the United States and the immigrants. While they criticized the liberal oligarchy for its materialism, cosmopolitanism, and shallow belief in progress, unlike Chilean nationalists they did not propose specific economic or political measures to address its shortcomings. Most shared with Lugones—and with the positivists whose teachings they theoretically spurned—a belief in the rule of a talented elite and in racism.[21] Thus the idealists drew from the positivistic liberalism they claimed to reject.

The Church, Women, and Social Reform

Like the idealists, and as in Chile, the church opposed yet overlapped liberalism. In the 1880s the liberal state secularized public education, marriage, and the civil registry. Catholics justified their opposition partly by referring to the clause in the otherwise liberal Constitution of 1853 mandating government support of Catholicism. They criticized official incursions into education and the family as interfering with the "liberty" of the church and individual Catholics and as increasing the power of the state. Such language overlapped with liberal notions of freedom and limited government. Moreover, by denouncing the self-serving, corrupt PAN oligarchy, Catholic spokesmen set themselves up as moral leaders of the republic. Nevertheless, fearing that mass rule would unleash anarchy, Catholic deputy José

Manuel Estrada favored governance by an austere Christian elite that expressed the will of the people. He decried the sacrifice of the poor to capital and natural selection; in his opinion, liberal economics meant the egoism of "Jewish monopolies." Yet he rejected the leveling process that socialism entailed. Estrada's views, and Catholic thought as a whole, combined liberal and antiliberal tenets.[22]

Catholic criticism of the governing elite led to participation in the Revolution of 1890, which overthrew the anticlerical president, Miguel Juárez Celman, who had presided over the stock market crash. Out of this revolution emerged the Radical Civic Union party (UCR), the main vehicle for electoral democracy. The presidents who followed the ousted Juárez Celman, however, were conciliatory toward Catholics and helped reconcile them with continued oligarchical rule. The perceived threat from below also brought Catholics closer to the government.

By this time, as in Chile, the struggle with the liberal state prompted the rise of Social Catholicism and workers' circles.[23] In 1912 there were seventy-seven circles with 23,000 members, led mostly by priests and wealthy men. The state extended juridical recognition and subventions to some circles, indicating its proximity to the church at least on the social question. Some among the hierarchy and the elite, however, regarded the circles as subversive for supporting improved working conditions, although the circles viewed strikes ambivalently and at times supplied strikebreakers.[24]

The Liga Democrática Cristiana (1902–8) created even more suspicion. It sponsored discussion of the social question, organized roughly 5,000 workers in confessional unions, and trained Catholic antisocialistic labor leaders. One of these unions carried out a strike in 1906, arousing the hostility of wealthy Catholics, the circles, and the hierarchy and contributing to the downfall of the Liga and most Catholic unions.[25]

Social Catholic women played a more important role in Argentina than in Chile. Here, upper-class women had administered the most important charitable institutions since the 1820s. As the numbers of immigrants and inhabitants of the capital increased in the late 1800s, so did the social programs directed by women, many of which aimed to Christianize and employ impoverished females. They also enlisted recipients to work for these charities and teach their sisters to be pious and orderly. While welfare afforded women a public outlet for their energies, they were not welcome in rightist cultural circles.[26]

Beginning in the 1890s, Social Catholic projects for women continued these gender notions and, as in Chile, added the goal of keeping female workers, some of whom had participated in strikes and Socialist and anarchist groups, out of the left. Social Catholics inaugurated apprenticeships and other forms of aid to protect young working-class women from anti-Christian influences, while the Liga de Damas Católicas Argentinas, created in 1911, encouraged young female laborers to save money and prepare for marriage. In 1904 the Liga Democrática Cristiana organized a weavers' union, and the following year upper-class women formed a short-lived auxiliary of the workers' circles. Another outlet for activism was the antileftist Hijas de María, which participated in the mass and parade of May 21, 1910.[27]

Social Catholicism was relatively weak and paternalistic. Despite the split between Catholics who regarded the Liga Democrática Cristiana and even the circles as radical and those who favored such approaches, both sides condemned class conflict.[28] Still, this division indicated debility, as did the small numbers of adherents, even in comparison to Chile, which, with its tiny population, enrolled nearly as many in its Catholic labor groups as Argentina. Nor did Argentine Catholics enjoy the backing of a political party, although Chilean Conservatives were hardly united behind Social Catholic principles.

Yet Social Catholicism influenced upper-class opinion on reform. As a government statistician, the circle leader Alejandro Bunge supplied information on working and living conditions to Social Catholic deputies. The devoutly Catholic Manuel Gálvez published a sympathetic study on workers' everyday lives in 1913. Also influenced by Catholicism was the statesman Carlos Ibarguren, of a leading family of Salta, who wanted the government to head off a leftist revolution by reinforcing existing mutual aid organizations, harmonizing with the organic processes that had created these associations, rather than artificially imposing new ones. Circles and Social Catholics collaborated with the Museo Social Argentino, founded in 1911, which conducted studies and spread information on the social question.[29]

As in Chile, Catholics played an important role in sponsoring legal change, often working with Socialists. Catholic deputy and circle member Santiago O'Farrell and Socialist deputy Alfredo L. Palacios, who had once belonged to a circle, were instrumental in passing a Sunday rest law in 1905, and Catholics and Socialists also cooperated in securing regulations on female and child labor in 1907. Catholics and circle participants favored a national labor code, but Socialist and employer opposition, along with the indifference of President Julio Roca (1880–86, 1898–1904), caused its defeat in 1904.[30]

The Military and the Ligas

The social question preoccupied not only Catholic upper-class reformers but military officers, whose strikebreaking duties and antileftist sentiments resembled those of their Chilean counterparts. As mandated in the law of 1901, which followed Chile's by one year, universal conscription was supposed to "Argentinize" and diminish the revolutionary ardor of immigrants as well as secure national defense. Nevertheless, the officer corps included many who sympathized with the UCR campaign for democracy, some of whom participated in that party's revolt of 1905. Moreover, the strong German influence on both the Argentine and Chilean military was not necessarily antidemocratic.[31]

Between 1898 and 1901, Argentina and Chile nearly warred over a series of border incidents, triggering patriotic feeling. The conscription law and other military reforms, as well as the procurement of naval vessels, indicated the widespread concern over the country's defenses. So, too, did the nationwide rise of Ligas Patrióticas, which trained men to drill and use arms, reinforced patriotism, and supported government efforts to seek concessions from Chile and strengthen the armed forces. For their part, married and single women formed Ligas Patrióticas de Señoras and Señoritas, respectively, which helped raise money for weapons. The membership of the Ligas was diverse, including military officers, members of the native-born and immigrant elites, and Social Catholics. The local groups coalesced into the Liga Patriótica Nacional, which sponsored rallies and public demonstrations. In one meeting Estanislao Zeballos, a longtime social Darwinist exponent of Argentine expansionism, emphasized the need for strengthening the military, the nation's influence abroad, and internal cohesion through democratic reforms. Other Liga members, however, tended to divide immigrants into the good ones who collaborated with the Liga and the bad ones who did not, and they blamed the second group for national disunity and weakness. Such rhetoric helped create the climate for vigilante actions in 1910.[32]

Conclusion

All the threads led back to the interconnected immigrant and leftist threats perceived by an incipient, largely upper-class extreme right. It identified immigrants with the left and *argentinidad* with native-born supporters of the status quo. The overwhelmingly foreign character of the working class and the Creole composition of the upper class permitted this identification. In contrast, it was difficult for the more plebeian Chilean precursors to make this connection in their country, where workers were overwhelmingly native-born. Nor did the emerging extreme right hesitate to use violence when it perceived a threat from the formidable labor movement and from Jews. Nationalism in prosperous Argentina was largely cultural in character, whereas in its poorer neighbor it was heavily economic. The strong export economy buttressed liberalism and the liberal ruling party, the PAN, which had no genuine Catholic conservative rival. Radical rightist sentiments in Argentina were tied more closely to the church and its marginalized supporters than in Chile, where Catholics had their own party base. Both Chileans and Argentines regarded womanhood as a metaphor for internal dissolution and foreign domination, yet this did not preclude female roles in Social Catholicism and, in Argentina, the secular Ligas. Although the military was by no means monolithic, its antileftism and ties to the Liga Patriótica Nacional indicated its potential support for the extreme right.

CHAPTER 3

Brazil: A Fractured Republic

As in Argentina and especially Chile, Brazilian precursors denigrated the prevailing economic model and political system as inattentive to local needs. Other targets of criticism were foreign capitalism, labor, and immigrants, although antisemitism was less pervasive than anti-Portuguese sentiments. Authoritarian, nationalist, and centralizing notions gained popularity among military officers, the middle sectors, and some disenchanted upper-class elements. Brazil's racial composition, monarchist tradition, church-state disestablishment, and late shift to a republic distinguished it from the other countries and affected the evolution of the extreme right.

Prado and Monarchism

After the military toppled the empire in 1889, Brazil became a republic under a constitution similar to that of the United States. In practice, the two countries' polities differed considerably. In Brazil, landowners and bosses dominated the rural areas, and the governors of the most powerful states chose the presidents. The former ruling parties, the Liberals and Conservatives, ended along with the empire; to remain active, some of their members joined the Republicans, who splintered into state-level parties that spoke for local oligarchies. The national government represented shifting alliances of these state elites. Given the limited electorate and federal authority, these oligarchies exercised considerable control over their states. Behind these structures stood the military.[1]

During the difficult transition that marked these changes from the empire to the republic, some Brazilians clamored for a return to monarchy. They included politicians and officeholders of the imperial era, members of traditional rural elites, and Catholics. Among these monarchists was Eduardo Prado. A conservative Paulista (of São Paulo state), unlike other restorationists he had not occupied any official role in the old regime, and his family's wealth stemmed from the dynamic coffee sector. Only when the empire fell in 1889 did the longtime Parisian resident turn to political writing and activism.[2]

In *Fastos da dictadura militar no Brasil* (1890), Prado praised the former regime for promoting civilian rule, limiting the power of the military, and preventing regional rivalries, revolutions, and *caudilhos* (strongmen) from undermining national unity. Now, however, Brazil was in danger of splitting apart, as had so often happened in Spanish America. Republican corruption and financial mismanagement contrasted markedly with the empire's sound fiscal standing.[3]

Prado's monarchism was not of the counterrevolutionary European mode, for in many ways he identified with liberalism. He contrasted the new United States of Brazil, whose citizens paid taxes to a government they did not choose, with the free and dignified United States of North America. (That the tiny Brazilian electorate had voted only for the deputies under the empire seemed to escape him.) More strikingly, Prado denounced the republic's dictatorial bent and arbitrary deportations and imprisonments. The monarchy deserved praise for upholding "liberal institutions" and abstaining from violence against citizens. The choice was between liberty and tyranny, Prado affirmed, clearly identifying liberty with the empire.[4]

Prado's liberalism did not completely extend to religious matters, but even his views on this subject were moderate. He claimed that the republic had not truly separated church and state, since it had awarded primacy to the positivist "religion of humanity." Seemingly criticizing any official creed, Prado excused the Catholic Church's former status by pointing out that it had represented millions of the faithful, while the few positivists were mostly seekers of public employment. Increasingly pious in his later years, in subsequent works Prado praised the church for uniting the races under one faith and otherwise contributing to Brazilian colonial development. Prado never discussed the disagreements between Pedro II (1840–89) and the church, perhaps to avoid criticizing the emperor he admired. Nor did he seem familiar with the leading European Catholic writers of the day.[5]

Prado's second book, *A ilusão americana* (1893), was more conservative than the first. Although he still revered the empire and Pedro II for putting liberal ideas into practice, he emphasized that the desire to conserve the best features of the past had led the founders to retain the monarchy and other colonial structures. While the parliamentary system and the constitution were new, to a certain extent they, too, resembled historical institutions. Thus Prado downplayed the influence of revolutionary European ideas on the independence era.[6]

Prado faulted republican leaders for imitating the U.S. model, noting that one could not import another "race's" institutions. Moreover, the United States disdained Latin America and wanted to dominate it—a goal that the republican government, with its romantic notion of hemispheric unity, was unwittingly helping to fulfill. Prado condemned the United States for its violence against Indians and blacks; nor was its pragmatic, utilitarian nature to his liking. His most telling critique of that nation focused on its class relations. Bourgeois republics permitted capitalist abuses on a scale unseen in other types of states, he claimed. In the United States, the "plutocratic class" ruled "with greater rigor and more tyranny than the czar of Russia," and its privileges outweighed those of the clergy or nobility in medieval Europe. This class had appropriated the freedoms won under the revolution of 1789, and there were no effective limits on its power. Industrial protectionism, the bribing of politicians, and the use of private armies against strikers enabled capitalists to control and impoverish the rest of society for their own benefit. Given these conditions, as well as the fact that the working class included the most capable and ambitious European laborers, the U.S. proletariat probably represented a greater threat to order than the European.[7]

There was an additional reason why the social question threatened the United States more than Europe. European monarchs understood that social instability could undermine not only their personal rule but the very form of government itself; thus it was in their interest to promote the welfare of all. This spirit of conservation did not characterize leaders of republics, who ruled in a transitory and individualistic fashion and tended to postpone troubling social issues. Thus in his opinion monarchies had carried out the great social reforms in history.[8]

Prado noted that the social question had characterized all time periods, and there was no permanent solution to it. In the ancient world, Christianity had relieved some of the suffering of slavery. Now slavery had ended, but the belief in the hereafter had also diminished, leaving workers impoverished and despairing. Ignoring Otto von Bismarck's authoritarianism and anticlericalism, Prado praised his alliance of crown, labor, and church against greedy capitalists as a new means of facing the social question. Reinforced by Social Catholicism, such an alliance was Prado's hope for the age.

Prado's Catholicism as well as his distaste for bourgeois materialism may well have influenced his prejudice against Jews. The Portuguese novelist José Maria de Eça de Queiroz described his friend's sentiments as those of the medieval church rather than modern France, despite Prado's long residence there. Still, contemporary currents of French antisemitism may have led Prado to identify Jews with the hated economic system; in *A ilusão americana* he divided capitalism into the categories of "semite or not semite." This identification was also apparent in a letter describing a business trip to London, where Prado resolved his financial matters by wandering the City from "Jew to Jew." Whether the motive behind his antisemitism was economic or religious, as for Julián Martel and Nicolás Palacios it had little to do with Jews in his country, who amounted to a handful in the Amazon and the northeast and about three thousand in Rio de Janeiro by 1900. This tiny collectivity received little national attention, although a few had become visible as businessmen in the capital. Thus, the frankness and intensity of Prado's views made him unusual among Brazilians of the era.[9]

Aside from his antisemitism, Prado was not an easy figure for the right to claim. He defended liberalism against an authoritarian state, and moderation tempered his Catholicism. His monarchism had little lasting impact, since this movement faded over time, although many extreme rightists would share Prado's fondness for the empire. Prado's devotion to tradition and slow organic change, his opposition to the United States and other foreign models, his piety and desire for a harmonious social order, and his antisemitism further inspired future activists. So, too, did his indictment of capitalist materialism and exploitation, one unaccompanied by any critique of the private ownership system from which his family had handsomely profited. Finally, Prado's critical dissection of the republican form of government ironically convinced many readers that liberal institutions promoted national weakness.[10]

Nativism and Nationalism

Economic difficulties beset the young republic and prompted nativist sentiments. Droughts and the abolition of slavery resulted in declining food production, and an unfavorable exchange rate increased the cost of food imports. Because wages did not keep pace with the soaring prices of the early

1890s, the urban working and middle sectors faced hardship. Some members of these groups blamed immigrants for their problems. Between 1872 and 1930, 2.2 million foreigners settled permanently, about the same number as in Argentina between 1870 and 1910. Immigration did not have as dramatic an effect on Brazil, however, as it had a much larger base population than Argentina and the newcomers entered over a longer period. In 1900, only 7 percent of the Brazilian population was foreign-born, compared with a third for Argentina in 1914. Still, immigrants accounted for a large share of the population of São Paulo state and the federal capital, the economic centers of the nation: respectively, 23 and 26 percent in 1900. In Rio de Janeiro, the Portuguese constituted 24 percent of the population and owned about 50 percent of the retail shops in 1890. A Portuguese diplomat in the 1890s estimated that his fellow citizens controlled perhaps 70 percent of financial, commercial, and real estate investment in the city. Their dominant position in business led many to blame the sharp price increases on the Portuguese, as did a long history of such charges dating back to the 1700s.[11]

Political instability also contributed to Lusophobia and nationalism. Military uprisings and disorders filled the early republican era, and the most serious of these, the naval revolt of 1893–94, won the support of Prado and other monarchists. President Marshal Floriano Peixoto (1891–94) and his forces suppressed this attempted revolution, aided by civilian "patriotic battalions" fomented and armed by the regime. When two Portuguese ships in Rio's harbor took in members of the naval conspiracy and refused to surrender them, Peixoto broke relations with Portugal. The assumption of the presidency by Prudente de Morais (1894–98), a representative of the Paulista coffee elite, troubled the Lusophobic republicans, for they regarded him as soft on monarchism. The president's renewal of relations with Portugal in 1895, after that country arrested the officers responsible for giving asylum, confirmed their beliefs.[12]

Willing to go to extreme lengths to defend the republic against attack, real or imagined, the Jacobinos consolidated during and after the naval revolt. This amorphous movement included patriotic battalions and republican clubs, which had spread throughout cities of the interior. The young officers, enlisted men, students, store owners, and clerical and other workers who filled Jacobino ranks wanted a forward-looking republic that would take power from the landed elites and implement policies enabling fellow native-born urbanites to advance. Jacobinos publicized their views in Congress, their own newspapers, and demonstrations. Violence against the Portuguese accompanied their fiery rhetoric.[13]

More sweeping than that of the Chilean Ligas, Jacobino discourse re-volved around ethnic nationalism. Jacobinos blamed the Portuguese for con-trolling prices, rentals, exchange rates, and prostitution. By introducing slav-ery and delaying independence and later the republic, the Portuguese had impeded Brazilian progress. Jacobinos proposed confiscating Portuguese-owned real estate, but their prescriptions went beyond simply reining in this group. They advocated expelling the foreign-born from the military and state bureaucracy, as well as exiling aliens who criticized Brazil. Ironically, the Jacobinos also wanted to expel Brazilian families who allowed their children to marry Portuguese residents. For dominating international trade and sup-porting the Brazilian monarchy, Great Britain earned their dislike. So did Europe as a whole, as the source of monarchical institutions. This anti-Europeanism pushed the Jacobinos to the Pan-American stance that Prado had lambasted.[14]

The Jacobinos managed to implement their slogan of "Brazil for the Brazilians" in concrete ways. They supported protecting local manufactur-ers, and Peixoto offered industries financial aid and exemptions from duties on raw materials and machinery. These policies, along with existing high tariff barriers, contradicted the lower prices also favored by Jacobinos. Peixoto's administration, however, facilitated the sale of inexpensive food-stuffs and the construction of cheap housing, thus meeting Jacobino con-cerns over the high cost of living. Partly for these reasons, Jacobinos revered Peixoto and created a cult around him after his death. However, Congress failed to pass a Jacobino bill to "nationalize" retail commerce, that is, to put it under private local control, as some had also urged in Chile.[15]

The Jacobinos' support for obligatory primary education and their ha-tred for the upper-class law school graduates who dominated government indicated their desire for equality. One of their newspapers, *O Jacobino*, claimed to defend the "national proletariat" by seeking the eight-hour working day, lower prices, and help for native-born Brazilians, goals shared by unions. Paternalism and a sense of distance, however, marked Jacobino sympathy for workers. A number of labor activists criticized Peixoto's poli-cies, noting that workers could not afford the new housing his regime spon-sored, nor could the marshal's distrust of foreigners and radical workers have pleased them. Yet some leaders of the fledgling union movement in Rio had Jacobino origins and shared the Jacobinos' paternalist and posi-tivist tendencies.[16]

This style of egalitarianism and economic nationalism assumed prior-ity over democracy. To protect the republic and Peixoto's programs, Jacobinos initially favored a strong executive and a weak legislature, but eventually they called for doing away with Congress and setting up a military dictatorship. Neither civil liberties nor the Catholic Church—suspect because of its ties to the monarchy—received Jacobino support. The struggle between soldiers and rebels in Canudos, Bahia, in 1896–97, immortalized by the journalist Euclides da Cunha, fanned fears of monarchism. In this apprehensive climate, some Jacobinos tried to kill the president they distrusted. This unsuccessful plot of 1897 gave Prudente de Morais an excuse to suppress the movement, although Jacobinos remained active in politics and participated in another fruitless revolt in 1904.[17] Anticlerical and egalitarian in certain respects, the Jacobinos nevertheless formed a precedent for the extreme right. Their protectionism and centralism set them and their heirs apart from the conservative landowning state oligarchies, as did their desire to incorporate the urban masses into politics under firm authoritarian rule. Also foreshadowing future opinion was their tendency to attribute problems to certain ethnic groups, although they recognized the faults of the economic structure.

Positivism

Another important group, the positivists, influenced and overlapped the Jacobinos. Found among the middle class and the bureaucracy, positivism had a particularly strong base in the military, whose leaders received positivist-inspired teachings in military schools. Other influential adherents included governors in the southernmost state of Rio Grande do Sul and ten other states between 1890 and 1915.[18]

While different schools of positivist thought existed in Brazil, most agreed on certain core beliefs. Primary among these was the belief in the rule of a technocratic elite drawn from professionals and the military, which would guide the masses from a Catholic to a modern scientific outlook. Many espoused a centralist state capable of subduing chaotic regionalism and potential class conflict. Like the Jacobinos they accepted the notion of private property but criticized economic liberalism, assigning the state the job of encouraging industrialization. Some positivists supported immigration, but others believed that former slaves, rather than foreigners, should work the land.[19]

Positivists hoped to integrate the proletariat into society in order to ensure their vaunted "order and progress." Educating the masses, raising wages, and improving working conditions would help accomplish this task.

Preoccupied with the family as the base of society, positivists advocated paying men salaries sufficient to permit women to remain in the home and strengthen it. According to Raimundo Teixeira Mendes, a leading positivist philosopher, this required the "moralization" of rich and poor alike: the rich would fund the general welfare and the poor would accept the status quo. The positivist governors of Rio Grande do Sul implemented some of these policies. Júlio de Castilhos (1893–98) established universal elementary education, and Antônio Augusto Borge de Medeiros (1898–1907, 1914–28) instituted the nation's first workmen's compensation law in 1919. During the labor agitation that surrounded World War I, Borge de Medeiros also raised the wages of state workers and encouraged private employers to imitate him, which many did.[20] In this manner, positivists left an important paternalistic legacy.

Positivists viewed Catholicism as outmoded and supported the separation of church and state. Despite the enmity between positivists and the church, they agreed on many issues. Both emphasized safeguarding the family and infusing morality into society, thus ensuring social harmony, hierarchy, and private ownership of property. Both attributed contemporary problems to individualism and favored authoritarian over liberal rule. Positivists accepted the right of a disestablished church to hold property and assume a role in public life. Their rejection of positivistic thought notwithstanding, church spokesmen at times recognized that the movement defended their institutional interests.[21]

The Church and Women

Unlike in Chile, where the long-lasting party system neatly split along proclerical and anticlerical lines, the Brazilian church was not tied to any particular party. Catholicism had been the state religion under the empire, and despite the fact that Pedro II was a tepid Catholic and a strong regalist, the church had backed him, except during a conflict in the 1870s. The new government separated church and state, ending patronage and authorizing civil institutions and secular public education. Because the Republicans and the anticlerical Jacobinos did not support the besieged church, Catholics created their own party. Although expanding the church's role was its main aim, at least one branch combined economic nationalist with antisemitic sentiments.[22]

Voter fraud, divisions among Catholics, and particularly opposition from the hierarchy kept such efforts from prospering. This dissension re-

flected the institution's difficulties in reorienting itself after the disestablishment. Most priests bitterly opposed the republic and other aspects of modernity. An exception was Father Júlio Maria, who criticized the clergy for isolating the church from the people and the currents of change. He argued for
embracing democracy and the republic, which afforded the church autonomy and the opportunity to expand its institutional network. The task was
to inject religion into the republic by changing its laws, educational system,
and flag and reducing positivist influence. Moreover, he asked the clergy to
substitute an alliance with the people for the former empire's protection. The
church should no longer admonish the poor to be patient and resigned. Instead, it should follow Leo XIII and "subject the despotism of capital to the
laws of equity," securing for labor the dignity and justice it deserved.[23]

A paternalist at heart, Father Maria's support for the poor coexisted
with a belief in all classes accepting their station in life. While he favored
democracy and urged the church to spread a new message throughout society, he directed his words to the elite. This prefigured the model of church
collaboration with the upper class and the state that prevailed in the 1920s
and 1930s. Perhaps for these reasons, as well as for the "virile" stand he
urged priests to take, radical rightists of the 1920s would regard him as a
precursor. Still, most of the hierarchy and clergy in his lifetime considered
him subversive, in the same way that many of their Argentine and Chilean
counterparts viewed Social Catholics. Although they gradually reconciled
themselves to the republic's existence, they continued to oppose liberal
democracy and greater ties to the poor, preferring to cultivate their following among the upper and middle classes.[24]

The church started to organize groups for women. As in the other
countries, it stressed women's roles as educators and helpmates in the family and as philanthropists and guardians of purity in society at large. Here,
too, these efforts began in the Catholic schools, where nuns influenced pupils to work in such groups as the Asociações das Damas Católicas and Fil-
has de Maria. A teacher, philanthropist, poet, and contributor to Catholic
newspapers, Amélia Rodrigues founded the short-lived Liga das Senhoras
Católicas Bahianas (later called the Liga das Senhoras Católicas Brasileiras)
in 1909. Resembling its counterparts, yet also in tune with the positivist focus on moralization, the Liga tried to sanitize carnival celebrations, fashion,
and the mass media, and it opposed feminism, which was beginning to recruit among the growing numbers of female professionals. A Catholic
women's group also existed in Minas Gerais, the center of Catholic mobilization in Brazil before the 1920s, and perhaps in other states.[25]

Responding to Leo XIII's call and the growth of militant unions, laypersons and priests founded workers' circles and other labor organizations after 1900 in Recife, São Paulo, and other cities. Six thousand laborers had joined the circles by 1915. The numbers of Catholic workers were low compared with those of Argentina and Chile, reflecting the slower development of the Brazilian labor movement and church resistance to Social Catholicism.[26] Permitting the formation of cooperatives and syndicates without government authorization, the law of professional associations (1907) stimulated the growth of Catholic mutual aid societies and unions. Influenced by papal doctrine and Bismarck's legislation during his studies in Germany, the prominent industrialist Jorge Street believed that government should recognize legally constituted labor unions and regulate working conditions. Employers also had the duty to pay just salaries, reduce working hours, and offer educational, medical, and day-care services, which Street attempted to implement in the worker town he began to construct in São Paulo in 1912. Street's views, however, were hardly typical among employers.[27]

Probably influenced more by positivism than Social Catholicism, reformers passed other protective legislation. In 1891 the national government issued a decree regulating child labor in the federal capital, and the São Paulo authorities did the same for their state. A national decree in 1905 guaranteed the rights of farm laborers to their wages. Rarely, however, did officials enforce these laws.[28]

Opposition to Labor

One could not say the same of repressive measures. Police and state armies frequently suppressed strikes. For its part, management, like its counterparts elsewhere, used strikebreakers and other techniques, sometimes coordinated through employer associations, to weaken organized labor.[29]

As in Argentina, politicians and employers wielded the immigration issue against labor. In the 1890s, although only 10 percent of the national male workforce was foreign-born, 79 percent of the industrial workforce in São Paulo and 39 percent of that in Rio fell into that category, as did most unionists in these cities. Partly owing to the activists' links to Europe, São Paulo had a stronger anarcho-syndicalist base than Rio, where there was a greater tendency toward reformism among workers. Expedited by the federal deportation law of 1907, São Paulo and other states ejected foreign workers considered subversive. Brazil had expelled about 550 by 1921, and the mere threat of expulsion probably dampened militancy. Employers pitted native-born, often Afro-Brazilian strikebreakers against foreign-born laborers. Writers described unionists and labor radicals—whatever their ideology or background—as foreign conspirators bent on destroying the nation. As was the case in Argentina and Chile, they also insisted that the social question was foreign to Brazil and that socialism did not apply to this setting.[30]

Race

Like Argentine liberals, Brazilian leaders had hoped to attract immigrants in order to build the economy and "Europeanize" the society. Even more clearly than in underpopulated Argentina, in Brazil both aims were racist. Instead of training and settling former slaves, state and federal governments subsidized immigrants' travel fares and sold land cheaply to foreign colonists. This manifested not only their interest in lowering labor costs by creating a surplus but also their preference for whites over blacks. Influenced by social Darwinism and scientific racism, the upper class viewed Brazilians of color as inferior and blamed them for local problems. While some pessimists like Raymundo Nina Rodrigues, a doctor described as mulatto, interpreted the racial structure as an inherent impediment to progress, most of the elite believed that gradual "whitening" of the population, achieved partly through immigration, would enable the country to advance.[31]

By the turn of the century, some intellectuals were reconsidering the questions of immigration and race. The positivist stress on factual evidence gathered through observation of reality influenced them to study the Brazilian people rather than simply accept foreign dogma; however, sometimes this method led to equally racist conclusions. New European and U.S. theories emphasizing environment over race slowly filtered into Brazil in the early 1900s, although as yet they convinced few. Immigrant commercial prowess in Rio and immigrant union membership in São Paulo inspired resentment. So, too, did their mobility: foreigners owned 15 percent of rural properties in São Paulo in 1905 and 22 percent on its western coffee frontier. In reaction, writers began to criticize immigrants and extol native-born Brazilians, as did their Argentine peers.[32]

The classic study of Antônio Conselheiro's religious movement, *Os sertões* (1902), illustrated this racial ambivalence. The author, Euclides da Cunha, praised Conselheiro's mixed-race followers for adapting to the barren environment and at least implicitly regarded this group as the core of the future nation. Yet he defined these *caboclos*, or backwoodsmen, as mestizo, slighting the African contribution to their makeup; indeed, he denigrated mulattos and blacks. He also feared that miscegenation produced unstable people and therefore could promote chaos. Racist assumptions tempered his admiration for the inhabitants of the interior.[33]

Although literary critic Sílvio Romero acknowledged the indigenous and particularly African contributions to the economy and to a mixed race suited to local conditions, he concluded that progress required whitening. He therefore supported the immigration of Europeans, especially Germans. But he also wanted the government to focus colonization efforts on the former slaves and the native-born poor, joining similar calls by positivists. Most of all, Romero wanted Brazilians to build their own future confidently without recourse to foreign models.[34]

Some monarchists shared Romero's confidence in the homeland. In *Porque me ufano do meu paiz* (1901), the aristocratic conservative historian Afonso Celso eulogized the empire and listed among the glories of Brazil the achievements of Afro-Brazilians and *caboclos*. Eduardo Prado did not treat Afro-Brazilians in his works, but he respected the Indians and *caboclos* of the colonial era. He elevated what he saw as these true Brazilians over the "artificial cosmopolitanism" of the city of São Paulo.[35]

Also critical of foreigners, Alvaro Bomilcar was far more racially tolerant than other authors. A mulatto, this future radical rightist leader considered racial prejudice "the principal factor of all our social evils." Since little evidence supported the belief in white superiority or pure races, Bomilcar called for eschewing foreign racial doctrine and conducting serious empirical research on the aptitude of Brazilians. Hardly free of racial stereotypes, Bomilcar nevertheless believed that one could not blame people of color for Brazilian problems; the descendants of the Portuguese had ruled the country, he said, and they bore responsibility. The least cultured and, ironically, the "most mestizo" of Europeans, the Portuguese had brought racism to Brazil, and the Jacobino-tinged Bomilcar condemned their legacy and the Portuguese immigrants who nourished it. Instead of abandoning its own people, the government should ease their entry into commerce and industry and open the schools and naval officer corps to people of color and humble origins.[36]

Alberto Torres

The foremost nationalist of this period, Alberto Torres, also was relatively tolerant on race. A federal deputy, governor of Rio de Janeiro, and supreme court judge, Torres agreed with da Cunha, Romero, and Bomilcar on the need to avoid theories and immerse oneself in local research. In his positivist-influenced view, the belief in racial inequality, based on faulty foreign science, only served imperialist ends. All nations were ethnically diverse, and the achievements of the various races and racial mixtures in Brazil demonstrated their worth. At the same time, Torres cautioned against *mestiçagem* (race mixing), arguing that it did not help the groups involved and that it might harm them.[37]

However inconsistent these words, Torres sympathized with native-born Brazilians and opposed whitening. Well suited to the environment, indigenous and Afro-Brazilians would advance according to the laws of evolution. Brazil's problem was social, not racial; the masses lacked food, housing, and education. By reforming the economy, the government could inspire in them the same ambition and hope that enabled immigrants to succeed. Subsidizing immigration at the expense of the native-born was a "monstrosity," a policy that only enabled the planters to earn quick profits. Torres also opposed subsidizing immigration because it interfered with the natural processes that operated in harmony with the physical and social milieu to form the nationality, a belief in organicism reminiscent of the Argentine Carlos Ibarguren.[38]

Unlike other nationalists, Torres thought that Brazil should remain an agrarian nation, but he did not support the status quo. Recognizing that coffee exports had stimulated economic development, he also discerned a dangerous dependence on this commodity. Torres proposed that Brazil continue to produce for the foreign market, using export earnings to purchase goods unavailable locally, but that it shift toward smallholder production for the domestic market. Policies favoring small farmers would be the best means of feeding and employing the people and promoting stability. The government had to undo the long legacy of "depredating colonization," characterized by latifundia, the exhaustion of natural resources, inadequate food cultivation, and the extreme exploitation of labor. It should distribute land, tools, seed, and farm animals to needy residents, but he did not explain how the government would acquire the property. Among other measures, Torres advocated irrigation works, conservation, high taxes on unproductive and absentee-owned holdings, agricultural tariffs, and free primary and agricultural education to renew the rural areas.[39]

Torres viewed modern industrial urban life suspiciously. He opposed industrial protection partly because it encouraged migration to the cities, which were centers of dissolution and cosmopolitanism containing extreme wealth differences that threatened the social order. Revolutions could not

heal these ills, for they offered only "subjective panaceas" and sometimes resulted in new problems. For example, the individualism of the French Revolution had subdued state despotism only to create a capitalist variety that
abused the poor and set them against the rich. Nor was socialism any better
because it reduced incentive and portended another form of dictatorship.
Torres opposed utopian notions and did not expect the uneducated masses
to initiate reform: "The body feeds; it does not inspire, nor direct, the
brain." Instead, enlightened leaders should guide the nation along a middle
route between individualism and socialism. This was the path of social justice, which would ensure popular welfare yet maintain the natural inequalities between individuals. Torres regarded this and other aspects of his program as a "conservative and reorganizing restoration" that would stave off
revolutions.[40]

Foreign domination exacerbated Brazil's problems, Torres believed.
Foreign loans and credit subordinated the heavily indebted Brazil, as did
foreign companies and workers. Precluding exchange within the interior,
colonialism had oriented production and transportation completely toward
exports. Thus, trade enriched the metropoli yet impoverished Brazil. In
fact, Brazilian businessmen and bankers collaborated with foreigners in
draining the country of resources and capital. As a partial remedy, Torres
proposed requiring foreign companies to set up local headquarters and employ Brazilians. His indictment of imperialism stretched to include local intellectuals' "almost idyllic adoration for the foreign," which he identified as
the main obstacle to national consciousness and initiative.[41]

This adulation extended to the imitation of foreign political institutions. Brazil had experienced a surfeit of reforms based on vague utopian
theories, especially under the republic, but none had altered the grim reality. Liberals, "expert in destruction," had failed to organize the nation, while
reactionaries contentedly allowed the people to live in misery. Shifting back
and forth between the two extremes, Brazil had not progressed. Propelling
the country forward required abjuring exotic—and indeed all—models.
This meant replacing the foreign-inspired constitution with one grounded
in local realities. It also meant subjecting partisan politics—divisive, self-
serving, personalistic, and doctrinaire—to "an organic politics . . . of the
whole, of harmony, of equilibrium."[42]

Torres believed that "government of the people by the people" was a
"fiction"; it was "time to substitute for it 'government of the people for the
people.'" Recalling aspects of the monarchy, his proposed constitutional reforms aimed at preventing democracy, harmonizing representative govern-

ment with the permanent interests of society, and organizing a chaotic nation. A system of largely indirect elections would select most officeholders, and various interest groups would choose the rest. Consisting of certain local officials and others nominated by high-ranking leaders, the Coordinating Power would occupy terms for life.[43] Through these means Torres intended to put enlightened nonpartisan statesmen in power, although it was unclear how the new process would ensure institutional reform.

Torres envisioned a powerful centralized state between "radical individualism" and "utopian collectivism." It would take such powers as taxing exports from the states. The Coordinating Power would authorize federal interventions in the states under many more conditions than the republic, and it would also resolve conflicts between different levels of authority, determine policies, and foster national consciousness. An Institute for the Study of National Problems would research local conditions to influence policy.[44]

Torres's "ideology of the state," as Bolivar Lamounier called it, set the radical rightist agenda for the future. This agenda included an antiliberal, corporatist state and an organic society that overrode class and other divisions. A benevolent dictatorship would solve social problems through technocratic planning.[45] Future extreme rightists would share Torres's faith in institutional change and a "third position" between socialism and liberalism. His disdain for abstractions and utopian solutions would appeal to them, as would his opposition to racism, immigration, imperialism, and the class conflict and diverse ethnic composition of cities.[46] Torres's qualms about economic dependence on coffee combined with support for private property also heralded radical rightist thinking.

The Military

Sharing with Torres a marked positivist influence, many military officers agreed with him on the need for a centralized, authoritarian, and technocratic state. Floriano Peixoto and his Jacobino allies saw the citizen-soldier as one who rid the nation of corrupt politicians. When this moralizing task failed, and especially once military training began in Germany after 1905, some officers formulated a new mission resembling that of their Chilean peers. The only stable institution in a chaotic nation, the army would not only suppress disorder but help develop the country and educate its people. This project predisposed its advocates toward an authoritarian nationalism.[47]

The army had assumed great prominence when it overthrew the mon-

archy and initially presided over the republic. Officers occupied more cabinet posts and congressional seats after 1889 than before. The existence of the
state-level militarized police forces, as well as the oligarchies' opposition to
a strong federal army, however, limited its power and fed resentment. These
factors also increased the army's dislike for the federal system.[48]

Workers' opposition to impressment, to the inadequate treatment of
soldiers, and to the law of obligatory military service (1908) probably alienated some military leaders from the laborers' cause. Still, the Brazilian army's
image was not as unpopular as that of the Argentine or Chilean armies. The
Força Pública of São Paulo and other police units, rather than the army, repressed labor struggles. Moreover, some positivist officers sympathized with
labor's economic demands. Thus military authoritarianism was not necessarily antiworker.[49]

Conclusion

The fragmented, unstable, and impoverished state of the republic prompted
nationalist concern. Influenced by positivism or monarchism, writers and
activists denounced liberalism and foreign domination. Some went on to
construct visions of a centralist authoritarian state, a project shared by military officers. These figures set themselves apart from the state oligarchies
complicit in the liberal federalist system. Hatred for Portuguese-owned enterprises helped inspire the nationalist Jacobinos in the 1890s. Regarding
racism as a foreign import, some precursors viewed the black component of
the population relatively tolerantly. Reflecting the weakness of organized labor and the church, Social Catholicism as yet barely influenced Brazil, and
women played but a minor role in this small religious movement. Some
Catholics, however, were beginning to move toward nationalism.

CHAPTER 4

Conclusion

Precursors of radical rightist movements in Argentina, Brazil, and Chile agreed on many issues. They feared dissolution—which they attributed to immigration, labor protest, inept administration, imperialism, or other foreign threats—and the concomitant loss of national power and prestige. Among these dangers the foreign presence loomed largest in the eyes of the Chilean Ligas Patrióticas, Argentine vigilante groups, and Brazilian Jacobinos. The precursors opposed aspects of liberalism such as its weak model of government, corrupt partisan politics, and economic abuses, yet this ideology influenced them, as did positivism, particularly in Brazil. Officers of the three countries envisioned an important role for the military, as a reformist institution above pernicious political divisions, in forging a modernizing state. Although many precursors, especially in Argentina, belonged to the elite, they denounced it as greedy, cosmopolitan, and indifferent to local problems. In doing so they redefined the ruling class in terms of state of mind rather than control over production and government. This would become part of a strategy to defeat or offer an alternative to leftist thinking. Another important component of the alternative to the left would be the notion of helping the poor within a reformed capitalist system, a middle route between socialism and individualism, as heralded by Social Catholics and Alberto Torres. Greater local control over the national destiny without discarding private enterprise would also be part of this program.

These ideological threads set their spokespersons apart from the upper-class establishment, which benefited from the existing state of affairs and wanted to maintain it. Everywhere its wealth and power were based on land. The strength of the agrarian export sectors in Argentina and Brazil, and of their rural political base in Brazil and Chile, were the aristocrats' main concerns. The state possessed sufficient weapons to control organized labor, except in Argentina in 1909–10. Thus liberalism usually met upper-class interests. On religious matters the elites parted ways. The secularism of wealthy men in Argentina and Brazil reinforced their liberalism, but the Conservatives among the Chilean aristocracy were confessional. With these general concerns, elite parties and groups would solidify into the moderate right after 1914 in Argentina and Chile. Brazilian moderate rightists remained fragmented into regional groupings.

Apart from these similarities, one notes many differences. Upper-class Argentine precursors directed themselves against foreign-born rivals below them. Chilean and Brazilian precursors were of broader social composition. With their middle-class components, the Brazilians and Chileans were more willing to denounce the prevailing economic model than the Argentine landed elite, which profited heavily from it. That the benefits of export-oriented growth were not as evident in Brazil and Chile also affected radical rightist rhetoric.

In addition, nativist currents reflected the impact of immigration and conquest. Opposition to the Portuguese was marked in Brazil. The Peruvian residents of the north, rather than the scant numbers of Europeans, were the main target of ire in Chile, although antisemitism and other forms of prejudice were present. Antisemitic sentiments were more pronounced in Argentina, with its large Jewish community, than in the other countries. Still, as succeeding chapters will demonstrate, demography does not account fully for the patterns of prejudice.

Race was a more critical issue for Brazil than for Argentina and Chile. The mass arrival of Europeans had whitened much of Argentina, so its extreme rightist precursors paid relatively little attention to the issue of people of color, compared with other Argentines and with their Brazilian and Chilean peers. Despite Francisco Encina's pessimism, other Chileans manipulated social Darwinist ideas to prove the superiority of Chilean mestizos. Brazilian authors could not ignore the many impoverished Afro-Brazilians who only recently had attained freedom. Although the elites generally favored "whitening" the population, a few thinkers such as Torres and Alvaro Bomilcar, while not discarding social Darwinism, moved toward racial tolerance.

The strength of the labor movement and the left was another variable.

Workers appeared to pose a greater threat to the status quo in Chile and especially Argentina than in Brazil, giving the incipient far right in Argentina a concern to rally around. Thus the Argentine far right was closer to consolidation than the forces in the other nations.

A reaction to the working class, Social Catholicism, was more vigorous in Argentina and Chile than in Brazil, as was female participation in it. In general, the church in Argentina and particularly Brazil was alienated from the state. Eventually this dissatisfaction would push local Catholic militants to the extreme right.

Women were barely beginning to enter the political arena and the incipient far right. Only in Argentina did they join a secular right-leaning group in this period. Nevertheless, gendered imagery enriched the precursors' language in Chile and Argentina. Here, writers identified weakness with femininity and strength with masculinity; in view of these links, it is not surprising that radical rightist movements would be heavily male in composition.

Political traditions also affected the development of the extreme right. Chile had the best-established party system of the three countries. In Chile, the moderate right had a natural home in the Conservative Party, a base lacking in the other nations, and to a lesser extent in the Liberal Party. As will be seen, the ruling party of Argentina, PAN, was divided. The end of the Brazilian monarchy also witnessed an end to its two major parties, and the Republicans split into state-level groups. Thus there would be more space available for rightists in Argentina and Brazil to form new extremist factions than in Chile.

In this early period the extreme right had not yet consolidated. Writings, programs, and ephemeral groups contained elements of this type of thought and action and hinted at future developments. Nativist violence, opposition to liberalism and the elite, and an emerging alternative to leftist thinking distinguished some precursors from moderates, but the distinctions were not firm. Still, Argentina and Brazil already showed greater potential for rightist extremism than Chile.

PART 2

The Era of the Ligas: World War I to the Mid-1920s

World War I and its aftermath was a period of turmoil in Latin America. In this climate of instability and democratic challenge, rightists shifted from rhetoric and episodic acts to forming extraparliamentary groups. Usually catalyzed by labor mobilization, these groups began to formulate an alternative to the left. Their nationalism consisted of opposition to immigrants, foreign dangers, and leftist internationalism. The extremists' interests and personnel often overlapped the military, government, and moderate right, yet relations among them were sometimes ambivalent. Women increased their involvement, as did the Catholic Church, which left its imprint on radical rightist ideology.

The differences among the three countries sharpened during this period. Besieged by laborers and political reformers, the moderate right in Argentina was the least secure. Represented by the Conservatives in Chile, the church still felt alienated from the political arena in Argentina and Brazil. For these reasons the extreme right evolved the furthest in Argentina, with Brazil in second place and Chile in third.

CHAPTER 5

Chile: Defending the Fatherland

This was a turbulent period in Chilean history. Workers, leftist students, and reformers mobilized for social and political change throughout the country. They clashed with rightists of all hues who resisted the threats from the left, from Chile's neighbors, and from presidential candidate Arturo Alessandri. Catholics and women continued their social welfare activities and participated in the opposition to labor, to Alessandri, and, in effect, to democracy. Nevertheless, the moderate right retained vigor, and the extreme right did not coalesce into strong and lasting organizations.

These events occurred within an erratic economic climate. The nitrate industry on which Chile depended first experienced a severe depression from 1914 to 1915, then rose to the height of its production from 1916 to 1918 before undergoing another crisis from 1919 to 1923. During the first and third periods, businesses slashed wages and laid off thousands. At the same time, the cost of living skyrocketed. The average working-class family in Santiago and Valparaíso spent an average of 64 percent of its income on food in the years 1912 to 1925, and the price of food rose 138 percent between 1913 and 1919 alone. According to Bergquist, in terms of inflation, the duration and depth of the postwar depression, and the oscillating demand for labor, world economic forces affected Chile more than any other South American nation. The economic crisis reinforced criticism of economic liberalism, already widespread before 1914.[1]

59

Border Tensions, Labor, and the Ligas

The conflict among Chile, Bolivia, and Peru over Tacna-Arica flared anew during World War I. Bolivia and Peru aligned with the United States in the war, astutely distinguishing themselves from neutral Chile. The Peruvians linked the settlement of Tacna-Arica with Woodrow Wilson's belief in self-determination, and Chileans feared that the League of Nations would award the entire territory to Peru.

In this context, anti-Peruvian nativism and Ligas Patrióticas emerged from dormancy in northern Chile. During Liga rallies in early November 1918, crowds in Pisagua and Iquique vandalized Peruvian-owned property. On November 23 in Iquique, after greeting the arrival of a Chilean journalist expelled from Peru, a throng pounced on Peruvians, their social club, and their businesses. The local Peruvian consul, Santiago Llosa Arguelles, had already demanded guarantees of Peruvian safety; now a mob assaulted Llosa as he headed to the intendant's office to protest the latest violence and forced him to board a ship for Peru. Accepting the vigilantes' action, local authorities confined the consul to the vessel. In response, Peru repatriated its consuls; Chilean consuls had already begun to leave Peru.[2]

Thus far the government had not responded to northern demands for action. Indeed, the governor of Tarapacá warned the local Liga to abstain from further demonstrations and violence, and the foreign relations ministry asked the press not to push the nation into war. Yet "patriots" such as Anselmo Blanlot Holley urged that strong national measures be taken against the supposed Peruvian threat. A veteran of the War of the Pacific, leader of the Balmacedista Liberal Democrats, deputy from Tarapacá, and a participant in anti-Peruvian rallies, Blanlot denounced the presence of disloyal foreigners and Peruvian agents in the north.[3]

Privileged Chileans faced an internal as well as external threat. The organizational efforts of the working class had risen to new heights during the war. Founded by Conservatives in 1909, the Federación Obrera de Chile (FOCh) turned from mutualism to struggle when it came under the control of the Socialist Workers Party in 1917. In 1921 FOCh affiliated with the Communist International, and the next year the Socialist Workers Party became the Communist Party. FOCh, together with the anarcho-syndicalist International Workers of the World (IWW), which reached Chile in 1919, and other militant groups, carried out at least 229 strikes in Santiago and Valparaíso alone between 1917 and 1921. Labor activism posed more of a threat to the nitrate export sector in the north and the coal and ranching areas in the south than to the elite's stronghold in the central valley.[4] Nevertheless, given the revolutionary climate in Europe and state dependence on mineral revenues, such activism anywhere alarmed the upper class.

The Asamblea Obrera de Alimentación Nacional (AOAN), organized by FOCh, mounted an impressive display of labor unity and strength in Santiago on November 22, 1918. Between 50,000 and 100,000 members of unions, mutual aid societies, and Catholic, student, and women's groups marched to La Moneda, the presidential palace, to demand lower food prices. *El Mercurio*, the voice of the establishment, praised the generally peaceful event, albeit patronizingly, and President Juan Luis Sanfuentes (1916–20) forwarded several AOAN proposals to Congress.[5]

Some members of the ruling class, however, regarded the demonstrators as impertinent and disrespectful of authority. That the AOAN petition defined patriotism to include feeding people and stimulating industry struck Blanlot and others as subversive. Deputy Nolasco Cárdenas of the pro-labor Democratic Party agreed with the AOAN that patriotism was not just a matter of war but of helping the poor, predicting that laborers would no longer automatically go into combat "at the sound of the bugles." Although some leftists came to his defense, the Chamber of Deputies censured Cárdenas and forced him to resign his position as its vice president. A residence law prohibiting the entry of subversive foreigners and facilitating their deportation had been introduced in Congress after a general strike in Valparaíso in 1917. Now Blanlot clamored for passage of this bill, which *El Mercurio* claimed would prevent foreign labor agitators from exploiting Cárdenas's words. It became law in December 1918.[6]

Yet foreigners accounted for only 3.2 percent of the Chilean population and 4.5 percent of the industrial workforce in 1920. Immigrants formed a larger component of the inhabitants in the extreme north and south—27.5 percent in Tacna, 15.3 percent in Tarapacá, 9.1 percent in Antofagasta, and 21.5 percent in southern Magallanes. Still, native Chileans made up 86–90 percent of those employed in the northern nitrate industry between 1919 and 1924, the remainder consisting largely of temporary migrant workers from Peru and Bolivia. Foreigners amounted to only 5.1 percent of workers in Valparaíso and 3.5 percent of those in Santiago, and labor leaders were native-born.[7]

Ignoring the paucity of foreigners, the fact that some workers and students had criticized Cárdenas, and the deputy's claim that he was a loyal Chilean, "patriots" identified laborers and their student allies as foreign opponents of nationalism. A group of wealthy citizens in southern Punta Arenas, a labor center, declared the need for a Liga Nacional that would halt foreign propaganda. Upper-class youths in Santiago suggested forming Ligas Patrióticas to combat the workers and socialists who agreed with Cárdenas.[8] The perceived Peruvian and worker dangers thus came together.

In the next few months Ligas emerged from hibernation and sponsored a flurry of events throughout Chile. While the extent of coordination between the groups is unclear, they shared aims and conducted similar activities. The Liga Patriótica Militar y Círculo de Oficiales Retirados (LPM) organized a parade through Santiago on November 30 that attracted groups of employees and Catholic workers and the Asociación Nacional de Estudiantes Católicos (ANEC), as well as reserve officers. Founded in 1915 as an alternative to the progressive Federación de Estudiantes de Chile (FECH), the Social Catholic-leaning ANEC included Catholic students and white-collar youth. FECH turned down an invitation to the parade, and nationalists accused FECH of pacifism and pro-Cárdenas sentiments. The LPM also hosted a reception honoring Blanlot on December 2. Over 60,000 attended the demonstration of the Liga Patriótica of Valparaíso on December 7, making it the largest event in the city's history. Rallies against Cárdenas and Peru spread to other cities.[9]

The Ligas attacked Peruvians rhetorically as well as physically. Liga newspapers in the north described Peruvians in the ugliest of racist terms and endangered their lives by publishing lists of, and derogatory articles on, "cholos" who were deemed offensive. They also listed Chilean merchants and professionals, encouraging people to patronize only these businessmen. Trying to appeal to labor, the Ligas berated "Jewish Peruvian" slum landlords for high rents. As in the past, they claimed that nitrate company managers favored Peruvian over Chilean workers and the expulsion of the former would help Chileans advance. The Ligas blamed Peruvians for the widespread view of Chilean workers as alcoholic and insolent. They attributed the spread of antinationalist doctrine among laborers to Peruvians as well, insisting they used all means possible to cultivate hatred against Chile.[10]

As one of their organs put it, the Ligas tried to "remove the anarchic blindfold" that "enemies of our fatherland" had placed on workers. Administrators and employees in several *oficinas* (nitrate installations) formed Ligas; in one of them, foremen pressured workers into attending Liga functions. *Liguistas* attacked the carpenters' union headquarters in Valparaíso, expelled Socialists from Oficina Sargento Aldea, and destroyed a leftist press in Iquique. In the last episode, the police detained Socialists rather than the assailants, indicating collusion. For their part, Socialists accused Blanlot of instigating the border conflict to promote his party and safeguard his sub-stantial real estate and sulfur-processing investments in the north. The AOAN added that the Balmacedista was trying to distract public opinion from the food issue.[11]

At least one Liga leader attempted to formulate a radical rightist ideology. The prestigious lawyer Belisario Salinas, who headed the Liga Patriótica y Unión Social of Antofagasta, called for returning to the "old values" of honor and work, and he blamed liberalism as well as communism on Peruvian bribes. Salinas tried to broaden the Liga's constituency by recommending such measures as subdividing property and lowering food prices. His program, however, did not expand membership beyond the retired officers, professionals, white-collar workers, government employees, and upper-class youth who filled the Ligas.[12]

A national strike wave in early 1919 brought the military into the political arena. Fearing a social revolution, several generals planned to offer support to President Sanfuentes if the May Day celebrations turned violent. They favored naming officers as intendants and governors, as well as lobbying Congress for military projects. Dedicated to these ends, the Sociedad Ejército de Regeneración held its first meeting in April 1919. In a parallel action, fifty naval and army officers adhered to a military junta, which wanted the president to suppress "political anarchy" and push through labor, fiscal, and military legislation. It seemed as if the junta would install a military dictatorship if the president faced opposition or refused its aid. The likely beneficiary of a coup was Arturo Alessandri, a Liberal senator from Tarapacá and presidential aspirant who attended junta meetings. Congressional immunity protected Alessandri from prosecution, but sixty officers were found guilty of plotting against the government.[13]

Left Versus Right

Whether as traditional politician or conspirator, Alessandri was equally objectionable to the elite. In the electoral campaign of 1920, as the candidate of the Liberal Alliance, which included Radicals, Democrats, and some Liberals, Alessandri advocated an income tax, arbitration of labor disputes, a ministry of labor and social prevision, and the separation of church and state. Except for the last proposal, the Conservatives, Nationals, and Liberals who made up the opposing National Union claimed to favor similar measures, so the platform did not make him controversial. Nor did his background, which was less august than that of his opponent, Luis

Barros Borgoño, the president of the exclusive Club de la Unión, but hardly modest. The Liberal Alliance, however, had somewhat less prestigious credentials than the National Union, which regarded Alessandri's supporters as upstarts. Alessandri's support for the residence law and other antilabor measures indicated his essential conservatism, yet his impassioned appeals to his *chusma querida* (beloved rabble) and his denunciation of the oligarchy repelled the elite. His upper-class detractors accused him of promoting class hatred and thus weakening Chile to aid Peru; indeed, they claimed he was in Peru's employ. They feared that his populist style and his followers' attacks on vote-buying augured their political decline. Their control of the countryside and the overrepresentation of these areas in Congress had made Conservatives the supreme party, and they particularly dreaded this change. Alessandri won the bitterly fought election of June 25, 1920, but so narrowly that Congress asked a tribunal to verify the results.[14]

Barros Borgoño's supporters seized upon the volatile border issue to try to divert attention from the unresolved election. On July 13 a coup overthrew the Bolivian government, which had been negotiating with Chile. Although the new Bolivian ruling party gave assurances of peace, some feared that Bolivia and Peru would take advantage of the divisive political situation in Chile. Rumors of Peruvian troops amassing on the border strengthened such anxieties. Only three weeks after the election, Minister of War Ladislao Errázuriz, an adherent of the National Union, mobilized the army and refurbished northern garrisons, shipping many pro-Alessandri officers to the border. Supporters of the Liberal Alliance saw in "Don Ladislao's War" an official attempt to steal victory from their candidate.[15]

In the ensuing weeks, a wave of patriotism engulfed the country. Even newspapers that had expressed moderate views on the border dispute, such as *El Mercurio*, shifted to an extreme nationalist position. Regaining notoriety, Ligas held huge demonstrations in Santiago and other cities, and new Ligas mushroomed—in at least one case formed by the government. The governor of Coronel province invited the heads of the political parties, officials, and other prestigious persons to form the Liga Patriótica of the department of Lautaro.[16]

Inactive since 1918, members of the Liga Patriótica de Valparaíso reconstituted the group in mid-July 1920, now calling themselves the Liga Patriótica Chilena. Its culminating event was a parade on July 24 attracting over 100,000 marchers, including municipal and provincial authorities, army and naval groups, professionals, laborers, and businessmen. One U.S.

diplomat believed that while this and other patriotic displays genuinely represented Chilean opinion, the government used them to curb class conflict; another thought that officials sought to divert attention from the resolution of the election.[17]

The Liga Patriótica Chilena applauded the provincial intendant for ordering all foreigners, starting with Peruvians, to sign a police register. Apparently this was not enough, for the Liga forced over 500 Peruvians in Valparaíso out of the country by early August. Similar expulsions took place in Iquique and Antofagasta. Although officials denied government complicity in the expulsions, police in Iquique arrested Peruvians on charges of involvement in the IWW.[18]

The electoral campaign and Don Ladislao's War had polarized political opinion. For students in Santiago there was no middle ground: they had to choose between left (FECH) or right (ANEC). Viewing Alessandri, a Mason, as the Antichrist, and fearing Conservative decline, ANEC supported the nominally Catholic Barros Borgoño, as well as the Ligas and the mobilization. Although its socialism, internationalism, and pacifism put it to the left of Alessandri, FECH backed him. On July 18 FECH asked the government to justify the mobilization and calm down the country. The ministry of justice and public instruction admonished the students for their impertinence; regarding FECH as nothing less than traitorous, rightist youth went further and attacked its Club de Estudiantes the next day. This "white guard" also destroyed the Numen press, which had printed IWW works opposing the mobilization, and assaulted its director, Santiago Labarca, a FECH member. Police arrested about twelve of the perpetrators, only to set them free at the station.[19]

The conflict between right and left escalated on July 21. A throng of men and women had accompanied the first reservists departing for the north to the train station. The young men in the crowd then passed by La Moneda, where they offered their services to Sanfuentes. Standing next to the president, Senator Enrique Zañartu, a Balmacedista member of the National Union, denounced FECH for selling out to Peru. A mob headed to its club, overwhelmed the police guards assigned by the government, and ransacked the premises. Alliance congressmen claimed the police, who did not call in reinforcements, and military officers participated in the assault. The fact that security forces detained four FECH members yet none of the perpetrators seemed to confirm official complicity.[20]

That same evening, leftist youths neared a group of rightists who were parading downtown. Perhaps avenging the attack on FECH, a leftist shot and killed Ignacio Alfonso, a Liberal, and Julio Covarrubias Freire, scion of an upper-class Conservative and Social Catholic family, who was carrying the Chilean flag. All the leftists but one eluded the police, who had not been present at the scene.[21]

Reactions to the violence divided along partisan lines. LPM leaders proposed a statue of Covarrubias, and the Chamber of Deputies paid him homage. Some Aliancistas denounced both the sacking of the club and the murders, but other congressmen excused the first action. "When the question of defending the fatherland arises, no one has the right to raise the flag of antipatriotism," pronounced Conservative senator Gonzalo Bulnes. Ironically, Zañartu declared that he could not justify the raid, adding that he could not reproach those responsible, either.[22]

Covarrubias's funeral on July 23 celebrated the elite's notion of national unity against the leftist threat. Representatives of government and upper-class, business, and Catholic groups marched to the cemetery, symbolically claiming the city streets for their views. Invited by *El Mercurio*, society women turned out in unprecedented numbers. A reporter praised them for their patriotism, observing that "the woman, when she lets herself be carried away by her marvelous instinct for danger, which is always an instinct for love, rarely errs." Through the presence of 3,000 upper-class women, many of them Red Cross volunteers, the right appropriated female purity, maternal feeling, and selflessness for the national cause. Deemed untrustworthy, workers were absent from this display of nationalism.[23]

Responding to these events, FECH announced it did not need lessons in patriotism from "illiterate sportsmen." FECH regretted Covarrubias's death, yet it also protested the arbitrary imprisonment of the four students who had defended the club. It demanded that the government ground the mobilization in reality instead of lies. Responding to the Ligas' requests, the government annulled FECH's juridical personage on July 24 and arrested FECH leaders. Authorities continued to harass students and workers in Santiago and Valparaíso.[24]

Meanwhile, workers were mobilizing in the far south, under the auspices of the Federación Obrera de Magallanes (FOM), formed in 1911. Tied to FOCh, FOM organized laborers in the ranches, meatpacking plants, urban skilled trades, and ports. It pressured employers into signing collective contracts, hiring union members, and paying cash wages, and it also restricted sales of alcohol. By 1920 the FOM had about 4,000 members, representing half of the population of Magallanes; it boasted a press and two newspapers, a vibrant institutional network, and ample strike funds. During a general strike from late 1918 to early 1919, union members briefly took control of Puerto Natales. Battles took place between Carabineros and FOM militants, with losses of life on both sides and considerable property damage. Businessmen and officials blamed FOM, particularly its few foreign members, for driving up production costs, dictating terms, and spreading leftism. Authorities were determined to repress the troublesome labor organization, which Senator Bulnes called an "international soviet."[25]

Their opportunity came during Don Ladislao's War. Landowners, businessmen, professionals, government officials, and police and military officers, including the commander of the Magallanes battalion, formed a Liga Patriótica in Punta Arenas on July 24. Its patriotic rally the next day, which featured a speech by Governor Alfonso Bulnes, nephew of the Conservative senator, attracted a large crowd. Angered by labor's absence, young Liguistas headed from the demonstration to FOM, where they tried to provoke an incident. Unsuccessful, they marched to *El Magallanes*, a newspaper critical of the patriotic wave, but the police prevented them from attacking the building. As Democratic deputy Manuel O'Ryan later pointed out, the governor must have understood the Liga's aims, but planned nothing to protect workers.[26]

Indeed, the authorities were involved in the subsequent violence. The evening of July 26, Commander José Barceló Lira and Lieutenant Eduardo Cristi of the local battalion, acting Police Prefect and Army Major Aníbal Parada, and other Liga members met in the Club Magallanes to map out an attack. Parada, also known as "El Macho," had helped repress labor in Iquique and, according to the U.S. consul, was stationed in Punta Arenas to do the same. Early on July 27, armed youth, police, Carabineros, and masked military personnel in plainclothes swarmed the streets around FOM headquarters. Parada and Cristi, as well as other leading policemen, were present, and one eyewitness claimed to have recognized Bulnes, sporting false sideburns. The throng fired shots at the wooden edifice, while police entered the premises, killing workers and destroying the printing press of *El Trabajo*. The building soon burst into flames; officials attributed the fire to explosions of FOM's supposed dynamite caches. Police and army units prevented firemen from approaching the building and turned off the water until FOM and the surrounding structures were smoldering ruins. Twelve Federados and one policeman perished. In a separate action that night, assailants beat the director of another FOM organ, *El Socialista*, and his wife, and demolished their home and the newspaper office.[27]

A news blackout and virtual state of siege followed these events. FOM declared a five-day general strike, and Carabineros and soldiers patrolled the streets, breaking up groups, keeping workers from leaving Punta Arenas, and detaining FOM leaders. Reports of torture and killings later surfaced. Deputies complained that the authorities in Magallanes screened telegrams and the mail, keeping news from reaching Santiago. The two major local papers did not appear for three days after the fire, and when they did, the authorities pressured them into silence about the incident. Eventually congressmen pieced together the story using dispatches from Argentina and letters from eyewitnesses.[28]

In the meantime, the government's version dominated the press and Congress. Governor Bulnes's report, approvingly read by Minister of the Interior Pedro García de la Huerta in the Senate, claimed that either gunfire within FOM or Federados firing on "patriots" outside began the episode, and Parada and the police rushed there after the shooting began. Whatever its causes, Bulnes added, the fire had "sanitized the territory."[29]

Bulnes's statement and callous conclusion only raised questions and provoked anger among Democrats and Radicals. These doubts forced García de la Huerta to change his story. Now he insisted that the late hour had prevented authorities from arriving quickly to stop the shooting between nationalists and antinationalists. Blaming the incident on foreign radicals, the minister argued for permitting the governor of the southern territory to deport such persons, which the administration quickly authorized.[30]

These shaky justifications did not hide official complicity. Military, police, and civilian leaders belonged to the Liga, attacked FOM, and tried to cover up the event. If not an actual party to the violence, Bulnes at least approved of the Liga and its actions, as did the national administration. As in the cases of Numen and FECH, no one ever prosecuted the assailants. Bulnes resigned his office but assumed another government post, and Barceló Lira and Parada eventually received promotions.[31]

Border and labor tensions subsided temporarily with the resolution of the election. The absence of Peruvian and Bolivian troops on the border and the abysmal conditions for Chilean soldiers had discredited "Don Ladislao's War." So, too, had rumors of corruption. Meanwhile, the electoral tribunal, fearful of Alessandri's *chusma querida* (beloved rabble), confirmed his victory on September 20. With this announcement, the mobilization ended. After Alessandri took office in December, he appointed a new governor and police prefect in Magallanes, who leaned toward labor, and this helped assuage FOM's feelings.[32]

During the peak of left/right conflict in July and August 1920, *El Mer-*

curio had argued that Chile needed a permanent nationalist organization. A new group attempted to fulfill this role. The municipal government of Santiago designated a committee to plan a commemoration of the battle of Iquique for May 21, 1921. When the event proved successful, some of its organizers proposed a permanent nonpartisan body to sponsor patriotic celebrations, stimulate nationalism, and repel foreign subversion. The self-styled Comité Patriótico Permanente met with government officials and representatives of the LPM and two upper-class women's groups—the Liga de Damas Chilenas and the secular Club de Señoras, founded in 1915, which hosted social events and encouraged women's intellectual development through courses and lectures. Nevertheless, the organization languished.[33]

Nor did the Ligas fill the gap. Under Sanfuentes, the elite had received ample official support against leftist students and workers. The upper class still perceived a leftist threat, but this threat did not force extraparliamentary rightist groups to consolidate. Nor had the Ligas and Comité conceived patriotism broadly enough to make it appealing to wider segments of the population. In addition, the negligible foreign presence among workers rendered hollow the right's attempt to identify the left with non-Chileans. Despite the Ligas' comments about Jewish Peruvians, the right had even greater difficulty tying radicalism to that community, consisting of only 2,100 to 3,300.[34]

Labor, the Elite, and President Alessandri

The elite was less sure of Alessandri's position on labor than it had been of Sanfuentes's, so the election of June 1920 prompted the growth of employer associations. The first was the Unión de Comerciantes in Valparaíso, later called the Asociación General de Comerciantes, founded by shipping and commercial interests during an IWW port strike in July 1920. Police Prefect Enrique Caballero and other authorities cooperated with it extensively. Caballero broke the strike, but continued union activity and IWW militancy prompted the Asociación to organize a lockout in the port on August 18, 1921. Asociación affiliates would hire only those who had signed its registry and agreed to obey its regulations, which forbade membership in the IWW. Disagreeing with these measures, the Alessandri administration tried to arbitrate the dispute, but the Asociación, sensing victory, refused. The depression and the existence of a large labor reserve enabled the Asociación to win. Employers' groups in Antofagasta and Talcahuano, the nitrate and coal-handling ports, respectively, and other harbor cities followed the Asociación's example. Despite his declared sympathy for workers, Alessandri did not challenge the powerful business associations.[35]

Describing the local employer association, U.S. Consul Homer Brett in Arica observed that "some of its most prominent members quite openly state that they are out to 'smash' the labor unions." The association's activity was timely; business would lose little because there was a recession, labor had no savings left and was defenseless, and soldiers did not regard themselves as workers. Moreover, while laborers thought Alessandri favored them, Brett believed that the government had ordered local officials not to yield to them.[36]

The Unión Agraria, a society of landowners founded in the postwar years to oppose rural labor organizing efforts, envisioned a national-level group sponsoring "freedom of work" in all economic realms. This deceptive term meant detaching laborers from unions. The Unión broached this idea with employer associations and large firms, and the result was the foundation of the Asociación del Trabajo (ADT) in October 1921. To it the landowners' society contributed funding, personnel, and facilities. The ADT claimed that 1,122 firms employing 127,390 workers were affiliated by 1924. Caballero's links to business, the police, and the upper class, through his membership in the Club de la Unión, made him an appropriate director of the organization. Some members of the ADT affiliates were also active in the National Union.[37]

Caballero insisted that the group had not organized itself "in a warlike manner," although his actions in Valparaíso belied his words. Unlike labor agitators, he claimed, the ADT hoped to attain social peace by instilling modern industrial relations ideas in employers and "sentiments of order, economy, and solidarity" in workers. The ADT's lectures, publications, and library would educate *patrones*. These published works included *El régimen socialista*, a predictably negative view of socialism by the nationalist Guillermo Subercaseaux. An Alessandri supporter and holder of several government offices during the 1920s, Subercaseaux nevertheless had become more rigidly antileftist during the postwar era. Such projects as a placement agency and medical clinic in Santiago, which the ADT planned to extend to the provinces, would teach laborers to cooperate with employers and avoid "dissolvent and anarchical elements."[38] While these plans did not materialize, the ADT's job registry, which excluded labor militants, imparted the same message in a more coercive fashion.

Caballero did not believe that Chile faced an imminent leftist threat; the army, police, and Carabineros could easily suppress a revolution. However, the former police official no longer regarded simple repression as sufficient. Leftism would thrive in Chile's festering conditions if businessmen did not dispense welfare measures in workplaces. Such programs would illustrate the need to "maintain the capitalist regime that has realized the progress and civilization of the world." Yet the organization's notion of how to maintain capitalism was narrow. The ADT favored employer reform efforts on a voluntary basis rather than the labor laws that politicians were debating at this time.[39] Nor did the ADT spread broad ideas of economic nationalism. Still, it represented an initial attempt at a corporatist solution to the capital-labor conflict.

The ADT's lobbying efforts and provision of strikebreakers, along with the depression and official actions, helped weaken the labor movement by 1921. Thousands of unemployed nitrate workers were streaming into the central cities, aggravating the dismal outlook for jobs and wages. During the first half of 1921 Alessandri resolved some conflicts to labor's benefit, but troops massacred 70 nitrate workers at Oficina San Gregorio and jailed 130 others in Antofagasta province in February. The president became impatient when unions continued to go on strike, despite his actions on their behalf. Pressured by the right, he resorted to the repressive tactics used by previous administrations.[40]

Students as well as workers were disappointed with the president. Alessandri released FECH leaders from jail, and the organization resumed its activities. When the president began negotiations with Peru, however, Carlos Vicuña Fuentes, a Radical professor and FECH leader, called for returning Tacna-Arica to Peru and conceding to Bolivia an outlet to the sea. His statement outraged military officers and the National Union, some of whose members pushed the government into removing Vicuña from teaching. Although it did not adopt Vicuña's views, FECH mobilized students, professors, and Radicals in his defense, even demonstrating outside La Moneda. Alessandri refused to back down. Angry at FECH for defying him, he set up the competing Federación Nacional de Estudiantes, to which he awarded a building and facilities. Engineering students and youth tied to the upper class or governing circles joined the new group, weakening FECH, as the president had intended.[41]

The economic downturn and political circumstances kept Alessandri from fulfilling his promises of reform. The president inherited a virtually bankrupt treasury, and only new taxes could finance a welfare program. The aristocratic opposition that dominated the Senate refused to pass a tax bill or any other piece of Liberal Alliance legislation. Union activism had forced

Alliance and Union legislators to agree on the need for state supervision of capital-labor relations, but their alternative versions stalled in partisan maneuverings. After he posted police and military officers at the polls in March 1924, Alessandri secured an Alliance-dominated upper house. The divided Alliance forces in the Senate, however, proved incapable of passing Alessandri's long-delayed reforms, preferring instead to discuss a congressional salary bill. Moreover, military supervision of the election had tainted these proceedings, in the opinion of the Union, which believed that its candidates should have won. Angered, some Union members began to plot with the military.[42]

The Military

Military officers had long agreed that civilian administrations were corrupt and incapable of dealing with pressing social problems. Their participation in "Don Ladislao's War" had politicized them further. Rejecting their customary strikebreaking role, they wanted the state to devise new means of controlling unions, which had renewed their activity in 1924. In this regard the younger officers admired Benito Mussolini for restoring order in Italy, although their politics were more amorphous than fascist. They also resented Alessandri for assigning them to monitor the polls and for meddling in military affairs.[43]

Some senior naval and army officers, including Generals Luis Altamirano and Juan Pablo Bennett, joined with National Union politicians and Catholic youth to form a secret society, Tenacidad Entusiasmo Abnegación (TEA), in 1924. Its civilian leaders, who included Liberals Oscar Dávila and Ladislao Errázuriz, wanted to avenge the 1924 election and restore the aristocracy's influence. TEA held clandestine indoctrination meetings for its 1,500–2,000 civilians, many of them ANEC activists, and carried out provocative acts, such as placing bombs in the home of the Masonic grand master, beating up the minister of war, and creating incidents along the presidential route to Congress for the annual opening ceremony on June 1. A leading participant in these ventures was the young judge Jorge González von Marées, the future chief of Chilean National Socialism, who bore the title of "Legionnaire" in the organization. TEA's civilian campaign of terror shifted to military plans to overthrow the president in November 1924 and call for new elections.[44]

TEA, however, did not garner support from middle- and junior-level army officers. Majors Marmaduke Grove and Carlos Ibáñez and their peers supported Alessandri's proposed reforms and found the newly elected Senate's unwillingness to pass them inexcusable. In view of the fact that military personnel, teachers, and government employees had not received paychecks for months, the congressmen's preoccupation over their own salaries infuriated the lower-ranking officers.

The reformers preempted the plans of their superiors. In early September, the young officers notified Alessandri of their demands for military and social legislation and their opposition to the salary bill. The president vetoed the congressional salary law and named Generals Altamirano and Bennett and Admiral Francisco Neff to the cabinet. Congress passed the military's program, including the labor code, consisting of workmen's compensation, social security, and regulations governing child and female labor, strikes, and workers' organizations. These laws did not apply to agriculture, and Union and Alliance members alike contributed regressive provisions, including state control of union finances, strike procedures, and elections.[45] Although Alessandri might have used the junior officers to achieve his reforms, he resigned when he realized that the military intended to remain in power. The military conservatives in the cabinet ousted the civilians, closed Congress, and formed a junta.

Divisions within the military soon sharpened. True to TEA aims, the junta appeared to favor the Union's presidential candidate, Ladislao Errázuriz. Calling for a new constitution and additional social legislation, Ibáñez, Grove, and other junior officers did not want to return to oligarchical politics. The junta tried to suppress the reformers, who countered by ousting the former on January 23, 1925. The new junta invited Alessandri back to finish his term; in the meantime, it cultivated support among women and laborers. Feminist groups such as the Consejo Nacional de Mujeres (1919) and Partido Cívico Femenino (1922) had petitioned Alessandri for civil and political rights, and the junta responded to some of their requests. Faced with rent strikes and the formation of tenant leagues, it also freed political prisoners and lowered rents.[46]

Fearful of labor's renewed vigor, the new junta's progressive tinge, and Alessandri's possible return, aristocratic elements formed resistance groups. Men created white guards, which also were a response to the Guardia Republicana, founded by Radicals to support the junior officers and Alessandri's return to office. A putsch attempt by former TEA members and rightist officers in late February failed. Never confident in Alessandri, rightists also lost their faith in the military. Instead, they began to envision a reliably antileftist civilian armed force, larger and more permanent than the white guards and Ligas. For their part, upper-class women in 1925 founded Acción Nacional de Mujeres de Chile, their first secular rightist group. It stood for protecting the family, helping abandoned women and children, and securing female suffrage. Implicit was its opposition to the junta and Alessandri—as well as its notion that if they could vote, women would support the church and the right.[47]

Alessandri regained the presidency in March 1925 in a climate of worker militancy. He dispatched troops to the north, where they arrested over 1,000 activists and, at La Coruña nitrate camp, slaughtered between 600 and 800 strikers. Union politicians and even the Alessandri administration accused northern workers of accepting Peruvian money. Despite the government's show of force, Ligas Patrióticas briefly reemerged. Official terror spread from the north to the coalfields and central cities, ending the labor mobilization of 1924–25.[48]

Supported by military reformers, Alessandri implemented the constitution of 1925. The new document curbed congressional authority in favor of the executive, thus lessening the possibility of legislative stalemates. It also assigned the state the task of protecting laborers' rights and well-being and gave priority to the national interest over individual property rights. At the same time, it separated church from state.

The Union had little choice but to accept the constitution, given military backing and public approval. This coalition, however, disliked the document for reducing the political power that the oligarchy had exercised through Congress. Not surprisingly, Conservatives opposed the disestablishment of the church. This party also regarded secular authority over welfare as a potential threat to itself and the church, as Radicals increasingly controlled the state bureaucracy and would use its expanded jurisdiction to reap political rewards.

The Church and Women

Nor did Conservatives necessarily agree with the move away from economic liberalism, as the experience of Jesuit Father Fernando Vives Solar demonstrated. Vives taught Social Catholic doctrine in the aristocratic Colegio San Ignacio, where a circle gathered to discuss these ideas. Starting in 1916, his followers organized workers' syndicates, which did not go far beyond the class collaboration of the workers' circles. Vives's group also edited *El Sindicalista*, critical of a church tied to the rich. These activities angered some priests and Conservatives, who forced Vives into exile from 1912 to 1914 and again from 1918 to 1931. His second departure dampened youthful interest in the social question, although some continued their involvement.[49]

Some of his disciples leaned far to the right. Santiago ANEC members demonstrated this bent through their membership in TEA and a marked interest in Italian fascism. Recognizing the need for workers to organize to secure higher wages, an associate of Vives, Father Guillermo Viviani, proposed subsuming capitalism under a hierarchical organization of manual and intellectual labor. This belief eventually led Viviani to admire Mussolini's corporatist system and to conclude that the future belonged to fascism. Viviani's corporatism prompted him to found the Casa del Pueblo, a worker center, in 1917, and the laborer-led Confederación de Sindicatos Blancos in 1925. Constrained by the hierarchy, neither group prospered.[50]

Archbishop Crescente Errázuriz of Santiago (1919–31) opposed democracy, socialism, and worker autonomy, although he believed that the "proletarian" deserved a decent living and abode. Like Vives, the archbishop understood that as long as the church remained tied to the Conservatives it could not make inroads among the poor. Clerical partisanship not only alienated the people but corrupted priests and gave the party power over the church. Widely regarded as a friend of the Alliance, Errázuriz urged churchmen to abstain from the 1920 campaign, although most ignored his admonitions. On inauguration day he invited the president to a service, where he noted that the church, like Alessandri, favored reforms to help the lower and middle classes. The invitation and the message outraged many clerics, as did his 1922 pastoral explaining that the church could not represent any political party. Alessandri's separation of church and state wounded him deeply, although after the disestablishment, the relationship between the two men resumed a cordial tone. Despite the archbishop's move away from the Conservatives, clerics still supported the party.[51]

The church was slowly changing course with regards not only to Conservatives but also to women, whom it was beginning to mobilize in novel ways. One new group was the Asociación de la Juventud Católica Femenina (AJCF), founded in 1921 by Bishop Rafael Edwards Salas. Like its male counterpart, ANEC, AJCF included members of diverse class origins. By 1924 it had organized 174 centers around the country with 6,123 members, whose main activity was to study religious and social ideas. A branch of the AJCF, the Sindicato Blanco de Labores Femeninas—the "white" indicating its anticommunism—visited the sick, sold goods made by impoverished women, and taught religion and other subjects to children and working women. Despite its emphasis on philanthropy, the AJCF was nontraditional in some respects. Using uncharacteristic martial language to refer to a female group, Edwards defined it as "an army inured to war" for Christ. The AJCF also held large assemblies and annual conventions attended by women from the entire nation. By emphasizing the intellect and holding national meetings, it broke with the usual female role, and the travel and Edwards' warlike imagery served as precedents for radical right-wing women of the 1930s.[52]

Catholics also organized female workers. Although the percentage of women in the labor force was declining, women were moving into factories; between 1916 and 1940 one-quarter of industrial laborers were female. A significant presence in unions, women were involved in 47 percent of all strikes from 1917 to 1921.[53] To prevent further leftist and feminist inroads, Catholic women wanted to ground female laborers in the faith. Accordingly, in 1914 the Liga de Damas Chilenas founded a syndicate of female business employees and office workers, and in 1915 another of seamstresses. By 1928, 535 women had joined the first and 350 the second. A syndicate of factory employees arose in 1924 under the auspices of the Sisters of Charity, attracting 220 members by the late 1920s. Although they favored better salaries and hours, retirement benefits, and profit sharing, there was little indication that their goals or mutual aid activities antagonized employers.[54]

Conclusion

The church's halting efforts to appeal to a wider class spectrum and establish an alternative to the left bore little fruit during this period. There were other signs of potential extreme right-wing weakness. Nationalists could not convincingly tie labor radicalism to the tiny foreign or Jewish presence. Sympathetic to the Ligas, the military nevertheless was divided ideologically by the mid-1920s. Finally, Chileans of diverse political persuasions found fault with liberal economics. Extreme rightists could not lay exclusive claim to this territory, and they showed little interest in such a subject during these years.

The radical right paramilitary groups did not command a broad, lasting appeal. No carefully framed ideology linked the Ligas, white guards, TEA, and employer associations, or separated them from the moderate right. These groups were arms of the elite and hence overlapped the moderate right, representing its radicalization in a moment of crisis. Yet the moderate right—the National Union, Social Catholics, and women's groups— was strong enough to protect its interests without a permanent radical rightist organization. The working class mounted a vigorous challenge, but only in 1920–21 and 1924–25 did the upper class have reason to fear that the state might mobilize and conciliate popular groups, and these concerns were temporary. Generally the authorities, even under Alessandri, cooperated with the elite and business to repress workers and leftist students. For these reasons, the organizations of this tendency remained small, fragmented, and transitory.

Still, by the end of the period there were signs of change. The very fact that the military and many politicians felt the need to legislate a labor code indicated the workers' force. The parliamentary system had upheld the aristocracy's power, but its collapse in 1924–25 and the rise of military reformers augured new threats to the established order. In response, extreme rightists would create stronger organizations in the 1930s.

CHAPTER 6

Argentinizing Labor

In contrast to Chile, Argentina offered propitious conditions for an extreme right-wing movement. The landowning elite lost political weight in a newly democratized system, and it faced a significant challenge from workers. The perceived severity of the danger, coupled with uncertainty about the government's labor policy, prompted the formation of a violent group outside existing political channels—the Liga Patriótica Argentina. The support it received from influential politicians, the military, and the church helped make it the most powerful manifestation of the extreme right in this period.

The Moderate Right

The Argentine oligarchy's political influence decayed in the early twentieth century, more than that of the Chilean upper class. Agriculture in the Chilean central valley required many permanent workers, and the landowners' domination over them helped ensure their political power. Argentine landowners lacked a comparable rural base, as they employed only small numbers of peons to work on their ranches, and their tenant farmers were transient and foreign-born. Furthermore, personal rivalries and disagreements split the oligarchical National Autonomist Party (PAN) into provincial groupings. In the meantime the Radical Party, drawing upon upper-class dissidents and the middle class, organized at the precinct level. Concern over the growing labor threat prompted leaders of the old ruling class to attempt to consolidate the upper sectors and appeal to the native-born. They also reasoned that co-opting the Radicals' platform would enable them to retain office. These deliberations resulted in the law of 1912 providing for effective universal male suffrage. While broad segments of the populace had previously participated in politics, with this reform their votes exerted greater sway. The Argentine system now was appreciably more democratic and inclusive than the Chilean, although both excluded workers—in Argentina, because foreign workers rarely became citizens.[1]

The PAN splinters mainly served as vehicles for local strongmen and elite interests. What they stood for—beyond greed for power—was unclear. Argentines commonly grouped the Conservative Party of Buenos Aires (founded in 1908) and other provincial factions under the conservative rubric, but these parties were not conservative in the traditional sense. Most of their adherents inherited PAN's regard for laissez-faire economics, immigration, public secular education, and other aspects of nineteenth-century liberalism, including its skepticism toward democracy. Few embraced the clericalism that typified Chilean Conservatives. The elite began to call itself conservative during the time of the electoral reform to indicate its desire to conserve society against leftist onslaught.[2] Thus, allegiance to old ideas and antileftism defined the moderate right from its onset. Another characteristic was its use of any means necessary, however fraudulent or violent, to hold or regain power. The question was whether the elite would learn to repackage its views and practices in a way that appealed to a mass electorate.

Some of its members understood that victory over the Socialists, with their platform of socioeconomic change, and especially over the Radicals, with their democratic rectitude, required the formation of a modern national party. Accordingly, conservative reformers founded the Progressive Democratic Party (PDP) in 1914 and selected Deputy Lisandro de la Torre of Santa Fe as presidential candidate for 1916. Drafted by reformer Carlos Ibarguren, the PDP platform stood for economic nationalism, democratic principles, and social welfare. It advocated tariff protection, government regulation of working conditions and support of mutualism, and even land reform. The PDP statement demonstrated greater interest in such issues than the Radicals, who did not even have a platform. Torre's fierce anticlericalism and aristocratic manner repelled potential supporters, but regional fragmentation and the ambitions of other conservative leaders proved even greater impediments to his ability to unite the elite.[3]

Divided, the moderate right could not exploit electoral opportunities as the reformers of 1912 had predicted. The Socialists won the federal capital in the 1914 congressional elections, and the Radicals triumphed in the 1916 presidential contest, electing their candidate, Hipólito Yrigoyen (1916–22, 1928–30). Despite their control of the Senate, the conservatives pulled little weight in a system dominated, unlike the Chilean, by the executive branch. Their impotence bred disgust with democracy and a willingness to consider extraparliamentary forms of political power. Thus, the fortunes of the extreme right would be inversely related to those of the moderate right.

The Economy, Labor, and Yrigoyen

World War I and the immediate postwar period witnessed a severe economic crisis. Trade and investment dislocations threw Argentina into a depression between 1913 and 1917 that probably was worse than that of the 1930s. Grain exports did not fare well during the war, unlike livestock products. By 1918, a slow recovery began in the urban areas, but the foreign market for meat and wool exports shrank. The demand for grain briefly rose and declined anew. In the war years, salaries in the capital dropped 38 percent, while the cost of living rose 71 percent. Urban and rural workers faced a large gap between their wages and the cost of necessities, and unemployment climbed to at least 30 percent in 1917. Tenant farmers in the grain region experienced high indebtedness and eviction rates.[4]

Reacting to these conditions and to the revolutionary tide in Europe, workers launched an impressive mobilization drive. The number of strikes and strikers in Buenos Aires alone grew from 80 and 24,300 in 1916 to 367 and 309,000 in 1919, respectively. About 16 percent of the labor force in the capital adhered to the anarcho-syndicalist Federación Obrera Regional Argentina (FORA) IX, the most active of the labor federations, in early 1919; this percentage increased to 24 percent by the end of the year.[5] As succeeding events would indicate, the labor movement was not as strong as it seemed. Unlike in the Chilean nitrate fields, the dispersed and transient nature of the labor force in the livestock and grain sectors had inhibited community and, in turn, union building. The foreign origins of most militant workers and their inability to call liberalism into question also were liabilities.[6] Still, strikes in the meatpacking plants, ports, and railroads between 1916 and 1918, along with the creation of the first unions of landless rural workers, directly threatened the export economy and alarmed landowners and foreign managers.

Before Yrigoyen assumed office, the elite had not feared that he would threaten its class position. The willingness of several conservative leaders to withhold support from Torre, or even extend it to the Radical candidate, demonstrated this lack of concern.[7] Yrigoyen's social proposals created little controversy, although the opposition-dominated Congress passed few of them. The president's populist image and initial dealings with organized labor, however, like Alessandri's, differed from those of previous presidents. Seeking social peace and votes from workers, the Radical leader met with union representatives, and his administration helped resolve some large wartime strikes to labor's benefit. Before 1919, the government did not deport militants or call a state of siege, and it did not resort heavily to using the police and the army during capital-labor conflicts. Nevertheless, its support of foreign companies in the meatpacking strike of 1917 illustrated the administration's limits.

Not taking government hostility against unions for granted, however, businessmen created a permanent strikebreaking group. Delegates from the major economic sectors, representing local and foreign firms, the Unión Industrial Argentina, and the Sociedad Rural Argentina, the prestigious ranchers' association, formed the Asociación Nacional del Trabajo (ANT) in July 1918. Its first president was Pedro Christophersen, a Norwegian shipper, landowner, and head of the stock exchange. Like its Chilean offspring, the ANT insisted that it favored economic benefits for workers, but its principal aim was to destroy the union movement and restore management's control over labor.[8]

The president's *obrerismo* (workerism), as they viewed it, was not the only trait that annoyed conservatives. Lacking a firm base in Congress and the interior, Yrigoyen had entered the presidency from a position of weakness. To gain control of the legislative branch, he intervened in the conservative-dominated provinces to prevent electoral fraud and pursued a confrontational strategy in Congress.[9] Indignant conservatives denounced his partisan maneuverings, ignoring the fact that PAN had resorted to similar tactics. Fearing their political demise, they responded with obstructionist behavior of their own.

Yrigoyen's neutrality also perturbed young members of the elite. Influenced by the idealistic reaction against positivism, upper-class youth longed to submerge their individual identities in a noble cause. Many Argentines regarded the war as such a cause, and they blamed Yrigoyen for denying them the opportunity to participate in it. While a few future extreme rightists supported Germany, most favored the Allies, and they set up organizations on its behalf. One such group was the Comité Nacional de la Juventud, including cultural nationalists Ricardo Rojas and Leopoldo Lugones, which arose in October 1918. Its activities had barely gotten under way when the war ended. Searching for a new avenue for its energies, the Comité renounced existing parties and prepared to launch itself into politics.[10] Before it could do so, however, a labor crisis erupted.

Laborers, Vigilantes, and the Military

A strike brewing in the capital since December 1918 developed into a general strike on January 9, 1919. For the next week, the Semana Trágica, a bloody struggle raged, pitting workers against capital and the state. The strike wave spread to the provinces of Buenos Aires, Santa Fe, Córdoba, and Mendoza. On January 9, *La Época*, the government's mouthpiece, warned laborers to stop the disorders or the government would do so by force. That evening and into the next morning, Radical general Luis J. Dellepiane led troops into Buenos Aires, eventually quelling the worker-led violence. Officials and union leaders resolved the original strike a few days later. Evidently Yrigoyen hoped that the repression would mollify conservatives and the mediation would soothe labor.[11]

For upper- and middle-class residents of the capital, however, the repression began too late. Conservatives and the ANT had asked for severe law-and-order measures since the beginning of the crisis. Fearing that the government had lost control, the elite regarded the situation as the logical outcome of Yrigoyen's *obrerismo*. Rumors that Dellepiane decided on his own to move into the city may have confirmed their belief.[12] The worldwide context of labor militancy and leftist activism led the well-off to predict that a revolution was imminent. They identified this revolution with the Jews, most of whom were of Russian origin.

Acting on these fears, members of the Comité Nacional de la Juventud, young Radicals, and other civilians joined policemen to attack Jewish and working-class neighborhoods from January 10 to 14. Demolishing Jewish-owned property and community organizations, as well as labor institutions and newspapers, they mauled, shot, and arrested thousands. Some observers thought that Dellepiane tried to restrain the forces of order, but his attempts appeared unconvincing. The vigilantes resembled the Policía Civil Auxiliar, which the general had organized in 1910, and they used army weapons distributed with Dellepiane's and perhaps Yrigoyen's authorization. The disproportionately high arrest rates among Jews and the detention of the Jewish leaders of a supposed "soviet" indicated that the authorities, as well as the bourgeoisie, equated Jews with revolution. (The government subsequently released the suspects for lack of evidence, although Social Catholic priest Gustavo Franceschi and others continued to blame the disorders on Jews.) Official complicity turned the repression of Jews into a genuine pogrom. White guards also attacked Jews in Rosario and perhaps other cities.[13]

In the meantime, civilians and military men were openly forming white guards. Comité members, older citizens, and military officers met in police precinct offices to set up neighborhood patrols. To those interested in creating an officially recognized force, Dellepiane suggested that they turn to the Centro Naval, an officers' club where vigilantes had met throughout the Semana Trágica and received training. The Liga Patriótica Argentina would later claim that the government had appointed one of the instructors, Captain Jorge Yalour, to form the neighborhood patrols. Rear Admiral Manuel Domecq García invited Comité members and other civilians to the Centro on January 12 to establish a permanent citywide guard. Informing Dellepiane of his actions, Domecq García contacted the Círculo Militar, the army officers' club, to help plan the new organization.[14]

Publicly Dellepiane maintained distance from the guard, but there is little doubt he approved of it. Chillingly foreseeing the practices of the dictatorship of 1976–83, Dellepiane later told the U.S. ambassador that the administration could have prevented the Semana Trágica by having the labor "ringleaders silently disappear one by one, without any open arrest."[15] Yrigoyen's refusal to use this method may have inclined the general toward a paramilitary organization that did not share such scruples.

That the military mobilized a radical right-wing movement was not surprising. Presidents had usually called on the army to suppress laborers, and Yrigoyen had ordered the marines to break up the meatpacking strike of 1917. Dellepiane and other officers moved back and forth from the military to the higher echelons of the federal police, another force used to repress strikes. Like their Chilean peers, Argentine officers disliked being used for this unpopular purpose, particularly by a president who distanced himself from such policies to curry favor among workers. Yet most officers fiercely opposed the left, and their opposition grew when they uncovered two soviets in army ranks. Perhaps they, like the conservatives, thought Yrigoyen had mishandled labor policy. Indeed, a group of retired officers asked Dellepiane to lead a coup as he entered the capital, but he refused. Why the navy took the initiative, however, is not clear. Perhaps the naval leaders' class origins—higher than those of army officers—and pro-Allied

sentiments facilitated their ties to the Comité.[16] Or it may have been un-
seemly for the army, charged with the official repression, to coordinate an
unofficial one.

The military bestowed prestige, legitimacy, and power on the fledgling
rightist movement. It stamped the extreme right with an imprimatur of patriotism. Military leadership of the white guard indicated the unity of the
conservative classes and the forces of order against the leftist threat—and
perhaps against the government.

While civilians patrolled the streets of Buenos Aires, registered in the
new guard, and formed paramilitary units in the provinces, others solicited
donations for the families of men killed or wounded by workers. The most
important of these endeavors was the Comisión Pro-Defensa del Orden,
headed by Domecq García. Conservatives and future Anti-Personalist Radicals (who later split with Yrigoyen) joined the organization, as did prominent Catholics; members of the Comité, neighborhood patrols, and ANT;
and Dellepiane, Yalour, and other high-ranking officers.[17]

The Liga Patriótica Argentina

Domecq García incorporated the Comisión, Comité, and other groups into
the new civil guard, the Liga Patriótica Argentina (LPA). A committee that
he directed invited politicians, army and naval officers, members of upper-
class clubs, and priests to attend the first meeting on January 20 in the Centro Naval. Major Justo Diana represented the Círculo Militar and Captain
Jorge Yalour the Centro Naval. Monsignors Agustín Piaggio and Miguel de
Andrea, the Social Catholic leader, served as church delegates. The Asociación de Damas Patricias also sent observers.[18]

The LPA indicated it would do more than safeguard neighborhoods. To
ensure "respect for the law, the principle of authority, and the social order,"
Liguistas would form neighborhood groups to repress anarchist activities.
Encouraging laws and labor organizations that would guarantee "social justice" and "proletarian" welfare within the given order would be among the
LPA's tasks. The LPA favored naturalizing several categories of immigrants,
such as those who owned property and businesses, but it excluded opponents of the constitution. Harking back to cultural nationalism, five of its
fifteen aims concerned "Argentinizing" the schools. Domecq García described the LPA's mission as one of promoting a broad nationalism that
would fight the abuses of the greedy rich and the violent poor. Representing
a middle ground, the LPA would restore harmony to the nation.[19]

Argentinidad to the LPA meant accepting the given order. Laborers could legitimately aspire to better economic and working conditions, but not necessarily strive to obtain them; instead, the LPA would secure these goals for the poor. Dispensing such favors to the people, as well as moralizing and educating them, resembled church projects. Militant workers and other dissenters did not fit the LPA's notion of working within the given order, and therefore they were "foreign." The immigrant backgrounds of most workers reinforced the LPA's distinction between bourgeois "nationalists" and their "alien" opponents. As had Social Catholics and Alberto Torres, the LPA staked out a third position between unrestrained capitalism and labor radicalism.

That the LPA was able to claim this space suggested the weakness of the state. The ideological and order-keeping roles it had appropriated properly belonged to the government. Congress, however, was mired in partisan obstructionism, and the LPA lacked confidence in the administration's willingness to restrain labor. Estanislao Zeballos, a conservative, former minister, and proponent of the Liga Patriótica Nacional of 1901, blamed Yrigoyen for coddling "delinquent workers," yet he also deplored the "spectacle" of the patriotic "sportsmen" who had replaced official personnel in the streets. Zeballos regarded the use of "irresponsible popular police" as a sign of governmental decay.[20]

Perhaps his reverence for nationalism and order overrode his misgivings, for Zeballos soon joined the LPA. He, Monsignor de Andrea, officers from both services, and Radical and conservative politicians formed a provisional governing body, headed by Domecq García, that presided over the LPA's initial membership drive and consolidation of its organizational structure. The neighborhood and provincial guards became, in the LPA's military language, "brigades." There were forty-three brigades in the forty-five police precincts of Buenos Aires. Occupational groups, professional associations, and branches of the Sociedad Rural Argentina established their own brigades. Anxious to demonstrate their patriotism and distinguish themselves from leftist Jews, Jewish businessmen formed a small short-lived brigade. Landowners, merchants, and civic leaders in the interior created brigades, as did LPA organizers; all formed "free labor" brigades as counterweights to militant unions. Further illustrating the LPA's goals, brigades in cities set up "neighborhood defense commissions," and those in the countryside created "commissions in defense of rural labor."[21]

Domecq García decided to relinquish his post to a civilian, and on April 5 the brigades elected Manuel Carlés president, a position he occupied from 1919 until his death in 1946. A friend of both conservative reformers and Radicals, particularly future Anti-Personalists, the former deputy was also known for his patriotic oratory at Police Chief Ramón Falcón's funeral and other occasions. Yrigoyen had named Carlés to head the 1918 intervention in Salta, and in February 1919, as the LPA was forming, he contemplated appointing Carlés naval minister. The Conservative Coalition of Buenos Aires also considered him for its list in December 1919. His ties to various political factions and to officers, whom he taught in the Higher War College and other military schools, enhanced his leadership.[22]

Carlés reigned over a tightly knit organization. The Junta Central included eighty people chosen by the brigades of the federal capital and one representative from each of the provincial brigades. In turn, the Junta elected eight officers who, with seven others, formed the Consejo Ejecutivo. Although elections occurred every two years, the composition of the Junta and Consejo varied only slightly throughout the 1920s. The Consejo formulated policy, officiated over the brigades, and administered funds. The Junta discussed LPA ventures, conferred with brigade leaders, and sent representatives to the provinces to gather information and establish new chapters. It also named commissions to raise funds and study national issues. The Junta invited brigade delegates to attend annual LPA congresses, beginning in 1920, to present papers on national issues and listen to commission reports.[23]

The organization eventually encompassed the entire country. Its core consisted of about 550 male brigades with perhaps 11,000 permanent members, who were represented at the annual congresses and mentioned in the press throughout the 1920s. Most brigades were located in regions where unions were active, such as the federal capital, littoral ports and lowlands, grain-raising areas, and Patagonia.[24]

Women in the LPA

Generally, neither the former ruling class nor LPA leaders favored female participation in politics. Nevertheless, the state of emergency demanded that women's roles in charities, education, and the family be harnessed to the LPA's mission. The LPA's organizing committee had invited a women's group to attend the first meeting, and the statutes permitted the recruitment of both sexes. When Carlés became president, he began to spread the LPA's message to women in churches and their associations, an activity he continued throughout his life, and to welcome women's groups to LPA headquarters. The Consejo Nacional de Mujeres, a federation of upper-class charities and clubs, and the Asociación Nacional Pro-Patria de Señoritas announced their support for the LPA, and similar organizations sent the LPA letters of praise. The LPA invited the Asociación Pro-Patria, Asociación de Damas Patricias, Sociedad de Beneficencia, and the Congregación de la Santa Unión, a nuns' order that administered an elite girls' school, among other women's groups, to its independence festivities on May 24, 1919. Carlés and his female guests led a parade through the streets of the capital, an unusual public appearance for women that paralleled their march with de Andrea in 1910. A reporter observed that the female presence lent "a delicate note of beauty" to the procession.[25]

The Junta invited delegates of upper-class charitable groups in Buenos Aires to the first meeting of the Liga Patriótica de Señoras on June 29, 1919. Carlés and several prestigious female philanthropists addressed sixty-five matrons and twelve girls. On July 20, the Señoras chose a Junta Executiva and a president, Julia Elena A. de Martínez de Hoz, a sponsor of Catholic charities and the wife of a prominent landowner and LPA member. In early October, the young women separated from their elders, founding the Liga Patriótica de Señoritas.[26] This split mirrored the distinction between the roles of married and unmarried women in the larger society.

Women then organized their own brigades—a title they retained, despite its martial connotations. In August, the Señoras' Junta assigned members to establish brigades in eighteen capital precincts. Catholic parish and other groups became the brigades of their neighborhoods or cities. Sometimes the Señoras in Buenos Aires asked male brigade leaders to set up women's auxiliaries, or male brigades suggested to women of the same locality (often their wives and relatives) that they create such groups. The Señoritas centered most of their chapters around their principal activity, factory schools for female workers.[27]

Women also belonged to other sections of the LPA. Since few women took part in important workers' conflicts after the LPA's birth, there were only a handful of female free labor brigades. Suggestively, when female department store employees carried out a strike in Buenos Aires in 1919, a brigade of this occupational category arose. Women formed the Liga Patriótica del Magisterio Argentino in January 1920, although male teachers filtered into it. Teachers' brigades were organized along gender lines in the capital and the provinces of Buenos Aires and Mendoza. Like the employees' brigade, the Mendoza brigade originated during a teachers' strike.[28]

Male and female Liguistas envisioned important roles for women within the organization. When she announced the adherence of her Asociación Nacional Pro-Patria de Señoritas to the LPA, President Mercedes Pujato Crespo, a writer of modest origins from Santa Fe, declared the group would work for the nation by eliciting respect for its sacred symbols, laws, and institutions. Now was the time for Argentine women to join the "defense movement" against those who wished to destroy society, said the Córdoba female brigade. Justo P. Correa, a member of an old Catamarcan family and of the Magisterio, wrote that by incorporating women, the LPA was rounding out its mission and utilizing "the beautiful and the affective" to obtain victory.[29] Forty-one permanent women's brigades with 820 members, plus the Señoritas' school groups, agreed with these aspirations.

Carlés affirmed women's importance to the LPA by noting their position within the family, which he regarded as the bulwark of the nation. With its hierarchically arranged and differentiated roles of husband, wife, and children, the bourgeois family modeled and reinforced class society. In this ideal household, women taught their offspring obedience, religion, morality, patriotism, and reverence for work. Disorganized immigrant homes and secular education threatened to undermine such values, as did feminism, which Carlés defined as "the fight against men in order to masculinize women." The postwar years witnessed much debate over female suffrage, the object of a determined effort by Socialist and middle-class feminists. Although feminists did not win the vote at this time, their loud campaign alarmed Carlés and may have prompted his outreach to women. Instead of voting, he thought women should moralize foreign families and strengthen the social fabric.[30] But would such tasks weaken their femininity, families, and society? Would this mean incorporating women into the male sphere of politics?

The LPA found ways around this problem. It carefully described itself as a moral and patriotic association, rather than a political one. This claim not only reaffirmed the LPA's nonpartisanship, but it legitimized female activity. The LPA also prudently assigned women duties similar to the ones they exercised within the household and the church. Moreover, it separated men from women within the organization, preventing dubious contact between the sexes, and ensured male control. Throughout the 1920s, the president and most of the leaders of the Magisterio branch were women, but their main spokesperson was male. The LPA permitted female teachers, Señoras, and Señoritas to choose their own leaders, but they did not vote in the elections for the male authorities to whom they reported. Thus the LPA supported male supremacy in the nation as a whole and retained it within the group.[31]

The LPA's Base and Relations with the Government

Its broad gender and social composition strengthened the LPA. About 69 percent of the male central authorities were upper-class, as were almost all the Señoras and Señoritas, who were linked by kinship to each other and to their male peers. Half of the male leaders owned land or came from landed families, and at least 31 percent had held office before 1916, suggesting their ties to the old ruling class. The social backgrounds of male brigade members were not as august. Only 18 percent of brigade delegates to the annual congresses were upper class, and 19 percent were landowners or members of landowning families. Since it was doubtful that the "free laborers," hired by Liguistas to break strikes and unions, chose freely to join the LPA or adhere to its ideology, the middle sectors formed the popular base of the organization—perhaps 31 percent of the male national leaders, 82 percent of the delegates, and an even larger percentage of the male ranks and the teachers' brigades. The average male Liguista in 1920 was forty-seven years old, probably at his professional and economic height.[32]

Its military following also enhanced the LPA. Seventeen percent of LPA leaders and 8 percent of the entire sample consisted of military officers. Six months after the LPA's inception, it claimed 6 generals, 18 colonels, 32 lieutenant colonels, 50 majors, 212 captains, 300 lieutenants, and over 400 sublieutenants—and this was only the army contingent. Members of the armed forces publicly adhered to the LPA, military aviators flew LPA officials and spread its propaganda, and officers went to the interior on missions for the Junta, founded brigades, and attended LPA lectures. When one lone officer dared to criticize this role publicly, the army disciplined him and thus probably silenced others. Concerned about the extent of military participation, in July 1919 the government forbade active military personnel from joining or publicly supporting any patriotic association. The next month the government prohibited Liguistas from recruiting policemen or meeting in police stations. But it was unable to break the links between the LPA and the official forces of order. Angered by Yrigoyen's meddling in military affairs, his use of troops against strikers, and other grievances, active and retired officers remained in the LPA or cooperated with it, as did policemen. Throughout the 1920s, over 100 military officers served in the Junta and Consejo and as brigade delegates to the annual meetings. Dellepiane himself joined by 1926.[33]

The issue of the military underlined the ambiguous relationship between the LPA and the government. During the Semana Trágica, the administration dispersed arms to the vigilantes, who included Radicals, and initially permitted them to meet in police stations. *La Época* approved of the civil guards and the early LPA, and Radicals sometimes spoke out in the LPA's favor in Congress.[34] Military involvement in the LPA, however, raised doubts within the administration. So did the LPA's ability to attract thousands of adherents across the country, including the president's upper-class opponents inside and outside his party. Yrigoyen probably perceived the LPA as a rival for power, a potential national conservative party.

However, LPA leaders recognized that partisanship would drive away many of their diverse followers, who had united solely around the social question. Perhaps they understood that their aristocratic backgrounds would prevent them from winning elections against the Radicals. Instead of becoming a party, the LPA secured its goals on its own and by acting as a pressure group.

Liguistas Against Workers

Without serious interference from the administration, the LPA set out to maintain order. As noted, it attempted to control the labor supply by forming free worker brigades. The LPA's Dirección de Gremios registered workers, gave them identification cards, and placed them in jobs—often with LPA employers. Workers' brigades were supposed to provide their members with the only union-style services that Liguistas considered legitimate— mutual aid, education, and the gradual improvement of working and economic conditions. Whether they did in fact fulfill these functions is doubtful. The LPA theoretically recognized the right to strike for limited economic reasons, but in only a few instances did free workers actually protest and never with their leaders' consent.[35]

The LPA's free labor brigades strikingly resembled those of the ANT, and the two organizations signed up members at the same address. The LPA and ANT overlapped in other respects as well, including membership. The two groups worked together to break strikes and cripple organized labor by introducing scab workers and resorting to violence.[36]

The ANT and LPA cooperated in the simultaneous port and taxi drivers' disputes.[37] Seconded by the federal police under its chief, Elpidio González, a leading Radical, the LPA and the ANT-affiliated Liga Propietarios de Automóviles Particulares conducted a relentless strikebreaking campaign against the militant taxi-drivers' union between late May and early June 1921. The Radical intendant agreed to the LPA's request that the city revoke the licenses of "undesirables." The LPA also asked the municipality to hire chauffeurs only from its approved list. Defeated by combined LPA, ANT, and official actions, the taxi drivers returned to work on June 7.

The waterfront, a vital nexus of the export economy, had witnessed almost continual conflict since 1916.[38] The Federación Obrera Marítima (FOM), the main port union, had won government backing and some control over hiring, and its successes enabled it to lend support to other Federación Obrera Regional Argentina (FORA) IX affiliates. These victories in turn strengthened the resolve of employers, the ANT, and the LPA to force a showdown in the port. Their opportunity came in early 1921 with a dispute among rival dockworkers' unions, prompting the LPA and ANT to introduce their newly created stevedores' brigade into the port. The government was unable to solve the jurisdictional conflict, and it experienced heavy pressure from ANT members, U.S. and British diplomats, and foreign shippers, who vowed to boycott Argentine ports if free laborers could not work there. Moreover, elections were approaching, and the president wanted to shore up his base among well-to-do Argentines. For these reasons Yrigoyen tilted away from FOM toward capital and opened the port to all laborers on May 23.

Fights between unionized workers and LPA-ANT strikebreakers began the next day. Killed in one of these incidents was the bodyguard of ANT president and LPA member Joaquín de Anchorena. The administration sent in troops, commanded by General José F. Uriburu, and reinforced the police, while members of the LPA and Liga Propietarios de Automóviles Particulares escorted the stevedores' brigade to the port and guarded it during work. FOM responded with a general port strike on May 31, but a severe wave of repression forced unionists to return to work. The LPA and ANT freely attacked FOM stevedores and prevented them from being hired. Aided by the government, LPA, and ANT, employers had crippled FOM and reassumed control of the port.

Aside from the taxi and port strikes, the LPA usually left labor matters in Buenos Aires to the ANT. It took charge of such matters outside the capital, although the ANT provided the LPA with financing and strikebreakers.[39] In the interior, where rural laborers were organizing in areas critical to the export economy, the LPA had its biggest confrontations with workers.

An early clash was in Las Palmas del Chaco Austral, a huge estate in northeastern El Chaco that produced cattle, sugar, and tannin for export. The company's owners and directors included Argentines and Englishmen, and its president was Carlos T. Becú, a prominent Radical. Its Creole, Indian, Brazilian, and Paraguayan peons earned meager wages paid in scrip redeemable only at company stores. Living in an isolated area had encouraged a sense of community among the workers. Helped by FOM and FORA IX, they formed a union and struck late in 1919, winning higher wages to be paid in cash, among other benefits. The company, however, insisted on charging a fee for this "service."[40]

Unwilling to accept a union, management began its counterattack in early 1920. The LPA and ANT sent mercenaries who terrorized inhabitants and provoked scuffles with union members. By May a company administrator, Alberto Danzey, had organized these agents provocateurs into a brigade. When Becú and the local administrators dismissed union complaints against the LPA and cut off union and FORA attempts to negotiate, the union called a strike, demanding the firing of Liguistas and an end to charging fees for wages paid in currency.

The strike was long, bloody, and indecisive. Battles took place between workers, on one side, and Liguistas, police, and company guards, on the other. Captain Gregorio Pomar, Radical commander of the Ninth Infantry Regiment, imposed a cease-fire and a settlement favorable to workers in August. After the troops departed, however, the firm disavowed the agreement and the strike resumed. Overwhelmed by hunger, LPA terrorism, and an influx of workers fired from other estates in the ailing region, the union ended the strike in June 1921. Aided by the Unión Sindical Argentina (USA), the successor to FORA IX, the union achieved the right to be paid in pesos without fees two years later. A national law passed in 1925 affirmed this right for all Argentines. Having attained its goal, the union declined; the Las Palmas brigade outlived it, lasting until at least the late 1920s. This particular clash with the LPA had resulted in a rare but slight victory for laborers.

Landless workers in the grain zone also were forming unions tied to the syndicalist and anarchist federations by 1919. A large strike in December 1919 prompted government repression and the creation of LPA brigades throughout the pampas. Rural protest continued in 1920 and 1921, as did LPA mobilizations. By 1921 the Federación Obrera Comarcal (FOC), affiliated with FORA IX, had organized seventy-four unions in Entre Ríos province; on the other side were fifty-one LPA brigades.[41]

In January 1921, a union of peons and manual workers in Villaguay department, located in the region of Jewish agricultural colonies, struck against farmers and threshing machine owners. Liguistas attacked the union secretary; the police, some of whom were LPA members, jailed him and other militants. The union, the Socialist local, and FOC planned a rally on

February 11 in Villaguay to protest these actions. Gunfire broke out between protestors, on one side, and police and Liguistas, including the local conservative leader, on the other. Most of the thirty-five casualties were laborers. The detention of seventy-six workers and Socialists—but no Liguistas—also demonstrated the LPA's control of the battle. Afterwards, the LPA continued to intimidate workers and Socialists, even targeting Deputy Fernando de Andréis, dispatched by the party to defend the prisoners.[42]

The Villaguay brigade, newspapers, and a Radical deputy from Entre Ríos, Eduardo Mouesca, saw the clash as one pitting "Jewish revolutionaries" against "orderly Creoles." The fact that the union secretary and eighteen of the jailed were Jewish immigrants lent credence to such views. Yet Jews figured on both sides of the conflict. The majority of the prisoners were Creoles, while Jews numbered among local Liguistas. Whether they belonged to the LPA or not, the interests of Jewish colonists, who outnumbered Jewish landless workers, resembled those of the organization. For these reasons, national LPA leaders did not comment on the identity of participants in the incident. Either agreeing with the LPA's aims or fearful of identification with the left, Jews joined the LPA in increasing numbers after the Villaguay episode. By May at least twelve of the thirty brigades in the Jewish colony area had Jewish members.[43]

Despite LPA threats and lack of cooperation from Radical authorities in Entre Ríos, Andréis finally secured the prisoners' release. By this time the provincial brigades had shifted their eyes to the port city of Gualeguaychú, where FORA IX–affiliated unions had been active. Businessmen, farmers, ranchers, conservatives, and Radicals feuding with the provincial government had formed a brigade in late 1919. Its statutes proclaimed "freedom of labor" and the independence of capital as "fundamental principles," and refused to accept unions. The brigade tried to fire and blacklist union members and other critics of the LPA. These efforts increased in early 1921, and violence broke out between the two sides.[44]

The wrangle culminated on May Day. The LPA tried to appropriate this symbol of the international labor struggle and transform it into a national holiday of free labor, as Nazis would do in Germany. Brigade authorities noted that May 1 commemorated Justo José de Urquiza's pronouncement against Rosas in 1851 in Entre Ríos. Whereas Urquiza had defied Rosas's tyranny, Argentines today faced one imposed by unions. *Entrerrianos* would defeat evil European ideas and the "red rag," as they had vanquished Rosas's red flag at Caseros in 1852. Thus the LPA recast a patriotic event to symbolize cohesion against labor militancy. The government authorized the LPA celebration in the remote hippodrome in the morning and the workers' usual festivities in the central plaza in the afternoon. By separating the times and places, it hoped to avoid violence.[45]

The LPA's "Day of the Argentine Worker" began when brigades of Gualeguaychú and twelve other towns, including Jewish colonies, paraded with their free laborers to the hippodrome. The horsemen, many dressed in gaucho style, carried blue and white banners as they rode through the town, receiving applause and flowers from the multitude. The parade recalled the cultural nationalists' panegyric view of bygone rural class relations. Their garb and use of Argentine colors appropriated the national mantle for their cause. The well-executed choreography of the procession and the review outside the hippodrome symbolized the orderly, quasi-military society the LPA desired. Carlés arrived by airplane, adding a modern note to the otherwise "traditional" proceedings. After patriotic songs, speeches, and Carlés's departure, the rally dispersed.[46]

Disorders outside the planned rally revealed more of its meaning. Some LPA members headed to the workers' demonstration, where the few available policemen could not stop them from surrounding the crowd. Mounted Liguistas and people inside the buildings circling the square fired a huge volley of shots into the throng. Policemen risked their lives protecting workers from the shooting, and one died as a result. When the gunfire stopped, only Liguistas and the fallen—at least six dead and twenty-eight wounded, few of them LPA members—remained in the square. Speciously claiming he did not know who fired the first shot, Carlés praised it as one "directed against an apostasy."[47]

Unlike the Villaguay episode, the provincial government responded initially in an impartial manner. The controversy over the previous incident, the national press coverage, the LPA's obvious guilt, and the relative absence of the Radical Civic Union's Socialist rivals helped explain the difference, as did the presence of opponents of the administration in the Gualeguaychú brigade. The police detained several union members and four Liguistas, including a conservative leader, but quickly freed the workers. Governor Celestino Marcó claimed that the LPA undermined government authority and blamed it for the shooting, as did the national Radical press. However, when Socialist leaders arrived to represent the families of slain workers against the LPA, and press coverage waned over the course of the lengthy judicial proceedings, the government shifted its stance. Gualeguaychú policemen, who had initially accused the LPA of the crime, now said they knew nothing or blamed the workers. Fearing LPA reprisals and lacking official protection, three judges recused themselves from the case. The fourth judge freed the Liguistas on the basis of insufficient evidence. Policemen resumed their usual harassment of labor militants, and the LPA managed to impose free laborers in job categories once dominated by FORA IX affiliates.[48]

Since 1918 FOM and FORA IX also had helped organize unions in Chubut, Santa Cruz, and Tierra del Fuego, which affiliated with the Federación Obrera Regional (FOR) of Río Gallegos. In response, businessmen, ranchers, and ranch managers, many of them European-born or representatives of foreign companies, formed about seventy-five brigades, with additional branches in the interior. The LPA and ANT reinforced these groups with free laborers. As elsewhere, the foreign-born joined both sides of the struggle, a fact the LPA tried to obscure by distinguishing foreign *capitalists*, who contributed to the national economy, from foreign, mostly Chilean *radicals*, who in its view did not.

Liguistas cooperated with authorities in repressing a vibrant labor movement and one of the largest rural strikes in Argentine history. Called by FOR in November 1920, the peons' strike aroused great anger among large sheep ranchers. LPA vigilantes pushed strikers off the ranches and hunted down workers they blamed for disorders. Lieutenant Colonel Héctor Varela, the Radical commander of the Tenth Cavalry Regiment, helped resolve the dispute to the benefit of labor, but when landowners disavowed the agreement, workers resumed the strike. Urging the government to step in again, the LPA and employers pushed Yrigoyen into sending Varela back in November 1921. The LPA patrolled Santa Cruz and joined the army in its sweep through the interior. Furnishing vehicles, fuel, housing, and provisions, the LPA helped the military slaughter as many as 1,500 striking ranch hands by January 1922. Once Varela's men had demolished the Patagonian unions, the LPA organized workers in the area into free labor brigades. The episode was the LPA's most important victory over workers.[49]

The Patagonian brigades and Carlés congratulated Varela for his successful mission. Concerned that the massacre had undermined his support among workers, Yrigoyen did not praise the commander or publicize the event. His silence irritated army officers, who thought that the president was seeking to shore up his image at their expense. It also bothered members of the elite, who believed that he had repeated his dilatory response to the Semana Trágica. Yet the ruling party also tried to appeal to the upper class. Radical deputies helped defeat a Socialist attempt to form a commission to investigate the Patagonian killings, just as they had done to a Socialist request to ask the minister of the interior to explain the Las Palmas episode.[50] One should also recall the Radicals' lack of sympathy for the taxi drivers and workers in Villaguay and their flip-flops over Gualeguaychú. In these instances partisan interest and a desire to appease the elite tilted the ruling party toward capital.

Thus, like the Chilean ADT and Alessandri, the LPA and ANT forced Yrigoyen part of the way back to the old means of repressing labor. The government continued to court native-born, less contentious, politically unaffiliated workers. Yet it also prohibited some leftist rallies and authorized police to imprison labor militants, enforce the residence and social defense laws, and ban the display of anarchist and Socialist flags.[51]

Aided by the LPA, the ANT, and the government, as well as a gradual lowering of inflation and a labor surplus, employers won the contest with labor. Union membership and the number of strikes and strikers declined markedly in the 1920s. FORA IX fell apart in 1922, and the weaker and smaller USA replaced it. The left also split when some Socialists joined the Communist Party, founded in 1920. Seemingly so strong in 1919, labor and leftist groups were in disarray.[52]

Gender and the LPA

While male Liguistas suppressed laborers, their female colleagues sought to "Argentinize" them, drawing upon their philanthropic experience and Social Catholic conceptions of social justice. Their main targets were women, who constituted about 22 percent of the national labor force in 1914 and as many as 30 percent of industrial and manual laborers. Some of these women belonged to unions and female anarchist and Socialist centers. Although female workers were almost equally divided between Argentine- and foreign-born, the Señoritas deemed it necessary to bring all into the nation. To this end they established tuition-free schools in greater Buenos Aires. Nineteen such schools attracted over nine thousand students by 1927, and as late as 1950 the LPA claimed that over fifty were operating.[53]

Carlés described the schools as "exclusively Argentine." Classes in reading and writing, arithmetic, secretarial skills, and sewing and other vocational arts, and access to reading materials in the library annexes gave women opportunity to move upward within the given order. Instruction in hygiene, home economics, childcare, and first aid prepared them for tasks in the home. The schools also provided an alternative to such unhealthy activities as flirting with men, drinking, dancing the tango, or watching immoral films. Lessons on the catechism, patience, modesty, love, family, and work reinforced the schools' moral mission. Students learned to be content, courteous, punctual, and respectful toward authority—"Argentine values" attractive to management. Lectures on Argentine history, geography, and civics emphasized patriotism, as did other parts of the curriculum. María Lea Gastón, a student at the Gratry factory school, reported that her teacher taught them to sew and sing patriotic songs at the same time.[54] The school's Argentine nature meant submission to the gender and class structure.

The Señoritas' overriding goal was to prevent subversives from exploiting female workers' ignorance, as Elisa del Campillo, first vice president of the Señoritas, saw it. A factory school teacher, Carmen Lasse, assuaged male Liguistas' possible fears by telling an LPA congress that educating the woman did not mean filling her with "abstract science," but teaching her to be a "conscientious mother" and to hate disorder.[55] Whether women transmitted their lessons to their children and husbands was unclear, although small numbers of male workers attended the schools as well.

Although they assigned instructional tasks to hired teachers, the Señoritas played important roles in the schools. They set the curriculum, provided role models for the young workers, solicited space from employers, collected funds and books, and publicized their efforts at the LPA congresses and throughout society. This work may have brought them closer to their charges; as President Jorgelina Cano of the Señoritas learned, these pitiful youngsters were "our sisters." Another Señorita, Marta Ezcurra, moved from the LPA to a career in social work. While it is not clear whether these examples were typical, it is evident that the Señoritas administered the LPA's most important social project. They also set up a home for juvenile delinquents, led fund-raising drives for male brigades and needy children, and organized neighborhood libraries.[56]

The Señoras also directed most of their efforts toward strengthening the immigrant family and integrating it into the nation. They organized day-care centers, free clinics, schools, patriotic celebrations, and distribution of food, books, clothing, and cradles in poor areas, along with benefits to finance these activities. In doing so they cultivated skills like those of the Señoritas. The Señoras' best-known project, however, did not involve foreigners. From 1920 through at least the 1930s, they held annual expositions and sales of textiles produced by Indian and Creole women in their homes in the northwest. The Señoras intended to help an economically deprived and truly Argentine group of women and enable them to remain in their households. Also, as Señoras president Hortensia Berdier pointed out, the project exemplified the LPA's belief in stimulating industries using local raw materials.[57]

The female social endeavors aimed to ameliorate specific problems faced by the proletariat, without increasing its agency. The textile fairs also represented awareness of a more abstract issue—the need for a long-term solution to underdevelopment. Manifesting concern for broad issues, women (and men) of the Magisterio brigades railed against Bolshevik and secular influences in education and, like the cultural nationalists, sought to promote its "Argentine" character. For the most part, however, female Liguistas left theories and abstractions to men.

Ironically, although LPA women sharpened their talents in the organization, they did not take a public stand on feminism. Their speeches never referred to women obtaining the vote at the local level in Santa Fe in 1921 and San Juan in 1927 or additional rights in the revised civil code of 1926. Indeed, their privileged yet nonprofessional backgrounds, top-down notion of charity, and ties to the church set female Liguistas apart from leftist women and feminists.[58]

Male Liguistas also were involved in social works, especially after they helped repress the strike wave by 1922. Primary schools, vocational classes for workers, free clinics, and children's tours of the capital were among their projects. They also sponsored homages and awards for policemen, firemen, and soldiers, patriotic commemorations, and activities with nationalistic or local themes. Some of these events infused customary practices with new meaning, such as the "rustic dinners" often hosted by brigades. Serving typical foods in a rural atmosphere, these meals reminded guests of the social peace and national virtue once supposedly found in the countryside.[59]

Yet these endeavors were not as important as the female ones, which fit the LPA's and society's notions of gender. Señorita President Cano ascribed "peace, love, and resignation," as well as idealism, faith, intuition, will, and perseverance to women. These mythic qualities suited women's duties as mother, helpmate, teacher, and caregiver within the family, LPA, and nation. The male personality that the LPA envisioned lent itself to men's roles as fighters, publicists, lobbyists, and ideologues. The LPA constructed men as benevolent yet authoritarian heads of family and the public sphere, to whom women, children, and their social inferiors owed respect and deference. Austere and Christian, these *caballeros argentinos* would protect honor, home, property, and country with arms, if necessary. In times of conflict, Liguistas resorted to martial language; Gualeguaychú brigade members described men of their province as brave *hidalgos* (noblemen) with a "strong arm and fist." Carlés warned, however, that "violence is an exception, not a system; it is a form of national defense that can never take on the character of vengeance." A teacher in military schools, the LPA president advocated the "intelligent violence of warriors, not of evildoers." An observer interpreted Carlés's "cult of heroism" to mean civic virtue rather than martial discipline.[60]

Carlés and the LPA equivocated on whether force was an essential quality of manhood. The LPA sponsored a lecture series in 1923 by Leopoldo Lugones, who had no such doubts. His desire for the people to unite in spirit with the military against its enemies, including democracy and leftism, surpassed Carlés's mild militarism. The poet proclaimed that Argentines had to "virilely" face the task of "cleaning the country" of radical immigrants, either through repression or expulsion. In a famous speech the next year (this one unrelated to the LPA), Lugones announced the arrival of the "hour of the sword." Four action verbs, "to arm, combat, command, teach," defined the complete life. The first three were "expressions of conquest and force"; indeed, "life itself is a state of force." The true man would assume the higher calling of duty, sacrifice, heroism, and other martial virtues.[61] More radical than the LPA's conception of manhood, Lugones's view formed a bridge between the vitalism of the Comité Nacional de la Juventud and the far right of the 1930s.

LPA Ideology

The LPA charged men and women with injecting morality into society. Indeed, notions of purity and propriety obsessed Carlés. Like author Julián Martel, he did not want foreigners to "pollute" Argentina or "contagion in immoral homes" to infect children. Carlés defined the immoral home as one that was outside matrimony or followed leftist belief; to him, the two seemed identical. The LPA's task, he noted, was to "moralize the home and guard the people" from "immoralities and perversions" brought by immigrants. Such immorality even extended into the political system, where "evil political breeds . . . stimulated all the concupiscence of the low social levels in exchange for the electoral vote." Argentine mothers defended "the purity of morals" by training their children to resist the passions that weakened reason; male Liguistas did so through arms, ideology, and the example they set. Carlés's preoccupation with bodily control betrayed his concern for social control. In his view, evil from the outside threatened society, the body writ large; cleanliness stood for the expulsion of this foreign threat.[62]

LPA men wove morality into their ideology of class conciliation. Carlés claimed that before mass immigration, Argentines had accepted the world as it was, unequal and hierarchical. Respecting family, property, and authority as the basis of society, they had progressed in an orderly manner through hard work and saving. Ungrateful "guests," however, had overturned moral politics in favor of their immoral version, polluting the nation that had welcomed them. They denied the world as it was in favor of the way they wanted it to be. Utopians, anarchists, socialists, and syndicalists—all were "human dregs without God, country, law," or family. Against those who wanted to construct society using a theoretical blueprint, the LPA hoped to secure the general welfare through natural means, according to what was "humanly possible." One could not eliminate distinctions among people; all individuals would retain the positions "natural" to them and take only what was rightfully theirs. At the same time the LPA favored laws that curbed the abusive rich and labor militants alike and helped the poor. Such reforms "humanized" leftist ideals by removing their theoretical coating and converting them into real possibilities. Carlés called them examples of "practical Christianity" or "practical humanitarianism."[63]

The LPA disagreed with the leftist view of class as well as leftist utopianism. It regarded nations, rather than classes, as the primary social units. Some Liguistas denied the existence of classes in Argentina, while others claimed that they were not as rigid as in Europe. Whether classes existed or not, most LPA members agreed that the possibility of upward mobility robbed them of significance. Liguistas offered their own "Argentine" definition of workers as including all producers and thinkers. This definition permitted the LPA to call its first three annual meetings "Congresses of Workers." As would German National Socialists, Liguistas obscured leftist terminology or sought to replace it with their own.[64]

Members and guests discussed means of implementing practical humanitarianism in the LPA congresses. They debated the merits of social security, labor regulations, maternity leaves and other benefits for female workers, public housing, cooperatives, profit sharing, and land reform. Many of these proposals harked back to Social Catholics and conservative reformers, and members of these groups presented papers and helped draft commission reports. Although some Liguistas were foreign-born businessmen or worked for foreign companies, speakers manifested concern for economic nationalism. One explained that the industrialized nations maintained a trade balance favorable to them, confining primary product producers "to an economic slavery which keeps them in a plane inferior to countries prepared to control their destinies." He wanted Argentina to assert control over its own resources and economic life. LPA members encouraged Argentines to invest locally and the government to raise tariff barriers, curb foreign investment, reduce the external debt, and establish a merchant marine, public investment fund, and state meatpacking plant. Inevitably, the LPA tied economic nationalism to the social question. It viewed industrialization as a means of raising employment and thereby reducing labor dissatisfaction. Some Liguistas blamed underdevelopment on worker-led disturbances, giving them another reason to regard labor as antinationalistic. Similar to Ricardo Rojas, Carlés linked radical immigrants' exploitation of Argentina to that of foreign capital; both, in his view, required a nationalistic solution.[65]

Liguistas avoided criticizing the landowning elite and local capitalism by casting blame elsewhere. Not only foreign business and labor, but middlemen, colonizing companies, and representatives of finance capital were targets of LPA ire. Yet the congresses did not single out Jewish merchants and financiers.[66]

Corporatism, as advocated by a prominent jurist and member of the Junta Central, Arturo Pallejá, offered a potential solution to the problems of social disorder, political decay, and usury.[67] Although the LPA president found much fault with civil liberties, universal suffrage, equality, and Yrigoyenist "demagoguery," until the late 1920s Carlés considered corporatism tyrannical and did not call for a change in the political system.[68] Unlike in Chile, where fear of social instability prompted labor legislation in the mid-1920s, in Argentina, after the defeat of labor in 1922, few Liguistas were willing to consider such sweeping changes to preserve the essentials of the social order.

Familiar with corporatism, LPA members also were acquainted with rightist movements elsewhere. Carlés praised the Italian Fascist land distribution program as a bulwark against Bolshevism and compared the LPA to various European antileftist groups, with which the LPA corresponded. A Liguista even visited Action Française, a group founded by the premier European radical rightist of the day, Charles Maurras. Nevertheless, the LPA's annual meetings and pamphlets never mentioned Maurras and rarely referred to any European organizations. The only foreign influences the LPA president acknowledged were positivism and Catholicism. Again, this enabled him to distinguish the LPA's *argentinidad* from the "exotic" doctrine of class conflict, which Carlés believed did not apply to an underdeveloped country.[69]

Diversity within the organization impeded consensus on issues other than the need to tame workers. Speeches at the congresses, however, reflected the growing willingness of the upper and middle sectors to consider antiliberal economic ideas. The economic uncertainties of the postwar era led some members of the elite, within and outside the LPA, to contemplate a limited industrialization program that would not transform the socioeconomic structure.[70]

Despite the LPA's anti-Jewish and anti-immigrant origins, its congresses devoted little attention to such issues. The statutes had recommended excluding immigrants who disagreed with the constitution, and a few speeches at the meetings advocated restricting the entry of immigrants. Most Liguistas, however, seemed to favor Argentinizing and controlling foreigners rather than excluding them. Nor did antisemitism make its way into official LPA ideology, although the flow of 67,000 Eastern European and Middle Eastern Jews into Argentina from 1921 to 1930 may have concerned Liguistas. Their interest in maintaining a labor surplus tempered their nativism. Still, probably most LPA members believed in keeping Argentina as white and Christian as possible. An invited speaker, the essayist Lucas Ayarragaray, emphasized the need to maintain the country's racial heritage, particularly by preventing an Asian influx. Occasionally Liguistas referred to means of enhancing the Creole race. A suggestion to keep victims of certain diseases from marriage was one of the rare examples of social Darwinism within the organization.[71]

The LPA's mild stance on immigration and race indicated its essentially moderate views. It represented the radicalization of the moderate right during the postwar crisis. Once the crisis had diminished, its members shelved their violence and threatening rhetoric and reverted to conservatism. The LPA's submergence of antisemitism was a mark of its declining radicalism. Strident criticism of Jews could lead to broader questioning of the economic system, as seen below (see Part 3), broader than the LPA wished to entertain.

The Church

The LPA's partner in conservatism was the Catholic Church. Five priests and at least eleven staunch Social Catholic laypersons appeared in the sample of male Liguistas, and there were other signs of overlap. Father de Andrea belonged to the provisional governing body and first Junta, and he and Father Piaggio attended the first LPA meeting. The archbishop of Buenos

Aires was honorary president of the eighth congress, and the bishops of Corrientes, Salta, and Tucumán visited the ninth. Other highly placed clerics such as Father Gustavo Franceschi, Monsignor Dionisio Napal, and Nicolás Fasolino, vicar general of the Archbishopric of Buenos Aires, delivered addresses at the LPA's annual meetings. Napal and Father Saravia Ferré were brigade members, and the Franciscan Juan B. Lagos served in the Junta Central. Significantly, the priests tied to the LPA tended to be military chaplains, indicating the links between the three institutions.[72] That Carlés gave talks in churches also signaled the hierarchy's approval.

Why the church befriended the LPA is not immediately evident. Many Catholics belonged to the Radical Party and admired Yrigoyen's philosophy, which contained ideas that were Catholic in nature or resembled Catholic thought. Like the church, he assigned to the state the duty of mediating among social groups and promoting harmony, and he appealed to morality and frequently resorted to Christian metaphors. The president favored a labor code and other social measures reminiscent of Social Catholicism, although they stalled in Congress. Yrigoyen donated his presidential salary to Catholic charity, opposed attempts in Congress to legislate divorce, and chose prominent clerics for ceremonial roles. The church must have found these aspects of Yrigoyenism attractive. However, the hierarchy probably agreed with Franceschi, who believed that the president had not sufficiently braked labor militancy.[73] The church's lingering suspicion of the state may also have motivated its ties with a private institution of order.

Catholicism and the LPA overlapped in significant ways. At LPA congresses priests spoke on such issues as labor legislation, nationalism in the church, and the church's social mission, indicating the LPA's receptivity to these views. Carlés consistently supported Social Catholic positions, "Christian morality," "practical Christianity," and "the school with God." The LPA's insistence on its nonpolitical character probably also mollified clerical concern about offending the government.[74]

The response of the predominant current within the hierarchy to the Semana Trágica resembled the LPA's co-optative side. Similar in theory if not practice to the free labor brigades, the eighty-five workers' circles attracted 36,000 members by 1919. In April of that year, a new organization, the Unión Popular Católica Argentina (UPCA), dedicated itself to invigorating the Catholic social conscience, "the nationality, and, more concretely, . . . Argentinism," according to de Andrea. Its directorate included three lay Liguistas, de Andrea, and Fasolino. A fund-raising drive, whose slogan was "Give and you will conserve," was its most important activity. De

Andrea was its spiritual leader, and most members of its financial committee were Liguistas, as were other organizers and contributors, including eighteen women. The proceeds financed four small worker neighborhoods, a vocational school for female workers, and other projects.[75]

As the use of these funds suggested, Social Catholics continued to mobilize women—and in ways that resembled the LPA. The Sociedad La Cruz de Obreras Fosforeras, founded by a priest in 1917, attracted workers from other industries and set up fifteen locals with 650 members in Greater Buenos Aires. Meanwhile, guided by Father Gustavo Franceschi, upper-class girls established the Centro de Estudios Blanca de Castilla in 1916. The Centro organized seamstresses, retail employees, and other female laborers into three Catholic syndicates, which by 1919 had 719 members. Like their counterparts founded by the Chilean Liga de Damas, the syndicates and La Cruz respected religion, country, family, and property and emphasized education and mutual aid. In 1922 de Andrea's explicitly antirevolutionary Federación de Asociaciones de Empleadas (FACE) absorbed all four groups; nine years later FACE included eighteen unions with 7,000 members.[76]

Perhaps their agreement on class conciliation allowed the hierarchy to overlook less Christian aspects of the LPA. One such aspect was Carlés's tendency to deify the nation. He invoked the "fatherland" as the "deity" that had "consolidated the peace, secured justice, promoted the general welfare and assured the blessings of liberty." Appropriating Catholic terms for political use, he entitled another speech "Catechism of the fatherland doctrine."[77] Such statements did not harmonize with church teachings; the Vatican would criticize Action Française, Italian Fascism, and German Nazism for putting nationalism above religion and substituting one for the other. Nor did the LPA's violent acts conform to church notions of social peace.

Miguel de Andrea epitomized church links with the LPA and with a Catholicism that was more patriotic than spiritual. While some, particularly in the elite and hierarchy, regarded him as leftist, others found his ambitions, top-down leadership style, and ties to politicians and the upper class repugnant. They accused him of alienating the poor by casting the Social Catholic programs as means of avoiding revolution, rather than simple social justice. The controversy that enveloped him helped doom his nomination for archbishop of Buenos Aires in the mid-1920s. After the Vatican rejected him, de Andrea gave up his candidacy, but President Marcelo T. de Alvear (1922–28) refused to accept his resignation. When a delegation of Catholics asked Alvear to change his mind, he instead cut government funding for the church. Finally the president accepted the resignation but declared the nuncio and his secretary persona non grata. The dispute ended in 1925, when the Vatican ratified Alvear's new choice.[78]

Alvear's actions rankled many Catholics and reminded them that they lacked influence over the secular state. For this and other reasons, some turned against democracy. Franceschi advocated moving toward a corporatist system, in which the legislature would represent economic groups rather than political parties, and only male family heads would vote. In the meantime, Franceschi and de Andrea tempered their suspicions of democracy with the belief that the church could tame and moralize it.[79]

A movement rejecting democracy altogether grew out of attempts to form a young Catholic elite. Catholic students had already mobilized against the university reform movement, which advocated a greater role for students in university governance, along with other changes in administration and curricula. To Catholics this movement endangered social hierarchy and religious values. Founded in 1922 as a response, the Cursos de Cultura Católica trained upper-class youths in orthodox theology and philosophy. Reading secular rightist thinkers such as Charles Maurras, Ramiro de Maeztu, Nicolai Berdiaev, Osvald Spengler, Maurice Barrès, and Werner Sombart, students began to envision a hierarchical corporatist society. The participants regarded themselves as rebels against the Catholic bourgeois establishment. "Dissident toward tradition and toward the right, but dissident" nonetheless, they initiated a Catholic "revolution" that would transform the right in the late 1920s.[80]

Conclusion

The LPA had reached its apogee by 1922. During the next six years, unions declined and the LPA was content with President Alvear, a moderate Radical who appointed Carlés as interventor in San Juan in 1922 and Domecq García as naval minister. From this position, the first LPA president could impose free labor policies in the port. The government was once again in the hands of aristocrats whom the elite trusted to protect its interests. Thus the LPA remained quiescent until the end of the decade.

Still, postwar Argentine conditions, in contrast to Chile, had nurtured an extreme right-wing movement. Labor had imperiled the oligarchy's economic base, and members of the middle as well as upper classes, male and female, feared for their property and privileges. Divided and weakened, conservative forces had lost control of the state in this most democratic of Latin American countries, and they suspected the reformist government of leniency toward workers. These motives pushed them toward the extreme right. The moderate right—aristocratic women, employers, conservative parties, upper-class Radicals, and most Social Catholics—shared the basic tenets of the LPA and ANT, the extreme rightists. So did the predominant factions in the church and the military. The fact that the LPA never set itself apart from conservatives or Radicals by establishing itself as a political party permitted this overlap. The LPA and ANT drew their membership from the moderates; all that separated moderates from extremists in this crisis was the extremists' willingness to use force and in other ways work outside the political system. Thus the extremists served as the moderates' armed guard. The end of this period, however, witnessed new Catholic-inspired radicals whose beliefs would differ markedly from those of moderate rightists.

CHAPTER 7

Against Anarchism: Brazilian Nationalism

From 1915 on, "nationalism invaded Brazilian culture,"[1] although not always in a clearly rightist fashion. Ideologies were not as well defined in Brazil as in Argentina and Chile, and here the ruling parties stood for little but oligarchical power. While some of the new movements seemed liberal democratic, they overlapped with and contributed ideas to others much further to the right. The military continued to furnish support for change along authoritarian lines. Extreme rightists also drew upon the anti-Portuguese and corporatist legacy left by the previous generation. Antisemitism and reactionary Catholicism distinguished them from moderates and most precursors. Unlike the other cases, the radical right was at odds with the conservative oligarchies that controlled the state.

Economy, War, and National Defense

As in Argentina, nationalist groups consolidated during an economic crisis. Industry expanded during World War I, and coffee fared well until 1917. The rubber sector collapsed during the war, however, and coffee prices sank after 1918. Declining imports of food, industrial inputs, and other goods limited manufacturing efforts, cut tariff revenues for the federal government, and increased the cost of living. The inflation rate was 125 percent from 1914 to 1924; food prices alone tripled between 1914 and 1920. Yet until 1919 wages fell precipitously. These conditions spelled hardship, and they reminded intellectuals and policymakers of Brazil's dependence on foreign markets, capital, and imports.[2]

In Brazil as well as in Argentina, there was considerable sympathy for the Allies. In March 1915, the distinguished spokesman for liberal democracy, Ruy Barbosa, poet Olavo Bilac, jurist Pedro Lessa, and others formed the Liga Pro Aliados, which pressured the government to enter the war on the Allied side. Like the Argentine Comité de la Juventud, Liga members wanted to take part in an elevating cause. The Liga also campaigned against the Teuto-Brazilian community's use of the German language and loyalty to Germany. Its concern over German cultural isolationism expanded into a general preoccupation with assimilating immigrants and spreading patriotism. Similar sentiments lay behind anti-German riots in 1917. Tied more closely through trade and diplomacy to the United States than were Chile and Argentina, Brazil entered the war in October of that year after Germany torpedoed four of its ships, and it suspended German-language publications and schools. The Brazilian military, however, played only a limited combat role.[3]

Even before Brazil entered the war, members of the Liga and the upper classes demonstrated concern over preparedness. The idealism stirred by the conflict as well as an older fear of Brazilian weakness influenced this attitude, which was embodied in Olavo Bilac. During a speaking tour in October 1915, the poet admonished São Paulo law students for leaving "Brazil devastated without war and decrepit before old age." In Europe, virile young men were marching off to fight, but apathetic Brazilians were inert. Self-interest, a "hideous foreignism," infected the educated elite and threatened to widen into an epidemic, whereas the rest of the population, malnourished and unschooled, was scarcely human. Government did nothing to help the masses or to integrate the immigrants into the nation. Bilac claimed that if it were enforced, the universal conscription law of 1908 would promote democracy, civic pride, unity, patriotism, and, by implication, manliness. The military also would turn the poor into healthy, literate citizens. Hence the draft would strengthen order and the nationality at a time when they were besieged. He urged youth to work toward this goal, asking medical students to heal their sick country. Common among Brazilian intellectuals, Bilac's penchant for metaphors of the body and disease revealed anxiety over internal decay as well as external threat.[4]

The internal threat that he, like Alberto Torres, envisioned was one of disintegration. Conflicts and economic inequalities among the states, along with political corruption, could tear the country apart. Bilac recommended civic education, based in schools and the military, to combat fragmentation. The elite would have to cultivate its civic virtue before it could prepare the public or solve Brazil's economic problems.[5]

The Ligas

Bilac found an outlet for his ideas in the Liga da Defesa Nacional (LDN), deliberately named after a prestigious military journal, which he helped found in 1916. The LDN attempted to consolidate a citizens' army by supporting the draft and military training in schools and other institutions, scout troops, and the formation of reserve units. Spreading patriotism and the cult of heroism through speeches, publications, celebrations, and prizes was another activity. Talks given by Bilac and other leaders received widespread coverage, especially in the nationalist *Revista do Brasil*, published in São Paulo from 1916 to 1925. Like its predecessor, it promoted instruction in Portuguese and the building of national schools in foreign colonies. The national president served as the honorary chief, and each state president headed the local regional directory, thus cementing ties between the government and the Rio de Janeiro–based organization. Indeed, the founders picked the ministers of war, the navy, and finance, along with a prominent cleric, as officers, although the LDN insisted on its independence from partisan politics. Pedro Lessa became the first LDN president; Miguel Calmon, a distinguished statesman from the Bahian elite, vice president; and Bilac secretary-general. Members of the Liga Pro Aliados figured prominently in the group.[6]

The LDN won adherents from influential sectors. Military officers furnished Bilac with materials to document his case and attempted to win over the army to his ideas. They as well as eminent businessmen and professionals were among the leaders, and the educated middle class filled the ranks. Jorge Street and other wealthy notables contributed funds, and Cardinal Joaquim Arcoverde de Albuquerque Cavalcanti of Rio de Janeiro and archbishops and bishops lent their support, as did monarchists such as Afonso Celso.[7]

Support for the LDN, however, was not universal, even among nationalists. For Alberto Torres, the defense of Brazil required constitutional and administrative reform, fiscal prudence, and economic nationalism more than a citizen army. One might also have criticized the LDN's voluntary training for enabling participants to claim the status of reservists and secure exemption from the draft, seemingly defeating Bilac's purpose of unifying the country. At any rate, the LDN helped convince the administration, already pressured by the military and wartime fears of unpreparedness, to enforce the draft law.[8]

Bilac coupled the LDN's military pursuits with martial rhetoric. Life consisted of "constant combat," and those who did not defend themselves weakened and perished. Brazilians had to protect not only their bodies and material goods but also their honor and history. Yet Bilac was no full-blown social Darwinist. He thought education and better nutrition would improve Brazil's mixed race, which he did not regard as inherently inferior.[9]

For LDN members, nationalism implied antiliberalism as well as manly heroism. Deputy and novelist Henrique Coelho Neto advised Brazilians to welcome foreigners proudly, not submissively, and not to allow them to acquire land, the repository of the nationality and wealth. Another LDN member, Belisário Penna, a well-known hygienist and eugenicist, pointed out how disease, malnutrition, and ignorance weakened Brazilians and prevented them from working efficiently. The government needed to provide vocational and hygiene instruction to the masses and settle them in an organized fashion in the interior. This task of *saneamento* (sanitation) would be difficult, for local oligarchies had taken advantage of the republic's excessive liberalism and promoted anarchy. Yet the generalized state of "illness" required urgent attention.[10]

LDN president Augusto Olympio Viveiros de Castro, minister of the Supreme Federal Tribunal, agreed. Thanks to excessive individualism, citizens ignored their civic duties, employers treated laborers like machines, and workers issued ruinous demands. Egoism also accounted for paternal abandonment of families and the use of birth control, which deprived the state of population and degraded marriage. This form of individualism was related to the problem of sensuality, especially evident in the capital, where women were no longer chaste. The family would disintegrate if Brazilians did not restore the old moral code.[11]

Other LDN members shared Castro's concern for hierarchy and family. To claim that one was a citizen of humanity, rather than of one nation, was utopian and ridiculous, thought Bilac: Was there a world confederation? Were there citizens of the planetary system? Those who denied the fatherland were "moral monsters" who denied all social and moral life. Everyone belonged to a family, a fatherland, and humanity, which were intertwined; one could not reject one without rejecting the other two, and if he lacked these, a man lacked a self. According to Coelho Neto, only the imprudent contemplated overthrowing "those who are on top without remembering that the fall of the higher ones exposes the weakest ones to misery and the entire edifice to ruin." Because the family imparted such admirable traits as discipline, order, hard work, and obedience to one's superiors, the stronger the family the stronger the nation and the social fabric.[12]

Coelho Neto made these remarks against the backdrop of labor mobilization. Inflation, inspiration from abroad, and increased consciousness and organization led workers to mount an unprecedented number of strikes between 1917 and 1920. Anarcho-syndicalists helped lead two major waves of activity in 1917 and 1919. Roughly 50,000 laborers took part in a general strike in São Paulo in 1917 that sparked strikes throughout the country. Militancy peaked in 1919, with sixty-four strikes in the city of São Paulo, fourteen in that state, and seventeen in Rio de Janeiro. Constituting 36 percent of all industrial laborers in 1920, women were important participants in these actions. Indeed, a strike by female textile workers in São Paulo had precipitated the general strike of 1917.[13]

The government asked the LDN to contemplate responses to the strike wave. Offering official support, in April 1920 Minister of Justice Alfred Pinto suggested that the LDN should plan "repressive action" against anarchism and Bolshevism. Coelho Neto promised that his organization would call on the "conservative classes" to help spread "patriotic propaganda," following the model set by the Liga Patriótica Argentina. It would aim its propaganda at native-born workers, showing them that foreign subversives pushed them to the front line and hid behind them. The fact that 60 percent of industrial laborers in 1920 were immigrants tended to reinforce such views, as did the continuing predominance of foreigners among labor leaders. The LDN created a commission to study the labor question and devise means of ensuring social peace.[14] Repression by civilians proved unnecessary, however, for the official forces of order quelled the unions.

Debilitated by his speaking tours, Bilac died in 1918. The elite who had responded enthusiastically to the draft during wartime increasingly evaded it by 1920, a fact that did not escape the nationalists' or the military's attention. By the mid-1920s, the LDN had faded from public view.[15]

Bilac's campaign had inspired the formation of another nationalist group, however. Since the early 1900s, a reformist circle had formed within the Paulista Republican Party (PRP), the ruling party of São Paulo. Led by Júlio de Mesquita Filho, co-owner of *O Estado de São Paulo* and a founder of *Revista do Brasil*, these intellectuals and professionals favored popular electoral participation and mass education. This group arranged for Bilac to inaugurate his nationalist speaking tour in the São Paulo law school in 1915.

The poet urged Mesquita Filho to mobilize his fellow law students, many of whom were related to the PRP dissidents. Conversations among pupils and professors led to the founding of the Liga Nacionalista (LN) in 1916.[16]

Mesquita Filho agreed with Torres that Brazil lacked a sense of nationality: "In our borrowed civilization there is not even adaptation: there is simply a copy." By disparaging what was native, Brazilians weakened confidence and civic attitudes, which in turn led them to put their individual, class, and regional interests above those of a country that barely existed. Mesquita Filho agreed with Bilac on the need to stem this "social anarchy" by ridding the leading classes of apathy and pessimism. The (soon fascist) poet Filippo Tommaso Marinetti's emphasis on masculinity and vitalism, which had already inspired the *Revista do Brasil*, also resounded in Mesquita Filho's aim of preparing a new generation of patriotic, energetic youth. This generation would create a united nation "conscious of its force, free of . . . economic tutelage and the squeeze of foreign capital."[17]

The LN declared itself to be a nonpartisan group dedicated to national solidarity. It supported implementation of the draft law, scouting, and reserve units, yet it emphasized suffrage and education. The LN advocated the study of national problems and the obligatory teaching of the Brazilian language, history, and geography by Brazilian-born teachers in all schools. Its "solidarity" had its limits, for only native-born men were eligible for LN membership. This exclusion revealed a xenophobic streak, as did criticism of foreigners and Afro-Brazilians by Mesquita Filho. The fact that the organization did not select its leaders democratically was another indication of elitism. Headed by law professor Frederico Vergueiro Steidel, the group was filled with educators, law students, and journalists. Directing itself toward the "superior classes," the LN had attracted only 1,004 members by 1917.[18]

In many ways the LN resembled the LDN. The two groups arose out of the same wartime context and nationalist campaign, their leadership coalesced in an authoritarian fashion, and their themes overlapped. Both aimed at regenerating the elite. The LDN's emphasis on military service, however, differed from the LN's focus on education and suffrage. The LDN's concerns reflected its origins in consultations among intellectuals and military and national political leaders, and its headquarters in the federal capital reinforced its ties with the last two groups. The wealthiest state in Brazil, São Paulo, had the largest middle and working classes, and the LN represented the dissident sector within the ruling party that envisioned integrating these classes into the existing order through the vote.

Fear of revolution permeated the LN's views on political change. In the LN-sponsored *O que o cidadão deve saber* (1919), Antônio de Sampaio Dória, professor at the normal school of São Paulo, warned against anarchism or other forms of cosmopolitanism. Mesquita Filho argued that democracy could strengthen the social order, but if workers were not incorporated into electoral politics, a revolution would destroy the nationality.[19]

While it sponsored other activities, the LN mostly worked for electoral change. It urged citizens to vote and helped them register. The organization lobbied for the secret obligatory ballot, but it did not favor extending the vote to women or illiterates. Instead, it believed that educating the male masses would enable them to qualify to vote and make independent choices on election day, thus eliminating corrupt political machines and oligarchies. Moreover, teaching immigrant workers to read would nationalize them. To further this goal, the LN assisted some immigrants in the naturalization process.[20]

In pursuit of these aims, the LN created night schools for workers, many of them immigrants, in São Paulo and the interior. The state provided materials and space, sometimes in existing schools, and the LN paid for electricity, personnel, and printing. The Asociação Comercial of São Paulo also donated funds, and industrialists permitted the LN to establish schools in their factories. The curriculum, which included civics, hygiene, and morality, resembled the program of the Liga Patriótica Argentina, as did the LN's decision to name them "nationalist schools." As of 1918, 624 men and 232 women were enrolled in such institutions, and in 1919 at least nine schools were operating. The night school for women may have been the first of its kind in Brazil.[21]

The LN also backed broader educational change. São Paulo state president Washington Luís (1920–24) appointed Dória director of public education, and he devised a reform package strongly supported by the LN. Previously, the state had obliged children to attend school for four years yet failed to adequately finance their education or assure their presence. Doria's new law cut the four-year obligatory schooling to two years yet raised educational funding, enforced attendance, and incorporated scouting into school programs. The reform reinforced the rigid social structure. Two years were not enough to impart literacy, and the law discouraged pupils by setting a fee for the next two years. At any rate, the reform was short-lived. In 1925, Luis's successor restored the four-year program.[22]

LN support of the status quo was evident in its reaction to workers. In October 1919, the Federação Operária planned a general strike to protest police harassment of militants, unions, and the labor press. In response, the

LN warned foreign workers that "Brazil is ours," and that only Brazilians could participate in politics. It cautioned Brazilian laborers against adhering to combative unions or to militants whom the LN accused of hoodwinking them. A few days after this patronizing and xenophobic statement, on October 31, students arrived at the law school to find a provocative article from A Plebe plastered on a wall. It joked that "our Catholic city" could not live without prostitutes, the "defenders of public morality," who supposedly were about to go on strike. Enraged by this affront to their manhood, law students destroyed the editorial and printing offices of the anarchist organ, and they carried out a mock burial of printed materials they found there. The mob tried to attack the prolabor Diario Español, but a police guard, conspicuously absent from A Plebe, prevented the students from entering. Perhaps state authorities feared the diplomatic consequences of assaulting a Spanish press. Since most LN members were law students, they probably were among the vigilantes.[23]

Hoping to bridge the gap between left and right, Afonso Schmidt addressed the LN in A Plebe. The leftist journalist insisted that only those freed from wage slavery could "sanitize" the interior and end illiteracy; only a libertarian-style commune could develop the civic engagement and spirituality that Bilac had desired. Criticizing the LN for overlooking abuses of foreign capital and for its partnership with government, Schmidt asked the movement to create with the left a nationalism that would free Brazil from the foreign yoke. The LN ignored Schmidt, however, and lost interest in labor matters after authorities quelled the 1919 strike.[24]

Governments and businessmen cooperated in repressing labor. Employer associations worked with the public forces of order to break strikes and smash unions. Federal legislation passed in 1921 made it easier to deport foreign-born militants, and, beginning in 1919, the maritime police in Rio de Janeiro kept radicals out of the country. Presidents Wenceslao Braz (1914–18), Epitácio Pessôa (1919–22), and Artur da Silva Bernardes (1922–26) repressed workers, Braz and Bernardes under states of siege that lasted from November 1917 through 1918 and from 1922 until 1926, respectively. These measures, together with a bleak economic situation and splits in the movement, weakened labor in the 1920s.[25]

Once union agitation declined after 1920, military restlessness became evident. Enthusiastically supporting Bilac's campaign, officers hoped to create a stronger army that would regenerate Brazil. President Pessôa accentuated their discontent by appointing civilians to head the military ministries and vetoing a pay hike. The arrest of army leader and former president

Marshal Hermes de Fonseca (1910–14), the temporary closing of the Clube Militar, and the victory of the official presidential candidate, Bernardes, whom officers suspected of slandering them, further alienated the military. Junior officers rebelled in Copacabana in 1922 and São Paulo in 1924, beginning the Tenente movement. Influenced by the military positivists of the early republic, the Tenentes stood for a vaguely defined nationalism, a strong central government, and an end to corrupt oligarchical rule. Although some Tenentes sympathized with workers, in general they did not favor democracy.[26]

Ironically, the LN was a casualty of the military uprisings. During the revolt of 1924, rebel soldiers occupied São Paulo for three weeks, while troops loyal to the federal government bombed the city, which had been abandoned by civilian authorities. The LN stepped into the vacuum, setting up a municipal guard to enforce law and order, distributing supplies, and coordinating medical services. Although the organization protested the rebels' assault and blocked their overtures to São Paulo workers, it aroused government suspicions. When loyalists retook the city, they arrested LN leaders, and Bernardes closed the LN and its schools. Some former LN members joined the PRP, but many others founded the opposition Democratic Party, which favored electoral reform, in 1926.[27]

Nativist Catholic Nationalism

Another nationalist current was developing in Rio de Janeiro alongside the Ligas. It first manifested itself in *Brazílea* (1917–18), edited by Arnaldo Damasceno Vieira, an army captain and engineer; Alvaro Bomilcar, the antiracist author; and Jackson de Figueiredo, the Catholic writer. For *Brazílea* as for the Jacobinos of the 1890s, Brazil's biggest problem was its enslavement to European and especially Portuguese culture and business. It even regarded the "conservative classes" as foreign, although whether it meant in origin or perspective was unclear.[28]

Drawing sustenance from the LDN and LN, *Brazílea* also advocated military service and civic regeneration and distrusted foreigners, and its moralism resembled the LDN's. However, the Ligas were much less Catholic than the magazine and did not single out the Portuguese for criticism. Influenced by Bomilcar, the publication did not see the masses as racially inferior. Furthermore, it perceived the poverty in which most Brazilians lived and which the government did little to ameliorate, and it accorded social justice and economic nationalism a much higher priority than did the LDN and LN. *Brazílea* reflected the concerns of middle-income Cariocas (residents of Rio de Janeiro), many of whom still blamed inflation on the Portuguese, who owned 43 percent of the commercial establishments and 74 percent of the factories in Rio de Janeiro in 1920.[29] In contrast, the Ligas drew from the upper and upper-middle classes and from cities in the interior, although the LDN was based in Rio.

The *Brazílea* circle created Propaganda Nativista (PN) in 1919 as another expression of their beliefs. Dedicated to the Jacobino hero Floriano Peixoto and composed exclusively of native-born Brazilians, the organization attracted a small group of intellectuals, professionals, and bureaucrats from various states. PN favored nationalizing retail commerce and the press, limiting foreign acquisition of real estate, and raising internal loans to pay off the foreign debt and create financial independence. To emancipate Brazil politically, PN opposed the notion of foreigners, even naturalized citizens, holding government positions. It denounced the notion of a Luso-Brazilian confederation as an infringement on Brazilian sovereignty. Proposed by the Portuguese government, the confederation would standardize the language spoken in the two countries, extend citizenship rights to Portuguese residents, and recognize Portuguese degree holders. Inspired by Torres, PN advocated a council of notables to study national problems and provide a sense of unity. Moving the capital to Goiás would also help unify the country and move the population away from the coast facing Europe. The organization would defend Catholicism, the majority religion, and lobby to mention God in the constitution. PN would also work for a law favoring immigrants who would work in agriculture. By promoting racial equality, lower rents, and labor input into regulating food prices, PN hoped to help workers, despite its "attitude of combat against anarchism." Federal authorities had established the Comissariado da Alimentação Pública in 1918, along with other measures, but had not been able to control rising costs. PN also wanted to incorporate women, neglected by the military-leaning Ligas, into the nationalist cause.[30]

The group's anti-Portuguese sentiments took concrete form. On July 20, 1919, PN members tangled with Luso-Brazilian confederation advocates at a rally in the Largo da Carioca. PN distributed nationalist fliers in the streets, at meetings, and on streetcars. It lobbied for Deputy Camilo Prates's bill requiring that Brazilians compose at least half of the personnel of foreign-owned firms, a plank in the PN platform.[31] PN members also contributed articles to the anti-Portuguese journal *Gil Blas*, founded in February 1919 by Alcibiades Delamare, a government functionary.

Representatives from PN, LN, LDN, and other nationalist organizations attended the inaugural meeting of Ação Social Nacionalista (ASN) on February 13, 1920, at the prestigious Instituto Histórico e Geográfico Brasileiro in Rio de Janeiro. Afonso Celso, monarchist, LDN member, *Brazílea* contributor, and head of the Instituto, was named president. The ASN, he declared, was neither religious nor partisan. "Purely conservative and defensive," it would unite existing groups dedicated to safeguarding the nationality. Prates, Bomilcar, and Senator Justo Chermont were officers, and board members included Treasury Minister and LDN president Homero Baptista, LDN members Coelho Neto and Street, and two congressmen. As had the LN and LDN, ASN organizers chose the leaders behind the scenes. Pedro Lessa of the LDN, three priests, Jackson de Figueiredo and other prominent Catholics, and three generals, an admiral, and other military officers numbered among the ASN's first members.[32]

Over 1,500 guests, including Cardinal Arcoverde, military officers, women, and delegates from the federal and state governments, attended the installation ceremony on April 21. Echoing Bilac and Coelho Neto, Celso told the distinguished crowd that "the family was the tiny fatherland; the fatherland was the large family." A man who lacked or did not love family was a miserable aberration, as were people who did not love the nation. The ASN president referred to Alfredo Pinto's speech to the LDN against immigrant agitators. Celso favored expelling the foreign subversives who corrupted Brazilian workers, just as heads of households expelled disrespectful members.[33]

An ASN affiliate situated this goal in the ideological spectrum even more explicitly than Celso. The Liga Rio-Grandense Nacionalista identified itself as a conservative force supporting the authorities against anarchism and as a "patriotic" solution to the social question. The French counterrevolutionaries Maurice Barrès and Charles Maurras were its inspiration.[34]

The ASN adopted the platforms of the Ligas and especially the PN. To these it added support for labor legislation, which would safeguard capitalism, eliminate the problems of strikes and lockouts, and help the oppressed within a climate of order. Yet its motto, "Against anarchism: nationalism," indicated it would fight subversion. The ASN opposed the concentration of foreigners in agricultural colonies and "parasitic" immigrants in the cities. It supported close relations with the American and especially South American republics. "Sanitizing," developing transportation, and spreading the catechism would improve life in the interior. Although Celso had insisted the ASN was not religious, *Gil Blas*, its mouthpiece, advocated voluntary religious instruction in the public schools and frequently invoked Catholicism. The ASN also aimed to emancipate the Brazilian woman through moral, practical, and civic education, and elevate "her true role as primordial factor of our moral greatness."[35]

Drawing upon Bomilcar, Torres, *Brazílea*, and PN, the ASN praised race mixture and denounced racial prejudice, which set it apart from moderate rightists. The elite tended to regard people of color as hopelessly inferior and as an impediment to development. Through immigration and the dying out of the supposedly weaker races, the population would become whiter, thus alleviating Brazil's economic and political problems. Law professor and social commentator Francisco José de Oliveira Viana was the most influential spokesperson for these views in the 1920s.[36]

On race and other matters, the ASN was more popular than moderate rightists and the Ligas. The appeals to women and native-born workers indicated its desire to transform public consciousness and organize a broad following. By 1921 the ASN loosely grouped over 180 local associations claiming 250,000 members. These figures were probably exaggerated, and it was doubtful that all the adherents of these institutions considered themselves militant nationalists. Nevertheless, the ASN was larger than the Liga Patriótica Argentina in numbers and as a percentage of the population. Primarily middle-class, the affiliates included organizations of professors, employees, shopkeepers, bureaucrats, retired officers, Catholics, women, and maritime interests. People of color figured in photographs of ASN affiliates and functions.[37]

As evinced by the participants at its early meetings, the ASN received military backing. Police, firefighters, civil guard, and military personnel visited its offices and offered support. Major João Cezimbra Jacques wrote a series of articles on the worker threat for *Gil Blas*, and General Pedro Carolino de Almeida spoke at several nationalist gatherings.[38]

Even more evident was government favor. President Pessôa met several times with Celso and Delamare to assure them of his support, and in May 1920 he accepted the post of honorary president of the organization. A fervent admirer of the "nationalist president," as he called Pessôa, Delamare sent him copies of *Gil Blas* and wrote to him frequently. The president awarded him a succession of administrative positions and appointed Bomilcar and at least one other prominent ASN member to government offices. President Bernardes of Minas Gerais sent a telegram of adhesion to the ASN's installation meeting in April 1920 and backed the organization when he served as president of the nation.[39]

The ASN also received support from the Chamber of Deputies. To enhance its prestige and give it government mailing privileges, ASN deputies Ildefonso Albano of Ceará and Prates introduced a resolution declaring the group to be of public utility. The resolution passed and Pessôa signed it into law in November 1920. Thanks to this measure, the following month the city administration of Rio de Janeiro announced plans to construct headquarters for the organization.[40]

However, some deputies disapproved of the ASN. Labor advocate Maurício de Lacerda castigated it for its Lusophobia and lambasted the president for serving as its honorary leader. When Pessôa pointed to his friendship with Portuguese residents, Lacerda rejoined that they included only the wealthy. Like the Chilean Socialists who criticized the Ligas, the deputy regarded ASN and government diatribes against foreigners as means of dividing and conquering workers. Some congressmen also pointed·out how one of the ASN's cherished goals hurt poor people. When the government decided to enforce an 1897 law nationalizing the fishing industry, as the ASN favored doing, this dispossessed the largely impoverished community of Portuguese fishermen.[41]

Several deputies objected to ASN extremism. Lacerda condemned naval commander Frederico Villar, ASN member and enforcer of the fishing law, for delivering a violently anti-Portuguese speech at an ASN demonstration in October 1920, and he criticized marchers for insulting anti-ASN federal deputies. In his opinion, Villar and other naval participants had broken military discipline. To demonstrate the group's fanaticism, Deputy Gonçalves Maia of Pernambuco read aloud a letter Villar had written to LN president Steidel, published in the press, in which the commander chided the LN for criticizing ASN anti-Portuguese attitudes and ignoring "Portuguese insolence." In 1921, Maia read to the chamber a flier in which the ASN urged readers to "kill the Galician" and threatened to imitate the example of fascism. Denying these words came from his group, Prates nevertheless was forced to admit that non-Portuguese businessmen also exploited Brazil. Alvaro Baptista, brother of the LDN president and deputy from Rio Grande do Sul, denounced the ASN's brand of nationalism as intolerant, divisive, and even anachronistic. Lacerda tried to humiliate the ASN by legislating payment to its leaders of salaries equivalent to the minimum ones earned by state workers, but his attempt to make a point about low wages failed.[42]

Anti-Lusitanianism split nationalist forces. The LN had sent representatives to the ASN's first meeting but absented itself thereafter from its functions. Unlike the ASN, the LN accepted foreigners and Portuguese as collaborators (but not members). It accused the ASN of chauvinism, which the latter denied, although it admitted that its focus on curbing foreign economic control differed from Bilac's on the draft, education, and civic virtues. The ASN reminded the LN that the Portuguese presence was much greater in Rio de Janeiro than in São Paulo; the LN should not judge the nationalisms of other states by its criteria. Pointing to signs of Portuguese influence, the ASN noted the Portuguese ancestry of Mesquita and other LN members, as well as LN's support for Brazil's Latin brothers in the war, a goal favored by Portuguese merchants, who competed with the Germans. One ASN member warned that "the accommodating, sleep-inducing narcotic of Lusitanianism" drugged the LN.[43]

Like the LN, the church initially supported the ASN. Cardinal Arcoverde, the vicar general, and Monsignor Fernando Rangel, the leading organizer of Catholic workers, attended the installation meeting, and Monsignor Joaquim Soares de Oliveira Alvim represented the church at the group's first anniversary celebration. The ASN received support from Archbishop João Becker of Porto Alegre and other high-ranking clerics, and Archbishop Silvério Gomes Pimenta of Minas Gerais contributed an article against Protestant missionaries to *Gil Blas*. Male and female ASN members staffed the commission overseeing the project to build a statue of Christ the Redeemer on Corcovado Mountain, completed in 1931.[44] The church's interest in expanding its flock among the middle sectors helped explain this collaboration. So, too, did its agreement with the ASN on social harmony, religion, morality, the family, and especially Catholic instruction in the schools.

Archbishop coadjutant and future cardinal Sebastião Leme of Rio de Janeiro privately told Delamare in 1921 that he applauded his patriotic campaign; if not for his official position, he would join it himself. The nationalist leader learned, however, that Leme vetoed his name for the statue commission, arguing that he would alienate the Portuguese colony. Nor did Leme invite Delamare to the Eucharistic Congress of 1922.[45] The canny archbishop used the nationalists to advance the church's causes but avoided embracing them, actions he would repeat in the 1930s.

Nevertheless, *Gil Blas* increased its devotion to Catholicism, which offered a foundation for Brazilian unity and a means of promoting order. In the midst of "corrupting internationalism," the church understood the benefits of nationalism and could discipline the people. As Delamare noted, one could not separate nationalism from Catholic morality. Accordingly, *Gil Blas* cited Eduardo Prado, Júlio Maria, and other Catholics as inspiration.[46]

Within the ASN, the Centro Católico Nacionalista reinforced this link.

It defended the interests of nationalism and Catholicism against Protestantism, its supposed anarchist offspring, and decadent U.S. films and readings. The Centro promoted priestly vocations and Catholic private education and opposed the teaching of positivism in public schools. The perception that the church was taking over the ASN prompted criticism and some resignations. In response, the Centro dubiously insisted that the ASN welcomed non-Catholic patriots, although it considered them ignorant, and it intended to free Brazil of religious diversity.[47]

Gender and the ASN

Its Catholic orientation may have enabled women to view the ASN as a logical extension of their customary church activities. So, too, may have Delamare's appeal to women to emulate Joan of Arc as a model of Christian nationalism and self-sacrifice. One who made this transition, the Catholic activist Amélia Rodrigues, had established the Aliança Feminina in Rio de Janeiro in 1919. Its goals of preparing women for the vote and opening all careers to them resembled those of feminism, although the Aliança carefully stated that it hoped to accomplish these without masculinizing women. Its additional aims of injecting morality into the media, promoting patriotism, and helping laborers resembled the intentions of the ASN, which Rodrigues joined in 1920.[48]

A few female groups also affiliated with the ASN. These included the Asociação Feminina Beneficente e Instructiva, which ran a girls' school; Legião da Mulher Brasileira (LMB), a charitable organization; Grêmio Dramático Nacionalista; and Centro Pedagógico Nacionalista, which may also have had male educators as members. The teachers and professionals who belonged to these institutions, along with the Catholic women and wives and female relatives of male leaders who joined the ASN, probably were of the same middle-class extraction as the rest of the group.[49]

Women joined the ASN for gendered patriotic reasons. Delamare asserted that their goodness, constancy, and Christian resignation made women compatible with the ASN's nationalism of love. LMB president and writer Anna César added that the love of the mother, wife, sister, and daughter invigorated nationalism, referring to ASN women only in terms of their relations to men. Further tying nationalism to prevalent views of the female personality, she added that women wanted to cultivate their patriotic sentiments with the same care they used to cultivate their gardens and appearance. Another ASN member, Rachel Prado, appealed to Brazilian women—

daughters, sisters, wives, and especially mothers—to work for nationalism and against the foreigner who abused local hospitality. She widened the female role by urging women to promote patriotism in schools, offices, and factories as well as among their children in their homes.[50]

A letter published in the newspapers asked women to ignore racial and class divisions and join the ASN's "redemptive work of economic and financial emancipation." The 115 signatories, several of whom were married to ASN male leaders, considered themselves heirs to a tradition set by courageous *brasileiras* since the colonial period. Their predecessors had fought alongside their husbands against the Dutch and helped convert the Indians.[51]

Few women, however, took an active part in the ASN. Unlike the Liga Patriótica Argentina, the group did not run charity projects, thus eliminating a likely arena of female participation. Perhaps the timely state repression of workers obviated the need for independent action among the female proletariat. The women's infrequent activities included fund-raising for ASN affiliates. For example, the poet and teacher Maria Rosa Moreira Ribeiro, who belonged to the LMB and Centro Pedagógico Nacionalista, organized a benefit for the Centro Marítimo Nacionalista in the Teatro Municipal of the federal capital in 1921. She and the young women of the Grêmio Dramático Nacionalista, which she headed, wrote and presented skits for the program. The Grêmio may also have exemplified the ASN's interest in developing Brazilian theater. Women collected donations for the statue of Christ the Redeemer, and Maria Junqueira Schmidt, Delamare's cousin and a young professor and ASN member, spoke on the project at the Biblioteca Nacional in June 1921. They also attended ASN functions and at least one demonstration; female and male delegates met President Pessôa at the train station in May 1921 and applauded his speech defending his nationalist record.[52]

Schmidt and Ribeiro were the most prominent women in the ASN. The director of Academia Feminina, an institute of higher learning for women in the country, Schmidt had studied in Switzerland and participated in Catholic affairs. Twenty years old in 1920, she would enjoy a distinguished career in education and social service. Ribeiro belonged to the Red Cross and other women's groups outside the ASN. The state government of São Paulo had assigned her to work with the nationalist organization. Both women gave speeches for the ASN, and Ribeiro also served on *Gil Blas*'s editorial staff and wrote articles for it.[53] This publicist role, an unusual one for women in this period, made Schmidt and Ribeiro more conspicuous than the Argentine upper-class rightist women. The ASN's middle-class character enabled it to appeal to a few educated, native-born career women, and it granted them visible roles.

Sensing women's increasing prominence in society, the ASN was interested in forging a female constituency that reached beyond the home and school. Women's roles were receiving much attention in public forums, and the main current of Brazilian feminism, the Federação Brasileira pelo Progresso Feminino (FBPF), with its relative conservatism and bourgeois character, was gaining ground among male politicians. Breaking with other feminists, the FBPF carefully avoided criticizing the church and the patriarchal family. This contrasted with the ties among feminists, immigrants, and leftists in Argentina, which alienated rulers and the upper class, although few feminists espoused radical ideas on the family or sexuality. The FBPF presented women as peacemakers and moderate reformers who could help heal the wounds of the strife-torn political system of the 1920s and early 1930s. Thus Brazilian feminists slowly garnered support for female civil and political equality, even among the right.[54]

Little distinguished Ribeiro's speeches and articles from FBPF pronouncements. The leader of the female current of nationalism, as Delamare described her, praised feminism as well as the nationalist efforts of the educated Brazilian woman, freed from "the antiquated ideas that the woman should not leave the home, where the man created for her a chimeric throne, separating her, with that treacherous flattery to her weakness and vanity, from the sacrosanct battle of aggrandizing the loved Fatherland." She called on women to use their capacity for love, charity, and the giving of life to promote the nation. To this end, single or childless women, or those who had raised their offspring, should work alongside men, remaining within an appropriate orbit of action. The female activist would lose the throne "that only exists in sick imaginations," but she would gain "an altar in the hearts of worthy, sensible persons." Women should build their own thrones, through their goodness, and without humiliating male adulation.[55] Ribeiro's exclusion of women with children, her vague admonitions on proper female behavior, and her religious allusions struck a conservative chord, but her critique of the cult of domesticity was progressive.

Schmidt's views were more conservative. Deriding the notion that women could support themselves only through marriage, she commended Bertha Lutz, a civil servant, scientist, and head of the FBPF, and favored women's entry into education and public administration. Yet ironically the professor viewed the ideal woman as mother, salon organizer, and philanthropist. Capable of ruling the country, women should nevertheless aim at ruling the home. Nor should feminism "exteriorize" women, who were destined for an intense inner life. Schmidt defined feminism narrowly as raising one's children to be patriotic.[56]

Some of Schmidt and Ribeiro's male colleagues also advocated women's rights. The ASN's mouthpiece praised Bertha Lutz and her feminist movement, although it criticized female groups that appeared to oppose Catholicism. Identifying motherhood as women's primary role, Justo Chermont of the ASN nevertheless introduced a female suffrage bill in the Senate in 1919. One writer for *Gil Blas* supported female suffrage, insisting that since the female sex reasoned as well as the male, confining it to the home made no sense; if men could combine citizenship and parenthood, so could women. Stronger and more moral than men, women would vote in a manner that benefited the country.[57] He, like Ribeiro, was willing to entertain female activity outside the home.

Bomilcar combined Catholic apologetics with sympathy for the women's movement. The church had condemned sexuality, luxury, vanity, and other sinful qualities as a reaction against the corrupt ancient world; by identifying these sins with women, it had given its ideas force. Bomilcar admitted these actions had harmed women, but he insisted that Christian morality had also helped them. Liberals, however, had passed laws that hurt "the most suffering and hence most deserving part of humanity." For example, by depriving married women of the right to dispose of their property without their husbands' permission, the Brazilian civil code confined women to "prolonged captivity." As most women were single or orphaned, they needed jobs "conforming to their dispositions" and wages equal to those of men. His proposed first step toward this goal, training for domestic labor, however, was hardly innovative. Women also should receive an education that prepared them for entering public life and filling government posts. Bomilcar hoped Brazilian women would reach, "with the restrictions adequate to our affectionate and sentimental nature, a situation of equality closer to the North American type." Once women attained equality with men, the nation would climb to the pinnacle of South American civilization.[58]

Their middle-class origins and openness on women's issues notwithstanding, ASN members differed from feminists. Feminists wanted to extend the liberal democratic ideals of equality and rights to include women, whereas Bomilcar and other ASN members criticized liberalism and moved toward authoritarianism. For feminists, freeing women was the highest goal; for Bomilcar and even Schmidt and Ribeiro, female emancipation was subservient to nationalism. Bomilcar wanted women to replace male Brazilians in the bureaucracy so that men would move into commerce and industry, thereby diminishing the preponderant role of foreigners in those sectors. While most feminist leaders did not confront the church, neither did they embrace it; the ASN, however, was firmly Catholic. In its emphasis on the church, morality, and proper female comportment, the ASN's views resembled those of the Aliança Feminina or *Revista Feminina* (1915–27) more than it did those of the FBPF. The most popular female magazine of these years, the *Revista* advocated a more active role for women, albeit one still tied to Christian morality and the home.[59]

Although ASN members thought women would enhance nationalism, they usually described the cause as masculine. Ironically, Ribeiro depicted the organization as "proud and manly." Contradicting the "nationalism of love" designation, *Gil Blas* declared that its nationalism was a "violent" reaction to Portuguese attempts to "unman" the nationality. Perhaps ASN men and women could not imagine another manner of expressing power and strength. Whatever the motive, this discourse related to the ASN's construction of masculinity. Ribeiro portrayed men as courageous, martial, and filled with vitality. Combining racial tolerance with considerations of masculinity, *Gil Blas* regarded the mixed-blood *caboclo* as the "manly type of our race." The carefully preserved distinction between masculinity and femininity, male prowess and female abnegation, hinted at the ASN's devotion to other social distinctions and hierarchies, such as those among classes.[60]

The ASN Confronts Laborers and Foreigners

For Bomilcar and the ASN, people's origins instead of the economic structure explained Brazilian social problems. The author distinguished between workers who followed "foreign" theories and the national "proletariat of color." Concerned only about the latter, Bomilcar blamed its poverty on foreigners who dominated the economy, thanks to "excessive constitutional liberalism" rather than capitalism per se. According to the ASN, foreign industrialists exploited Brazilian workers; foreign merchants, landlords, and loan sharks overcharged them; foreign retailers refused to hire them; and foreign professionals blocked their advancement. Instead of following a liberal policy of universal solidarity that undermined the fatherland, the government should exclude immigrants from jobs as long as native-born workers were available. Bomilcar distinguished patriotism, a "natural" sentiment, from the vague, unrooted notions of cosmopolitanism, anarchism, and radical socialism. Foreign laborers and "agitators dazzled by the beauty of egalitarian theories" devised elsewhere could not solve local problems. Instead, Bomilcar favored a socialism that was Catholic in its moderation and gradualism and devoted to native Brazilians.[61] Although he did not label it as such, this was a "national socialism" that offered an alternative to leftist thinking.

Yet a socialism predicated on class conflict appeared inherently foreign to Delamare. "Flashing blood in dilated eye sockets and sweating vengeance and hate through all the pores," undesirable immigrants had come to deceive local workers. Here, Delamare aimed the venom normally reserved for Portuguese against all alien leftists. Several *Gil Blas* authors, however, attributed radicalism solely to Lusitanians. The magazine inaccurately claimed that 79 percent of local anarchists were Portuguese.[62]

The ASN castigated leftists and most militant unions. Delamare advised government, society, families, and individuals to fight the revolutionary left in a "war without respite." Favoring several strikes that it considered orderly (and that were directed against foreign firms), *Gil Blas*, however, denounced other strikes it saw as politically motivated.[63]

The ASN supported not only Pessôa's repression of labor but also ongoing government efforts to contain its militancy. After the strikes in São Paulo in July 1917, the state legislature added provisions to the sanitary code regulating female and child labor. A federal law of 1919 provided for mandatory accident insurance in transportation, construction, and factories using machinery. President Bernardes recognized May Day as a holiday and created a national labor council to advise the government on work and social welfare matters; two of its twelve members were representatives of organized labor. Yet the council had less power than a labor ministry proposed by Lacerda. Under Bernardes, Congress also created a pension fund for several categories of workers and mandated paid vacations for industrial laborers and commercial and bank employees. The laws were poorly enforced, however. In addition to these kinds of measures, the ASN backed a labor code, stalemated in Congress, and advocated adding coverage of agricultural workers to the workmen's compensation law of 1919. These Social Catholic–style reforms were what ASN members approvingly called "cooperativist syndicalism" or, in Bomilcar's parlance, socialism.[64]

A May Day celebration in 1920 hosted by the Brazilian-owned firm Pereira Carneiro in Niterói, Rio de Janeiro, earned the ASN's praise. The festivities included paternalistic pronouncements by company spokesmen, a mass, and a speech by Monsignor Rangel, in which he declared that devotion to God would resolve all social problems. Reminiscent of the LPA, employers, with ASN backing, tried to strip the holiday of its revolutionary and international connotations.[65]

Jorge Street, president of the Centro Industrial do Brasil, applied Social Catholicism to his business, and the ASN generally applauded his vision. Only employees and their families could live in his factory town, Vila Maria Zélia, and while the housing was cheaper and cleaner than elsewhere, residents were subject to strict supervision. Attendance at Sunday religious services was mandatory, as was abstinence from alcohol. Girls received embroidery lessons, and their mothers had to accompany them to dances. Union publications did not circulate in the *vila*, except for the social events section; workers accused Street of promoting the local Centro Católico over the union. In these ways the industrialist sought to impart bourgeois notions of femininity, work habits, and piety and to limit class consciousness. The company provided day-care, charity, and other services to workers, encouraging them to view Street as their father, protector, and boss all in one. Few other industrialists were as paternalistic as Street, although some provided bonuses and services for reliable employees. Street's opposition to accident compensation, paid vacations, a labor ministry, and the labor code, however, was all too common.[66]

The ASN also concerned itself with other economic matters. Suspicious of costly protectionism and urban culture, unlike the Jacobinos the group did not advocate a dynamic role for the state in promoting industrialization. Instead, it followed Torres in proclaiming that the nation was and should remain agricultural. Accordingly, it advocated improving transportation in the interior, reducing railroad freight charges, facilitating credit for farmers, and setting up rural savings banks, but it did not address land reform. The ASN also favored better salaries for agricultural workers and extending to Brazilians the same privileges that foreign colonists received. It approved of government measures restricting coastal fishing and the merchant marine to the native-born, establishing open-air urban markets to reduce food prices, and limiting foreign investment and the repatriation of profits in some sectors in the early 1920s. Such ASN proposals as nationalizing employment in foreign-owned enterprises failed to pass Congress.[67]

Anti-Lusitanianism, however, drowned out the ASN's concrete economic proposals. It also alienated most of the upper class, which found such attacks crude, radical, and damaging to Brazil's relations with Portugal. Moreover, powerful landed interests profited from immigration. Disgusted with the governing elite's cosmopolitanism and unwillingness to support most of its program, the ASN followed an independent path. It launched two political parties in the postwar era, the Partido Republicano Nacional and Legião Republicana, but both failed, as did Delamare's campaign for the Chamber of Deputies in 1921.[68] The last issue of *Gil Blas* appeared in 1923, and by 1924 the ASN had faded.

In 1924 Delamare and other former ASN members, such as Celso, Villar, Prates, Bomilcar, Homero Baptista, and Jackson de Figueiredo, along with deputy and future minister Francisco Campos and the racist writer Oliveira Viana, tried to revive its concerns under a new rubric, the Academia Brasileira de Ciências Econômicas, Políticas, e Sociais. Pessôa assumed the presidency, and President Bernardes, who proclaimed that he was an "integral nationalist" opposed to "dissolvent cosmopolitanism," was its honorary leader. Consisting of only thirty active members, fifteen honorary ones, and sixty correspondents, the Academia aimed to be Alberto Torres's council of national studies. By examining economic and social issues from a local perspective, the organization hoped to further national autonomy. Bernardes persuaded the Academia to study immigration, the cost of living, coffee valorization, and the revolts that were convulsing the nation. The Academia invited Bernardes, federal and state officials, Cardinal Arcoverde, and Archbishop Leme to the opening ceremony in the Círculo Católico. Perhaps tainted by its links to the defunct ASN, however, the Academia was short-lived.[69]

Catholic Authoritarianism

Meanwhile, former ASN members were inching toward authoritarianism. This current of nationalism had already criticized liberalism, and it had upheld religion, tradition, and order against the left. Now it further questioned the current form of government and the ideology that legitimized it. Possibly disillusioned by his electoral loss, by 1924 Delamare believed it was a mistake to base the political system on the vote in a country lacking unity, prosperity, authority, an honest bureaucracy, and parties oriented by ideas. He suggested the reunification of church and state, the insertion of religion in public education, and the creation of a dictatorship to forestall social disorganization. Delamare wanted Brazil to emulate the examples of Primo de Rivera and Mussolini, who combined nationalism, hierarchy, and collaboration with the church.[70]

Jackson de Figueiredo followed a similar path. A lawyer and journalist from Sergipe, the devout *Brazílea* editor and PN and ASN member was "a declared enemy of Revolution, in all its aspects." For him, political morality originated in Christianity, which decreed submission to authority, the law, and peaceful change. Not necessarily an armed movement, revolution manifested dissatisfaction with the social order and insubordination against profound truths. Leftists, liberals, democrats, feminists, atheists, and non-Catholics fit under this sweeping heading. Troubled by Brazil's independence from Portugal, Figueiredo denied that this struggle met the definition of a revolution, for it had not swept away religion or other national dogmas.[71]

Figueiredo revered the French monarchist Charles Maurras as the most lucid opponent of revolution. Maurras blamed the Reformation for questioning the need for a priestly intermediary between God and humanity and a papal intermediary between God and kings, thus fomenting egoistic individualism, liberalism, and democracy. Liberalism had undermined authority at all levels and, through the French Revolution, had destroyed the monarchy, social equilibrium, the church's prestige, and national glory. Maurras viewed democracy as a government of numbers, in which the ignorant majority prevailed over the capable few. Ultimately this meant rule by the rich, for they financed the politicians and the press that manipulated the masses, and their domination accentuated the differences between classes. Figueiredo concluded that democracy represented "the most sordid of falsehoods" and incited the basest tendencies of the lower class. Nor had it brought peace or social benefits to any country.[72]

For both Figueiredo and Maurras, leftism was yet another loathsome consequence of Protestantism. Figueiredo noted that the untamed ideas of the French Revolution made the nations it contaminated more susceptible to Bolshevism. The abuses of an atheistic and greedy liberal bourgeoisie had pushed laborers toward revolution. If bourgeois governments treated them leniently, workers would assume that they were weak and try to overthrow them. If these administrations oppressed them, however, they created martyrs and strengthened the radical cause. Thus the anti-Christian revolutionary order resulting from the Reformation contained the seeds of its own destruction.[73]

However approving of his analysis, Figueiredo did not endorse all of Maurras's solutions. He agreed with the Frenchman's notion of a hierarchical, corporatist, and regionally based system of representation. Like Maurras, he favored a Christian monarchy, but in his view the Brazilian empire had not fit this model. Figueiredo praised some of the republican presidents and seemed to regard an authoritarian republic, stripped of liberalism, positivism, and democracy, as consistent with order. He also approved of Maurras's notion that each society follow a single religion, believing that Brazilian nationalists should be Catholic and intolerant of other faiths. But Figueiredo understood that Maurras loved Catholicism as a pillar of order and a symbol of French identity rather than for its spiritual content. He disassociated himself from the Frenchman's subordination of the church to nationalism and politics, a position subsequently condemned by the Vatican in 1926. Nor did the Brazilian Catholic identify with Maurras's positivism, a cold and un-Christian doctrine, although he admitted that it was in part a reaction against excessive liberalism. Probably he agreed with his friend and disciple Hamilton Nogueira, a medical hygiene professor, that positivism at least was a doctrine of order.[74]

Figueiredo discerned problems other than the ones outlined by Maurras. The so-called conservative classes had abandoned this ideology for radical ideas. Brazilian democracy distrusted power, lacked coherent principles, and possessed no programmatic parties, not even liberal ones. Since the nation was undisciplined, so, too, was the military, whose revolts Figueiredo strongly denounced. Given these conditions, the widespread penchant for political "messianisms" was understandable.[75]

"Death to Revolution!" was Figueiredo's battle cry. His ideal was "a column of fire," a counterrevolution, or the opposite of a revolution. Brazil needed a "party of order" to defeat revolution by spreading discipline, authority, and spiritualism; that he had chosen the title adopted by early-nineteenth-century Brazilian Conservatives was, perhaps, no coincidence. Figueiredo saw an embryo of such a group in the examples of Pessôa and Bernardes. Since one could not create order through disorder, counterrevolutionaries should not try to overthrow the decadent republic by using arms but by organizing a disciplined movement for change, similar to Italian Fascists and Primo de Rivera.[76]

According to Nogueira, Brazil was undergoing a clash between "revolutionary Satanism," represented by anarchism and other dissolvent influences, and the "party of order." Nogueira judged that order was winning, but it would have to continue its "reactionary action" long after victory, for revolution would inevitably resurge. The party of order could rely only on Catholic precepts to stamp out revolution, using the example of the stable Catholic Middle Ages. Earlier, the church had freed the slaves by converting them, not by inciting them to revolt against their owners. This was the "true liberty" of submission to God that Nogueira preached, not the "liberty" that followed the Middle Ages, which had led to killing, destruction, and tyranny.[77]

Catholic nationalists equivocated on the issue of foreign influence. Figueiredo and Nogueira saw no contradiction between their nationalism and foreign sources of inspiration. Suspicious of U.S. Protestant influence, however, and reminiscent of Eduardo Prado, Figueiredo scorned what he termed Bomilcar's "Americanophilism." He criticized the Portuguese presence and, like Bomilcar, blamed Brazilian liberals for permitting members of this group to control the press and commerce. Still, he broke with Bomilcar and Delamare by insisting that Portuguese imperialism was no worse than other imperialisms. The greed that this collectivity had displayed in Brazil contradicted its own Christian values, with which Figueiredo identified.[78]

Antisemitism

As Catholic nationalists reclaimed kinship with the Portuguese in cultural and religious matters, they deepened their readings of European and especially French counterrevolutionaries. These considerations led them to substitute the Jew for the hitherto despised Lusitanian. The use of the term *métèque* illustrated this change. Employed by Maurras, this pejorative word dated back to the Greek *metoikos*, the foreign merchants whose commercial prowess antagonized the ancient Athenians, who segregated them and denied them citizenship. *Gil Blas* had hurled this word against Lusitanian businessmen; Catholic nationalists now identified it with Jews. Nogueira lambasted the Jews' "denationalizing *metequismo*," crediting Eduardo Prado for having warned of the materialistic Yankee civilization, a "*métèque* society of Jews and *arrivistas*."[79] After 1922, such views replaced anti-Portuguese sentiment among Catholic nationalists.

As early as 1919, Jackson de Figueiredo referred to an international conspiracy of hate-ridden, diabolically intelligent, wealthy Jews, "foreign to the civilized world." In succeeding years he concluded that by weakening Brazil internally, liberalism would increase the domination of "elements without a fatherland, . . . the universal force of money, . . . the hard ambitions of a plutocracy of an eminently anti-national character." This was the "universal imperialism of a plutocracy of Jewish origin or of a spirit of absolute conformity with it."[80]

Bomilcar, who had fallen out with Figueiredo, nevertheless shared his Catholicism and antisemitism. Great Britain and other countries used what he called the "Jewish method" to subordinate weaker ones: corrupting certain classes, bureaucrats, and politicians; dominating commerce, industry, and the press; and distorting the historical record. More powerful than any army, the Jewish method was that of a vampire, which kept its victim alive only to suck out more blood. The nations that employed this means represented a "Jewish order" of materialism and confusion, which Bomilcar contrasted with his preferred "military order" of religion, heroism, fatherland, and family.[81]

These themes also surfaced in Delamare's and Nogueira's writings. The *Gil Blas* editor thought that North American Protestantism disguised a Jewish desire to control the Brazilian economy. Competitive and hate-ridden, Protestantism was "the Judaizing spirit of the Old World allied to ambition, the delirium of money . . . that intends to divide, through religious conflicts, the Brazilian family." Operating within commerce, industry, and the halls of government, the Jewish order created depressions and manipulated "fictitious financial agonies." To the Jewish conspiracy, Nogueira added antipatriotic propaganda "of a certain internationalism of a frankly Jewish character," referring to leftism. He also traced modern liberty and tolerance back to Judas; both, in his view, were evils that weakened the nation and the faith.[82]

Catholic nationalists equated Judaism and capitalism as dominating, materialistic, and international. They regarded socialism as cosmopolitan and tied to the "stomach," and they attributed it to liberalism (another Jewish invention) and capitalism, drawing further links between these ideologies and Judaism. Figueiredo believed that the Russian Revolution had reconciled itself with capitalism per se, if not with individual capitalists. Only a religious ascetic movement, allied with corporatism, that would remove people's attachment to materialism would truly challenge capitalism or socialism.[83] Such movements would emerge in the 1930s.

The growth of the Jewish community may have heightened Catholic apprehensions. Estimates of the Jewish population in 1920 range from 6,000 to 8,000, with perhaps 2,000 residing in Rio de Janeiro. Between 1921 and 1925, when most of the antisemitic writings appeared, 7,139 Jews arrived in Brazil, followed by 23,000 over the next five years. Mostly from Poland, Rumania, and Lithuania, the immigrants settled primarily in the largest cities. Many impoverished Jews entered the economy through peddling and extending credit to their customers. By the mid-1920s, these activities and Jewish concentration in certain neighborhoods attracted criticism, and not only from Catholic radical rightists. Yet Brazilian Jews in the early 1920s or even at the end of the decade, when many had climbed out of poverty, scarcely resembled the powerful conspirators of extremist propaganda.[84]

Perceptions of modern life more than of actual Jews pushed these Catholics toward antisemitism. Unlike the LPA, which had initially identified Jews with leftism, Brazilian extreme rightists saw them as symbols of hated yet antithetical aspects of modernity.[85] The strong European counter-revolutionary influence on the Brazilians, and their alienation from the status quo, accounted for the difference. It was easier to blame the Jewish phantasma for economic problems than the class hierarchy, the agrarian export economy, or capitalism itself. Although Catholic nationalists disapproved of capitalism, they targeted its international nexus and greed instead of its main characteristic, the private ownership and control of property. With its partial critique of capitalism, antisemitism could serve as an alternative to the broader leftist critique. The Jewish conspiracy was not the main theme of Catholic nationalist writings, but its intersection with other important issues made it a central theme. Figueiredo, Nogueira, Delamare, and Bomilcar gave radical antisemitism a place in the extreme right, one heralded elsewhere by Julián Martel and Nicolás Palacios.

The Church

Catholic nationalists participated in the church's revival of the 1920s. As archbishop coadjutant of Rio de Janeiro, Sebastiao Leme launched an ambitious program of consolidating support for the church and strengthening its public role. This program included Christianizing intellectuals to form a counterweight to anticlerical members of the ruling class. Leme's friend Jackson de Figueiredo founded *A Ordem* in 1921, which became the official organ of the Centro Dom Vital, organized by him, Nogueira, and Perillo Gomes in 1922. Leme strongly supported both efforts. Identified with the antimodernist current of "integral Catholicism," *A Ordem* overlapped the Catholic nationalist writings discussed above. Claiming Júlio Maria and Eduardo Prado as its precursors, the Centro sponsored discussions and prayer meetings, published books in its Prado collection, and organized libraries. Like the Argentine Cursos de Cultura Católica, it guided intellectuals in a reactionary direction—one that Júlio Maria might have disavowed—but it had a greater impact than the Cursos in this period. Delamare and former PN member Artur Gaspar Viana also belonged to the Centro, and *A Ordem* published works by these figures, the monarchist Plínio Correia de Oliveira, and future members of Ação Integralista Brasileira.[86]

The church expanded its activities and prestige in the 1920s. It propped up the social and political order through its school network, support for state repression of strikes and military revolts, and participation in the nationalist campaigns for military service, civic pride, and educational reform.

Some priests even assumed political posts. In return, the church sought Bernardes's approval of constitutional amendments on obligatory religious education in public schools and on recognizing Catholicism as the religion of the people, but the president refused to give it. Leme also united existing male and female Catholic groups in the capital under the Confederação Católica, which he founded in 1922. Two years later, the Confederação had grown to include 400 affiliates, and in the 1930s it expanded into Ação Católica Brasileira. Through these efforts the church garnered significant middle- and upper-class support.[87]

More interested in his contacts with the state and upper sectors, Leme left the organization of labor to others. By the early 1920s, Rio de Janeiro had its own Confederação de Trabalhadores Católicos, as did Minas Gerais. Such groups were explicitly antirevolutionary. The Centro Operário Católico Metropolitano of São Paulo, for example, pledged its support for the government and the "conservative classes" during strikes in 1919 and 1920. The title of the Minas confederation's newspaper, *O Operário*, was the same as that of a long-standing anarchist paper, indicating a desire to confuse and divide the latter's readers.[88] These were the types of labor groups favored by the ASN and Catholic nationalists.

Intellectual Trends

New currents of rebelliousness set off another rightist reaction. The year 1922 witnessed both the birth of the Communist Party and the Semana de Arte Moderna in São Paulo. Here, artists, musicians, and writers proclaimed their independence from traditional styles and their dedication to a truly national art. Verdeamarelismo, which took its name from the colors of the Brazilian flag, split off from the modernist movement. Its spirituality, ruralism, and opposition to racism and leftism recalled nationalist rhetoric; indeed, *Brazílea*, the *Revista do Brasil*, and LN had influenced its leading figure, Plínio Salgado, a writer, PRP state deputy, and future head of Ação Integralista Brasileira. These "modernists of order," as Antônio Arnoni Prado called them, praised fascism.[89]

Other authors advocated new political directions. Disillusioned by the nation's economic backwardness and political fragmentation, a group of writers published *A margem da história da república* (1924), an influential critique of the republic. Citing Torres, the authors recommended the scientific study of Brazilian reality and the formulation of Brazilian solutions to local problems, ones carried out in a context of order. They echoed Torres's disdain for foreign theories and the disorganized state of the country. Reflecting his corporatism and European rightist influence, one contributor favored a syndicalist state governed by producers.[90]

Perhaps the most famous contributor was Oliveira Viana. In his article and other works of the 1920s, Viana, like Torres, regarded the constitution and liberal democracy as imports unsuited to local realities. A communist-style redistribution of income made no sense in a nation without sufficient wealth, production, or inhabitants. Nor did liberalism, which translated into bossism and clientelism. Like Torres, he advocated a strong centralized state to educate, discipline, and dominate local elites, organize the country, and impose order. In contrast to his mentor, however, Viana believed that the racial defects of the populace made a dictatorship necessary. He also wanted the government to harmonize corporate interests and stimulate the creation of a smallholding agrarian class, although Viana did not say how it would do so. Nor did he explain how such a state would arise, given oligarchical opposition and his belief that the masses were incapable of such a task.[91]

Conclusion

By the mid-1920s, Catholic nationalists had reached political conclusions similar to Viana's, although their religious perspective contrasted with his secularism. The path to these beliefs had been a long one. The LN and LDN contributed to the extreme right the vitalism and virility of their combat motive, the identification of immigrants with the left, a sense of urgency, and devotion to the fatherland, hierarchy, and unity. Although at first glance the Ligas seemed liberal democratic, their fear of dissolvent influences—regionalism, individualism, military revolts, foreigners, and leftists—pushed them into the forces of order; the LDN, after all, affiliated with the ASN. Catholic, xenophobic, and increasingly authoritarian and antisemitic, *Brazílea*, the PN, ASN, Academia, and Centro Dom Vital were more obviously of the extreme right. Imbued with a more popular spirit than the Ligas, they constructed an alternative to the left, one of nationalism, paternalism, racial tolerance, opposition to foreign capitalism, inclusion of women, and scapegoating of foreigners and Jews that prefigured the views of Ação Integralista Brasileira of the 1930s. The Catholic current drew not only from the Ligas but from European thought and such local precursors as Torres, the Jacobinos, monarchists, and positivists.

The groups enjoyed the adherence of moderate rightists, the church, and the military. The church backed the LDN and, less strongly than might have appeared, the ASN. It was more enthusiastic about the Centro Dom Vital, a movement it controlled. The military strongly supported the LDN, and some officers joined the ASN. The ASN and Catholic nationalists, however, condemned the Tenentes and barracks revolts, even though the rebels shared some of their views. Members of the government were found in the LDN, ASN, and Academia, and LN member Dória was in the São Paulo state administration. The ruling class, however, was unwilling to take the anti-Portuguese campaign as far as the ASN wanted. Members of the elite joined the LN and LDN, but not as many belonged to the ASN, which mainly consisted of middle-class men and women. Extreme rightist groups in Brazil were not militias of the upper class, as they were in Argentina and Chile. Their ideas and, in the case of the ASN, class composition, rather than the practice of violence, distinguished them from moderate right-wing forces.

Several factors limited the extreme right. The strength of the conservative oligarchies obviated the need for such a movement. Unconcerned about broadening its appeal, the state repressed unions and the left on its own, leaving no role for an independent strikebreaking organization. In any case, the leftist threat was not as great as in Argentina. The relative debility of labor robbed extreme rightists of a rallying call and extreme rightist women of a mission.

CHAPTER 8

Conclusion

Extreme rightist groups in the three countries during the age of the Ligas shared some features. Arising in the wartime context, they wanted to express their manhood and energy in an inspiring cause. For Brazilians and Argentines, this initially meant participating in the conflict, and for Chileans, it meant protecting the country against supposed Peruvian subversion. Radical rightists soon reinterpreted their nationalist mission as one of preventing labor unrest, which they traced to revolutionary Europe (or Peru). They opposed the remolding of society to fit utopian dreams, which they regarded as destructive, misguided, and un-Christian—and a threat to their own positions. As an alternative to leftism and militant unions, the Liga Patriótica Argentina (LPA) and Brazilian Catholic nationalists constructed an ideology based on opposition to foreign businesses and inhabitants, a third position between capitalism and socialism, and roles for both genders.

The military had many ties to extreme rightists in all three countries. Active and retired officers helped organize the various Chilean Ligas, the LPA, and the Liga da Defesa Nacional. At the same time, Brazilian and Chilean extreme rightists opposed reform currents within the military. Ironically, these military insurgents upheld some beliefs similar to those of the extreme right, such as the need to end oligarchical rule while simultaneously curbing and uplifting the undisciplined masses.

The numbers of radical rightist women expanded in the three countries, as did their sphere of activity. Women moved from strictly church-related organizations to right-wing nationalist groups under secular leadership, although the Catholic orientation of the LPA and Ação Social Nacionalista (ASN) facilitated their entry. Their participation in demonstrations in Chile and Brazil and editorial tasks and speeches to primarily male audiences in Brazil represented new departures. Still, the female mission in the LPA was the customary charitable type. The nature of their political involvement notwithstanding, women and men, with some Brazilian exceptions, usually justified it in domestic terms.

The very need to justify female activism partly reflected women's circumscribed roles in the larger societies. It also indicated the ambivalence felt by movements largely constructed as male. Radical rightists tended to equate masculinity with strength, honor, and the martial virtues they were beginning to revere; incorporating women, therefore, threatened to undermine the groups' image of power and valor. Such tensions would not disappear with time.

Differences among the three countries were also marked, particularly with respect to labor and the left. Labor activism caused the greatest panic among the propertied classes in Argentina. Here and to a lesser extent in Brazil, demographic factors lent cogency to the rightist equation of foreigner with radical. Partly for these reasons, the LPA formulated the most effective project and organizational structure of the groups in this period. The perceived gravity of the worker threat helps explain why Social Catholicism appeared stronger in Argentina and Chile than in Brazil. It also helps account for the philanthropic nature of the female role in the LPA and the relative importance of its female contingent.

The groups responded differently to feminism. In Chile, a movement favoring female equality and political rights had barely begun, but Brazilian extreme rightists aligned themselves with it while the Argentines opposed it. The conservatism of mainstream Brazilian feminism, contrasting with the progressive affiliations of the Argentine variant, helped determine this alignment. So, too, did the differing class affiliations of women in the Brazilian and Argentine extreme right. Devoted to society, church, and charity functions, female aristocrats found the Argentine and Chilean radical right-wing movements attractive. More likely to approve of feminist goals, some native-born middle-class female professionals adhered to the ASN.

This in turn points to class distinctions among the men. While the major movements of the three countries recruited from the middle and upper classes, the aristocratic leadership of the Chilean and Argentine groups, and the tension between them and the democratic reformist governments of

Alessandri and Yrigoyen, respectively, gave them an elitist tone. In contrast, the ASN tried to appeal to native-born middle sectors.

Another variable was the strength of conservatism. The Brazilian oligarchies remained firmly in control of the state and federal governments during this period. Not needing to mollify the weak reform forces or attract labor support, they suppressed the union movement. Displaced from the presidency by democrats, the Chilean and Argentine elite no longer occupied as secure a position. Under these circumstances, an extraparliamentary right attracted Argentines who feared a permanent loss of power and administrations favorable toward labor. Dissatisfied elements in the church also drifted toward the LPA. The weakness of conservatism, along with the variables discussed above, made the Argentine extreme right the strongest in the Southern Cone, the one most able to exert influence on government and society.

Despite its loose organization and premature demise, the size and influence of the ASN indicated Brazil's second-place status. As Charles Hale has noted, the "strength and longevity of the Old Republic had the anomalous dual effect of inhibiting liberal democracy and socialism and yet inviting criticism of the republican system."[1] The obvious failure of the liberal economic and political models inspired calls for change. The weakness of progressive forces helped dictate that change would come from the right. Moreover, the extreme right included members of middle sectors—in larger numbers than the LPA—as well as disaffected elements of the elite. Uncomfortable with its status in the republic, the Brazilian Catholic Church furnished support and arguments for the extreme right, which expressed the earliest full-blown right-wing corporatist critique of liberalism in the three countries, complete with antisemitic features.

Extreme rightist forces in Chile were the weakest. Linked with the still-prominent Conservatives, the church had little reason to support an extraparliamentary right. Foreigners were conspicuously underrepresented in the ranks of labor and the left. Once Alessandri assumed the presidency, the oligarchy realized that he would repress the workers' movement, although perhaps not as resolutely as preceding administrations, and it could continue to exert influence through Congress and the top echelons of the military. The Ligas and other groups proved incapable of uniting or broadening their appeal.

At least initially in this period, moderate and radical rightists in the three countries were closely allied. Not organized as political parties, the Argentine and Chilean movements served as the arms of conservative factions rather than as their competitors. These organizations represented the radicalization of the moderate right in a time of crisis. The main distinction between moderate parties and extremist groups was the latter's propensity for violence. Only in Brazil did ideology—Catholic, xenophobic yet racially tolerant, authoritarian nationalism—distinguish extremists from moderates, although a Catholic reactionary current was beginning in Argentina and to a lesser extent in Chile. Only in Brazil did extremists create political parties that briefly attempted—and failed—to challenge those of the oligarchies; they would mount a greater threat in the next decade. Relations among rightists would not always be as close in the 1930s as they were in the 1920s, at least in Argentina and Chile.

The Era of Fascism:
The Late 1920s to 1939

To many Latin Americans, the Great Depression symbolized the bankruptcy of the liberal economic and political project. In search of solutions to the crisis, some turned to the extreme right. Inspired by European fascism and integral Catholicism, extreme rightists attained their zenith, forming important movements that reached out to the popular sectors during this era. Moderate rightists even borrowed ideas and practices from radical rightists; the dividing line between them was none too clear.[1] Yet the moderates helped check the power of the extremists.

In the 1930s, the Chilean Movimiento Nacional Socialista, Ação Integralista Brasileira, and Argentine Nacionalistas occupied the extreme position in the right because they offered the most radical means of fighting the leftist foe.[2] The Brazilian and Chilean movements and many members of the Argentine fell under the fascist category. Building upon the past, they devised an alternative to socialism, one emphasizing social justice within national boundaries and change within order. They planned to alter the meaning of life rather than the social structure. By defining capitalism as greed, usury, monopoly, and especially international finance, rather than private property, they could present themselves as its opponents. Such evil traits they often associated with Jews, and antisemitism substituted for class struggle. They recast the Marxist struggle of proletarians against capitalists as that of proletarian against capitalist nations. They emphasized the creation of a strong corporatist state ruled by moral individuals rather than a specific economic program. Their focus on masculinity, youth, and violence appeared revolutionary. There was much rhetoric and even some action against the bourgeoisie—not against the class per se but against its "spirit." Presumably neither capitalist nor socialist,[3] fascist doctrine was ambivalent and deliberately so, a useful trait for a movement that sought a broad following.

Their shared beliefs did not completely disguise the differences among the movements, some of which carried over from the past. The most salient difference was the continued prominence of the Argentine radical right. In Argentina the church, the military, and conservatives ultimately lent more support to the extreme right than in the other countries. Only in Argentina did this movement attain power, however briefly, over two provinces and over the country, and return to power in the next decade, after its Chilean and Brazilian peers had declined.

CHAPTER 9

Chile: Socialism for the Twentieth Century

Political and economic crisis in the early 1930s provoked a level of instability that spurred the formation of right-wing paramilitary organizations. The principal movement of the extreme right, the Movimiento Nacional Socialista (MNS), hoped to bring order out of chaos without returning to the past. It was only one of many competing rightist factions and parties. The MNS's ambiguous relationship with other rightists, as well as with the government, the church, and the military, would eventually contribute to its fall.

The political crisis was tied to military intrusion into government, starting with Carlos Ibáñez del Campo, one of the younger officers who had deposed President Arturo Alessandri in 1924 and General Luis Altamirano in 1925. Ibáñez took control of the army and used it to support constitutional reform and buttress his ambitions. Disconcerted when Alessandri returned to office, Ibáñez pressured him and then his successor, Emiliano Figueroa Larraín (1925–27), into resigning the presidency, and got himself elected instead. An authoritarian reformer and modern-day Diego Portales in the eyes of his admirers, Ibáñez modernized administration, implemented public works and land distribution programs, and expanded education. Protective tariffs added to his nationalist credentials, although the reliance on foreign capital and loans detracted from them. The settlement of the border dispute with Peru removed that issue from the nationalist agenda. The regime also suppressed the left and political leaders and disregarded civil liberties and Congress. It sought to dominate the labor movement by consolidating laws into a labor code and creating an officialist fed-

eration. Some aristocrats praised Ibáñez's measures, while others denounced them as socially radical or dictatorial. Whether they supported
him or not, the former oligarchs recognized that Ibáñez had broken with
the old order.[1]

The pitfalls of overdependency on nitrate and copper exports and the
large foreign debt became apparent with the advent of the Depression.
Chile defaulted on its foreign loans in 1931 and could not secure additional
financing; meanwhile, government revenues dried up. In percentage terms,
the nation experienced the worst foreign trade loss in the world between
1929 and 1932, as sales of minerals plummeted and Chile was unable to purchase imports. Thousands of unemployed miners left the north and joined
the ranks of the jobless in Santiago and other areas. Ibáñez slashed government expenses to balance the budget, thereby aggravating unemployment
and dissatisfaction.[2]

The Depression sparked political instability. Demonstrations by groups
demanding a return to constitutional rule provoked government repression
and killings. The overwhelming economic crisis and dissension that could
be controlled only through bloodshed forced Ibáñez to resign in July 1931.
Political chaos ensued for the next year and a half, as military and civilian
leaders alternated in power. None proved able to manage the economy or
mobilize support.

Although Ibáñez had decimated independent labor organizations,
several events convinced the upper classes that the crisis had restored the
left. A Communist-influenced naval mutiny broke out in September 1931,
followed by an attack by unemployed workers and a few Communists on
the Copiapó regiment in December, both suppressed by the government.
Then came the twelve-day "Socialist Republic" in June 1932, whose leading
figure was Marmaduke Grove, one of the reformist conspirators of 1924
and 1925. Its vague plans to install a corporatist-style welfare state bespoke
paternalism rather than socialism, and its disorganization and lack of mass
support enabled the military to overthrow it. For three months Carlos
Dávila and his government attempted to impose a more conservative
brand of corporatism before the armed forces removed him from power.[3]
The naval mutiny and the Socialist and Dávila regimes heightened the
elite's fear of the left and strengthened its identification of revolution with
the military.

Instability, economic crisis, military involvement in politics, and the
perceived leftist threat sparked reactions from the right. When Ibáñez fell,
civil guards arose to prevent looting and disorder. Prestigious civilians and

retired officers, including Jorge González von Marées, joined the Unión Cívica de Nuñoa. After the naval mutiny the authorities, working with the police, army, and Carabineros, set up the Legión de Reservistas. The Guardias Cívicas of Copiapó and Vallenar took part in the repression of December 1931.[4]

Nacismo

Observers pondered ways of moving the country away from disorder and possible revolution. One was Guillermo Subercaseaux, the Nationalist Party leader of the teen years, whose regard for a national socialism and a government above parties led him to admire early German Nazism.[5] Another was Jorge González von Marées, a young jurist who had written a law thesis blaming the selfish plutocracy and especially undisciplined workers for the social question. To help them acquire better habits, González founded several institutions for worker education. His membership in the Tenacidad Entusiasmo Abnegación (TEA) and in a civil guard, his admiration for Carlos Ibáñez and Diego Portales, and his reading of Nicolás Palacios, Francisco Encina, and Osvald Spengler edged him toward authoritarianism.[6]

González helped shape a new movement in early 1932. To do so he sought out Carlos Keller, a middle-class Ibáñista bureaucrat of German descent and educational background. Keller's book, *La eterna crisis chilena*, which advocated economic nationalism and rightist authoritarianism, had impressed González. In March, retired general Francisco Javier Díaz Valderrama, who had trained in Germany, served in the German army, and helped depose Alessandri in 1924, invited Keller and González to his home. Díaz had translated the Nazi program into Spanish for publication by his press, La Cruz Svástica, and he urged the formation of a similar group. González assured the general that such a movement was coalescing. On April 5, 1932, the anniversary of an important independence battle, Keller and a few others met with González and listened to him read his National Socialist program. This was the first meeting of the Movimiento Nacional Socialista (MNS, Nacis, or Nacistas).[7]

Disseminated soon thereafter, but redrawn and recirculated after the Socialist Republic, the manifesto urged Chileans to replace the democratic ideal, which had degenerated into demagoguery, egoistic class conflict, immorality, and anarchy. This was the moment for Chile to regenerate its political system, starting with expelling Communists and lackeys of foreigners. Nacistas wanted a strong government of order, hierarchy, and social justice that would unite the people and impose the national interest. It would be democratic in that any capable citizen could aspire to leadership, but not in the sense of suffrage, partisan politics, or leveling, all of which the Nacistas rejected. While they expressed their admiration for Portales and Ibáñez in other contexts, they made it clear that a Nacista state, based on popular mobilization, would differ considerably from a state under these two leaders. Rejecting "reactionary and absorbent capitalism" and "irresponsible and anarchic communism," Nacistas supported private property that benefited the nation and productive rather than parasitic capital.[8]

Nacistas hoped to reorganize the country politically and economically. They advocated replacing popular with functional representation, granting equal political rights and duties to both sexes, and decentralizing and improving the efficiency of the bureaucracy. The MNS wanted the state to nationalize public utilities, banks, and inadequately exploited foreign-owned mines, thus providing sufficient credit and permitting these enterprises to operate in Chile's interest. The state should control foreign trade so as to prevent imbalances and protect industry without driving up the cost of primary consumption items or local production. It should also expropriate, subdivide, and colonize latifundia, form agricultural cooperatives, and prohibit the rental of agricultural property. All Chileans should have the right to work and own their own land. Besides land reform, Nacistas proposed profit sharing, limited inheritance rights, and an obligatory year of national service to bring the classes together. Lowering the mortality rate and taxes on large families would help increase the population. Finally, Nacistas wanted to exclude undesirable immigrants.

The movement was an idealistic, hierarchical "disciplined force" led by men "of strong, self-sacrificing, determined spirit."[9] In keeping with the military-style organization, Nacistas wore a gray shirt, tie, and cap, and a ribboned brown leather strap over the shoulder. They copied the fascist salute and the führer principle. Like a military commander, Jorge González von Marées wielded supreme power as *el jefe*. The membership belonged to nuclei grouped into larger units at the communal, district, and provincial levels, headed by "commissars" selected by González. Directly below *el jefe* were administrative departments and the Tropas Nacistas de Asalto (TNA). A clear imitation of Nazi and fascist paramilitary squads, the TNA served to teach obedience, self-sacrifice, and a strict moral code to its youthful members—a code which did not forbid murder. Naci youth also received training first in the Juventud Nacional Socialista and later in the Grupo Nacista Universitario (GNU).[10]

Milicia Republicana

Meanwhile, a rival rightist group was forming. Opposed to the left and to military intervention in politics, many members of the civil guards and of the upper and middle classes found the coup that had installed the Socialist Republic abhorrent. They coalesced into small, clandestine circles throughout central Chile; the most important was the Milicia Republicana, which formed on July 24, 1932. Led by Eulogio Sánchez Errázuriz, a civil engineer, businessman, and Ibáñista functionary, the Milicianos swore to impose and uphold democratic republican rule and fight any form of tyranny. Instructed by retired officers, they gathered secretly to train and organize themselves in military fashion, wearing a dark blue coverall and cap and a leather belt.[11] The Milicia united opposition circles and grew rapidly in the next few months.

By this time, military involvement in politics had brought Milicianos and other Chileans to the boiling point. On September 13, 1932, the Santiago garrison overthrew Carlos Dávila and implanted General Bartolomé Blanche, a former Ibáñez official. Even some officers feared Ibáñez's return and resented the military adventurers for tarnishing Chile's image. They wondered if Blanche would accept the results of elections scheduled for October 30. General Pedro Vignola, head of army forces stationed in Antofagasta, demanded on September 26 that Blanche reestablish civilian rule. Milicianos and other civilians rallied around Vignola, forcing Blanche to hand over power to the president of the Supreme Court, Abraham Oyanedel. Street fights between soldiers and civilians manifested popular revulsion against the armed forces. Imbued with the same antimilitary sentiments, the new civilian authorities quietly authorized the transfer of arms from the army to the Carabineros and from the Carabineros to the Milicia.[12]

The Milicia safeguarded the election. On the eve of the balloting, it issued its first press statement, insisting on its nonpartisan and nonclassist character and pledging support for any freely elected government. On election day, armed Milicianos in plainclothes stationed themselves throughout the capital to prevent disturbances. Yet peace reigned as Alessandri regained the presidency—backed by Radicals and his former enemies on the right. A Communist-inspired mutiny attempt in an army regiment in Viña del Mar on January 24, 1933, prompted the Milicia to activate its units in that area. Authorities arrested the plotters, however, before they mounted a coup.[13]

The mutiny provided further evidence of growing leftist power. Marmaduke Grove won second place in the 1932 presidential race, and various leftist factions consolidated into the Socialist Party in April 1933. The Socialists would combine worker demands and nationalist goals with an appealing populist style. To defend themselves against the Milicia, unions in central Chile began to organize their own "red guards" and militias in early 1933. Forsaking his beloved *chusma*, Alessandri immediately secured extraordinary powers and cracked down on the left. The government's decision to allow the Milicia to hold a parade on May 7 sharpened leftist fear of repression and of official collusion with the Milicia.[14]

This parade demonstrated the Milicia's strength and connections. A huge, mostly favorable crowd watched between 13,000 and 14,000 uniformed members march through the streets of the capital. The police, however, arrested others for hurling leaflets criticizing the "white terror." Although the government had ordered Milicianos to be unarmed, the trucks that accompanied each "regiment" contained weapons and tear gas, and about 1,000 armed Milicianos placed themselves at strategic points along the route. Members of the British and other foreign communities marched, as did Radical Minister of Education and Justice Domingo Durán and Alessandri's nephew, Gustavo. The president, ministers, and congressional leaders greeted the marchers as they passed by La Moneda. Alessandri spontaneously addressed the Milicia, declaring it would buttress republican institutions and serve as the "foundation of law and order." Describing the Milicia as well within the constitution, he gave it his official approval and support. As one Miliciano succinctly put it, the president loved the organization because "he felt we protected him."[15] In effect, the Milicia protected not only Alessandri but also an elitist political system and government austerity policies that hurt the poor.

Backed by the president, the Milicia extended its membership under bourgeois control. It grew to an estimated 40,000 to 50,000, with units throughout Chile.[16] Milicia leaders were mostly professionals and businessmen "desirous of peaceful conditions in order to carry on their affairs profitably," as the U.S. military attaché put it. Half of the General Staff and many other officers were members of the aristocratic Club de la Unión. Tied to the oligarchy, technocratic in orientation, and previously inactive in politics, prominent Milicianos thought they could promote constitutional rule better than corrupt politicians. This stance attracted support from wealthy and influential men such as Alessandri's powerful treasury minister, Gustavo Ross, an orthodox economic liberal. The Sociedad Nacional de Agricultura and foreign and national companies placed ads in the group's magazine, and some private concerns donated money. A finance committee of eminent businessmen solicited funds from companies and wealthy individuals, apparently suggesting appropriate amounts for particular foreign-owned firms to pay. Considering the weakness of the state in the early 1930s, businesses felt obliged to pay such sums as an "insurance premium." Firms pushed their employees to participate in the organization.[17]

The Milicia also recruited women and the less privileged. Impressionistic sources indicate the presence of teachers, minor bureaucrats, small farmers, white-collar and retail employees, independent artisans, and manual workers—perhaps unorganized. Sporting white uniforms, small numbers of women joined the Red Cross sections of various regiments and attended rallies.[18]

Yet there was little space for women in a group so heavily devoted to military-style functions and rhetoric. The Milicia focused on its men, particularly on their masculinity, more so than previous groups. With the coups and instability, according to one Miliciano, Chile had lost "all notion of virility, of arrogance, of dignity." Milicianos had to take action because "we want to be men before eunuchs." A poem by one Miliciano described his peers: "The forehead very high, the chest erect . . . they march arrogant as lions." The organization exalted youth as a state of mind representing valor, adventure, and an appetite for life and ideals.[19]

Miliciano Julio P. Bravo Hayley called the group's ideology "republicanism," a term also used by the Liga Patriótica Argentina (LPA). Good republican government meant elected authority, adequate social legislation, class cooperation, and "liberty in order" (another LPA phrase). Repeatedly condemning class struggle, the Milicia claimed that its mere presence deterred attacks on the social order. The alternative to a republic was a tyranny that, like communism or fascism, hated freedom and violently imposed its views. Milicia republicans opposed all governments of force, yet Bravo's denunciation of the British Labor Party administration raised doubts whether they would also oppose a democratically elected leftist government in Chile.[20]

The Milicia portrayed itself as a model of social relations for the nation. An employee and his supervisor might be in the same unit: "In the office, one is the chief. In the militia, the other is the chief." It noted that true democracy required the cooperation of "capitalists and employers, workers and employees, of those who possess and those who have nothing." The "humble overall of a worker," the symbol of labor, conveniently obscured the class origins of the Milicianos. The "democracy" of the Milicia resembled the notion of the equality of soldiers at the front, so cherished by Nazis.

Significantly, as in the armed forces, it did not include popular decision making; generally of high social rank, the top officers determined policy.[21]

In other ways the Milicia betrayed ambivalence with liberal democracy. The very existence of an armed civilian guard seemed outside the constitution. A magazine cover featured Diego Portales, known for his creation of an authoritarian state, and the periodical referred to the decay of political parties. Yet the Milicia did not move substantially beyond political liberalism before mid-1935. In this sense it was a transitional group between the Ligas of the 1920s and the fascists of the 1930s; in fact, a few members had belonged to TEA and earlier movements. Like the LPA, it opposed leftism through a show of force (although it never actually used it) and formed an alternative to unreliable authorities. The organizations drew upon similar social strata and included members of different parties: in the Chilean case, moderate rightists—Conservatives, Liberals, and smaller parties included in Alessandri's coalition—and centrist Radicals. Both represented the radicalization of the moderate right in a time of crisis. Recognizing the similarity, the Milicia praised the LPA and referred to its "related aims."[22] Yet the Milicia's military-style organization, uniforms, and cult of forceful manhood—so characteristic of fascism—set it apart from the earlier group.

In these last respects the Milicia resembled the local National Socialists, but there also were differences. Distinguishing between the two movements, the MNS leader compellingly described the Milicia as a semiofficial militarized group, armed and even staffed by the government, dedicated to protecting an antiquated system. He pointed out that fascism was popular and the Milicia, mostly composed of the well-to-do, was not. Perhaps Milicianos belonged to different parties, but they professed the same socioeconomic ideas. Milicianos and Nacistas shared anticommunism, but their means of fighting this ideology differed: the Milicia's approach was material and coercive, while Nacismo, as a fascist movement, aimed at changing the popular mentality. González insisted that the Nacistas' heroic brand of violence to create a new order varied from the Milicia's threat of force to defend oligarchic economic interests. To drive home this point, "Nacismo Is Not a White Guard" appeared in large letters in the MNS newspaper, *Trabajo*, in May 1933. *Trabajo* also noted that the Milicia itself disclaimed fascist tendencies and instead linked fascism and communism.[23] Another Nacista considered the Milicia's promotion of order one of the most "virile" acts in Chilean history yet hollow and lacking in content.[24]

Regarding it as potentially receptive to Naci doctrine and vulnerable to Naci control, the MNS infiltrated the Milicia. The Milicia's ample supply of arms also made it attractive to the Nacistas. One Miliciano discovered that a third of his regiment, that of Viña del Mar, was Naci. For their part, Milicianos who found their organization bourgeois and vacuous became Nacistas. The MNS welcomed the assurances offered by Julio Schwarzenberg Lobeck, physician and president of the General Staff, to González in mid-1933, that the Milicia would accept a fascist government if it achieved power through constitutional means.[25]

Yet a quarrel soon started. When Nacistas began to fight Communists in the streets in August 1933, the General Staff ordered Milicianos to leave the MNS. The Milicia decided not to permit its resources to serve an armed political group that planned to destroy other parties—even if they were leftist. In turn, Nacistas accused Milicianos of aiding the government, spreading political propaganda despite their supposed nonpartisanship, and, in 1936, selling arms they should have returned to the authorities. They even charged Milicianos with forcibly preventing Nacistas from selling their newspaper.[26]

Relations between the Milicia and fellow moderate rightists remained cordial. Most Liberals and Conservatives supported it. Fearing socialism more than the Milicia's secular stance, the church lauded this patriotic "reaction of the fatherland's health against the gangrene that was threatening to destroy it." The church did more than praise it; the Milicia's headquarters in Santiago occupied property owned by the archbishop.[27]

Not surprising was the firm opposition of the left, consisting of Communists, Radical Socialists, Socialists, the various splinters of the Democratic Party, dissident Radicals, and Social Republicans, who had left the Radical Party because of its complicity with Ibáñez. They regarded the Milicia not only as a bourgeois reaction against the proletariat but as seditious and unconstitutional. After the parade of May 7, Social Republican deputy and former student activist Carlos Vicuña Fuentes asked the Chamber to pass a resolution dissolving the Milicia and prosecuting its leaders. Socialist senator Eugenio Matte presented a resolution stating that the armed forces were sufficient to guarantee order, which other armed groups only imperiled. Milicia supporters easily defeated these resolutions. Ruling against leftist arguments, the appeals court of Santiago declared that the Milicia was legal.[28]

Tensions between the Milicia and the left threatened to explode. Menacing statements by Milicianos confirmed suspicions that they opposed even those leftists operating legally in the political arena, such as Marmaduke Grove, who was elected to the Senate in 1934.[29] In July 1933, authorities uncovered a leftist plot against the Milicia as well as the government.[30]

Until 1934, the president aided the Milicia. The authorities allowed the movement to import arms and arrested its most vociferous opponents, and semiofficial agencies placed ads in the *Boletín*. A British diplomat estimated that the government provided 4 million pesos annually in subsidies, although this sum may have included the value of arms transfers, discussed below. These means of support, however, also translated into means of control and vigilance: Alessandri could receive information on the Milicia from colleagues, two nephews, and a son who were members, and he could withdraw government recognition and favors as easily as he bestowed them. Indeed, the president instructed the investigations branch of the Ministry of the Interior to watch the Milicia carefully.[31]

Alessandri continued the weapons transfers that had begun under the previous administration. The ministers of the interior under Oyanedel and Alessandri ordered the army to deliver large quantities of arms to the Carabineros, who in turn put them at the disposal of the intendant of Santiago, Julio Bustamante, former director of the Carabineros and Milicia officer. Bustamante handed these weapons to the Milicia through the target practice clubs that many Milicianos joined. Arms worth an estimated 25 million pesos, or approximately $2 million, changed hands.[32]

The Milicia enjoyed cordial relations with most of the forces of order. A militarized police corps used by Alessandri as a counterweight to the unreliable army, the Carabineros were the natural allies of the civilian guard, although they harbored some suspicions toward it. Policemen, firemen, and especially the traditionally conservative and apolitical navy were also the Milicia's friends.[33]

Initially agreeing with the Milicia's goals, some army officers helped the movement by training its members and transferring arms. By the parade of May 7, however, their opinions had hardened against the Milicia, which had come to embody upper-class and administration hostility toward the army. The fact that Alessandri aided the group yet cut the army's budget was particularly annoying. The army also felt excluded from the friendships that knit the Milicia and other forces of order.[34]

Commander in chief Vignola made his dislike for the Milicia plain. After the parade of May 7, he declared that soldiers and officers could neither belong to the Milicia nor discuss it. In October 1933, Vignola demanded behind the scenes that Minister of Defense Emilio Bello Codesido force the Milicia to return its weapons to the army. The minister told him to withdraw his statement or resign, and the general apparently dropped the demand. Two months later, in a letter addressed to Bello Codesido, Vignola claimed that Milicianos, alerted by rumors of a possible revolt, had spied on an army maneuvers camp and he requested Carabinero support. He asked the minister to leave the army alone and to prevent similar acts in the future. *El Debate*, whose three directors were prominent Nacistas, published this letter, which Vignola had never mailed, without his knowledge. This act reinforced reports that Nacistas, closely tied to Ibáñista officers, were stirring up dissension in the barracks. Alessandri forced the general to resign and ordered the detention of two of the Naci journalists. To dispel the rumors of Naci plots, González threw them out of the MNS. For its part, the Milicia hotly denied it had been watching the army.[35]

With the appointment of General Oscar Novoa Fuentes to take Vignola's place, the president began to tilt toward the army. A firm advocate of military professionalism who had remained aloof from the military coups and governments of 1924–32, Novoa managed to pry army officers from political involvement. Confident that the army was under control and aware of its dislike for the Milicia, Alessandri reconsidered his support for the civil guard.

Another incident called this support into question. After Carabineros dissolved several worker gatherings and broke a May Day strike, bombs exploded in Schwarzenberg's house and other Milicia targets, as well as in the offices of *El Mercurio* and *La Nación* in early May. Enraged, the Milicia wrote Grove and thirteen other leftist leaders, including senators and former ministers, accusing them of at least indirect responsibility for the attempted assassination of the Milicia commander. It threatened to hold them accountable for such acts in the future.[36]

This letter had important political consequences. It aroused dissension within the Milicia and may have sparked some resignations. Backed by their parties, the fourteen leftists answered that the note broke the Milicia's oath and placed its members outside the law. Even parties that had favored the organization and contributed personnel to it, such as the Radicals, were disturbed. The largest party and "swing" group in Congress, Radicals formed part of Alessandri's coalition. After the letter, prominent Radicals called for disbanding the Milicia and ordered party members to resign from it. Although the party did not push the matter, the Milicia could no longer count on it. The Radicals' shift on the organization coincided with their general move to the left, away from Alessandri's emphasis on austerity and repression and toward reform.[37]

Nacistas responded in uniquely populist fashion. They agreed that the Milicia was outside the constitution, but this did not bother them. Instead, they castigated the organization for singling out leftist leaders, insisting that "those of the right deserved equal punishment. There are, among them, some that merit more punishment than many of the left."[38]

Most important, the letter turned the administration against the Milicia. Notifying Schwarzenberg of his support and concern over the attack, Alessandri nevertheless admonished the group to leave law enforcement to the authorities. In response, the General Staff resigned, although Schwarzenberg remained president, and he publicly accepted Alessandri's dictate. Over the opposition of the minister of the interior, the army, and the Radicals, the Milicia held its largest parade—of about 37,000—on October 13, 1934. Significantly, Alessandri stood along the parade route but did not greet them at La Moneda, as he had done in May 1933.[39]

Recognizing that the Milicia had outlived its usefulness for the administration, Schwarzenberg announced on July 24, 1935, the organization's third anniversary, that it had completed its mission and would slowly demobilize. Yet the Milicia still held reviews, published its journal, and retained its arms. Confused and disillusioned, many members lost their enthusiasm and left. Believing that the leftist threat still required the Milicia's presence, some officers of the Santiago garrison called on the leaders to reactivate the organization. After a well-publicized dispute that further weakened the Milicia, Schwarzenberg expelled four of the protesting officers.[40]

The formation of the Popular Front, consisting of leftists and Radicals, in March 1936 finally prompted Milicia leaders to dismantle the rapidly shrinking movement in July and plan a new party.[41] In October 1936, Milicianos created National Action; two months later it fused with the Republican Union (1932), another party with many Miliciano members, to form Republican Action (AR). Opposing class conflict, the party desired voluntary cooperation among management, labor, and employees to strengthen the capitalist system, with only limited state intervention. AR advocated a rightist form of politics based on selection, authority, traditional values, and an emphasis on duties instead of rights. This "true democracy" would rest upon plural voting and converting the Senate into a corporative chamber. A novel aspect of the program was its call for incorporating women into political life on an equal basis with men.[42]

Winning only two seats in the Chamber of Deputies in the 1937 elections, Republican Action had little electoral appeal. Evidently many within and outside the Milicia thought it would duplicate other moderate rightist parties. A more extreme alternative was the Legión Cívica de Chile, founded by former authorities of the cadet school on the day the Milicia was disbanded. These Milicianos had moved toward a more explicit rightist stance after the demobilization, a shift reflected in *Caupolicán*, the successor to the *Boletín*. Growing to 4,000 by 1937, the Legión attracted some of the Milicianos expelled over the demobilization issue as well as corporatist-leaning businessmen. The Legión openly pitted itself against electoral politics.[43]

Politics and the Nacista "Revolution"

As the remnants of the Milicia edged toward corporatism and authoritarianism, they resembled more and more the Nacistas they claimed to despise. Like the Milicia, Nacistas owed their early growth to the reaction against the Socialist Republic. At this time, Naci leaders moved to the right and distinguished their program from the government's, which they characterized as virtual communism. Although it initially called for subdividing latifundia, the MNS now claimed to oppose confiscations, demagogic attacks on private property, and even social legislation; it did not want "the appetites of the low depths of society" to feed off the wealthy. Nacistas denounced only parasitic and exploitative capitalism, not the economic system as a whole. To brace "order, peace, and work," the movement would not hesitate to engage "the extremist hordes." Only open combat "without mercy" could vanquish anarchy or communism, not academic talks or politics as usual, for one could not reason with criminals.[44] Fearing leftism, wealthy youths joined the MNS. Their dues enabled the fledgling movement to disseminate its views over radio and in *El Imparcial*, beginning in July 1932, on a weekly and later biweekly National Socialist page.[45]

Naci refusals to denounce the military or engage in traditional politics, however, alienated some upper-class adherents. So, too, did the movement's criticism of parasitic capitalism and speculators who had handed the economy over to "international Judaism." To some, this sounded a bit radical.[46]

Nacistas equivocated on whether they were revolutionary. They claimed their movement was the "antirevolution," the opposite of revolution, serving to confront it, condemn it, and substitute for it in the hearts of the people. Not conformist, however, Nacismo was also revolutionary; in fact, González declared the MNS a revolutionary and defensive movement at the same time. Unlike the leftist materialistic version, the Naci "authentic revolution" sought the "spiritual conquest" of Chileans. Using radical means to defeat revolution and take its place was quintessentially fascist, as Nacistas readily conceded.[47] In contrast, the Milicia and its heirs sought to overcome revolution through more moderate means and certainly not to replace it.

Nacismo continued to expand after Alessandri became president. It opened its own newspaper, *Trabajo*, in April 1933 and turned to the provinces, holding the first Nacista congress in Chillán in mid-October. Naci rallies attracted Guillermo Subercaseaux and other prominent observers. Increasing its visibility through provocative behavior, in March 1933 the MNS began to disrupt Communist rallies, and in June such scuffles spread to the University of Chile. Communists and workers took their revenge on August 7 at the Nacistas' first public meeting at the Teatro Providencia and in the parade that followed. The fracas resulted in six wounded Nacistas and ten casualties among their opponents. One of the founding Nacistas, the lawyer Mauricio Mena, recalled proudly that the episode attracted new members. It also indicated that leftists were willing to answer Nacistas in kind.[48]

The next incident was more serious. About 1,000 Nacistas and sympathizers attended the movement's second gathering at the Teatro Iris on August 27. Gunfire broke out between Nacistas and labor militants waiting outside the theater. A Socialist construction worker died, two workers were gravely wounded, and there were four other casualties. Carabineros detained at least one Nacista and five other unidentified men.[49]

The violence sparked debate in the Chamber of Deputies. Radical leader Gabriel González Videla considered Nacistas a menace to democracy that the government had not addressed, partly because wealthier interests liked the movement's anticommunism. Amidst a flurry of resolutions, Communist Andrés Escobar called for dissolving and disarming Milicianos and Nacistas because they threatened labor.[50]

Moderate rightists found much that was positive in the MNS. While he insisted he did not support Nacismo, Conservative Ricardo Boizard, a former member of TEA and of the Catholic student organization ANEC, praised its idealism. To defeat the MNS, Boizard favored incorporating some of its ideas into political practice, such as ridding Chile of universal suffrage and other "anachronistic" democratic principles and suppressing dissolvent ideas. Fellow Conservative Rafael Moreno agreed that these Naci political views found much favor among the "parties of order," which, however, disliked the MNS's socialist-like statism, its attacks on political parties, and its dictatorial stance. Moreno did not explain how this stance differed from the authoritarianism that the moderate right favored.

Liberal Alejandro Dussaillant described Nacismo as a reaction against the powerful Communist threat in particular, as well as against political corruption, a mediocre bureaucracy, and universal suffrage. (Curiously, he,

Boizard, and Nacistas ignored the fact that suffrage was far from universal.)
Dussaillant preferred the idealistic, self-denying, intelligent Nacistas to the
Communists, although he admitted that some found the former's patriotism too extreme. Their undemocratic nature did not seem to bother the
Liberal deputy, who praised Italy and Japan for their recent economic ad-
vances. In his opinion, Nacismo had a right to participate in political life, at
least until communism disappeared and the political system changed.

Seeking a middle ground, González Videla presented a resolution stating that the Chamber condemned Nacista and Communist activities that
threatened to overturn the political and social system, and it favored legal
means to sanction them. The Chamber approved his resolution, although
forty-four deputies abstained. Many of the abstainers were leftists, but some
were rightists who did not want to equate communism with Nacismo.

This debate set a pattern. Often equating the MNS with the Milicia, the
left was its steadfast enemy until 1937. Before they joined the Popular Front,
Radicals also denounced the movement but frequently linked it with communism. Moderate rightists accepted many Nacista ideas and mainly demurred over tactics.

The 1934 Nazi assassination of Austrian chancellor Engelbert Dollfuss,
an authoritarian Catholic, prompted Conservative criticism of Nacismo for
its destructive and revolutionary tendencies. However, Boizard also saw the
MNS as a "natural reaction" against the tolerance toward communism—
and this was the attitude that prevailed until 1937. As long as Nacistas confined themselves to attacking leftists, moderates usually praised their extremist cousins with faint damnation.[51]

In 1933–34 the administration's position on Nacismo was only slightly
more hostile than that of its moderate rightist parliamentary allies. Under a
periodically renewed law of extraordinary powers mainly directed toward
the left, the government censored some articles in *Trabajo* and occasionally
shut it down. It regulated some Nacista rallies and prohibited others. Yet the
administration allowed the Milicia and the Nacistas to hold parades of
armed men, despite the fact that the same law prohibited such displays. Nor
did the Ministry of the Interior implement the Chamber's resolution. Opponents of the liberal democratic system and, at least implicitly, of the existing administration, the Nacistas did not receive the accolades and favors
that the president lavished on the Milicia. Nor did they experience the harsh
repression that workers did. Instead, the administration initially accepted
them as a tacit partner against leftists, all the while closely watching *el jefe*.[52]

Nacistas in the University of Chile tested the government's position. In

June 1934, violence broke out in the law school between the tiny Grupo Nacista Universitario (GNU), headed by Javier Cox Lira, an aristocratic law student, and young Socialists and Communists. Forty to fifty TNA members, mostly nonstudents, came to the GNU's aid, breaking windows in university buildings and injuring five leftist students. A day after the attack, anti-Naci students disarmed Cox, stripped him of his outer clothing, and forced him to leave university grounds, whereupon they returned his garb. The court briefly imprisoned González, Cox, and several others for their roles in the onslaught. The incident also sparked the creation of the Milicia Universitaria Anti-Fascista, one of the first Chilean left-wing militias of the 1930s.[53]

The administration could not ignore an armed attack on a public facility. On June 22, Minister of the Interior Luis Salas Romo declared the TNA illegal, for only the armed forces or those with official permission could carry weapons. He instructed intendants and governors to dissolve all meetings of the MNS and similar groups, confiscate their guns, repress their violence, and detain those responsible for it. Accordingly, the government canceled several public Naci functions, and Carabineros forcibly halted TNA exercises in Concepción in September, wounding twelve. Yet the efforts of law enforcement officials, who allowed Nacistas to conduct peaceful activities, seemed halfhearted.[54]

Nor did the government prevent further confrontations between Nacistas and leftists. Campaigning in the municipal elections, Nacistas clashed with Communist Left and Leninist Youth brigades in March and April 1935 in Santiago. Young Socialists and Nacistas continually skirmished in Valparaíso, particularly over the selling of their respective papers, *Consigna* and *Trabajo*. *Trabajo* was a daily, but Nacistas only hawked it in the streets on Saturdays, the day the Socialist weekly was published. Their intent to provoke their rivals and invade Socialist territory was clear, as was the Socialists' will to defend their turf. Nacistas swung their belts against their opponents, the metal buckles producing serious head wounds, and Socialists responded with rubber-covered clubs reinforced with metal or electrical cables. On the evening of June 13, 1935, the antagonists fought with even deadlier weapons. When Socialists knifed several Nacistas, the gray shirts fired their guns. Three Nacistas died, and five Socialists and four Nacistas were wounded, all of them young workers. Arriving late, Carabineros detained four Socialists but no Nacistas.[55]

Leftists were determined to deny the MNS supremacy over the streets. Well aware of the Fascist and Nazi records against workers in Europe, they felt themselves to be victims even before Nacistas attacked them. They also regarded Nacistas as interlopers seeking to conquer their well-earned space. "Manly" dignity and a sense of territoriality dictated that each side meet the other's actions with a similar display of resolve and force.[56]

Such motives were evident in the independence festivities of September 1935 at the Parque Cousiño in Santiago. As Alessandri made his way through the park after the customary military review, leftists attacked Pablo Acuña Carrasco, a nineteen-year-old TNA sergeant, for shouting, "Long live Nacismo!" A veteran of battles with the left, Acuña perished of knife wounds and instantly became a martyr in the Nacista pantheon. The death of this upper-class youth at leftist hands led *El Diario Ilustrado* and *Revista Católica* to applaud Nacista patriotism and decry Communist fanaticism.[57]

Over the objections of leftists and union members, Alessandri permitted the MNS to hold its second national rally in Concepción, a labor stronghold, on October 13–14, 1935. Boding ill for the event, gunfire erupted between laborers and Nacistas on a train from Santiago to Concepción on October 12, gravely wounding the Nacista nephew of the bishop of Concepción. Carabineros met the train at its destination and conducted Nacistas to their lodgings, clearing angry workers out of the way. That night Nacistas shouted slogans and fired shots into the air. The next day was a long, bloody one that witnessed many incidents of combat between Nacistas and leftists. In the worst of these, Nacis killed a local Socialist leader and participant in the 1931 naval mutiny in his home. Police arrested five Socialists and Communists but no Nacistas.[58]

The Concepción episode sparked renewed criticism of the MNS. Socialist deputy Rolando Merino filed a criminal complaint against the movement, and even Boizard decried the Nacis' use of force, although he blamed Communists for doing the same. Minister of the Interior Luis Cabrera announced that the administration would enforce a decree of June 21, 1932, prohibiting militarized subversive groups, adding that the Carabineros would break up demonstrations by uniformed members of such organizations lacking official permission to wear their garb.[59]

When Carabineros arrested uniformed Nacistas in downtown Santiago, however, an appeals court overturned Cabrera's order and freed the prisoners. The Senate rejected a Nacista accusation against Cabrera, but it agreed with the court that uniforms were legal and the arrests contradicted liberty of political expression. Leftist senators voted with the majority because they did not want the administration to use the decree against their own militias. Thus the government could no longer detain uniformed civilians.[60]

The next important episode of violence occurred in Valparaíso. After weeks of Naci-Socialist provocations there, *Trabajo* and *Consigna* vendors once more faced off on June 13, 1936. Three Nacistas died, and three others plus five Socialists and one unaffiliated bystander were wounded, all of them workers. Arriving late, the Carabineros detained only Socialists, again seemingly colluding with Nacistas. The Ministry of the Interior promptly forbade public meetings of armed individuals who predicated violence against the established order or government—a measure it could employ against either side.[61]

Moderate rightists and the church commended the MNS for fighting communism. *El Mercurio* admitted that Nacismo carried out "antiseptic, hateful, but necessary work." Blaming the bloodshed on the odious freedom of the press, *La Revista Católica* added that the incident had created sympathy for the Nacista cause. Deploring the violence, Conservative deputy Enrique Cañas Flores nevertheless asked the government to punish those who killed the humble, honest, and nationalistic Nacistas. Yet foreshadowing the future, the president of the Conservative Youth, Bernardo Leighton, dissented from the party elders. He assigned responsibility for suppressing communism to the government and judicial system, not to armed vigilantes.[62]

Composition of the MNS

The casualties in Valparaíso indicate Nacista support in the lower classes. Suggesting as much, the anarchist Federación Obrera Local of Osorno described Nacistas as those who "defended the bourgeoisie, betraying their comrades of labor." Guillermo Izquierdo Araya, a future fascist activist, believed that 60 to 70 percent of Nacistas were of humble origins; González estimated that 70 percent were laborers. A journalist saw a few "elegant" persons in the MNS headquarters, but mostly young "modest people, . . . well-groomed workers, lower-level employees, university students." Reinforcing these observations, Nacistas received a higher percentage of votes in the first district of greater Santiago, which included many workers, than in the rest of Chile, winning about the same fraction of their total votes in that district as the Socialists. The importance of youth and workers made the MNS similar to the Romanian Iron Guard and Hungarian Arrow Cross fascist movements.[63]

There are other signs of the relatively modest and young backgrounds of Nacistas. As discussed below, on September 5, 1938, a group of Naci volunteers attempted in vain to overthrow the government, and sixty-three perished. Nacista hagiographers supplied biographical sketches of fifty-six of these dedicated militants. About 41 percent were in the middle or upper sectors, and 55 percent were in the lower-middle sector or below. Twenty-seven percent were university or professional school students; 35 percent were workers; 22 percent were employees, technicians, or functionaries; and 6 percent were employees of higher status. The average age of the deceased was twenty-two. The average age of Nacistas as a whole may have been higher, since young men were more likely to volunteer for a bloody confrontation.[64]

That half to two-thirds of the movement came from the lower and lower-middle classes should not obscure the higher status of the rest. There were aristocrats such as lawyers Mauricio Mena and Diego Lira Vergara and landowner Ricardo Cox Balmaceda. Gustavo Vargas Molinare, a deputy from 1937 to 1945, owned two estates and was a director of several firms. Many Catholic students found Nacismo attractive, and they tended to come from the upper sectors; 23 percent of the martyrs had attended Catholic schools or were at least very devout. Moreover, some MNS nuclei divided their members into occupational groups, such as those of lawyers, doctors, and workers, indicating the adherence of professionals. The presence of religious youth and aristocrats also typified Eastern European fascism.[65]

There is also the question of German involvement. Six of the martyrs claimed some German ancestry, as did González, Keller, and other prominent Nacistas. One of two Nacista newspapers outside the capital was located in Valdivia, a heavily German-populated area. German Chilean businesses contributed to the MNS and placed ads in the Nacista journal *Acción Chilena,* and a German-owned press published *Trabajo.* Nevertheless, *el jefe* insisted that only 5 percent of party members were of German descent. Backing up his claim, Nacista candidates in Valdivia and Llanquihue, another German population center, lost the 1937 election, and only 20 percent of the Naci vote came from the south.[66]

With its broad composition, Nacismo had organized at least 2,000 nuclei throughout Chile by 1937, and that year the electorate chose González and two other Nacista deputies. *El jefe* received 40,000 votes, the largest majority attained by any deputy from Santiago. The MNS claimed 30,000 members in 1938, but Potashnik estimated that at its height there were only 20,000. This compared unfavorably with the 60,000 Socialists and 25,000 Communists, although Nacis attracted more adherents than the AR or other small rightist parties.[67]

The Alternative to the Left

Naci ideology was suited for mobilizing men of various classes, if not huge numbers of them. González proclaimed that the MNS formed part of fascism, a global movement against the social decomposition left by liberal democracy. Fascism, he declared, stood for the supremacy of blood and race over internationalist and materialist doctrines, and for the dominance of the able few over the mediocre. As fascists, Nacistas were neither right nor left "exclusively"; events guided their leaders (like those of Germany and Italy) in one direction or another.[68]

In 1932 they emphasized their reactionary character, but to compete with the strong leftist parties and attract support, Nacistas sometimes placed themselves in the vanguard. They criticized the wealthy for living comfortably in the capital on incomes derived from their properties, instead of residing on and investing in their estates. Echoing their precursors, Nacis blamed the decadent upper class for forfeiting control over the economy and permitting foreigners to step into the vacuum. Chileans had to restrain foreign capital so that it could serve as a tool of development rather than as a means of conquest. This and other necessary changes might reduce the upper-class standard of living and result in "general poverty," but it would be "a healthy poverty . . . on which one could construct a new social edifice, more just, more humane, more perfect." Led by those who worked—the most able laborers, industrialists, farmers, businessmen, and artisans—rather than indolent aristocrats, the new society would guarantee work and social justice for all, the abolition of parasitic capitalism, and the protection of productive activity. Because they sought to end the terrible poverty that afflicted the country, they claimed to be leftist. One should not confuse fascism, a popular movement, with reaction, said Trabajo, for fascism and Marxism were "brotherly enemies" who parted ways only after a certain point along the barricade. It predicted that "reaction would be suffocated by Nacismo."[69]

Sometimes reactionary, sometimes revolutionary, Naci ideology appealed to diverse groups. Many youths appreciated the movement's elevation of action over verbiage, feeling over reason, and energy over theory. They perceived that fascism was in vogue; its socialism was twentieth-century, unlike the old-fashioned Marxist kind. These features and the MNS economic program also drew unorganized workers, who were a special target for Nacistas and other fascist movements.[70] Resentful of the elite and fearful of sinking into the proletariat, members of the lower-middle to middle classes responded to the Nacista critique of these sectors and its promise to open the economy and the state to individual advancement. The Naci critique of class conflict, universal suffrage, and widespread mediocrity found support among aristocrats disenchanted with existing parties— and even adherents of these parties. Naci spiritualism and opposition to materialism and leftism appealed to some Catholics. Nacismo offered something to many.

Nacista socialism attracted opponents of the "Muscovite" version. Unlike the opposing brand, it rested on the cooperation of all social groups to maximize national welfare, predicating the "material and moral elevation of a race" rather than the domination of a class. Individuals would assume the posts in society that they could best perform; the quality of their work, rather than the prestige of their occupations, would determine how people judged them. National gain would override and replace the profit motive, and individuals would serve the state and abide by strict discipline. MNS socialism was, therefore, a "synonym of order, of selection, of renunciation of the individual to the benefit of the collectivity," and as such it could draw from the entire class spectrum.[71]

As did other fascisms, Nacismo set itself up as an alternative to the left, claiming it was as radical, uncompromising, and concerned about the poor as the "other socialism." One component of this alternative was its populist economic program; another was the displacement of class struggle. Unlike some precursors or moderate rightists, Nacistas did not deny or decry the existence of classes, but they often obscured social boundaries by grouping different categories of wage laborers and capitalists under "producers" or "workers of the mind and muscle," as did their European peers. A Nacista state would not abolish classes, a natural and necessary feature of society; rather, it would ensure decent wages and a reasonable return on investment. To replace an aristocracy they saw as depraved, Nacis were creating a new one based on hard work, integrity, and patriotism instead of on money and lineage. These values superceded but did not annul the old social distinctions, just as the uniform concealed one's status without destroying it. They proposed a state-controlled syndicalist organization of producers that would subsume unions and capital. Thus, the Nacistas would replace the strife-ridden vertical social structure under a corrupt, selfish elite with a horizontal one in which all classes, each considered equally honorable, would cooperate for the common good and contribute personnel to the leadership.[72]

The movement and its programs illustrated some of these notions. The

TNA and, in general, the military character of the MNS blurred class lines and emphasized a hierarchy based on effort and talent, as did the Work Service. Modeled on a Nazi program, the Service sent young Nacistas out to clean up impoverished neighborhoods and help the community. Like the Catholic workers' circles, in this manner privileged Nacistas developed some ties with and understanding of the poor. At times the Service inverted the usual hierarchy. Lower-class Nacistas showed their wealthier "comrades"—a term they used purposefully—how to use tools and often directed the work details. Nacistas also addressed each other on the same level, using the formal *usted.*[73]

Nacistas recommended that the state adopt an obligatory year of service for all eighteen-year-olds except those who joined the military. It would also include other volunteers, those who would benefit from the program, and the unemployed, all of whom might receive a small wage. Aside from promoting social solidarity, the service would train people in work habits and build needed housing and infrastructure. Workers fulfilling their year of service would help construct their own abodes and pay part of the value; *campesinos* receiving government land would help clear it. Unmarried women would also take part, but without leaving their homes for extended periods. Instead, they would work in nearby hospitals, schools, and impoverished households.[74]

The Nacistas' folkloric parties, or *machitunes*, celebrated social solidarity, inverted hierarchy, and utilized national customs. At these outdoor events, the local *jefes* handed over the proceedings to a *cacique* who officiated over a traditional meal, a songfest, the national dance (*la cueca*), and jokes at the leaders' expense. One of the movement's favorite *caciques*, however, was Otto Krahn, *jefe* of the social action department. Insofar as it went, the humorous inversion of hierarchy alleviated tension and strengthened authority within the movement.[75]

More radical than *machitunes* was Naci extremism of the word and deed. Wild, exaggerated claims and threats abounded in *Trabajo* and González's speeches. This intemperate rhetoric often resulted in the government shutting down the Naci paper and jailing or suing its editors. Nacistas thought that the existence of "extremist hordes" and an antinational regime justified their words and actions. Bloodshed would not only purify Chile of leftism but regenerate the perpetrators. Violence also channeled the potential radicalism of the lower, the frustrations of the middle, and the fears of the upper classes. It represented a means of rejecting bourgeois behavior without spurning the social order.[76]

Pageantry was another integral part of the strategy to appeal to a large following and supplant the left. The Nacista concentration in Concepción in December 1934 was illustrative. A curious public watched 2,000 uniformed, torch-bearing Nacistas march through the streets, claiming this space for their militarized and hierarchical concept of order and community. "The spectacle is magnificent and applause is not scarce," commented a reporter. The next day González and other speakers addressed 3,000 Nacis and 4,000 spectators in the stadium, their affirmation of mystical faith and authoritarianism striking a chord in their listeners. The event was much more beautiful than the "stage setting of political parties," wrote the same observer.[77] Nacistas hosted other impressive ceremonies, such as the swearing in of new members. These choreographed rituals, as well as the insignias and uniforms, gave onlookers and participants alike a sense of belonging to a larger, quasi-religious cause, one whose emotional and dramatic qualities overrode what Nacistas saw as the cool, theoretical nature of leftist appeal.[78]

Emotion and violence helped define the virility that was part of the Nacista alternative to the left. The Naci writer José Sánchez praised those who "have the manliness to go to the streets, forming the battalions of the warriors of national liberation." The movement, according to *Trabajo*, was preparing the way for the rule of "the strongest and best gifted," who contrasted with the "flabby, pampered, capricious" bourgeois male; Nacistas would rid society of this "subhuman." Their ideal man embodied strength and their concept of individual freedom, which meant embracing spiritual values and self-improvement. Nacistas deemed their "male" and hence true sense of liberty "immensely superior to feminine liberty, sentimental and susceptible to flattery and corruption, daughter of our liberal regime."[79] As for Nicolás Palacios, feminine meant weak and despicable whereas masculine meant strong and admirable.

Ironically, this male revolutionary was supposed to accept the bourgeois "patriarchal virtues of old Chile." Obliged to love their parents and siblings, young Nacistas were to honor the family hierarchy. Nor were they to swear, smoke, or drink. Men should choose between responsible fatherhood within marriage and "the sublime love of pure and intact virginity."[80]

Carlos Keller's thinly disguised treatment of the MNS in his novel *La locura de Juan Bernales*, however, portrayed a different facet of manliness. He used composite features of González and himself to construct *el jefe* Bernales. Ascetic and principled in other respects, like the puritanical González, Bernales nonetheless smoked and drank in private. Keller approvingly described Bernales's means of beginning a relationship with a lower-class woman, Inés: he simply raped her. From that moment the weak, soft, and yielding woman was his. Perhaps the author lifted this episode from his own life, as he had a mistress and *el jefe* did not. Although Keller wrote that a real revolutionary must bury his bourgeois prejudices, Bernales, at Inés's urging, did not marry her because of her humble origins. Or perhaps he did not marry her because he had given up bourgeois customs. Either way, Bernales's conquest of Inés reflected a more revolutionary sense of masculinity. As was the case for other fascisms, the emphasis on "orderly" families uneasily coexisted with a less conventional focus on youthful virility, symbolizing a desire to both tear down and maintain bourgeois society.[81]

Anti-imperialism was another ingredient of Nacismo's alternative to the left. Nacistas described fascism as a reaction to the liberals' subordination of the world to international capitalism. The creditor nations reduced the borrower nations' ability to pay their obligations by limiting the entry of their exports. Accordingly, the movement targeted the debt policy. Ibáñez suspended payment on the foreign debt in 1931 and Gustavo Ross resumed it in 1935. The government financed these remittances by taxes on foreign mining concerns and general sales and by contributing its share of nitrate earnings. Nacistas—along with Radicals and leftists—complained of the tax burden on the poor and the fact that the administration was sending these revenues overseas rather than using them to improve the economy. With González observing that "we should not pay, because we are hungry," in 1937 Naci deputies presented a bill suspending the debt payment. The MNS urged Chile to forge a Latin American bloc, aided by Italy and Germany, that would trade for mutual advantage, fight for independence against the "Yankee economic yoke," and refuse to pay the debt service. It praised nationalistic movements such as those of Augusto César Sandino of Nicaragua, the ruling Partido Nacional Revolucionario of Mexico, and the Alianza Popular Revolucionaria Americana of Peru.[82]

Some critics charged that the MNS's and particularly *el jefe*'s nationalism was superficial. In 1930 the Ibáñez government had placed González on the commission charged with formulating a new contract with the U.S.-owned Compañía Chilena de Electricidad, and the young lawyer had written most of it. When observers condemned the proposal as a sellout to foreign capital, González had defended it and guaranteed its acceptance. In 1933 *La Nación* denounced the contract for awarding the company the right to set exorbitant rates and a ninety-year concession, excessively long even by

Latin American standards. The Naci leader replied, somewhat disingenuously, that these rates were not in the contract and that the government, which the newspaper backed, had recently approved a rate hike. Ironically, in 1937 González lashed out against the administration for having allowed the company to export foreign exchange four years before—something his contract must have permitted.[83]

Still, Nacistas' slurs against Ross and the administration's economic policies strengthened their nationalist and popular credentials. So, too, did their economic program, which included such proposals as raising the tax on copper exports.[84]

Nacista antisemitism also fit within this strategy of co-opting anticapitalist and anti-imperialist sentiments. Although prejudice against Jews had appeared in Catholic writings and speeches, it had not figured prominently in Chilean rightist ideology and practice since Palacios. The fact that antisemitism was in vogue among European fascists partly explained its resurgence in Chile. The severity of the Depression also may have awakened a desire to find scapegoats. The most important reason, however, was that the economic content of antisemitism enabled the MNS to appear radical—an aim foreign to earlier rightist groups.

Change within the Jewish population was another motive. Small groups of Sephardics and Eastern Europeans trickled into Chile in the 1920s, when most Jews were involved in peddling, retail commerce, and the needle trades, although a second generation was entering the university. Estimates of the Jewish population in 1930 ranged from 3,697 to 6,000. After 1933, increasing numbers from Germany and other Central European countries fled to Chile, where some manufactured textiles and other consumer goods. Three Jews won seats as deputies in the 1937 elections, while others founded institutions and protested events in Germany. By 1941 there were as many as 20,000 Jews, 18,000 of them residing in Santiago. Although the figures were small, representing only about 0.4 percent of the total population and 2.6 percent of that of the capital, the Jewish community was clearly growing in size and prominence.[85]

Chileans outside the far right commonly tied Jews to money.[86] Yet anti-Jewish leftists inserted these statements within larger critiques of capitalism. In contrast, for Nacistas as for Brazilian Catholic nationalists, antisemitism substituted for such a critique. Nacis reserved their ire for finance and international capital, rather than the entire economic structure at home and abroad, and for Jewish entrepreneurs and bankers rather than all capitalists. While it is true that they criticized some non-Jewish businessmen, they found fault with their greediness and not their control. The MNS thought it possible to separate materialism from private ownership and to do away with the first (which, significantly, they identified with Judaism) while retaining the second. Moreover, they also censured Jews for reasons other than their supposed economic prowess.

A curious dichotomy on antisemitism reigned within the movement until mid-1937. The Nacista press was the main outlet for its anti-Jewish sentiments. Nacistas also shouted anti-Jewish slogans in their assemblies and as they sold *Trabajo*. Yet MNS platforms, books and pamphlets authored by leaders, and the journal *Acción Chilena* rarely displayed these views.[87] Nacis evidently decided that antisemitism might appeal to a popular audience, but not necessarily to the better educated, wealthier readers of their more academic expositions. While it fit into their broader ideology, it was expendable.

Nacistas voiced antisemitic sentiments early on, but such expressions were cursory. In 1933 the Nacista nucleus of Temuco explained that because the Jews in Chile did not monopolize more than their share of economic activities—unlike Jews in Germany—Nacismo need not concern itself with them. *Trabajo* confined itself to brief statements usually related to economics. When the newspaper began to focus on the economy and Ross's policies by October 1934, however, it increased its discussion of Jews.[88]

Nacista antisemitism reached a high point between 1935 and mid-1937, precisely when the movement conducted its bloodiest forays against the left and simultaneously set itself up as a radical alternative to it. Furthermore, as *Trabajo* noted, Jews were increasingly entering the country, its commerce, and its professions; thus, they were not totally imaginary creatures for Nacistas. *El Rayo*, the Naci voice of Valdivia, ran a series entitled "Chronicle of International Judaism" describing the possible ramifications of such incursions in 1935. It described a Jewish state-within-a-state that used money, liberalism, communism, and other tools to achieve world power.[89]

Not surprisingly, *El Rayo* praised Germany for treating the Jews, the worst enemies of humanity, as they deserved. Naci author Juan Gamboa, however, claimed Germans were not persecuting Jews but simply were liberating themselves from "outside" interference, permitting both to develop their cultures separately and autonomously. Gamboa seemed to accept Nazi racial criteria, as did Javier Cox, who wrote that for Germans, the Jewish problem was one of blood. Cox, however, thought such views did not apply to Chile, for Catholicism did not permit racial discrimination.[90]

Keller rejected German racism while retaining antisemitism. In his view, Nazi racial laws were simply a reaction to the rapid and overwhelming Jewish "penetration" of professional and cultural life. Although racism had restored German pride, Keller criticized it. The Nazi racial theorist Alfred Rosenberg insisted that race determined spirit, a view as materialistic as Marx's claim for the conditions of production. That the spiritual determined the material would be more in keeping with fascism. Moreover, racial classifications were arbitrary, responding to a felt need rather than scientific precision. The Nazi exaltation of racial purity was misplaced, for racial mixing was healthier than endogamy, which led to degeneration. Thus German racial ideology was faulty. Keller accepted the restrictions on Jews, which "indisputably corresponded to a necessity," but such restrictions did not require a racial grounding. Using Spengler's ideas, Keller concluded that the Jews had exhausted their cultural creativity and that materialism exhibited the "Jewish mentality." This spiritual type of reasoning would serve as a better basis for handling the Jewish question.[91]

Feigning moderation, González insisted that Chile lacked a Jewish problem. He applauded the Jewish immigrants who had applied initiative and creativity to their endeavors. Nacistas would oppose them only if they refused to submit to national needs; they would also oppose "race imperialism" imposed by Jews or any other group. *El jefe* seemed to regard these as genuine possibilities. Perhaps thinking of his own background—his paternal great-grandfather was Jewish—he noted that there were many families with Jewish blood and they formed part of the nationality. In short, Nacistas would never persecute other faiths or carry out the kind of antisemitic policies necessary in Germany. As the last statement indicated, antisemitism lay beneath González's seeming benevolence. One must stress the word *seeming*. The Naci leader himself referred to deals with supposed Jewish banks as examples of "Judaic imperialism," and all Naci publications were subject to his ultimate approval.[92]

Nacistas paid keen attention to government discussions of Jewish immigration in June 1936. Deputy Vicuña Fuentes advocated permitting more Jews into the country, but Minister of Foreign Relations Miguel Cruchaga refused, insisting that they would displace local merchants rather than enter the more vital areas of agriculture and mining. Applauding Cruchaga, the Nacista press observed that Jews had never used their financial skills to serve humanity. Instead, they worked to enrich themselves, spread communism, and in other ways assert control over the world. Only Communists wanted Jewish parasites in Chile.[93]

Trabajo carried these conspiratorial arguments to the extreme. Responding to a "directive" of conquest, the Jewish world was moving quietly and indirectly to dominate the Christian world. Even when Jews intermarried with Catholics, they did so to advance their cause by hiding their identity and even feigning antisemitism, before revealing themselves at the right moment. *Trabajo* despised the "spirit of usury" that Jews expressed in their economic and political dealings. Despite these characteristics, the few who had inhabited Chile until recently had posed no danger. Mass arrivals of Jews, however, would intensify the anti-Christian struggle and constitute a "grave threat."[94]

As evidence of this threat, *Trabajo* cited the abuses of Ross, the Guggenheim mining interests, certain black marketers and leftists, and Agustín Edwards, the publisher of *El Mercurio*. Most of the figures it named were not Jewish, and *El Mercurio* frequently criticized Jewish immigration. Still, the Naci daily perceived the existence of a hostile Jewish front behind its enemies' activities.[95]

This alleged conspiracy dwarfed the power of any institution or country. Jews not only controlled banking, commerce, and the media. They also infiltrated government, starved people, and fomented discontent, strikes, and rebelliousness. Jews were synonymous or allied with communism, liberalism, and Freemasonry; together they were the great enemies of morality, the family, the fatherland, and spiritualism, for Jews had wanted Jesus to establish an earthly rather than a heavenly realm. Even when offered by pious young Conservatives, criticisms of Nacismo embodied the "international Jew."[96]

This radical antisemitism did not manifest itself in violence. The only clash before 1941 was accidental. In December 1935, TNA members battered their way into the pool of the Estadio Militar and exchanged blows with the swimmers, including a Jew, until Carabineros threw the Nacistas out. *Trabajo* blamed the Jew for the episode and threatened reprisal, but I found no record of one.[97]

Despite its radical nature, the Nacistas' antisemitism was not violent or biological like the Nazi type. Nor did their broader views on race coincide with those of their German peers. Drawing from rightist precursors, they praised the Chilean mestizo "race" and its Spanish and Araucanian progenitors and spoke of improving it. While González and other Nacistas affirmed such social Darwinist notions as natural selection and racial inequality, Keller and *Trabajo* criticized racism as a materialist doctrine. The principal MNS author on such matters, José Sánchez, rejected racial distinctions as ideologically divisive. Unlike Germany, where Sánchez blindly insisted there were no victorious or submissive races, Chile, a conquered nation, contained Creole masters and Indian and mestizo serfs. The paternalist veneer of these relationships did not hide their power dimension, and capitalism had only widened the gaps between these groups. Downtrodden people of color had joined the left to fight the "reactionary" Creoles. Thus the left had "a racial and atavistic base: the hatred of the Indian for the conqueror." Instead of organizing politics along racial lines, the MNS wanted to substitute an aristocracy of merit for one grounded in genealogy. In this regard, Sánchez concluded, it resembled Italian Fascism more closely than German Nazism. Photographs of the MNS reveal it included men of indigenous descent.[98]

Women and Nacismo

Women posed more of a dilemma for Nacismo than did racial issues. Initially the movement limited itself to men, for, as González put it, its vision of life was essentially "virile and manly." Drawing upon Catholic and bourgeois notions, Nacistas emphasized the importance of a well-organized home for their movement and the nation. In it men and women, each characterized by certain intrinsic traits, remained within their respective sphere of duties. Intrepid, muscular, and warlike, the man supported his family, while her physique and delicate, sedentary nature oriented the woman toward motherhood and homemaking. She was the base of the family and hence of the social structure. Educating children and forming their souls was her task, one which the man could not perform. Political participation would remove the woman from the home and therefore did not suit her; such activities fell within the male domain, although the MNS frowned on them for either sex. However, Isabel Carrera de Reid, who wrote for the Nacista press, insisted that the woman, no longer a "useless doll," deserved the municipal vote, since the city was the prolongation of the home and their problems were interrelated. Thus the husband and wife complemented each other and worked together, raising offspring for the fatherland. This form of family embodied the values of hierarchy, order, and harmony that, according to the MNS, had inspired traditional Chile and served as a model for the ideal Naci society.[99]

Nacistas feared that men and women were invading each other's natural territory or otherwise failing to play their proper roles, thus endangering the species. In the name of liberty, men availed themselves of prostitutes, thereby corrupting both sexes. Modern women, especially of the upper classes, devoted themselves to luxury, drinking, and shameless sensuality rather than the home. The liberal economic system had also impoverished the people and forced women into the workforce, lowering male salaries and employment as well as the birthrate. Frustrated male breadwinners had turned to alcohol and gambling. Yet Marxism masculinized women even more than liberalism. In the Soviet Union women took on male jobs and avoided maternity through birth control, while in Chile an army of "red women" incited women to leave the home to falsely lift their status, compete with men, and, like Eve, obey the "serpent." The "red women" probably meant the Movimiento Pro Emancipación de Mujeres de Chile, which from 1935 on fought for the political, legal, and economic equality of women, birth control, and, in general, a leftist program.[100] Nacistas believed that these forces threatened to wipe out the distinctions between the sexes, preventing men from becoming husbands and fathers and preventing women from becoming wives and mothers.

The MNS's goal was "the liberation of the woman." This did not entail granting her more "rights," which it saw as illusory. Rather, it meant going back to nature—to the masculinization of the man and the "feminization of the woman, returning her to the home and her basic function: maternity." To implement this objective, which recalled Manuel Carlés's views, the MNS wanted to convince men to fulfill their obligations and treat women respectfully. It also hoped to educate women to dedicate themselves to marriage and children. Through the Work Service, upper-class girls would train the less fortunate to remain in the home and become better wives and mothers; at the same time they would give up frivolous pleasures and assume social responsibilities. If extreme poverty or lack of male relatives—the only justifiable reasons—forced them into the paid labor force, women should dress modestly and avoid men as much as possible. Eventually the MNS would end exploitation, making it unnecessary for women to hold jobs. It would also promote housing construction, legalize illicit unions, and otherwise enable women to bear more and healthier children within matrimony. Nacistas would permit women in the future society to acquire knowledge, teach others, and administer to the needy, but they justified these roles in terms of motherhood and saintliness.[101] Keeping the sexes separate and distinct would safeguard the social order.

While pretending not to do so, Nacistas shifted their views on women. In December 1935, González announced that to reflect the makeup of the nation and respond to their pleas, the MNS would admit women. A spiritual and emotional movement should include them, especially since their membership had nothing to do with politics. They would not deliberate in assemblies or further their ambitions; of course, Nacismo also prevented men from doing so. Nacista social action required the female touch, for helping the poor was an "intuitive art," not a science, in which the Naci woman could engage without losing her feminine attributes. Unlike feminists, she would not compete with her male comrade, but would work alongside him as a "sister, wife, and mother." First she would "feminize herself," cultivating her delicacy, discretion, patience, and feelings, and then help poorer women perfect their femininity.[102]

The timing of women's entry contradicted their supposed nonpolitical role. That women had attained the municipal vote in 1934 was not lost on the Nacistas, nor was the birth of Acción Nacional de Mujeres that year. Led by Adela Edwards de Salas and other upper-class Social Catholics, this group sought to mobilize conservative women. Its activities and the fact that the new female electorate favored moderate right-wing parties in the election of April 1935 suggested a potential base of support for the MNS. Nacis amended their statements to say that women should not engage in regular politics, but it was their duty to participate in the MNS brand, which was exclusively concerned with the common welfare. Perhaps prompted by the election of twenty-five women to municipal office, *Trabajo* now insisted that Nacistas engaged in "feminist politics." Their feminism, however, did not involve changing traditions imposed by nature or converting women into men, but rather restoring the female "throne" overturned by male selfishness and female childishness and laziness.[103] Justifying female participation strained Naci ideology.

Unwilling to give up the movement's masculine orientation completely, Nacistas denied women their voice and identity. *Trabajo* rarely supplied the names of female members, and such pseudonyms as Sureña, Chiribiri, and Recluta appeared under articles purportedly written by women. Among the few exceptions were the writer Isabel Carrera de Reid and Berta Loeser, who directed women's charity work.

That the MNS ultimately attracted few women is not surprising. Before González announced their eligibility for membership, young women formed the first "feminine brigade" in Valparaíso in November 1935, and the first swearing-in ceremony took place a month later. Feminine brigades also arose in Puerto Montt, Valdivia, Concepción, Temuco, and eight districts of Santiago, but Nacista women numbered only in the hundreds.[104]

Resembling women of the Liga Patriótica Argentina (LPA), female members appeared to be of higher social rank than the movement as a whole. As wives, mothers, and sisters of Nacistas and Naci martyrs, some had answered entreaties to support their male relatives. Evidently they agreed with the organization's goal of conserving the bourgeois family and the social structure. Their duties in the movement were in keeping with the tasks that upper-class women had carried out for the church. Nevertheless, the MNS did not appeal to women's Catholic sentiments; indeed, it had to overcome fears that it was anti-Catholic. To do so, it often referred to women's spiritual mission in the movement.[105]

Like the LPA, Nacistas duplicated the gendered division of labor in society. Men formulated the ideology, battled their enemies, served in Congress, and headed their families. *El jefe* even appointed a man as provincial director of the Santiago feminine brigade. Although men also helped the poor through the Work Service and other means, women were primarily responsible for welfare projects, mostly oriented toward other Nacis. They provided food, medicine, and clothing for hospital patients and needy Nacista families, as well as candy, toys, and parties for children of poor MNS members. The feminine brigade of Santiago operated an employment agency for Nacista laborers and employers that in its first year placed 116 men and women, including four maids and three laundresses. Women and men of the movement donated blood for emergency hospital cases. Nacista medical students and women staffed a free clinic in Santiago, established by an upper-class Nacista, and the female brigade of Santiago also founded a dental clinic. By preparing meals and organizing services for male comrades, Naci women served as their helpmates. They held their own *machitunes*, meetings, and funerals. To pay for their activities, they requested donations and organized social functions, sales, and raffles.[106]

The "feminine page" that *Trabajo* inaugurated in April 1936, containing articles on childcare, domestic tasks, and gender ideology, along with ads for cosmetics and other "female" products, reminded female Nacistas of their place. Yet they also stepped outside that place. Wearing uniforms may have seemed mannish, and the gray-shirted women participated in predominantly male events, such as patriotic celebrations and concentrations. Breaking with custom, several hundred women traveled from their homes to march in a parade of 7,000 Nacistas in Concepción in December 1936. In November 1936, they joined the funeral procession of Raúl Lefevre Molina, an eighteen-year-old Naci electrical worker slain by leftists. Forestalling possible criticism, an anonymous female Nacista explained that the sacrifice of a comrade had wounded their delicate hearts, compelling them to share the pain of Lefevre's parents. The writer insisted that onlookers exclaimed

over their uniforms, which the women wore with elegance and "natural co-
quetry." She also praised them for an instinctive knowledge of how to step
in time. Combining martial and customary female imagery, *Trabajo* referred to female members as "the falanges of future mothers of the Nacista
State" and "the soldiers" or "legions" of the Nacista "spiritual crusade."[107]
Such attempts to reconcile femininity with participation in a militarized
movement, however, were fraught with tension.

The Moderate Right Turns Against the MNS

The men of the militarized movement continued to engage the left in street
battles. Perhaps the most notorious encounter took place on August 22,
1936. That evening witnessed a noisy debate between young Nacistas and
members of the Socialist Youth, including Héctor Barreto, a nineteen-year-
old writer, at the Café Volga, a leftist hangout. The discussion degenerated,
and Barreto and the Socialists threw the Nacistas out of the café. They returned with TNA reinforcements, and one Naci challenged Barreto to a
fight in the street. The match had barely begun when a Naci bullet killed the
young Socialist. The authorities later arrested a few Socialists and eight
Nacistas, with the Socialists claiming to have forced the police's hand by
bringing in two of the MNS perpetrators.[108]

The murder outraged many and raised questions about the government's responsibility. What helped make it a cause célèbre was the victim's
stature as a poet and young worker who was valiantly seeking a higher education while supporting his family. Even Conservatives praised Barreto and
denounced the killing. Whether the government could prevent such acts
was the issue—and the Ministry of the Interior declared it could not.
Alessandri insisted that the earlier ruling, which wrongfully permitted
Nacistas to wear uniforms, limited what he could do. Scornfully rejecting
such claims, Senators Guillermo Azócar of the Socialist Party and Manuel
Hidalgo of the Communist Left wondered how the security forces managed
to keep workers from meeting peacefully yet somehow could not control a
provocative armed group.[109]

Nacista leaders chillingly defended their movement. In a radio speech,
González assumed responsibility for Barreto's death, attributing the bullet
that hit the youth and all others fired by Nacistas to his "personal inspiration." His movement had used violence and would continue to do so when
"collective conservation" dictated. Such violence was an "organic manifestation of life"; to condemn it was a sign of "degeneration," an indication

that the society was too weak to defend itself. After all, life was a constant struggle against death, which came when an organism ceased to resist it. Chile had almost reached that point, thanks to the historic political parties that had drowned it in corruption and partisanship. Marxists had no reason to attack the right, which would never fight in the streets or attract the masses; hence it targeted Nacismo, the only virile response to the crisis. Keller agreed with González that self-defense had mandated taking a life, and many more deaths might follow. "But who has said that there is no right to kill?"[110]

The investigations unit jailed González for his alarming speech, and Barreto's mother sued him for inciting bloodshed. The courts dismissed both cases, however, and freed *el jefe* and the Nacistas originally detained for Barreto's murder. Even the official *La Nación* complained of the judiciary's inaction. Minister of the Interior Cabrera ordered intendants and governors to direct the police to search uniformed party militants for weapons.[111] These measures did not stop the violence.

The administration's tolerance finally ran out. On November 15, 1936, the train that González, Keller, and other Nacistas were taking stopped in Rancagua. A shouting match between Nacistas and Popular Front members on the platform led to gunfire, wounding bystanders and gravely injuring a child. Carabineros detained some Nacistas in Rancagua and arrested those on the train when it reached Santiago. Law enforcement officials returned González, Keller, and eighty-five other detained Nacistas to Rancagua for judicial proceedings and rifled *Trabajo* offices and Nacista headquarters for evidence. This energetic government response contrasted markedly with earlier episodes.[112]

Risking official displeasure, Nacistas pointed their fingers at the government. The Naci press and fliers claimed that policemen had fired on the train and into the crowd, which explained why there were MNS sympathizers among the wounded. The government swiftly punished Nacistas for assigning it the blame. Declaring that *Trabajo* had broken the law by spreading false information designed to undermine public order, authorities confiscated the newspaper for eight days, arrested the vendors, and intercepted the fliers. On the day of the illegal story, the administration sent a new internal security bill to Congress, worded in such a way as to authorize the repression of the left as well as Nacismo. The length of the bill, and the speed with which it was introduced, awakened speculation that the government had prepared it long before.[113]

Finally moderate rightists joined the anti-MNS chorus. "One need not confuse virility with barbarism," intoned the hitherto sympathetic *El Diario Ilustrado*, asking the government to repress this "excessively fanatic" movement. Accordingly, Democratic senator Pradenas and his Conservative colleague, Rafael Gumucio, proposed asking the government to repress Nacismo. Liberal Guillermo Portales, however, added all violent political groups to the resolution; by not naming them, he made it possible for the Popular Front senators to accept it. This resolution and a similar measure in the Chamber passed. So, too, did the internal security law, over the Popular Front's opposition.[114]

Some moderate rightists, however, still spoke up for the MNS. Three prominent Conservatives—Senator Carlos Aldunate, Social Catholic Alejandro Valdés Riesco, and law professor Alfredo del Valle—pointed out that most of the wounded were MNS sympathizers; moreover, the configuration of their injuries made it unlikely that the shots had come from the train. While they did not subscribe to Naci ideology, the three Conservatives appreciated its support of family, religion, and fatherland in this dissolvent climate. An old friend of the movement, Liberal deputy Dussaillant, agreed with their analysis of the incident, declaring that only the "well-inspired" MNS, "so unjustly persecuted," could liberate the country from the left.[115]

El Diario Ilustrado reproached Aldunate, Valdés, and del Valle for standing up for what it now called the harshest critics of Conservatives. They dared to defend a socialist, totalitarian movement that included antireligious people. The newspaper considered them disloyal to the party, to its principles of Catholicism and antisocialism, and to a government that included two Conservative ministers.[116]

The court eventually accepted some of the points made by the Nacistas and the three Conservatives. In March 1937, a judge ruled that shots fired from the train only could have caused two of the five injuries. Of the ninety-seven Nacistas originally jailed, the judge cleared ninety-one of all charges, fined five for carrying weapons without a permit, and sentenced one to forty days in prison for slightly wounding a bystander.[117] The uproar over Rancagua had ended in a fizzle. Yet the episode finally pushed the administration against the MNS.

The same events also showed that other rightist sectors had shifted away from the Nacistas. As *El Diario Ilustrado* suggested, one sore point was religion. Like the Chilean Ligas and the Milicia, the movement, at least initially, did not embrace Catholicism, enabling it to recruit German-Chilean Protestants and nonreligious persons. In fact, the MNS seemed to profess an alternative religion with its own mystical beliefs, rituals, asceticism, and sense of purity and self-sacrifice. Nacistas asserted that they alone possessed the truth and could "save" the country. Graced with the "eternal baptism" of traditional doctrine, Nacistas believed in Chile above worldly things. González solemnly added each slain Nacista to the pantheon of the "martyrs of the cause," which resembled that of Christian martyrs. According to Javier Cox, the martyrs' "purifying blood" promoted the "redemption" of Chile: "From this blood of heroes will come the reign of Social Justice." *El jefe* predicted that the three Nacistas slain in Valparaíso would experience "resurrection" in thousands of new recruits. The "dead and the living" would bring about the "miracle of national resurgence."[118]

The clearest expression of this alternative religion was the "Nacista prayer." Approaching the "altar" of the *Patria* with the "most intense faith," Nacistas offered Chile their enthusiasm, worldly goods, and physical bodies, expecting nothing in return. Their faith would help "light in the hearts" of citizens "the sacred flame of patriotism." Nacistas would take up arms when necessary to fulfill their "crusade," but the bloodshed, which would ensure that the fatherland remained "immaculate and whole," would not sully the "immaculate purity" of the flag. To die on behalf of one's country was no sacrifice; it was an honor Nacis would value "beyond the tomb!"[119]

Nacistas constantly defended themselves against the suspicions that their eschatology and cult of the state awakened in Catholics. *Trabajo* insisted that Nacistas did not intend to create a new religion as fascists had in Germany and Italy. The MNS respected the "brake on the passions" and other Catholic contributions to national development. The church and the movement both opposed communism, class conflict, and the exploitation of the poor. Apart from these points of agreement, it made no sense for Nacistas to target the church; they were not savages, and they sought to avoid divisive struggle.[120]

Conservative deputy Boizard criticized fascist political expediency in religious matters. In response, González admitted that fascism elevated politics over religion. Approximating Maurras's position, which was condemned by the church, *el jefe* and Diego Lira Vergara insisted that a Nacista state would recognize and support religion as the strongest defense against disorder. But González and Lira claimed that Nacistas, unlike Conservatives, would not judge which religion was correct. *El jefe* slyly added that since Catholics believed their faith was the true one, they had no reason to fear it would decline under fascist rule. In fact, in 1937 he denounced Hitler's policies toward Protestants and Catholics.[121]

Nacistas disagreed with clerical involvement in politics and what they saw as Conservative advocacy of state subservience to the church. They pointed out that the Vatican did not want the church identified with any political party. Lira noted that like Jesus, Nacistas left heaven to God and statesmanship to Caesar. Nacista Rodrigo de Baena insisted that those who tied church to state and religion to fatherland imitated the Jews, who demanded of Christ a worldly rather than a spiritual kingdom.[122]

Nacistas might not have defined themselves as Catholic, but they had no trouble appropriating the church's social doctrine. They praised the ideas of Leo XIII, claimed to uphold a Christian sense of property ownership, and mourned the death of a Social Catholic leader, Father Fernando Vives. In fact, Lira criticized the Chilean church for not doing enough to promote Social Catholicism. If rich Catholics could ally with atheists to protect their interests, declared one Nacista, Christian workers could join with nonbelievers in the MNS to advance theirs. A Nacista flier entitled *¡Católicos!* claimed that through its support of family, morality, and religious education the MNS was closer to the church than any Catholic party—a dig at the Conservatives. Only Nacismo could implant a social Christian order.[123]

To capitalize on the passions aroused by the Spanish Civil War and to compete with the Conservative Youth, described below, in mid-1936 Nacistas began to identify themselves more closely with Christianity and Catholicism. A Nacista pamphlet of that year described the abnegation and spirituality of the movement as Christian-inspired. Contradicting other MNS pronouncements, it insisted that Nacistas' primary goal was the "Reign of God through Christ." Christianity is part of our doctrine, said *Trabajo*, and we submit to it. González announced that Nacismo defended Christian civilization against liberalism and Marxism and represented its political fulfillment. He characterized himself as Catholic, adding that the movement's concept of life dictated that the MNS chief had to be Christian. Yet when asked what he believed in besides himself, González omitted God from his answer of destiny and the Chilean people.[124]

Nacistas derided Conservatives for "defending" religion by mixing it with politics and deviating from papal encyclicals. Indeed, few Conservatives welcomed Pope Pius XI's encyclical *Quadragesimo Anno* of 1931, a successor to Leo XIII's document on capital-labor relations. Nacistas pointed to the fact that Conservatives who favored reforms had to fight their leaders to get them accepted. Moreover, Conservatives flouted Cardinal Eugenio Pacelli's famous pronouncement on the church and politics. Speaking for the Vatican, Pacelli declared that the clergy should not identify with any party, nor could any party claim to represent the church and all Catholics. Catholics could participate in any party that did not oppose religion and the church. Conservatives and even the local church tried to ignore this statement, or to claim that Chilean Catholics could belong to this party alone, for only it gave adequate guarantees to the faith. Nacistas underlined the obvious contradictions between such attitudes and Pacelli's words. With justification they claimed that by inserting the church into partisan politics, Conservatives had sullied its image and alienated the people from it. In contrast, Nacismo would help restore the church's prestige by removing it from the political arena.[125]

Yet Nacistas faced a rival in a new generation of young socially minded Catholics. In the late 1920s Bernardo Leighton, Eduardo Frei, Jaime Eyzaguirre, and other students who had participated in Social Catholic study circles transformed ANEC, the Catholic student organization, into a dynamic intellectual forum. Some joined a succession of tiny Catholic groups and parties advocating social reform, thus distinguishing themselves from other moderate rightists. Repelled by the Conservatives' *politiquería* and reactionary stance, core ANEC members nevertheless decided that renovating this party from within offered the best possibility of legislating papal social doctrine. Still, the resulting Centro de Estudiantes Conservadores, founded in 1933, maintained some independence from the larger party.[126]

The Centro indicated its authoritarianism by calling its newspaper *Lircay* (1934–40), in honor of the battle of 1829 that thrust Portales into leadership. Renamed the Movimiento Nacional de la Juventud Conservadora in 1935, the organization asserted its Christianity, nationalism, and solidarity with Spanish America and its desire to strengthen the Chilean economy and defend it from imperialist encroachment. Respecting human integrity, its ideal state was neither a liberal democracy nor a socialist or fascist dictatorship. The Juventud envisioned a corporatist system based on freely organized syndicates, a type of society epitomizing "liberty within order." Pointing out the social function of property, it wished to extend property ownership to as many as possible. It also advocated a family salary and acknowledgment of the human factor in labor. The program's emphasis on Christian education, the rejection of divorce, and the assertion of parental rather than state authority over children followed church strictures. It would organize its members in a hierarchical and disciplined fashion, inspiring them to serve the nation and God with a sense of abnegation.[127]

The young Conservatives' beliefs overlapped those of the MNS. The main areas of disagreement related to their respect for autonomy vis-à-vis the state and, perhaps, the educational role of the church. Their allegiance to the institutional church also set them apart from the Nacistas' division of loyalty between a vague Christianity and their alternative faith. The distinction between the Juventud's authoritarian and a Nacista-style dictatorial state was unclear. The young Conservatives cited Dollfuss as a model, yet the Austrian chancellor had suspended elections and Parliament, censored the press, and ruled repressively. Dollfuss's government-controlled union, which had replaced mostly socialist ones, hardly epitomized the freely organized corporatist system built from the bottom up advocated by the Juventud. In the Juventud's vision, the church, family, and other intermediary institutions would safeguard some freedoms, but the MNS also promised to buttress them. It was difficult to imagine how the Juventud's ideal polity would be much more democratic in practice than the Nacistas'. The Juventud's charge that foreign doctrine had inspired only its rival lacked credibility.[128]

With greater justification, the Juventud Conservadora cited other differences. One was the Nacistas' exaggerated nationalism, which Frei described as a harmful individualism applied to the level of the nation. The Juventud also criticized the Nacistas' provocative rhetoric. Most important was the group's disgust with Nacista violence. It believed that the "club" would only push workers into counterviolence or a "tyrannical" Popular Front–type government like that of Spain.[129]

Nacistas blasted back at the young Conservatives. They saw their rivals as *jovencitos bien* whose approach to social justice was paternalistic at best. The MNS questioned the Juventud's commitment to Social Catholicism, noting that its parent party was the most "antisocial" and "retrograde" in Chile. To warm up its "cold concept, with the smell of the tomb" and counter Nacista inroads, the party had brought in the young Catholics. Sometimes Nacistas conceded their good intentions, but they saw them as Conservative tools nonetheless. According to the MNS, the Juventud's belief in liberal democracy—which the latter denied—separated the two organizations, as did its devotion to a legality that permitted plutocratic abuse. When Leighton said that ideological differences should not lead to street fighting, *Trabajo* rejoined that "the political struggle is . . . nowhere but the street," adding that Leighton's indifference to communism explained his passivity.[130]

Still, both movements were spiritual, hierarchical, antileftist, and corporatist, and the affinity of ideas meant fierce competition for the same constituency. By 1936 the spirited debates between Conservative youths and Nacistas threatened to degenerate into violence. To defend itself and, perhaps, to attract the type of young men who joined Nacismo, the Juventud organized its own uniformed militarized unit, the Falange. Leighton claimed that the name came from Alexander the Great's Macedonian brigades, but its insignia of a red arrow piercing two lines symbolized the third way between capitalism and socialism and resembled the yoked arrows of the Spanish fascist group. The terms Juventud Conservadora and Falange became interchangeable, and in November 1936 the entire movement officially adopted the title Falange Nacional. Nacistas scornfully noted that the Movimiento Nacional de la Juventud Conservadora not only had imitated the Nacistas' name, ideas, and symbols; now it had copied the TNA. The uniform was meant to erase class differences, not to attract *niñas bien*. But then the Falangistas knew no workers, save waiters and servants. Despite their paramilitary formation, Falangistas lacked the bravery, conviction, and rebelliousness of those they mimicked, claimed Nacistas.[131]

The Naci appeal to young Catholics did not appear to alarm the church hierarchy, although it inevitably drew them away from Conservatism. Instead, *La Revista Católica* criticized young Conservatives for attacking Nacistas more than Communists. Nacismo and communism were the two extremes that threatened representative government, but if disorder occurred, it sided with Pius XI's preference for fascism over communism. According to the periodical, Communists promoted their ideas and hatred of fascism through the Falange. Regarding Juventud support of the social encyclicals as leftist, the hierarchy distrusted and feared the Falange more than the MNS.[132]

The rivalry between the Falange and MNS sparked a few incidents, none of which approached the ferocity of the clashes between Nacistas and leftists. In October 1936, members of the Juventud Nacional Socialista swaggered into Conservative headquarters, where one Naci youngster pulled out an old revolver—one that supposedly lacked a trigger—and frightened Conservatives into lifting their hands and turning over party pamphlets. Conservatives complained to the authorities, who arrested six of the culprits but freed them shortly thereafter. The MNS promised to return the pamphlets if Conservative Carlos Lira Infante gave back the 1,800,000 pesos it accused him of stealing from the Caja de la Habitación Popular. The Falange took revenge by attacking young Nacistas. Accusing young Conservatives of hurling tear gas bombs into an MNS gathering in La Serena in early November, Nacistas broke up a meeting of their rivals in Santiago. Then in February 1937, during a Falange march in Concepción, the local TNA leader knocked Bernardo Leighton to the ground. The Conservative

Party president spoke to the minister of the interior, and perhaps for this reason the government detained 150 Nacistas a few days later.[133]

The Falange had the last word. It won seven seats in the Chamber in 1937, compared with the Nacistas' three, and Leighton briefly served as minister of labor that year. The Falange received more favor from voters and the government than the Nacistas.

The Naci Shift to the Left

The Rancagua episode pushed the other rightist parties away from the MNS. It also forced Nacistas to redirect their aggressions from the left toward the now hostile Alessandri regime. Using the internal security law passed after the episode, the security forces cracked down on the movement. On May 21, 1937, they arrested six Nacistas for hurling tear gas bombs at the official parade opening the congressional session. This incident finally stirred the church into denouncing the MNS.[134]

The changed political realities dictated a reformulation of tactics. Government repression and moderate rightist distaste for their violence forced Nacistas to shift their sphere of activity from the streets to Parliament in 1937. This move, however, entailed new problems. By the mid-1930s the well-developed Chilean party system was a crowded field, especially on the right. The fact that Nacismo had entered the political arena late, as was characteristic of fascism, limited its ability to garner electoral support. Curtailing its extraparliamentary actions made it less unique and perhaps less likely to win votes. By 1937 most parties had joined the pro-Alessandri right or the Popular Front; to exercise any influence the electorally weak Nacistas would have to do the same. They seemed to choose their side by taking seats in the extreme right of the Chamber, against the Conservatives' wishes. Yet the MNS perceived the left's growing prowess. Recognizing that Alessandri was their common adversary and that the Popular Front had a good chance of winning the next presidential election against the hated Gustavo Ross, Nacistas confounded expectations and joined the opposition. González declared that while the MNS was neither left nor right, at least the left wanted justice for the people.[135] Surely this was the only example in the world of a fascist movement aligning itself with antifascist Popular Front forces.

Leftist deputies had qualms about welcoming their former enemy. Socialist Julio Barrenechea and Communist Marcos Chamudes recognized the Naci leader's opposition to Ross, whom Barrenechea judged as even more fascist than González, but they questioned the Naci leader's newfound com-

mitment to the masses. When his fellow Socialist deputies accused González
of ties to Germany and U.S. imperialism, Ricardo Latcham hit *el jefe*, who
in turn punched Socialist Emilio Zapata. For his part Zapata aimed a glass
vase at the Naci leader but missed. "Nacismo does not fool us, its popular
clothes and anti-imperialist bells conceal the preparations for its next
treachery toward the people," warned Socialist Efraín Ojeda.[136]

As Nacismo tilted toward the left, moderate rightists continued to distance themselves from their former ally. Boizard claimed that unlike the
MNS, Conservatives and their youth section stood for democracy and nonviolence. Even while attacking Nacismo, which he insisted was not a true
mass movement and expressed nothing, he betrayed sympathy for fascism,
for in the same breath he justified Fascism and Nazism for uniting and invigorating their countries. *El Mercurio* denounced the MNS for abandoning
its anticommunist rhetoric and working with its former enemy. It con-
tended that the personalistic Nacista chief's whims and resentments dictated all the policies for his party.[137] González's authoritarianism and capri-
ciousness had not bothered the newspaper before, when it fought the left.

González's followers regarded him as courageous and radical, but at
times *el jefe*'s behavior struck others as unbalanced. On one such occasion
in January 1938, he told the Chamber that constitutionalism was a sham,
citing Alessandri's internal security laws and arbitrary acts. In his opinion
the Chamber had debated these infractions endlessly to no effect, for it
lacked the moral authority to judge executive abuses. When the head of the
Chamber could not convince González to retract his words or stop speaking, the Nacista warned, "We will come to remove you with bayonets." Instead, the Carabineros dragged him out.[138]

González helped create even more commotion in the Chamber on May
21. The Popular Front unsuccessfully sought a meeting with Alessandri to
request guarantees in the forthcoming presidential election. Fearing the
Frentistas would disrupt his speech opening the congressional session, the
president packed the hall with policemen. As he approached the lectern, dynamite exploded outside near the entrance. Before the president could
speak, González Videla, as head of the Popular Front, asked permission to
read the petition for electoral guarantees. Rightist congressmen and hundreds of agents drowned him out, prompting Frentistas and Nacistas to
leave the hall. In this tumult, a fistfight broke out involving *el jefe*, rightists,
and agents that drew in the Popular Front, while Nacistas set off tear gas in
the hall. Several adversaries fell on the Nacista leader as he fired his revolver,
causing the bullet to hit the wall above the president. Many thought he had

aimed for Alessandri, but González claimed to have fired to scare off his attackers and halt the proceedings. Earlier he had told another Nacista that he would fire in the air to cause a disturbance. The Carabineros disarmed him and beat him severely, injuring his leg, and also beat and arrested several Frentistas and Nacistas. When González Videla attempted to prevent authorities from arresting *el jefe*, agents detained him as well, although both were freed. The court stripped the Naci of his parliamentary immunity and sentenced him to one and a half years in prison for his actions.[139]

The events of May 21 brought the MNS and Popular Front closer. Representatives of the two groups pointed to the massive presence of policemen and prior warnings as evidence that the government was responsible for the disturbance. Together they protested the officials' intrusion into Congress, violation of parliamentary immunity, and brutal treatment of congressmen.

González affirmed that the incident had united popular forces against the regime, overcoming the hatred that had once divided them. Political circumstances had changed, and Nacismo, like any "living organism," could not remain static. Thus the movement no longer identified with fascism, although, as *Trabajo* insisted, it still wished to install a "dictatorship of the people" in place of the existing "plutocratic dictatorship." The Nacista chief disconnected the MNS from German Nazism and antisemitism. Symbolizing this ideological shift, the Nacista deputies moved to the left side of the Chamber.[140]

The right scorned its former ally. Republican Action warned that political demagoguery had "contaminated" Nacismo. Boizard accused the MNS of abandoning its original ideals and betraying its martyrs. Some Nacistas left the movement, protesting González's denial of fascism, his alliance with the left, and his "insipid declarations . . . with respect to Judaism."[141]

Indeed, González had already softened the movement's antisemitism when he moved the MNS parliamentary delegation into the opposition. Nacistas were less anxious than before to distinguish themselves from and substitute for the left—and perhaps their leader realized that radical charges against Jews did not resonate among most Chileans. Thus, after March 1937, *Trabajo* drastically reduced its mention of Jews. This shift on the Jewish question further demonstrated Nacista opportunism.

MNS antisemitism, however, did not completely disappear. In January 1938, Ecuador considered expelling Jewish immigrants who had not entered farming or industry. The Chilean Chamber of Deputies resolved to ask the Ecuadoran government not to evict them, but the Nacista deputies voted against this measure on the pretext of not intervening in the internal policies of another country. González added that he did not want to exclude individuals from entering Chile simply for belonging to certain groups, unless their culture varied markedly from the local one or they would not adapt themselves—hinting at Jews. These pronouncements, however, drew upon the stereotypes of traditional antisemitism rather than the conspiratorial notions of the radical variety. Nor were they the most extreme views expressed during this and other debates on Jewish immigration.[142]

Distinctions between the MNS and the left remained. Nacistas continued to criticize their former foes, although in muted fashion. More important, *el jefe* could not bring himself to support a Popular Front candidate for president. Realizing that he could never win that office, whether as a leftist or a rightist, González put his movement behind Ibáñez in October 1937, but the general maintained his distance. After the Popular Front nominated conservative Radical Pedro Aguirre Cerda as its standard-bearer in April 1938, Ibáñez approved the formation of the vehicle for his candidacy, the Alianza Popular Libertadora, which included the MNS. Vaguely reformist, nationalist, opposed to the government and to communism, the Alianza offered a means of perpetuating the MNS and its mission.[143]

For its part, the right had already nominated Gustavo Ross at its convention in December 1937. Politically inept at best, and unfeeling at worst, Ross once said that "one had to treat the native in our country with the slavers' whip." Many of the wealthy agreed with him and admired his financial wizardry. Republican Action overcame its scruples and its concern for social justice and joined the Rossistas. The "whip" separated Ross's supporters from the Falange, which had submitted its own choices for president for the right's consideration. The Falange's presumption and its decision to allow its members freedom of action in the campaign infuriated Conservatives.[144]

Nevertheless, the division in the opposition seemed to promise a rightist victory. Ibáñistas and Frentistas also thought that Alessandri might use the powers of his office to interfere with the voting if it went against the regime's candidate. Acutely aware of these problems, the Nacista leader feared that if Ross won he would repress the MNS; that result was possible even if Aguirre Cerda were victorious. In either case, González faced a prison term. The only way out seemed to be a coup; thus, with Ibáñez's knowledge and support, *el jefe* and a select group of MNS militants and army officers planned one. Under the circumstances, González had nothing to lose except his credibility, for he had always insisted that he opposed a putsch. However, his frequent shifts had already weakened his credibility.

The rebels would set up a new government to preside over free elections. They believed that, without the administration's support, the Ross candidacy would fade away and Ibáñez would defeat Aguirre Cerda. This route offered González not only a way of surmounting his difficulties but an appealingly revolutionary means of attaining power in place of the customary bourgeois electoral pacts.[145]

The Military, the Putsch, and Its Results

Although the military was ideologically diverse, radical rightist doctrine attracted some officers, particularly among those who had trained in Germany. After facilitating the rise of the MNS, one such officer, General Díaz Valderrama, founded Acción Nacionalista de Chile in 1932. Composed of military men, this group advocated functional representation, repression of revolutionary strikes, and commercial ties within Latin America to free the region "from the claws of International Judaic capitalism." Retired officers formed the kindred Legión Social Nacionalista in late June 1932. Reacting against the Socialist Republic, it favored a "genuine socialism" respecting the social function of property and social justice within order. The Legión wanted to rid Chile of "destructive and dissolvent doctrines" and restore the armed forces' legitimate role of foreign defense.[146]

After the early 1930s, officers expressed their views more discreetly as the administration moved to depoliticize the armed forces. Still, continuing contacts with the German military and local German Nazis may have moved Chilean officers toward the right. Perhaps building on such connections, Nacistas attempted to recruit among the military and stir up dissension within it against the Milicia. These efforts to gain a military following achieved some success. General Carlos Vergara Montero and other military personnel helped train the TNA, and Vergara Montero, General Aníbal Godoy Castro, and former director of the Academia de Guerra Aníbal González González, all retired, were Naci candidates for city councilmen in the elections of 1935. Many retired officers, including Ibáñistas, were found in the MNS, which had nuclei in the navy and army. When Nacismo joined the Alianza, it strengthened its ties with Ibáñista officers, some of whom helped plan the coup. Retired colonel Caupolicán Clavel served as the intermediary between the MNS and these elements.[147]

When his appeal was denied in late August and he realized that the government knew of the plot, González decided to schedule the putsch for September 5, the anniversary of the 1924 coup. Claiming to favor a later date,

Ibáñez refused to commit himself. On September 4, Alianza supporters held a march in Santiago whose size alarmed Frentistas and Rossistas alike and suggested that the general might win the election after all. Ibáñez's campaign manager, retired colonel Tobías Barros Ortiz, thought that the very possibility of an electoral victory disturbed González, who was determined to carry out his dramatic plan. To some observers, however, the event foreboded a coup.[148] The next day, a group of Nacistas took over the Caja de Seguro Obligatorio building, killing a Carabinero, and fired from its balconies on the presidential palace. A few blocks away, another group took control of the main building of the university. Yet another contingent attempted to cut the electrical supply to the capital. When Clavel told Ibáñez that the coup was under way, Ibáñez sought asylum in the unsympathetic Infantry School, which delivered him to the authorities. No one informed the specific regiments committed to the plot that it had started.

Anticipating the worst, Alessandri worked out a plan for defeating the rebels with Commander Novoa, Carabineros director General Humberto Arriagada Valdivieso, and other officials. Carabineros and soldiers managed to win back the university building, a battle in which six Nacistas died and several Carabineros were wounded. Alessandri ordered the security forces to march the survivors to the Caja to convince the Nacistas there to surrender. After some mishaps and casualties, the Nacis capitulated. Then, however, the Carabineros shot all the prisoners in cold blood in the Caja building. Who ordered the slaughter was unclear. Some blamed Arriagada, others blamed Alessandri, and while both denied culpability, the president took responsibility. For his part González gave himself up and assumed responsibility for the putsch, temporarily exonerating Ibáñez. Two Carabineros and sixty-three Nacistas had perished. Four Nacistas had survived the massacre, lying wounded under the corpses.[149]

The coup attempt convulsed the political scene, although not as González had anticipated. Even before receiving extraordinary powers from Congress, the authorities began to repress Nacismo and the Alianza. All political groups but the Nacistas condemned the coup: the left because the government used it to justify a state of siege that could affect the election, the moderate right because it was directed against the administration, and even the Alianza because it made Ibáñez look bad.[150] The details of the massacre, however, alienated the public from the administration and Ross. Recognizing that Ibáñez could not win now and perhaps having made a deal with Aguirre Cerda for a pardon, González instructed his movement to support the Popular Front. Reluctantly, the general withdrew his candidacy.

The authorities exonerated Ibáñez and released him from prison two days before the election, hoping his presence would divide the vote, but to no avail. The Popular Front won by a tiny margin of about 3,000 votes, the MNS having supplied enough votes to edge Aguirre Cerda into office. In one of the first acts of his presidency, Aguirre Cerda pardoned several Nacistas, including González, who had received a sentence of twenty years. Although many Falangistas wound up supporting Ross, the Conservatives blamed them for his defeat. As a result, the Falange Nacional became independent of the Conservative Party in December 1938 and in 1958 renamed itself the Christian Democratic Party.

Further disconnecting itself from fascism, in early 1939 the MNS changed its name to the more Creole and leftist-sounding Vanguardia Popular Socialista (VPS). The VPS disavowed racial supremacy and totalitarianism and favored the liberal freedoms. It created a new democratic structure for the party, placing some limits on *el jefe.* The Alianza Popular Revolucionaria Americana's anti-imperialist salute replaced the fascist one. Significantly, the VPS recognized class struggle as a reality, although it did not exalt it, and put itself on the side of the exploited. In place of the partial nationalizations it once had advocated, it now supported the takeover of all foreign-controlled sources of national wealth. Illustrative of these egalitarian changes was the new stance on women. After September 5, *Trabajo* devoted more coverage to female activities in the VPS and named the women involved.[151]

Yet there was carryover from the past. The party still saw a role for private enterprise, assuming it accorded with popular needs, and it dedicated itself to spiritual values. The VPS equivocated on violence and ominously opposed groups unwilling to assimilate—a category that could include Jews. While displaying concern for their plight, González's famous critique of the selling of visas to Jewish refugees manifested his usual preoccupation with corruption and "inappropriate" immigrants. Moreover, *Trabajo* accused Jews of involvement in this scandal and exaggerated the numbers entering the country. The VPS leader's suggestion that the Corporacíon de Fomento de la Produccíon, the new public development corporation, be financed through a tax on the copper exported by U.S. companies resembled the levy he had previously proposed. Sympathetic to the Popular Front, the party nevertheless kept some distance from it and particularly its Communist component. Thus its identity was ambivalent.[152]

The putsch and the move to the left had alienated many Nacis. The coup turned out so horribly, said Keller bitterly as he left the movement,

that it was good that González blotted out the tragic past by creating the an-
tithesis of the MNS. Angered by *el jefe*'s rejection of fascism, ex-Nacistas
had founded the Partido Nacional Fascista (PNF) in October 1938. Antisemitic, armed, and aggressive, the party copied its precursor's original program. Meanwhile, ex-Milicianos created the Frente Nacional Chileno in
mid-1939, some of whose members were implicated in General Ariosto
Herrera's unsuccessful coup attempt of August 1939. A number of PNF
members and more recent VPS defectors founded the Movimiento Nacionalista de Chile (MN) in February 1940, which again duplicated MNS
doctrine. Its honorary leader was Herrera, an admirer of Mussolini.[153]

Soon the VPS rejoined the extreme right. Aguirre Cerda's lackluster
record and his pardoning in 1940 of Arriagada and other Carabineros jailed
for the massacre angered the party. So, too, did the administration's reluctance to award it cabinet posts. By October 1940, VPS militants were back in
the streets fighting Communists, and the VPS, MN, Frente, and moderate
right-wing parties were holding rallies to denounce the government and
Communists. Its poor showing in the elections of March 1941 further frustrated the VPS, which turned *Trabajo* loose against Jews, democracy, and
the left. Tying himself to what he saw as the antidemocratic wave of the future, González declared his support for the Axis. For the first time, Chilean
fascists intentionally attacked Jews, when in July 1941 VPS and MN militants
invaded the Círculo Israelita, the Jewish community center, damaging the
premises and injuring three people. After Vanguardistas killed one person
in an attack on Radical Party headquarters in May, the authorities locked
González up in an insane asylum. *El jefe* quickly obtained his release, but
now that the public viewed him as a lunatic, the VPS leader lost the little
stature he had left, and his party further declined.[154]

Conclusion

Was González crazy? Young men died for him, whereas they only voted for
others, as one journalist pointed out.[155] Yet he never awakened the same enthusiasm in most Chileans. González's problem was that of the extreme
right as a whole, for Chile did not present the conditions for this current to
prosper. The lack of foreigners and Jews, the strength of moderate rightist
parties and institutions, and the vitality of the party system robbed radical
rightists of potential appeal and a space in which to operate; for these reasons such movements developed slowly. By the time they emerged in the
1930s, leftists had already appropriated the banner of economic nationalism

and tied it to a critique of capitalism, one that proved compelling in the country most affected by the Great Depression. Thus they occupied the nationalist space. The left had even influenced the army, cutting into the extreme right's potential base.

Within these limits, extraparliamentary rightists took two main paths. A transitional group between the Ligas and fascism, the Milicia emphasized repressing leftist threats to order. Once Alessandri, with the Milicia's help, did just that, this organization lost its reason for being.

Taking a more extreme path, Nacistas fit the description of fascism offered by Stanley Payne, a specialist in European fascism. They opposed liberalism, leftism, and conservatism, although they sometimes allied with the last, which is characteristic of this tendency. They wanted to create a new type of authoritarian state and a corporatist system. Fascists aimed to recast their nation's relationship with other countries; so, too, did the MNS, through anti-imperialism. Creating an idealistic, spiritual new culture was another goal. Nacistas also embraced violence, youth, male dominance, the führer principle, and the use of myths, symbols, and rituals. Militarizing politics through uniforms, marches, martial values, and violence, they sought to mobilize a broad following.[156]

Mario Sznajder, a student of Nacismo, however, concludes that this movement was not fascist. Its adherence to church and family and its view of Portales as a precursor, in his opinion, were conservative elements that separated the MNS from full-blown fascism. Yet its Catholicism was sporadic and opportunistic, and at any rate some fascist movements, particularly outside Germany, absorbed conservative and religious elements. Besides, although Nacistas admired Portales, they recognized his limitations as a model for twentieth-century activists. Sznajder also claims that anti-imperialism distinguished Nacismo from European fascism, but Italians and Germans, despite their own expansionism, criticized English imperialism.[157] Thus, despite Sznajder's arguments, the fascist label holds.

In addition, the MNS fit the definition of fascism as a movement seeking to gain support and defeat the left by imitating it in some ways and cultivating a radical appearance, albeit one opposed to Marxism. The weak economy and powerful leftist presence help explain why the MNS was more worker-oriented, violent, extreme, and opportunistic than groups elsewhere. This slant toward the popular sectors did not, however, succeed in recruiting large numbers, nor did it involve a strong appeal to women, at least before the movement's temporary turn to the left. The attempts to include women faltered, for they seemed to conflict with the MNS's emphasis on masculinity, which was part of its alternative to the left—ironically, a feature which the left seems to have shared.

Nacismo's antileftist stance initially won friends among moderate rightists and clergy, although the church retained its loyalty to the Conservatives. Moderates adopted part of the extremists' theory and practice, such as the uniform and other aspects of the militarization of politics, the distaste for universal suffrage, and the belief in hierarchy and corporatism. As historian John Weiss notes for Europe, the Chilean case demonstrates that during crises conservatives approximate "the radical revolutionaries to their right," without resorting to the same ferocity.[158]

Ultimately, however, conservatives helped limit Naci power. MNS violence eventually alienated moderate rightists and the church, and the movement completely lost its allies when it joined the opposition. Government and party hostility boxed the Nacistas into a losing strategy. Incapable of winning control for themselves, Nacistas instead helped win it for another group, the Popular Front.

CHAPTER 10

Argentina: For Fatherland, Labor, and Social Justice

Argentina entered this period with the strongest legacy of radical rightist activism of the three countries. The far right's ties to the oligarchy hampered its ability to attain popular support, however. Nor was the perception of a leftist threat as strong as it was in 1919 or in Chile in 1931–32. Moreover, the once-fragmented conservative forces consolidated to a certain extent after 1930. These factors seemed to limit space for extremists, and internal divisions also weakened them. Still, they built upon their long-standing identification with the church, the military, and nationalism to increase their influence. Only rigged elections and military backing kept the conservatives in power, resulting in a legitimacy crisis that gave extremists opportunities to spread their views. Stamping the 1930s with their violence and intrigues, here radical rightists gained access to power at the national and provincial levels, unlike their Chilean peers.

Nacionalismo and the Struggle Against Yrigoyen

The evolution of rightist movements was intimately related to the ruling Radical Civic Union's (UCR) record. By recognizing the university reform movement and enlarging the bureaucracy, Hipólito Yrigoyen helped open higher learning, the professions, and government service to middle-class Argentines of recent arrival, who became avid Radicals and won office on the UCR ticket. The creation of the state oil monopoly, Yacimientos Petrolíferos Fiscales (YPF), further widened government patronage and attracted nationalist support. The president continued to appeal to syndicalist and unorganized workers. At the same time, he created many enemies by intervening widely in the provinces to remove local conservatives and even Radical competitors from power. The aristocratic Marcelo T. de Alvear, who assumed the presidency in 1922, soothed relations with the oligarchy and tried to cut the bureaucracy, thereby alienating much of his party. The Radicals split into the largely middle-class Personalists, or Yrigoyenists, and the more elitist Anti-Personalists, who identified with Alvear's policies although he did not join them. Pledging to nationalize the oil industry under YPF control and attacking U.S. oil interests and restrictions on Argentine exports,[1] Yrigoyen won the 1928 election. His strong victory and the fruit of his previous interventions enabled his party to win a majority of deputies. Only the Senate rested in the opposition's hands.

All rightist factions disliked Yrigoyen and feared that his tactics and popularity would prevent them from regaining power. The Anti-Personalists, various conservative parties, Liga Patriótica Argentina (LPA), and young members of the elite increasingly interpreted democracy as a permanent loss of political control to the despised offspring of immigrants. They identified the Radical caudillo's seemingly perpetual rule with dictatorship.[2] Since the people had consented to his rule and the growth of executive power, his was what they called a dictatorship of the masses, one that resembled or could lead to communism.

The LPA, whose conception of liberty had always been narrow, led the movement away from democracy. By suppressing worker gatherings, the LPA had mocked freedom of thought and political association, and its emphasis on authority and lower-class deference contradicted the democratic ideal of equality, another concept omitted from the LPA's ideology. LPA president Manuel Carlés once had employed the term *democracy* to refer to "a state of justice for all," but by the late 1920s he preferred *republic* to *democracy*, noting that the founders of Argentina had established only the first. In his restrictive republic "discipline, the principle of authority, the security of the individual and in one's work, and civil peace reigned."[3]

Recalling Yrigoyen's earlier *obrerismo*, Carlés and other members of the elite feared that Personalist democracy contained the seeds of disorder. In April 1928, just after the Radical's reelection, Carlés secretly convened the presidents of the brigades of the capital to ensure that they were prepared to act if the new government did not take firm action against labor conflicts. Following Yrigoyen's inauguration in October, the Porteño brigades approved Carlés's proposal to reconstitute the militias. Citing labor unrest in

Santa Fe, aristocrats complained that the authorities were too weak to fight Bolshevism, even though Yrigoyen sent federal troops there to quell strikes. Indeed, despite internal divisions and the legacy of LPA and employer actions, labor agitation grew in the late 1920s, and the Unión Ferroviaria attracted almost 71,000 workers by 1930, becoming the largest union in Argentine history to that point. Carlés and others attributed this renewed activism to Yrigoyenism. The LPA president insisted that the university reform movement, promoted by Radicalism, had weakened discipline and authority in education and helped disseminate leftist ideas. He also believed that the administration had concluded a pact with anarchist leaders.[4]

By this time Argentina was in an economic crisis. In 1928, capital left the country and exports began to drop; once the Depression began, the capital flight and decline in export levels and prices proceeded in earnest. The wholesale prices of meat, grains, and linseed fell by 50 percent from 1929 to 1933, and the gross domestic product declined 14 percent between 1929 and 1932. While severe, the crisis did not have as pronounced an effect as the postwar slump.[5]

Nevertheless, Yrigoyen seemed unable to cope with the economic difficulties, the chaos within his administration, and his diehard opposition in the Senate. Austerity measures prompted by the Depression cut his following, as did the administration's image of corruption, divisiveness, and lethargy. Violence between Personalists and their opponents provided evidence of political decay that the septuagenarian president was powerless to halt or to which he may have contributed. Rent by partisan disputes, Congress was equally helpless. Yrigoyen's continued interventions in the provinces to weaken local elites, gain control of the Senate, and push through his oil nationalization bill deepened the polarization. Within this context, the LPA, conservatives, and Anti-Personalists began to contemplate overthrowing the government and setting up a new order. The Independent Socialists, who had broken away from the party in a struggle for internal power in 1927, joined this emerging coalition. So, too, did some military officers, disturbed by Yrigoyen's partisan (and dilatory) handling of their concerns.

The most extreme of these conspirators became known as Nacionalistas. Their ideas had begun to take form in the early 1920s. The same postwar labor conflicts that had activated the LPA had prompted Juan Carulla and others to search for new means of ensuring order. Carulla's wartime experiences as a doctor for the French army, which taught him the dark side of human nature and the fallacy of utopianism, had already led him to discard his youthful anarchism. Carulla's inaccurate perception that Socialists had not aided the war effort pushed him toward the right, as did the temporary alliance between George Sorel's syndicalists and Charles Maurras's monarchists, which proved to him that rightist nationalism could be revolutionary.[6]

Poet Leopoldo Lugones had reached a similar conclusion. After his martial speeches of 1923 and 1924, he rejected the leveling tendency of democracy, communism, and Christianity, as well as their aim of universal brotherhood. The war had demonstrated the failure of rationalists and religious believers to order life according to metaphysical concepts; instead, the concrete realities of biology, race, nation, force, and hierarchy prevailed. Most Nacionalistas spurned the poet's paganism and social Darwinism, although they admired his authoritarianism.[7]

Nacionalismo became intertwined with Catholicism. Young Nacionalistas read European Catholic and counterrevolutionary works in the Cursos de Cultura Católica and its spin-off discussion circles, Convivio and Baluarte. Participants in these groups also contributed to the influential Catholic periodicals *Criterio* (founded in 1928) and *Número* (1930–31). Like the Centro Dom Vital in Brazil, these organizations and journals aimed at molding upper-class youths into a Catholic authoritarian elite.[8]

Nacionalistas claimed foreign sources of inspiration. Although some were suspicious of Mussolini's autocratic tendencies, most approved of his strong corporatist government, repression of the left, and cordial relations with the church.[9] But Charles Maurras was the most important model for this emerging counterelite, as he was for the Centro Dom Vital. Like Maurras, Nacionalistas regarded liberalism, democracy, and Marxism as linked and dissolvent. Since they agreed with Maurras that liberalism had launched the process of decay, it rather than leftism initially was their main target. Like Maurras, they favored a strong state under the rule of a capable elite; as sons of the disinherited political class, they were more self-interested than the plebeian Frenchman. A corporatist "functional democracy" should replace the present version of democracy, dominated by plutocrats, the unschooled masses, and demagogic politicians. Opposed to the immigrant working and middle classes, Nacionalistas shared the Frenchman's xenophobia. And, increasingly after 1930, Nacionalistas envisioned a Maurras-style conspiracy directed from abroad, pitting liberals, democrats, leftists, Jews, and foreign capitalists against "true" Argentines. Yet their admiration was not uncritical. Most Nacionalistas rejected monarchism, and the Vatican's condemnation of Maurras tempered their respect.[10]

The principal mouthpiece of such ideas from 1927 to 1931 was *La Nueva República* (*LNR*), founded by Carulla and Rodolfo and Julio Irazusta, among others. The Irazusta brothers came from an Anti-Personalist family of Entre Ríos that had lost much of its land after World War I, and their uncle had been an officer in the LPA's Gualeguaychú brigade. Hostile to Yrigoyenism, *LNR*'s main concern before September 1930 was to convert the ruling class from liberal to counterrevolutionary doctrine.[11]

This task meant convincing its readers that democracy conflicted with the nation's traditions and welfare. "Democracy is not in the Constitution," wrote Rodolfo Irazusta, because it meant disorder. The founding fathers preferred republicanism, which, unlike democracy, stood for the national interest rather than individual interests, the rule of law rather than the rule of the masses, federalism rather than centralist dictatorship, and representation of the vital forces rather than political parties. True nationalists, therefore, were republican.[12]

Carlés, whom Rodolfo Irazusta hailed as a precursor, had influenced *LNR*'s republicanism.[13] Nacionalistas agreed with Carlés on the need for religious values, "seeing the world as it is," and subordinating liberty to the national interest. Both criticized liberalism, socialism, and partisan politics and identified Argentina's enemies as foreign. By this time Carlés, like the Nacionalistas, lumped liberal democrats with leftist workers as agents of dissolution.

Both advocated the rule of the elite, but *LNR* did so more ambivalently than Carlés. While admiring the stability and prosperity imposed by the oligarchy, *LNR* writers also criticized it for its partisanship and liberalism. They denounced the elite for universal suffrage and Conservatives for competing with Radicals for mass support. Through opportunism and lack of doctrine, Conservatives were not resisting the left adequately and thus were forfeiting the right to govern.[14] Nevertheless, Nacionalistas would seek recruits among Conservatives.

Even before Yrigoyen's reelection, Nacionalistas decided to end the reign of democracy. Rodolfo Irazusta and Carulla asked General José F. Uriburu, who had favored the German side in the war and supported Nacionalista publications, to lead an uprising in late 1927, but he demurred. Concluding that the Yrigoyen regime would open the way to anarchy, the general changed his mind about leading a revolt after he retired from active duty. Not long thereafter, Carlés became the first prominent figure to openly call for Yrigoyen's overthrow. Meanwhile, Rodolfo Irazusta and Roberto de Laferrère, a member of a patrician family and a writer for the pro-Nacionalista and Conservative *La Fronda*, had created a youth militia, the Liga Republicana, to undermine the government.[15]

As the LPA turned against democracy, it radicalized its notion of manhood. By the late 1920s Carlés had turned from mild praise of martial values to extolling the "virile" Creole race, which had overturned tyrants, and the "warlike and impassioned" members of earlier generations, "whose countenance[s] seemed to carry a sword and . . . a defiant expression."

These words presaged a coup.[16] Various forces conspired to topple the president. The diehard anti-Yrigoyenism of Carlés, provincial elites, Conservatives, Anti-Personalists, and Independent Socialists helped create the conditions for a *golpe*. The Liga Republicana carried the ideological battle into the streets, demonstrating against the government, disseminating propaganda, and fighting police and Radical stalwarts. In the course of their action, *LNR* and Republicanos altered their political thinking. Originally they had supported the constitution as a republican document, but now they endorsed only its preamble; evidently it was more democratic than they had thought. On the eve of the revolution, in August 1930, the Legión de Mayo joined the struggle. Unlike the Republicanos, the Legionarios lauded the "democracy" that had existed before mass suffrage. They mouthed the opinions of Conservatives, who simply hoped to regain power, and as such drew *LNR*'s criticism. United under Conservative deputy and Legionario Alberto Viñas, the thousand-odd Republicanos and Legionarios papered over their differences. Although the Legión turned against electoralism after the coup, this conflict foreshadowed future tensions between Nacionalistas and Conservatives.[17]

Yet the army was primarily responsible for the revolution. Nacionalistas helped convince Uriburu not only to overthrow Yrigoyen but to impose a corporatist system. Most officers sympathetic to a coup, however, inclined toward Anti-Personalist general Agustín P. Justo, who favored working with the opposition and returning to constitutional rule as quickly as possible. To win Justo's backing, Uriburu promised not to impose a new political order coercively. Uriburu commanded a small number of troops to march toward the presidential palace, accompanied by Legionarios and Republicanos. Few officers took steps against the column, which more and more units joined when it became clear that the authorities were paralyzed. These actions forced the president and vice president to resign. The military conspirators had accomplished their goals with remarkable ease, thanks to Yrigoyen's loss of popularity. The revolution may not have awakened much support, but few actively opposed it.

Nacionalismo and the Uriburu Regime

Most Argentines hoped the new regime would address the economic crisis and quickly reinstate a constitutional government. Uriburu, however, interpreted popular compliance to mean agreement on the need for a corporatist authoritarian regime. Yet only his closest allies endorsed his plans to amend the constitution, nullify the male suffrage law, and suppress the opposition.

The Depression and nationalism prompted the government to overturn traditional liberal economic policies. It cut expenditures and raised taxes in order to balance the budget, although it was careful not to slight the military's share. In a more innovative manner, it levied a 10 percent surcharge on the tariff and some additional duties. An exchange control commission set priorities on imports and the use of hard currency in order to restrain capital flight and ensure debt service. To help relieve the agricultural crisis, the government authorized credits for corn producers and stimulated the construction of grain elevators. It inaugurated public works programs and studied means of diversifying the economy and fomenting industry, even expanding the official oil monopoly in the process.[18]

Restoring order in the political realm was, however, the new regime's priority. Uriburu's cousin, conservative reformer Carlos Ibarguren, and his Nacionalista appointees created the bases for a "functional democracy" during Ibarguren's intervention in Córdoba province. Lugones, Carulla, and other Nacionalista advisers, including at least thirty named to government posts, urged the president to do the same. They were suspicious of Uriburu's oligarchical appointments, although Minister of the Interior Matías Sánchez Sorondo and Carlos Meyer Pellegrini, interventor of Buenos Aires, both Conservatives, tried to reassure them by denouncing the old political system. Bound by his promises to Justo and influenced by the partisan-minded Sánchez Sorondo, the president decided to restore constitutional government in stages, beginning with elections in the provinces deemed least likely to favor Radicals. Eventually an elected Congress would convene an assembly that would vote on the proposed constitutional amendments. Conservatives backed the president's electoral plan with the proviso that they would form the backbone of his envisioned new political movement. Thus their arena, Buenos Aires, became the site of the first election on April 5, 1931—and of the plan's ignominious defeat. The Radicals won the election, and the embarrassed government nullified it.[19]

The regime had already taken coercive measures. Declaring a state of siege, it censored the press and shut down unsympathetic newspapers, obstructed habeas corpus, and restored the death penalty, executing two anarchists and three others. Cooperating with Italian authorities and local Italian Fascists, it detained large numbers of workers, students, and Radicals, including Yrigoyen, and deported some of them. The government harshly repressed strikes and other disturbances, which it blamed on Personalists. As head of the political order section of the federal police, Leopoldo Lugones, son of the poet, helped lead the offensive against democrats and leftists. He and his section tortured many prisoners; others accused of torture or complicity in it were Uriburu's friend, Lieutenant Colonel Juan B. Molina; Alberto Viñas, director of the penitentiary; Sánchez Sorondo; and the president himself. After the April defeat and a Radical military revolt in July, the repression stiffened. The authorities closed Radical offices and publications, exiled Alvear and other Radical leaders, and restricted them from running for office.[20]

At least initially the government was divided on labor matters. One side, including the police, favored blind repression. Although they were willing to suppress combative unions, Uriburu's fascist-influenced appointees in the Labor Department advocated resolving capital-labor disputes through state-sponsored mediation efforts. The corporatists lost out to the advocates of brute force, who smashed anarchist, Communist, and other worker organizations. Although Uriburu claimed he favored the corporatist side, he did not mobilize labor in even a controlled fashion as a first step toward a corporatist system. His policies made the regime popular with employers, but they also demonstrated how far it was from being genuinely fascist.[21]

With the failure of the electoral strategy, Uriburu faced a difficult choice. He could step down from power or make further compromises to the Justo faction, as it demanded. Or he could move further to the right, to a "government of force," as Nacionalistas urged. Uriburu combined the second and third alternatives. He conciliated Justo by removing Sánchez Sorondo, scheduling new elections, and discarding the notion of corporate representation, which angered some Nacionalistas. Nevertheless, he still urged the passage of other constitutional amendments.[22]

In January 1931, Uriburu had helped sponsor a new paramilitary organization, the Legión Cívica Argentina (LCA), to unite existing Nacionalista groups and defend his regime. Led by Dr. Floro Lavalle, a landowner and LPA member, the LCA absorbed the Legionarios and Republicanos and added more brigades. Supporting the proposed reforms, it would promote nationalism, create social harmony, and combat the government's enemies. Thousands of Legionarios with blue and white armbands paraded in military formation before the president on April 26. Moving toward the alternative of a government of force, a month later the government officially recognized the LCA as its partner in "institutional reconstruction," authorizing the army to arm its members and instruct them in military installations; indeed, officers would head many LCA brigades. Uriburu justified this measure by claiming that creating this reserve unit helped the state, which could not afford a large military draft.[23]

LCA ties to the regime were evident. Uriburu praised it in speeches, met with its leaders, and attended some of its exercises. Its members held functions in schools and other official buildings, used the post office's press to print signs and fliers free of charge, and wore gray uniforms furnished by the War Ministry. The intendant ordered the municipality of Buenos Aires to contribute 10,000 pesos to the LCA's ceremony commemorating the anniversary of the revolution. High-ranking Uriburu appointees used their positions to publicize the LCA within the national bureaucracy and provincial interventions, and the Buenos Aires police lent support. Socialists and other opponents accused Legionarios of forcing government workers to join the organization and attend its parades, which the LCA denied.[24]

Whether through coercion or attraction, the LCA grew in numbers. It reached a height of 30,000 in the capital, and although its base was Buenos Aires and Córdoba, it had members throughout the nation. Additional brigades of women and primary- and university-level students helped make the LCA the largest Nacionalista group of the early 1930s.[25]

The LCA provoked strong criticism from many quarters. Scoffing at Uriburu's claim that the organization was apolitical, observers cited its cooperation with the Conservative Party of Buenos Aires, with which it shared an address in La Plata, and local conservatives in at least one other province. Even the establishment press objected to its official status and political links. The LCA spied on and attacked Radicals, students, union members, and other opponents of the regime. Many suspected that the president would use the organization to prolong his rule or put the Conservatives in power. Criticizing the LCA's lumpen composition, Laferrère withdrew the Liga Republicana from the LCA, and other Nacionalistas followed.[26]

The LCA roused opposition from the military. Although they and their predecessors had supported the LPA, some officers thought the new, more militarized group usurped their authority, its military overseers notwithstanding. They also saw the LCA as a poorly disciplined mob. Allied with

Justo, these officers disapproved of military participation in an organization buttressing a government of dubious allegiance to the constitution. The LCA presented an unhealthy reversal of roles in which civilians involved themselves in military activities while soldiers dabbled in politics. Collaborating with it would corrupt the military as an institution. Nor did these officers approve of the LCA's fascist leanings, although their own adherence to liberal democracy was shallow.[27]

Carlés had harsh words for the LCA and the government. The LPA president condemned the regime for assigning officers to train "phalanges" of public employees to attack dissidents. Although he did not object to quelling labor, Carlés could not accept the level of repression against the upper and middle classes. He publicly rebuked Uriburu for limiting freedoms he now admitted that some had a right to exercise. In his view, the government had only increased popular sympathy for the martyred Radicals and diminished respect for the military. The president responded by preventing his old friend from speaking in churches at Sunday mass, whereupon Carlés advised Uriburu to return to retirement and the military to return to the barracks. In July 1931, Carlés resigned his chair of civic morality in the Colegio Nacional de Buenos Aires, which he had held for forty years, asserting that he could not teach the subject under a regime that disregarded it. Even leftists applauded his defiance. Returning to simple antileftism and his Radical origins, during the 1930s Carlés censured extremists of the left and right and supported Alvear's efforts to consolidate the Radical Party. He referred to democracy and liberty more frequently than in the previous decade, although he still defined them narrowly.[28] No longer of the extreme right, the LPA lingered on but was only a shadow of its former self.

Some Nacionalistas were equally disenchanted with the government, albeit for different reasons. In their view, rather than using unpopular Conservatives as collaborators, the administration should have installed a new political system appealing to the Radicals' constituency, thus eclipsing both parties. Instead, Uriburu's dictatorship had simply frightened the public and subverted the constitution without changing it.[29]

Nacionalistas urged the government to extend its economic program and cast off colonial subjugation. The short-lived Acción Republicana, founded by Lugones and members of the *LNR* circle in 1931, proposed that the administration set meat and grain prices, shipping charges, and land rents and provide farmers with credit. It asked the state to stimulate the building of nationally owned grain elevators and meatpacking plants and find Latin American markets for Argentine goods. Acción Republicana also advocated nationalizing electric power, protecting industries based on local raw materials, and erecting a Platine economic union. Uriburu's disinterest in the fate of locally owned meatpacking plants like the one in the Irazustas' hometown, however, convinced the group of government apathy and even hostility toward national capital.[30]

LNR writers perceived a conflict between the revolutionary plan, however limited in scope, and plutocratic interests. Foreign firms ruled the country through the oligarchs they employed as lawyers and local representatives. "Liberalism on the payroll of foreign enterprises cannot conceive of permitting that we ever have national industries but that we should content ourselves with being a cattle-raising and agricultural nation," wrote Fausto de Tezanos Pinto, an aristocratic journalist. Undermining control from abroad required overturning the liberal democracy that had caused social dissolution and handed national wealth to the foreigner: hence the need for Uriburu's program. But this the elite could not permit because it would hurt it financially. According to Rodolfo Irazusta, democracy simply meant the predominance of parasitic administrators, linked to foreign business, immigrants, and cosmopolitan cities, over producers.[31] Thus, it spelled dependence.

Nacionalista Social Composition

Most Nacionalistas in the early 1930s were part of the oligarchy they criticized. About 61 percent of a sample of members of Nacionalista groups were upper-class. Many Nacionalistas came from interconnected elite families; 35 percent of the group studied were closely related to other Nacionalistas. Only 3 percent had participated in the LPA, but 14 percent were closely related to members of that group. Averaging thirty-three years of age in 1930, very few figured in government before 1916. Yet close relatives of 32 percent of the sample had served in office before the Radicals assumed power. Over half, or 53 percent, owned land or belonged to landowning families.[32]

Some groups differed from the general profile. The most dedicated Nacionalistas, those who belonged to more than one organization, were the most blue-blooded; 78 percent were upper-class. The small *LNR* circle, however, was distinctly lower in status, as only 33 percent pertained to the elite. A bare 11 percent of these writers were closely related to other Nacionalistas.

Nacionalistas differed from the LPA in some respects. The average one was sixteen years younger than his LPA counterpart of 1920. Even though more of the LPA leaders were upper-class, the Nacionalistas' popular base was smaller than that of their predecessor. There was a similar degree of participation in oligarchical governments, either through their own political offices or those of their families. Yet even this similarity suggests a distinction: a group that considered itself robbed of its birthright for fourteen years was more dissatisfied with the status quo than one that had lost power only a few years before, as was the case for some Liguistas in 1919.

Nacionalismo and the Political System Under Justo

These disinherited young men shared Uriburu's bitter reaction to the return to a pre-Radical version of politics, which he characterized as "embezzlement, robbery, pillaging." Justo had forced Uriburu into relinquishing any further claim on the presidency, to which he himself aspired. The provincial conservative factions had reconsolidated in the National Democratic Party (PDN) in 1931, while maintaining their local party identities. The PDN, Anti-Personalists, and Independent Socialists formed the Concordancia, Justo's civilian coalition. When Uriburu vetoed Alvear's candidacy, Radicals decided to abstain from the campaign. Some Radicals supported the reformist Civil Alliance, which ran PDP leader Lisandro de la Torre for president and Socialist Nicolás Repetto for vice president. Aided by fraud and limitations imposed under the state of siege, Justo easily won the election and assumed office in February 1932.[33]

Suspicious of Justo as an agent of the oligarchy and enemy of Uriburu, Nacionalistas unhappily acquiesced in his victory. Many would unfavorably compare his record with Uriburu's, which became enshrined in what Ronald Dolkart calls the "myth of September." Uriburu's death in April 1932, which some Nacionalistas perceived as a martyrdom, accentuated the myth. Seemingly diminishing the Nacionalistas' space of activity, the merger of conservative forces only papered over the clash of individuals and strategies among moderate rightists. The play of ambitions, shifting political circumstances, and the ruling coalition's corruption and lack of legitimacy provided extreme rightists with ample opportunities to carp, meddle, and gain influence.[34]

Justo provided Nacionalistas with such an opportunity in the economic realm. Fearing that the Depression would force the British to favor beef and grains from its empire and curtail purchases of Argentine goods, the government signed the Roca-Runciman Pact in 1933. The British pledged to keep their meat purchases at the 1931 level, erase the tariffs on grains, and allot 15 percent of the meat trade to Argentine meatpacking plants; for its part Argentina offered sweeping import duty and trade concessions. Many Argentines perceived the treaty as a humiliating display of national subservience. They also charged that it protected the core of the elite, the cattle fatteners, at a high cost to the rest of society.[35]

The pact did not have the harmful consequences that many anticipated. The devaluation of the peso and the low prices of Argentine exports limited purchases from abroad and provided impetus for import-substitution industrialization, which may not initially have been the government's aim but increasingly became one. Justo also succeeded in undermining another degrading accord, which threatened to permit the British tramways to create a transportation monopoly in the federal capital. Contemporary observers could not predict these results, however, and many regarded the administration as a shameful lackey of imperialism.

In Chile the left, with its native-born working-class base in the foreign-dominated mining sector, led the struggle against foreign capital. This was not true of Argentina. Until the 1930s, birthplace and other allegiances tied most workers to Europe. Like other groups, Socialists praised the ability of the export economy to generate wealth. Their internationalist views, desire to attract a broad urban following, and opposition to industrial employers led most to emphasize free trade and consumers' rights. Furthermore, they tended to reject economic nationalism as the core of fascism. Socialists pointed out the abuses of foreign capital and loans, and unions sometimes resorted to nationalist arguments to win government favor, especially under Uriburu, but neither group supported industrialization or economic nationalism in a unified, sustained fashion.[36]

Nor had center or center-left politicians produced much economic nationalism. Yrigoyen had denounced U.S. oil firms and trade policy, but his cultivation of economic ties with the British weakened his nationalist credentials. In the late 1920s, an Yrigoyenist public prosecutor and enemy of the LPA, Manuel Ortiz Pereyra, had denounced the dependence on foreign companies and European ideas. His ardent defense of democracy had set him apart from Nacionalistas, but some of his notions, such as opposition to immigration and "exotic" class divisions, resembled theirs. In the early 1930s, another Radical, Ricardo Rojas, supported repudiating the foreign debt and nationalizing foreign companies. Yet Yrigoyen's death in 1933, the subsequent leadership of the relatively conservative Alvear, government crackdowns, and the failed Yrigoyenist military conspiracies of the early 1930s created disorder within the party and delayed and marginalized Radical nationalism. Another democratic nationalist was Lisandro de la Torre. From the Senate he continued the PDP's tradition of defending national industries, but his rigidity and inability to appeal to the public hampered his campaign.[37]

Extreme rightists, then, retained their claim on economic nationalism, as their appropriation of the title of nationalism indicates. The Roca-Runciman Pact provided the occasion for the Irazustas to strengthen this identification. In a book published a year after the treaty, they traced back to 1806 a pattern of elitist compliance with British efforts to control Argentina's economic destiny and relegate it to a position of raw materials provider. Excessive adulation of and subservience to Europe characterized the oligarchy, which the Irazustas defined as a vehicle for certain ideas and practices rather than a class. So, too, did its elevation of abstract liberal concepts—now considered antiquated elsewhere—above national independence and greatness. This tendency had severely damaged Argentina, as had the elite's disdain for the Spanish Catholic heritage. Only Rosas and, much less consistently or effectively, Yrigoyen, had departed from this colonial pattern, but the coup the Irazustas had supported had restored the oligarchy in its full force.[38]

The Irazustas held the liberal elite responsible for the nation's problems. Not simply mistaken or misguided, the oligarchs were traitors. This book and earlier *LNR* statements suggested a division in Argentine society between those who sided with foreigners—leftist laborers, liberals, import-export interests, government administrators, lawyers employed by foreign firms—and those loyal to the nation, mainly producers. Ignored were the many liberal landowners. This formulation would serve Nacionalistas as a radical alternative to class concepts.

Rightist responses to the book varied. Carlés endorsed it tepidly, while Hispanist Manuel Gálvez praised it highly. Carlos Ibarguren (junior) and *Bandera Argentina*, founded in 1932 by Carulla, admitted that the revolution had reinstalled the oligarchy but claimed this had not been Uriburu's intention. Most of the establishment, including many Nacionalistas, simply ignored the disquieting treatise. When the Jurado Municipal de Literatura of Buenos Aires voted to award it a prize, the government, possibly pressured by the British embassy, forced it to change its mind, thereby proving the Irazustas' point.[39]

The Irazustas no longer fit comfortably in some Nacionalista circles. Having learned that one could not easily impose a revolutionary program from above, and determined to join the opposition, they returned to the Radicals, the only mass party. While the brothers still criticized the UCR and democracy, they were willing to accept them as means of attaining a strong antiliberal and anti-imperialistic government. The Irazustas and Gálvez, who was gathering materials for a sympathetic biography of Yrigoyen, belatedly recognized that the former president possessed some nationalist traits. Still, the brothers maintained ties with Nacionalista groups.[40]

The Irazustas' retreat to the UCR was only one of the splits in Nacionalismo. The 1930s witnessed an astounding proliferation of Nacionalista groups and periodicals. Personal ambitions and rivalries accounted for some of the divisions, but so did genuine differences of opinion. The LCA and Acción Nacionalista Argentina/Afirmación de una Nueva Argentina (ANA/ADUNA) remained loyal to Uriburu, whereas the Irazusta circle discerned his faults. Baluarte and Restauración placed greater emphasis on Catholicism than other organizations. The LCA, the largest group of the early 1930s, and the Alianza de la Juventud Nacionalista (AJN), the largest of the late 1930s, attempted to attract a popular following, while the Liga Republicana spurned one. The smaller organizations, however, wielded an intellectual influence that the more sizable ones lacked. Some groups embraced the fascist label, although most Nacionalistas obscured their ties with this ideology. Finally, the militarized LCA and various legions differed from civilian-style associations.[41]

Efforts to unite all Nacionalista groups under one rubric invariably failed. In fact, quarrels among Nacionalistas sometimes degenerated into fist fights. At the fourth anniversary celebration of the revolution, the virulent anticommunist and antisemitic high school teacher Carlos Silveyra reproved many Nacionalistas for their "exotic" uniforms, Roman salutes, and other foreignisms. Violence broke out between his opponents and supporters, and police broke up the event.[42]

Accordingly, some authors have placed the groups in categories.[43] Without ignoring distinctions, I focus on the immense overlap among them—one which Nacionalistas recognized. To some extent all professed Catholicism (except Lugones), corporatism, and Hispanism, and all criticized liberalism, electoral democracy, imperialism, feminism, leftism, cosmopolitanism, and Jews. Many moved from one group into another or belonged to several. Despite their petty jealousies and differences, the movements cooperated with each other, held common functions, and participated in joint forays against their enemies. Rather than divide Nacionalismo into mutually exclusive factions, it is best to see it as a coalition of shifting extreme rightist forces, some more radical than others. The importance lies in the whole, rather than in the individual groups.[44]

As a whole, Nacionalistas entered an ambiguous relationship with Justo. The new president lifted the state of siege, freed the ailing Yrigoyen, and permitted other UCR leaders to return from exile. After a rally to welcome the exiles home on February 27, 1932, about a thousand Radicals attacked *La Fronda* and the armed Republicanos inside in the early hours of the next day. Shooting from both sides resulted in four deaths and twenty-five wounded, and the police detained Radicals and Republicanos. The Republicanos thought that the government hoped the troublesome antagonists would kill each other off.[45]

Yet the new government cooperated with and used Nacionalismo to a certain extent. Despite numerous requests, the administration never rescinded Uriburu's decree of January 1932 giving the LCA legal status. Justo even awarded LCA leaders Carulla and Lavalle minor government posts and permitted the LCA to continue to use government buildings and mailing privileges. The wily Justo deployed the LCA in his maneuvers to set left against right and Uriburista against Radical officers—usually to the right's benefit. At the same time, to the democratic forces he offered his administration as the only alternative to Nacionalismo.[46]

In the early Justo era, Nacionalistas began to shift their focus from the UCR to leftism. Socialist strength in the capital, a strike wave in 1932, the presence of the Soviet commercial and consular office Iuyamtorg, which Nacionalistas charged with spreading propaganda, and the Socialist-inspired congressional debate over inaugurating relations with the Soviet Union influenced this change. So, too, did events in Chile and government labor initiatives such as paid vacations, a half day of rest on Saturday, state mediation efforts, and occasional support for strikers. Such moves to win Socialist favor convinced many Nacionalistas that Justo was moving leftward, despite continued deportations and torture of labor militants, the creation of the antileftist special section of the federal police, and various reimpositions of the state of siege.[47]

To coordinate Nacionalista efforts against communism, Carlos Silveyra founded the Comisión Popular Argentina Contra el Comunismo (CPACC). CPACC planned a rally in the Plaza del Congreso to convince the government to expel Iuyamtorg and foreign subversives, declare communism illegal, and abjure relations with the Soviets. For several days before the event, rumors spread that CPACC would attack Jews physically as well as communism rhetorically. Minister of the Interior and former LPA member Leopoldo Melo assured a Jewish delegation they would receive police protection, but Socialist deputies questioned the worth of such guarantees. Joining the minister in praising CPACC, PDN deputy Abraham de la Vega insisted that the charges against it were exaggerated and the authorities had the situation under control. In fact, the rally on August 20, which attracted only five to six thousand, was peaceful.[48] The exchange set the tone of national debate in the 1930s, in which the Concordancia congressmen generally favored the Nacionalistas, and the PDP and Socialists opposed them.

A public meeting against reaction hosted by the Federación Obrera Local Bonaerense, an affiliate of the anarcho-syndicalist Federación Obrera Regional Argentina, at the Parque Patricios on December 3, was not as tranquil. Invading labor's space, LCA and perhaps ANA/ADUNA members fired on the crowd, killing one worker and wounding another. The police detained several laborers but none of the perpetrators, prompting protests from Socialists, students, and unions. When delegates of other parties in the municipal council blamed labor rallies for inciting violence, Socialists asserted that Nacionalista pronouncements favoring dictatorship, unchecked by authorities, were far more subversive.[49]

Debate continued in the Chamber of Deputies, where Repetto called for the dissolution of the rightist militias. National Democrat and former LPA member Manuel Fresco, however, took notice of the national and moral reserves that contained leftist-instigated violence. Openly admiring the perpetrators, his party mate, Francisco Uriburu, cousin of the former president and director of *La Fronda*, predicted that "if Communists want to finish with the Nation, Argentine youth will finish with communism." Uriburu claimed to know who the assailants were, but refused to divulge their names, even when a judge requested them. The men remained in impunity.[50]

By early 1933 the Socialist-controlled municipal council passed a resolution asking the government to dissolve the armed Nacionalista groups, over the opposition of the PDN sector, which claimed that the matter did not fall within the council's jurisdiction. Melo admonished the council to leave the legions to the judicial branch. Two deaths in a tangle between Nacionalistas and Radicals on May 25, however, strengthened the Socialists' resolve.[51] In the Chamber of Deputies, Repetto asked for an interpellation of Melo in order to question him on the government's stance. Despite support even from Independent Socialists, the Chamber narrowly defeated the request. PDN member Uberto F. Vignart explained his vote by insisting that the legions were healthy responses to the Radical threat and claiming that the PDN stood for most of their ideas.[52] Here as in Chile, the moderate and extreme right overlapped.

Córdoba was another scene of Nacionalista violence. Long-standing opposition to the university reform movement, a Catholic revival in the 1920s, and the Ibarguren intervention had helped make Córdoba a Nacionalista center. Luis Guillermo Martínez Villada, a professor in the local law school and in the Colegio Montserrat, attracted students with his lectures on Catholic and counterrevolutionary doctrine. His followers, including his colleague, the young philosopher Nimio de Anquín, founded the Instituto San Tomás de Aquino in 1929. Resembling the Cursos de Cultura Católica in Buenos Aires, the institute contributed articles and manifestos to *Número* and *LNR*. Ibarguren's provincial government supported this circle and strengthened its ties to Nacionalistas in the capital. The Anquín group joined the Partido Fascista Argentino (PFA, 1932), or Fascismo Argentino, which had broken away from the Partido Nacional Fascista (1923). Founded by Italian immigrants, these fascist parties were distinctly less oligarchical than other Nacionalista groups of the early 1930s. Argentine-born Nicolás Vitelli headed the PFA branch in Córdoba, and when he died in 1934, Anquín assumed the leadership.[53]

The PFA's main allies in Córdoba were the LCA and ANA/ADUNA. Dr. Pablo Calatayud, Ibarguren's former minister of government and ANA/ADUNA leader, declared that the groups were extending the work of the intervention by countering democratic and Communist threats. Members of the ruling Democratic Party, a PDN affiliate, also had begun to enter Nacionalismo during the intervention, as did some police and local government employees.[54]

Uniformed PFA members in Córdoba routinely attacked cinemas showing political films they judged offensive, fired weapons in the streets, and threatened leftists and Radicals. Their excesses annoyed the provincial administration, which closed PFA offices in March and June 1933. The PFA's enemies retaliated by assassinating one of its members, a bricklayer, in June and bombing PFA headquarters in July.[55]

Nacionalistas focused their ire on Socialist provincial deputy José Guevara, an outspoken critic of the extreme right. After an anniversary celebration of the coup of 1930, attended by Nacionalista leaders and Governor Pedro J. Frías, uniformed Legionarios scuffled with Guevara and six other Socialist provincial deputies. A few days later, when Guevara found the door of his house aflame, he denounced the LCA and PFA as thieves, degenerates, and worse. Infuriated by these affronts to their masculinity, two Legionarios assaulted the deputy, which prompted Guevara to ask the governor to guarantee his security. Frías ordered police chief Julio de Vértiz to take precautions, but this fascist sympathizer freed the LCA assailants the next day, claiming lack of evidence.[56]

A few hours after the LCA members received their freedom, Guevara and other Socialist speakers held an antifascist rally. A shouting match between Socialists and Nacionalistas led to gunfire, killing Guevara with a shot in the back and severely wounding two others. Vértiz and other policemen stood nearby but did little until after the shooting, when they arrested Vitelli and twelve other fascists and three Legionarios. They also arrested a Socialist, Bernardo Movischoff, whom they treated brutally. First Nacionalistas avowed their innocence, but the evidence weighed so heavily against them that they then claimed that Movischoff's and Guevara's antipatriotic statements had provoked the shooting, which they described as "self-defense." The police shut the LCA and PFA headquarters and detained other Nacionalistas.[57]

Breaking the pattern for cases involving Nacionalistas, the Democratic authorities achieved some results. They identified Rodolfo Odonetto as the probable murderer. The thirty-two-year-old, native-born former police employee had left the Democrats for the LCA, allegedly because he did not receive the government job the party had promised him. He had four previous arrests, including ones for forced entry and drunken disorderliness. His background indicated the plebeian and lumpen character of many Legionarios. The fact that the dean of the law school defended him and two other detainees in court also suggested Nacionalismo's continuing upper-class base. Odonetto achieved his release from prison after only nine months, the judge deciding, rather dubiously, there was not enough evidence to hold him. Nor did his accomplices or superiors receive punishment. Socialists derived some satisfaction from the fact that, amidst charges of complicity, Vértiz resigned. When an official investigation "cleared" Vértiz, however, the ANA criticized the Frías administration for not trusting him, and forced it to appoint a Nacionalista, Manuel Villada Achával, to his post.[58]

The Democratic response to Nacionalismo was mixed. The party newspaper covered it extensively and favorably. Members of the ruling party expressed their sympathy with Nacionalismo and defeated Socialist-proposed resolutions to dissolve the Nacionalista groups in the municipal council and provincial Chamber of Deputies. Yet Democratic leaders and national deputies condemned the killing and, reversing an earlier stand, declared that party members could not belong to an antidemocratic group. This decision prompted Manuela Torres Castaño, widow of a former Democratic governor, to resign from the vice presidency of the local LCA feminine brigade. Democratic president José Heriberto Martínez counterposed Nacionalistas who opposed democracy and the law, provoked disorder, and held "carnivalesque" parades with his party's true democratic nationalism. His indictment of communism and praise for Uriburu did not keep the local ANA chapter from regarding this "inheritor" of the revolution as cowardly and treacherous. The ANA must also have scorned the Democrats who adhered to a nonpartisan front against the extreme right.[59]

Opposition forces in the national Chamber of Deputies used the incident to demand change. Repetto asked, should Socialists create a militia of their own to defend themselves? Melo wondered what Repetto wanted from the administration, which had to respect people's rights. Act like a real government and "put on your pants" was the reply. Withdrawing official recognition of the LCA and using article 22 of the constitution outlawing armed civilian groups were among the specific measures suggested by Socialist Juan A. Solari. In response, PDN deputies Fresco and Vicente Solano Lima insisted that the Socialists were exaggerating the danger and wasting time discussing it. Socialist Silvio Ruggieri and Progressive Democrat Julio Noble disagreed, pointing out that what was permissible for the Nacionalistas was not for Socialists and Radicals: the government assigned the legions to judges and the parties to the police. The crux of the matter, according to Noble, was that the government feared the legions because of their roots in the army, but if it repressed them it would attract popular support.[60] A government born of a coup and fraud, however, could not risk losing its military support.

Aside from indicating the partisan division on Nacionalismo, the incident showed that there was a consolidated extreme right. Nacionalista groups in Córdoba, such as the PFA, LCA, and ANA/ADUNA, worked together and supported each other. These and other groups continued to attack laborers, students, and Socialists throughout the country.[61]

Another site of such occurrences was Buenos Aires province, where the LCA had organized many brigades and enjoyed ties with Conservatives. The LCA had invaded the labor stronghold of Santos Lugares, a railroad center outside the capital, setting up a chapter there in early 1934 that soon began to attack workers. In response, two railroad unions, La Fraternidad and the Unión Ferroviaria, hosted a massive anti-LCA rally on July 28. When it dispersed, a group headed toward the LCA office. Legionarios fired on those who reached the building, seriously wounding a female passerby and killing a railroad worker.[62] Provincial Minister of Government Rodolfo Moreno, a

PDN moderate, visited Santos Lugares, closed the LCA local, and ordered police to arrest civilians in uniform. However, he and Interior Minister Melo did not dissolve the armed bands, as requested by the unions and the Confederación General del Trabajo (CGT), the labor central formed in 1930 with which the Unión Ferroviaria was affiliated. Provincial and local policemen detained thirteen Legionarios, but a judge set them free, dubiously claiming lack of evidence.[63]

In the wake of this murder, the sixth committed by Nacionalistas, Socialist deputies again requested an interpellation of Melo. Joining the chorus of PDN objections, PDN deputy Uberto F. Vignart argued that the meager Nacionalista forces merited little attention; the Socialists were creating "storms" out of "drops of water." The death of a worker, replied Socialist Luis Ramiconi, was not a mere drop of water. Tiburcio Padilla of the PDN praised the LCA as an "institution of order" filled with upstanding people. Leftists in Santos Lugares had deliberately provoked it, he claimed; if the LCA should be dissolved, so should the Socialist Party, for workers also killed their enemies. With these arguments conservatives defeated the interpellation.[64]

Despite the PDN's disclaimers, Nacionalista influence extended to high levels in the party and in government, particularly in Buenos Aires. Its governor, Federico Martínez de Hoz, a wealthy Conservative landowner related to several Nacionalistas, had won his post in the fraudulent elections of 1931. Out of ideological affinity or acknowledgment that he owed his situation to the revolution, Martínez de Hoz attended a ceremony in Lobos naming the municipal park after Uriburu in September 1933—a change to which many local citizens objected. Lieutenant Colonel Emilio Kinkelín, a Germanophile LCA leader and close associate of Uriburu, told the Legionario-studded crowd that he had the military might to keep the UCR out of power. Socialists questioned the governor's presence at this alarming event. Then in 1934 Senator Sánchez Sorondo, the governor's ally, proposed that the new provincial constitution should mandate religious instruction in the schools and restrict freedom of the press. Moreno kept these measures out of the document, but Martínez de Hoz's congratulatory message to Sánchez Sorondo deepened existing divisions within the PDN and pegged him as a Nacionalista.[65]

These divisions precipitated a crisis in early 1935 that engulfed Martínez de Hoz's governorship and embroiled the Nacionalistas. After negotiations with national and party dignitaries, the governor agreed to leave office for the good of the Conservatives but then changed his mind, enlisting Nacionalista support to remain in his position. Their disdain for politics notwithstanding, Nacionalistas responded to the call, detecting an opportunity to gain access to power, spread their militarized groups throughout the province, and challenge Justo, who by now also wanted to oust Martínez de Hoz. Backed by Sánchez Sorondo, Martínez de Hoz forced his cabinet ministers to resign (Moreno had already departed) and in early March replaced them with three Nacionalistas: Marcelo Lobos of the LCA; Carlos Ribero, a high-ranking LCA leader, retired naval officer, and former member of Uriburu's cabinet; and Raimundo Meabe of Nacionalismo Argentino, the interventor of Buenos Aires province who had officiated over the bogus electoral contest of November 1931. About 150 Nacionalistas applauded the swearing in of the new cabinet. Martínez de Hoz issued a manifesto, possibly drafted by Nacionalistas, in which he adhered to Uriburu's goals and claimed that as governor he stood above any one party.[66]

In previous instances most PDN figures had tempered their criticism of Nacionalismo and downplayed its strength. Now that it threatened their power, they reacted differently. Party forces in the provincial legislature impeached Martínez de Hoz on several counts, including naming to his cabinet persons who publicly opposed the constitution and the existing form of government and advocated violence.[67]

The provincial government moved to the right, and Nacionalistas assumed a visible and defiant presence. The first act of the newly constituted government, on March 8, was to sack and close the offices of the Unión Obrera Local in La Plata. Hundreds of armed Republicanos, ANA/ Adunistas, and Legionarios swaggered in and around the Casa de Gobierno, guarding the governor, monitoring bureaucrats and journalists, and issuing orders to policemen. According to the Socialist newspaper *La Vanguardia*, the only administrative business that was proceeding normally was the daily payment of wages to the "fascist army." When the legislature asked Martínez de Hoz to give up his post, he remained in his office shielded by Nacionalistas. On March 14, the Justo administration dispatched another federal interventor and troops to La Plata. Knowing he had lost, the governor gave the Nacionalistas a farewell address. Nacionalistas escorted him and his entourage to cars waiting outside the Casa de Gobierno, peacefully ending their brief experience in power. The LCA invited delegations from all the Nacionalista groups that had participated in these events to a "creole meal" in early March, commemorating the first Nacionalista cabinet after Uriburu.[68]

The episode had broad repercussions. Sánchez Sorondo left the PDN, although he retained his Senate seat until 1941. At last the administration considered revoking the LCA's official status, but it never did so.[69] The incident hurt Justo's and the PDN's prestige. It also demonstrated that conservative and Nacionalista elements would use or lash out at each other, depending on the needs of the moment. As long as Nacionalistas targeted leftists, Radicals, and workers, the administration and most PDN members found it useful and saw little need to interfere with it. Moreover, in this manner Justo mollified Nacionalista sympathizers in the army and other influential circles. Only in instances such as the Martínez de Hoz episode, when Nacionalistas threatened the PDN, or the Guevara killing, when they simply went too far, did moderates attempt to restrain them. The fact that Nacionalistas did not participate in electoral politics, unlike their peers in Chile, facilitated the overlap between moderate and radical rightists and an ambiguous, shifting relationship.

Tensions between rightists and the opposition escalated in 1935. Radicals reentered the political process and mounted fierce campaigns for the November balloting. Unprecedented fraud in Buenos Aires enabled Manuel Fresco to capture the governorship and the Concordancia to maintain its control over this vital province. The UCR candidate Amadeo Sabattini, however, narrowly won the governor's race in Córdoba, where the overconfident Democratic machine had not deemed it necessary to use dishonest methods. Sabattini's success revived popular hopes for democracy, as did the triumph of the Popular Front in Spain and France. Collaboration among Progressive Democrats, Socialists, Radicals, union members, and Communists in early 1936 seemed to herald an alliance of democratic forces similar to the European. Meanwhile, laborers entered a period of mobilization, carrying out 69 strikes in 1935, 109 in 1936, and 82 in 1937, in contrast to 42 in 1934. Horrified by the prospect of a unified and strengthened opposition, rightists of different hues proposed a rival National Front. Independent Socialist and Finance Minister Federico Pinedo penned its manifesto, in which he borrowed from Nacionalismo by denouncing democracy as the leftist, demagogic fruit of the vote of the ignorant masses. Predictably, the manifesto called for electoral changes that seemed likely to perpetuate the regime. Laferrère declared that while Nacionalistas also opposed individualistic democracy, they could not support this effort to prop up Justo's corrupt antinational administration.[70]

Partisan rifts and opportunism within each camp kept both fronts from materializing. Nevertheless, reinforced by the Spanish Civil War, the battle lines between rightists and democrats hardened, and nowhere more so than in Córdoba. There, the PFA had allied with the ANA and LCA to form the Frente de Fuerzas Fascistas de Córdoba in 1935 under Nimio de Anquín, changing its name the following year to the Unión Nacional Fascista (UNF); in this important province the principal Nacionalista groups embraced the fascist label. Once relatively critical of Nacionalismo, Democrats sought means of regaining control, and under these circumstances some of them saw the UNF as an ally.[71]

In his inaugural address, Sabattini pledged to dissolve antidemocratic armed bands. Accordingly, police began to crack down on Nacionalista demonstrations. In mid-August, while Justo was vacationing in Córdoba, a dynamite blast ripped through the doors of the Salesian Colegio Pío X in the provincial capital. Finding an identical explosive in the headquarters of the Fourth Army Division in Córdoba, authorities arrested three Nacionalistas. Observers speculated that Nacionalistas and their Democratic allies were hoping to create a disorderly climate, attract the president's attention, and provoke an intervention. Justo refused to comply, and bombings continued.[72]

In late August, scuffles broke out in the law school as Nacionalistas, including Anquín and former police chief Manuel Villada Achával, tried to force students to sign a statement of support for General Francisco Franco. This turmoil prompted a police crackdown on Nacionalistas. Ironically, Anquín and other UNF leaders complained to the ministers of war and the interior of a lack of constitutional guarantees and of police brutality. They insisted that the local administration was coddling Communists while repressing patriots. The provincial minister of government, Santiago Castillo, initiated a criminal case against UNF authorities for insulting the police.[73] These actions indicated what the Justo government could have done had it been serious about quelling Nacionalismo.

The Democratic bloc in the Chamber of Deputies questioned Castillo on the government's attitudes toward communism and the social order. Castillo and the leader of the UCR deputies, Reginaldo Manubens, responded that the only danger to the social order was the local *fascio*, which Manubens said represented the "disguised Democratic Party." Among the pro-Nacionalista Democrats, he claimed, was their president, José Heriberto Martínez, who had reversed himself. Several Democratic deputies, however, insisted that these persons did not speak for the party, and the Democrats filed out of the Chamber in disgust. Castillo later contrasted the weak communism of a few workers with the fascism brewing "in the petit . . . [and] high bourgeoisie, in capitalism, and in the university." He claimed to have photographs of former provincial bureaucrats and employees and other prominent Democrats taken at Nacionalista functions.[74]

Conflict still raged in the university and the Colegio Montserrat in 1938. Divisions among democratic students enabled the extreme rightist minority, influenced by Anquín and other Nacionalista professors, to win the directorship of the law students' organization. When the Federación Universitaria insisted on voting on whether to accept the new leaders, Nacionalistas charged it with seeking to overturn the election. Angry words led to an exchange of bullets around the voting table, killing two Nacionalistas and wounding others on both sides. One of the slain was Benito de Santiago, a devout and poor young member of Acción Católica, the umbrella association of church lay groups, and a UNF student leader at Montserrat. The other was Dr. Francisco García Montaño, an upper-class lawyer and ANA member.[75]

Authorities never could identify the perpetrators, yet some observers blamed Nacionalistas for provoking the violence, as the episode gave them cause to demand a federal intervention as well as an end to democratic procedures in the university. Not all radical rightists favored national government involvement, however. The Nacionalista organ *Crisol* warned Democrats who wanted to use an intervention to return to power that Nacionalistas had not shed their blood for "political filth."[76]

The incident became a cause célèbre for Nacionalistas around the country. Condolences and statements of solidarity from extreme right-wing groups streamed into UNF headquarters. Santiago's funeral gave them an opportunity to display their feelings. The cortege paraded through the streets, with many youths praying with their rosaries as they marched. The Argentine flag and the Nacionalista banner of a blue cross on a white background—uniting the national colors with a religious symbol—draped the coffin. Thus mourners appropriated religion for their cause and claimed city streets for both. The speakers included *Crisol* editor Enrique Osés, Acción Católica figures, Nacionalistas from other provinces, and Anquín. Osés and Anquín lambasted the bourgeoisie for its complicity and cowardice, but the murderers, according to the UNF *jefe*, were "communism, Judaism, and degenerate Radicalism." To honor the martyr, Anquín asked the mourners to lift their arms in salute while they swore "by God, honor, and the fatherland to return the homicidal bullet." He declared that Nacionalistas were ready for combat, influenced not by hate but by their love of religion and homeland. *Clarinada*, Silveyra's monthly, urged its readers to heed Anquín and pit "Christian violence" against "red violence."[77]

The Alternative to the Left

These Christian references distinguished Nacionalista rationalizations from those of Nacistas, although both movements used violence to demonstrate their radicalism. Other Nacionalistas, however, regarded bloodshed in a manner resembling their Chilean peers. A Liga Republicana and ANA/ ADUNA member of a prominent landowning family, Luis F. Gallardo, declared that to carry out their revolution—which meant replacing "semitic capitalism," politics as usual, and all manifestations of leftism with "nationalist socialism"—Nacionalistas were willing to kill the roughly two thousand leaders of opposing groups. Fascismo Argentino of Córdoba defined its fascism as the "violent restitution of the spiritual." Kinkelín of the LCA agreed with Nacistas that "one does not bring about nationalism only with ideas, or one does this less with ideas than with the club." Feigning moderation, *Crisol* asserted that repeated provocations in the face of official passivity forced citizens to take matters into their own hands. Like Nacistas, however, it defined "provocations" broadly to include insults against Nacionalismo and the military, UCR and socialist activism, and communism in the schools.[78]

Nacionalista rhetoric matched the Nacistas' in savagery. When Senator de la Torre courageously exposed official lies during investigations of the livestock industry in 1935, a gunman killed his friend Enzo Bordabehere in the Senate. Because the murderer was a PDN member and some thought he was also a Nacionalista, many observers blamed the crime on the two groups. The Unión Nacional Corporativa Argentina, however, angrily disassociated Nacionalismo from "political filth," insisting that conservative ruffianism alone was responsible for the slaying. Not that the Unión foreswore bloodshed; if such acts would help free Argentina from liberal sellouts, the Unión would start by assassinating the ministers of agriculture and finance. It warned its enemies that it would avenge their attacks with greater force; "for this we are Creoles."[79] Such intemperance of word and deed and bitterness toward conservatives enabled Nacionalistas, like Nacistas, to portray themselves as radical.

Their uncompromising hatred of leftists also seemed radical. As Osés put it, "The total repudiation of red internationalism is the predominant sentiment . . . in *nacionalismo*," one which he traced back to the LPA. Osés's friend Silveyra, founder of CPACC, emerged as the Nacionalista "expert" on leftism. He underwent numerous lawsuits for spreading his venomous opinions, recruiting for Nacionalista organizations, and persecuting Jewish and dissident students in his secondary school classroom, as well as defaming public figures and inciting violence in his magazine *Clarinada*, which was extreme even by Nacionalista standards.[80]

Silveyra's and other Nacionalistas' loathing for communism knew no limits, although they did not seem to know what it was. They labeled any plea for social justice as communist, except when it came from their lips. Silveyra defined communism as materialism and destruction of the family and of Christian civilization. In his opinion, university reform advocates, Jewish community periodicals, and those who referred to Nacionalistas as fascists and agents of the special section as torturers were Communists. So, too, were youth groups that encouraged comaraderie, for this was but a first step toward sexual relations, so common among Communists. Freedom of meetings was merely a means of permitting communism to spread.[81]

Silveyra not only denounced Communists; his organization and magazine rooted them out. CPACC held street-corner lectures on the evils of communism and encouraged its constituent groups to break up leftist meetings and search leftist centers for subversive literature. Silveyra published information gathered through these surveillance and "counterespionage" activities in *Clarinada* and also traded data with the authorities. Thus he influenced government repression of leftist and democratic groups, and officials used him as a publicity organ for such deeds. The YPF, which his brother headed, and other official agencies such as the Banco de la Nación Argentina, Caja Nacional de Ahorro Postal, Banco Hipotecario Nacional, Junta Nacional de Granos, and Banco Municipal placed advertisements in the periodical, indicating backing from some government quarters.[82]

CPACC helped propel the various attempts to outlaw a very broadly defined notion of communism. Sánchez Sorondo presented this bill after the CPACC demonstration of 1932, but the Senate did not consider it. When he resubmitted it in 1936, the measure passed only the Senate. Not long after assuming the governorship of Buenos Aires in 1936, Fresco issued a decree outlawing communism, a measure that his police used to suppress various opposition groups. Eight other provinces passed similar laws.[83]

Silveyra encouraged the state to adopt further anticommunist measures. To promote contact between the two, he suggested placing children's recreation centers next to military barracks. Military officers, he thought, should secretly monitor library collections. The government should expel all leftists from teaching, control student groups, detach unions from politics, and establish "Argentine syndicates" of employers and workers under the leadership of the native-born. The employer syndicates would "help" their labor counterparts in order to eliminate "red" unions, and the labor syndicates would create "defense groups" against communism—proposals resembling the LPA.[84]

Initially, not all Nacionalistas were as interested in helping workers as Silveyra. The U.S. ambassador may have overstated matters when he claimed in 1937, "Perhaps no country is suffering less from world problems than Argentina," but the Depression had created less hardship there than in the two other nations, and the recovery was quicker and less painful. Under these circumstances it was more difficult—and not only for Nacionalistas—to entertain the notion of state intervention than for Brazilians and Chileans.[85]

In the early 1930s, Manuel Gálvez criticized most of his peers as upper-class reactionaries with little interest in social justice. In contrast, he supported a "practical socialism," one divested of Marxism and class struggle that worked within a context of order and hierarchy. Fascism, which he advocated, was rightist only in its opposition to democracy and revolutionary socialism and in its advocacy of religion; in economic and social matters he claimed it was leftist. Agreeing with Gálvez, the Agrupación de la Juventud Acción Social Nacionalista observed ruefully in 1934 that Nacionalismo had made few inroads among youth because its leaders, backed by the conservative oligarchy, were in the service of capital. It did not occur to them to criticize "egoistic, arbitrary, and absorbent capitalism."[86]

Like Nacistas, some Nacionalistas rebutted this charge. Osés insisted that he and his allies were neither defenders of unjust privileges nor the "police of the possessors before those who do not possess." We love workers and want to help them, unlike their leaders who use them as instruments, he claimed.[87]

As did their Chilean peers, most Nacionalistas eventually favored a strong corporatist state marked by hierarchy and collaboration that would limit economic individualism in the interest of the community. It would also eliminate class warfare, delegating capital-labor disputes to special tribunals. Nacionalistas generally assigned the state the duties of nationalizing credit, helping the unemployed and elderly, and setting a livable wage level, although ANA/Adunista Luis Gallardo wanted to delegate social security and health programs to labor syndicates. Some asserted that all Argentines deserved to own houses, and Gallardo proposed taxing excessive wealth to finance worker housing. Guardia Argentina suggested government-sponsored projects to provide jobs so that, as in Germany and Italy, all would work and no one would go hungry. Nacionalistas agreed on the need to help laborers move into the middle class and widen property distribution. For example, Guido Glave of the Unión Patriótica Argentina suggested expropriating latifundia and redistributing the land to smallholders, providing them with a long-term payment schedule, credit, and technical assistance. Nacionalismo Laborista advocated means of guaranteeing all tenant farmers the right to own the land they cultivated. This group favored taxing unearned incomes, excess profits, inheritances, and money invested abroad.[88] These points formed part of the Nacionalistas' alternative to the left.

Fresco tried to put some of these ideas in practice as governor of Buenos Aires. In 1935 in that province there were 10,385 industrial firms with 128,278 workers; by 1946 there were 23,745 firms and 326,623 workers. These increases, along with the strike wave of 1935–37 and Communist labor activism, raised elite fears about social instability, and Fresco responded to these apprehensions. His aims of helping yet controlling workers resembled those of the LPA to which he had belonged, although he had the additional goal of attracting political support. The governor launched a public works program to increase employment, provide housing and health clinics, and improve infrastructure. Another program distributed land to the rural poor, although not always expeditiously. Fresco reorganized the labor department and gave it more power to regulate capital-labor relations and enforce legislation. He supported the organization of rural workers into "safe" unions, increased their wages, and regulated their working conditions. Under his labor code of 1937, which mandated compulsory arbitration of labor conflicts, the government settled hundreds of disputes, often in favor of unions, including Communist ones. He had less success in compelling unions to register with the government. Fresco extended his unionization efforts toward teachers, forcing them to join his Corporación Nacionalista de Maestros de Provincia. Resembling the LPA's teacher brigades, it upheld "social confraternity" and "Argentinism" against "exotic and disaggregating tendencies." Through another decree of 1937 he, like other extreme rightists, attempted to "nationalize" May Day, which he exhorted workers to celebrate peacefully under the Argentine flag. The governor summarized his program as one of "social pacification."[89]

Fresco also fulfilled other parts of the Nacionalista agenda. These included religious instruction in the public schools and the practice of voting in public, or the *voto cantado*.[90] These measures, the repression and fraud, and his open support of European fascism cut into the popularity he might otherwise have attained through his social programs. Some Nacionalistas scorned him as an officialist politician with ties to foreign railroad companies, while some Conservatives distrusted his authoritarianism and labor policy. More important, he fell prey to the plans of Justo's successor, Roberto Ortiz (1938–40), to clean up the electoral system. Ortiz first weakened Fresco and then removed him from power through an intervention in 1940.

Fresco's ties to foreign capital put him at odds with most Nacionalistas, who, by the late 1930s, made anti-imperialism part of their alternative to the left. Their goals included stimulating locally owned industry through tariff protection and other means. They advocated the creation of a merchant marine to transport Argentine goods, particularly to the South American countries with which Nacionalistas, like Nacistas, were anxious to improve commercial ties. Lugones, the Irazustas, and other Nacionalistas saw the cultivation of economic relations with neighboring countries as a first step toward establishing regional hegemony, which they thought Argentina would have exercised since the early 1800s if not for liberal defeatism. Luis Gallardo urged the state to regulate meatpacking plants and market grains in order to better deal with foreign monopolies. To further aid local producers, he wanted the government to establish agrarian cooperatives and grain elevators.[91]

Economic nationalism involved limiting foreign economic activities. Nacionalismo Argentino proposed that the state take over foreign utility, mining, and transportation companies. Some wanted to abstain from new foreign loans and suspend the foreign debt service. Much like the Brazilian Ação Social Nacionalista, Guardia Argentina wanted to compel foreign companies to employ a certain percentage of Argentines. It also suggested keeping shareholders, lawyers, and anyone employed by or in debt to foreign companies out of government.[92]

Some extreme rightists combined economic nationalism with revolutionary-sounding appeals to laborers. The Federación Obrera Nacionalista Argentina (FONA) advised workers to organize unions not just to demand economic gains but to attack capitalism, and particularly its foreign version, which enslaved both the "proletariat" and Argentina. Workers would enjoy their rights only in an independent nation, so they should strive for the liberation of both. Thus the socialist notion of international labor solidarity was a myth, for the proletarian struggle acquired a "transcendental" revolutionary sense only under the national flag.[93] This formulation, and indeed much of the Nacionalista socioeconomic program, foreshadowed that of Peronism and leftist nationalist groups decades later, although it also harkened back to the LPA's views on the necessary collaboration of labor and capital in underdeveloped countries.

Suspicion of foreign capital led naturally to hostility toward the British. In the opinion of journalist Ramón Doll, newly independent Argentina, populated by a heroic Catholic Spanish-Creole race, had threatened the emerging capitalism of Protestant England. Hence the latter had divided the Platine region and subordinated it to its will, aided by local liberals. As Ernesto Palacio, another member of the Irazusta circle, noted, the Protestant United States had helped the British seize the Malvinas. The foremost symbols of *entreguismo*, the islands had to be retaken. This desire to alter relations with other countries was a prime characteristic of fascism and another part of the Nacionalista alternative to the left.[94]

When Nacionalistas scanned Argentine history, they found that only one leader, Rosas, had challenged the British and other imperialists. But Rosas was attractive to them for other reasons as well. They admired his traditionalism and what they saw as his Catholicism; some, however, may have quietly respected his religious realpolitik, so similar to Maurras's. They applauded the shift from mercantile to landed interests—from the hated financial and commercial capital to the vaunted "productive" capital tied to the soil—that Rosas's rise to power represented. Rosas's huge ranch and the society he dominated embodied the paternalistic social relations that many Nacionalistas wanted to re-create. His love of rural life cemented his ties to Creole Argentina and distanced him from the immigrant Argentina and foreign influences they despised. Rosas's mass support demonstrated to Nacionalistas that a strong antiliberal leader could be popular. Unlike the present rulers who enriched themselves in office, Rosas lost his immense wealth. Nacionalistas had no quarrel with Rosas's suppression of liberals and dissidents, nor with his lack of interest in theories or constitutions. Some saw him as the model for a contemporary dictator, although Julio Irazusta, for one, regarded this notion as anachronistic.[95]

The recognition of Rosas helped revive historical revisionism. The reaction against immigrants and leftism that had fueled the previous wave of revisionism continued, but behind the current wave was a generalized concern over national decline and subservience to foreign countries. Antiliberal influences from Europe also made authoritarian leaders like Rosas more appealing. This revisionist current began with Carlos Ibarguren's timely publication of an admiring biography of Rosas in 1930, based on lectures he had given in 1922, and continued with the Irazustas' book of 1934. That year Rodolfo Irazusta and others formed a committee to seek the return of Rosas's remains from England. Already having begun research on the dictator, in the mid-1930s Julio Irazusta started to give talks on the subject. Fi-

nally in 1938, two revisionist centers arose: the Instituto de Estudios Feder-
alistas in Santa Fe, including José María Rosa (junior), and the better-
known Instituto Juan Manuel de Rosas de Investigaciones Históricas in
Buenos Aires. The Irazustas, Doll, Palacio, Laferrère, and Gálvez—who
would shortly publish his own biography of Rosas—were among the directors of the second Instituto, which has sponsored research, lectures, commemorations, and publications to this day.[96]

Although the Rosistas' authoritarianism did not necessarily sway the
public, some of their other themes did. Many approved of their critique of
the oligarchy, which seemed radical, even though the Irazustas and other revisionists defined it as the standard-bearer of liberalism rather than as a social class. The respect for the masses, not identified with Sarmiento's barbarism; the praise for a leader who stood up to the foreigner; and the condemnation of a "liberal system of *entrega*," in Ricardo Font Ezcurra's words,
appealed to many Argentines. Indeed, many revisionists delighted in knock-
ing down such liberal icons as Sarmiento. They offered something not
found in official histories: an explanation of why Argentina had not assumed its place in the sun, as many would have predicted before 1930—
namely, the machinations of foreigners and their oligarchical allies. These
views struck a chord in the Argentine public, disgusted by the corruption
and fraud of the 1930s, or what Osés called the "clear and continuing treason to the moral and material interests of the fatherland." However reduc-
tionist and conspiratorial, this theory became the most popular ingredient
of the Nacionalistas' alternative radicalism.[97]

The Fuerza de Orientación Radical de la Joven Argentina (FORJA)
joined Nacionalistas in revising historiography. Beginning in 1935, its members studied Argentine economic relations with Great Britain and applied
their insights to attempts to reform the Radical Party. Unlike Rosistas,
FORJA supported popular sovereignty and a self-styled leftist, albeit non-
Marxist, nationalism. That FORJA qualified its nationalism as leftist indicated that radical rightists had already appropriated the title. Yet its condemnation of the liberal elite, class struggle, and communist and socialist
cosmopolitanism resembled rightist nationalism. Indeed, one of its main
figures, Raúl Scalabrini Ortiz, was a close friend and admirer of the Irazustas. José María Rosa (junior) later claimed that FORJA's only quarrel with
Nacionalismo was its dislike of lingering Uriburismo.[98]

Their anti-imperialism notwithstanding, Nacionalistas, like Nacistas,
accepted the core of capitalism and criticized only its trappings. Such formulations drew upon Catholic as well as European fascist doctrine. The

most important Argentine to address this topic was Father Julio Meinvielle, the chaplain of Baluarte and a prolific author. Similar to Brazilian Catholic nationalists and the Nacistas, Meinvielle defined capitalism as an "economic system that seeks the unlimited growth of profit through the application of mechanical economic laws," a definition that did not mention private property. Meinvielle drew some distinctions between liberals, who reserved the profits for the oligarchical few, and Marxists, who reserved profits for the proletariat or the state. Identifying materialism as the essence of capitalism, however, enabled him (and Nacionalismo) to conflate this economic system, liberalism, and Marxism. In capitalism, finance regulated production and production regulated consumption; a Catholic conception of the economy mandated that consumption regulate production. Meinvielle saw nothing wrong with accumulating wealth, as long as the entrepreneur reinvested much of it to provide jobs and products that met human needs. Too often, however, capitalism promoted ruinous competition, which demolished enterprises, employment, and the bonds that united and protected people, leading to extreme inequality.[99] This was the Nacionalistas' justification for claiming that capitalism destroyed families and stability (with which leftists would agree) and even private property (an argument that leftists would see as contradictory).

According to Meinvielle, the products of land and industry were the genuine riches. Sterile and unproductive, money was only an instrument of exchange and possessed no real value in itself. For this reason the church opposed charging interest for loans. Capitalism, however, had implemented this idea, thereby dividing humanity into two classes, oligarchical speculators and impoverished producers. The Irazusta group and other Nacionalistas had adopted this view, which obscured the differences between employers and workers. Citing Werner Sombart, the cleric blamed Jews for usury and all the evil that flowed from it.[100]

Judaism had erred in visualizing the Messiah as an earthly figure who would create a triumphant Jewish empire rather than a kingdom in heaven. Thus Jews had not only committed deicide but carnalized "the divine Promises." Since the Crucifixion, the world had been divided into two: Jewish carnality and greed, and Christian spirituality. All human forces grouped around the first, the side of Satan, or the second, the side of God; those who were not of or for Christ were for the Jews. Thus anything that contradicted or conspired against Christian principles was by definition Jewish, even if the perpetrators were Gentile. This included many disparate forces, for the Jewish hostility to Christianity was "universal, inevitable and terrible."[101]

The cleric's analysis of "Jewish" malevolence followed his inexorable Manichean logic. Since by definition they wanted to destroy the Christian world, they were of necessity responsible for all that befell it. Without directly citing the Talmud, Meinvielle claimed it encouraged Jews to rob and hurt Christians and offer Christian blood as sacrifice. They persecuted the early Christians, enslaved their descendants through usury, and incited all heretical groups. The church kept Jewish malice in check during the Middle Ages by isolating Jews in ghettos—a fate which Jews brought upon themselves by refusing to assimilate, convert, or abjure conspiracies. The Renaissance, Reformation, and Enlightenment all echoed Jewish ideas and benefited the Jews. The French Revolution, which undermined Catholicism and its defender, the monarchy, freed Jews from the church's restrictions to carry on their war against Christianity in earnest. Using liberalism and capitalism, both of which they invented and controlled, Jews robbed from those who had nothing; socialism, another Jewish doctrine, robbed from the wealthy. Thus Jews created class conflict and set Christians against each other. With communism, financed by Jewish gold, Jews would control Christians even more implacably. Finally, Zionism would make Jerusalem the capital of a Jewish-dominated world. Feigning moderation, Meinvielle claimed he did not intend to create a "malignant god" out of Judaism, evasively blaming weak Christians for allowing themselves to be used by Jews. Yet he saw Judaism as the first and primary cause of anti-Christian events.[102]

This Jewish conspiracy resembled the one depicted in the Protocols of the Elders of Zion. Perhaps aware of the fact that courts in several countries had ruled the Protocols to be a forgery, Meinvielle wrote that he did not know if this document was authentic. He added, however, that it undeniably explained all that had happened between Jews and Christians.[103] Nacionalistas would echo his equivocal statement.

Despite their all-encompassing tactics, Meinvielle considered it possible to defeat the Jews. The main means was to unify and strengthen Christianity, but another was to repress Jews with the sword, as in Spain, if necessary. Like Anquín, the cleric believed violence that served the "Truth" was compatible with Christianity. Fascism, he thought, would restore a Christian sense of economy. His aim was a society of small producers based on collaboration rather than avarice, in which the church would regain its supremacy and end usury and Jewish domination.[104]

Most Nacionalista periodicals and groups professed anti-Jewish views, which intersected with issues of critical importance for them. Antisemitism was the central theme of *Clarinada* and of *Crisol*, which called itself the "anti-Jewish newspaper." As was true for Nacistas, antisemitism substituted for a critique of the class system. The fact that some powerful grain exporters were of Jewish origin seemingly reinforced the Nacionalista identification of Jews with imperialism.[105] Unlike their Chilean peers, Nacionalista anti-Jewish attitudes did not wax and wane according to political circumstances. Since the early 1930s, most Nacionalistas have been antisemitic.

Criterio epitomized the convergence between Catholicism and Nacionalismo on Jews, among other issues. It contained a variety of positions on Judaism, all hostile. Manuel Gálvez's articles represented a traditional antisemitic perspective. In 1931 he estimated there were 800,000 Jews in the country, a wildly exaggerated figure many Nacionalistas would cite. As the large size of their community and the small host population would prevent assimilation, he favored restricting Jewish immigration. If the Jews worked hard and did not conspire against the church or the nation (phrasing suggesting he regarded the opposite as a genuine possibility), Gálvez predicted that Argentines would treat them well. The fact that Jews who converted to Catholicism found warm welcome indicated there was no antisemitism, which he seemed to define in racial terms.[106] Many Jews would have disagreed.

Far from Gálvez's inflated statistic, there were only about 191,400 Jews in Argentina in 1930. But as in Chile, the fact that their numbers and mobility were increasing helped explain Nacionalista apprehensions. Despite immigration restrictions partly influenced by antisemitism, thousands of mostly Central European refugees arrived in Argentina during the Nazi era. Some of them, along with earlier arrivals, moved into industry, setting up textile and other tiny factories, while others joined the ranks of small businessmen. Jews also became more conspicuous in professional and intellectual life. There were 254,400 Jews in Argentina in 1940, or about 1.9 percent of the population. Despite these signs of prominence and prosperity, in 1939 most Jews were still in the working class.[107]

Even before this immigration wave and evidence of mobility, Father Gustavo J. Franceschi, Social Catholic activist and editor of *Criterio*, complained of "implacable semitic penetration." In 1933 he claimed not to be a "violent antisemite"; by 1934 he insisted he was not an antisemite at all, for hatred was anti-Christian. While he condemned the German persecution, he believed that Jews must have done something wrong to prompt it; he admitted, however, that Jewish crimes did not merit such a response as the Kristallnacht of 1938. Perhaps a Christian devotion to martyrdom led him to predict that "the best among the Jews will humble themselves and accept this test destined to purify them." Franceschi advised Catholics to pray for Jews but not open the country to them, for he wanted to maintain Argentina's Catholic Latin character.[108]

Kristallnacht provoked little change in the cleric's attitude. Franceschi approvingly cited the young Hitler when he returned from the front and concluded that Jews, "with their poorly groomed beards, their long and dirty coats, their sharp noses and elusive eyes," could not be authentic Germans. Unlike Meinvielle, he did not attribute capitalism and communism to a Jewish conspiracy, yet Franceschi believed that their materialism led Jews to these positions, which hurt Christian society. The problem was that Jews remained Jews, opposed to Christians, who had to defend themselves. Argentines should not imitate Hitler, who had gone to ludicrous extremes. For example, one should confiscate only the property that Jews had acquired improperly, although Franceschi did not suggest taking away the property of unscrupulous Catholics. He emphasized strengthening Christianity, keeping Jews out of government, and converting them.[109]

Father Virgilio Filippo, who would offer masses at Peronist functions and serve as a Peronist deputy, denounced Jews over the airwaves and in such Nacionalista publications as Clarinada. Going further than Franceschi, he, like Meinvielle, warned of a multifaceted Jewish plot. Filippo tied together as Jewish Marx's threat to the social system, Freud's threat to the family and religion, and Einstein's threat to faith and certainty, a formulation repeated by spokesmen for the military dictatorship of 1976–83. He even questioned attempts to assimilate, claiming that Jews who encouraged their children to enter Catholic society simply were undermining it from within. Like Franceschi, Filippo urged closing Argentina's doors to Jews: "Either we control them or they devour us."[110]

The best-known statement of radical rightist antisemitism was the novel El Kahal-Oro (1935). Its author, Gustavo Martínez Zuviría, had served as a PDP national deputy but left the party over its leader's anticlericalism. Now director of the National Library, he regarded the Jews as the "diabolical race" of the Antichrist; like Meinvielle, he teasingly admitted that the Protocols might not be true but that its provisions had been "marvelously fulfilled." Disagreeing with the priest, however, Martínez Zuviría believed that Argentina instead of Jerusalem might be the future capital of a Jewish-dominated world. The truly diabolical plot of El Kahal-Oro outlined how some Jews supposedly planned to bring this about. The author concluded that as two nationalisms could not coexist in the same country, the phrase "Kill the Jew" was interchangeable with "Long live the fatherland."[111]

This popular novel aroused a storm of controversy. The Jewish writer César Tiempo noted that an obscure poet had received a jail sentence for penning a leftist poem, but Martínez Zuviría's "monstrous accusations" and incitement of murder met with official silence, perhaps because he was related by marriage to Minister of Justice Iriondo. Indeed, Ministry of Justice stamps appeared on the advertising for his book. Tiempo and others demanded his dismissal from his government post. The Nacionalista press fit these complaints about a "very patriotic" and "brave" book, as Doll called it, into its framework. In its view the criticism and the refusal of Jewish advertisers to publicize the book only proved the power of the Kahal, the secret Jewish leadership. *Criterio* blamed the detractors for not presenting evidence disproving the author's thesis. It even warned Jews not to complain too loudly, lest their "petulance" bring down "popular hatred" on them.[112]

Usually Nacionalistas were cruder than the clerics. *Crisol* published scurrilous lies in its "Jewish news column," rivaled only by *Clarinada*'s series on "Who is this Jew?" which printed grotesque caricatures of Jews as devils, spiders, and other monsters resembling Nazi cartoons. The LCA journal *Combate* issued the following "commandment": "War against the Jew. Hatred toward the Jew. Death to the Jew." Unión Nacionalista de Estudiantes Secundarios (UNES, the LCA's student branch), Acción Antisemita Argentina, and other groups put up antisemitic posters around the country. One read: "Kill one Jew a day and you will clean our loved fatherland of this sore." Meeting a Jewish request, the Sabattini government forbade the UNF from displaying such posters, but crackdowns were rare.[113]

Unlike in Chile, Nacionalistas took out their rage on flesh-and-blood Jewish prey. They stormed theaters showing Jewish or anti-Nazi films and assaulted those they judged to be Jewish. In August 1934, for example, Laferrère and other Nacionalistas attacked a movie house for showing *The House of the Rothschilds*, which they judged philosemitic. The audience fought back until police arrested the perpetrators. Mostly aristocratic, the ten Nacionalistas quickly obtained their release and paid small fines.[114] Observers charged the police with excessive tolerance or even complicity in such events.

Synagogues also were targets. In March 1934 in Buenos Aires, one of the Congregación Israelita's usual broadcasts of its evening services took place on Good Friday. Two explosions interrupted the radio program and caused a few mild injuries among the congregation of roughly six hundred, who had to leave the building. This time the police arrested five men. Justifying the bombing, *Crisol* complained that it was not enough that the Jews controlled the cereal trade, the universities, the left, and traffic in women; now they had insulted Catholics and abused the nation's hospitality, and Argentines had had to answer them in kind. Nacionalistas vandalized the same synagogue during the Jewish New Year of September 1934.[115]

Nacionalistas and German Nazis collaborated in some actions against Jews and critics of the German regime. One example was the series of attacks on the Teatro Cómico of Buenos Aires for presenting *Las Razas*, a translated version of an anti-Nazi play by Ferdinand Bruckner, a Jewish playwright expelled from Germany. When the German embassy complained about the play, the government ordered the removal of certain scenes. This was insufficient not only for Nazis but for Nacionalistas, who condemned the play for defending the Jews. On December 16, 1934, a large group tried to interrupt the performance. Fighting broke out several times between anti- and pro-Nazis, and the police arrested about fifty of the second contingent. On December 20, police found a youth tossing tear gas into the theater. Finally on January 13, the authorities detained seven Legionarios for carrying incendiary bombs and inflammable liquids into the premises. They in turn implicated other LCA members and Hans Hermann Wilke, a German-born employee of a German bank.[116]

This was one of the few cases of Nacionalista violence that resulted in a trial and sentencing. Defendants Wilke and Florentino Martín Rocha, a former government employee and LCA member, had hired and paid the fifteen Argentines, all lower- and lower-middle-class Legionarios, to attack the Teatro Cómico and other targets. Wilke had belonged to the NSDAP and the LCA, although he insisted he had left both, and he probably was a German agent. The group also confessed to assaulting the anti-Nazi *Argentinisches Tageblatt*, two synagogues, and several Radical and Socialist installations, among other sites. After their appeals ran out in 1937, the Argentines received short sentences and Wilke a somewhat longer one, although Wilke may have escaped to Brazil, perhaps with German assistance.[117]

While Argentines outside the extreme right did not physically attack Jews or engage in radical antisemitic rhetoric, they were not free of prejudice. The elite continued to exclude Jews socially, and even some Socialists and FORJA members displayed insensitivity to Jewish concerns. Perhaps responding to Nacionalista pressures, the government fired Jewish professors, doctors, and other professionals from public institutions in the 1930s. In a clear example of such pressure, José María Rosa of Nacionalismo Laborista urged leaders in San Juan province not to appoint "the Jew Goldstein" as magistrate, but it is not clear whether they heeded his words. Numerous allegations by Sánchez Sorondo and Silveyra, however, led police in 1937 to raid and close eleven Yiddish schools in the city and province of Buenos Aires and arrest twenty-two teachers on charges of communism, although they lacked a judicial order. When they found no evidence, the authorities reopened the schools and freed the teachers. Nacionalista antisemitism may also have influenced the restrictive immigration policy. Yet one must note that, reluctantly or not, Argentina admitted more Jews in the 1930s on a per capita basis than any country but Palestine.[118]

Generally Nacionalistas did not base their antisemitism on biological grounds. As had Nacistas, most rejected German-style racism as materialistic, pagan, and even anti-Catholic; in fact, they accused Jews, with their supposed separatism, of being racists. One exception was *Frente Argentino*, which described Jews as an inferior and useless race and favored its extinction. Similarly, although strictures against immigration and foreigners holding public office abounded in their programs, Nacionalistas rarely criticized immigrants for racial reasons. They extolled the Creole "race," but this was more of a cultural construct than a biological one, consisting largely of Catholicism, martial virtues, and other traits inherited from Spain. Unlike Nacistas, they did not recognize the contributions of people of color to this "race," which they vaguely considered white. Still, in contrast to Sarmiento and other Argentine liberals, Nacionalistas generally did not denigrate the inhabitants of the interior, many of whom had indigenous roots.[119]

By offering antisemitism as a solution to all their problems, Nacionalismo was expanding into the "lowest layers of the population," warned *Mundo Israelita* in 1935.[120] Yet antisemitism was only part of the Nacionalistas' alternative radicalism that accounted for this trend. This radicalism also included hatred of oligarchs and imperialists, the revisionist explanation of Argentine ills, love of the "race," a belief in social justice, a violent sense of masculinity, and opposition to materialism, "nonproducers," and Jews rather than capitalists per se.

As Nacionalista ideology and practice radicalized by the late 1930s, it diverged from the tendencies of national-level conservatives, as represented in the PDN and Concordancia. Few moderate rightists had any use for Rosas, for they traced their liberal ideological lineage back to the dictator's opponents and particularly to the anticlerical Roca. Usually they were unwilling to contemplate replacing parliamentary democracy and liberal freedoms— no matter how incomplete—with the Nacionalistas' ill-defined corporatist system, although some expressed interest in regressive electoral "reforms" likely to benefit themselves. Their elitism led conservatives to be more explicitly racist, although less openly antisemitic, than Nacionalistas. Unlike Nacionalistas, moderate rightists revered ties with Great Britain and assigned priority to meat and grain production, as well as the interests of the rich, whom the Nacionalistas despised. Most looked to trickle-down economics rather than redistribution to help the poor. Yet to counteract the Depression and prevent social conflict, the Concordancia departed from liberalism by stimulating industrialization and regulating capital-labor relations. The conservatives' pragmatism contrasted with the Nacionalistas' rigid principles and conspiratorial notions. This flexibility, however, did not translate into forging a national project to attract the electorate. Reserving power for themselves, maintaining stability, and preserving the alliance of provincial conservative parties were their main goals.[121] Although Fresco, Sánchez Sorondo, and others straddled the two camps, generally conservatives rejected the Nacionalistas' alternative to the left. The mutual opportunism of the first half of the 1930s was punctuated by mutual dislike by the end of the decade.

Paradoxically, there was more ideological overlap within the Chilean than the Argentine right. The Chilean elite and Conservatives had no difficulty accepting the cult of Portales; the Naci view of him drew upon Encina and other establishment historians and in no way questioned the aristocracy's power. The deficiencies of Chile's export economy, the severity of the Depression, and the strength of the left made moderate rightists more willing to consider state interventionism, economic nationalism, and corporatism than their Argentine counterparts, although they were generally liberal. The commonalities were especially marked between Nacismo and the Falange. These shared traits, however, spurred competition and conflict between extremists and moderates, particularly since the former, unlike the Nacionalistas, constituted a political party.

The Popularization of Nacionalismo

In the early 1930s, the LCA and such labor-oriented groups as Fascismo Argentino and the FONA began to use their alternative to the left to attract the public.[122] Such efforts culminated in the Alianza de la Juventud Nacionalista (AJN), a coalition of student groups whose largest component was UNES, the LCA's affiliate. When it arose in 1937, in effect replacing the moribund LCA, the AJN announced its aim of converting to Nacionalismo "thousands of young workers" who might otherwise fall to Marxism. The AJN became the most dynamic radical rightist organization of the late 1930s and early

1940s, attracting between 30,000 and 50,000 adherents throughout the country. The core consisted of energetic men in their early twenties like the former UNES chief Juan Queraltó, but it also included older figures like Ramón Doll and Juan B. Molina.[123]

Like Chilean Nacismo, the AJN repackaged the Nacionalista message into radical, forward-looking rhetoric. AJN members revered the Catholic faith and the values and leaders of the past, but as revolutionaries they envisioned new responses to local problems. They placed themselves against not only Marxism but "liberal, capitalist, and bourgeois society" and the decadent aristocracy. Their "strong and ethical" corporate state would achieve total economic independence, divide latifundia and government lands among the rural poor, provide generous social welfare benefits for workers, and eliminate the agro-trusts and meat export monopolies. Unusual among Nacionalistas, the AJN wanted to make higher education more accessible for those outside the elite. "Neither merchandise nor an insult," labor possessed dignity; it was a right the state should guarantee and a duty all should perform. Against the notion of social classes, the AJN asserted the unity of all Argentines who contributed with their "labor of the brain or of the muscle" to the nation. The AJN flag of a black condor holding a hammer in one talon and a pen in another depicted these bonds; its red and black colors hinted at anarchism (and the Spanish Falange). The condor evoked the German eagle and an image of power. With its wide range in South America, it also suggested interest in enlarging Argentine influence, which the AJN wanted to achieve by recovering the Malvinas and strengthening the military and ties with Ibero-America. More predictably, the AJN regarded the "Jewish problem" as "one of the gravest" in Argentina, and it hoped to end the Jews' "harmful influence in government, the economy, and culture."[124]

The AJN carried its radicalism to the streets and schools. It particularly recruited among the elite and upwardly mobile students who attended Catholic institutions. It also put up posters and gave street-corner talks in mostly working-class neighborhoods. The AJN directed a national billboard and lecture campaign in 1938 against the United States and the upcoming Pan American Union conference in Lima. One poster criticized Yankee imperialism for taking Panama, through U.S. control of the Panama Canal, and half of Mexico, through its victory in the U.S.–Mexico War in 1848; killing the Nicaraguan guerrilla leader Sandino; subjugating the circum-Caribbean region; and promoting U.S. oil companies through the Chaco war (1932–35), a struggle between Bolivia and Paraguay over an oil-rich region. Another described the Good Neighbor Policy as a mask for imperialism, insisting that at the conference the United States would try to en-slave Argentina. Expressed in campaigns, rallies, and fliers, these anti-U.S. sentiments, demands for the Malvinas, and denunciations of official corruption resembled FORJA's views.[125]

Other activities, however, were explicitly antileftist. One was the March of Liberty on May Day 1938, offered as an alternative to the Socialist-CGT festivities. As had the LPA and Fresco, the AJN hoped to nationalize this holiday. Some of the gray-shirted Alianza marchers bore signs declaring, "We fight for the Fatherland, Labor, and Social Justice"; all gave the fascist salute to the applauding crowds. Female sympathizers shouted such refrains as "The Jews and the English are Siamese twins." The march ended at the Plaza San Martín, where Aliancistas commemorated a Nacionalista martyr killed by leftists in 1934, Jacinto Lacebrón Guzmán. Noting that Nacionalismo was no longer the patrimony of a few, President Queraltó of the AJN spoke of lifting the "Argentine laborist conscience." *Crisol* estimated that 30,000 attended this event, which in subsequent years the AJN renamed the "March of Argentine Labor."[126]

Another spectacle designed to appeal to a large audience and offer a contrast with the left was the AJN's torchlight independence parade on July 8, 1938. Intended to dwarf the Federación Universitaria's small torchlight rally of May 25, the event drew between 10,000 and 20,000, according to the Nacionalista press. Uniformed Aliancistas led musical bands, trucks with loudspeakers, and marchers carrying huge posters communicating nationalistic and antisemitic slogans to "comrades" and well-wishers.[127] In the 1940s, the AJN held "Marches of Sovereignty" reclaiming the Malvinas. These parades were the most important Nacionalista attempts to draw a popular audience.

Like other Nacionalistas, the AJN also used violence to attract a diverse following. The press reported the usual skirmishes and mutual provocations between the Alianza and the left, especially at the Universidad de Buenos Aires, but it overlooked many shooting sprees in working-class neighborhoods. The fact that the AJN was more plebeian than other Nacionalista organizations and deliberately challenged laborers in their space may have rendered such encounters particularly bitter.[128]

Gender and Nacionalismo

The AJN shared the youthful masculine style that was the essence of Nacionalismo as well as Chilean Nacismo and European fascism. Nacionalistas expressed a sense of military manliness in their aggression against the left, as well as in their many references to youth, war, and potency in writings and speeches. Fascismo Argentino defined its ideology as the "path and force of youth" and the "virile action" of defending the fatherland. The title of the Nacionalista organ *El Pampero* referred to a Creole breeze that swept across the pampas: not "an old wind / but a young macho wind!" Argentines, who acted like old men, complained Gálvez, had to wake up from their long "siesta." The country needed tough youths, filled with "heroic ardor, impatience, faith, enthusiasm." As if referring to LCA storm troopers, he noted that the "youthful man does not smile: he curses, he screams, he hits."[129]

Nacionalista Santiago Ferla declared that his comrades wanted "a strong, audacious man" and "a delicate, conciliating woman." Like Nacistas, Nacionalistas thought that maintaining these gender distinctions would guarantee the social order, and they consistently affirmed that a woman's place was in the home. They praised Mussolini for curtailing female participation in the labor force and trying to increase the birthrate. But certain dangers undermined this construction of gender and family. According to Osés, liberalism debased men by diminishing their masculinity and vibrancy. Ferla believed that the United States deliberately exported feminism to induce passivity so that men in other countries would not fight imperialism or set up strong military governments. Many Nacionalistas pointed out how capitalism had weakened the home by paying men low wages and pushing women into offices and factories. FONA and other Nacionalistas agreed with Nacistas that socialism threatened the family and customary gender roles, and female "equality" in the Soviet Union destroyed femininity. Likewise, socialist opposition to private property and inheritance could keep fathers from providing for their families.[130]

After women in San Juan province achieved the right to vote in municipal and provincial elections in 1927, Juan Carulla observed that contrary to accepted belief, women were conservative only within their own sphere and could not counter the ill effects of universal suffrage. Outside the home they were more likely than men to fall into moral decay, as they were doing in San Juan by voting for Radicals and attending political events. That women labored inappropriately in factories was bad enough; now "demagogic elections" would take them out of the home altogether. Thus feminism was but one more manifestation of the revolutionary dissolution that threatened the world.[131]

Throughout the 1930s, Nacionalistas continued to challenge feminist concerns. On the extreme was *Bandera Argentina*, which considered the woman's vote an "insanity," and Uriburu, whose interventor in San Juan suspended female suffrage. Seemingly more moderate, Juan P. Ramos of ANA/ADUNA coyly claimed not to oppose female suffrage, for it could never be as bad as male suffrage, but he urged giving priority to other issues such as the economic crisis. Faced with a Nacionalista-influenced climate of hostility, the most prominent feminist organization of the early 1930s, the Asociación Argentina del Sufragio Femenino, asked Congress in 1932 to give the vote only to native Argentine women who were literate, mature, and capable. This coincided with the Nacionalistas' view of the "qualified vote" for men, when they favored any kind of vote at all. But women did not achieve even this limited right, much less suffrage for all females, as advocated by Socialists and feminist groups of the latter half of the decade. President Justo even supported an unsuccessful effort to return married women to their pre-1926 civil status.[132]

Even more than Chilean Nacistas, Nacionalistas excluded women. They opposed female public roles, their publications rarely mentioned women, and their emphasis on violence, heroism, and virility left little room for female participation. So, too, did their relative disinterest in the poor until the late 1930s, except for the LCA. Since women could not vote at any level, unlike in Chile, Nacionalistas had even less reason to mobilize them. At any rate, the difficulty of entering a system of a few well-established parties, along with the prevalent fraud, kept most Nacionalistas from participating in elections. One could argue that their opposition to voting determined this abstention, but the same belief did not prevent Nacistas from fielding candidates when they judged it opportune.

Still, some women tried to break into Nacionalismo. Several thousand marched down the Avenida de Mayo to the presidential palace in support of the coup of 1930 a few days afterwards. The most important manifestation of female Nacionalismo in the early 1930s was the Agrupación Femenina de la LCA, formed in June 1931. Adhering to the revolution, Legionarias promised to inculcate love for the armed forces and respect for order, authority, and hierarchy in the home and school. Through aid to the poor they would help create social peace. They described these tasks as outside the political and military realms, but this disclaimer did not prevent La Prensa from condemning their participation in a partisan militarized organization. For their part, male LCA leaders kept the Agrupación under their control by assigning it a male "technical adviser," Colonel Julio A. López Muñiz.[133]

About 700 women joined the Agrupación, creating branches at least in Buenos Aires and Córdoba. Of a sample of seventy-one Legionarias, 79 percent were upper-class, a higher figure than for male Nacionalistas of the early 1930s. Yet the statistic represented a decline from the nearly 100 percent aristocratic female Liguistas, indicating the widening appeal of radical rightist ideas among women. They set up soup kitchens, housing for the jobless, and centers to teach women crafts that could help them support their families while remaining in their homes. Like those of the LPA, the projects were to promote social harmony and spread bourgeois notions of female roles. Legionarias also held benefits, attended some male gatherings, invited Nacionalista and Catholic men to address them, and hosted tearful remembrances of Uriburu. Occurring in a context of union weakness, their activities received much less publicity than those of LPA women, who were active at the height of labor radicalism.[134]

Women participated in other Nacionalista groups. Fascismo Argentino had *fascios femeninos* that served as auxiliaries to the male *fascios*. The Asociación de Damas Argentinas "Hogar y Patria," an upper-class organization independent of men, was formed in Buenos Aires in June 1932, a month before CPACC, to fight communism and dissolvent ideas; in line with these views, it explicitly opposed female suffrage. It, too, celebrated September 6, the date of the 1930 coup, and other events in the Nacionalista calendar and set up at least one school that taught vocational and homemaking skills to women. The Damas also helped sponsor the ANA's radio talks on Nacionalista topics.[135]

Isabel Giménez Bustamante, a member of an upper-class family and, eventually, of the female branch of the Asociación Nacionalista de Estudiantes Secundarios, challenged some of the Damas' views on ANA radio in 1932. Praising women for their efforts in the home, work, education, and politics, including, ironically, female opposition to the "tyrant" Rosas, Giménez added that with the vote, women would be the main guarantee of stability in Argentine society. Agreeing with the Asociación Argentina del Sufragio Femenino, Giménez advised Congress to award suffrage only to the literate Argentine-born woman, who wanted to "elect her rulers, conserve her religion, defend her home, educate her children." In contrast, naturalized citizens, who included Communists, had brought the old hatreds of Europe with them. Although antileftist, this address demonstrated that female Nacionalistas held a variety of opinions.[136]

Young women, probably mostly upper-class, continued to join Nacionalismo. They formed such groups as the Comisión de Damas de la Junta de Recuperación de las Malvinas in 1939 and the Comisión Femenina Pro Homenaje a los Héroes de la Reconquista de Buenos Aires in 1940. The

latter celebrated the Argentine overthrow of the British in 1806, which resonated deeply among Nacionalistas. According to Marysa Navarro, the AJN
included 3,000 women by the early 1940s, although the Nacionalista press
largely ignored them.[137]

Señorita María Esther Méndez of the Unión Nacionalista Santafesina
exemplified Nacionalista women's concerns. Addressing her female "comrades" in Rosario in 1941, she noted that theirs was not a group of "niñas
bien" who had teas and were mentioned in the social pages; if this were our
goal, "we would not be nacionalistas." Instead, they helped male Nacionalistas working to create a "free fatherland, without Yankee ideas, without Jews
or politicians," and to halt the Soviet tide, which victimized women by removing them from the home. She contrasted her comrades, who collected
clothing and goods for underprivileged Argentines, with the upper-class
Junta de Damas de la Victoria, which sent the proceeds of its charitable
works to the Allies. On one side were the humble girls of the Unión, with
their faith in God and nationalism, who helped the people of their own
country. On the other were "old grotesque figures, Jews, Communists, who,
to kill their unhealthy idleness, meet for a 'cocktail' or 'bridge' to send aid to
the Russians." The speech contained the typical Nacionalista blend of traditional and radical rhetoric. Certainly Méndez did not mince words about
Jews and oligarchs.[138]

A photograph of female Unión members depicted young women
dressed in full white aprons. Like the male uniform, the apron concealed
distinctions in dress and the appearance of wealth. It symbolized their willingness to work for the nation and made them seem to be laborers, if not of
the mind or muscle, then of the hearth. It also recalled the smocks that female teachers and pupils had worn in public schools since the late 1800s,
and thus tied women to customary roles in education. Furthermore, the
color white evoked female purity.[139] Accordingly, Nacionalista women appeared more conventional than the uniform-clad female Nacistas. They
made even less impact than their Chilean peers on a movement that prided
itself on its virile revolutionary character.

The Nacionalista Base Among Civilians and Officers

Nacionalistas had widened their following in terms of class if not so much
gender. In 1939 the U.S. military attaché described the men among them as
mostly "sons of moderately rich parents, students, conservatives, and men
of the middle class who wish to secure for themselves government jobs." My

study of 174 men who figured among the adherents to the neutralist Frente Patriótico of 1941, which drew from many Nacionalista groups, confirms their lack of prominence. No information was available for 59 percent of the sample. Only 25 percent belonged to the upper class and 21 percent owned land or were of landed families, compared with 61 percent and 53 percent, respectively, of the earlier Nacionalista sample. A healthy sprinkling of Italian names appeared in the list of 1941, suggesting that Nacionalistas were recruiting the descendants of immigrants. Nacionalismo was no longer a tightly knit family grouping, for the percentage of those related to others in the survey declined from 35 to 14 percent. That 19 percent were related to members of the earlier sample or were in it, however, indicates continuity in the ranks. The Frente Patriótico did not seem to include AJN members; if it had, the results might have been even more plebeian.[140]

It is difficult to estimate the total number of Nacionalistas, for many belonged to several groups, some belonged to no groups, and the groups rarely supplied credible membership statistics. In 1933 the German embassy calculated that there were roughly 100,000 Nacionalistas; a U.S. official in 1940 estimated 300,000. Even allowing for exaggeration, these estimates—which centered on Buenos Aires—suggested that Nacionalismo had grown.[141]

It also had spread in the military, facilitated by the overlap between Nacionalista and military values. The former's exaltation of hierarchy, discipline, and duty resembled military beliefs; indeed, Nacionalista paramilitary groups patterned themselves on the armed forces. In lectures and writings specifically directed to officers, Nacionalistas praised the military and advised enlarging its role and budget. For their part, military men increasingly disdained corrupt civilian rule and published Nacionalista-influenced articles in military journals.[142]

Nacionalistas tried to convince officers to take up the mission that Uriburu had left unfulfilled: to overthrow the government and establish a truly antiliberal state. In a pamphlet distributed to the military in July 1936, ANA/Adunista Luis Gallardo praised the values that set the military apart from—and above—liberal democracy, noting that the soldier was "subject to moral principles superior to any law." To forestall imperialism or communism, the military should create a new regime governed by Christian nationalist ideals. Insisting that the military order was the highest expression of citizenship, Nacionalista professor Jordán Bruno Genta sought to convince army officers to carry out this extreme right-wing mission. He continued to lecture the military on this duty until the 1970s.[143]

To reinforce these messages, Nacionalistas secretly circulated fliers within the army and navy urging a coup. A notice of June 1936 warned that legal measures alone could not keep Radicals out of power. Once there, Radicals would create such chaos, as they were doing in Córdoba, that communism would inevitably follow. Only the armed forces could prevent this debacle.[144]

Military personnel joined and plotted with Nacionalistas. Retired and active officers belonged to the LCA, AJN, and other groups. Uriburu's war minister, General Francisco Medina, and Admiral Carlos Daireaux were leaders of the ANA, and three retired, high-ranking army officers headed Defensa Social Argentina, which claimed over 10,000 reservists. An LPA supporter in 1919 and fervent Uriburista, General Francisco Fasola Castaño, formed the less important Concentración Popular Argentina after Justo expelled him from the military for publicly criticizing him. Admiral Abel Renard and Generals Fasola Castaño, Benjamín Menéndez, Nicolás Accame, Emilio Kinkelín, and Juan B. Molina, among other officers, conspired with Nacionalistas.[145]

Molina was a perennial conspirator. Justo sent him to Germany in 1933 as military attaché in order to pry him away from the LCA and frequently assigned him to Europe in the following years. There his admiration for Hitler and all things German increased. When he returned to Argentina in 1936, he headed a Nacionalista plot to overthrow Justo, but the president outwitted Molina and transferred him and his subordinates before the planned date of the rebellion. Instead of punishing Molina, the president promoted him to brigadier general and in 1937 permitted his election as president of the Círculo Militar.[146]

Whatever the president's motives, by not directly confronting Molina and other Nacionalista officers, he ceded them ideological control over the military and isolated his own supporters. Justo left it to his successor to check Molina, which Ortiz did by removing him from his post as director general of the army engineers in July 1938. Six months later Molina retired, but he continued to plot against civilian rule, now as leader of the AJN. Ortiz also transferred other Nacionalistas and appointed moderates to command. Still, Nacionalista influence grew within the military, as the revolution of 1943 would demonstrate.[147]

The Church and Nacionalismo

Another critical sector tied to Nacionalismo was the church. The overlap was so marked that it was unclear which way the influence went; Nacionalistas adopted Catholic views and many prominent clerics and laypersons approximated Nacionalista positions. Nacionalista periodicals published articles by Meinvielle, Filippo, and other priests, while the writings of Rodolfo Irazusta, Doll, Gálvez, and the Italian Fascist Gino Arias, much admired by Nacionalistas, appeared in *Criterio*. Several generations of Nacionalistas received training in Catholic thought in the Cursos de Cultura Católica in the 1920s and 1930s. The magazines *Baluarte* (1932–4) and *Sol y Luna* (1938–43) and such individuals as Martínez Zuviría, Anquín, César Pico, and Alberto Ezcurra Medrano combined Catholicism and Nacionalismo in a way few Nacistas duplicated. Although Nacionalistas celebrated their own calendar and cult of martyrs, they did not erect a substitute religion like their Chilean peers; allied with the church, they did not need one. The only Nacionalista who was openly anticlerical was Lugones, and he may have been reconsidering his stance before he committed suicide in 1938.[148]

The very upper-class Restauración, founded in 1936, epitomized Catholic Nacionalismo. Heavily influenced by the Spanish Civil War and the Spanish Falange, Restauración inserted "With the cross converted to sword, we will restore the national faith" into its anthem. Its leaders, who had participated in the Cursos, aimed at furnishing Nacionalismo with a spiritual base. To the usual Nacionalista platform, Restauración added a greater emphasis than other groups on church aspirations for control over its own sphere of activity, more say in family and educational matters, and a Catholic-inspired economy.[149]

The Eucharistic Congress in Buenos Aires in October 1934 inspired Nacionalistas and other Argentines to move in a more Catholic direction. Over a million received Communion and many returned to the fold, while others felt their faith strengthened. Young Nacionalistas helped organize the congress, formed contacts with priests and Catholic groups, and grasped the church's ability to unite Argentines of diverse backgrounds. The Vatican envoy to the congress, Bishop Roberto Tofanelli of Luca, reinforced this message when he spoke at LCA headquarters on how Catholicism and Fascism, joined in a common struggle, were restoring Italian greatness. The congress also showed the increasing power of the church, not only among the hitherto skeptical elite but in government. Justo's support and attendance signaled his desire to gain church backing.[150]

There was other evidence of the church's growing standing. The number of parishes in the capital rose from 39 in 1929 to 105 ten years later. Created in 1928 to coordinate all lay activities, Acción Católica boasted of 80,000 members in 1940 and many more sympathizers. Some of these adherents were cadets and officers, recruited in military schools. Indeed, clerics such as Monsignor Dionisio Napal, a former LPA member and general vicariate of the army, tightened relations between these two influential elites; they saw the military as a preferred vehicle for attaining a Catholic-influenced state. This organizational base enabled the church to lobby effectively for its goals, as seen in the defeat of the divorce bill in the Senate and Fresco's authorization of religious instruction in provincial schools.[151]

The church assigned greater priority to its educational and family agenda than to rightist politics per se, although its admonitions against voting for anticlerical parties hurt the Socialists and the PDP. Thus, Nacionalismo and the church were not one and the same. Miguel de Andrea, for example, opposed Nacionalismo and some aspects of the Concordancia. Criticizing electoral fraud and governments of force, the bishop of Temnos denounced attempts to transplant fascism to Argentine soil and suppress freedom. He saw reforming men through Christianity rather than reforming the constitution as the vital task. Hardly a progressive, however, de Andrea lambasted the left and universal suffrage, calling for a corporatist state whose adherence to democracy was dubious. Nevertheless, his brand of elitist liberalism was not the predominant sentiment within the hierarchy or Acción Católica.[152]

The majority sided with Franceschi. He noted that Catholics supported the family, religion, private property, and the fatherland, not in their present form but as they should be. Unlike liberals—the true conservatives who wanted things to remain the same—Franceschi and other Catholics opposed the current order in favor of an "integral" restoration of Christian life.[153]

Although Franceschi's position resembled the Nacionalista one, he and Meinvielle had some concerns about the movement. They were suspicious of its predilection for autocracy and for figures like Maurras and Rosas, who saw religion as the handmaiden of government. They feared that Nacionalistas might convert the state into an autonomous power, an ultimate end, or even a divinity, thus repeating and even magnifying the errors of liberalism, which had glorified individuals and disconnected them from society. Franceschi and other clerical sympathizers hoped to prod Nacionalistas in a Catholic direction.[154]

Alberto Ezcurra Medrano tried to reassure them. In his view the church represented divine truth; nationalism was partial and human but still a truth. Nacionalismo must be Catholic and naturally tended toward it, while the church was indifferent to political forms and should not be Nacionalista. Admitting that there were good and bad nationalisms, Ezcurra Medrano put Nazism, which placed the state over God, in the second category, but he claimed that all liberalisms and socialisms were bad. With their Christian inspiration, Franco, Dollfuss, and Oliveira Salazar would be better models for the Argentine movement than Hitler. Yet the Italian rapprochement with the church demonstrated that fascism could evolve into a Christian nationalism.[155]

Catholic spokespersons were ambivalent about fascism before World War II. They criticized fascist statism, Nazi anti-intellectualism and social Darwinism, and Hitler's conflict with the church. At the same time, they applauded aspects of Italian Fascism and Nazism, such as their economic policies and corporatism.[156]

Meinvielle eventually leaned toward approval. Initially critical of fascism, by 1937 he had decided that the Italian type, which he did not define as totalitarian, was moving from paganism toward Catholicism and had performed some worthy tasks. Fascist violence was necessary to defeat communism, and it could help prepare a new generation for the final battle between Christian and anti-Christian forces. Indeed, the fascist countries were already doing so by helping Spain return to Christian ways. Strongly affected by the Spanish Civil War, as were other Argentine Catholics, Meinvielle exalted the Spanish Nationalists' purifying war under the Cross. The cleric was much more critical of pagan Nazism, but even it fit within his apocalyptic version of history. Once World War II began, Meinvielle predicted that the Axis would fulfill a Catholic mission by destroying a skeptical France and weakening a Protestant England. Then the other world powers would defeat a satanic Germany, enabling it to convert and lead other nations along a similar path.[157]

In an article published in Argentina, the influential French cleric Jacques Maritain rejected fascism. Contrasting with the radical right's third way between liberalism and communism, his "integral Christian humanism" was a third way between the extremes of right and left. Maritain opposed Catholic alliances with fascists to defeat the left, the imposition of an ideology through civil war, and the savagery of both sides in Spain.[158]

Disagreeing with Maritain, César Pico regarded Catholic participation in "strong movements of reaction . . . against the revolutionary current," including fascism, as legitimate and expedient. The upper-class Cursos leader and *LNR* contributor called for the destruction of all the principles underpinning communism, which he traced back to the Renaissance. This exhaustive struggle justified Catholic collaboration with—though not commitment to—fascism. Pico made light of fascist totalitarianism, Machiavellianism, and voluntarism, characteristics that Maritain had criticized, and he related fascist views of human nature to the Catholic notion of original sin. In his opinion, Catholics could accept the bolstering of the state up to a certain point, as long as it did not hurt the church. They could not, however, accept German paganism, or religion as the state's tool, although Pico, emphasizing the Italian case, thought the latter improbable. Maritain feared that by tying religion to oppression, fascism, as in Spain, would drive the people from the church. To this Pico asked if it was better to allow a leftist victory or simply to tell Catholics to take refuge in their religion. He insisted, without evidence, that workers in fascist countries supported the regimes. Catholic participation might also move fascism toward Catholic regimes combining authority, corporatism, social justice, and traditional law. Pico even thought that Maritain's third force could be a "Christianized fascism."[159] It was unlikely that Maritain would have agreed.

Fascism and Nacionalismo

Other Nacionalistas were more reluctant to admit collaboration with or ties to fascism. Carlos Silveyra complained that opponents tried to rob Nacionalismo of legitimacy by labeling anyone opposed to liberal democracy as fascist: "We are not fascists, because we are not Italian; nor are we National Socialists, because we are not German, nor Falangists, because we are not Spanish. We are Argentines, patriots." He conceded, however, that Nacionalistas admired these other groups, as was apparent in the Nacionalista press and other writings.[160]

Here and elsewhere Nacionalistas narrowly interpreted fascism and National Socialism as movements specific to Italy and Germany, respectively. They did this partly to dispel the simplistic notion, spread by various antiracist groups, a congressional committee investigating anti-Argentine activities, and later the Allies, that Nacionalismo was a Nazi or Fascist creation. Even in this limited sense, however, there were links between Europe and Nacionalismo, spotlighted by the expression *nazionalismo con zeta*, such as the Fascist-Nacionalista alliance in Córdoba and Nazi involvement in the Teatro Cómico bombing.[161]

These linkages were one matter; whether Nacionalismo was fascist was another. Federico Ibarguren insisted that his comrades were "Lugonians" rather than fascists. The origins of fascism, he wrote, lay in nineteenth-century socialism, whereas he traced Nacionalismo back to Catholicism and the Hispanic cult of personality. Ibarguren ignored the fact that of all Nacionalistas, Lugones most closely approximated the Nazi paganist, Ceasarist, social Darwinist model. He also overlooked how Catholics like Anquín, Meinvielle, and Pico championed fascism, and how the European right had contributed to it. A Cursos and Baluarte participant, Mario Amadeo, assigned greater importance to the Argentine elements in Nacionalismo, such as the defense of national sovereignty, historical revisionism, and economic nationalism, than to those of foreign inspiration, such as the uniforms and salutes. Amadeo did not recognize that the first and third of these "Argentine" traits were vital to fascism everywhere.[162]

Bandera Argentina believed that Nacionalistas had imitated fascism to their detriment. It observed that the movement upheld the notions of fatherland, economic nationalism, and an order based on authority, discipline, and force; it also denigrated liberal democracy, bourgeois parliamentarianism, and Marxism. Simple reflections of universal fascism, these ideas were insufficient to create a national movement.[163] At the time of this writing, historical revisionism and the AJN, the most popular manifestations of Nacionalismo, had not yet crystallized. Nor was it evident that the traits mentioned were necessarily foreign in origin. But the editorialist situated Nacionalismo within fascism, although he thought that it had not adapted itself successfully to local conditions.

Historians have reached different conclusions on Nacionalismo. Marysa Navarro regards Nacionalistas as too Catholic and insufficiently violent to be fascists; my descriptions of street fighting should dispel the second point. David Rock considers them too clerical and elitist to fit this designation, and taking his cue from Nazi and Fascist diplomats, Ronald Newton sees them as too antipopulist. While Navarro, Rock, and Newton judge Nacionalismo according to one or two isolated traits, comparing it point by point with European movements, Cristián Buchrucker and Alberto Spektorowski conclude it was fascist. Mario Nascimbene and Mauricio Neuman disagree with Buchrucker and Spektorowski, but they eliminate the LCA, AJN, and the most radical Nacionalista leaders from their considerations.[164]

I would argue that by the late 1930s, at least those Nacionalistas of the LCA-UNES-AJN, FONA, *Crisol,* and *Clarinada* strains fit Nolte's definition of fascism as a movement trying to subdue the left and attract a broad following through radical means. The Nacionalistas' radical alternative to leftism consisted of historical revisionism, social justice, anti-imperialism, antisemitism, the cult of virility, and criticism of the oligarchy. Meeting Payne's criteria, they also used ceremonies, the "myth of September" and other symbolic elements, and a militarized political style to mobilize support, although they did not go as far in this regard as the Nacistas did. Nevertheless, Argentine extreme rightists made the issue of economic nationalism their own, in contrast to the Chileans. The fact that most Nacionalistas came from outside the elite by the end of the 1930s attests to their success in popularizing the movement. Only the Catholic influence on its notion of an idealistic and spiritual new culture distinguishes Nacionalismo from Payne's view of fascism—and from Nacismo. However, the many pious Italian Fascists, the very Catholic Belgian Christus Rex, the devoutly Orthodox Romanian Iron Guard, and clerical participation in the Croatian Ustasha show that fascism, particularly outside Germany, could absorb Catholics and Christians.[165]

Comparison with Payne's typology demonstrates not only Nacionalismo's largely fascist character but also its failures. According to one of his criteria, Nacionalistas emphasized an "authoritarian, charismatic, personal style of command."[166] They may have wanted a führer, but never found one. General Uriburu had alienated some Nacionalistas even before death removed him from the scene. Officialism and fraud tainted Fresco and Sánchez Sorondo, and Molina was shadowy and frequently absent from the country. Osés was too much of an ugly rabble-rouser, and Lugones lacked charisma and political skills. For better or for worse, González von Marées united Chilean Nacistas, but Argentines had no comparable figure.

The lack of leadership was related to the divisions in the movement. The 1930s—and later years—witnessed the rise of many extreme rightist groups that experienced difficulties in uniting.[167] The diversity within the movement, however, also widened its appeal and thus was a strength as well as a weakness.

As Julio Irazusta later observed, another problem was that Nacionalismo "did not surge from below, from the people, but from above, from officialism." The Irazusta brothers and Carulla also blamed Nacionalistas for fomenting coups rather than mobilizing wide support. Partly thanks to the efforts of first the LCA and later the AJN, the Nacionalista constituency broadened over time, but it did not include large numbers of poor people or women. Nacismo had fewer members, even as a percentage of the population, but a higher proportion of workers. The fact that Nacionalistas did not exercise great mass appeal did not set them apart from most fascist movements, but it was a shortcoming.[168]

Yet Nacionalista ties to important elites were also an asset in an increasingly authoritarian country. Nacionalistas made many friends among priests, whose influence grew in the 1930s, and officers, the most prominent political actors in Argentina. Links to the armed forces and members of the ruling coalition helped Nacionalistas acquire government resources and avoid persecution. Although their relations with moderate rightists in and out of government at times were acrimonious, the fact that extremists did not have their own party, unlike in Chile, permitted some cooperation. Through Uriburu, Fresco, Martínez de Hoz, and the Ibarguren intervention, Nacionalismo attained public office and helped frame policy. Nacionalistas were latecomers to the political scene, but the moral and intellectual bankruptcy of the PDN and Concordancia left them a larger space in which to operate than the Nacistas occupied. These factors, along with the widespread perception of Argentine decline, would enable Nacionalismo to exert power through the military coup of 1943 and influence politics for years to come.

CHAPTER 11

Brazil: A Revolution of the Heart and Soul

In the 1930s, Brazil contained the single largest radical rightist group in the ABC nations, in terms of numbers if not percentage of the population. Ação Integralista Brasileira (AIB) drew upon themes of earlier rightist groups and their ties to elites. More than in Argentina and Chile, its belief in order, nationalism, and a consistent ideology resonated in a country afflicted with regionalism, conflict, and personalist rule. Ironically, the AIB moved into the relatively empty space of mass politics, becoming the first nonproscribed national and popular party in Brazil. Adding to its following, it mobilized women more effectively than its Argentine and Chilean peers. Yet this broad support proved insufficient to assume control in a country where moderate rightists held sway over the state and national governments and, in the end, won the backing of the military and the church. While using the AIB for its own purposes, by the late 1930s the state had destroyed the once-powerful movement.

The Revolution of 1930 and the Rise of the AIB

The AIB evolved within the context of economic crisis and political uncertainty. Even before 1929, the overproduction of coffee spelled high valorization expenses, which the government financed through mounting foreign loans. With the world crash, coffee prices fell sharply, as did the nation's gold reserves. In 1931–32, imports dropped to a third of their value in 1928, and exports to one half.[1] Extremely dependent on a single export commod-

248

ity, Brazil was more severely affected by the Great Depression than Argentina although less than Chile. The economic situation weakened the legitimacy and power of the oligarchies that had ruled the Old Republic.

This debilitation manifested itself in the crisis surrounding the election of 1930. The outgoing president, Washington Luís, chose another Paulista, Júlio Prestes, as his successor. Accustomed to sharing power with São Paulo, the elite of Minas Gerais felt slighted, and those of the other states did not want yet another Paulista as president. Prestes's opponents created the Liberal Alliance, which also attracted Tenentes (junior officers) and other reformers. It nominated Governor Getúlio Vargas of Rio Grande do Sul for president and João Pessôa of northeastern Paraíba state for vice president. Predictably, Prestes won the election, but when a gunman assassinated Pessôa soon thereafter, the Liberal Alliance, probably inaccurately, blamed his death on the government and rose up against it. To prevent civil strife, the military deposed Luís and handed the presidency to Vargas in October 1930.

The revolution provided an opening for new political groups. Many applauded the break with the past; Brazil could not return to the discredited political structures of the Old Republic. There was a sense that reformers were starting over from scratch, and in the turmoil of the early 1930s the direction of change was as yet unclear. In this context extreme rightists found room to formulate a project and aspire to leadership.

Several factors lent weight to their endeavor. One was the widespread revulsion against liberal democracy and economics, which many intellectuals identified with the overthrown regime, although it had hardly encouraged mass participation. Regional divisions and the lack of programmatic parties lent cogency to pleas for authority, unity, and discipline. The dispersal of labor in the coffee export sector, coffee workers' access to land, the small size of the urban proletariat, and official repression had tended to inhibit leftist organizations. Demonstrating little awareness of the realities of life for the poor, voices of the middle sectors leaned toward authoritarianism. Even some reformers whom historians have placed on the left mixed progressivism with elitist and corporatist precepts.[2] Thus the main beneficiary of the antiliberal reaction would be the right.

The Vargas administration in Rio Grande do Sul between 1928 and 1930 offered a model of rightist reform. Aided by his interior secretary, Oswaldo Aranha, the governor tightened official control over the state. Rejecting economic liberalism, the administration organized producer cartels and cooperatives and mediated among them. Vargas spoke of the need to structure society through groups based on class and economic activity, citing such influences as Benito Mussolini and author Oliveira Viana. He also drew upon the positivist legacy left by his predecessors, characterized by a centralizing executive, a weakened legislature, and a concern for workers and "progress."[3]

Vargas's ideas resembled those of the Tenentes, his allies in the revolution, who continued to manifest economic nationalism and disdain for politics as usual through the Clube 3 de Outubro and the Legiões Revolucionárias that arose in São Paulo, Minas Gerais, and Rio de Janeiro. Aranha, who helped lead the revolution and became minister of justice, promoted this organizational effort to lend support and ideological coherence to the provisional government. Common to the various legions was a desire for strong central government, corporatist representation, and a political structure that reflected Brazilian reality, notions dating back to Alberto Torres. The Legiões and Clube also wanted the government to eliminate latifundia and harmonize workers and employers. Despite their supposed hostility to foreign models, these groups were influenced by Italian Fascism. This was particularly true of the uniformed Minas legion, led by Francisco Campos, state education minister and former member of the rightist Academia Brasileira de Ciências Econômicas, Políticas, e Sociais.[4]

Other groups were more clearly rightist. The tiny Ação Imperial Patrianovista Brasileira or Pátria Nova (1928) aimed to reinstate the monarchy, but the new empire, unlike the old, would be staunchly Catholic, corporatist, and antiliberal. Embracing the statism that the devout Pátria Nova spurned, Ação Social Brasileira (ASB, 1930) intended to convert itself into a fascist party, but journalist Osorio Borba noted that the "butterfly" that emerged from the ASB "larvae . . . died before flying."[5]

Some nationalist precursors hatched short-lived butterflies. *Brazílea* reappeared in 1931 but faded in 1933. The Academia de Ciências Econômicas, Políticas e Sociais briefly revived in Minas Gerais in 1932 as the Social Nationalist Party, headed by former president Artur Bernardes. Of greater importance was the Sociedade dos Amigos de Alberto Torres, which arose in Rio de Janeiro in 1932. Among its founders were Oliveira Viana, the rightist author Plínio Salgado, and Belisário Penna, formerly of the Liga da Defesa Nacional. Strongly linked to government circles, the Sociedade analyzed national issues along Torres's lines. It also lobbied policymakers to restrict the immigration of Japanese, Jews, and other groups it disliked.[6]

Olbiano de Melo's fascist party did not even reach the larvae stage. A member of the elite of Minas Gerais and formerly of its ruling party, Melo concluded that liberal democracy was outmoded. To influence the as-yet-directionless revolution, he wrote a series of books proposing a Brazilian fascist state and a National Syndicalist party, which never came into being.[7]

The only kindred movement attracting popular support was the Legião Cearense do Trabalho (LCT). Severino Sombra, its founder, was an army lieutenant and disciple of Jackson de Figueiredo. Imprisoned for not participating in the revolution, which he initially condemned as liberal, Sombra, like Melo, came to realize that the new regime lacked content. He hoped to influence it by organizing a labor movement in Ceará, an impoverished northeastern rural state with few unions. In August 1931, he officially launched the LCT, which united existing mutual aid societies and Catholic worker groups, one of them led by the newly ordained priest Hélder Câmara. About 15,000 joined the LCT. Like Social Catholicism, its aim was a corporatist state that redistributed income and celebrated authority, family, and religion. The LCT's martial-sounding title, uniforms, and hierarchical structure, however, suggested fascist influence.[8]

Meanwhile profascist intellectual groups were coalescing in Rio de Janeiro and São Paulo. Law students of this persuasion in Rio formed the Centro Acadêmico de Estudos Jurídicos (Caju) in 1930, and affiliates sprang up in other states. Caju, Patrianovista, and other rightist authors congregated around the journal *Hierarchia*, inspired by the Fascist periodical of the same title. Caju and *Hierarchia* admired the Italian regime, although Fascist conflicts with the church perturbed some of the young thinkers.[9]

A contributor to *Hierarchia*, Plínio Salgado, was the leading rightist literary figure. His nationalism had led him to the works of Torres, Euclides da Cunha, and Oliveira Viana. Moving from Verdeamarelismo, in 1927 he helped found another nationalist literary movement, the Revolução de Anta, which praised Indians and *caboclos* and decried European racism. At the same time, Salgado warned that Brazilians would not uphold their status as a masculine people if they did not strengthen the nationality.[10]

Salgado traveled in Europe, meeting Mussolini in Italy, and returned to Brazil an admirer of fascism. A member of the ruling party of São Paulo, he supported the Prestes candidacy. Like Melo and Sombra, however, he came to see the revolution as malleable. Salgado adhered to the Legião Revolucionária de São Paulo, through which he intended to disseminate his authoritarian ideas. Oswaldo Aranha invited Salgado, along with Aranha's cousin, Alfredo Egídio de Sousa Aranha, publisher Augusto Frederico Schmidt, Minas legion leader Francisco Campos, and San Tiago Dantas and other Caju members to his house to discuss fascism, the legions, and the revolution. Here Salgado made contact with future Integralistas. Sal-

gado had written a statement in Europe melding the major features of
Tenentismo with *brasilidade*, which he published as the manifesto of the
São Paulo legion of March 1931. *Brazílea* proudly linked Salgado's document to the nationalist doctrine it had pioneered, referring to its own writers as "the first legionnaires." Containing diverse views, the legion, however,
gave the statement little support. Suspicious of the revolution, Salgado and
other future Integralistas broke away from Aranha's project and the col-
lapsing legions.[11]

In February 1931, Salgado wrote Schmidt of the need for a radical nationalist newspaper that would coordinate common points of conservative
thought. He used *conservative* for the lack of another word, for he did not
want to conserve liberal democracy and he considered himself revolutionary. This paper would be *A Razão*, founded in São Paulo in June 1931 by
Sousa Aranha, who had also financed Salgado's trip to Europe. Edited by
Salgado and Dantas, *A Razão* referred frequently and admiringly to Oliveira
Salazar, Mussolini, and Hitler. Yet Salgado advised Brazilians to adapt fascism to local conditions, using Torres as a model. The newspaper staff also
understood that its desired revolution would fail if it excluded laborers. Indeed, Salgado in *A Razão* criticized the bourgeoisie more harshly than leftist workers.[12]

The various fascist-leaning circles converged early in 1932. Salgado began to lecture at the prestigious law school of São Paulo, and some of his listeners joined his Sociedade de Estudos Políticos (SEP), as did several Patrianovistas and Caju members, including Dantas. SEP was dedicated to a new
order grounded in authority, national unity, class conciliation, and knowledge of Brazilian conditions. Salgado founded a subgroup, Ação Integralista
Brasileira (AIB), to spread SEP's principles throughout society, and Sombra
and Melo agreed to join forces with it. Salgado prepared a document to
serve as the basis for the new national organization, and the three met in
Rio in July 1932 to discuss plans, but the Constitutional Revolution in São
Paulo cut the meeting short.[13]

The dissension in São Paulo already had interfered with this project.
The Democratic Party, some career military officers, and particularly the local elite resented the Tenentes's radicalism and the extension of federal
power under Vargas's interventors. The Democrats and the oligarchical
Paulista Republican Party called for elections and a return to constitutional
rule, the Democrats for liberal democratic reasons and the Republicans to
reassume control over the state. During demonstrations in May 1932, re-
gionalist students burned down *A Razão*, the focus of SEP/AIB activity and

the newspaper of the Legião Revolucionária. The revolution, which broke out in July, attracted support from some oligarchical leaders in other states and from Sombra. The Vargas regime suppressed the revolt, forcing Sombra into exile, and young army lieutenant Jeová Mota and Father Câmara took over the LCT, eventually bringing it into the AIB. Salgado did not publish the AIB's statement of ideals, the October Manifesto, until after the revolution, when he disseminated it throughout Brazil. He established the first AIB center in São Paulo, and Melo founded the second in his hometown of Teófilo Otoni, Minas Gerais. SEP faded away, absorbed by the AIB.[14]

Better written and less bellicose than Nacionalista and Naci declarations, the October Manifesto offered a similar vision. Fractious states, contending parties, warring classes, and greedy individuals precluded national strength and prosperity. A system of representation through professional associations and indirect elections would provide Brazil with needed unity, hierarchy, and discipline, and it would end domination by a few in favor of the interests of all. Unity also entailed ridding the nation of cosmopolitanism, which Salgado defined as the nefarious tendency, particularly of the elite, to revere the foreign and denigrate the local, especially *caboclos* and blacks.[15]

Nationalism also signified opposition to such foreign notions as communism, which was growing within the body of the country "like a cancer." Communism could not solve the social question, for it was based on the same ideas as capitalism, differing only in that it would reduce the number of employers to one and exploit the workers through a few bureaucrats recruited from the bourgeoisie. It destroyed "the family, to better enslave the worker to the State; . . . the human personality, to better enslave the man to the collectivity; . . . religion, to better enslave the human being to the instincts"; and private initiative, in order to sacrifice "all of humanity to a falsely scientific dream" it hoped to realize in the distant future. Integralism accepted private property, which it thought capitalism damaged, but under state regulation. It offered workers and peasants the possibility of upward mobility through collective contracts, adequate wages, and corporatist representation. The AIB "does not destroy the 'person,' like communism; nor do we oppress it, like liberal democracy: we dignify it." It would transform the worker into the "hero of the new fatherland."

Integralistas met in São Paulo on April 23, 1933, to begin building their movement and march through the streets. Despite its hostility to politics, the AIB registered as a party a few days after the meeting in order to participate in the elections for the constituent assembly that would write the new constitution. Its only successful candidate was Mota, who achieved victory on the ticket of the Liga Eleitoral Católica (LEC), a national pressure group that screened candidates on their church-related views.[16]

Nevertheless, Integralistas had started the first large nationwide political party in Brazil, rivaled only by the Communist Party. In 1927 Communists had created the Workers' and Peasants' Bloc, an electoral front, and then in 1929 formed the General Labor Confederation, which boasted 60,000 members. Internal feuding and waves of government repression, however, limited the party's spread.[17]

Demonstrating that it was a model of organization, the AIB meticulously constructed a movement, municipality by municipality. First it spread propaganda in the target area, particularly among teachers, clerics, and other influential citizens, who attracted others to the cause. Heralded by a publicity campaign, prominent Integralistas then visited the town. A typical flier declared, "I am a Brazilian. . . . I want to be an Integralista." Other fliers invited youths, "working classes," and other groups to welcome the dignitaries. Many of these places were small, isolated localities, and the arrival of AIB figures often aroused great enthusiasm. For several days such speakers as Salgado, Gustavo Barroso, the flamboyant writer and head of the Academia Brasileira de Letras and the Museu Histórico Nacional, and Miguel Reale, the bright young legal expert on corporatism, gave talks and led rallies. Generally these events were part of longer regional tours known as "Integralista caravans" or "*bandeiras*," cleverly appropriating the term referring to the legendary Paulista expeditions into the interior to claim territory for Portugal during the colonial era. Similarly, Integralistas hoped to conquer the particular region for their movement. The early *bandeiras* were frugal affairs, sponsored by Sousa Aranha and other wealthy members, but contributions from larger numbers of Integralistas added to the panoply of later ones. Shortly after the caravan or individual left for the next stop, an AIB "nucleus" would form. Nuclei in the larger towns would send *bandeiras* of their own into the hinterland to establish new centers or subnuclei.[18]

The AIB scheduled a national congress in late February to early March 1934 in Vitória, Espírito Santo, to consolidate itself and show the country it had arrived. Internal dissension, however, threatened to derail the event. Sombra had returned from exile to find Salgado, who had proven his organizational and oratorical skills, ensconced as Chefe (chief). Sombra wanted to broaden the leadership and include himself in it, and he wanted to delay the conference to allow discussion of his revisions to the proposed statutes. Although Salgado tried to conciliate him, he refused to relinquish his position or postpone the meeting. When Sombra publicly criticized Salgado, the chief threw the lieutenant out of the AIB.[19]

The congress illustrated the AIB's emphasis on ideas, which Salgado claimed set the movement apart from Brazilian *caudilhismo*. Committees gave reports on various topics, including syndicalism and feminine organization. A reading list for participants included works by Salgado, Barroso, Sombra, Oliveira Viana, Torres, the Catholic leader Alceu Amoroso Lima, the Tenente Virgínio Santa Rosa, the Nazi Gottfried Feder, and Henry Ford, indicating a mixture of Brazilian, foreign, and antisemitic influences. Over time the AIB reinforced its doctrinal focus by adding to the reading list and offering courses to train leaders and indoctrinate members. To those who might have complained that the führer principle contradicted the centrality of ideas, Salgado characterized the Chefe as an idea, not an individual. His assertion that the doctrine rather than the Chefe reigned supreme, however, seemed somewhat contrived.[20]

A statement of Integralista aims circulated on the eve of the convention. Heading the list of "what the Integralista wants" was an "Integral State" identified with the nation rather than a particular party or class. Second was a strong corporatist government. Political centralization and administrative decentralization based on the municipality rather than the separatist states would unify Brazil. The government would oppose usurers and intermediaries who impoverished productive forces, trusts and other capitalist attacks on private property, and the enslavement of consumers and producers to Jews in New York and London. While Integralistas distinguished this "manly attitude" from communism, in which the state was the sole capitalist, employer, and enslaver, they wanted the state to take over the mines, transportation, electricity, dams, and eventually banks. This proposal went beyond placing such enterprises in Brazilian hands, as recommended by earlier groups. The state would exercise a monopoly on the sale of basic foods to prevent price gouging, as nationalists of the 1920s had urged, and it would protect Brazilians preyed upon by foreign companies. The statement overlooked the low wages paid by Brazilian employers, although it referred to the need to provide economic support for families. It advocated phasing out almost all taxes, leaving the financing of a future Integralista state and its nationalizations uncertain. Other goals were free education at the primary and secondary levels and lowered tuition for universities. The church and Integralista state would cooperate to further Christian ideals but within a climate of religious freedom. Removing domination by Jewish capital and Moscow, the state would oversee culture and the mass media. It would strengthen the armed forces and eliminate harmful political influences on them. Radical in some respects, the document neglected social welfare issues.[21]

The list of aims seems to have provoked some dissension. One reworking of this statement, published in the *Monitor Integralista*, omitted the references to Jews, while another, penned by Barroso, restored them. Barroso also added "What Integralism Combats." This long list included the usual targets of democracy, leftism, materialism, liberalism, and usury, along with foreign loans and Jewish international capitalism. The inclusion, removal, and reinsertion of opinions on Jews indicated disagreement. Moreover, a provision on religious freedom, as well as the focus on the Integralista state, disturbed some Catholics. Barroso annoyed them further by placing sectarianism in his enemies list, falsely claiming that Integralism drew upon all religions.[22]

Approved at the Vitória congress, the statutes provided for a hierarchical organization. The nuclei, further subdivided into districts in the urban areas, were grouped into state or "provincial" jurisdictions—the Integralistas used the imperial term, hinting at monarchist sympathies. There also were provinces of the sea, including the merchant marine and navy, and of Brazilians living abroad. The congress declared Salgado "perpetual and unsubstitutable" in the role of national chief, who had nearly absolute powers. He chose the provincial chiefs, who picked the municipal ones, who in turn nominated those at the district level. The national chief also picked the heads of the various national secretariats, who formed the Supreme Council, which in turn selected the Chamber of Forty, a consultative body. Provincial delegates made up the Chamber of 400, envisioned as the corporatist chamber of a future Integralista state. The Corte do Sigma, the most important AIB body, consisted of the Supreme Council, Chamber of Forty, provincial chiefs, and a few others selected by the Corte. The provinces and nuclei had departments and councils resembling those at the national level. The unimportance of elections led one to question the AIB's sincerity about the electoral system it proposed for the nation. The concentration of authority in the hands of the Chefe also cast doubt on its claim of division of power in the Integralista state.[23]

New members went through the swearing-in ceremony, paid a contribution of their choice as an initiation fee, and received identity cards and pins depicting the Greek letter sigma drawn over a purple map of Brazil surrounded by silver. They also provided personal data on membership cards, which the nuclei kept on file. This information, including the individual's educational level, occupation, and affiliations, enabled the nucleus to monitor its members' lives and determine their duties.[24]

By donning the Sigma, the new members embraced the AIB's "totalitarian concept of the Universe," which referred not to a system of domination, although it advocated one, but to an understanding of the world and the individual as totalities with spiritual, intellectual, and material dimensions. Claiming that liberalism overlooked material needs and communism equated humans with their economic and sexual desires, the AIB prided itself on regarding humans in their totality, although it set their spiritual aims above the others. The word *integral*, meaning a whole, was related to this "total" vision. In mathematics, an integral was a sum of an infinite number of tiny parts. An organism was an integral of millions of cells; the nation was the integral of all cells of the social organism. Thus its government must be total, representing all the cells, or people, through their corporations. Similarly, Integralismo was a whole, a totality. Used by the mathematician Gottfried Wilhelm von Leibnitz to refer to the sum of small things, the sigma manifested Integralismo's concern with "adding all together, considering all."[25]

Popularizing the AIB

Preoccupied with the totality of existence, the movement itself was almost a total way of life. Intricate rituals and symbols played an even more important role in the AIB than in Nacismo. Integralistas greeted each other by raising their right arms and saying, "*Anauê*," repeating the term three times to greet the Chefe and twice to greet other officials. The salutation supposedly came from the Tupi word for "good," thus tying Integralismo to what was indigenous, yet the arm gesture obviously was the Italian Fascist one. Distinctive ceremonies marked important events in an Integralista's life. The AIB celebrated its members' graduations from the university, marriages, and deaths, as well as the baptisms and birthdays of young Integralistas, or Plinianos. In the Plinianos, girls mainly prepared for their duties as future mothers, whereas the boys' training emphasized physical exercise, scouting, and military-style drills. The AIB had its own sports teams, social gatherings, and charitable services for impoverished Integralista families. That there were national secretariats dedicated to such matters as education and art indicated the movement's broad scope. Led by *A Offensiva* of Rio de Janeiro (1934–38), over 100 periodicals supplied the organization's view of the world. Symbols reached into the home; despite its supposed antipersonalism, the AIB provided large round plastic pictures of the Chefe for attachment to tabletops and walls.[26]

The *bandeiras*, rituals, symbols, and mystical language attracted many men and women whose only previous involvement outside home and work was religious. Such practices also were useful means of appealing to illiterates. The rites, distinctive speech, and shared customs made participation exciting and meaningful and provided a sense of identity and unity in the movement.[27] No other national party or institution offered these inducements, except the Catholic Church. This indicated another possible area of conflict between Integralismo and Catholicism.

Integralistas also set themselves apart from other Brazilians by their dress. There were Integralista hat pins for women and belt buckles and swords for men. The essential part of the uniform was a green shirt for men and green blouse for women; thus men were called Camisas Verdes and the women Blusas Verdes. Their right sleeves and caps bore the insignia. For Barroso the uniform was a public profession of the Integralista creed; Reale recalled it was a means of attracting the masses, one that some AIB leaders initially feared was demagogic.[28] As in the other cases, it unified the movement, papered over class differences, and heightened its military élan.

The militia epitomized this military spirit. "Commander" Barroso headed the paramilitary force, seconded by army Captain Olympio Mourão Filho, whose formal rank within Integralismo was chief of staff. Concern over Communist inroads into the armed forces led Mourão Filho, who had opposed the Tenentes and the revolution of 1932, to join the AIB in late 1932. The AIB expected all male Integralistas between the ages of sixteen and forty-two to serve in the militia in some capacity. Perhaps only a tenth, however, became active militiamen.[29]

Admitting that the militia resembled fascist assault troops, the Chefe nevertheless denied any violent intent. He insisted that while Germany and Italy were organized nations with a nationalist spirit, Integralismo and the militia had to create them. Reassuring the armed forces that the militia was no rival, Dantas claimed that it inculcated love of military service in the men and trained them to defend the nation against internal subversion. Indeed, in these respects the militia recalled the scouting and military preparedness campaigns of Olavo Bilac, the Liga Nacionalista, and the Liga da Defesa Nacional, and it linked the AIB to this nationalist tradition. But not all of its purposes were benign, as Dantas hinted. The militia contained a section that planned military operations, whose goal must have been to prepare a revolution or war against its enemies. Headed by Mourão Filho, a secret service gathered information on Jews, leftists, Masons, and liberal democrats, which Integralista police shared with law enforcement officials. The many parades of militiamen and other uniformed Integralistas signaled their combat readiness to the government and potential foes alike. The participation of about 4,000 Camisas Verdes, including militiamen, in the Independence Day military parade in Rio de Janeiro on September 7, 1934, also demonstrated official approval of the AIB, an impression reinforced when Vargas and General Pedro Aurélio de Góes Monteiro returned the Integralista salute.[30]

The AIB and the Political System

The AIB and its militia represented a threat to labor and to democratic government, as leftists understood. Despite claims of nonviolence, in November 1933 Integralistas began to assault workers by targeting a meeting of the Liga Operária Independente in Fortaleza and an antifascist gathering in São Paulo. In July 1934, an antifascist article in *O Socialista* of Barra do Pirai, Rio de Janeiro, provoked Integralistas to attack its editorial office. Such encounters prompted the first debate on Integralismo in the newly organized national constituent assembly. Condemning fascism for persecuting workers, Deputy Armando Laydner, a railroad union member, urged the assembly to outlaw militias and the use of uniforms by political groups. Jeová Mota and Luis Sucupira, a fellow Catholic deputy of Ceará, successfully defended the AIB against this proposed measure.[31]

The early 1930s witnessed the mobilization of workers and leftist groups. Vargas's labor laws encouraged the organization of unions not openly tied to leftist parties. By 1935, over 500 unions existed, and the numbers of unionized workers had increased considerably since the revolution. Nevertheless, police continued to harass and suppress labor militants and strikers. A host of leftist groups—anarchist, Communist, Trotskyist, and others—competed for followers, which they often found among the intelligentsia rather than among workers. Internal divisions and official repression further weakened them. Despite these problems, leftists and reformers joined a popular front organization, the National Liberating Alliance (ANL), in March 1935. Organized by the Communist Party, the ANL was headed by the famous Tenente Luís Carlos Prestes, who had turned to communism. Although it included laborers, military officers and members of the middle class were its base. More radical than that of the AIB, the ANL platform favored nationalizing public services, subsoil rights, and uncooperative foreign enterprises. It also supported land redistribution, a moratorium on the foreign debt, an eight-hour working day, wage increases, social security, civil liberties, women's rights, and racial justice. At its height it attracted between 70,000 and 100,000 members.[32]

The battle lines between left and right hardened, and many believed it necessary to choose one side or the other. Determined not to let the events of Italy and Germany repeat themselves in Brazil, leftists and workers organized to fight the AIB. On October 3, 1934, they fired on Camisas Verdes, including Salgado, who were parading through Baurú, São Paulo, killing two policemen and an Integralista railroad functionary, and wounding several other Integralistas. Police arrested a few anti-AIB labor militants but freed them for lack of evidence.[33]

Despite pressure from police, who feared another Baurú, the AIB insisted on holding a march through the streets of São Paulo and a rally in the Praça da Sé on October 7. The left interpreted the AIB intrusion into the working-class center of the country as a challenge to its manhood and power. Led by the Communist Party, unions and leftist factions defiantly invited the public to an antifascist gathering in this central plaza at the same time as the Integralistas' scheduled event. When the police denied them a permit for that time, leftists vowed they would assemble with or without permission.[34]

The resulting fracas surprised no one. The first to arrive in the Praça were uniformed members of the newly formed feminine department of the AIB, who moved to the top steps of the cathedral. Leftists regarded this self-styled "honor guard" as a cowardly means of protecting Salgado and other chiefs, who were supposed to stand directly in front of it once they arrived in the parade. Shooting broke out between the hundreds of policemen and civil guardsmen in the square and leftists screaming anti-Integralista slogans, and several grenades exploded. Lifting their arms in the salute and singing the national anthem, female Integralistas won the admiration of many onlookers, including persons outside the movement. The shooting died down, but it resumed when the marchers, numbering between 8,000 and 10,000, began to enter the Praça, and now Integralista militiamen joined the battle. The conflict raged for several hours, resulting in the deaths of one member of the Brazilian Socialist Party, two policemen, a civil guardsman, and two Integralistas, and over thirty other casualties. The police detained leftist and labor leaders and broke up the antifascist rally that began after peace returned to the Praça in the late afternoon.

The incident revealed fissures within the right. Disagreeing with the

Chefe, who pointedly blamed the police for the conflict, Deputy Morães Andrade of the Constitutionalist Party, the voice of the Paulista elite, insisted policemen had done what they could against leftist snipers shooting from rooftops. The Constitutionalist deputy nevertheless attributed much of the fault to Integralistas for advocating force to suppress communism and change the given order.[35] The Paulista and other state oligarchies shared the AIB's antileftism, yet they distrusted the Integralistas' populism and propensity for violence. To the conservative elites, this radicalism was unnecessary to stem the leftist threat. Their desire to retain local control conflicted with the AIB's call for centralized government and national unity. For their part, Integralistas lambasted oligarchical liberalism as materialistic, destructive, and elitist.

At the federal and state levels, governments began to take precautions against the extremes. In November, Interventor Juraci Magalhães of Bahia barred members of the state Força Pública, which formed part of the army reserve, from joining the AIB. But leftists were the main target of official action. Only nine days after the Praça da Sé incident, Vargas decided to seek a law repressing the "dissolvent wave." Early in 1935 the regime proposed the National Security Law, giving itself special powers to combat vaguely defined subversive acts. Although the government primarily directed the bill against the left, Salgado feared it would regard the AIB as subversive.[36]

By the time the administration submitted this bill, Congress had split into a pro-Vargas majority and anti-Vargas minority. Primarily made up of conservative oligarchs anxious to preserve their power, the opposition also included a few progressives. Together the opposition supported liberal rights, the oligarchs largely out of a desire to check Vargas's centralization of authority and the progressives for genuinely democratic reasons. This minority attached to the bill some provisions targeting the AIB. One proscribed organizations with differing ranks of command and formations, and another permitted only the states to have militias. An amendment prohibiting unofficial groups from wearing uniforms, however, was defeated. The legislature passed the amended bill, and Vargas signed it into law in early April.[37]

Even before this law, the AIB saw itself as besieged in the state of Rio Grande do Sul. The movement had grown rapidly in the south, particularly among Brazilians of German and Italian descent. The organization's strength awakened concern among rival parties and local administrations, which helped motivate an incident at São Sebastião do Cai on February 25, 1935. Integralistas from around Rio Grande do Sul joined the nucleus for a rally in the main plaza, where a scuffle broke out between an elderly Camisa Verde and the son of the city treasurer. Gunfire between AIB members and the police, whom the AIB had blamed for harassment, killed an Integralista hotel manager and two policemen and wounded eleven others, including the chief of the Cai nucleus. Claiming to have found large quantities of hidden arms, the police arrested over 100 Integralistas. The state interventor, Antônio Flores da Cunha, who had previously permitted the AIB to organize freely and loaned Salgado a place to speak, closed down AIB centers and prohibited AIB rallies to avoid further violence. As the mayor of the town belonged to the state ruling party, the local and state administrations seem to have cooperated in using the incident to limit the AIB.[38]

The National Security Law and Flores da Cunha were on the minds of Integralistas at their second national congress in Petrópolis in early March. With their usual pageantry, Camisas Verdes festooned the streets with streamers and propaganda and filled an "Integralista Museum" with books and other memorabilia. Local Integralistas greeted the nearly 1,000 delegates from all of the Brazilian states with anauês and dropped flowers on them from balconies and windows as they marched through the town. Provincial Chief Dario Bittencourt of Rio Grande do Sul received a loud ovation. The state delegations brought fistfuls of dirt, which they mixed together to symbolize the desired national unity and the wholeness of Integralismo. Preceded by a motorcycle squad, Salgado came by car from Rio de Janeiro, and an Integralista cavalry unit welcomed him and escorted him to his hotel. In a speech he predicted that whether "the oligarchs, pseudo-owners of Brazil and the caudilhos" liked it or not, the Integralistas would rule within ten years. These bold words notwithstanding, the AIB seemingly obeyed the National Security Law by converting the militia into the Department of Education and Physical Culture.[39] The change fooled no one.

Under the National Security Law, the authorities could prosecute the AIB not only for its de facto militia but for its opposition to the form of government. AIB member João C. Fairbanks made this opposition clear when he assumed his seat as São Paulo state deputy in April 1935. Obliged to swear to faithfully fulfill his mandate and work for the common good of São Paulo, within constitutional limits, the uniformed Fairbanks stopped with the words São Paulo and replaced the rest with a promise to weaken liberal democracy. Many fellow deputies protested his defiance, but the national government did nothing.[40]

Predictably, the ANL and AIB clashed on various occasions. After a rally, ANL members paraded through Petrópolis on June 9. When they passed by AIB headquarters, an attack broke out in which Integralistas killed one worker and wounded between seven and eleven others. The bullets removed from their bodies came from the same type of arms used by the military, and observers suspected that here and in other places, the police, who received weapons from the army, had passed some along to the AIB. Opponents of the AIB demanded an investigation. Protesting the incident, the ANL called for a two-day general strike and boycott of businesses owned by or employing Integralistas.[41]

The ANL's increasing militancy promoted conflicts with the AIB and the government in June and July. The ANL battled the AIB in Belo Horizonte, Juiz de Fora, the state of Santa Catarina, and Penha, a working-class suburb of Rio de Janeiro. Over the parliamentary minority's opposition, Vargas shut down the ANL in July. After this point, ANL activity was covert and mostly carried out by Communists.[42]

The suppression of its rival left the AIB as the only legal, nationally organized party. But some of its statements seemed to run afoul of the National Security Law. Salgado allegedly said 400,000 Camisas Verdes were awaiting his order to take over the country and that the strong Integralista sector in Santa Catarina was preparing for the revolution, although he disclaimed these remarks. When the government closed the ANL, Barroso apparently boasted that it lacked the force to do the same to his group. Anti-Integralistas seized upon these stories to try to extend the federal ban on extremists to the AIB. Seeing no indication that the Integralistas planned disorder, Vargas refused.[43]

Despite the suppression of the ANL, the violence did not abate. Gunfire broke out between leftists and Integralistas heading by train to a congress in Cachoeiro de Itapemirim, Espírito Santo, in early November. Three leftists died, and nine of their number and three Camisas Verdes were wounded.[44]

The opposition in the Chamber of Deputies called for closing the AIB. Asserting that Integralismo was far worse than the ANL, José do Patrocínio, a deputy representing the transport employees, chastised the government for allowing Camisas Verdes to march in the streets, retain a militia, and taunt their opponents and the authorities. Agreeing that official inaction amounted to complicity, Abguar Bastos, a combatant of 1930 and former ANL member, noted that the administration had ignored the chamber's request to explain its tolerance of the AIB.[45]

When other deputies claimed that Barroso and Salgado advocated the armed route to power, Jeová Mota responded that his party had removed references to violence from its program. Patrocínio wondered if the Integralistas reserved one set of statements for external and another for internal use. Several deputies pointed to the AIB's propensity for bloodshed, which Mota insisted did not reflect his party's means of spreading its doctrine but simply the clash between two opposing currents. Alexandre José Barbosa Lima Sobrinho, a member of the Sociedade dos Amigos de Alberto Torres and an ANL opponent, asserted that the state must defend itself from such conflicts.[46]

A Tenente and an ANL sympathizer, Domingos Velasco, presented a resolution asking the president either to close down the AIB or halt the repressive measures against the ANL. Favoring freedom for all political currents, a few deputies opposed this resolution, as they had the National Security Law. Several others were against it because they denied that Integralismo, unlike the popular front organization, was subversive. Edmundo Barreto Pinto, an anticommunist deputy representing public employees, questioned whether the legislative branch had the right to suppress a political group. Mota added that the executive branch dealt with political violence, so the resolution was unnecessary. Annoyed by persistent Integralista heckling from the galleries, deputies narrowly approved the measure. The government simply ignored the resolution, but AIB leaders realized that Vargas could use it whenever it suited him.[47]

The ANL exited loudly from the political scene. The morning after the congressional debate, persons probably from this organization dynamited the entrances to several AIB centers in Rio de Janeiro. A few days later, Communist-inspired army contingents in Natal, Recife, and Rio de Janeiro rebelled in succession. Poorly coordinated, these insurrections lacked broad civilian or military support. Some military and police officials had received advance information on the revolts from their internal spy networks, which included Integralistas. In particular, General Pantaleão da Silva Pessôa, head of security for the presidential palace, chief of staff of the armed forces, and president of the anticommunist Liga da Defesa Nacional, maintained close links with the AIB and its intelligence sources. The government suppressed the rebellions so easily that some observers wondered if the Machiavellian administration had instigated them.[48]

Probably it had not, but it took advantage of the situation. Vargas obtained a state of siege decree from Congress, which extended it regularly through the following year, as well as amendments tightening the National Security Law. As it had done on and off since 1930, the administration censored the press. The military expelled suspected leftists from its ranks, and the police imprisoned ANL members, dissident intellectuals, and even progressive deputies, deporting those who were foreign-born. Directed by Federal Police Chief Felinto Müller, law enforcement officials systematically tortured detainees, who numbered between 5,000 and 15,000. Aiding the police was the witch-hunting National Commission for the Repression of Communism, created by Vargas and headed by Gaúcho deputy Adalberto Corrêa, an AIB supporter. In 1936 the National Security Tribunal, which judged cases of supposed treason, joined the arms of repression. Vargas even resorted to Integralista-style anticommunist and hyperpatriotic rhetoric. Thus the president managed to eliminate the left, enlarge his powers, and strengthen his base in the military.[49]

The repression of the insurrections helped define the Vargas administration, which previously had zigzagged toward authoritarianism. The president had devoted much energy to dealing with the states: ending squabbles in some, taming and winning over leaders of others, and suppressing recalcitrants. Social welfare and labor legislation, particularly the creation of a ministry of labor and a structure of government-recognized unions and employer groups, manifested his corporatism. His desire to consolidate power in the federal government—and himself—also flouted Brazilian liberal theory. Catholic and corporatist ideologues—including Oliveira Viana, Francisco Campos, and Gustavo Capanema—rose within the ministries, while Tenente influence subsided. Vargas's support of suffrage for literate men and women suggested democratic sentiments, but his coercive treatment of labor and hierarchical view of the family belied them. With the Communist uprisings, the government moved further to the right. Next to the rabble-rousing Integralistas, the nonmobilizing Vargas regime appeared conservative, but its antileftism, corporatism, centralism, and repressive measures overlapped their views.[50]

Like Vargas, Integralistas seemed to profit from the insurrections. Salgado grandiloquently offered Vargas 100,000 Camisas Verdes—from the supposedly nonexistent militia—to put down the rebellions. While the president declined the offer, it lent the AIB prestige. The events reinforced AIB notions of the Communist threat and gave some weight to its proposed solutions. General Pessôa and other military leaders welcomed the organization as an anticommunist collaborator, and Vargas saw it as a useful means of propagating the authoritarian ideas that bolstered his rule. The AIB's continuing involvement in disorders would also enable the wily president to tighten the national security apparatus and consolidate a dictatorship.[51]

In actuality the AIB was in a difficult position. If it took any decisive steps toward revolution, Vargas could repress it, as he had the ANL, although top government, military, and police officials sympathized with In-tegralismo. For this reason Salgado accommodated the AIB to the regime. But if the AIB relied on the electoral route, it would be difficult to reach power in the short run. In 1934 AIB voters elected one federal and six state deputies and by 1936 four more state deputies, twenty mayors, and almost 3,000 city councilmen. The growth in votes was impressive but did not promise a presidential victory in the near future. Furthermore, by empha-sizing electoralism and submitting to the National Security Law, Salgado alienated the radicals in his movement. One Integralista privately com-plained that the Chefe "cloistered the movement within clubs and theaters. He separated it from the people. He lost the notion of how a movement like ours needs to be more virile, more dynamic, more revolutionary."[52]

These comments reflected tensions within the movement. The AIB may have been a single organization, but, like Nacionalismo, it was not mono-lithic. Reale and Melo later divided it into three factions. They placed them-selves in the first, which focused on socioeconomic matters and a syndical-ist reorganization of society. Salgado's faction, according to Reale, empha-sized Catholicism and spiritualism; Melo described it as one that sought a bourgeois accord with the government. Reale noted that the Chefe was sus-picious of the first group's "socialism," which might make the AIB seem Marxist. Barroso and other militiamen formed the third wing, which Melo designated as anti-imperialist and Reale as irrationalist and antisemitic.[53]

In reality these groupings overlapped considerably. Barroso's anti-semitism had much economic content, and anti-Jewish and anticolonial notions were not limited to him or his faction. Anxious to obscure the an-tisemitism of his youth and of the AIB, Reale tried to set Barroso off from the rest of the movement, but he overdrew this distinction. The more radi-cal anti-imperialist and syndicalist wings opposed ties to the regime, con-testing the views of Salgado's conservative faction.[54]

To the extent that it existed as a separate bloc, the Chefe's conservative current was the dominant one. Still, except at a few decisive moments, he permitted these differing tendencies to express themselves. Whether by de-sign or accident, this tolerance strengthened the movement by enabling In-tegralistas to attract diverse groups.

Integralistas had much to offer well-off conservatives. First, they re-sisted socialism and worker autonomy and ardently defended private prop-erty. Catholics must have harkened to the movement's puritanism, ex-pressed in its repugnance for sensual behavior, drugs, Hollywood movies, and "savage" music like jazz. Undoubtedly, they approved of rules such as the one that barred members from wearing uniforms when they gambled, attended carnival, drank alcohol, or danced in non-Integralista settings. The AIB's devotion to a hierarchical family, which its ideologues often expressed in explicitly counterrevolutionary terms, must also have appealed to them.[55]

AIB members were indeed "extremists of the 'right,'" as Dâgmar Cortines proudly proclaimed. Chief of the feminine department of Bahia, Cortines saw nothing wrong with extremism in defense of God, family, and fatherland. At the end of time, humanity would divide into the band of Satan on the left and that of God on the right. The gospel did not mention a middle, for Jesus had said that those who were not with him were against him. Playing on words to denote these leanings, other Integralistas said that they would straighten out (*endireitar*) Brazil, a word which contained *direita*, or right.[56]

The AIB's Alternative to the Left

Ação, the voice of the syndicalist wing, admitted the movement was on the right but distinguished it from reaction. It criticized those prosperous Brazilians who erroneously took the AIB's defense of traditional values and private property to mean that it also supported their banks, latifundia, and exploitation of workers. The movement was really one of right-minded ("*direita*") people from below, who labored, suffered, and hated those who did not have to work. "We are angry with the reactionaries, with the stupid ones who speak of glories that did not exist."[57] Rightist yet populist, such views helped define the AIB's alternative to the left.

The Chefe denied that the AIB was rightist, for he rejected what he considered the nineteenth-century framework of left, right, and center. It was necessary to destroy the "reactionary right," "the left that calls itself revolutionary," and the opportunistic parties of the center. The AIB fought not the bourgeoisie but rather the spirit of the century that produced this class. Like his peers elsewhere, Salgado suggested it was not averse to this group's control of wealth and power, only to the way it exerted this control. Nor did the AIB oppose the legitimate aspirations of the proletariat, which it wanted to separate from the beliefs that subjected it to oppression; evidently beliefs rather than social conditions were responsible for exploitation. The Chefe explicitly denounced Marx's idea of the proletariat independently carrying out its own revolution against the bourgeoisie. Instead, the Integralista revolution was that of the twentieth century against the nineteenth, a totalitarian revolution that socialists, liberals, and even reactionaries of the extreme right could not comprehend.[58]

Other Brazilian political groups had emerged in the last century and were outmoded. Only Integralismo expressed the mood of the times and the youthful spirit. Salgado labeled his principal ideological rival conservative, basing his conclusion on the notions that Marxism reflected the bourgeois determinism of the 1800s and that its vision of the future society was static. In contrast, Integralismo was the only revolutionary force, for its voluntarism broke with determinism and it embraced a dynamic and total view of continual material and spiritual renovation. The future Integralista state, the Estado Novo, would constantly change and thus would represent a "permanent revolution"; here the Chefe borrowed a Marxist term while altering its meaning.[59]

Nor was this the only item Salgado borrowed from Marxism. He recommended using the Marxist method to study Brazilian history as the best means of comprehending the liberal economy. British and local liberals had freed the colony from Portugal in order to enslave it to international capital and the incipient national bourgeoisie. Particularly under the Old Republic, the dominant economic forces used regional autonomy to reinforce their privileges and fragment the nation. Salgado's conclusion that this experience justified an Integralista revolution, however, departed from Marxism.[60]

Despite their enmity for Communists, Integralistas admired them. Similar to Naci leaders, Salgado declared his love for his badly informed "Communist brother" who fought Integralistas in the streets, while cowardly liberal democrats watched these battles from the sidelines. Custodio de Viveiros considered opportunistic liberal democrats the worst enemies of the Sigma, rather than honest and brave Communists. The socialist *A Platéia* claimed that as Integralistas used a language that was 75 percent Marxist, they could not help but excite the laborers they addressed, who knew little about Marxism.[61] Through such words the AIB displayed its radicalism and attempted to recruit workers.

At times the language indeed sounded leftist. Father Hélder Câmara, for example, blasted bourgeois pedagogy, which recommended treating rich and poor children equally and inculcating them with class harmony. What was the good of such teachings in view of the massive social inequality outside the school? What was the point of intellectual education when workers were mere machines lacking human rights or the ability to think? Could aesthetic education beautify the lives of those who did not really live? Instead of education, only the organization of all groups under a vigilant Integralista state could ensure the reign of true social harmony, in which no particular class predominated.[62] Ignoring the influence that the wealthy could wield on a corporate state, Câmara's prescription fell short of Marxism.

Integralistas positioned themselves as an alternative to the left they hated yet admired, aiming at those searching for a national brand of socialism. The Chefe described his revolution as one "of the proletariat, of students, of humble ones, of the young in spirit." The most far-reaching statement came from Reale, who wrote of the universalization of fascism after 1929 as a full-fledged social revolution with its own beliefs and program. Fitting Integralismo within this framework, Reale saw it as the "true proletarian revolution." Influenced by the wartime exaltation of voluntarism and a heroic conception of life, the proletariat had nationalized itself and begun to demand rights in the name of the fatherland rather than exclusively its class. For Reale this nationalized proletariat was the genuine one, and its expression was Integralismo.[63] Resembling the views of the Federación Obrera Nacionalista Argentina (FONA), Reale's writings, however, expressed more solidarity with workers.

Integralistas affirmed another sense of revolution akin to that of their Argentine and Chilean peers, one of changing humanity instead of social structures. For Salgado, the Integralista revolution was a profound alteration in the people and the state that occurred "in the secret mysterious dominions of the Spirit." In the short term, the Integralistas would establish their self-styled totalitarian state. The long-term change was a interior one, in which people would put aside their selfishness, prejudices, and skepticism and train themselves in humility, discipline, self-control, and faith. They would learn to accept the leadership of a comrade from a lower social class than their own and correct their own faults before criticizing the nation. Only after this interior revolution of the heart and the soul against materialism, atheism, and bourgeois and foreign enemies, as J. Venceslau Junior described it, could Integralistas proceed to overthrow the reign of international bankers.[64]

In the Integralistas' sense of the term, they opposed capitalism. They believed that all should aspire to private property, which was legitimate if acquired through honest labor and consonant with the national interest. For Barroso as for the Argentine Julio Meinvielle, capitalism meant the abuse and destruction of property. Only evil property owners fell under the rubric of bourgeois or capitalist, according to Paulo Fleming, as might an egoistic laborer. Thus the bourgeoisie was not a class but a malignant spirit condemned by the AIB and its South American peers. In place of bourgeois rule by the wealthy, Barroso advocated government by a new elite comprising members of all classes who had proved their worth through study, work, sacrifice, and struggle, much as did Nacistas and Nacionalistas.[65]

The AIB did not carry this critique of capital, limited and anti-Marxist as it was, to its full potential. Though in theory Integralistas denounced low wages and poor working conditions, they tended to praise and support producers. For them as for other fascists, the true malefactors of wealth were "parasitic" international financiers. The AIB expert on economic matters, Reale, identified three stages in the development of capitalism in the nineteenth century. In the first, capital removed the state from the economy in those countries where a "free market" served its interests. The second was the stage of state tariff protection for nascent industries, capitalist penetration of lesser developed countries, and colonialism. Reale called this the imperialist stage, but he disagreed with Lenin's belief that it represented the highest phase of capitalism. Instead, he added a third stage, in which capitalism "internationalized itself, dominating all the States." In this stage of "financial supercapitalism," capital had separated itself from, and imposed its will on, producers. Bound by loans, the nation was "a simple employee of the supernational-capitalist State, whose prime ministers were almost all of the Judaic race."[66]

National liberation meant fighting capitalism, now organized as the "supernation of capital without a fatherland." This also involved freeing the ideal of social justice from class struggle, historical materialism, and economic internationalism. In this context, anticapitalism no longer was the exclusive domain of the proletariat, as under Marxism, but of the entire nation. Its standard-bearers were Fascism, Nazism, Integralismo, the New Deal, and to a certain extent Stalinism. Extending Reale's argument, Salgado noted that the AIB hoped to free a "proletarian Brazil from imperialist hands." He and Reale transposed the concept of class conflict to an international scale, as did Italian Fascists, the Liga Patriótica Argentina, and the Argentine FONA.[67]

According to Reale, Marxism could not solve the problems of capitalism. Karl Marx showed how capitalism destroyed small property, but he nevertheless supported its demolition instead of defending property against capitalism. Marx's "critique" of capitalism was really an apology for it, which enabled Reale to understand the seemingly paradoxical ties "between the high masters of Jewish finances and the no less semitic red agitators." To capitalists Marx offered a useful means of destroying family, property, religion, and the sovereignty of the state, which Reale regarded as the only factors that reinforced liberty. Furthermore, the notion of laborers freeing themselves entailed a battle with capitalists and intelligentsia, which could lead to a Bolshevik state that took capital's place. Finally, Marx had not foreseen the willingness of some employers to pay their laborers higher wages or encourage them to purchase stock in the companies, measures that promised workers a better life within the framework of private property.[68]

Since the main characteristic of capitalism, as the AIB defined it, was the entrepreneur's freedom to use capital, Reale, citing Mussolini, concluded that the solution was to limit this freedom. Accordingly, Integralismo would establish producer organizations to guide production, with the state settling disputes among them and looking out for the national interest. Addressing the issue of finance capital, Reale praised Hitler's attack on speculators and bankers, whom he and the Nazis agreed were Jewish. Reale also approved of the German practice of financing public works and small enterprises through bonds and cooperatives, measures that avoided charging interest on loans.[69]

The party program of 1937, issued during the presidential campaign, addressed these and other points. It proposed a national banking system to provide credit to all producers and greater state control over financial matters. The Integralista state would attempt to liquidate public debts and set up production, credit, and consumption cooperatives. The program called for nationalizing mines and hydroelectric plants, reviewing public utility contracts with foreign companies, eliminating interstate taxes, and rationalizing import duties. It did not specifically discuss industrialization, foreign investment outside the areas mentioned, or dependence on coffee. The assumption was that a strong and ethical corporate state would automatically solve economic problems and capitalist abuse. It would end the type of regime in which "he who robs little is the thief, he who robs much is the baron," as Victor Pujol put it. Yet perhaps because of growing state authoritarianism, the program was less radical than earlier AIB statements. It did not even heed the call of Frederico Villar, formerly of Ação Social Nacionalista and now of the AIB, to restrict fishing to Brazilians.[70]

Another glaring omission was the problem of latifundia, although there were a few discussions of this topic in *Ação*. While claiming there was excessive "antilatifundiary romanticism" in Brazil, the newspaper admitted that oversized estates promoted monoculture, extreme exploitation, and *caudilhismo*. It was vital to weaken the large landowners by centralizing power and supporting small proprietors through cooperatives, lower taxes, and credit. One article attacked the notion that abundant vacant territory forestalled the need for land reform; one had to solve the problem where people lived, rather than force the poor to wander. Another commended state governments in the south for giving land to farmers. Although several writers agreed that the state should encourage the spread of small farms, few explicitly favored the division and redistribution of large properties.[71]

Integralistas focused more heavily on the social question than on landownership or industry. As Barroso put it, one of their primary tasks was to win labor from communism.[72] The Integralista press was one instrument in this campaign. *A Offensiva* had a "syndical page," *Século XX* a "syndicalism and laborism" segment, and *Ação* a "proletarian" section. Of the three papers, *Ação* contained the most coverage on labor, economics, and sports—matters that its editors judged to be of interest to São Paulo workers, the most militant in the country.

Not surprisingly, the movement took a dim view of strikes. It admitted that liberal capitalism allowed laborers few means of defending themselves except through work stoppages. But even *Ação* believed that "reds" usually led them. The popular-oriented magazine *Anauê!* featured a short play by Victor Pujol, "The Striker," in which João, a Communist, was involved in a long strike. His Integralista wife, Maria, urged him instead to find another job and trust in God, to which he countered that faith in God and the Virgin did not put food on the table. In João's absence, a doctor tried to heal their sick child, but the light went out, dooming his efforts. João returned home, boasting of cutting the electricity to the city, and his wife informed him that he had killed his offspring. The story demonstrated the AIB view of strikes as cruel and irresponsible. A rare one the AIB officially supported was that of sailors in the merchant marine, some of whom belonged to the movement. It was quick to say, however, that under an Integralista state strikes would not be necessary, for there would be no exploitation, labor would have representatives in power, and the state would oversee contracts.[73] Nor would strikes be tolerated.

Integralismo claimed that its future state would give workers social justice, which it did not want workers to win for themselves. Set in an antiliberal, antisocialist, hierarchical, and nationalist framework, the labor program was enshrined in Barroso's Carta Brasileira do Trabalho and numerous articles in the Integralista press. According to these statements, all workers had a right to a decent life, which meant acquiring land, a house, tools, or other types of property. The Integralista state would organize all "laborers"—capital, manual, intellectual, and technical—in syndicates; unlike existing laws, it would not exclude rural workers. Only this type of structure could ensure class collaboration and effective social reforms. The AIB advocated the eight-hour day, with a six-hour day for workers in hazardous occupations, although at times it said it would permit the needy to work longer hours. A minimum wage based on the notion of a family salary would allow women to remain home, but Integralistas nevertheless favored the principle of equal salaries for men and women who worked at equivalent jobs. All workers were entitled to vacations, medical aid, profit sharing, social security, consumers' cooperatives, and educational and cultural programs. But in the long run, Integralistas hoped that questions of maximum hours, minimum salary, and social aid would become obsolete. A corporatist government would gradually phase out the wage system in favor of payments to all producers proportional to the wealth they created. Reale admitted that there would always be differences between individuals, but the state would attempt to "present equal opportunities to naturally unequal beings."[74]

Contradictory in some respects, this labor program still was more visionary than that of Nacis or Nacionalistas. With the important exception of the governmental structures of control, the future economy approximated the anarchist dream of a union of small producers. Nor did the Argentines or Chileans concern themselves with equal pay for women. The reason for this difference was that the Brazilian constitution of 1934 already contained this provision, as well as suffrage rights for women, whose allegiance the AIB was therefore interested in winning.

The Chefe asked Integralistas to join unions, become officers in them, and unite with like-minded workers to subdue Communist influences. Such maneuvers took place in the Alliance of Workers in Civil Construction. Founded in 1931, this group included Integralistas and non-Integralistas alike, all of whom favored an AIB-style nationalist corporatism and opposed Marxism. Other workers' organizations refused to have anything to do with the alliance.[75] Such activities harmonized with Integralista infiltration of and espionage against Communist groups.

Like the movements in the other countries, the AIB tried to nationalize workers. In 1937, for example, Jeová Mota announced that all nuclei would celebrate May 1, and the AIB magazine *Anauê!* dedicated its May issue to labor. *A Offensiva* told workers that "fatherlands are eternal. The social justice of Integralismo will take form within the Brazilian fatherland. You are not workers of the world. You are workers of Brazil." Reale reminded laborers that they would only prosper within a rich country, implying they should reserve their allegiance for the nation and produce without complaint.[76]

The movement's efforts to attract workers increased after the suppression of the ANL and the attendant expansion in political space for the AIB. Mota, the principal figure in this campaign, organized the movement's first syndicate, that of bank clerks in Rio de Janeiro, in April 1935. The AIB then proceeded to organize nine categories of professionals, twenty-six of white-collar workers, and sixteen of blue-collar workers in the federal district. Mota officiated over the first AIB syndicalist convention in January 1936 in Rio de Janeiro, whose participants included a variety of workers, employ-ees, and professionals from the federal district and the states of Rio de Ja-neiro, São Paulo, and Espírito Santo. Among other topics, the delegates dis-cussed the nonenforcement of labor laws, the need for unions to voice their concerns to government, and the unequal treatment of Brazilian versus for-eign workers. Workers expressed interest in courses to make unions more effective, and Mota began to offer such instruction for Integralista leaders involved in labor matters in July 1936. Mota told the assembly that Inte-gralistas had to support labor and that AIB workers should be active union members. Referring to himself as the "highest Integralista proletarian," a contradiction in terms, Salgado tempered Mota's militancy by cautioning the delegates that one could resolve labor problems only within the totality of national problems.[77]

In late August 1936, Mota announced the opening of a Syndical Corpo-rative Service. Workers and Integralistas from the southern half of Brazil at-tended its convention in December, where they approved the AIB's labor program, including syndical unity and "autonomy." It was not clear whether the last term signified freedom of action or freedom from leftist politics or Jewish capitalism, which the convention and Integralista labor statements condemned.[78]

Although Mota never departed from Integralista beliefs, his syndical-ism skirted the edge. Regarding Mota as too leftist, in early 1937 the Chefe removed him from the syndical service by naming him provincial chief of São Paulo, and the AIB's labor efforts abated. In June, the disgruntled dep-uty resigned from both the Chamber and the movement, complaining that he could not express his revolutionary aims in Integralismo. He had entered the AIB because of his dislike for capitalism and economic oppression, but there was no room for "intense proletarian syndical action" within it. Mota now professed support for democracy and opposition to fascism, messian-ism, and the notion of salvation coming from outside or above the people. Stung, *Ação* retorted that "whoever is not an Integralista would become or must be a Communist." Although Mota's departure pleased some Camisas Verdes, who disliked his critical attitudes, it dealt the movement a severe blow. It reduced its radicalism and opening to workers, and it prompted an exodus from the organization. Angry Integralistas physically assaulted some of these deserters, further damaging the AIB's image.[79]

Antisemitism

Mota's exit, however, did not remove another important component of AIB radicalism—its antisemitism. Prejudice against Jews did not make Integralismo unique in Brazil, especially among rightists. Such sentiments had characterized Eduardo Prado, Ação Social Nacionalista, and the Centro Dom Vital, and the Centro continued to publish radical antisemitic articles in *A Ordem* by such authors as Plínio Corrêa de Oliveira, an LEC activist and former member of SEP, the AIB's precursor, and Arlindo Veiga dos Santos of Pátria Nova. Elsewhere, Centro Dom Vital leader Alceu Amoroso Lima blamed Jews for spurning Christ and for "modern semitism, not religious, but economic and political, cosmopolitan and antinational or pseudonational," although he admitted that some exaggerated it. A nationalist of the Minas Gerais elite, Afonso Arinos de Melo Franco, described the Jews as "a race at once infernal and divine, creator and assassin of ideas and religions, race of announcers of God and of deicides."[80] Integralistas built upon these formulations.

One is tempted to attribute some of this parlance to the growth and heightened stature of the Jewish population. From 1926 to 1930, about 22,000 Jews, mostly from Eastern Europe, entered the country, a threefold increase over the early 1920s. Brazil adopted immigration restrictions after the onset of the Depression, but from 1931 to 1942, over 27,000 Jews arrived. By 1940, 20,379 resided in São Paulo state and perhaps 1,000 less in the federal district. In that year, Brazilian Jewry numbered 55,666, representing a tiny 0.136 percent of the population. Many of its members were prosperous shopkeepers and small manufacturers, and the arrival of German, Austrian, and Italian professionals and businessmen in the 1930s added to the community's stature. The Jewish proletariat was far smaller than that of Argentina, although this did not prevent antisemites from blaming Jews for Bolshevism.[81]

All three movements used antisemitism as a means of demonstrating their anticapitalism and nationalism, as was the vogue in Europe, often without reference to the Jews who inhabited their countries. Still, local conditions had weight. It is no accident that antisemitism had long characterized the rightist spectrum in Argentina, where immigrants and Jews formed the largest percentages of the population and the working class of the three countries, and nationalism overlapped Catholicism. The Nacistas' distance from the church, the weakness of anti-immigrant sentiments in Chile, and the vagaries of the political context helped account for the inconsistency of their antisemitism. If one went by demographic factors alone, one might expect the Integralistas to duplicate the Chilean pattern. Chilean Jews composed a slightly higher but still miniscule percentage of all inhabitants. In Chile and Brazil, the Jewish presence grew rapidly in the 1930s, and Jews tended to concentrate in the middle class and in one or two large cities. Yet unlike Nacistas, most Integralistas were unflaggingly anti-Jewish, thanks to the legacy of Catholic nationalism and anti-immigrant sentiments.

A devout Catholic and member of a traditional Cearense family in economic decline, Barroso was the Integralista best known for radical antisemitism. He headed the Integralista Centro de Estudos Anti-Judaicos as well as the militia. Feigning an open mind, Barroso told the Jewish newspaper *Civilização* that the AIB opposed racial and religious prejudice and other disaggregating tendencies. But he added that if racial or religious groups contributed to dissolution by trying to create a state within a state, the movement would fight them. Clearly this was how Barroso regarded the Jews.[82]

They were more than a state within a state; Barroso identified them with all he disliked about modern civilization. "At the bottom of capitalism, we find the synagogue"; Jews were the "priests of capital." He regarded Brazil as a colony of the Rothschilds and Simonsens, a part-Jewish Paulista family; yet neither he nor other Integralistas blamed specific non-Jewish Brazilian entrepreneurs. Judaism meant "systematized destruction" of all institutions in society. Jews destroyed property by dispensing international loans, increasing taxes, devaluing currency, speculating and carving out monopolies, and encouraging class conflict. By fomenting prostitution, birth control, and the love of luxury, they undermined the family. Jewish cosmopolitanism and dislike of tradition weakened the nation; Jews' materialism, atheism, and hatred of Catholicism destroyed religion; whereas their subversive education, immoral entertainment, and other vices corrupted the youth. Soviet communism, controlled by Jews, further damaged these institutions, and Franklin D. Roosevelt's presidency (which Reale praised) was equally Jewish. Through feminism, "Judaic vermin" had set women against men; by inventing the slave trade and creating the Frente Negra Brasileira, a civil rights group, Jews pitted blacks against whites. The Jews were also racist because they did not mix with others. Insisting that he countered Jewish racism with the Christian sense of equality, Barroso claimed that racism was justified in Germany but not in Brazil, where many races coexisted. That he considered Jews a race that included Christians like Roosevelt—who would not identify themselves as Jews—indicates that the Integralista was much more racist than he admitted. So, too, did his belief that reprehensible behavioral traits characterized this "race."[83]

Barroso acknowledged that Jews could make these inroads into Christian society only with help from upper-class allies. Still, he, like Meinvielle, insisted that the Jews directed a worldwide conspiracy, as outlined in the Protocols of the Elders of Zion, which he translated into Portuguese. Jewish intellectuals ridiculed Barroso's belief in the Protocols, which the Integralista claimed had come to pass. When President Isaias Golgher of the União Israelita of Belo Horizonte proposed a mock trial of Barroso for his antisemitic accusations, Barroso declared he would accept such proceedings if a trial of Jews preceded them.[84]

The Jewish question was not so much Reale's focus as it was Barroso's, nor did the young jurist blame the Jews for all that was evil. He declared that Integralismo would accept, even as members, those of the Jewish "race" who did not hold themselves apart, oppose Christian values, engage in usury, or serve as instruments of international finance or the Soviet Union—qualifications demonstrating his prejudices. (In fact, a handful of Jews, at least in Santa Catarina, did join the movement.) The cases of Gino Arias, Henri Bergson, Benjamin Disraeli, and Jacques Maritain demonstrated, said Reale, that Jews could embrace notions of discipline and organic society. Since of the four only Bergson professed Judaism, and he had strong Catholic leanings, it was clear that Reale looked kindly only on those Jews who gave up their religion. Reale repeatedly insisted that he and his movement were not racist. One should not oppose Jews only for being Jewish, for this would entail "judging men by their exterior and material aspects of color and of cranial formation, which repels a spiritualist." Evidently racism meant theories of racial superiority and inferiority, which he, like Nacista Carlos Keller, rejected as materialistic and partial, unsuited to a spiritual and totalitarian view of life. Yet both Reale and Barroso defined Jews as a race with harmful attributes.[85]

According to Reale, it was clear that "semites" had "absolute hegemony" among the most important representatives of "supercapitalism." The struggle against this economic system thus was one against "certain sectors of Israel." But this did not mean Integralistas believed in a racial doctrine; the problem was an economic and particularly a moral one. The fight against capitalism did not require distinguishing between "the Jewish moneylender and the moneylender who calls himself Christian," he wrote, suggesting that usury was Jewish by nature.[86]

Reale also spotted Jews behind liberalism and leftism. Jewish bankers manipulated the Constitutionalists of São Paulo and other liberal parties. The "semite press" created sympathy for Communists after the Russian Revolution. Reale praised Hitler for eliminating the Jewish Communist threat to Germany, and he believed that the strikes that had plagued Brazil before martial law had facilitated "Judaic domination."[87]

Jews were even less important for the Chefe than for Reale, but the two shared a similar view of them. Salgado's novels of the early 1930s contained repugnant Jewish characters, including a white slaver and another who planned to undermine Brazil. Referring to "the Jew Adam Smith," Salgado identified Jews with liberalism. Also tied to Jews, communism would bring "masses of Russian workers, Jewish administrators and executioners" to Brazil. Freeing the country from its economic chains meant driving out U.S., French, English, "or, what is worse, international Jewish" influences. He blamed international Jewish capitalists and Communists for wanting to defeat the AIB.[88]

Concerned about AIB antisemitism, Chief Rabbi Isaiah Raffalovich, who had long worked with Jewish refugees, met with Salgado in October 1934. The rabbi told the Integralista leader that it was unfair to blame the diverse Jewish community for the opinions of a few. Since some Jews had fled the Soviet Union for Brazil, how could one accuse them all of being Communists? He challenged Salgado to name one Jewish foreign bank manager in the country. The Chefe insisted that Integralistas were not racist and did not oppose Jews on racial or religious grounds. Honest Jews, like honest Brazilians (evidently these were two separate groups), deserved their praise. But Integralistas opposed Jewish political methods of achieving domination, and they responded to attacks by "semites" who abused the laws. Salgado and Raffalovich agreed that Jews and the AIB would stop criticizing each other. Some prosperous Jews even contributed to the AIB when it agreed to remove offensive passages from its literature. Yet the movement broke these promises, and its antisemitism continued.[89]

Salgado issued his definitive statement on the Jewish question in 1936. He noted that Integralistas wanted Jews to intermarry with Christians and other races, for "an intelligent race should not continue to maintain barbarous prejudices." The Chefe asserted that Jewish capitalism did not exist as such and was the same as the Christian variety; it was a "coincidence" that the Jews controlled 60 percent of international money lending. Since the Integralista state would eliminate international capitalism and Brazilian subservience to the Rothschilds, there was no reason to wish the Jews ill for being "the principal ones responsible for the economic-financial disorder that torments peoples, especially the semicolonized like us, of South America." One could not hate the race of Jesus, for antisemitism was anti-Christian and the popes had condemned it. Eventually Jews would build their own nation, free of the fear that had led them to isolate and "encyst" themselves in other countries.[90] Circular and even cynical, this writing revealed an antisemitism not as bombastic and absolute as Barroso's but radical nonetheless.

Salgado had permitted Barroso to air his brand of antisemitism in AIB publications. Still, disagreement on this issue and conflicting ambitions sparked rivalry between the two. These surfaced in early 1936, when Barroso submitted an article to *A Offensiva* in which he attributed financial crimes to certain local Jewish businessmen. José Madeira de Freitas, the editor, had some Jewish friends and refused to print the article; he accepted diatribes against the imaginary international Jew but not specific Brazilian Jews. Barroso then published this and related pieces in *Século XX* in March, and one of the businessmen in question sued this periodical. Advised by his former mentor, Sousa Aranha, to silence Barroso for the good of the movement, the Chefe closed *Século XX* and kept Barroso out of the Integralista press until September. The antisemitism of the main AIB newspaper temporarily abated a bit, but articles about Barroso and advertisements for his books continued to appear. Salgado issued the statement discussed above in this context as an answer to Barroso. Meanwhile, unknown assailants briefly kidnapped and terrorized Ovidio Cunha, Barroso's secretary and chief of the AIB's "section of repression of Judaism," in Rio de Janeiro in June. Cunha attributed the action to his support for Barroso and anger against Salgado. Rumors persisted until 1937 that Barroso would leave the AIB to set up a rival movement, but in private he humbled himself to his Chefe.[91]

Most Integralistas were radical antisemites who, unlike Barroso, did not necessarily criticize individual Brazilian Jews. Years later, the former chief of the feminine department of Porto Alegre, Aurora Nunes Wagner, insisted that the Protocols were accurate and that Jewish financial and economic control was a "plague." Hélgio Trindade found that 61 percent of surviving local leaders and members agreed strongly with the statement that "the Jewish spirit is a permanent threat to humanity," and another 21 percent agreed somewhat. The corresponding figures for national leaders were only 36 and

20 percent, indicating they were less antisemitic than their followers—or clever enough to realize that such views were no longer fashionable.[92]

Popular-oriented Integralista publications provide further evidence of the movement's antisemitism. Violent denunciations of Jewish capital, revolutionaries, movies, prostitution, immigration, and journalism filled the pages of *A Offensiva*. It and other AIB newspapers carried a regular column, "International Judaism," seeking to authenticate the Protocols. Fifteen of the twenty-four Integralista periodicals I surveyed contained anti-Jewish pronouncements, ranging from traditional antisemitic critiques of Jewish acquisitiveness to radical charges of capitalist–Communist collusion. The more worker-oriented *Ação* had less anti-Jewish content than *A Offensiva*, reminiscent of how Chilean Nacismo's antisemitism diminished when it moved to the left. Integralista authors other than Salgado, Barroso, and Reale also penned antisemitic works.[93]

Antisemitism affected AIB policies. I found only one possible case of Integralista violence against Jews, in which the bombing of a Jewish school in São Paulo in 1934 seriously injured several children. The Jewish community blamed the AIB for the explosion, as well as for threatening to blow up a Jewish theater in that city, but the movement disavowed involvement. Yet its nuclei reported to central authorities on the numbers and occupations of Jews in the area. The AIB's foreign relations department wrote kindred movements in the region on the need to coordinate actions against "Judaic bolshevist materialism." As in Argentina, its views influenced immigration and other government policies. Unlike Integralistas, however, the Vargas regime sometimes regarded Jewish stereotypes favorably, envisioning archetypally rich Jews as valuable immigrants.[94]

The AIB and Other Ethnic and National Groups

Integralistas did not exclude all minorities. Breaking with its Jacobino heritage but agreeing with Alberto Torres, the group issued qualified support for a selective immigration policy. Retention of their language and culture had not kept Germans and Italians from assimilating, the AIB claimed, even as it denounced Jews and Japanese for not mixing. Avid recruitment among the first two groups and its own racism must have influenced the AIB's contradictory rhetoric.[95]

AIB racial views generally echoed those of Alcibíades Delamare, who joined the AIB, and other nationalists of the World War I era. As a "nationalist proletarian movement," Integralismo was the expression of the mestizo masses, proclaimed *Ação*. Reale refuted the notion that racially mixed peoples were inferior without completely rejecting the "scientific" character of racism, while Salgado extolled Brazil's mixed racial heritage and especially its indigenous roots. Taking pride in his supposed Aryanism, Barroso marred this picture of tolerance. Still, the movement claimed to have recruited 5,000 Indians in the Amazon, and *Anauê!* printed photographs of some of them, including a few young women, bare to the waist, offering the Integralista salute. Other photographs displayed the mestizo and African backgrounds of many Integralistas. Except for Barroso's, these views resembled the racial openness of Nacistas but contrasted with the racism of Brazil's ruling elite, still heavily influenced by such thinkers as Oliveira Viana.[96]

The AIB had a shifting relationship with the nation's first black party. Born in 1931, the Frente Negra Brasileira dedicated itself to liberation and mobility for Afro-Brazilians in six states. None of its candidates won office, but the Frente forced the integration of entertainment sites and the civil guard and established social welfare programs in São Paulo. Some of the Frente's branches affiliated with the ANL, prompting the AIB to criticize the Frente's racial exclusivity and Barroso to blame it on Jews.

The preferential treatment of immigrants, the racism of the planter oligarchy, and the Depression-era squeeze of the native-born middle sectors, members of which presided over the Frente pushed the São Paulo center toward the extreme right. So, too, did the fact that its founder was Arlindo Veiga dos Santos, the antisemitic Pátria Nova leader. Thus the AIB embraced it, permitting the Frente to hold events in its São Paulo center. The Frente's shift to the right, however, alienated its mass constituency, forcing it to disband in 1938.[97]

Still, the AIB's acceptance of the São Paulo branch of the Frente indicated its racial tolerance, a component of its alternative to the left. Also part of this alternate radicalism were its pageantry, total way of life, militarized sense of manhood, national socialism, antisemitism, dynamic and spiritual concept of revolution, and openness toward workers. These notions overlapped the Nacistas' and Nacionalistas' alternate radicalism, but the other two groups were nowhere near as successful in creating a distinctive lifestyle.

The AIB's Membership

Its alternative to the left helped Integralismo attract a large following. Although the movement claimed to have a million members by late 1936, most observers cut this figure to about 200,000. Nevertheless, Integralismo was larger than the ANL had been; in terms of numbers, it was also the single largest organization under study and perhaps the single largest fascist group in the Americas. Nacionalistas may have outnumbered Integralistas, but they were divided into many associations. Significantly, however, in terms of percentage of the local population, Nacionalistas ranked first, at 2 percent, followed by Integralistas at 0.5 percent and Nacistas at 0.4 percent.[98]

The AIB's following was diverse as well as numerous. Trindade found that 11 percent of national leaders were of the high bourgeoisie and 88 percent were professionals, while 14 percent of regional leaders pertained to the high bourgeoisie, 64 percent to the professional class, 14 percent to the petit bourgeoisie, and 3 percent to the popular sector. Among the less prominent local leaders and members, 24 percent were professionals, 54 percent petit bourgeois, and 22 percent popular, including rural and urban workers. Trindade's survey is more complete than the information available for the other groups under study, impeding precise comparisons, but it seems that Integralismo included fewer workers than Nacismo and more than the Argentine groups. Its mainly middle-class character resembled Nazism and Italian Fascism more closely than its South American peers and harked back to Ação Social Nacionalista. Nor did the upward mobility of many Integralistas, as documented by Trindade and René Gertz, necessarily set them apart from European fascists.[99]

Most of those sampled by Gertz and Trindade were under thirty-one years of age in 1933. Like the other movements, Integralismo appealed to the young with its promise of a new world and its youthful, virile rhetoric. Disregarding the female members, *Anauê!* declared, "All Integralistas are young men"—at heart if not in actual age. According to *O Integralista*, the voice of AIB university students of São Paulo, "Young men cannot be liberals because they are not impartial and do not have fear. Fear is impotence. Impotence is senility." To be a youth, it continued, is to be free: free "to the point of warring with liberty and creating discipline."[100]

Gender and the AIB

Gender preoccupied the AIB, and allusions to manliness permeated its rhetoric. It wanted to create an "epic of strong men," noted *A Offensiva*. An AIB student paper, *Quarta Humanidade*, warned that the movement "is not a girls' high school. It is a school of men, who . . . are going to construct a great nation." Disputing this assertion, leftists derisively referred to Integralistas as *galinhas verdes* (green hens), suggesting they were cowardly and effeminate. The leftist press seized on Barroso's reaction to the Praça da Sé incident as evidence for its case. Bragging about Integralista courage, the militia leader allegedly crowed, "Eu sou homem para dez," by which he meant that he had the strength of ten men. *Jornal do Povo* of Rio de Janeiro, however, interpreted this ambiguous phrase as meaning he was man enough for ten. It characterized his boast as "Roehmic," referring to Ernst Röhm, the Nazi storm trooper and well-known homosexual, and gleefully published the story under the heading "Integralismo and Homosexuality." The AIB disavowed Barroso's embarrassing statement."[101] Evidently masculinity was equally important to the left and the extreme right.

Violence was part of the Integralistas' militarized concept of masculinity, and as such it belied the insistence of some spokesmen on peacefulness. Reale admitted that at least the first stage of fascism, when its standard-bearers combated evil, was violent. "This movement is of violence," Salgado frankly declared. Life is force and violence is a social need, wrote G. N. Tondella in the AIB organ *A Voz d'Oeste*; to disavow this would contradict the laws of nature.[102]

Nevertheless, the AIB was not as resolutely male in composition and character as the Nacionalistas and Nacistas. With its penchant for encompassing the whole, the movement planned to include women from the beginning. By December 1933, women had organized a uniformed group in Teófilo Otoni, Olbiano de Melo's hometown. Feminine sections or departments of local nuclei arose in the federal district and São Paulo by June 1934 and quickly spread throughout the country. The women's bravery at the Praça da Sé in October 1934 attracted others to the cause. By late 1936, perhaps 20 percent of the Integralistas were female, the largest such contingent in the three countries.[103]

Women joined the movement for interrelated reasons. Several Blusas Verdes testified to their desire to work for the greatness of Brazil, a new sense of life, and the glory of God. Some stressed protecting the Integralista trilogy from anarchy, materialism, and utilitarianism, while others focused on the movement's spiritual and Christian nature, which seemed a natural continuation of their religious education and upbringing. Aurora Nunes Wagner and others emphasized the Communist threat.[104]

Two-thirds of the men Trindade sampled also mentioned anticommunism as an important motive for membership. Yet this preoccupation had special meaning for female Integralistas, whose bonds to family made them fear its decline under communism. Echoing Naci and Nacionalista sentiments, Nilza Perez, editor of the women's section of *Anauê!*, blamed com munism for destroying private property, parental authority over children, and indissoluble marriage ties—the pillars of family strength. By eliminating individually owned homes, it threw families into mass housing, and this, in Perez's opinion, promoted promiscuity. Since Soviet citizens could easily obtain a divorce, the Soviet state had reduced marriage to an "officialized" form of prostitution, a temporary relationship meeting animal-like carnal needs, that left the woman without protection to compensate "for her weakness and powerlessness." The state substituted itself for mothers by sending infants to day-care centers where, Perez said, they received early sexual initiations. Other authors described Russian women as baby-making machines producing slaves for the Soviet system, contrasting this situation with that of Italy, where motherhood was sacrosanct and parents were "the owners of children."[105]

Whether the comparison was accurate or not, the last phrase strikingly evoked the desired hierarchical arrangement in the family and, by extension, society. These Integralista writers also made their distaste for sexuality clear. Despite their rhetoric extolling virility, they seemed to disapprove of male as well as female sexuality. Sensual pleasure bespoke an attachment to worldly things that did not suit a spiritual movement.[106] This contrasted with the mix of unconventional and respectable sexual behavior found in other fascist movements, including Nacismo. Perhaps even more explicitly than Nacismo and Nacionalismo, the AIB identified carnality with the bourgeoisie, Judaism, and communism; all, in its view, were devoted to the stomach.

Perez admitted that family life was not all it should be under capitalism. Only the restoration of the "patriarchal and Christian" family could ensure stability and happiness. She agreed with Barroso that paternal authority in an orderly, Christian home was the base of the ideal hierarchical society. To tie the AIB to this type of society, Salgado dubbed its revolution that of the family, distinguishing it from the French Revolution of the individual, the Russian one of class, and the Italian and German ones of the state. All three authors feared communism, but Perez expressed the concerns of middle-class women anxious to retain their role, security, and Marian image.[107]

Dr. Irene de Freitas Henriques, secretary of the national department of women and Plinianos (significantly grouped together), feared that if women did not enter politics, the family would disappear, and with it love, solidarity, and the entire basis of happiness. To prevent humans from thus turning into animals, women would have to become active in the type of politics that sought to strengthen the state, although not the low form that threatened their purity. Resembling Naci views, this function merely extended their role as "the great guard of the virtues of the home," as the Chefe's wife, Carmela Salgado, put it. As such it helped calm fears about female political participation.[108]

Friends and relatives often influenced women to join Integralismo. One male Integralista noted that it was rare for the wife of a member not to be a Blusa Verde. The AIB women's magazine, *Brasil Feminino*, related a fictitious tale of how a female friend and her attractive brother, both Integralistas, influenced a young woman to give up her frivolous ways and don the green blouse. A year later she and the handsome Integralista married. Further suggesting that joining the movement was akin to sexual conquest, *Anauê!* asked AIB women which aspect of the movement seemed "most seductive." In keeping with the manner in which many women became Integralistas, Carmela Salgado (head of a local feminine department before she married the Chefe), Dulce Thompson, and Iracy Padilha—all wives of AIB leaders—described their activities within the organization as those of wife, mother, companion, sister, and daughter.[109]

The wife usually followed the man's example. *Monitor Integralista* reported on a Blusa Verde who was leaving the movement because her fiancé opposed it. The Chefe asserted that her consideration of her future husband "is worthy of being imitated by all fiancées and wives of Integralistas who still have not dressed in the glorious green blouse, giving prestige, in this way, to the attitude of their bridegrooms and husbands."[110] Preserving male authority overrode even the AIB, although Salgado hoped the two would go hand in hand.

The emphasis on family helps explain the backgrounds of women in the movement. Female Integralistas included some professionals and workers: Wagner was a dentist, Albuquerque was an employee of the power company, Henriques had a higher degree, and Iveta Ribeiro, the editor of *Brasil Feminino*, and Rosalina Coelho Lisboa, an intermediary between Vargas and Salgado, were writers. Yet only a handful figured in biographical dictionaries, indicating that few engaged in any prominent activity outside the home other than Integralismo. The fact that many had male relatives in the organization suggests that their social origins were similarly middle-class, as had been true of the ASN. This contrasts with the higher status of Nacionalista and Nacista women.

The AIB's flattering interest also convinced women to join. It featured women's sections in its two major periodicals, *Anauê!* and *A Offensiva*, and in 1937 *Brasil Feminino* adopted Integralismo, becoming the lone radical-rightist female magazine of the three countries. Although the ANL had a women's auxiliary that addressed a mixture of feminist and middle-class concerns, the AIB's attention to women made it unique among male-led political groups of any ideology.[111]

Integralistas used radical-sounding language to describe the domestic role they envisioned for women. Perez noted that under Christianity, woman reached her height as "woman-mother, woman-saint, women-heroine, woman-educator." In recent times she had achieved rights and become a professional, but at the expense of her primary vocation. The same materialists who granted her political and civil prerogatives denied her a soul: liberals saw her as an adornment, or abandoned her to a base struggle for existence, and communists regarded her as a mere object of pleasure or a reproductive animal. A spiritual movement analogous to Christianity, Integralismo would restore woman to her proper place, "robbing her of 'Yankee' masculinity, pulling her out of her subaltern position as society's object, to make of her a revolutionary of hearts and ideas." Adding to this seemingly progressive rhetoric, Perez insisted that the movement would "liberate" women from stifling social prejudices and foreign bourgeois ideas. The revolution required women who would raise valiant sons with the traditional lullabies of black mothers rather than U.S. fox-trots. Thus they would help create a strong country, "as if it were a single happy and pure home," as AIB official Floriano Japeju Thompson Esteves put it.[112]

Yet the AIB extended domesticity to its limits. It believed that women with ability could become professionals, scientists, artists, bureaucrats, and even politicians, as long as they attended to their duties in the home and defended their virtue and dignity. According to Perez, the AIB wanted a "superior," cultured, yet "feminine" woman who would enter the university and work at man's side, but never forget that as "mother, wife, daughter" she should bestow warmth and affection on her loved ones. She would have "the brain of a man, the physique of a woman, and the heart of a child." Albuquerque claimed that the woman had to remove herself "from the submission in which she lives, of fear and timidity," and obtain a sense of her "autonomy, the certainty of her own worth." These writers allotted women space for independence and public activities, if they remained "feminine."[113]

Women played several roles in Integralismo. The publicity accorded to its female members helped obscure the movement's violence, as in the case of the Liga Patriótica Argentina. With her instinctive sense of harmony, the woman promoted what Salgado regarded as the AIB's mission of creating moral, spiritual, political, and economic beauty. The Blusa Verde inspired "her brother, fiancé, husband, son and grandson in the saintly crusade." As had the mothers of ancient Sparta, she defied the AIB's opponents and offered her progeny to the movement. She trusted the Chefe and obeyed orders without question; custom mandated that the female Integralista follow such strictures even more closely than her male peer. Spreading the AIB creed in the home, school, and workplace was another duty. She fought the materialist ostentation that so angered laborers, as well as immorality, the decay of tradition, and prejudice against the poor. Similar to LPA women, the female Integralista carried out much of this activity by providing a moral example, refraining from viewing degenerate Jewish films, smoking, drinking, reading lurid novels, or wearing revealing bathing suits. By devoting herself to her family and raising Christian, patriotic, and courageous children, the Blusa Verde strengthened the cult of God, family, and fatherland. She was the standard-bearer of *brasilidade* against cosmopolitanism, as well as the epitome of obedience, love, sacrifice, and purity—the values Integralistas held dear.[114] Finally, she helped complete and reproduce the AIB's total way of life.

As in the other movements, women's most important activities were charitable. Blusas Verdes regarded such acts as their Christian duty and as stopgap measures until an Integralista state truly helped the poor. They established libraries and schools to impart literacy, domestic arts, and vocational training to the impoverished, usually women and children, and at these schools they often distributed teaching materials and clothing to the students. Nursing courses helped prepare Blusas Verdes to work at AIB clinics and become Bandeirantes da Caridade, who visited hospitals, asylums, and homes of poverty-stricken Integralistas. Women founded inexpensive restaurants for workers, playgrounds, and milk distribution centers, or *lactários*. They dispensed toys and candy to children at "Christmas for the Poor" celebrations. *AO* claimed that by July 1937 female Integralistas had created hundreds of *lactários*, more than 1,000 clinics, and more than 3,000 schools, and given away goods to more than 5 million people. These figures were probably exaggerated, but women nevertheless accounted for most of the AIB's social welfare projects.[115]

Women formed part of the AIB structure. Initially some belonged to male nuclei and a few served as officers. As the numbers of women grew, however, they congregated in their own departments, which met weekly in the local headquarters at times carefully scheduled to avoid male meetings. The authorities wanted to keep the sexes apart for reasons of propriety and, perhaps, to symbolize the perfect order within the AIB "family" and future state. This separation, however, may have increased women's confidence in organizing themselves. At their meetings, women discussed Integralista publications and listened to talks on gender, political and financial matters, and AIB doctrine offered by men and women. (Occasionally women addressed male nuclei.) There was a female hierarchy that stretched from local and provincial Chefes to the head of the national secretariat, Dr. Henriques. Called the "first lady" of Integralismo, Carmela Salgado did not occupy an important formal position. Henriques, the lone woman in the Integralista Supreme Council, was the unrivaled female leader. Eventually Iveta Ribeiro, Dulce Thompson, and three other women served in the Chamber of 400. The small numbers of women at the top, as well as their subordination to Salgado and other male figures, indicated the limits to female independence in the AIB.[116]

Still, women held their own congresses, such as the one of October 1936 in the federal district that drew representatives from at least eleven states, and another in Petrópolis in June 1937, attended by delegates from the capital and state of Rio de Janeiro. At these proceedings—opened and closed by male leaders—women spoke on such topics as their administrative functions and tasks in the AIB; female religious, cultural, and political vocations; the communist threat; education; and the vices of smoking, drinking, and watching Hollywood films. These events provided opportunities for women from different areas to mingle, exchange ideas, and address large audiences. As did female Nacistas on occasion, many women broke with custom by traveling long distances from their homes to attend the congress of 1936, which lasted several days.[117]

Female electoral participation also broke with custom. Decades of feminist effort culminated in the acquisition of the vote in 1932. The main suffrage organization, the Federação Brasileira Pelo Progresso Feminino, had argued that voting would not remove women from their essential duties, would signal progress toward modernity, and would help stabilize the country. Vargas, the elites, and the Catholic Church accepted this moderate position, especially since its advocates were not leftist or anticlerical, unlike many Chilean and Argentine feminists.[118] That women could vote at all levels made Integralistas, with their electoral strategy, more interested in mobilizing them than their Chilean and especially Argentine peers. A few Blusas Verdes ran for office, and one won a city council seat in São Paulo state. For the presidential campaign of 1937, women taught potential voters to read, for only the literate could vote, and helped them register. The AIB estimated that women cast 50,000 out of 848,000 ballots in the internal plebiscite that overwhelmingly chose Salgado as its presidential candidate.

These statistics may have been inflated, but the low percentage of female voting (women composed 20 percent of the AIB but cast only 6 percent of the ballots) probably reflected reality. AIB reliance on their campaigning and votes boosted female self-esteem. Nevertheless, Salgado may have deflated such sentiments by reminding women that voting was outmoded and useless, implying that the decisions to play politics and mobilize women were opportunistic.[119]

Several AIB authors criticized feminism for obscuring the "natural" differences between the sexes and derided it as a false doctrine. One Integralista praised Nilza Perez for distancing herself from the "analytical, superficial, futile, cheap" feminism of the previous century. Perez considered it absurd for women to demand their rights when humanity was struggling for its existence against communism. To further divide a people already fragmented by partisanship meant handing Brazil over to the reds. Once Integralismo liberated the fatherland, it would assure Brazilian women of their rights, which Perez surely defined differently from feminists.[120]

The victories of feminism made it difficult to dismiss, however. Rather than completely reject its concepts, Integralistas, like Ação Social Nacionalista and Nacismo, preferred to modify them. While opposed to Socialist feminism, Dr. Dario Bittencourt believed that Integralistas could embrace a Christian feminism that accepted the distinct natures, duties, and rights of men and women. *Anauê!* applauded the "true feminism, Christian and Brazilian," of female Integralistas. To foment a "rational feminism" was a goal of *Brasil Feminino*, which endorsed the expansion of women's political and civil rights. At the same time it approved of the fact that married women did not enjoy as many liberties as widows or single women, as this assured order within the family.[121]

The tameness of its feminism notwithstanding, the AIB recruited more women and accorded them greater roles than did Nacismo, Nacionalismo, or most political parties in Brazil. Nor did female participation in Integralismo seem as contradictory as that in the other far-right movements, for it had to reconcile itself with the reality of female suffrage. Despite its violence and appeals to masculinity, the AIB's total way of life required the inclusion of women.

Relations with Other Rightist Groups and Ideologies

The AIB's relations with other rightist groups were more ambivalent than its relations with women. Some authoritarian precursors, such as Ação Social Brasileira, merged with it, but its ties with Pátria Nova were more complex. Sebastião Pagano and other Patrianovistas had participated in SEP and the early AIB. Integralistas, however, generally saw monarchism as foreign and outmoded, views which alienated the Patrianovistas. Nevertheless, AIB publications occasionally commended Pátria Nova, and an article by Pagano appeared in *Panorama*.[122]

The AIB coexisted amicably with the Liga da Defesa Nacional (LDN). The Integralista press applauded its programs, such as its series of anticommunist talks given in the Brazilian Academy of Letters, not coincidentally headed by Barroso, and the LDN's "Centers of Brazilianism" in schools, factories, and military units. Explicitly designed to fight communism, these centers spread Brazilian studies, love of God, and respect for the family and moral principles. For its part the LDN, under its president General Pantaleão Pessôa, welcomed Integralista cooperation. Pessôa told the AIB that as a soldier on active duty, he could not join it or any party, but he sympathized with its nationalism and civic achievements. He invited Integralistas to the LDN "Fatherland Day" celebration in 1936, whose speakers included Rosalina Coelho Lisboa and Vargas. At least half the audience was Integralista, and the Chefe himself was present.[123]

Relations with the Sociedade dos Amigos de Alberto Torres were not as cordial, despite Salgado's and Belisário Penna's early activity in it. The Integralista press commonly cited Torres and approved of the Sociedade's stand against Jewish and Japanese immigration. Yet Sociedade leaders feared that Integralistas wanted to take over the group. President Rafael Xavier, a lawyer and public functionary, hoped to keep the Sociedade nonpartisan, and he thought that the AIB's violence and opposition to individual liberties and electoral politics contradicted Torres's ideas. For these reasons, he fought the Integralista presence in the organization. Barbosa Lima Sobrinho, a Sociedade member and federal deputy, chastised the AIB in the Chamber.[124]

Also at issue were the philosophical links with Nazism and fascism. Integralistas openly admired Italian Fascism; their regard for Nazism was somewhat less obvious, except in Barroso's case. While not denying its fascism, to gain acceptance from Congress, the electorate, and the Catholic Church, the AIB distinguished its doctrine from the European ones. The Integralistas' republicanism and non-Catholic members separated them from Action Française, noted Reale, who also pointed out that the AIB accorded primacy to spirituality rather than the fatherland. Spokespersons dubiously claimed that the AIB, unlike the Nazi and Fascist regimes, opposed Ceasarism and recognized the essential rights of the human person and the autonomy of individuals and groups in relation to the state. They also criticized the German regime's paganism, materialism, and racism; the consensus was that its views on people of color might suit the German context but not the local one.[125]

Nevertheless, building upon the undeniable similarities with Fascism and Nazism, the AIB targeted Brazilians of German and Italian descent. "Of course you are a National Socialist, because of what it has done for Germany; join Integralismo because of what it will do for Brazil," read an AIB flier distributed in Florianópolis, and it directed a similar flier on Fascism and Integralismo toward Italo-Brazilians. Large numbers of Italo-Brazilians, especially among the middle class, responded to such inducements, and the movement was strong in São Paulo and the far south, where many Italians had settled. The Integralista appeal to Teuto-Brazilians, however, competed with that of the Nazis. Many of the first generation who wanted to assimilate, or could not join Nazism because it was limited to the European born, donned the green shirt, whereas the older colonists became Nazis. AIB electoral victories in the German colony zone of Santa Catarina in 1936, the fact that Santa Catarina contained the second largest number of Integralistas of all states, and the presence of 42,000 Camisas Verdes at the provincial congress of Blumenau in 1935 indicated the movement's success among German-Brazilians. So, too, did German membership in the AIB's "Foreign Legion," its contingent of foreign residents, which also included many Italians. Angry at the AIB for splitting German ranks and weakening cultural identity, community leaders and Nazis quietly allied themselves with state governments against the Sigma.[126]

Somewhat hypocritically accusing Integralistas of Nazi ties, southern state governments repressed them. They displayed little concern over the Nazis themselves, demonstrating that the real issue was not ideology or a German state within a state, but the fact that Integralistas, unlike Nazis, contested the authorities' power by running for office and criticizing their policies. This rivalry sparked numerous conflicts, as in Cai in 1935, after which Governor Flores da Cunha of Rio Grande do Sul clamped down on the movement from time to time. Governor Nereu Ramos of Santa Catarina closed AIB provincial headquarters in Florianópolis in September 1936 and detained the provincial chief. In May 1936, Governor Manoel Ribas shut down AIB nuclei and institutions in Paraná. Integralistas in São Paulo and Santa Catarina complained that governments prohibited their parades and functions while permitting those of Nazis.[127]

The AIB and the Political System

The Camisas Verdes' propensity for violence, opposition to regionalism and local elites, and subversive activities were compelling reasons for states to suppress them. These factors and the powerful motive of retaining power guided the actions of authorities throughout Brazil. In 1936 the government of Minas Gerais prohibited Integralistas from wearing uniforms in public and holding marches and other activities. Perhaps because of AIB successes at the polls, in the same year Espírito Santo also forbade the use of the green shirt and sent the police out to harass Integralistas.[128]

Persecution of the AIB reached a high in Bahia, the state with the largest number of Camisas Verdes. Bahia had received much attention from the AIB, which intended its local branch to serve as a model of racial democracy for the nation. Here, Tenente Juraci Magalhães, first as interventor and then as governor, forged ties with local oligarchs to construct his base. Unlike Magalhães, the AIB courted the people, becoming the first organized ideological movement in the *sertão*—and the first to criticize the landowners. However vague and religious, its call for change appealed to devout Bahians. After the government repressed the ANL and Integralistas began to enter local elections, they became the main opposition force in the state. Magalhães closed their nuclei in the interior from time to time and limited the wearing of uniforms. In September 1936, he claimed to have discovered evidence of an Integralista plot in correspondence between Provincial Chief Joaquim de Araújo Lima and the AIB national secretary of finance, Belmiro Valverde, which stated that if the Bahian government further hurt the organization it would abet communism, and the AIB would have to strike first before communists did. Magalhães ordered police to shut all nuclei, seize documents, and arrest AIB leaders, including several military officers, efforts which led to Integralista casualties. The police found papers that the governor claimed supported his case, such as plans to attack Communists, if necessary. They also found a map of military installations and a questionnaire from national AIB authorities asking about the strength of military forces, AIB militiamen, leftists, and Jews. Finding arms in his office, policemen arrested Valverde in Rio de Janeiro, but they released him shortly thereafter.[129]

Perhaps as a hint to the president, Magalhães warned it was criminal to favor the AIB in order to fight communism. He thought that Vargas "gave prestige to Integralismo. He was in love with Integralismo." Vargas considered Magalhães overly worried, for the AIB was not as strong as it pretended.[130]

Integralistas denied the coup allegations and characterized them as a pretext for persecution. Both points were probably true. The exchange between Lima and Valverde was vague, and the map, plans, and survey were part of the AIB's standard operating procedure. Perhaps for this reason, in March 1937 the National Security Tribunal freed the prisoners pending trial. Despite a clause in the National Security Law forbidding public gatherings, and protest from opposition deputies, no one prevented jubilant Integralistas from parading through the capital. In June 1937, when Vargas lifted the state of siege during the presidential campaign, the nuclei in Bahia reopened.[131]

The Bahia controversy renewed the debate on outlawing the AIB, and the Chamber deliberated on this matter in September 1936. Wildly applauded by Camisas Verdes in the galleries, Edmundo Barreto Pinto, who had just returned from a trip to Germany, asserted that only the electoral court could close a legal political party. For Oswaldo Lima of Pernambuco, who insisted that rightist extremism was necessary to protect Brazilian democracy against communism, another mark in the AIB's favor was its support for family and country. Father Pedro Macário de Almeida of the oligarchical opposition Mineiro Republican Party disagreed, arguing that AIB violence contradicted its belief in God, fatherland, and family. Adalberto Corrêa, head of the National Commission for the Repression of Communism, believed the government should put all anticommunist forces to use, including Integralismo, and patriots should unite behind the campaign against communism. Gaúcho João Neves da Fontoura, an opposition leader, countered that people should unite not only around anticommunism, but around the constitution and antifascism.[132]

Some of the discussion centered on the questions of arms and the military. Since it was illegal to possess weapons without police permission, Abílio de Assis, class representative of industrial employees and opponent of government repression, wondered how the armed AIB escaped prosecution. When Jeová Mota insisted that the arms found in Valverde's office were to protect the AIB against communist attack, others argued this was the job of official forces. Clemente Mariani, leader of the Bahian delegation and member of Magalhães's Social Democratic Party, read the captured AIB documents, emphasizing revelations of infiltration into the military. Mota claimed that Integralistas in the armed forces offset communist influence, to which Mariani responded that this was not the AIB's task.

The nub of the matter was how a democratic government should defend itself—Vargas's authoritarianism notwithstanding. Leopoldo de Diniz

Junior, once of the fascist Ação Social Brasileira and now of the majority, did not want the regime to shut down a legally recognized party, but others disagreed. Perhaps for pragmatic reasons, some deputies equated communism and Integralismo and thought the government should suppress both, rather than merely the first. Quoting Salgado as saying that democracy was the enemy because it led to communism, Tenente Augusto Amaral Peixoto, an opposition deputy, offered a resolution allowing the government to prohibit antidemocratic groups during states of siege. It passed in December 1936 but had no effect.[133]

The debate revealed that Pinto and Corrêa had joined the AIB camp. Pinto addressed a meeting of Integralista parliamentarians and officials the next month, and he and Mota gave the delegation a tour of the chamber. In 1937 Pinto read one of Salgado's speeches to that body, setting off a loud pro-AIB demonstration in the galleries eventually broken up by police. Backed by Corrêa, he tried to include the Chefe's words in the minutes.[134]

The AIB and Religion

As voiced by Father Almeida, the debate had also raised the critical issue of the AIB and religion. Integralismo, like Nacismo and Nacionalismo, greatly overlapped Catholic opinion. Salgado, Barroso, and Reale claimed the movement was based on God, although they maintained that it was not, strictly speaking, a religious one; for their part, Alceu Amoroso Lima and other Catholic lay leaders favored an inner spiritual revolution that resembled the Integralista type. Camisas Verdes derived much of their social program and critique of capitalism from church doctrine. The AIB's emphasis on piety, morality, family, authority, and corporatism was similar to that of the church, as was its opposition to liberalism, communism, Jews, and Masons. If Camisas Verdes did not promote the union of church and state, fearing one could become the instrument of the other, neither did many Catholics in the 1930s. Catholics must have also appreciated AIB support for a concordat with the Vatican.[135]

Appeals to Christian sentiment filled Integralista publications. The most compelling was Salgado's article on the "Christian meaning of Integralismo," printed in the shape of a cross. Even the barely literate could not fail to grasp this powerful image. Publicly professing his faith, the Chefe declared that the Integral State came from, was inspired by, and would work for and move toward Christ. A Offensiva carried a regular "Catholic column" to further link the movement with the religion.[136]

Through such appeals Integralistas elicited "the tacit and frequently open approval" of the clergy, according to the U.S. military attaché. Hundreds of priests affirmed their support and lent concrete aid to the Sigma; six were in the AIB Corte do Sigma and seven in the Chamber of 400. Twenty out of the 100 bishops and archbishops made pro-Integralista declarations. Bishop Manoel Nunes Coelho of Aterrado claimed that Integralismo was the only movement capable of preventing the end of Christian civilization. Integralismo was clearly superior to liberal democracy, noted Bishop José Maurício de Rocha of Bragança, and its program was the best he had seen in Brazil. Religious schools disseminated AIB readings and hosted chapters of Plinianos, while orders held retreats for the movement. Catholic seminaries used a text that praised Integralismo as the most spiritual and perfect force for change. Among Salgado's advisers were priests such as Father Leonel Franca, a respected scholar and Cardinal Leme's negotiator with the government.[137]

Prominent laypeople made their way into Integralismo or publicly supported it. Seven members of the Centro Dom Vital were AIB leaders, and others, such as Hamilton Nogueira and Jonathan Serrano, attended AIB gatherings. Jackson de Figueiredo's brother and the famous Catholic writer Tasso de Silveira, formerly of Propaganda Nativista, became Integralistas. Participants in Ação Católica, Juventude Católica, and the Círculos Operários, as well as other laypeople, joined Integralismo as a means of fighting communism, spreading Catholic values and social doctrine, and, as they saw it, deepening their faith.[138]

Catholics had reasons, however, to distrust Integralismo. One was the Integralista tendency to appropriate Catholic belief and substitute itself for that faith, as exemplified by the annual ritual commemorating the outlawing of the militia, the "Night of the Silent Drums." Each local chief began the ceremony at 11:00 P.M. by handing over the proceedings to the humblest and poorest Camisa Verde, who represented Salgado. In São Paulo, the widow of one of the martyrs of the Praça da Sé received this task. Those assembled sang the Integralista hymn, recited the names of Integralista martyrs and deceased nucleus members, and read sections of the October Manifesto. A speech followed. At midnight there were three minutes of quiet, representing the muffling of the drums, during which the Camisas Verdes silently asked for the happiness of their enemies in the "Prayer of the Drums." After an announcement that Integralistas throughout Brazil had observed this silence, a person read a poem on the meaning of the ritual. The assembled swore loyalty to the AIB statutes, sang the national anthem, and shouted *anauês* to Brazil and God. Finally, the nucleus telegrammed the Chefe that it had held the ceremony.[139] Through this ritual Integralistas bonded with their organization's history, and the telegrams and simultaneity of its celebration around the country demonstrated how the AIB united Brazil. Choosing a worker to officiate showed the movement's interest in the lower class (and, in this case, women); at the same time, the temporary inversion of hierarchy only reinforced it. Most important, the martyrology, mystical rhetoric, and greetings to God suggested that the AIB, like Nacismo, was establishing an alternative religion.

There were many other indications of this strategy. Salgado referred to the "apostles" or "evangelists" of the AIB's spiritual revolution. Integralistas commonly characterized their slogan as the trilogy or even "saintly trilogy." A large AIB parade, according to one writer, converted Brazilians into brothers "in this incomparable Eucharist of the Total Fatherland." The rituals and cult of martyrs resembled Catholic ones; members celebrated religious marriage, baptism, and funeral rites that also included Integralista features. In the funeral ceremonies, the highest AIB authority present noted that the deceased had gone to the "Militia on the Other Side." An adoring writer for *Anauê!* compared Salgado, the "salvation of Brazil," to Saint Paul: both emerged in decadent times, sacrificed everything for the cause, suffered from Jewish hatred and threats, and created "an enormous spiritual family" of diverse people. According to Deputy Clemente Mariani, effigies of Christ and Salgado were located next to each other on the walls of the Bahian nuclei. One *Anauê!* cover depicted the two side by side, with Salgado a bit higher. Such statements and practices ran the risk of sacrilege.[140]

Balancing its positive and negative attributes, Alceu Amoroso Lima issued a carefully nuanced endorsement of the AIB. How should Catholics react to a movement whose precursor was Jackson de Figueiredo? The Centro Dom Vital president saw the oath to the leader and exaltation of violence, will, and action as problems. The AIB's belief in freedom of religion was a perilous but acceptable temporary alliance against greater evils. (To the AIB it essentially meant, as it did for Nacistas, the ability to recruit German Protestants.) Also dangerous was the AIB's tendency to substitute itself for Catholicism or the possibility that Catholics would become too dedicated to the movement. Catholic Camisas Verdes might confuse liberalism with freedom, thus undermining the church's defense of the human person, and regard church organizations as passive. They might also criticize church tolerance of different parties and Catholics who remained outside Integralismo, and perhaps they might even see the movement as the church's savior.

The movement's statism and the chance that it might elevate the nation above religion troubled him, as Nacionalismo's similar tendencies had troubled Meinvielle and Franceschi. Yet since they shared allegiances and enemies, particularly communism, sympathetic understanding was the least that Catholics could offer Integralismo. They could also enter it, provided they subordinated the political to the spiritual, although Lima opposed the participation of priests or leaders of Ação Católica. He also was suspicious of female involvement in the AIB or any other political party. While the church had to retain freedom of action and could not identify itself with any political tendency, no party could fulfill Catholic political needs and social doctrine as completely as Integralismo.[141]

In later statements Lima sounded even more approving. The AIB was a "great force of resistance" to communism, "confessed or masked," and campaigns against "this growing and healthy" force were unpatriotic. Nor did he find it totalitarian or antisemitic; as shown above, Lima himself was prejudiced against Jews. Nevertheless, Lima never joined the movement, preferring to be a "soldier of Christ." AIB publications tended to edit out his qualifiers, yet Lima's less than complete support and his nonpartisanship dissatisfied Integralista leaders.[142]

Official nonpartisanship suited the church, which had constructed a congenial relationship with the Vargas government. Under Cardinal Leme's leadership, the institution offered itself as a bulwark of stability and a potential ally of the state in the chaotic 1930s. In this context the church expanded its organizational network and pressed its demands. Leme created Ação Católica and gave impetus to the workers' circles, which grew to seventy-five with a membership of 50,000 by the mid-1930s. As an antileftist project, the circles received the support of Federal Police Chief Müller and the Ministry of Labor, where Catholic personnel had achieved influence. Run by the Centro Dom Vital, the Liga Eleitoral Católica (LEC, 1932–37) was a political pressure group that negotiated with parties to make their platforms more favorable to Catholic interests, recommended candidates who favored Catholic demands, registered and mobilized Catholic voters, and lobbied the constituent assembly to insert its ideas into the constitution of 1934. The resulting document mentioned God in the preamble, prohibited divorce and recognized religious marriages, and provided for religious instruction in public schools during regular hours and religious aid to the military. The constitution also defended private property, recognized syndical pluralism, and included Social Catholic–sounding labor provisions. It represented a victory for the church.[143]

The church's changing status, as well as conditions in Germany, affected the hierarchy's views of the AIB. The anticommunist Archbishop João Becker of Porto Alegre, who had supported the ASN, initially praised European fascism and Integralismo, while advising the AIB to put more emphasis on Catholicism. In 1935, however, he encouraged Catholics to defend Vargas instead of Integralismo, for the constitutional order provided sufficient guarantees and rights to the church. The archbishop feared that Integralismo, like German Nazism, entailed risks of dictatorship and anticlericalism. In part, he may have been thinking of Integralista calls for the "nationalization of the clergy," or replacing foreign priests with Brazilians, reminiscent of Nazi attempts to Germanize Catholicism. These views led Becker to try, with little success, to revive Ação Social Brasileira as a nonpartisan rival to the AIB. Despite Becker's suspicions of the AIB, church publications in his diocese praised it.[144]

More consistently than Becker, Bishop Gastão Liberal Pinto of São Carlos fought Integralismo. He argued that the AIB substituted itself for Catholicism, put itself above the church, and denigrated Catholic organizations. Discouraging Pinto from publicizing his views, Cardinal Leme pointed to the AIB's spiritualism, opposition to communism and other anti-Christian forces, and allegiance to Catholic social doctrine. Leme not only applauded Integralismo but smoothed over the areas of conflict between it and the church.[145]

Some lay intellectuals added to Pinto's critique and Lima's cautions. The AIB's view that the church was weak and needed its protection, as well as its hints that Catholics who did not join were bourgeois hypocrites and cowards, angered many.[146] Some Ação Universitária Católica members mistrusted Integralismo for co-opting religious sentiments and energies. Questioning the church's uncertain role in the future AIB state, the Catholic law professor Alexandre Corrêia thought no existing party satisfied a Catholic consciousness. O Legionário of São Paulo agreed, fearing the danger of a movement that, like Maurras, mainly saw the church as the creator of useful social myths. Other Catholic authors decried its "divinization" of the state. Salgado's old rival, Severino Sombra, tried to attract pious youths from the AIB to a new legion throughout Brazil in mid-1937. It preached that the choice the AIB posed between communism and fascism, a doctrine troublesome to the church and laborers alike, was a false one. Peace, the constitution, and Catholic social doctrine were the best defense against communism, not Salgado's violent agitation. These conservative critics voiced not only Catholic concerns but those of local oligarchies fearing Integralista radicalism and centralization of power. The Centro Dom Vital, after all, had supported the São Paulo revolution of 1932. Perhaps most telling was Sombra's accusation that, through its support of a directed economy, recognition of the existence of class struggle, and a deterministic belief in revolution, the AIB approximated communism.[147]

Sombra had tried, unsuccessfully, to convince ecclesiastical authorities to condemn the AIB, and Father Câmara defended the movement against his charges. One of the priest's most effective tools was to point out that many of the criticisms Sombra leveled against the AIB also applied to Câmara and Sombra's old Legião Cearense. The open quarrel between two prominent Catholics displeased church authorities in Ceará. Over Leme's opposition, Câmara moved to Rio de Janeiro to become Salgado's secretary and assistant and eventually joined the AIB Supreme Council.[148]

The Câmara–Sombra debate was part of an ongoing polemic in which Integralistas at times appeared defensive and even hostile. Salgado complained of bourgeois Catholics carping about the oath while "my militiamen die defending the idea of God." Only communists benefited from Catholic–AIB discord, noted another Camisa Verde. Lúcio José dos Santos, a devout professor and AIB member, grumbled that Catholics condemned aspects of Integralismo that they tolerated in other parties. When the LEC issued the same approval for all parties that accepted a minimum of three of its points, Salgado angrily demanded special recognition for having agreed to all ten. The LEC's refusal left bitterness.[149]

Cardinal Leme handled the issue of Integralismo adroitly. His reply to Pinto indicated his sympathy with the movement; his grievance with Câmara revealed his distaste for obvious clerical participation in even a compatible party, but he accepted quieter though broad priestly involvement. A tradition of political neutrality, the priority accorded to the spiritual realm and to Ação Católica, and particularly the vital negotiations with the state dictated the cardinal's official nonpartisanship. Leme and the church reaped the benefits of the new constitution and of government favor, yet at the same time profited from Integralista antiliberalism and anticommunism. Furthermore, the church retained friendly ties with the movement in order to be able to influence and gain concessions from it should it reach power. This was, then, a two-tiered strategy.[150] On a spectrum ranging from the Argentine church, identified with Nacionalismo, to the Chilean, relatively distant from Nacismo, the Brazilian lay between the two but closer to the Argentine.

Vargas, the Military, and the Estado Novo

Facing the growing authoritarianism of the Vargas regime and harassment in various states, Salgado campaigned for the presidential election of January 1938.[151] Prevented by the constitution from seeking another term, Vargas appeared to be out of the running. Governor Armando Sales Oliveira of São Paulo, the candidate of the Paulista elite and hastily formed Brazilian Democratic Union, stood for regionalism and liberalism, with nods in the direction of fascist Europe. José Américo de Almeida, who was a Tenente, an ally of Juraci Magalhães, and a fervent anti-Integralista, appeared the popular choice, although the electorate played no role in nominating him. Although Almeida seemed to be the official candidate, his populism alienated Vargas, military officers, and elites. Salgado argued tellingly that he alone represented an established national party with a coherent ideology, rather than a momentary electoral alliance.

Violence marred the constitutional image that he sought, however. Gunfire broke up a parade of 20,000 Integralistas in São Paulo in July 1937, leaving one dead and eighteen wounded, seventeen of them Integralistas. A Jewish peddler and suspected Communist, the slain man was killed by Camisa Verde Eugenio Aducci, who claimed his victim had aimed a gun at Salgado. The police detained Aducci, a probable member of the AIB secret police. The shooting of a young Blusa Verde in Muguy, Espírito Santo, perhaps by Communists, immediately followed this episode. To opposition legislators, the incidents again demonstrated the AIB's violent and antidemocratic tendencies.[152]

The violence then spread to other cities. A battle between AIB members and opponents in Porto Alegre in early August left one dead and three gravely wounded. Integralistas then invited trouble by invading labor's space and scheduling a rally in Campos, Rio de Janeiro, a sugar mill town with an active union movement, on August 15. Shooting broke out when an AIB speaker ignored warnings by police to moderate his intemperate remarks. Believing they were under attack, policemen fired into the crowd. As the multitude fled the gunfire, an angry group chased down the hated Integralistas and forced some to strip off their green shirts. Altogether, thirteen to fifteen perished, including three or four Integralistas, and several dozen were wounded. Even a state police investigator agreed that law enforcement officials had erred, and the officers who had ordered the firing were detained. Salgado blamed the massacre on the authorities, who in turn pinned it on the AIB and closed its local headquarters. In September, Integralistas killed an Almeida campaign leader in the federal district.[153]

These incidents had repercussions for the movement. Salgado temporarily banned the uniform, and the police chief of Rio de Janeiro prohibited weapons at public gatherings and forbade police, many of whom were rumored to be Integralistas, from using political insignia. Formerly of the Liga Nacionalista, Minister of Justice José Carlos de Macedo Soares declared that defense against communism did not mean encouraging extreme rightist opponents of the constitutional regime like Integralismo. Indeed, the authorities should fight the AIB as well as communism. Anti-Integralistas in the chamber applauded the minister's remarks, the strongest yet uttered by a national official. With a little energy the government could repress Integralismo, advised José Tomás de Cunha Vasconcelos, a pro-Vargas deputy. In September, however, the Supreme Electoral Tribunal nullified Soares's words by recognizing the AIB's constitutionality and its right to wear uniforms and issue propaganda.[154]

Thanks to shared goals and AIB efforts, the military was much friendlier to Integralismo than the minister of justice and some deputies. Influenced by long-standing authoritarian currents in the military, most officers, particularly after the purges following the rebellion of November 1935, shared the AIB's anticommunism and devotion to hierarchy and order. Some officers may have been suspicious of the organization's militia, but others regarded it as a potential reserve under the army's control. Although they visualized an independent role for the armed body under an Integralista state, Camisas Verdes did not disabuse them of this notion. Integralistas obtained support through flattering articles on the military in the AIB press. Barroso taught classes in the Escola Militar, and Integralistas spoke to officers and posted articles from the AIB press in their mess halls. They described their recruitment efforts as a means of stemming communism in the ranks, which elicited approval from some military leaders. The AIB electoral program called for obligatory military service, increasing the military budget and popular support for the military, and nationalizing the state militias, points attractive to officers. When military officials balked at their men taking another oath or wearing another uniform, the AIB released the armed forces from these obligations. Responding to Chief of Staff General Góes Monteiro's opposition to military involvement in politics, Salgado claimed that Integralismo was not political in the usual sense of the word; moreover, it was a legally registered party and, unlike the liberal parties, contained no

disorderly or communist tendencies. Integralistas also conspicuously attended military parades and ceremonies, such as the memorial for the victims of the 1935 revolt.[155]

Frequent notices and photographs of military members in the AIB
press testified to its successful recruitment. There were twenty officers in the
Corte do Sigma, and four army officers and two admirals in the Chamber
of Forty. In 1936 the Chefe boasted of followers in all ranks of the armed
forces and state militias, claiming that 4 percent of male Integralistas were
military personnel. Whether this figure was accurate or not, according to a
War Ministry report as many as one-fourth of army officers and half of
naval officers were members or sympathizers. Indeed, the degree of support
in the navy may have been higher. Although they often belonged to ordi-
nary nuclei, army and military police officers even had their own nucleus in
Rio de Janeiro.[156]

The movement also enjoyed favor among high-ranking nonmembers.
Federal Police Chief Müller and General Pantaleão Pessôa admired the AIB,
and General Newton Cavalcanti, the Chefe's friend, delivered speeches in its
praise. General José Meira de Vasconcelos, commander of the Escola Militar, had a favorable review of Barroso's Brasil: Colônia de banqueiros printed
in its bulletin and ordered three copies of the book for its library. Military
organizations invited Integralistas to speak at their functions. Góes Monteiro commended the AIB's "Brazilian" character and gave a speech at the
inauguration of an Integralista school for workers in Niteroi.[157]

Yet support for the AIB was not unanimous among officers. An incident in September 1936, when antagonism between Integralistas expelled
from the military and several soldiers led to an AIB attack on the second
battalion of the Fifth Infantry Regiment in Pindamonhagaba, São Paulo,
could not have pleased them. The military had contained ANL adherents,
Tenentes, and other reformers who were enemies of the AIB. Among these
were Admiral and Deputy Augusto Amaral Peixoto and former Tenentes Juraci Magalhães and General Manoel Rabelo. Rabelo denounced the AIB's
ties to the church and thought the violent movement required disciplining.
A group of army officers in 1936 asked him to assure Vargas of their support
against Integralismo, but as the president had just invited some Camisas
Verdes to talk with him, the general decided the timing was poor and refused. A positivist, Admiral Américo Silvado censured Integralismo as monarchist, reactionary, and opportunistic. As the decade wore on and conservatives Góes Monteiro and War Minister Eurico Gaspar Dutra consolidated
power, these voices became fewer. Still, Góes Monteiro and even sympa-

thizers like Cavalcanti were suspicious of the AIB's militia, mobilization of the population, and fostering of multiple loyalties in the military.[158]

Military backing was vital for the Integralistas. It was unlikely they could win the election, for the electorate numbered about 3 million, and the 800,000 ballots supposedly cast in the plebiscite included those of illiterates not qualified to participate in the presidential voting. Nor had they yet created a popular movement capable of seizing power, although their efforts had been prodigious. Only through the armed forces could they achieve control, and it was unclear whether this body would back them to this extent. Vargas had cultivated the military by expanding its budget and greatly increasing the size of the army. Military leaders distrusted Almeida's populism and in general feared the unsettling effects of the divisive campaign. These views led them to favor the creation of an authoritarian regime under Vargas allied with Integralismo.[159]

Also critical was the president's stance toward Integralismo. Especially after the Communist revolts, Vargas favored the movement. His government repressed the ANL but did not use the tools provided by Congress to hinder the AIB, and public officials except for Soares praised the AIB or remained neutral. Vargas accepted the state governments' anti-Integralista actions but did not extend them to the federal level. The Integralistas' fierce campaign against democracy, politicians, and communism helped create acceptance for a coup that would eliminate these forces, although the left after 1935 was only a phantasma. Thus the extreme right served Vargas's purpose of maintaining himself in power. Aware of military sympathy for Integralismo, he did not want to move against the AIB until he was sure of support from the armed forces. At the same time, by eliminating the AIB's rivals, he cleverly positioned himself as the strongest alternative to fascism.[160]

The creation of Defesa Social Brasileira (DSB) in October 1937 hinted that Vargas was moving away from the AIB and gathering conservative forces around him. The leaders of this semiofficial anticommunist organization included military officers and Federal Police Chief Müller; Minister of Justice Soares and Cardinal Leme attended the installation ceremony. Upper-class male and female, business, and government circles around the country rapidly adhered to it. Its duplication of some of the AIB's role, and Severino Sombra's presence in the DSB's council, suggested it was the movement's rival. At the same time, sensing that the authorities were moving toward a dictatorship, Leme lent his support by issuing a pastoral letter urging his flock to unite behind the government and against communism.[161]

Nevertheless, contacts between Vargas and the Integralistas increased as the fateful month of November approached. In June Vargas cordially received an AIB delegation presenting Salgado as a candidate. On his orders, Minister of Education Francisco Campos consulted with Salgado several times in September. Campos informed Salgado of the coup planned by Vargas and top military leaders and asked for his support, as well as his opinion of Campos's draft of a new fascist-inspired constitution. Sensing the Chefe's hesitancy, Campos assured him that Integralismo would form the base of the new regime. Müller and General Dutra gave Salgado further assurances, and Cavalcanti urged him to meet with Vargas to allay his fears. The president suggested that a coup would be better than an Almeida victory for the AIB, for the populist was hostile to the Integralistas. He seemed to promise the movement the Ministry of Education, which would control the AIB militia. Concluding he had no other alternative, Salgado accepted Vargas's plan.[162]

Meanwhile, the head of the AIB secret service, Olympio Mourão Filho, had drafted a plan of a possible Communist rebellion in order to prepare an Integralista response. This antisemitically labeled "Cohen Plan" made its way into the hands of the army General Staff, which revised and released it to the press as the description of an actual plot. The day after its release on September 30, Congress voted to grant Vargas his requested state of siege. Knowing the document was untrue, Salgado nevertheless announced that it demonstrated the impossibility of protecting the nation against communism under the existing constitution, and he pledged full support to the president and armed forces. Moderates like Minister of Justice Soares left the government. The suspension of constitutional freedoms, the criticism of democracy, and the climate of fear blocked the electoral campaign and accelerated the movement toward the coup.[163]

Vargas's maneuvers exposed the weaknesses within Integralismo. Its bourgeois wing supported Salgado's decision, but the syndicalists and anti-imperialists opposed it, and some of them favored a countercoup. The Chefe decided to put on a show of force to impress Vargas and reassure the more belligerent members. The AIB claimed that 50,000 Camisas Verdes marched in the parade of November 1 through downtown Rio de Janeiro to Guanabara Palace, where they saluted Vargas. Others counted only 17,000 to 20,000 participants, confirming the president's view that observers had overestimated Integralista strength.[164]

The trio of Vargas, the military, and Integralismo that Salgado had hoped for became a duo. Supported by the military, Vargas dissolved Congress, installed the new constitution, and proclaimed the Estado Novo on

November 10. Campos failed to inform Salgado of the date, which authorities had moved up from November 15, and the president did not even mention the Integralistas in his speech announcing the new order. Controlled by the government, the press attacked Integralismo and then ignored it. Salgado soon learned that the post of minister of education was contingent on the dissolution of the AIB, and he delayed accepting it. He had thought the movement would be the regime's political base, but the decree of December 2 closing political parties and militias and forbidding the use of uniforms and symbols affected it as well. The government shut down AIB centers, broke up their meetings, and even detained members. To survive, the AIB and other political groups had to change their names and become cultural organizations, divested of military members. The government, however, did not recognize Salgado's new Asociação Brasileira de Cultura, or ABC. Now that Integralismo had served its purpose, Vargas wanted to destroy this independent source of power, despite its ideological affinity.[165]

Reale, Barroso, and other Integralistas believed that Salgado had lost control of events. All along, voices within and outside the movement had criticized his irresolute leadership, and his faults were now painfully obvious. Some thought that after the coup mayors in the interior might have been willing to hand over their posts to the local chiefs, whom they considered allied with the new regime, but Salgado never gave the order. Barroso and Reale wanted the Chefe to accept the ministry as a means of keeping power, but Belmiro Valverde and others opposed this notion out of distrust of Vargas. Meanwhile Rosalina Coelho Lisboa mediated between the president and Salgado. After two months of vacillation, the Chefe finally refused the post in late January 1938. Incapable of exploiting the moment, Salgado let the initiative pass to Vargas. Years later, however, Reale wondered if the proper moment had ever really arrived.[166]

Government actions against the AIB provoked rumblings in the church and military. The policy troubled Cardinal Leme and AIB member Father Câmara, but eventually the administration and the church mended relations. The problem with the military was more serious. In his resignation letter to Dutra, Cavalcanti decried official policy and the betrayal of his assurances to Salgado about the coup. Altogether the authorities forced ten pro-Integralista generals to resign.[167]

Some disgruntled military men found their way into the two Integralista conspiracies against the president. As early as October 1937, Barroso attempted, unsuccessfully, to secure arms from Italy for a possible revolution. Salgado approved the plans for a coup but kept his distance from them, assigning leadership to Belmiro Valverde. Financed in part by Flores da Cunha, whom Vargas had forced out of the governorship of Rio Grande do Sul, the conspiracy also drew upon Sales Oliveira and other oligarchical and democratic opponents of Vargas, and General José Maria de Castro Junior directed the military operation. Scheduled for mid-March 1938, the leaders called it off at the last minute when problems arose with the naval contingent. Informed of the plot, the government arrested some of the conspirators and released them shortly thereafter. Valverde, Castro Junior, and others planned a second attempt for May 11. Naval lieutenant and non-Integralista Severo Fournier led an assault on Guanabara Palace, while other groups attacked the naval ministry, the homes of Góes Monteiro and Felinto Müller, and several radio stations. After a two-and-a-half-hour delay, the military unenthusiastically rescued the president. Authorities arrested about 1,500 people, including Integralistas and low-level navy officers. It sentenced some to prison terms of one to ten years, but freed most before they completed their sentences. The moderate rightist civilian conspirators went into exile, as did Salgado, who boarded a German ship for Portugal.[168]

Conclusion

The repressive measures before and after the coup attempts left Integralismo a shambles. Yet its prospects had already dimmed before the Estado Novo. Its attempt to attract a broad following and subdue the left through radical means manifested its fascist character. The AIB's alternative to leftism included nationalism and anti-imperialism, an opening to workers, antisemitism, criticism of the oligarchy, racial tolerance, a cult of violent masculinity, and an all-encompassing style of life. The AIB also fit Payne's criteria for fascism, except for the Catholic influence. Mixing conservatism with radicalism, as was typical of fascism, and employing a populist style new to Brazil, it mobilized a larger segment of the populace than any other party. To a greater extent than was true of Nacionalismo and Nacismo, women entered a movement that otherwise exalted its masculinity. This popular support, however, was insufficient to propel Integralismo into power.

To have done so, the AIB would have needed additional assistance from conservatives, the church, and particularly the military. Indeed, it amassed considerable support in the church, the armed forces, and the administration, although all three had reservations about its extremism. Alienated by its centralizing and mobilizational tendencies, the state oligarchies reacted more strongly against the movement. In their view the government's antileftism obviated the need for the AIB's more radical program. The crafty Vargas managed to outwit the Integralistas and use them to create his own right-wing dictatorship. Ultimately, albeit grudgingly in some cases, most members of the elite, the Catholic hierarchy, and the military found the stability and favors offered by Vargas more attractive than the dangers of a green-shirted revolution. The strength of conservatism spelled the weakness of the extreme right.

CHAPTER 12

Conclusion

Chilean Nacistas (MNS), Brazilian Integralistas (AIB), and Argentine Nacionalistas believed that they were living through a transitional moment in which their brand of radical nationalism would displace degenerate liberalism, conservatism, and socialism. The extirpation of these ideologies, their representatives, and the decay they had fostered figured prominently in what Roger Griffin calls the extreme right's "nebulous but radical moral and social revolution." The goal of this revolution was to set up a hierarchical and dictatorial state, inspired by a cult of heroism, that would unify and purify the nation. These traits, according to Griffin, were the essence of fascism.[1]

There was much carryover from the past to this project. Earlier activists had opposed liberalism, leftism, and militant unions, and they questioned democracy. The sense of willful activism and manhood of the wartime period contributed to the more radical cult of heroism of the 1930s. Catholic thought, whose influence on the right was growing in the late 1920s, permeated the views of hierarchy, corporatism, social justice, and Jews. Especially in Argentina and Brazil, radical rightists inherited and adapted the anti-immigrant and antisemitic sentiments of previous movements. Indeed, the groups of the 1930s fulfilled Jackson de Figueiredo's and Hamilton Nogueira's dream of a radical ascetic spiritual force opposed to a "Jewish" materialist, sensual, and revolutionary order.

The movements shared a common belief in what their members saw as a third way, between capitalism and socialism, that fit neither in the left nor the right. In reality, their devotion to hierarchy and private property, antagonism toward labor autonomy and the left, and provisional alliances with conservatives placed them in the right. Their pronouncements on gender and the family offered the clearest evidence of their right-wing identity. The nation was the family writ large: an orderly home, ruled by male and parental authority, with masculine men and feminine women, meant an orderly society.

Nevertheless, the ambiguity of their message helped them maximize their appeal. On the radical side, they formulated an alternative to the left, a revolutionary project of the twentieth century that, they claimed, superseded a left born in the 1800s. Their violent militarized version of masculinity and emphasis on youth, pageantry, and, in Brazil, an all-encompassing lifestyle formed part of this alternative, as did the grudging respect that accompanied their anticommunism. Injecting values into society and governance and establishing a corporatist state, in their opinion, would solve pressing economic and social questions, although they favored Social Catholic policies. By redefining capitalism as greedy and parasitic behavior and the bourgeoisie as a materialistic, antinational spirit, radical rightists could pit themselves against these malevolent forces. They substituted the struggle of proletarian against capitalist nations for that of proletarians against capitalists within each nation. Antisemitism also replaced notions of class conflict. Although sometimes composed of different elements, an alternative to the left was characteristic of fascism everywhere.

Another similarity among the movements was the failure of leadership. This problem was most obvious in Argentina, where no effective figure emerged to unite the various groups. González von Marées appeared unstable, yet the crowded Chilean political space gave him little choice but to shift from one side to another, looking for opportunity. Despite his considerable intellectual, oratorical, and organizational abilities, Plínio Salgado proved indecisive in the moment of crisis. However, Vargas and political circumstances also limited his room to maneuver.

The various governments had similar relations with extreme right-wing groups. Alessandri, Justo, and Vargas, all moderate rightists, tended to coddle the movements because they found their antileftism useful. In addition, the AIB helped Vargas by fostering an authoritarian climate propitious to the consolidation of his dictatorship. The president who most overlapped with the extreme right, Vargas, also maintained good relations with Integralismo until the Estado Novo to satisfy elements in the armed forces. Anxious to retain the military's favor, keep the various opposition groups off balance, and monitor Nacionalistas, Justo rarely cracked down on the far right. Once the movements lost their utility, as in Brazil after November 1937 or in Chile by late 1936, the regimes persecuted them. Still, these relations demonstrated the degree to which the moderate and extreme right coalesced in times of crisis and uncertainty. Local governments in Argentina and Brazil, especially those controlled by rival forces, were often more hostile to radical rightist groups than the national ones.

None of the movements obtained a huge popular following, although compared with other Brazilian parties, the Integralistas came the closest. In Argentina and Brazil, however, power rested in the military rather than in votes. Radical rightists found substantial support in the armed forces, but it was insufficient to gain control of the countries until 1943 in Argentina.

Even more than in the past, the movements emphasized masculinity, now in a militarized sense of the term. The task of incorporating women was therefore fraught with tensions and contradictions. The groups sought to reduce such strains by separating the male and female sections, asserting male leadership over women, and defining female roles in domestic terms. Still, particularly in Brazil, female activists attempted to carve out duties permitting them more independence and initiative than male leaders may have intended.

The movements differed in other respects, such as social composition. In the Argentine case, the percentage of Nacionalista aristocrats declined markedly by the early 1940s, yet it still appeared more upper class than its peers. The AIB was primarily middle class and the MNS middle to lower class, albeit with some leaders from the elite. Female activists seemed to be more aristocratic in Argentina and Chile than the male, although the extreme right in Argentina was widening its appeal. In Brazil, as was true of the post–World War I Ação Social Nacionalista, female Integralistas appeared to come from the middle class.

This information on social composition had broader implications. It indicated that the Brazilians and Chileans, with their enthusiasm for theatrics and other aspects of mass politics, presented their alternative to the left more effectively than the Argentines. The left was relatively weak in Argentina in the early 1930s, and the largely aristocratic Nacionalistas offered more of a single rightist message than a dual revolutionary-rightist one. Since economic conditions were better in their country than in Brazil or Chile, Nacionalistas found it harder to divorce themselves from liberalism and formulate a radical economic project than their counterparts. In contrast, the threat posed by Chilean leftists in the early 1930s and, to a lesser extent, by the Brazilian National Liberating Alliance (ANL) in the mid-1930s, prompted Integralistas and Nacistas to emphasize their radical side. In doing so, they also drew upon a stronger antiliberal legacy than the Argentines. Responding to this leftist surge, the Nacistas were the most violent and revolutionary of the three movements. By the late 1930s, labor and reform forces had revived somewhat in Argentina, and some Nacionalista groups became less unequivocally fascist in nature. Brazilian and Chilean activists, however, seemed more willing to admit to being fascist, or radical, than the Argentines. Thus in their heyday the AIB and MNS were more popular in composition and style than Nacionalismo, which learned how to exploit its appeal more effectively in the second half of the decade.

Of the three cases, the AIB recruited the most women and afforded them the largest role. This reflected the viability of an electoral strategy in a context where women had the vote. Moreover, the tensions involved in mobilizing women were less marked among Integralistas, who needed them to create a total way of life. When women won suffrage at the municipal level in Chile, Nacistas began to include them in their once exclusively male movement. The strength of feminism in Chile and especially Brazil led Integralistas and Nacistas to try to appropriate this term while altering its meaning. In Argentina, where feminism was weak in the 1930s, women lacked the vote, and various factors precluded an electoral strategy, only the most popular-oriented groups mobilized women on a limited basis.

As in the past, the extent of racism varied from country to country. Integralistas and Nacistas were more tolerant than Nacionalistas toward people of color. For all three groups, radical antisemitism was an important component of the alternative to the left; attacks on supposed Jewish greed and financial control largely took the place of attacks on capitalism. When Nacistas moved to the left, their antisemitism diminished, for the economic system and Alessandri's policies became their targets. The Chileans' shifting stance demonstrated that factors other than the demographic primarily explained prejudice against Jews. Still, it is noteworthy that only in Argentina, the country with the largest Jewish community, did radical rightists physically assault Jews before 1939. Here, at least, Jews were more than imaginary figures to the extreme right.

The three cases also differed with regard to the Catholic Church, although all tried to co-opt Catholic sentiment. Nacistas went the furthest in their secularism, ecumenicalism, and alternative religion. Nevertheless, the hierarchy praised the MNS until it moved to the left, although it sided with the Conservatives and the government. In contrast, Nacionalismo overlapped the church, although not all of the clergy favored it. Yet the Argentine Catholic Church also improved its relations with the state and the elite, enabling it to achieve some benefits. The insertion of religion into public education, however, still eluded it. Nacionalistas did not formulate an alternative religion; with influential clergymen on their side, they did not need one. Brazil falls between the two other cases. More Catholic than Nacismo, the AIB also included Protestants and set forth an alternative religion. While the church had an affinity for Integralismo, Leme's friendship with the government resulted in concessions long sought by Catholics. For this reason the church acquiesced in the regime's destruction of the Sigma. In all three countries the church was on the right, but it was closer to the radical right in Brazil and especially Argentina.

This situation resembled that of the military. In the early 1930s, the armed forces of the three countries contained diverse political tendencies, but the Chileans had the strongest reformist current; the Brazilians, with the Tenentes, were in second place. All three moved to the right over the course of the decade. Backed by the public, Alessandri brought the military under control so that it was not the kingmaker in Chile that it was in Argentina and Brazil. Although the MNS had some support in the army, it was more Ibáñista than Nacista, and ultimately more *civilista* than either. Nacionalista influence was growing in the Argentine army. For all Justo's maneuverings, Nacionalista views gained prestige among military men disillusioned with electoral fraud and corruption. Between these two cases, many Brazilian military men sympathized with and belonged to the AIB, as the coup attempts of 1938 indicated. Most, however, chose Vargas over an Integralista revolution.

Given the overlap in their beliefs, one might ask why the radical right did not achieve more sway over the armed forces in this period. Even military supporters often distrusted the extreme right's militias, popular mobilization, and radicalism. Generally they preferred the moderate right, especially one that, as in Brazil, incorporated some features of the extreme right.

The movements also differed with regard to their place in the political system and in the right. Chile possessed a lively array of parties, including the still-powerful Conservatives and diverse rightist groups. On the other side of the spectrum was the Popular Front, the strongest reform coalition of the three countries, which appropriated economic nationalism and change as its issues. A political latecomer, the MNS found little space for activity. As long as it mainly expressed a desire for order and opposition to the left, it found allies among the moderate right. Indeed, the smaller rightist parties and the Falange copied features of the Nacista program and style. Eventually, however, Nacista violence, duplicity, and demagoguery alienated the rest of the right. The conflict between the moderate right and Nacismo, and the crowded nature and vitality of the political system, helped make the Chilean extreme right the weakest and smallest of the three, as in the past, despite its invaluable boost to the Popular Front in 1938.

The Brazilian movement was still second in importance, and it was second in relative size. As the first legal national party, Integralismo encountered a nearly empty political field. Those members of the middle class who inclined toward the center or right found few alternatives to the AIB, and many joined it. Nor did the besieged left offer much of an alternative for change, especially after 1935. The revolution of 1930, however, had not swept away the regional oligarchies, who approved of the AIB's anticommunism but distrusted its nationalism and populism. Some Catholics shared these suspicions, however much they appreciated the movement's devotion to order. Like the church and the military, these conservatives ultimately sided with Vargas, rightly concluding they could maintain more power under his dictatorship than an Integralista one.

The largest of the three, the Argentine movement continued to be the most prominent. Several factors made up for the Nacionalistas' status as political latecomers. The structural debilities of the left prevented it from offering a compelling revolutionary project. Partly for this reason, the extreme right appropriated the nationalist banner. Moderate rightists, reunited in the National Democratic Party (PDN) and the Concordancia, ruled the country, but they owed their prowess largely to fraud and military backing. Their lack of legitimacy and of a message left much space for Nacionalista activity. Nacionalistas usually spurned electoral participation, and since they did not compete with the PDN for votes, they could ally with it. Alone of the three cases, the Argentine movement utilized its ties with conservatives and the military to reach power under Uriburu, Martínez de Hoz, Fresco, and the Ibarguren intervention in Córdoba. Some conservatives adopted Nacionalista positions and counted on Nacionalista support to retain or recapture office; Fresco, for example, was as much a Nacionalista as a PDN member. At times Nacionalistas served as the armed wing of conservatives, as had the postwar Liga Patriótica Argentina. Conservatives and Nacionalistas often demonstrated their hatred of each other, especially as the 1930s wore on, but they also held their noses and used each other. Nacionalistas may have been less united than their peers, but this diversity and decentralization also enabled them to influence different sectors, including some within the moderate right. These conditions enabled Nacionalismo to survive past the late 1930s, when the other movements were in disorder.

In Brazil and to some extent in Chile, radical rightists lost out to strong conservative groups, to which they had contributed aspects of their thought and practice.[2] Moderate rightists ruled Argentina, but only by suppressing what had been the most democratic of the three polities. Their relative weakness afforded Nacionalismo the opportunity to retain identity and strength, despite the overlap between extremists and moderates.

One might point out that the radical right in the ABC countries exercised little control, even at its height. Nacionalistas only attained influence over one short-lived national administration and several provincial ones. Few fascist movements in the world, however, achieved long-lasting domination; the Italian Fascists and German Nazis were the exceptions, not the rule. The ultimate test of the extreme right's power lay in its legacy, and that is the topic of the next chapter.

The Legacy

In a televised debate between presidential candidates during the 1989 campaign in Chile, a reporter observed that Hernán Büchi, Augusto Pinochet's (1973–90) heir, used the term *modern* in place of *the right*. Hinting that Büchi was disguising his ideology, the panelist asked why "no one wants to be of the right" in Chile. Büchi claimed that Marxists had created a negative image of the right and given the word *right* a bad meaning.[1] My answer to this question is more complex than Büchi's. Nevertheless, this episode indicates that now as before World War II, the Chilean right—and particularly the extreme right—faces certain liabilities. It suggests that old patterns live on in the three countries.

In this final chapter I will briefly survey the extreme right after 1939 and attempt to gauge its influence on populism, historical thought, the military, and the church. The exercise demonstrates the legacy of patterns forged in the early 1900s, indicating the continuing strength of radical rightist elements in Argentina, compared with Brazil and Chile. The beliefs and composition of the extreme right after 1939 call for a full, detailed treatment, but this chapter should provide scholars with questions to ask and a hypothesis to test.

Based largely on secondary sources, my tentative conclusions require grounding in primary research. I must add that the analytical literature on the right that informs my view is scanty in some respects. Tellingly, the coverage is the best for Argentina. Since the late 1980s and the decline of Pinochet, scholars have begun addressing the topic for Chile. Except for their

315

involvement in the coup of 1964, however, Brazilian movements have received little attention. Nor have researchers analyzed women's participation beyond the groups that helped oust Presidents João Goulart of Brazil (1961-64) and Salvador Allende of Chile (1970-73).[2]

The Extreme Right After 1939: Trajectory and Continuity

In this section I explore the evolution of extreme rightist doctrine and the rise of new groups in the three nations. I also discuss the relationship between radical and moderate rightist factions. Finally, I trace the activities of extremists prominent before 1939. The object is to judge the strength of radical rightist movements and their links with the past.

Changing international conditions after World War II forced extreme rightists to reevaluate their ideas. For some, the defeat of the Axis spelled the failure of fascist-style dictatorships, corporatism, and economic nationalism, although others continued to advocate such policies, often in seemingly more benign forms. Some softened their antisemitism, at least in public. The beginning of the cold war persuaded many to view the United States more kindly, now that the materialist colossus of the north had assumed leadership of the global anticommunist struggle, although they still suspected its imperialist designs. The realization that stability and development could hinge on good relations with the United States, the major lender, military trainer, market for raw materials, and supplier of imports for many Latin American countries, affected their opinions.

In this context the right underwent some changes. The polarized climate of the cold war legitimized the far right's opposition to leftism. At the same time, however, the cold war pitted democracy against communism, and extreme rightists found themselves incongruously in the first of these camps. Some continued to criticize democracy, but they did so more subtly than in the past. Rightists as a whole were divided over economic issues, with some upholding nationalist and redistributive policies, and others espousing the free market. Which view constituted the extreme is not immediately clear. The advocates of free-market economics—known as "liberal rightists," regardless of their often dubious support for civil liberties—were extreme in that their policies hurt the poor and parted company with the past. Specifically, they broke with the populist model established by the Popular Front in Chile (1938-41), Juan Perón (1946-55) in Argentina, and Getúlio Vargas's second presidency (1950-54) in Brazil, which had attracted large constituencies in each country. Liberal rightist elitism also departed from the radical rightist mobilization tendencies of the 1930s. Indeed, such views recalled those of moderate rightists before 1939, although this connection deserves additional study.[3] On the other hand, one could argue that authoritarian supporters of statist programs, which bucked the United States and the postwar liberal trend, attempted to assuage worker discontent, and possessed some popular and nationalistic appeal, were the extreme. As did their precursors, these rightists sought to limit and control capitalism, which they blamed for fostering instability and greed, and they continued to offer a radical alternative to the left. I think the second group is the extreme, although historians need to examine this matter carefully.

CHILE

From the 1940s to the mid-1960s, radical right-wing forces in Chile appeared weak. Reconverted to fascism, the Vanguardia Popular Socialista merged with the Movimiento Nacionalista de Chile to create the Unión Nacionalista in 1942, which lasted only three years. Some ex-Nacistas joined with former adherents of the Milicia Republicana and members of diverse parties to form Acción Chilena Anticomunista (AChA, 1946–48). The primary mission of Los Estanqueros (1946–54) also was anticommunism, which the group combined with devotion to Portales and Spanish traditions. Spanish and Catholic influences were even more marked in the Movimiento Revolucionario Nacional Sindicalista (MRNS, 1947–60s), which claimed Nacismo and the Spanish Falange as its precursors. Thus for the first time Hispanism and Catholicism permeated Chilean radical rightist organizations, probably to replace the discredited fascist banner as a means of mobilization. Los Estanqueros and military associations such as Línea Recta (1955) decried *politiquería* and called for a stronger executive and a corporatist state; members of these groups and another military faction, PUMA, participated jointly in the second administration of Carlos Ibáñez (1952–58). Ex-Nacistas and others in the Agrarian-Laborist Party (PAL, 1945–58), discussed below, echoed this message and also were influential in that government. After the breakup of the PAL, Nacistas regathered briefly in the Popular National Party. Meanwhile, Los Estanqueros and other extreme rightists formed National Action (1963–65), a vehicle for propelling their leader, Jorge Prat Echaurren, into the presidency. Its electoral efforts, however, failed. Like other far right groups of the 1940s to early 1960s, National Action had only a small following.[4]

Until the mid-1960s, the extreme right waned; afterwards, it waxed. Not coincidentally, its fortunes paralleled those of the left. Mounting economic difficulties, the adoption of the secret ballot, rural–urban migration, and increased literacy among the lower classes prompted their mobilization and the electorate's shift to the left by the late 1950s. The growth and radicalization of the left set off a reaction within the right. The church's increasing progressivism and the drastic reduction in the moderate right's constituency resulting from the electoral reform further alienated the right. So, too, did Christian Democrat Eduardo Frei's (1964–70) and, particularly, Socialist Salvador Allende's expropriations of the oligarchy's landholdings. Weakened by the loss of votes and congressional seats, and angered by agrarian reform, Conservatives and Liberals fused with National Action to form the National Party in 1966. After Allende's election, this rightist alliance radicalized and turned against democracy itself, proving once again that in moments of crisis, distinctions within the right disappear. Its violent arms were the Frente Nacionalista Patria y Libertad and the Movimiento Rolando Matus, which fought Allende supporters in the streets. Women of the National Party helped create Poder Femenino, which mobilized housewives against the government and taunted military officers to overthrow it. The associations of employers, landowners, small property owners, professionals, and relatively privileged workers organized in the Movimiento Gremialista fostered crippling strikes.[5] With help from the United States and centrist sectors of Chilean society, united and radicalized rightist forces created the climate for the military coup.

It is noteworthy that former Nacistas dispersed throughout the political landscape rather than join one or another of these extreme rightist groups. An illustrative example is Jorge González von Marées. Disavowing extremism, functional representation, dictatorship, and government economic controls, the former Naci leader became a Liberal in the 1940s. He wrote some editorials for *Estanquero*, but they were unsigned and unacknowledged. Other Nacistas retraced their steps to Ibañismo and corporatism through the PAL. When it collapsed, José Foncea Aedo, Javier Lira Merino, and other ex-Nacis moved into the Christian Democratic Party. Among the Nacistas who joined the National Party was Sergio Onofre Jarpa, a former member of the Nacista youth, PAL, and National Action. Oscar Jiménez Pinochet, *El jefe*'s lieutenant in the attempted coup of 1938, became prominent in the PAL, serving as a cabinet minister during Ibáñez's second presidency (1952–58). Claiming the MNS/VPS had always stood for socialism, Jiménez resurfaced in Allende's cabinet. Sergio Recabarren Valenzuela, another Nacista militant and PAL member who was a minister under Ibáñez, ran as the left's candidate for deputy in 1962 and lost to Gustavo

Monckeberg Barros, the ex-MNS candidate of the right (and, later, of the National Party). Except for their participation in PAL and perhaps the Popular National Party, the trajectory of former Nacistas lacked consistency.[6]

Nacistas did not align themselves with the most dynamic current in the right—that of the free-market Catholics. Jaime Eyzaguirre and other nonpartisan Catholic thinkers since the 1930s had favored corporatism and social justice. The exchange program between the University of Chicago and the Universidad Católica, however, promoted free-market views among Catholic scholars and students. Initiated in the mid-1950s, this program gathered steam as an effort to counteract Christian Democrat and leftist statism. Rightist Catholic intellectuals managed to reconcile these seemingly contradictory influences. As had corporatists of the past, they continued to advocate a society based on intermediate institutions, including functional groups, or *gremios*, instead of political parties. Unlike their precursors, they placed private companies among the beneficent intermediate groups, and they blamed the reformist state for suffocating the rationality and natural spontaneity of individual economic endeavors. Thus they melded hierarchy and order to economic liberalism. Starting in the late 1950s, such groups as Opus Dei and Sociedad para la Defensa de la Tradición, Familia, y Propiedad (TFP) spread these notions, along with intransigent antileftism, among military officers and the middle and upper classes. The most important advocate of these ideas was Jaime Guzmán, a member of TFP and the founder of the Movimiento Gremialista, centered in the Universidad Católica.[7]

Guzmán was largely responsible for the Declaration of Principles (1974) of the military government, led by Pinochet, which overthrew Allende in 1973. This document expressed the synthesis of neocorporatist and liberal views explained above. It also incorporated ideas attractive to radical rightists, who approved of its prohibition of political parties, appeals to the Hispanic past, and vision of the state as the embodiment of the nation.[8]

To differing degrees, all of these rightist currents allied with and influenced the regime, which displayed a brutality against leftist and democratic forces unparalleled in Chilean history. Yet fissures emerged within the right when liberal rightist views won over the administration. The extremists favored Pinochet's antileftism and stern authoritarianism but could not accept free-market economics.[9] The downsizing of the state and the seeming success of the liberal model further marginalized radical rightists.

Rightist forces regrouped and jockeyed for influence in the 1980s. Pinochet first banned and then, in 1987, reauthorized partisan activity, and new rightist parties emerged. Jarpa, who briefly served as minister of the interior under Pinochet, and other National Party politicians congregated in National Renovation (RN), which portrayed itself as democratic, whereas the free-market economists and technocrats who formed the Independent Democratic Union (UDI) embraced Pinochet's dictatorship. On the eve of the presidential race, a maverick businessman, Francisco Errázuriz, founded the Union of the Center-Center. Despite his party's name, Errázuriz made some appeals to the far right by criticizing liberal economics and emphasizing anticommunism. The genuine voice of the radical right, however, was Avanzada Nacional (1983–90), founded by members of Patria y Libertad as a pro-Pinochet movement and backed by the secret police. The smallest and most extreme of the rightist parties, it favored economic nationalism and even greater authoritarianism. Factionalism within the right, along with a popular thirst for democracy, enabled Christian Democrat Patricio Aylwin to defeat Büchi, backed by RN and UDI, and Errázuriz in 1989. A Pinochet law and support from those who had fared well under the dictatorship, however, ensured a significant rightist presence in the new Congress—one far greater than before the coup.[10]

The right lost another presidential election in 1993, although RN and UDI retained weight in Congress. Beginning with this race, the rightist parties formed an alliance, yet divisions plagued it as well as its constituent parts. Within and outside the rightist coalition, the far right had little support.[11] From 1990 to late 1998, the main pattern observed before 1939 again prevailed, assuming that one does not define UDI as the extreme: a relatively strong moderate right leaving little space for radicals.

Another weakness of the Chilean extreme right is its contested link to nationalism. Citing their kinship with Portales, Nicolás Palacios, and Francisco Encina, Los Estanqueros and other extremist groups called themselves "nationalists," and observers tended to accept this self-designation. Some Catholics and Pinochet followers also claimed this title. Cementing their connection with Palacios (and, perhaps unwittingly, with his social Darwinism), elements close to Pinochet reprinted this author's *Raza chilena*. These rightists explicitly omitted Nacismo from their list of nationalist precursors, criticizing its foreign inspiration, personalism, and faulty leadership.[12] Probably the Nacistas' attempt to attract a popular following also repelled them. The extremists' elitism and the Catholics' free-market sentiments, however, kept most Chileans from identifying them with nationalism, a banner long assumed by the left. This factor helped marginalize the extreme right.

BRAZIL

Vargas's Estado Novo (1937–45) in many ways incorporated features of AIB ideology. It was a corporatist state that regulated class relations and restricted freedom. As had most Integralistas, the government recommended domestic roles for women and subordinate ones for laborers, although these groups did not necessarily follow its prescriptions. Laws providing maternity benefits and child care facilities for female workers did not contradict the view of woman as mother above all else—and at any rate employers often evaded them. Vargas attempted to centralize political authority, but took much less power from the state oligarchies than Integralistas would have liked. However, they would have approved of his developmentalism, embodied in the creation of the state iron and steel installation, and his emphasis on religion, patriotism, and physical fitness in the schools. An Integralista state might have established an agency resembling Vargas's Department of the Press and Propaganda, which inserted nationalistic messages into the media. (Its head was Lourival Fontes, a former member of the AIB's immediate precursor, the Sociedade de Estudos Políticos.) Even the suppression of German Nazis and other foreign groups might have received the AIB's praise.[13]

Yet the regime differed from Integralismo in significant respects. An AIB government probably would have rejected the Estado Novo's "whitening" notions, shut the doors completely to Jewish immigrants, and persecuted the Jews who were already there, unlike Vargas.[14] The Estado Novo was not as antileftist as an Integralista regime might have been; once assured that they presented no threat, the pragmatic dictator allowed some leftists to publish their views. The president made little attempt to cultivate his charisma, although his labor laws and use of propaganda to publicize his *trabalhismo* heralded a move toward mass mobilization that would come to fruition after 1945. Vargas drew upon various influences, including European rightists, non-Integralista corporatists like Oliveira Viana and Francisco Campos, the Gaúcho positivist legacy, and his own realism. The mere fact that Campos and his colleagues were independent of Integralismo contrasted with the Argentine situation, where the Nacionalista movement engulfed the spectrum of authoritarianism.

After 1938 Integralismo fragmented. Already before this year Jeová Mota had led a syndicalist exodus from the Camisas Verdes. This army major, along with other adversaries of Vargas, participated in the Liga da Defesa Nacional in the 1940s as a means of opposing the dictatorship. When

Plínio Salgado left Brazil after the failed coups of 1938, he named Raimundo Padilha as the new Chefe. During Salgado's seven-year sojourn in Portugal, financed by Vargas, prominent figures abandoned the AIB. Disgruntlement over Salgado's leadership and his arbitrary choice of Padilha, acceptance of favors from Vargas, and awareness of the coming shift toward democracy contributed to their decisions. Brutal imprisonment under the Estado Novo may also have awakened doubts about fascism among some of the more socially conscious Integralistas. When the enemies of the dictatorship received amnesty in 1945, Salgado returned to Brazil to preside over the new Popular Representation Party (PRP). Its philosophy resembled that of the AIB, although it claimed to support democracy. Salgado gave the remaining Integralistas freedom of action, and many joined other parties. Bereft of the most capable Camisas Verdes and mired in old positions, the tiny PRP stayed afloat through alliances with other parties and political leaders. In return for Salgado's entering the 1955 presidential race and thus splitting the rightist vote, for example, President Juscelino Kubitschek (1956–61) named him head of the Instituto Nacional de Imigração e Colonização. Elected federal deputy in 1958, Salgado remained in Congress until he retired in 1974.[15]

The end of the Estado Novo and the return to democracy had sparked the creation of the PRP and other new parties. Liberal upper-class opponents of Vargas and of mass political participation streamed into the National Democratic Union (UDN). Vargas himself created the Social Democratic Party, which included his state-level oligarchical allies and other privileged segments, and the Brazilian Labor Party (PTB), which became more reformist and popular over time. Among the smaller parties, there were the tiny PRP and the populist Progressive Social Party (PSP) in São Paulo state.

By the early 1960s this system was breaking down. Frustrated by their inability to win votes, members of the UDN lost faith in electoral politics. Peasant mobilization and PTB reformism, which reached a high under João Goulart, pushed the upper sectors and military leaders to the right and into activities outside the political arena. The Escola Superior de Guerra inculcated civilians and military officers with national security doctrine, stressing anticommunism and authoritarianism. The Instituto de Pesquisas e Estudos Sociais (IPES) organized businessmen behind a military conspiracy against Goulart. IPES and the Instituto Brasileiro de Ação Democrática helped mobilize upper- and middle-class women in antigovernment "Marches of the Family with God and for Liberty"—one of which Salgado addressed. With civilian backing and U.S. acceptance, the military managed to overthrow Goulart in 1964.[16]

As discussed below, different rightist currents influenced the military regime (1964–85), which was hardly the captive of extremists. Unlike Pinochet, the Brazilian military did not ban political activity but channeled it into two approved parties: the pro-government National Renovating Alliance (ARENA) and the opposition Brazilian Democratic Movement (MDB). To curtail the growing power of the MDB, the government engaged in electoral manipulations and, in 1979, permitted the creation of new parties to split the MDB's vote. By the end of military rule in 1985, both the right and the opposition had fragmented into a host of parties. Yet a moderate rightist coalition managed to retain the presidency under José Sarney (1985–90) and Fernando Collor de Mello (1990–92) and, aided by the leading television network, to defeat Luís Inácio "Lula" da Silva, candidate of the leftist Workers Party, in 1989 and 1994. Moderate rightist forces in 1994 backed Fernando Henrique Cardoso of the center-left Brazilian Social Democratic Party as the candidate most likely to triumph over Lula. Suspicious of Cardoso's progressive past and nostalgic for the supposedly scandal-free and nationalistic military regime, extreme rightists gravitated toward the fascist-inspired Reedification of National Order Party (PRONA). With 7.4 percent of the vote, it registered third in the race, albeit far behind Cardoso and Lula.[17] Cardoso defeated Lula again in 1998, and the extreme right captured an even tinier percentage of the vote than in 1994. As in Chile, the extreme right declined after World War II, rose before the coup, and declined again thereafter. Yet the existence of PRONA suggests that weakness in the moderate right might prompt its radical cousins to rise again.

After 1945 many different parties and political tendencies attracted Integralistas. Salgado led the PRP and, after the government abolished it in 1965, moved into ARENA. Having left the PRP for the UDN in 1958, in 1966 Padilha also joined ARENA. Vice president of the PSP, Reale served in PSP administrations in São Paulo in the late 1940s and again in the early 1960s. Former SEP member Plínio Correia de Oliveira founded the Catholic counterrevolutionary TFP in 1960, the first of the branches in the three countries and the world. Within the PTB, Roland Corbisier concerned himself with labor legislation, and Rômulo Almeida focused on northeastern development and Petrobrás, the national oil monopoly. Another PTB member, San Tiago Dantas, served as minister of foreign relations (1961–62) and of the treasury (1962–64) under Goulart. Favoring an independent foreign policy, a Latin American free-trade zone, and democracy, he opposed the military uprising of 1964. Proponents of the *golpe* included Reale, Padilha, General

Olympio Mourão Filho, author of the Cohen Plan, and Admiral Arnoldo Hasselmann, a participant in the coup of May 1938. Mourão Filho and Antônio Gallotti were involved in IPES.[18]

Ex-AIB members continued to find themselves on opposing sides after 1964. Not surprisingly, many favored the military. Padilha served as an ARENA federal deputy and governor of Rio de Janeiro. Reale contributed to the Constitution of 1969, and Alfredo Buzaid was minister of justice from 1969 to 1974, the period of greatest repression. These and other Integralista collaborators with the regime joined Hora Presente, a Catholic counterrevolutionary group formed in 1968. Salgado became the vice president of the ARENA bloc in the Chamber of Deputies. An opponent of the military was Father Hélder Câmara, who began working in the slums of Rio de Janeiro in the 1950s and advocated liberation theology. Almeida and Geraldo Melo Mourão, a participant in the May 1938 coup attempt and a former PTB–PSP federal deputy, enrolled in the MDB.[19]

As in Chile, there was little continuity in the extreme right, and ex-Integralistas took no consistent political stand, although some expressed preference for different strands of populism. Its ambiguous ties with nationalism also hurt the far right. During the military dictatorship, officers who opposed free-market policies and political liberalization were known as "nationalists." Yet in the 1950s and beyond, Brazilians tended to identify nationalism with the left and with developmentalism, rather than with the extreme right, although former AIB members influenced some developmentalist currents, as discussed below.

ARGENTINA

Unlike the Chilean and Brazilian variants, Argentine Nacionalistas remained a coherent and distinct movement. Their belief in hierarchy, corporatism, *rosismo*, militant Catholicism, and economic nationalism, and their opposition to Jews, liberals, and leftists appear to have remained constant over time, despite some shifts resulting from the cold war. Whether Nacionalismo was indeed static, as the secondary literature suggests, however, requires further study.[20]

Ironically, Nacionalistas continued to fragment after 1939, indicating both weakness and an ability to influence diverse sectors. The largest group of the late 1930s, the Alianza de la Juventud Nacionalista, evolved into the Alianza Libertadora Nacional of the 1940s, which supported Juan Perón (1946–55, 1973–74). The next important Nacionalista organizations were the violently antisemitic Tacuara, formed in the late 1950s by members of

Unión Nacionalista de Estudiantes Secundarios (UNES), which dated back to the 1930s, and Tacuara's offshoots in the early 1960s, which attracted students and young Peronists. Father Julio Meinvielle served as Tacuara's adviser. Equally anti-Jewish but relatively pacific was the Guardia Restauradora Nacionalista of the 1960s, an upper-class refuge. In the same decade, groups such as the Ateneo de la República and Ciudad Católica reached out to military officers; they and the Argentine branches of TFP and Opus Dei also recruited Catholic traditionalists. (Founded in 1967, the very Catholic and Hispanist TFP did not regard itself as Nacionalista, although it acknowledged the overlap.) After Perón's fall, the Irazustas founded the Republican Union Party to voice their economic concerns rather than compete seriously for office. In addition, Nacionalistas congregated around such periodicals as *Azul y Blanco* (1956–57, 1967–69) and *Cabildo* (founded in 1974). These and other circles were small and ephemeral, but they did not encompass the totality of Nacionalismo, which maintained its strongholds in the church, military, universities, Instituto Juan Manuel de Rosas, and repressive apparatus of the state, and added new ones, especially among segments of Peronism.[21]

The endemic political instability after 1955 provided opportunities for extreme rightists. Civilian and military governments alternated in power up to 1983, and Nacionalistas played roles in most of them. As seen below, extreme rightists were more prominent in the Argentine military regimes than in those of Chile and Brazil. Even after democracy returned, Nacionalista officers, or Carapintadas, threatened Raúl Alfonsín's (1983–89) administration, and their leaders eventually created a party, Movement for Dignity and Independence (MODIN).

In the absence of a united, popularly based conservative party, the upper classes have worked through authoritarian civilian groups and the military to achieve their will, rather than through the democratic system. The founding of the Union of the Democratic Center (UCEDE) in 1983 seemed to break with the past. Its leaders rejected military-style solutions in favor of political as well as economic liberalism, and some of the party's youth contingent created an appealing popular style. The UCEDE briefly became the third electoral force in Argentina, after the Radicals and Peronists. Centered in the federal capital, however, its inability to forge a permanent alliance with provincial conservative parties limited its success. It provided support and administrative personnel for President Carlos Menem (1989–), who abandoned his Peronist roots for a free-market orientation. By seeking power at the top, the UCEDE neglected to develop its mass base and thus repeated the errors of its predecessors. Having melded its fortunes with Menem's, it did not field a candidate in the 1995 presidential race, and the Peronists absorbed its constituency and some of its leading activists.[22] The Peronists may become the conservative party, or conservative weakness may again leave space for Nacionalistas.

Nacionalistas did not fare particularly well in the 1995 elections. A dissident faction split away from MODIN, creating its own party, and neither attracted much support. Aldo Rico, MODIN's candidate for president in 1995, garnered only 1.77 percent of the vote, although the party won four congressional seats. Yet a Nacionalista general known for human rights abuses, Antonio Domingo Bussi, won the governor's race in Tucumán province. Furthermore, extreme rightist groups continue to operate outside the electoral arena, as in the bombing of the Jewish community center of Buenos Aires in 1994.[23]

The fragmentation of MODIN indicates that Nacionalistas continued to disagree over candidates, party labels, and strategies after 1939. The Alianza Libertadora Nacional and such figures as Ernesto Palacio, Manuel Gálvez, and Virgilio Filippo supported Juan Perón as the fulfillment of their ideals. Many were alienated, however, by the means Perón used to court workers, his cult of personality, the power he delegated to his wife, his eventual quarrel with the church, and other policies, not the least of which was his unwillingness to appoint Nacionalistas to office. The Catholic and elitist types in particular welcomed the overthrow of Perón in 1955. They and some Peronist Nacionalistas reunited under the rubric of the Federal Union Party, which participated with little success in the election of 1957. Many of these figures rallied behind Arturo Frondizi (1958–62) and his Intransigent Radical Party, a splinter from the UCR, but his positions estranged some of them. Meanwhile, the Irazustas criticized all administrations since 1946 for promoting economic dependency. Other Nacionalistas, however, supported the various military governments and Perón's return (1973) in order to restore unity and suppress leftists and militant workers.[24]

Despite these fissures, the contemporary Argentine extreme right appears stronger than its counterparts. By the 1960s the Irazusta brothers, Ernesto Palacio, José María Rosa, Mario Amadeo, Julio Meinvielle, Nimio de Anquín, Federico and Carlos Ibarguren (son), Marcelo Sánchez Sorondo, and others had participated in Nacionalista circles for thirty or forty years—a remarkable continuity unequaled in Brazil or Chile.[25] At the same time new members, some related to older ones, joined the fold. Thus Nacionalistas firmly retained their corporate identity. No less important was the fact that Nacionalistas had influenced governments from the 1930s to the early 1980s. Even in the 1990s, President Menem's minister of justice, Rodolfo Barra, revealed that he once had belonged to Tacuara; this disclosure, however, cost him his job.[26] Finally, Argentines still accepted the Nacionalistas' self-conferred title, adding the qualifier "leftist" to other strains of nationalism.

This overview of extreme rightist groups and individuals since 1939 has underlined the ongoing differences among the three countries. To highlight these disparities further, I turn to an analysis of some specific areas of thought and action. Radical rightists varied in the extent to which they influenced such important currents and institutions as the writing of history, populism, the military, and the church.

Historical Revisionism

The Argentine extreme right's nationalist credentials rest in part on its overlap with historical revisionism. Marysa Navarro points out that in anti-imperialism and the cult of Rosas the Nacionalistas found issues of genuine mass appeal. Historians and other writers of widely divergent political persuasions, many of them not affiliated with the Instituto, have drawn upon historical revisionism to construct the popular view of Argentine history. During the "Dirty War" of the late 1970s, Julio Irazusta observed ruefully that the military found his and other revisionist works in guerrilla hideouts. His disapproval of the revolutionaries notwithstanding, their use of *rosismo* demonstrated its resonance among varied groups. So, too, did the fact that President Menem brought back Rosas's remains from England in 1989, perhaps to win public favor before he enacted the unpopular measures of liberalizing the economy and pardoning military officers for human rights offenses and coup attempts.[27]

The identification between Nacionalismo and historical memory contrasts with the situation in Brazil and Chile. Although Gustavo Barroso, Hélio Viana, and other Integralistas wrote on historical topics, and the movement had some nostalgia for the empire, the AIB did not found its own historical school. However, Barroso's works influenced local views of economic dependency; his phrase "Brazil: a bankers' colony," only somewhat divorced of its antisemitic context, stuck.[28] Nacistas drew upon the already existing cult of Portales, reinforced by Alberto Edwards, Francisco Encina, and others. Nevertheless, they did not add historical writings to this body of works, and, at any rate, the famous Conservative's utility was limited. Nacistas revered him as the epitome of authority, statecraft, prag-matism, and self-sacrifice, but Portales, unlike Rosas, with his lower-class following, could not serve as a complete model for a movement based on mobilization. Portales did serve, however, as a model for the elitist Estanqueros and Pinochet's nonmobilizing dictatorship.[29] Thus the Brazilian and Chilean movements, unlike the Argentine, did not construct their own popular historical currents, which weakened their claims to the national-ist mantle.

Populism

After 1939, Nacionalistas and former Nacistas and Integralistas were inter-twined with populism. Peaking between 1920 and 1965, Latin American populism encompasses a variety of groups with certain broad traits in com-mon. As Joel Horowitz noted, populism "does not try to alter the basic eco-nomic structure, but seeks to make it fairer." Industrialization and redistri-bution of income are its main responses to underdevelopment and poverty. Such movements usually attract workers and other previously excluded groups, particularly from urban settings. Privileged and usually charis-matic, the leaders mobilize their followers through highly personal, emo-tional, paternalist, and nationalist appeals.[30]

In Chile, although there were other contributing sources to populism, the radical rightist influence was subtle and profound. This influence was at work in the Chilean populist Agrarian-Laborist Party. The PAL represented the fusion of Ibáñez's heterogeneous Popular Liberating Alliance and the Agrarian Party (1931–45), which had united southern farmers, businessmen, and corporatist thinkers. Los Estanqueros and former AChA activists also supported the PAL. It advocated corporatism, Hispanism, a third way be-tween socialism and capitalism, and a work service. The PAL admired Por-tales, Guillermo Subercaseaux, Nicolás Palacios, Francisco Encina, and Al-berto Edwards, yet it also favored the populist programs and mobilizational style of Juan Perón and the Bolivian National Revolutionary Movement. Opposing class conflict and *politiquería*, the PAL hoped its version of na-tionalism would overcome divisions between parties and between left and right. Although some of these elements were traditionally rightist, others smacked of Nacismo. It is not surprising, then, that "displaced Nacistas . . . formed and dominated the party," according to one Agrariolaborista, form-ing the Bandera Negra faction within the PAL. The Nacista impact on the second Ibáñez administration (1952–58) was especially striking. His cabinet included five former MNS militants: Pedro Foncea, Sergio Recabarren, Orlando Latorre, Oscar Jiménez, and Diego Lira Vergara.[31]

The rightist experiment with populism, however, was unsuccessful. The old general returned to office with his usual platform of nationalism, authoritarianism, and opposition to party politics and the oligarchy. With Socialist backing, the ruling coalition managed to legislate a minimum rural salary, government housing agency, state bank, ministry of mining, and other popular nationalistic measures. Ibáñez's shift toward liberal economic policies, however, not only failed to relieve stagflation but drove away his leftist and some of his PAL support.[32] The PAL splintered and outlived his administration by only two years.

In Brazil, former Integralistas also affected currents of populism. They participated in such populist parties as the PSP and PTB, and they also played prominent roles in a think tank that set the populist developmentalist agenda and became the ideological apparatus of the state in the 1950s and early 1960s. During Vargas's second administration, in 1952 ex-AIB members Miguel Reale, Roland Corbisier, Rômulo Almeida, Luis Almeida Sales, and Alberto Guerreiro Ramos joined other intellectuals, some with ties to Vargas, in the "Itatiaia group." This circle, which discussed development issues, evolved into the Instituto Superior de Estudos Brasileiros (ISEB) in 1955. ISEB was affiliated with the Ministry of Education and Culture, headed by Cândido Mota Filho, a former SEP member. Integralista participants in ISEB's early years included Reale, Almeida, Corbisier, Guerreiro Ramos, and San Tiago Dantas. A close collaborator of the movement, Augusto Frederico Schmidt, and a sympathizer, Alvaro Vieira Pinto, also participated. Most of these figures, as well as other founding members, had drifted away by the early 1960s, as the institute turned to the left. The military regime finally abolished ISEB in 1964.[33]

Despite their diverse membership, it is remarkable how these groups repackaged and updated the AIB's core concerns. Much as had earlier rightist generations, ISEB publications dissected the Brazilian "crisis." Corbisier and other ISEB writers concentrated on the nexus between underdeveloped and developed countries, instead of capitalism as a whole. Substituting nation for class, they regarded the former, rather than the proletariat, as alienated and deprived. In their view, national capitalism would liberate Brazil and convert it from object to subject status. When ISEB members addressed divisions within Brazil, they, like Integralistas, did so in a manner that obscured the class structure. The primary fissure they discerned was that of modern productive forces who represented the nation, including industrialists, the proletariat, and certain middle sectors, pitted against *latifun-diários*, merchants, and other nonproductive forces, who represented the antination. They tied the antinational traditionalists to imperialism, overlooking foreign investments in industry.[34] If one replaced "traditional" with "parasitic" and excluded agriculturalists from consideration, the formulation would sound Integralista. For ISEB, the struggle of modern versus traditional forces substituted for class conflict, again resembling AIB notions. The national/antinational dichotomy even recalled Argentine Nacionalista rhetoric.

Furthermore, the importance that ISEB placed on the state, capitalism, and intellectuals in the struggle for national development and autonomy suggested a top-down, authoritarian mentality. Indeed, many saw ISEB as the civilian counterpart of the military's Escola Superior de Guerra, both designed to train ruling groups. Elitist attitudes, however, were hardly confined to the right during these years.[35]

The far right exerted the most enduring influence on populism in Argentina, where its primary manifestation was Peronism. Juan Perón had links to the Liga Patriótica Argentina (LPA), and its president, Manuel Carlés, probably was one of his teachers in the Colegio Militar. A *golpista* in 1930 and 1943, Perón maintained strong ties with Nacionalista officers. His visits to Italy, Germany, and Spain in the 1930s affected his thinking, as did Catholic doctrine. Opposition to leftism permeated his thought and actions. As secretary of labor and as president, Perón tried to boost laborers economically yet control them, while he repressed the left. These policies were reminiscent of Manuel Fresco, and Eva Perón's projects among the poor and her organizing of female laborers recalled the activities of extreme rightist women since the early 1900s. Their program fulfilled goals of the LPA, Social Catholics, and Nacionalistas—but it also helped fulfill many workers' dreams of self-respect, economic gain, and political voice. Thus Peronism was multifaceted: it implemented radical rightist ideas yet unleashed a worker militancy that the right in general distrusted.[36]

Perón drew from Nacionalismo in other respects as well. His "Third Position" between liberal economics and communism came out of the Nacionalista lexicon, as did his platform of "political sovereignty, economic independence, and social justice." Other policies had a Nacionalista tinge: the corporatist structuring of business and labor groups, state control over marketing exports, denunciation of the oligarchy without destroying its economic base, discourse of class conciliation, and nationalization of communications, transport, and utility companies. Perón, however, rejected the cult of Rosas in favor of that of the less divisive San Martín, and although he held some antisemitic views, he recruited Jews into Peronism and appointed them to office. For these and other reasons previously mentioned, Perón alienated many Nacionalistas, but this does not deny their influence on him. As Mario Amadeo pointed out, Peronism took most of its concerns from his movement.[37] A more objective observer might add that the Peróns updated and popularized the Nacionalista agenda.

Insights gleaned from other movements, especially the UCR-affiliated Fuerza de Orientación Radical de la Joven Argentina (FORJA), facilitated this task. Members of FORJA began collaborating with Perón in 1943. To a far greater extent than Nacionalistas, this group identified itself with Perón, dissolving itself and merging with Peronism in 1945. Still, one must keep in mind the close relations between FORJA and Nacionalismo. European fascism, noncommunist unionists, and the legacy of union-state collaboration in the 1930s also influenced Peronism, but the first of these again overlapped Nacionalismo.[38]

Former members of FORJA, as well as many Peronists and Nacionalistas, supported Frondizi's populist campaign for the presidency. Running on a "national and popular" platform, this Intransigent Radical promised to rally Argentines of various political persuasions around his developmentalist program. Frondizi appointed far more Nacionalistas to his administration than had Perón, including two cabinet ministers (Alberto Tedín and Carlos Florit) and the ambassador to the United Nations (Mario Amadeo). Yet the president spurned the Nacionalista position on the economy, he moved back and forth on Nacionalista educational demands, and many Nacionalistas accused him of courting the left. As a result, these figures broke with Frondizi.[39] Nevertheless, the Nacionalistas' influence on the Frondizi regime confirmed their links with populism, stronger in Argentina than in the other two countries.

The Military

The extreme right also affected the military regimes in the ABC countries after 1939, although studies of the post-1964 "bureaucratic-authoritarian" governments, in particular, have largely ignored its impact. Instead, scholars have usually attributed such regimes to the economic and political legacy of populism, developments within the military, and the influence of U.S. and French military thinking. Yet the participation of military officers in extreme right-wing groups before and after 1939 suggests continuities.[40]

One might even ask whether the military in the 1960s through the 1980s took the place of civilian radical rightist movements or blended with them.

Officers in the Southern Cone represented a variety of rightist opinions. Conflict between moderate and extreme rightists marked the military governments, with varying results. Yet the definitions of moderate (also called liberal or soft-liner) and extreme (hard-liner or, significantly, nationalist) depended very much on the context. Both factions loathed partisan politics and deemed it necessary to repress leftists, workers, and other dissidents, although the soft-liners arguably were not as harsh as the hard-liners. Only under a severe dictatorship could moderates implement the free-market measures they usually preferred.[41] The extremists advocated coercion, not to facilitate such policies, for they favored economic nationalism and a corporatist state, but rather to cleanse the fatherland of what they saw as subversive antinational forces. As such, their views bore marks of radical rightist influence.

While it had contained diverse political tendencies, the Chilean military had a long history of involvement with extreme right-wing movements. Retired and active officers had joined the Ligas Patrióticas, Nacistas, Movimiento Nacionalista de Chile, and other groups and enjoyed close ties with such organizations as Los Estanqueros. They supported Ibáñez through PUMA and Línea Recta and participated in various conspiracies. The uprising of the Tacna regiment in October 1969, led by General Roberto Viaux, also manifested radical rightist sentiments.[42]

Given this heritage, one might have expected that hard-liners would dominate the Pinochet dictatorship. Indeed, the regime's antipolitical rhetoric and appeals to Portales evinced extremist influence. From their stronghold in the secret police, hard-liners wielded considerable influence over the repressive apparatus. Nevertheless, liberals prevailed, installing the most free-market oriented policies of any bureaucratic-authoritarian government. With a few exceptions, most officers finally accepted liberal economics, although they opposed the privatization of copper. Eventually soft-liners also convinced the dictator to loosen restrictions on parties and move toward a limited democracy, again over hard-liner protest. Yet moderates were hardly more lenient than extremists toward leftists.[43]

The two tendencies blurred more in the post-1964 Brazilian military administrations. The moderates were tied to the officers of the Força Expedicionária Brasileira in World War II. Their experiences in Italy taught them to be suspicious of extreme nationalism, fascism, and personalism, and to support cordial relations with the United States and foreign businesses.

They also were involved in the Escola Superior de Guerra (ESG), founded in 1949. Influenced by French and U.S. cold war thinking, the ESG developed national security doctrine, which addressed internal threats to the status quo. Its emphasis on buttressing the state and the national economy, however, also indicated possible Tenente and Integralista inspiration. Following from this doctrine, moderates instituted an anti-inflationary austerity program, attracted foreign capital, and promoted nontraditional exports, policies resembling those of Pinochet. Yet the moderate technocrats were not completely liberal, for the regime invested huge sums in industry, infrastructure, energy, and university education.[44]

The hard-liners tended to be officers who had not participated in World War II or the ESG. Less willing than moderates to accommodate politicians of any ideology, the extremists nevertheless wanted the government to appeal to the public by instituting land reform, antiprofiteering measures, development aid in the impoverished northeast, controls on foreign corporations, and an independent foreign policy. These stands were reminiscent of the AIB and its precursors, as were the hints of antisemitism in some of the extremists' repressive acts against civilians.

Moderates won out in Brazil, as they had in Chile, although with less ease. As in Chile, the extremists tended to control internal security, which strengthened them particularly between 1969 and 1974, the height of the antileftist campaign. Through threatened coups, participation in terrorist groups, and other means, hard-liners successfully pressured such presidents as Artur da Costa e Silva (1967–69) and Emilio Garraztazú Médici (1969–74) into appointing them to office, tightening repression, suspending representative government from time to time, and perhaps implementing such nationalist programs as land distribution in the Amazon and a nonaligned foreign policy. Yet soft-liners occupied more positions in the various governments and, as in Chile, determined the economic policies. Moreover, they maintained political parties, Congress, and elections, at least in form if not always in reality, and eventually moved the country back to democracy, all against the hard-liners' wishes.

In Argentina, Nacionalistas greatly affected the military governments, starting with that of 1943–46. The Grupo Organizador y Unificador, which planned the coup of 1943, consisted of Nacionalista officers. Its leader, Pedro Ramírez, eventually became president (1943–44), and another member, Juan Perón, began his climb to power. Such prominent Nacionalistas as José María Rosa (finance), General Luis Perlinger (interior), Gustavo Martínez Zuviría and Alberto Baldrich (ministers of justice and public instruc-

tion) occupied seats in the cabinet. Others assumed a host of lesser positions in the ministries, police, provincial interventions, and universities.
The imposition of religious instruction in the schools, dissolution of political parties, nationalization of some foreign-owned companies, and manifestations of concern for social justice, as well as crackdowns on Jewish organizations and leftists, revealed Nacionalista sentiments. When Ramírez
broke relations with the Axis powers in 1944, and his successor, Edelmiro J.
Farrell (1944–46), declared war on them in 1945, however, Nacionalistas felt
betrayed.[45]

The extreme right has influenced all of the numerous military regimes
since 1955, especially those of Eduardo Lonardi (1955), Juan Carlos Onganía
(1966–70), Roberto M. Levingston (1970–71), and the various administrations that composed the so-called Proceso de Reorganización Nacional
(1976–83). Lonardi, Levingston, and initially Onganía tilted their cabinets
toward Nacionalistas, who under Onganía drafted a corporatist document
to replace the constitution. The Cordobazo (1969), an explosion of labor
and student protest, however, halted this attempt at constitutional reform,
so reminiscent of Nacionalista aims in the 1930s. Although liberal rightists
predominated in Jorge Videla's (1976–81) cabinet, extremists controlled
much of the Dirty War during this most drastic phase. The Proceso's severe
persecution of Jews and antisemitic rhetoric also indicated Nacionalista influence. Significantly, such feelings did not pervade Pinochet's regime and
only rarely surfaced in Brazil. In yet another respect, the Proceso obeyed
radical rightist precedent. By "disappearing" suspected subversives, the authorities, probably unwittingly, were following the advice given by General
Luis J. Dellepiane in the Semana Trágica of 1919.[46]

Indeed, Nacionalistas helped frame the doctrine of national security
that prompted the coup of 1976. The primary figure was Jordán Bruno
Genta, who began addressing military audiences in the early 1940s and
served as interventor in the Universidad Nacional del Litoral after the 1943
coup. Throughout his career Genta insisted that opposition to communism
rested on Catholic principles, which he defined as authoritarian and hierarchical; an anticommunism embedded in liberalism, capitalism, or democracy, like that of the United States, was in his view a false one. U.S. entrance
into World War II facilitated what he saw as the victory of Communists,
Masons, and Jews. He predicated a "Counterrevolutionary War," directed by
a military dictatorship, that would mercilessly stamp out the Communist
threat that he believed permeated all sectors of society and would impose
Catholic and Hispanist values. As early as 1962, air force and army officers

took courses based on Genta's Counterrevolutionary War principles, and his book of the same title came out in the mid-1960s. Civilian and military members of the Legión Nacionalista Contrarrevolucionaria further spread these views. Recognizing his impact on the military, in 1974 the Marxist Ejército Revolucionario del Pueblo assassinated Genta. His Counterrevolutionary War began in earnest after his death.[47]

As in the other countries, soft- and hard-liners had their power bases. Even the more Nacionalista-inspired military governments tended to appoint moderates to the leading economic posts. From these positions, liberals imposed their agendas which, although they were not as consistently or radically free-market as those of Pinochet's "Chicago Boys," provoked the Nacionalistas' displeasure. Regarding certain state industries as essential to national security, extremists in the armed forces kept moderates from privatizing them.[48] Nacionalistas were not confined to the repressive forces and the Ministry of the Interior, as in Chile and Brazil. Hard-liners also applied their views to their labors in the Ministry of Foreign Affairs and Religion and the Ministry of Education and Culture, as well as in university administration. Liberals preserved some weight in the cultural realm, which may have kept the Proceso from embracing the cult of Rosas. Still, radical rightists achieved a broader influence in society than their peers elsewhere.

The Church

Elements of the Catholic Church had supported and even belonged to extreme rightist groups in all three countries before 1939. These links were weakest in Chile and strongest in Argentina. In recent years, the church's reactions to the bureaucratic-authoritarian governments have revealed striking differences between Chile and Brazil, on one hand, and Argentina on the other.

The respective hierarchies initially supported the coups of 1964 in Brazil and 1973 in Chile. The extent of terror in Chile, especially against Christian Democrats and Catholic spokespersons, however, convinced Cardinal Raúl Silva of the need to advocate human rights and offer aid to relatives of the disappeared. Although not all the bishops initially followed the cardinal's lead, over time the hierarchy became ever more critical of the dictatorship. The widening gap between rich and poor, along with the repression, particularly of Catholics, pushed the Brazilian bishops' conference into chastising the regime and organizing a human rights campaign. Cardinal Paulo Evaristo Arns of São Paulo even helped coordinate the secret and highly dangerous collection of data on torture and disappearances, which was published after the dictatorship ended.[49]

The Argentine hierarchy also supported the coup of 1976. Unlike their Brazilian and Chilean colleagues, the majority of leading clerics did not change their views, despite the disappearances of nuns and priests and the murder of two bishops. Military leaders consulted with bishops before the coup and maintained close contact with them afterwards. The religious and military hierarchies did not always have the same interests, for the regime wanted to control the church as well as other intermediary groups, and the church opposed such plans. Nevertheless, the two institutions' goals overlapped. Seemingly accepting the junta's claim that it was defending Western and Christian civilization, most bishops refused to meet with human rights organizations. With a handful of exceptions, their criticisms of the government were infrequent, narrow, and private, and clerical leaders offered little aid to victims of repression. Priests of the military vicariate justified the torture and killings and exempted their perpetrators from moral responsibility. Indeed, in 1995 former lieutenant commander Adolfo Scilingo charged that chaplains absolved naval personnel of guilt for throwing prisoners out of airplanes into the Río de La Plata. Only when the military left power did the hierarchy make its reservations public; only in 1996 did it finally admit shame over permitting the human rights abuses.[50]

Emilio Mignone argues that the hierarchy's dependence on the government contributed to its stance. Unlike Brazil and Chile, Argentina had never separated church from state, and the church received some official funds and pressed for concessions. Yet he also attributes the church's position to its right-wing ideology. The concrete manifestations of this ideology dated back to Social Catholicism and the years following World War I, when leading clerics, including chaplains of the armed forces, joined the LPA, which, like the Proceso, killed workers and leftists. These links grew in the 1930s, when the predominant ecclesiastical current regarded the military as the repository of antiliberal Catholic nationalism. The intertwining of the church, Nacionalismo, and the armed forces had borne fruit.[51]

In fact, the hierarchy castigated the democratically elected president, Raúl Alfonsín, more openly and severely. Feeling more besieged than it had under the Proceso, it accused his administration of fostering pornography and family disintegration after it had pushed a divorce bill into law.[52] The higher clergy found it harder to cope with the liberty and secularism of democracy than with the terror and Catholic-influenced authoritarianism of the Proceso.

A Weighty Legacy

In the introduction to this book I set forth a number of variables explaining the relative status of the extreme right in the countries under study. They included immigration, the fortunes and extent of local control over the export economy, the strength of labor and the left, the role of the church and the military, and the unity and influence of conservative parties and the political system. Here I will review these variables, demonstrating the relevance of the past to the present. Other scholars will need to determine the effect of the cold war and new variables that may have emerged since 1939.

Up to 1939, radical rightist movements in Chile were the weakest of those studied. The scanty presence of immigrants hampered efforts to blame them for leftism or economic domination, and Peruvians did not serve as targets after the settlement of the border dispute under Ibáñez. The inability of the foreign-controlled mining sector to generate economic stability, widespread prosperity, and industrial development reinforced leftist critiques of capitalism and provided leftist parties with recruits. Extreme rightists were distant from the church, which allied with Conservatives, although some clerics sympathized with Nacismo. The far right had military collaborators, but officers held diverse opinions and, at any rate, exerted less control over political events than their Brazilian or Argentine colleagues. The strength of established moderate rightist parties and the crowded and hardy political system left little room for radical rightist activity.

From 1990 until recently, extreme right-wing forces in Chile have remained the feeblest of the three countries.[53] Moderate rightists are powerful among soldiers and civilians, and the church is not connected to the extreme right. A full spectrum of parties resurfaced after the Pinochet years, and some of the leftist parties participated in the ruling coalition. Yet as this book neared publication in November 1998, Spain's attempt to extradite Pinochet and try him for human rights abuses altered the situation. Belligerently defending the former dictator and his legacy, RN and UDI blamed the threatened extradition on the Chilean left and claimed that the legal proceedings imperiled Chilean democracy and stability. In reality, rightist words and actions imperiled democracy and stability, as moderates and extremists alike tied their support for the political system to Pinochet's future. Leftists received death threats, and the extremist Patria y Libertad reemerged. Perhaps the image of a besieged and humiliated Pinochet undermined his moderate rightist supporters, who turned further to the right. Or one might argue that all sectors of the right united around Pinochet as a means of weakening the left, which had a strong candidate for the next presidential election.[54] Either way, the result is the same: as was true before, in moments of crisis the boundaries between moderate and extreme rightists fade.

Extreme right-wing influence in Brazil fell between that in Chile and Argentina before 1939. Radical rightists tied foreign workers to the leftist threat, although unions and the left in the Old Republic were not as strong as in Argentina or Chile. Planters exerted some control over the coffee export economy, but this was not a sufficient motor of development. Different movements contested the mantle of economic nationalism, rightists draping themselves with it throughout the 1930s, and leftist populists by the 1950s. Dissatisfied with its status, the church had close ties with extreme rightists, but in the 1930s it sided with the state, which gave it long-sought concessions. The military also cast its fate with the moderate rightist Vargas, despite its links to Integralismo and earlier groups. The outmoded local oligarchical parties and the dearth of national electoral vehicles left space for Integralistas. Moderate rightists, however, found other means of expressing their interests—through the military, the church, and especially the state.

Since 1939, Brazil largely has remained in the middle. Hard-liners are still prominent in the military, and they have a civilian following. These officers exerted more influence on recent military governments than their Chilean peers but less than the Argentine. The church, however, has largely moved out of the extreme right-wing orbit. The political system is still fragile, and conservative forces have splintered into several parties, some of them personalistic and transitory, yet they have managed to pull together to defeat leftists since 1985. Now as before 1939, they have little need to turn to extremists.

Radical rightists in Argentina formed the strongest of the movements studied. They succeeded in identifying immigrant workers and their views as foreign and dangerous, and they found niches in the military and the church, two institutions that grew in power as the polity weakened. Relative prosperity and local control of the meat and grain sectors delayed the onset of economic nationalism and, when it arrived, diverted criticism from capitalism toward simply the foreign nexus of the export economy. The fragmented conservative groups and political system gave extreme rightists space for action. The decision not to create an electoral party, which made sense in the context of voting fraud and military sway, widened their options and enabled some figures to straddle the moderate and extreme right.

Argentine extreme rightists have remained more prominent than their counterparts since 1939. They appropriated nationalism and strongly influenced populism. The Catholic Church sympathized with the recent military regimes, which bore the stamp of hard-liners, and it still harbors antidemocratic sentiments. Only in Argentina did the repression assume a clearly antisemitic character, and extremist elements continue to attack Jews. Moderate rightist parties again are weak and divided, although they have achieved their interests through President Carlos Menem, who may remold the Peronists into a national conservative party. Electorally Nacionalistas may be in eclipse, but modern Argentine history warns us that their marginalization may be temporary.

Although its legacy seems most apparent in Argentina, the far right left its mark on all three countries. Remnants of its thought and practice have endured, sometimes by mutating and resurfacing in unlikely carriers. The extreme right has influenced the church, historical memory, populism, and the military; it is through regimes governed by the last two forces that it has attained access to power. The most chilling sign of radical rightist prowess is its continuing role in the repressive arms of the state. Events in Chile in late 1998 demonstrated that perceived threats to moderate rightist power and prestige, or electoral opportunities, can quickly catalyze a shift to the extreme. The extreme right has left a weighty legacy indeed.

Reference Material

NOTES

I have divided the bibliography into four categories. The first three categories—archives, periodicals, and biographical sources—are further subdivided by country. Biographical information in the text comes from the respective biographical section for that nation, unless I indicate otherwise. When referring to biographical works in the notes, I generally cite them as a whole by country. All remaining works are found in the fourth category, including other primary and secondary sources, printed and microfilmed government publications, and interviews. Unless otherwise noted, all persons cited individually as authors come from the fourth category.

Introduction

1. Romero, *El pensamiento*, 16.
2. On the historiography of the Latin American right, see Hennessy; Payne, *Fascism*, 167-75. On Argentina, see Navarro Gerassi; Rock, *Authoritarian Argentina*; Deutsch and Dolkart. Brinkley has argued that the U.S. right has also received little scholarly attention, although other historians have disagreed. See Brinkley, 409-10; Ribuffo, 438-41.
3. The following authors have called for comparative examinations of Latin American history, including its political aspects: Skidmore, "Workers," 89; Mörner, Fawaz de Viñuela, and French, 63; Bergquist, 376-77.
4. See, for example, Bergquist, 15; Remmer, 3.
5. See Pinkney.
6. Bloch, a renowned French scholar, noted that "the primary interest of the comparative method is . . . the observation of differences." Cited in Woodward, 38.

7. That would be the subject of another book, as would the ties among the Latin American groups under study. Nor do I compare the right in the countries under study with that of the United States, for the European influence was paramount.

8. Nonspecialists might be tempted to equate these members of the right with Margaret Thatcher–style British conservatives. This would be an error, for many free-market rightists in Latin America have supported dictatorship rather than democracy.

9. The right carefully selects and in some cases invents these traditions. See Hobsbawm and Ranger.

10. On the difficulties of defining political terms, see Hale, esp. 59, 61. On the pitfalls of defining the right, see Romero, *El pensamiento*, 11; Eugen Weber, introduction to Rogger and Weber. See also Roger Eatwell, "The Nature of the Right, 2: The Right as a Variety of 'Styles of Thought,'" in Eatwell and O'Sullivan, 63. Yohn, 437, however, objected to seeing U.S. conservatism as "a reaction to a liberal norm that sets the terms of the debate." As any definition of the right reflects its character at the moment, I deliberately offer only a brief one here.

11. Payne, *Fascism*, 14–15; Waisman, 219, 227, 235; Hirschman, 3–6; Rogger and Weber; Eatwell, "Nature," in Eatwell and O'Sullivan, 62–76.

12. Weber, introduction to Rogger and Weber, 15–16; Mayer, 48–55, 59–71.

13. Influenced by Mayer, in my earlier work I used the term *counterrevolution* to refer to the entire constellation of rightist forces and to one of the three groups in this alliance. Here I use the word *right* to distinguish my views from Mayer's, because I now divide the Latin American right between moderates and extremists. For a typology of the Latin American right today, see Borón (in Chalmers et al.). Villagrán Kramer, 71, also used the terms *extreme* and *moderate right*, although his definitions differ from mine.

14. On the importance of studying the membership and actions of rightist groups, see Moore, xii.

15. Students of twentieth-century Latin America have only begun to analyze political speech from a gender perspective. A pioneering effort for one of the countries under study is Besse. On gender as a significant topic of study and a metaphor for relations of power, see Scott; on the gender connotations of nationalism, see McClintock.

16. On this overlap, see Robin; Soucy; Sternhill; and especially Blinkhorn. The definition of moderate or conservative, just like that of the right in general or the extreme right, also changed over time.

17. As Whitaker and Jordan noted (180), the "diversity of Latin America is reflected in the distinctive character of the unfolding nationalist process in each country." For a comparison of upper-class nationalisms, see Bagú.

18. Solberg, *Immigration*; Bergquist.

19. Related ideas were found in other countries at this time. On suspicions of immigrants, democracy, and a utilitarian elite, see also the Uruguayan writer Rodó, esp. 48–72.

Chapter 1 Chile: The Decline of a Manly People

1. On this turn-of-the-century "literature of crisis," see esp. B. Subercaseaux. See also Gazmuri Riveros, *Testimonios*; Ruiz; Godoy. Both Solberg, in *Immigration*, and B. Subercaseaux tie nationalism to the middle sectors, but Vargas Cariola, 214, identifies it with the elite.

2. Harold Blakemore, "From the War of the Pacific to 1930," in Bethell, *Chile*, 59–63; Bergquist, 25–37.

3. G. Subercaseaux, *Los ideales*, 5, 7. Although published in 1918, this work represents his earlier ideas. See also Vargas Cariola, 207–13; Zuleta Alvarez, *El nacionalismo*, 1: 51; Godoy, 38; Góngora, *Ensayo*, 92–94; Millar Carvacho, 22.

4. Encina, xx, xxiii, 309–14 (quote on 314); Pinochet Le-Brun, 11, 37. See also Ruiz, 131–32; Charles Griffin, 3. Biographical data on Pinochet and other individuals comes from the Chilean biographical portion of the bibliography. Pinochet had a progressive side, but I focus on the right-wing implications of his thought.

5. Charles A. Hale, "Political and Social Ideas in Latin America, 1870–1930," in Bethell, *Cambridge History*, 387, 389–90, 426. On Chilean positivism, see also Bader; Woll, "Positivism"; Yeager, "Elite Education."

6. Encina, 322; Pinochet Le-Brun, 5, 8, 10–11, 49.

7. Encina, 80, 82–84, 86–87, 93–98, 108–15, 139, 267–68.

8. Palacios, 2, 4–5, 7–8, 13, 19–20, 26, 64–65, 87–88, 188–90, 220–24. See also Gazmuri Riveros, "Notas," 236; and *Testimonios*, 20–21.

9. Palacios, 3, 10, 63, 87, 234, 248, 293, 301, 402, 405–6, 443–44, 446–47, 604, 612–14; B. Subercaseaux, 217.

10. Palacios, 560–61.

11. Ibid., 453, 469, 471; B. Subercaseaux, 218.

12. Gazmuri Riveros, "Notas," 232, 236; Godoy, 33–34. See also S. Lewis.

13. Solberg, *Immigration*, 36, 38.

14. Another work in the "literature of crisis" school similarly praised Germans while criticizing other immigrants. See Valdés Cange, 270–75.

15. Encina, 4, 29, 141, 151–53, 158, 160, 204, 309, 312, 332, 357–58.

16. Pinochet Le-Brun, 85, 86, 88, 104, 108, 113, 116, 126, 140, 144–45, 159, 164, 180, 193, 196, 204–5, 230, 235–36.

17. G. Subercaseaux, *Los ideales*, 21–28; Vargas Cariola, 207–13. Valdés Cange, 252–53, 255–57, also favored a strong executive and lambasted corrupt politics.

18. Solberg, *Immigration*, 69–72, 103–7.

19. Ibid., 70–71; Sater, "Race," 315, 318–19; Senderey, 56–57; population figure in Cohen, 128; Salinas C., "Cristianismo," 283, 300 n. 29.

20. This and the following paragraph are based on Palacios, 478–82.

21. On imaginary Jews, see Lesser, *Welcoming*, 3; on radical antisemitism, see Germani, "Antisemitismo," and Pulzer. Palacios's views fit Friedländer's model of "redemptive" antisemitism, in which to save one's race, one must fight the malevolent race of Jews.

22. Chile, Comisión Central del Censo, 37, 62–64, 66. See also González Miranda et al.; *La Voz del Sur* (Tacna), June 17, 1911, p. 2.

23. *La Voz del Sur*, May 29, 1911, p. 2, and June 17, 1911, p. 2; Monteón, 69.

24. *El Pacífico* (Tacna-Arica), June 9, 1911, p. 1, and June 20, 1911, p. 2; *El Grito Popular* (Iquique), June 2, 1911, p. 2; *La Voz del Sur*, May 27, 1911, p. 2; June 3, 1911, p. 2; June 5, 1911, p. 2.

25. *La Liga Patriótica* (Iquique), Jan. 5, 1919, p. 1; *La Voz del Sur*, June 3, 1911, p. 2; *El Pacífico*, May 27, 1911, p. 2; May 29, 1911, p. 2; June 8, 1911, p. 2; *El Comercio* (Pisagua), May 27, 1911, p. 2, and May 31, 1911, p. 2. See the photo of laborers at a Liga meeting in *Zig-Zag*, no. 355 (Dec. 9, 1911). The figure on Chilean nitrate workers comes from Stickell, 143.

26. *La Voz del Sur*, May 30, 1911, p. 2; *El Pacífico*, June 20, 1911, pp. 1–2.

27. *El Pacífico*, June 19, 1911, p. 2; *Zig-Zag*, nos. 328 (June 3, 1911), and 331 (June 24, 1911); *El Comercio*, June 7, 1911, p. 2.

28. *El Pacífico* (Tacna), July 18–19, 1911; Chile, Congreso, Diputados (July 20, 1911): 702, (July 21, 1911): 742.

29. *Zig-Zag*, no. 354 (Dec. 2, 1911); *La Voz del Sur*, June 17, 1911, p. 2; González Miranda et al., 59–60.

30. *El Grito Popular*, May 31, 1911, p. 2; June 2, 1911, p. 2; Aug. 9, 1911, p. 2; *El Despertar de los Trabajadores* (Iquique), Mar. 23, 1912, p. 2; *El Pacífico* (Tacna), July 6, 1911, p. 1; Monteón, 72, 75.

31. *Justicia* (Santiago), July 21, 1911, p. 2.

32. Izquierdo Fernández, esp. 66–67.

33. Sáez Morales, 1: 38–39; Quiroga and Maldonado, 101–5; Arriagada Herrera, 84–100; Somervell, 386–87. See also Nunn's works: "Emil Korner"; *Yesterday's Soldiers*, 139–40; *Military*, 98–100, 105–6, 115–17, 119–20.

34. Solberg, *Immigration*, 103–7; DeShazo, 144.

35. "Programa"; Charles A. Hale, "Ideas," in Bethell, *Cambridge History*, 390–91, 438–39; Pike, 112–18; Morris, 148–58, 164–68, 175–78, 184–90; Silva Vargas, 239.

36. S. Collier; John Lynch, "The Catholic Church in Latin America, 1830–1930," in Bethell, *Cambridge History*, 569–70. Mecham, 201–22, and Donoso, *Las ideas*, 174–326, trace the church-state struggle. See also Araneda Bravo, *El Arzobispo*, 153; Errázuriz, *Algo*, 183–84.

37. Ricardo Krebs, "El pensamiento de la iglesia frente a la laicización del estado en Chile 1875–1885," 19, 45, 60, and Sofía Correa, "El Partido Conservador ante las leyes laicas 1881–1884," 75–118, both in Krebs; Salinas C., "Teología." Woll noted that clerical historians defended the church's record on essentially liberal grounds in "Catholic Historian."

38. A. Cifuentes, 2: 148–53, 208–10, 249; Errázuriz, *Algo*, 291, 299–300; Silva Vargas, 243; Iñíquez Irarrázaval, 32; Araneda Bravo, *El Arzobispo*, 173; Magnet, 38–40; Landsberger, 78. On European Social Catholicism, see among other sources Camp; Moody; Fogarty; and Latourette.

39. Araneda Bravo, *Historia*, 600; Landsberger, 84–85; Silva Vargas, 247–49; Iñíquez Irarrázaval, 54–64.

40. On the influence of Social Catholic thought among Conservatives, see Iñíquez Irarrázaval, 65–67; Silva Vargas, 249–56; Araneda Bravo, *El Arzobispo*, 173; Morris, 122–34. On the measures, see Morris, 116–17; Iñíquez Irarrázaval, 121.

41. Valle, esp. 226–28; *Actividades femeninas*, esp. 317, 523, 585; Klimpel, 235–36; Verba, *"Liga,"* 1–4; Luis Barros and Ximena Vergara, "La imagen de la mujer aristocrática hacia el novecientos," in Covarrubias and Franco, 240–43. On working-class feminism, see Hutchison, "El feminismo"; Lavrin, "Women." For the figure, see DeShazo, 173.

42. Magnet, 39–43; see also Salinas C., "Teología," and "Cristianismo," 284.

Chapter 2 A Polluted Argentina

1. Collier and Collier, 131. Remmer's and Bergquist's works also influenced the analysis in this paragraph and the one that follows.

2. Romero, *A History*, 193; Chiaramonte, 121–44, 188; J. Irazusta, *Balance*, 53–77; Canedo, 81–82; Etchepareborda, *Zeballos*, 18–19.

3. Argentina, Dirección Nacional del Servicio Estadístico, 1: lxii, 1; Scobie, 273. See also Pomer.

4. Anti-immigrant and antisemitic passages are found in Martel, 13–14, 25, 34–36, 38, 115–28, 153, 205–8. See also Onega, 109–23.

5. Martel, 115–16, 238; population figure in Avni, *Argentina*, 27. See also Viñas, 231, 234; Masiello, 117–18; Onega, 111. On Jewish pimps and prostitutes, see Glickman, "Jewish White Slave Trade"; Mirelman, "Jewish Community"; and Guy, esp. 5–12, 17–23. Guy noted that Jewish pimps and prostitutes were found in Argentina as early as the late 1860s. See Gilman, 80–102, 119–27, on images of Jewish sexuality and sexual diseases.

6. Herrera, 49, 61–62.

7. Rojas, 115–18, 172–74, 179–81, 339, 342; Payá and Cárdenas, "Manuel Gálvez," 37–38, quote on 45. Payá and Cárdenas subsequently expanded this article into *El primer nacionalismo*. On educational nationalism, see Spalding, "Education."

8. Rojas, 13, 60, 116–17, 171–72, 185, 340.

9. Glauert, 4 n. 9; Onega, 202–3; Deutsch, *Counterrevolution*, 47–48.

10. On the events of 1909–10, see Deutsch, *Counterrevolution*, 33–38.

11. *La Nación* (Buenos Aires), Nov. 17, 1909, p. 6.

12. Andrea, *Oración*, 6–7; Sperber, 135.

13. McClintock, 273–74; Anderson.

14. To this discussion of white guards one should also add consideration of strikebreaking employer associations, such as the Sociedad Unión Protectora de Trabajo Libre (1905). See Adelman, "State," 81; Deutsch, *Counterrevolution*, 64.

15. Avni, *Argentina*, esp. 45, 48–49, 51, 77–78, 85–90, 91 (statistics); Solberg, *Immigration*, 87–89; Viñas, 253–55. See also Weisbrot; Mirelman, *Jewish Buenos Aires*;

Sofer; Centro de Documentación e Información sobre Judaísmo Argentino "Marc Turkow"; Jefferson, 154–55, 159.

16. Kroeber; Charles A. Hale, "Ideas," in Bethell, *Cambridge History*, 267–69; Brown, 270–75; Rojas, 135.

17. Slatta, 100–105; Kroeber, 10–11; Solberg, *Immigration*, 145–46; Canedo, 104–6. Lugones's lectures were published as *El payador* in 1916.

18. J. Irazusta, *Genio*, 7–8, 23–25; Canedo, 13–24, 95–97; Zuleta Alvarez, *El nacionalismo*, 1: 113–23.

19. Payá and Cárdenas, "Manuel Gálvez," 37, 40, 43–45, 47.

20. Gálvez, *El diario*, 101–3, 219–23; Gálvez, *El solar*, 13–19, 24, 41; and Gálvez, *Recuerdos*, 253–71, 320. See also Quijada, 23–29.

21. Glauert, 3–4; Gálvez, *El solar*, 41, and *Amigos*, 38–43, 57–75; Rojas, 117; Rock, "Intellectual Precursors," 274–77, 280–81, 283; Spalding, "Sociology," 50–59. An example of positivistic racism is Carlos Octavio Bunge. At this time in Argentina, racism characterized progressives even more than rightists, and therefore I do not see it as a specifically rightist trait; see Zimmerman.

22. C. Ibarguren, *La historia*, 56–57; Romero Carranza et al., 315; José Manuel Estrada, "Discursos sobre el liberalismo." On the nineteenth-century background to church relations with liberalism, see Bushnell, 63–66, 102; Mecham, 232–45; Lynch, "Church," in Bethell, *Cambridge History*, 341–42.

23. On these beginnings, see Auza, *Aciertos*, 1: 21–22, and *Los católicos*, 14–15, 27–33; Spalding, *La clase*, 509; Romero Carranza et al., 322–29, 352–62.

24. Sánchez Gamarra, 193–94; Ruschi, 78; Auza, *Aciertos*, 1: 24; Romero Carranza et al., 449; Furlong, 274; Spalding, *La clase*, 501, 529–30.

25. On the Liga and other Catholic activities, see Recalde, esp. 81–85, 89–90; Auza, *Los católicos*, 78–87, and *Aciertos*, 1: 68–70, 155–264; Spalding, *La clase*, 502–6, 543–49; Niklison, 18; Furlong, 280; Zuleta Alvarez, *El nacionalismo*, 1: 182–83; Zurretti, 386; Lynch, "Church," in Bethell, *Cambridge History*, 321.

26. Ciafardo; Gálvez, *Amigos*, 136.

27. Catholic women in the first two periods of rightist activity are discussed in McGee, "Female Right-Wing Activists," and Deutsch, "Catholic Church." See also Auza, *Aciertos*, 1: 116–18; Spalding, *La clase*, 535, 540. On female activism in labor and the left, see Carlson; Lavrin; Feijoó; and Navarro.

28. Recalde, 23–24; Auza, *Aciertos*, 1: 224.

29. Zuleta Alvarez, *El nacionalismo*, 1: 198–99; Rock, "Intellectual Precursors," 288; Gálvez, *La inseguridad*; Deutsch, *Counterrevolution*, 59–62. Before Bunge founded the nationalistic magazine *Revista de Economía Argentina* (1918–43), his research had already led him to support the protection of industries rooted in Argentine natural resources; see Imaz, "Alejandro E. Bunge." On upper-class opinion, see Eduardo A. Zimmerman, "Intellectuals, Universities, and the Social Question: Argentina, 1898–1916," in Adelman, *Essays*, 199–216.

30. Recalde, 21; Spalding, *La clase*, 525–26; Romero Carranza et al., 445–49, 453;

Auza, *Los católicos*, 100–107; Abad de Santillán, *La F.O.R.A.*, 123; Scobie, 145. On the state's alternating attitude of repression and co-optation toward labor, see Korzeniewicz, "Labour Movement," 32–39.

31. On German influence, see Nunn, *Yesterday's Soldiers*, and Schiff. See also Potash, 2–4, 9, 25; Rouquié, *Poder militar*, 1: 81, 83–84, 96. Civilian authors such as José Ingenieros also linked foreign affairs with the question of internal unity; see Brown, 141–42, 276–89.

32. *La Prensa* (Buenos Aires), Dec. 5, 1901–Jan. 19, 1902; *Caras y Caretas* (Buenos Aires), nos. 167 (Dec. 14, 1901), 168 (Dec. 21, 1901), 169 (Dec. 28, 1901); Zeballos, "Conferencia inaugural"; Bertoni, esp. 74–76; Scobie, 240; Sahni, 501, 506.

Chapter 3   Brazil: A Fractured Republic

1. Amaury de Souza, "El sistema de partidos políticos," in Jaguaribe, 1: 171, 175; Boris Fausto, "Society and Politics," in Bethell, *Brazil*, 266–75.

2. Janotti, 224–25; Hahner, *Civilian-Military Relations*, esp. 98–109; Levi, 119–20, 125–28; Pagano, 13, 68–69, 101, 130–31.

3. Prado, *Fastos*, 13, 16, 86, 102.

4. Ibid., 26–27, 37, 39, 47–48.

5. Ibid., 42–45; Villaca, 79; Pagano, 7, 70, 85–86, 180–81; Skidmore, "Eduardo Prado," 154, 160–61 n. 20; Rodrigues, esp. 64–75.

6. Prado, *A ilusão americana*, 66, 223.

7. Ibid., 67, 181–88, 190, 192–93 n. 1, 194, 197–200, 217, 222–23, 247.

8. On this and the following paragraph, see ibid., 188–96.

9. Levi, 119–20; Pagano, 253; Prado, *A ilusão americana*, 194; Eça de Queiroz, xxii, xxiv. On the Jews, see Lesser, *Welcoming*, 14–15; Lipiner, 114–15. On French anti-semitism, see Byrnes; Davies.

10. Skidmore, "Prado," 153. The failed rebellions of the 1890s discredited the already faltering monarchist movement, as did the overthrow of several European monarchies in World War I; see Lauerhass, 273; Hahner, *Civilian-Military Relations*, 108–9. Joaquim Nabuco's writings also helped convince right-wing readers of republican flaws and imperial virtues, although this Liberal's perspective differed from Prado's. See Needell, "A Liberal," 172–77.

11. For the statistics, see Merrick and Graham, 93–94; Warren Dean, "Economy," in Bethell, *Brazil*, 236; Brazil, Ministerio da Agricultura, Industria e Commercio, 4, pt. 1: lxiii; Klein, 318; Ridings, 64–65, 72–74; Carvalho, *Os bestializados*, 80; Topik, "Middle-Class Brazilian Nationalism," 96. See also Hahner, "Jacobinos," 127–31.

12. Queiroz, *Os radicais*, 17–80; Hahner, "Jacobinos," 131–33; Keith, 329.

13. Topik, "Middle-Class Brazilian Nationalism," 94; Queiroz, "Reflections," 184–85, and *Os radicais*, 24–25.

14. Hahner, "Jacobinos," 134–35; Queiroz, *Os radicais*, 99–107.

15. Topik, "Middle-Class Brazilian Nationalism," 96; Queiroz, "Reflections," 191–93; Queiroz, *Os radicais*, 107–8; Hahner, *Poverty*, 145. The constitution of 1891 al-

ready stated that nationally owned ships would control coastal trade, another Jacobino position. See Cavalcanti, 328. On industrialists and the state, see Luz, 88–101; Topik, "Economic Role," 127; Dean, "Economy," in Bethell, *Brazil*, 248–49.

16. Oliveira, *A questão*, 93; Carone, *Movimento*, 189–91; Needell, "*Revolta*"; Fausto, *Trabalho*, 41–62; Queiroz, *Os radicais*, 124–27; Hahner, *Poverty*, 135–39.

17. Hahner, "Jacobinos," 142–46; Needell, "*Revolta*."

18. Nachman, 14–15, 22; Carvalho, *A formação*, 28; Hahner, *Civilian-Military Relations*, 78–83.

19. Romano, 119–20, 122; Carvalho, *A formação*, 27; Nachman, 13–14.

20. Love, *Rio Grande do Sul*, 36, 179; J. C. Costa, 152–55; Vélez Rodríguez.

21. Romano, 120–36; J. C. Costa, 167.

22. Mecham, 266, 269–73, 275–77; E. V. da Costa, 209; Love, *São Paulo*, 110. On Catholic politics after 1889, see Lustosa, *Igreja e política*, 7–16, 48–50, and *A igreja católica*, 20–27; Wirth, *Minas Gerais*, 100–101, 125.

23. Júlio Maria, *A igreja*, 37–38, 44, 54–55, 57, 65; and *O catolicismo*, 240–42, 246–47.

24. Júlio Maria, *A igreja*, 36 (quote); Bruneau, "Power," 38; Beozzo, 107, 112, 115–17, 121.

25. Wirth, *Minas Gerais*, 199; Azzi, 11; Needell, *A Tropical Belle Epoque*, 58–60; Borges, *Family*, 175–79; Hahner, *Emancipating*, esp. 104–5, 119–20. Serrano, 198–200, cited a talk Júlio Maria gave to the Asociação de Damas Católicas of Juiz de Fora.

26. Wirth, *Minas Gerais*, 199; Hahner, *Poverty*, 222–23 (statistic on 222).

27. Teixeira, 2, 52, 65–69, 78, 80, 104. Street's worker town was not the first in Brazil (73), but it probably was the earliest one inspired by Social Catholicism.

28. Ibid., 105; Beiguelman, 11–12; Simão, 78; J. V. Freitas Marcondes, "Social Legislation in Brazil," in Smith and Marchant, 384.

29. Conniff, "Voluntary Associations," 68; Maram, "Labor," 255, 257; Beiguelman, 12–13; Hahner, *Poverty*, 267.

30. Statistics in Merrick and Graham, 105; Fausto, "Society," in Bethell, *Brazil*, 264; Michael M. Hall and Hobart A. Spalding Jr., "Urban Labour Movements," in Bethell, *Cambridge History*, 331. See also Michael M. Hall and Marco Aurélio Garcia, "Urban Labor," in Conniff and McCann, 167; Andrews, *Blacks and Whites*, 62–65; Paulo Sérgio Pinheiro, "O proletariado industrial na primeira república," in Fausto, *O Brasil republicano*, 2: 162–64; Maram, "Labor," 259–61; Hahner, *Poverty*, 265–66, 268; Carone, *Movimento*, 109–11, 117–20. Hall questioned the militancy of foreign laborers in "Immigration," 395–96, 399. For views on the social question, see Chacon, 138–39; Celso, 51; Ramos, *Introdução*, 60.

31. Andrews, "Black and White Workers," 495; Skidmore, *Black into White*, 57–61, 77; Borges, "'Puffy,'" 240–41; Peard, 36–38, 41–43.

32. Statistics in Holloway, 149. See also Skidmore, "Racial Ideas," 17–18; Andrews, *Blacks and Whites*, 86–87.

33. Cunha, esp. 50–54, 61–111; Skidmore, *Black into White*, 103–8; Brookshaw, 60.

34. S. Romero, 1: 30–32, 293–95; Brookshaw, 51; Eakin, 161–69.

35. Celso; Levi, 120; Skidmore, "Eduardo Prado," 155–57. On Celso as a conservative historian, see Rodrigues, 98–114.

36. Bomilcar, *O preconceito*, 34, 49, 51, 53, 56, 72–73, 75, 99, 101. This work was written in 1911. See also Bakota, 163; Skidmore, "Racial Ideas," 18.

37. Torres, *As fontes*, 7, 41; *O problema*, ix, 6, 8–9, 47–49, 65–75; *A organização*, 81. *O problema* and *A organização* were written before 1914. See also Lima Sobrinho, 128, 153, 232, 316–17; Marson.

38. Torres, *A organização*, 79–80; *O problema*, 76; *As fontes*, 36, 46.

39. Torres, *O problema*, 106; *As fontes*, 10, 12, 13, 19, 21–24, 28, 33; *A organização*, 209–15, 244. See also McLain, 30–31; Oliveira, "Ilha," 153.

40. Torres, *A organização*, 212–13, 240–42, 95–96, 104–5; *O problema*, 43, 87–88, 113, 128–29, 150. This view of the French revolution as counterproductive brings Hirschman's "perversity thesis" to mind; see 11–42.

41. Torres, *As fontes*, 30, 37–39; *O problema*, 108, 112, 123; *A organização*, 189, 208, 247–48. On the debt, see Dean, "Economy," in Bethell, *Brazil*, 222.

42. Torres, *O problema*, 11, 14, 28, 33–35, 145; *A organização*, ix–x, 139–42, 159.

43. Torres, *A organização*, 272, 277–79, 283–84, 286. Political institutions under the monarchy are described in Needell, "Brasilien."

44. Torres, *A organização*, 221–28, 243, 252–53, 255, 287, 308.

45. Bolivar Lamounier, "Formação de um pensamento político autoritário na primeira república: Uma interpretação," in Fausto, *O Brasil republicano*, 2: 358–59.

46. E. R. Gomes, 64–65.

47. Nunn, *Yesterdays' Soldiers*, 134–35; McCann, "Origins," 509, and "Formative Period," 741, 748–50.

48. José Murilo de Carvalho, "As forças armadas na primeira república: O poder desestabilizador," in Fausto, *O Brasil republicano*, 2: 226–27, 229.

49. Carone, *Movimento*, 122–23; McCann, "Nation," 229.

Chapter 5   Chile: Defending the Fatherland

1. Bergquist, 60; DeShazo, 64–67; Albert, 278–84, 317.

2. *El Mercurio* (Santiago), Nov. 3, 1918, p. 23; Nov. 4, 1918, p. 14; Nov. 25, 1918, p. 17; *La Prensa* (Buenos Aires) Nov. 6, 1918, p. 10, and Nov. 26, 1918, p. 9; Chile, Congreso, Diputados (Nov. 12, 1918): 418–19, (Nov. 25, 1918): 652–53; *El Diario Ilustrado* (Santiago), Nov. 24, 1918, p. 4.

3. *El Mercurio*, Nov. 13, 1918, p. 7; *El Diario Ilustrado*, Nov. 23, 1918, p. 5; *La Prensa*, Dec. 3, 1918, p. 11.

4. Hall and Spalding, "Urban Labour Movements," in Bethell, *Cambridge History*, 358. According to DeShazo, 194–95, it is difficult to estimate the number of union members.

5. DeShazo, 160–61; *El Mercurio*, Nov. 23, 1918, pp. 3, 17–18, and Nov. 26–27, 1918.

6. Solberg, *Immigration*, 107; *El Mercurio*, Nov. 23–24, 1918, Nov. 26–27, 1918,

Dec. 1, 1918, p. 3; *El Socialista* (Antofagasta), Dec. 12, 1918, p. 4, and Dec. 14, 1918, p. 4. Intellectuals of other Latin American countries defended Cárdenas in *Nosotros* (Buenos Aires) 30, no. 116 (Dec. 1918): 642. Administration impatience with the AOAN and growing repression resulted in the death of AOAN proposals in Congress and of the organization by 1920.

7. Chile, *Censo de 1920*, 277; Albert, 272; DeShazo, 22; Stickell, 143.

8. *La Prensa*, Nov. 27, 1918, p. 9; *El Mercurio*, Dec. 3, 1918, p. 21; Diputados (Dec. 13, 1918): 1212–13.

9. *La Liga Patriótica* (Iquique), Jan. 5, 1919, p. 1. *El Mercurio*, Nov. 6, 1918, p. 14; Nov. 28, 1918, p. 21; Dec. 1, 1918, p. 26; Dec. 3, 1918, p. 21; Dec. 6–8, 1918. On ANEC, see *Aliaga Roja*, 45. Having moved to the right, Catholic workers left the AOAN in early 1919, charging it had become too radical; see DeShazo, 162.

10. *El Mercurio*, Dec. 2, 1918, p. 14; *La Liga Patriótica*, Jan. 5–Mar. 11, 1919; clippings from *El Roto Chileno* (Antofagasta), n.d, n.p. I thank Jonathan Ablard for these clippings.

11. Quote in *El Roto Chileno*, n.d., n.p.; *El Socialista*, Dec. 10, 1918, p. 3; Dec. 12, 1918, p. 4; Dec. 14, 1918, pp. 3–4; Dec. 19, 1918, p. 1; Dec. 21, 1918, p. 3; Dec. 24, 1918, p. 3; Jan. 18, 1919, p. 2; Jan. 21, 1919, p. 4; Jan. 23, 1919, pp. 1, 4.

12. *El Socialista*, Jan. 28, 1919, p. 4; *El Paladín* (Antofagasta), Mar. 28, 1919, p. 1; Ramírez Necochea, "El fascismo," 11, 13.

13. Donoso, *Alessandri*, 1: 227–39; Nunn, *Military*, 121–23; Millar Carvacho, 57–62.

14. Houseman, 72–74; Yeager, "The Club," 546–48; Olavarría Bravo, 1: 89–90; Remmer, 71; DeShazo, 175–77; Donoso, *Alessandri*, 218, 243–46; Pike, *Chile*, 171. Politics of the period are well covered in Pinto Lagarrigue, esp. 87–100. The Liberal Alliance probably also bought votes. Since few laborers could cast ballots, however, they were not responsible for Alessandri's victory.

15. Chile, Congreso, Senadores (July 22, 1920): 467–68; Shea, Santiago, Telegram, July 24, 1920, 825.00/142, in U.S. Department of State, Records . . . Chile, 1910–1929; Donoso, *Alessandri*, 253–54; Nunn, *Military*, 125; Houseman, 76–77, 85.

16. *El Mercurio*, July 21, 1920, p. 14, and July 27, 1920, p. 16.

17. Deichman, Valparaíso, Telegram, July 25, 1920, 825.00/143; Shea, Desp. 576, Aug. 6, 1920, 825.00/160; *El Mercurio*, Jan. 30, 1919, p. 17; July 17, 1920, pp. 19–20; July 22, 1920, p. 18.

18. Shea, 825.00/160, Desp. 579, Aug. 20, 1920, 825.00/165, Desp. 583, Sept. 3, 1920, 825.00/169; Deichman, Desp. 139, Aug. 11, 1920, 825.00/163; Woodley, Antofagasta, Desp. 130, Aug. 23, 1920, 825.00/164; Brett, Tacna, No. 8, Sept. 3, 1920, 825.00/171; *El Mercurio*, July 19, 1920, p. 16.

19. Mayorga, "La difícil generación," 43; *El Diario Ilustrado*, July 20, 1920, pp. 1, 3–4; Barría Serón, 193–94; Magnet, 89–93; Diputados (July 30, 1920): 835–36, (Sept. 10, 1920): 1836; Kaempffer Villagrán, 177–78; Rivas Vicuña, 2: 208. See also testimonials in *Babel* 7, no. 28 (July–Aug. 1945): 13, 21, 25, 38–39.

20. Diputados (July 27, 1920): 763, (Sept. 24, 1920): 1900; Senadores (July 22,

1920): 466–67, 469; *El Mercurio*, July 22, 1920, p. 20; *El Diario Ilustrado*, July 22, 1920, pp. 1, 4; Magnet, 93–94; Kaempffer Villagrán, 182–88.

21. *El Diario Ilustrado*, July 22, 1920, pp. 1, 4; *El Mercurio*, July 22, 1920, p. 20; Magnet, 38.

22. Diputados (July 22, 1920): 687–92; Senadores (July 22, 1920): 468–71; *El Mercurio*, July 28, 1920, p. 15.

23. *El Mercurio*, July 23–25, 1920; Sperber, 119, 128–30.

24. *El Mercurio*, July 23–24, 1920; July 26, 1920, p. 12; July 28, 1920, p. 15; Diputados (July 27, 1920): 764, (July 30, 1920): 836–37, (Aug. 18, 1920): 1194, (Aug. 24, 1920): 1324, (Sept. 24, 1920): 1900–1901; DeShazo, 183–85.

25. *El Socialista*, Sept. 14, 1920, p. 2; Senadores (Aug. 18, 1920): 773, (Aug. 25, 1920): 849; Barría Serón, 188–91; *El Mercurio*, Oct. 4, 1920, p. 19; Oct. 13, 1920, p. 3; Oct. 18, 1920, p. 17; Manns, 47; Brady, Punta Arenas, Desp. 19, July 31, 1920, 825.504/10; Kaempffer Villagrán, 163–65. Labor and capitalist mobilization in Argentine Patagonia also affected the elite's perceptions; see next chapter.

26. *El Magallanes* (Punta Arenas), July 23–24, July 26, 1920, p. 3; *El Mercurio*, July 25, 1920, p. 23; Diputados (Aug. 25, 1920): 1350, (Aug. 28, 1920): 1512, (Sept. 3, 1920): 1646. Brady, 825.504/10, and Kaempffer Villagrán, 215–29, summarize the entire incident.

27. Diputados (Aug. 25, 1920): 1353, (Aug. 28, 1920): 1513–15, (Sept. 10, 1920): 1839; Mayorga, "Punta Arenas," 15; figures from Kaempffer Villagrán, 223–24.

28. Brady, June 29, 1921, 825.504/14; Mayorga, "Punta Arenas," 15; Diputados (Aug. 25, 1920): 1358, (Aug. 28, 1920): 1515, (Sept. 10, 1920): 1838–39.

29. Senadores (Aug. 25, 1920): 847–52.

30. The residence law only gave intendants this power, and there were none in Magallanes. See Diputados (Sept. 24, 1920): 1898–1900.

31. Kaempffer Villagrán, 228–29.

32. *La llamada movilización*; Brady, 825.504/14; Pinto Lagarrigue, 99; Nunn, *Military*, 125; DeShazo, 185–86.

33. *El Mercurio*, Aug. 1, 1920, p. 3, lauded the Liga Patriótica Argentina as a model and suggested that the government sponsor the effort. See also May 22–25 and May 31, 1921, p. 15; Verba, "*Círculo*"; *Actividades*, 573, 626–28; Klimpel, 236–37.

34. Figures in DellaPergola, 101.

35. Matthews, Antofagasta, Sept. 13, 1921, 825.504/15; Martin, Santiago, Desp. 716, Sept. 20, 1921, 825.00/205; Deichman, Valparaíso, Aug. 30, 1921, 825.5045/31; *El Mercurio*, July 16–17, 1920, and Jan. 14, 1921, p. 15; DeShazo, 183, 189–92.

36. Brett, Arica, Apr. 2, 1921, 825.504/13.

37. McConough, Concepción, Feb. 11, 1922, 825.504/18; *Memoria*, 19–23; figures from Morris, 202; Loveman, *Struggle*, 56–57; *El Mercurio*, Dec. 15–16, 1921.

38. Caballero C., *Balance*, 10–11; *Memoria*, 8–9; Pike, 341–42; Góngora, "Libertad," 17; *El Mercurio*, Feb. 13, 1922, p. 8; Guillermo Subercaseaux, *El régimen*. The Argentine Asociación del Trabajo and Liga Patriótica Argentina were models for the ADT.

39. Caballero C., *El capital*, 7–9, 13; Morris, 203.

40. Bergquist, 27, 64; DeShazo, 185–88.

41. Bonilla and Glazer, 42–44; Mayorga, "La difícil generación," 44, and "Los estudiantes," 44; Arriagada Herrera, 104; Vicuña Fuentes.

42. For the background to and the events of 1924–25, see Nunn, *Chilean Politics*; Yeager, "The Club"; Pike, 176–82; Millar Carvacho.

43. Arriagada Herrera, 93, 101–3, 106–7; Carlos Maldonado Prieta, personal communication.

44. Gómez Ugarte, 27–32; *Trabajo* (Santiago), July 20, 1933, p. 5; Tarr, 15–16; Nunn, *Chilean Politics*, 47–52; Millar Carvacho, 80–83; Bicheno, 362.

45. Morris, esp. 119–71; Collier and Collier, 189–91; Bergquist, 66–67.

46. Paz Covarrubias, "El movimiento feminista chileno," in Covarrubias and Franco, 627–28; Lavrin, *Women*, 290, 293–94; Nunn, *Chilean Politics*, 72; DeShazo, 222–26.

47. Strawbridge, 107; Klimpel, 339.

48. *Justicia* (Santiago), June 18, 1925, pp. 1–2, and July 21, 1925, p. 2; DeShazo, 227.

49. Araneda Bravo, *Historia*, 664–67; Grayson, 74, 81; Magnet, 59, 61–63, 72–74. Many Conservatives agreed with law professor José María Cifuentes, who argued that as Chilean workers were slowly advancing, little official intervention was necessary or desirable.

50. Viviani Contreras, *Sociología*; for his praise of fascism, see *Doctrinas*, 253–323, esp. 320. See also Moreno Beauchemin, 33–34, 47–49; Gómez Ugarte, 28; Magnet, 74; DeShazo, 205–6.

Propelled partly by Viviani, the Partido Popular Chileno, a social Christian "proletarian" party along the lines of the Italian Populares, arose in 1921, but worker disdain and Conservative opposition doomed it. See Juan Carlos González Ransanz, "La separación de la Iglesia y el Estado en la administración Alessandri," in *Siete ensayos*, 284–86; *El Mercurio*, Mar. 14, 1920, p. 28; Grayson, 82, 86.

51. Errázuriz, *Obras*, 3: 9–13 (1919), 37–47 (1921), 118–19 (1925), 216–18 (1924); Araneda Bravo, *Historia*, 699–701, 703–13.

52. Aliaga Roja, 57–59; *Actividades*, esp. 573, 575, 601–4.

53. Gaviola A. et al., 31–34; Covarrubias, "El movimiento," in Covarrubias and Franco, 621; Lavrin, "Women," 92, 96–101; DeShazo, 173.

54. Liga de Damas Chilenas, 14–15; Valle, 226; *Actividades*, 588–91; Verba, "*Liga*," esp. 6–7; Hutchison, "Working Women," 281–95.

Chapter 6 *Argentinizing Labor*

1. Alonso; Sábato, 139–63.

2. Cornblit, 605–6; Stimson, Buenos Aires, Desp. 737, Jan. 25, 1919, 835.00/164, in U.S. Department of State, Records . . . Argentina, 1910–1929; *La Mañana* (Buenos Aires), Jan. 30, 1915, p. 1. Note the difference between Conservative (a political party in Buenos Aires province) and conservative (a variety of parties and individuals of that persuasion).

3. Torre, *Obras*, 5: 29, 35–36, 43; Malamud; Deutsch, *Counterrevolution*, 30–32. The PDP also drew from the immigrant farmer-based Liga del Sur of Santa Fe.

4. Vásquez-Presedo, 2: 46; Shipley, 75; Tulchin.

5. Vásquez-Presedo, 2: 47; Rock, *Politics*, 190–91.

6. Bergquist, 102, 134–36.

7. Cornblit, 628.

8. *La Nación*, May 23 and July 13, 1918; *La Vanguardia* (Buenos Aires), May 15, 1919; Asociación del Trabajo, *Normas*, 3–4.

9. Azaretto, 65–67.

10. Deutsch, *Counterrevolution*, 70–72.

11. On the Semana Trágica, see Babini, 8–20; Bilsky; Godio; Rock, "Lucha"; "La Semana Trágica," *La Nación*, Jan. 9–19, 1969. See also Godio, 36, 48–49, 133; Ofelia Pianetto, "The Labour Movement and the Historical Conjuncture: Córdoba, 1917–21," in Adelman, *Essays*, 152.

12. Babini, 16; Bilsky, 73–75; Godio, 34–35, 181.

13. On antisemitism, see Avni, "Antisemitismo"; Sofer, 44; Solominsky, 17–21; Franceschi in *El Pueblo* (Buenos Aires), Jan. 26, 1919, p. 2; Rivanera Carlés (Manuel Carlés's grandnephew); Deutsch, "Argentine Right"; Mirelman, "Semana Trágica." On the vigilantes and militias, see *La Prensa*, Jan. 12–15, 1919; *La Nación*, Jan. 11–15, 1919; *La Época* (Buenos Aires), Jan. 10–12, 1919; *Caras y Caretas*, no. 1059 (Jan. 18, 1919); Romariz; Carulla, *Al filo*, 159–60; Piñero, 68.

14. Liga Patriótica Argentina (Liga), *La verdad*, 6–7; *Revista Militar* 19 (Jan. 1919): 198.

15. "A," Buenos Aires, no. 158, Aug. 2, 1920, copy of n. 1082, Stimson, Feb. 18, 1920, C-10-K, 12931, in U.S. National Archives, RG 38.

16. Cantón, 146–49; Bilsky, 74; Rouquié, *Poder*, 1: 150–51; Potash, 12.

17. *La Época*, Jan. 16–17, 1919; *La Razón* (Buenos Aires), Jan. 13, 1919, p. 2; *La Nación*, Jan. 14, 1919, p. 8; Godio, 183.

18. *Revista Militar* 19 (Jan. 1919): 199–202; *La Razón*, Jan. 17, 1919, p. 3; *La Época*, Jan. 20, 1919, p. 2; *La Prensa*, Jan. 20, 1919, p. 8.

19. Liga, *Estatutos*.

20. Zeballos, "Gobierno Radical," 273–80; Liga, *Primer Congreso*, 69; Collier and Collier, 148.

21. Araújo Salvadores, interview; Argentina, Policía, *Orden*; Liga, *Solemne homenaje*, 16. On the Jewish brigade, see *Vida Nuestra* (Buenos Aires) 3 (July 1919), n.p. The press exhaustively described brigade formation and the activities of Liga authorities and brigades.

22. *La Prensa*, Feb. 4, 1919, and Oct. 26, 1946; Pedro Maglione Jaimes, "Una figura señera—Manuel Carlés," *La Nación*, Jan. 12, 1969, 3d sec., 6; File 20137, Archivo de *La Prensa*, Buenos Aires; Rouquié, *Poder*, 1: 144; Zuleta Alvarez, *El nacionalismo*, 1: 193; Rock, *Politics*, 183.

23. Liga, *Estatutos*, 23–29. As Caterina (p. 84) pointed out, representatives from the capital dominated the leadership.

24. I calculated the number of brigades from the press and the congresses, and I based my estimate of core members on the fact that brigades averaged twenty officers. Each brigade had its own elected officers, junta, commissions, and treasury.

25. *La Prensa*, Apr. 15, 1919, p. 13, and May 25, 1919; Liga, *Octavo Congreso*, 410. On the Consejo, see Grierson; on views of female political participation, see Font.

26. *El Pueblo*, June 30–July 1, July 21–22, 1919; *La Fronda* (Buenos Aires), Oct. 8, and Nov. 1, 1919; *La Nación*, Nov. 4, 1919.

27. *La Fronda*, Aug. 10, 1920; *El Pueblo*, Aug. 10, 1919.

28. *El Pueblo*, Aug. 15, 1919; *La Prensa*, Jan. 12 and 31, 1920; *La Nación*, Aug. 13, 1920; *La Capital* (Rosario), Jan. 26, 1921; Spalding, *Organized Labor*, 65.

29. Pujato Crespo in *La Prensa*, May 13, 1919; Córdoba brigade in *La Voz del Interior* (Córdoba), Oct. 23, 1919; Correa in *La Capital*, Jan. 17, 1921. On Pujato Crespo, see La Palma de Emery, 192–93; and Auza, *Periodismo*, 299–300.

30. Liga, *Discurso de 1919*, 6, 9; Liga, *Catecismo*, 1–3; Font, 163; Liga, Comisión de Bellas Artes, Brigadas de Señoras, 7; Liga, *Sexto Congreso*, 44; Liga, *Octavo Congreso*, 53, 57. On feminism, see Carlson, 153–66; Lavrin, *Women*, esp. 266–77.

31. Not that the left was much better; indeed, it ridiculed the LPA's recruitment of women. See *La Voz del Interior*, Oct. 24, 1919; *La Protesta* (Buenos Aires), Oct. 29, 1919. On male resistance to female participation in labor and the left, see Lavrin, "Women"; and Navarro.

32. Information on the Liga's social composition is based on a sample of 146 brigade delegates to the annual congresses and 71 members of the Junta Central and Consejo Executivo, 1920–28. Sources are listed in the Argentine biographical section of the bibliography. Members of the Jockey Club, Sociedad Rural or other rural associations, prestigious social registers, and/or the Círculo de Armas were considered upper-class. I thank Néstor Tomás Auza and José Luis de Imaz for confirming the class backgrounds of the persons studied. On female backgrounds, see also *La Voz del Interior*, Oct. 24, 1919; *La Fronda*, Nov. 1, 1919; Liga, Comisión de Señoritas, *Sus escuelas*, 20. Most delegates to the congresses were officers of brigades, and their social standing probably was higher than that of the rank and file.

33. Figures in *Review of the River Plate*, July 25, 1919. See also *El Mercurio*, July 27, 1919, p. 22; *La Vanguardia*, Mar. 2 and June 11, 1919; *El Pueblo*, June 21–22 and June 24, 1919; Rock, *Politics*, 183, 198; Romariz, 171; Rouquié, *Poder*, 1: 151–57; Potash, 9–12; Caterina, 43–44, 46, 156–58, 290.

34. *La Época*, Jan. 11, 1919, p. 1, and Feb. 8, 1919, p. 1.

35. *La Fronda*, Mar. 15, 1920; *La Prensa*, Jan. 15, 1920; *La Vanguardia*, Dec. 15, 1921; *La Protesta*, June 14, 1923; Liga, *Tercer Congreso*, 153–54.

36. *La Vanguardia*, May 15–16, 1919; *La Protesta*, Apr. 29, 1922; *La Prensa*, Jan. 25, 1920; *Boletín de Servicios de la Asociación del Trabajo* (Buenos Aires) 1, no. 1 (Feb. 5, 1920): 1; Asociación del Trabajo, *¿Qué es la Asociación?*; Shipley, 293–97, 317–18; Riddle, Desp. 25, Apr. 10, 1922, 835.5043/1.

37. On these two cases, see Deutsch, *Counterrevolution*, 117–22.

38. Horowitz, "Argentina's"; Adelman, "State," esp. 89–102, and "The Political Economy of Labour, 1870–1930," in Adelman, *Essays*, 21–22.

39. *La Vanguardia*, Feb. 16 and May 5, 1921; *La Protesta*, Apr. 29, 1922; Shipley, 317; Argentina, Congreso, *Diputados* (Aug. 31, 1920): 652.

40. On Las Palmas, see *Diputados* (Aug. 31, 1920), 648; Domínguez; *La Vanguardia*, Aug. 12, 14, 17, 19, 24, 26, 30, 1920; Tissera; Cameron, 305.

41. Union figures in Gori, 242; G. Cuadrado Hernández.

42. On Villaguay, see *La Vanguardia*, Feb. 15–21 and 24–28, 1921; *Diputados* (Feb. 18 and 23, 1921): 311–16, 355–92. See also *La Fronda*, Feb. 27, 1921.

43. *La Fronda*, Mar. 3 and 14, 1921; *La Nación*, Mar. 2 and 14, 1921; Liga, *Primero*. On Jewish participation, see the entire issue of *Vida Nuestra* 4, no. 9 (Mar. 1921).

44. "Estatutos de la Liga Patriótica Argentina, Gualeguaychú," in Julio Irazusta archive, Papers, vol. 1; *La Fronda*, Nov. 15, 1919; *La Nación*, Mar. 23 and 31, 1921; Liga, *Primero*, 61–67; Argentina, Provincia de Entre Ríos, 2: 519–22.

45. Liga, *Humanitarismo*, 10; Liga, *Primero*, esp. 5, 9; *La Nación*, Apr. 19, 1921; Eric Hobsbawm, "Introduction: Inventing Traditions," in Hobsbawm and Ranger, 9.

46. On the events and pageantry of the day, see Liga, *Primero*, 29–32, 57–60, 70–72; *La Vanguardia*, May 2–4, May 6, and July 12, 1921; *La Fronda*, May 4, 1921; Entre Ríos, 3: 1026–27; *La Prensa*, May 2–3, 1921; Antonio A. Giménez, interview. See also Mary Ryan, "The American Parade: Representations of the Nineteenth-Century Social Order," in Hunt, 133–40.

47. Carlés in Liga, *Primero*, 85–86. Sperber, 116–17, noted the importance of studying "the interaction of planned and unplanned happening."

48. Entre Ríos, 2: 521, 523–24, 3: 1029–33, 1035–36; *La Vanguardia*, May 2–3, 8, 10, 16, and 27, 1921; June 15, 18, 22, 24, and 29, 1921; July 6, 12, and 18, 1921; Nov. 26, 1921; *La Fronda*, May 3, 1921; Marotta, 3: 39.

49. On the Patagonian episode, see Iscaro, 2: 189–91; Bayer; Fiorito; Liga, *El culto*; Borrero, 63–65. As Bergquist (104) pointed out, the shared Chilean identity of workers and isolated conditions under which they lived on the sheep ranches formed a strong basis for these unions.

On joint LPA-government actions to repress oil workers in Comodoro Rivadavia and Punta Arenas, Chile, see Iscaro, 2: 189; Solberg, *Oil*, 66–68; *La Vanguardia*, Oct. 23, 1919, and Feb. 27, 1920; *La Prensa*, Jan. 27, 1920.

50. Liga, *Campaña*; Diputados (Aug. 31, 1920): 648, (Feb. 1, 1922): 54–110; Rouquié, *Poder*, 149; Bayer, 2: 350–52, 3: 143–50.

51. *Review of the River Plate*, June 13, 1919; Rock, *Politics*, 197–98; Walter, *The Socialist Party*, 157, 160; Riddle, Buenos Aires, Desp. 44, May 10, 1922, 835.00/298.

52. Rock, *Politics*, 190, 214; Shipley, 292, 302–5; Vásquez-Presedo, 2: 47. Horowitz, "When Argentine Employers," however, partly attributes labor weakness in the 1920s to the failed general strike of 1924.

53. *La Fronda*, July 2, 1920; Liga, Comisión Central, *Memoria 1927*, 5; Auza, *Periodismo*, 130. LPA publications and the press mentioned nineteen schools; Liga, *La*

verdad, 11, cited fifty. Photos of the schools in the press and Archivo Gráfico de la Nación, and my interview with Baylac de Eizaguirre confirmed that these projects continued long after the 1920s. On women laborers, see Lavrin, "Women," 92, 101–2. Some industries, such as meatpacking, employed more immigrant than native-born women. See Lobato, 177.

54. Liga, Comisión de Señoritas, *Sus escuelas,* 21; Liga, Comisión Central, *Memoria de diez escuelas,* 44–50.

55. *La Fronda,* Jan. 27, 1921; Liga, *Séptimo Congreso,* 435; Liga, Comisión de Señoritas, *Sus escuelas,* 4.

56. Cano in Liga, Comisión de Señoritas, *Sus escuelas,* 12; Ezcurra, interview; Liga, Libro de Actas, Sept. 28, 1927, and Apr. 16, 1928, in Liga Patriótica Argentina archive; *La Capital,* Dec. 9, 1919; Liga, *Acción civilizadora* (1921).

57. *La Fronda,* July 25, 1920; Liga, *Tercera Exposición,* 1–5; Berdier in Liga, *Discursos pronunciados en el acto inaugural,* 2.

58. Hollander, 237; Carlson, 166.

59. Liga, Libro de Actas, May 18, 1927, and Apr. 1, 1930, LPA archive; Argentina, Policía, *Memoria,* 79–83, 102; Liga, *La verdad,* 15; *La Fronda,* Oct. 20, 1919, Feb. 12, 1920, and Dec. 14, 1920; Liga, *Acción civilizadora . . . 1922;* Hobsbawm, "Introduction," in Hobsbawm and Ranger, 6–7.

60. Cano in Liga, *Tercer Congreso,* 327–38; Liga, *Solemne homenaje,* 20; Carlés in Liga, *Quinto Congreso,* 38; Gualeguaychú brigade in Liga, *Primero,* 11; Liga, *Sexto Congreso,* 54. On the division of labor in the Liga, see McGee, "Visible."

61. Lugones in Barbero and Devoto, 55–56; Lugones, *La organización,* 11. Carlés supported the military and beefing up defense in "Diplomacia."

62. Carlés in Barbero and Devoto, 49; Liga, *Catecismo,* 14; Liga, *Octavo Congreso,* 52–53; Liga, *Definición,* 3; M. Douglas, 12, 16, 98–99, 169; Sander Gilman, "Plague in Germany, 1939/1989: Cultural Images of Race, Space, and Disease," in A. Parker, 180–83.

63. Liga, *Tercer Congreso,* 23, 29; *Catecismo,* 14–16; *Definición,* 3–4, 20–21; *Tercera Exposición,* 6.

64. Liga, *Séptimo Congreso,* 60–61; *Primer Congreso,* 41, 197–98; *Octavo Congreso,* 291; *Tercer Congreso,* 35; *Los Principios* (Córdoba), May 8, 1920; Kele, 10, 43–44.

65. Liga, *Congreso General,* 115; Carlés in Liga, *Noveno Congreso,* 79.

66. See, for example, Napal in Liga, *Cuarto Congreso,* 484; *Primer Congreso,* 45.

67. For Pallejá's ideas, see Liga, *Cuarto Congreso,* 93–107. I discuss corporatism in detail in Part 3.

68. Carlés in Liga, *Primer Congreso,* 44; *Sexto Congreso,* 39–40; and *Séptimo Congreso,* 69–70.

69. Liga, *Tercera Exposición,* 7; Liga, *Primero,* 37; Liga, *Humanitarismo,* 18; Liga, *Quinto Congreso,* 39–40; Stimson, Desp. 1422, Dec. 21, 1920, 835.43L62; *La Internacional* (Buenos Aires), Mar. 20, 1924, p. 1. On antileftist groups in Europe, see Mayer, "Postwar Nationalisms," 114–18; Diehl; Large. On LPA ties with such groups, see

Deutsch, *Counterrevolution*, 166–67; on its ties with the Chilean Liga Patriótica Militar, see Liga, *Solemne homenaje*.

70. Barbero and Devoto, 41; Falcoff, "Economic Dependency"; Murmis and Portantiero.

71. Liga, *Octavo Congreso*, 84–88; *Sexto Congreso*, 215–16; *El programa*, 15; Ayarragaray in *Noveno Congreso*, 473, 476. See also DellaPergola, 95 (figure); Caterina, 228–29.

72. On LPA ties with the church, see also Caterina, 285–88.

73. Franceschi in *El Pueblo*, Jan. 26, 1919, p. 1; Rock, *Authoritarian Argentina*, 61–63; Luna, *Yrigoyen*, 197–98, 201; White, Buenos Aires, no. 1567, June 1, 1921, 835.00/237.

74. Carlés in Liga, *Sociedad*, 6, and *Tercer Congreso*, 29; *Primer Congreso*, 132.

75. Figures on workers' circles in Niklison, 180, and on Colecta proceeds in Furlong, 282. See also Comité Ejecutivo; Andrea, *Pensamiento*, 85, 91, and *Obras*, 2: 81, 91, 99, 135; *La Fronda*, Oct.–Nov. 1919. Caterina, 288–89, found that the workers' circles, perhaps disturbed by the LPA's violence against unions, maintained some distance from it.

76. Andrea, *Obras*, 2: 111–13, 165; Esposito; File 46948, Archivo de *La Prensa*; Bayer, 1: 48–50; Auza, *Aciertos*, 2: 144–49, 3: 271–79.

77. Liga, *Primer Congreso*, 37; Liga, *Catecismo*.

78. *El Pueblo*, Nov. 16, 1919; Auza, *Aciertos*, 2: 399–401, 404; Comité Ejecutivo; Gálvez de Tiscornia, 36–37; Ivereigh, 69–70, 73; Caimari, *Perón*, 44; Furlong, 286–87; Zurretti, 394, 396–97; Ruibal, 66.

79. Franceschi, *Tres estudios*, 206–11, and *La democracia*; Andrea, *Pensamiento*, 60, 80.

80. Zuleta Alvarez, *El nacionalismo*, 1: 188–89; *Universitas* 9, no. 38 (July–Sept. 1975): 6, 13–14, 25, 46–47, 51.

Chapter 7   *Against Anarchism: Brazilian Nationalism*

1. Pécaut, 25.

2. Statistics in Topik, "Economic Nationalism," 289, and Albert, 263; see also Albert, 79–87, 90–91, 93–94, 194–98, 261–63; Department of Overseas Trade, "Report on the General Economic and Financial Conditions of Brazil for the Year 1919," in Great Britain, Parliament, 17: 13.

3. Luebke, 84–85, 104–6, 159, 176–80, 199–200; Bakota, 68. During the war, however, the U.S. supplanted Great Britain and Germany to become Chile's leading trading partner; see Harold Blakemore, "From the War of the Pacific to 1930," in Bethell, *Chile*, 68–69.

4. Bilac, *A defesa*, 4–8, 11–15, 39–41, 48, 56; Beattie, 443, 457; Borges, "Puffy," 235, 250–51.

5. Bilac, *A defesa*, 22–25, 34–35; *O Estado de São Paulo* (*OESP*), Oct. 24, 1915, p. 1.

6. *Revista do Brasil* (São Paulo) (Sept. 1916): 100–101; Topik, "Economic Nation-

alism," 262–64; Bakota, 68, 78; *Estatutos da Liga*, 3–6, 9; Instituto Histórico Collection, container 341, folder 67, Instituto Histórico e Geográfico Brasileiro (IHGB), Rio de Janeiro; Magalhães Júnior, 398, 403, 412; C. O'Neil, 42. Speeches hosted by the LDN included Barbosa, 2: 5–13, 17–34; Freire. I found no membership figures for the LDN.

7. *Estatutos da Liga*, 11–17; Instituto Histórico Collection, container 341, folder 27, IHGB; Magalhães Júnior, 390–92, 403; Pessôa, 34–36; Nagle, 45; C. O'Neil, 37.

8. For criticisms of Bilac and the LDN, see Nagle, 46–47; Magalhães Júnior, 394–97; Torres in Carone, *A primeira república*, 282–83, 296–97. See also Frank D. McCann, "Military," in Conniff and McCann, 59; Magalhães Júnior, 398, 403, 412; C. O'Neil, 42.

9. Bilac, *A defesa*, 126–32; Bilac, *Ultimas conferências*, 46, 50.

10. Coelho Neto, 87, 90, 148; Penna, 7, 14, 19, 36, 77–78; N. Stepan, 48, 92. Another LDN member, J. F. de Assis Brasil, explored educational and economic aspects of national defense, among other issues, 26–32, 38–40.

11. Bibliotheca da Liga, 12–13, 16–17.

12. Bilac, *A defesa*, 85–86, 133–34, 141–42; Coelho Neto, 12, 41–48, 53–60, 148. Bilac implied that, in defending family and fatherland, the military was assuming a manly duty; see Beattie, 461.

13. Figures on strikes in Fausto, *Trabalho*, 162–63; on women in Brazil, Ministério da Agricultura, Indústria e Commércio, 5: lxxix. See also Wolfe, *Working Women*, 16–25; Pena and Lima; Beiguelman, 83–111; French, 42–53; Dulles, *Anarchists*, 51–150.

14. Figures in Simão, 32; *OESP*, Apr. 16, 1920, p. 2; *Gil Blas* (*GB*) (Rio de Janeiro) 2, no. 62 (Apr. 15, 1920). *GB* is unpaginated.

15. Barbedo, Ministério de Guerra, Commando da Segunda Região Militar, Segunda Divisão, São Paulo, to Steidel, Mar. 25, 1920, Liga Nacionalista (LN) Papers, packet 2: B, Instituto Histórico e Geográfico de São Paulo (IHGSP); Bakota, 69; C. O'Neil, 81, 83–44. The LDN would reassume prominence in the 1930s and 1940s.

16. *OESP*, Dec. 18, 1965, Suplemento Literário, 3; Manor, pp. 321–22, 327–28, 330; C. O'Neil, 38–39.

17. Mesquita Filho in Carone, *A primeira república*, 276–82; Love, *São Paulo*, 98; Lima Sobrinho, 399–403.

18. Figure in *A accão*, 48; *OESP*, Dec. 16, 1916, p. 5; *Revista do Brasil* (Dec. 1916), 408; Dória, last page (unnumbered); Manor, 340; Nogueira Filho, 1: 69, 74–75; Mesquita Filho, 9, 11, 13, 21–23. Although published in 1925, Mesquita Filho's book suggests the LN mentality of a few years earlier.

19. Dória, 229; Mesquita Filho, 57–68.

20. Projeto de Regulamento Eleitoral da Liga Nacionalista, packet 2: B, and packet 1: A, D, LN Papers, IHGSP; *A accão*, 10, 20, 30, 49; *OESP*, Apr. 13, 1919, p. 3; Bandecchi, 62–67.

Among other activities, the LN also sponsored talks, patriotic celebrations, civic and health projects, and military training. See packets 2: B, and 1: E, F, H, LN Papers,

IHGSP; Brazil, Estado de São Paulo, 84–85; *A accão*, 19–20, 33–46; Nogueira Filho, 1: 55–57, 90–92; Bandecchi, 35–36, 45–46, 49–52, 75–77; *OESP*, Jan. 16, 1919, p. 5; Manor, 344.

21. Figures on students from *A accão*, 12. See also *A accão*, 12–15; Minutes of Meetings, Aug. 5 and 7, 1917; May 15, 1918; and July 26, 1918, LN Papers, packet 1: G, IHGSP; *OESP*, Apr. 3, 1919, p. 2, and May 29, 1919, p. 3; Bandecchi, 38.

22. Love, *São Paulo*, 94; Bandecchi, 40–43; C. O'Neil, 92–130; Luís to Steidel, Nov. 25, 1920, and Dec. 8, 1920, LN Papers, packet 2: B, IHGSP.

23. *El Mercurio* (Santiago), Oct. 29, 1919, p. 11, and Nov. 3, 1919, p. 11; *OESP*, Oct. 27, 1919, p. 2, and Nov. 1, 1919, p. 4; Maram, *Anarquistas*, 144–45; *A Plebe* (São Paulo), Oct. 30, 1919, p. 1. Authors have described *A Plebe* as anarchist or anarcho-syndicalist.

24. Schmidt, 7–13. This originally appeared in *A Plebe* in December 1919. See also Nogueira Filho, 1: 73–75. With regard to labor, the LN briefly corresponded with the Liga Patriótica Argentina; see *La Fronda*, May 30, 1920, p. 3.

25. Leme, 108–9; Momsen, Rio de Janeiro, Jan. 4, 1919, 832.00/169, U.S. Department of State, Records . . . Brazil, 1910–1929; Dean, 163–67; Love, *São Paulo*, 231; Simão, 123–24; Bakota, 88, 93; Luebke, 188.

26. McCann, "Formative," 763–64; Carvalho, "As forças," 210–14 (in Fausto, *O Brasil*); Boris Fausto, "Society and politics," in Bethell, *Brazil*, 296–300; Santa Rosa; Carone, *O tenentismo*; Wirth, "Tenentismo."

27. Love, *São Paulo*, 117–18, 349 n. 100; Manor, 347–49, 353; Bandecchi, 81–82, 84, 86.

28. *Brazílea* (Rio de Janeiro) 1 (1917): 3, 28, 238–41, 510; 2 (1917): 10.

29. Figures in Brazil, Ministério da Agricultura, Indústria, e Commércio, 5: xxxvi, lxii; Topik, "Economic Nationalism," 292. See also *Brazílea* 1 (1917): 4, 106, 195–98, 467, 470, 518–20, 544–46; 2 (1917): 9, 55–56.

30. *Jornal do Commércio* (Rio de Janeiro), May 9, 1919, p. 11; *GB* 1, nos. 33 (Sept. 25, 1919) and 34 (Oct. 2, 1919); *GB* 2, no. 127 (July 14, 1921); Beiguelman, 96; Albert, 265. On the Confederation, see *Revista do Brasil* 1 (Aug. 1917): 538–40; Brazil, Congresso Nacional, *Deputados* 8 (Aug. 23, 1921): 390.

31. *GB* 1, nos. 21 (Aug. 7, 1919), 35 (Oct. 9, 1919), 52 (Feb. 13, 1920); 3, no. 118 (May 13, 1921).

32. *GB* 2, nos. 52 (Feb. 13, 1920) and 54 (Feb. 19, 1920); *Correio da Manhã* (Rio de Janeiro), Feb. 14, 1920, p. 4.

33. *GB* 2, no. 64 (Apr. 29, 1920).

34. *O Nacionalista* (Porto Alegre) 1, no. 1 (July 1922): 1–3, 10–11; and no. 2 (Aug. 1922): 13–20, 25–26, 28.

35. Delamare, *As duas bandeiras*, 15–16, and *Línguas*, 190–95. President Lucídio Leite Pereira of the Liga Nacionalista Corumbaense emphasized his ASN affiliate's interest in emancipating women in his letter to Steidel, Aug. 29, 1920, LN Papers, packet 2: B, IHGSP.

36. Needell, "History," 11–20; Lesser, *Welcoming*, 29.

37. Topik, "Economic Nationalism," 98; for one such photograph, see *GB* 3: 101

(Jan. 13, 1921). The maritime interests were attracted by the ASN's support for nationalizing coastal shipping and fishing.

The ASN represented about 0.8 percent of the Brazilian population, whereas the LPA represented about 0.1 percent of the Argentine. These percentages, however, rest upon the ASN's probable overestimate of its membership and my own calculation of the LPA's militant core.

38. Topik, "Economic Nationalism," 266; *GB* 2, no. 82 (Sept. 2, 1920). The Jacques series began in 1, no. 58 (Mar. 18, 1920).

39. Delamare to Pessôa, esp. Oct. 20, 1920, July 28, 1921, Nov. 18, 1922, Feb. 12, 1923, folder 70, Alcibiades Delamare, Correspondence and press publications, 1920–26; Bomilcar to Pessôa, Nov. 7, 1922, folder 71, Alcibiades Delamare, Correspondence and press publications, 1926–41, Book 2, paper 170: Epitácio Pessôa archive, IHGB. See also *GB* 2, nos. 61 (Apr. 8, 1920), 64 (Apr. 29, 1920), 67 (May 20, 1920), 68 (May 27, 1920).

40. *Deputados* 1 (May 14, 1920): 601; 8 (Aug. 23, 1921): 393.

41. *Deputados* 6 (Aug. 28, 1920): 573–74; 9 (Oct. 5, 1920): 271, 276; 8 (Aug. 23, 1921): 396–97. See also Topik, "Economic Nationalism," 294.

42. *Deputados* 9 (Oct. 7, 1920): 389–95; 4 (June 28, 1921): 130–32; 4 (June 30, 1921): 233–55; 6 (July 27, 1921): 496–97; 8 (Aug. 19, 1921): 294–95; 8 (Aug. 23, 1921): 389–91, 400–403; 11 (Oct. 31, 1922): 638–40.

43. Manor, 342; *GB* 3, nos. 121 (July 7, 1921), 127 (July 14, 1921); 4, nos. 176 (June 24, 1922), 184 (Aug. 18, 1922).

44. *GB* 2, no. 65 (May 6, 1920); 3, no. 106 (Feb. 17, 1921); 3, no. 108 (Mar. 3, 1921); 3, no. 112 (Mar. 31, 1921); Delamare, *As duas bandeiras*, 14; A. de C. Gomes, 101–2.

45. Delamare to Leme, June 29, 1927, Pessôa archive, file 71, IHGB.

46. *GB* 2, nos. 55 (Feb. 25, 1920), 60 (Apr. 1, 1920), 85 (Sept. 23, 1920); 3, no. 109 (May 10, 1921).

47. *GB* 2, no. 70 (June 10, 1920); 3, no. 116 (Apr. 28, 1921).

48. *GB* 2, nos. 72 (June 24, 1920) and 85 (Sept. 23, 1920); Borges, *Family*, 179.

49. Hahner, *Emancipating*, 136; *GB* 2, no. 84 (Sept. 16, 1920); 2, no. 86 (Sept. 30, 1920); 3, no. 117 (May 5, 1921), 3, no. 118 (May 13, 1921).

50. *GB* 2, nos. 82 (Sept. 2, 1920), 85 (Sept. 23, 1920), 86 (Sept. 30, 1920); 3, no. 117 (May 5, 1921).

51. *GB*, 3, no. 130 (Aug. 4, 1921).

52. *GB*, 3, nos. 112 (Mar. 31, 1921), 117 (May 5, 1921), 118 (May 13, 1921), 119 (May 19, 1921), 125 (June 30, 1921); Delamare to Dantas, Feb. 27 and Mar. 18, 1932, San Tiago Dantas archive, Arquivo Nacional (AN), Rio de Janeiro.

53. *GB* 3, nos. 112 (Mar. 31, 1921), 126 (July 7, 1921), 147 (Dec. 1, 1921), 151 (Dec. 29, 1921).

54. On feminism and women's roles, see Hahner, *Emancipating*; Besse, 164–78; Alves.

55. *GB* 2, no. 77 (July 29, 1920); 3, no. 126 (July 7, 1921). On the links between feminism and female Ku Klux Klan members in the United States, see Blee.

56. *GB* 3, nos. 151 (Dec. 29, 1921), 152 (Jan. 6, 1922); 4, no. 192 (Dec. 8, 1922). On the ideology of motherhood, see Rago, 61–116.

57. *GB*, 1, nos. 31 (Sept. 11, 1919), 58 (Mar. 18, 1920); 3, no. 137 (Sept. 22, 1921); Besse, 168, 248 n. 119; Hahner, *Emancipating*, 145. Chermont's wife was president of the Aliança Brasileira pelo Sufrágio Feminino.

58. Information on Bomilcar in this and the next paragraph comes from *GB* 3, nos. 126 (July 7, 1921), 128 (July 21, 1921), 129 (July 28, 1921).

59. On *Revista Feminina*, see Hahner, *Emancipating*, 133–34; Besse, 183–90. The ambiguities of ASN views on women reflected the larger milieu, as described by Besse.

60. Ribeiro in *GB* 2, no. 77 (July 29, 1920) and 3, no. 120 (May 26, 1921); quote in 1, no. 52 (Feb. 5, 1920). See also 1, nos. 1 (Feb. 13, 1919), 33 (Sept. 25, 1919); 3, no. 118 (May 13, 1921); Scott, 1070–73. On the virility of mixed-sex organizations, see Nancy A. Hewitt, "The Voice of Virile Labor: Labor Militancy, Community Solidarity, and Gender Identification Among Tampa's Latin Workers, 1880-1921," in Baron, 142–67.

61. Bomilcar, *A política*, 11–14, 46, 48–49, 143.

62. *GB* 1, no. 1 (Feb. 13, 1919); 2, nos. 55 (Feb. 25, 1920), 77 (July 29, 1920). Only 19 percent of Maram's sample of anarchist leaders in Rio de Janeiro, Santos, and São Paulo were born in Portugal; most of the rest were Italian and Spanish. See Maram, *Anarquistas*, 21. Although this figure refers to leaders rather than all anarchists, it seems unlikely that the percentage of Portuguese among the latter (or among only Carioca anarchists) would be higher.

63. Delamare in *GB* 1, nos. 1 (Feb. 13, 1919), 38 (Oct. 30, 1919), 48 (Jan. 8, 1920). See also Jacques in 2, no. 59 (Mar. 25, 1920).

64. Hickerson, Rio de Janeiro, June 4, 1923, 825.504/7, in U.S. Dept. of State, Records . . . Brazil, 1910–1929, Microfilm Copy M519; Simão, 70, 78, 90, 94; *GB* 1, no. 15 (May 22, 1919); 2, nos. 58 (Mar. 18, 1920), 61 (Apr. 8, 1920), 101 (Jan. 13, 1921), 104 (Feb. 3, 1921). A few articles on labor in the early issues of *GB* seemed progressive, but they were not representative. See 1, nos. 2 (Feb. 20, 1919), 12 (May 1, 1919), 13 (May 8, 1919), 15 (May 22, 1919).

65. *GB* 2, no. 65 (May 6, 1920); Pinheiro and Hall, 2: 186–94.

66. Teixeira, 49, 69, 81, 84, 86, 88–94, 97, 100, 106, 108–113, 119, 141. *GB* criticized Street in an early progressive article in 1, no. 19 (June 19, 1919), but then reversed its stand in nos. 29 (Aug. 28, 1919) and 30 (Sept. 4, 1919). On changing employer practices and ideas in the 1920s, see Weinstein, 13–50.

67. *GB* 2, nos. 78 (Aug. 5, 1920) and 101 (Jan. 13, 1921); Bomilcar, *A política*, 81, 162–63; Topik, "Economic Nationalism," 277–79, 282; Debané, *Subsídios*. Debané, whose works were recommended by the ASN, previewed the group's economic views in *Economia*.

68. *GB* 2, no. 55 (Feb. 25, 1920); 3, no. 151 (Dec. 29, 1921); 4, no. 177 (June 29, 1922).

69. *Jornal do Commércio*, Nov. 11, 1924, p. 3; Nov. 14, 1924, p. 3; Nov. 23, 1924, p. 4; Delamare to Pessôa, Sept. 16, 1924, Sept. 21, 1924, Oct. 5, 1924, Oct. 17, 1924, Oct. 30, 1924, and dateless newspaper clippings, Pessôa archive, folder 70, IHGB.

70. Delamare to Pessôa, Nov. 4, 1924, Pessôa archive, folder 70, IHGB; Delamare, *As duas bandeiras*, 112-15, and *Línguas*, 37-41, 52-59.

71. Figueiredo, *A reaccão*, 12, 21; *Do nacionalismo*, 29; and *Affirmações*, 160-61. See also Sérgio Lobo de Moura and José Maria Gouvêa de Almeida, "A Igreja na Primeira República," in Fausto, *O Brasil republicano*, 2: 338; Nogueira, *Jackson*, 11, 199, 203. On Figueiredo see, among other works, Todaro, 58-182; and Iglesias.

72. Figueiredo, *A reaccão*, 40, 130, 193; "Epitácio Pessôa," 275-76; *Affirmações*, 276, 281-83; *A columna*, 72; *A questão*, 23, 25.

73. Figueiredo, *A columna*, 205; *A reaccão*, 22-24; *Affirmações*, 254.

74. Figueiredo, *Do nacionalismo*, 31; *Affirmações*, 271-73, 282-86, 290-93; *A questão*, 52; Nogueira, *A doutrina*, 35-37, 40, 43.

75. Figueiredo, *A questão*, 13-14; *A columna*, 25, 34, 91, 104, 115, 132, 134-35.

76. Figueiredo, *A columna*, 45, 50-51, 53, 101-2, 278; on the nineteenth-century party of order, see Needell, "Brasilien."

77. Nogueira, *A doutrina*, 33-34, 43, 47-71.

78. Figueiredo, *Do nacionalismo*, 9, 34, 42-45, 51-52, 56-57, 60; Delamare to Pessôa, July 28, 1925, and Nov. 11, 1928, Pessôa archive, folder 70, IHGB.

79. Hamilton Nogueira, "Reflexões contra-revolucionárias," *A Ordem* 5, no. 51 (July 1926): 218-19, and *Jackson*, 11, 209; Todaro, 80. I thank Ninon Schalk for explaining *météque*. On French right-wing antisemitism and its economic content, see Byrnes; Davies; Griffiths; Mosse, "French Right."

80. Figueiredo, *A questão*, 48; *A columna*, 138, 239.

81. Bomilcar cited in Delamare, *As duas bandeiras*, 131-33; *GB* 4, nos. 186 (Sept. 1, 1922), and 187 (Sept. 22, 1922). Bomilcar's manuscript, "A ordem militar e a ordem judaica," was never published.

82. Delamare, *As duas bandeiras*, 84-85, 102-3; Nogueira, *Jackson*, 199, and *A doutrina*, 183, 187.

83. Figueiredo, *A questão*, 61; *A columna*, 212. See also Ramos, *A crise*, 146. Gilman neglected the stomach, although one illustration (45) focused on it.

84. Lesser, "From Pedlars," 398-99, 404; "Pawns," 91, 130, 137, 146, 149; and *Welcoming*, 39-44. See also Sandberg, 56; Margulies, 325.

85. Thus for these extreme rightists they were "imaginary Jews," as Lesser put it in *Welcoming*. Needell reached a similar conclusion on Gilberto Freyre's antisemitism in the 1930s, in "Identity," 73-77.

86. Moura, 121, 123-24; Della Cava, 12; Nagle, 58; Santo Rosário, 180, 182; Velloso, "A Ordem," 123-30. On integral Catholicism, see Ivereigh, 86-91.

87. Miceli, 110-11; Santo Rosário, 144-45, 150-52; Della Cava, 12; Nagle, 60-61; Wirth, *Minas Gerais*, 126.

88. Dutra; A. de C. Gomes, 102; Santo Rosário, 103, 145; Love, *São Paulo*, 231; Dulles, *Anarchists*, 111, 115, 118, 133; Simão, 116, 207; Hahner, *Poverty*, 222.

89. A. A. Prado, esp. 46-50; Velloso, "A brasilidade," 62, 70-71, 73; Vasconcellos, 81-168; Nagle, *Educação*, 85-93; Love, *São Paulo*, 136-37; Lauerhass, "Getúlio," 93, 98.

90. See esp. the preface to *A margem da história da república*, 13–16; Pontes de Miranda, "Preliminares para a revisão constitucional," 181, 188, in *A margem*. Another contributor, A. Carneiro Leao, had played a role in the LDN; see Freire, v.

91. Francisco José Oliveira Viana, "O idealismo da constituição," in *A margem*, 137–60; *Pequenos estudos*, esp. 96, 126, 128, 187; E. R. Gomes, 74–82. Vieira, 71–79, compared Torres and Viana. See also Medeiros, 155–217; Needell, "History."

Chapter 8   Conclusion

1. Hale, "Political," in Bethell, *Cambridge History*, 437–38.

Part 3   The Era of Fascism: The Late 1920s to 1939

1. Blinkhorn, 9.
2. Nolte, 40; Irvine, "Fascism," 294–95.
3. Fascist movements believed in this "third way"; see De Grand, *Italian Fascism*, 81.

Chapter 9   Chile: Socialism for the Twentieth Century

1. On Ibáñez, see Drake, "Corporatism," 90–92; Bicheno, 366–69; Pike, 191–95; Loveman, *Chile*, 220–22; Nunn, *The Military*, 151–72; Houseman, 119–23, 129; Strawbridge, 145, 148–50, 162–66; Ramírez Necochea, *Origen*, 158–70.
2. Drake, *Socialism*, 60–63; Houseman, 126–28.
3. Somervell, 398–401; Sater, "Abortive Kronstadt"; Drake, *Socialism*, 72–83. Ortiz summarized clearly the confusing events of 1931–32.
4. Maldonado Prieto, *Milicia*, 18–34, 145–46; Valdivia Ortiz de Zárate, "Los civiles," 58–62, 99. A revised version of this thesis is Valdivia Ortiz de Zárate, *La Milicia*. See also Naval 'Attaché's Report, Sept. 3, 1931, 801-100, 825.1053/1, in U.S., National Archives, RG 59; Alliende González, 43.
5. G. Subercaseaux, *La política*.
6. Potashnik, 143–56.
7. Ibid., 113; Mayorga, "La fugaz violencia," 18; Nunn, *Military*, 137; Alliende González, 47–49; Keller R., *La eterna crisis*. Rather than join the MNS, Díaz formed his own group, described below.
8. Information in this and the following paragraph comes from Biblioteca Nacista No. 1 (1932). In *Pueblo*, 6, González von Marées faulted Ibáñez for rebuilding a state without rebuilding the people. González and Keller expressed their admiration for Portales in *Acción Chilena* 4, no. 1 (1935): 1–9, and 2, no. 5 (May 23, 1934): 129–60, respectively.
9. Biblioteca Nacista No. 1 (1932): 12.
10. Biblioteca Nacista No. 1 [*sic*] (1934): 18; Biblioteca Nacista No. 1 [*sic*] (n.d.): 18–19; Biblioteca Nacista No. 7 (1933); *Acción Chilena* 5, no. 2 (1936): 113–17, 139–44; Potashnik, 213–14, 216–24.

11. Mayorga Santana, 110–11; Mayorga, "La Milicia," 18; *El Mercurio*, July 25, 1935, p. 20. The uniform would change over time.

12. Hernán Millas, "Cuando Antofagasta hizo una revolución civilista," *La Época* (Santiago), Oct. 8, 1989, p. 20; Drake, *Socialism*, 83; Maldonado Prieto, *Milicia*, 44–47; Tarr, 155.

13. Chilton, Santiago, May 10, 1933, no. 72, FO 420/285, A1019/73/9, in Great Britain, Public Record Office, Foreign Office, Confidential File on Latin America (microfilm); Tarr, 158–59.

14. Alvarez Salamanca, Santiago, Mar. 28, 1933, no. 147, and Villablanca, Iquique, May 15, 1933, no. 25, in Chile, Archivo Nacional (ANC), Ministerio del Interior, Providencias confidenciales; Chilton, Santiago, Jan. 25, 1933, no. 71, FO 420/285, A1015/73/9; Drake, *Socialism*, 142–51.

15. *El Mercurio*, May 7, 1933, p. 17; May 8, 1933, pp. 12–14; Gunther, Santiago, No. 37, May 10, 1933, C-10-N, 16174-E, U.S., RG 38; Chilton, May 10, 1933, No. 240, FO 240/285, A4010/73/9; Andrews, Santiago, May 9, 1933, No. 15/33, FO 132/402, 106975, in Great Britain, Public Record Office (PRO), Foreign Office; Astorga, 10, (Miliciano's remark) 12; Alessandri in *Boletín Informativo de la Milicia Republicano* (*BIMR*) 1, no. 1 (July 24, 1933): 6–7.

16. Maldonado Prieto, *Milicia*, 59; Valdivia Ortiz de Zárate, *La Milicia*, 26; *La Opinión*, Nov. 14, 1936, p. 3. *BIMR* 2, no. 46 (July 24, 1935): 39, estimated the membership at 60,000.

17. *Hoy* (Santiago), no. 105 (Nov. 24, 1933): 2; Wooten, Santiago, Report 1603, Feb. 28, 1933, 825.1053/3, and May 8, 1933, 825.1053/4; Weeks, Santiago, Report 1772, Sept. 25, 1933, 2008-171-5, and Report 2040, Dec. 10, 1934, 2657-0-171/1, in U.S., National Archives, RG 165; Maldonado Prieto, *Milicia*, 159–60; Valdivia Ortiz de Zárate, *La Milicia*, 51–58; Thompson, Valparaíso, Dec. 14, 1933, and Dec. 29, 1933, FO 371/16568, A9441/73/9 and A9439/73/9, PRO; Chile, Diputados (Dec. 31, 1935): 1813; Mayorga, "Gustavo Ross," 19, and "La fugaz violencia," 18; *Vida Nueva* (Osorno), July 28, 1934, p. 4.

18. Andrews, May 10, 1933, no. 15/33, FO 132/402, 106975, PRO; Chilton, May 10, 1933, no. 240, FO 420/285, A4010/73/9; Wooten, May 8, 1933, 825.1053/4; *El Mercurio*, May 13, 1933, p. 11. See also *BIMR* 1, nos. 6 (Oct. 15, 1933): 27, and 7 (Nov. 1, 1933): 27; 2, nos. 30 (Nov. 5, 1934): 8, and 44 (June 20, 1935): 19–21; *Caupolicán* (Santiago) 3, nos. 53 (1st half Nov. 1935): 63–64, and 56 (2d half Dec. 1935): 35.

19. *Hoy*, no. 105 (Nov. 24, 1933): 2; *BIMR* 1, nos. 5 (Oct. 1, 1933): 1, poem in 6 (Oct. 15, 1933): 14, 14 (Mar. 1, 1934): 5; 3, no. 47 (Aug. 8, 1935): 3; *Caupolicán* 3, no. 51 (1st half Oct. 1935): 7. Yet the Milicia praised female participation in politics and the workforce. See *BIMR* 2, nos. 44 (June 20, 1935): 8, and 45 (July 5, 1935): 13–17; *Caupolicán* 3, nos. 52 (2d half Oct. 1935): 26; 64 (1st half May 1936): 7–9; 66 (1st half June 1936): 6, 52–53; 4, nos. 78 (1st half Dec. 1936): 5; and 80 (1st half Jan. 1937): 2.

20. Bravo Hayley; Cuadra Poisson, who previewed his organization's ideology; *BIMR* 1, nos. 2 (Aug. 15, 1933): 2, 3 (Sept. 1, 1933): 31, 4 (Sept. 15, 1933): 9, and 14 (Mar.

1, 1934): 19; Bravo in 2, nos. 31 (Nov. 20, 1934): 2, 32 (Dec. 5, 1934): 1, 35 (Jan. 20, 1935): 3, 36 (Feb. 5, 1935): 3.

21. *BIMR* 1, nos. 1 (July 24, 1933): 16, 21, 28; 2 (Aug. 15, 1933): 7, 28; 6 (Oct. 15, 1933): 27; 14 (Mar. 1, 1934): 1.

22. *BIMR* 1, nos. 4 (Sept. 15, 1933): cover and 4, and 6 (Oct. 15, 1933): 5; 2, no. 36 (Feb. 5, 1935): 1. *Caupolicán* printed an article by Carlés in 3, no. 67 (2d half June 1936): 27–30.

23. *Trabajo*, Apr. 20, 1933, p. 1; May 11, 1933, p. 1; May 25, 1933, pp. 3, 4. See also the comparisons between the Milicia and MNS in *Hoy*, no. 131 (May 25, 1934): 4–5; *La Protesta* (Santiago), Dec. 9, 1933, p. 4.

24. *Acción Chilena* 3, no. 1 (Oct. 1934): 1–4, 6–7.

25. Guarello, interview; Astorga, 11; Mayorga, "La fugaz violencia," 19; *BIMR* 1, no. 2 (Aug. 15, 1933): 5–6.

26. *BIMR* 1, nos. 4 (Sept. 15, 1933): 3–4, and 5 (Oct. 1, 1933): 8–11, 44; *Caupolicán* 3, no. 62 (1st half Apr. 1936): 43; *Trabajo*, Sept. 28, 1933, p. 1; Oct. 5, 1933, p. 1; Dec. 14, 1933, p. 3; June 14, 1934, p. 1.

27. Diputados (May 9, 1933): 2603; *La Opinión*, Dec. 12, 1933, p. 3; *La Revista Católica* 33, no. 750 (July 22, 1933): 139; 33, no. 758 (Dec. 9, 1933): 789; 35, no. 787 (May 25, 1935): 359; 36, no. 812 (July 11, 1936): 47; Tarr, 214–16; *BIMR* 1, nos. 1 (July 24, 1933): 1, and 7 (Nov. 1, 1933): 3; 2, nos. 42 (May 20, 1935): 27–28, and 46 (July 24, 1935): 1, 11–12, 37.

28. *El Mercurio*, May 10, 1933, pp. 9, 13; May 13, 1933, p. 13; May 17, 1933, p. 9; May 18, 1933, p. 9; July 8, 1933, p. 9.

29. Ibid., May 11, 1933, p. 17; *BIMR* 1, no. 17 (Apr. 15, 1934): 3, and 2, no. 23 (July 24, 1934): 9–10.

30. *El Mercurio*, July 21, 1933, p. 9. The Milicia offered to repress peasants embroiled in a complicated dispute with the government and private landowners in the Ranquil episode; see *El Mercurio*, June 29–July 8, 1934. The administration also considered mobilizing the Milicia during the railroad strikes of early 1936; see Mitchell, Santiago, Feb. 14, 1936, Desp. 61, FO 420/288, no. 53, A1483/74/9.

31. Mitchell, Oct. 16, 1934, Desp. 275, FO 420/286, A 8470/230/9, No. 89; Valdivia Ortiz de Zárate, "Los civiles," 246–56; ads in *BIMR* 2, nos. 29 (Oct. 20, 1934): inside cover, and 46 (July 24, 1935): 16; Mayorga, "La Milicia," 19; Alexander, *Arturo Alessandri*, 2: 537.

32. Cabrera, Oct. 16, 1935, no. 891, and Dec. 30, 1935, no. 1218, Ministerio del Interior, Oficios 1935, 2, and Fuenzalida Correa, Mar. 27, 1940, no. 39, Ministerio del Interior, Providencias Confidenciales 1940, ANC; Valdivia Ortiz de Zárate, *La Milicia*, 72–73; *Hoy*, no. 207 (Nov. 8, 1935): 16; Mayorga, "La Milicia," 19. For the extensive debate on the arms, see Diputados (Aug. 13, 1935): 2280–81, (Sept. 16, 1935): 3435–36, (Nov. 4, 1935): 254–60, (Dec. 23, 1935): 1622–31, (Dec. 30, 1935): 1765–86, (Dec. 31, 1935): 1805–35. To convert pesos into dollars, I used the exchange rate for 1934; see *World Almanac*, 623.

33. Chilton, May 10, 1933, FO 420/285, A4010/73/9; Andrews, May 18, 1933, FO 371/16567, A4222/73/9, no. 16/33; Mitchell, Oct. 16, 1934, Desp. 275, FO 420/286, A8470/230/9, no. 89, PRO; Maldonado Prieto, "Los Carabineros," 16–17; Somervell, 401–2.

34. Andrews, May 10, 1933, FO 132/402, 106975, PRO; Mariana Aylwin Oyarzún and Ignacio Alamos Varas, "Los militares en la época de Don Arturo Alessandri Palma," in *Siete ensayos*, 378; Orrego V., 86; Bravo Ríos, 54 *La Opinión*, Nov. 14, 1936, p. 3; *Hoy*, no. 204 (Oct. 18, 1935): 13.

35. Alvarez Salamanca, May 12, 1933, Novoa Fuentes, May 17, 1933, and Vignola, May 19, 1933, all in no. 516; Palma and attachments, Nov. 18, 1933, No. 530, in Ministerio del Interior, Providencias confidenciales 1933, ANC. See also Weeks, Report 1819, Nov. 28, 1933, 2008-171-6, U.S., RG 165; *El Imparcial*, Dec. 6, 1933, p. 1, and Dec. 21, 1933, p. 2; *La Opinión*, Dec. 12–13, 21–22, 1933; *El Diario Ilustrado*, Dec. 15–17, 1933; *Trabajo*, Dec. 21, 1933, p. 1; Alessandri Palma, 3: 20–24. The expelled Nacistas quickly helped create the short-lived Frente Nacional, which resembled yet bitterly opposed the MNS; see *Frente* (Santiago), Mar. 1–Aug. 16, 1934, Apr. 24–May 15, 1935; *El Frente Nacional*.

36. Weeks, Report 1916, May 9, 1934, 825.00/851; *BIMR* 1, no. 19 (May 21, 1934): 78; *El Mercurio*, May 2, 1934, p. 9, and May 6, 1934, p. 21.

37. *Hoy*, no. 129 (May 11, 1934): 11–14; *La Opinión*, May 7–9, 1934; Mayorga, "Fuego," 19; *BIMR* 1, nos. 9 (Dec. 1, 1933): 3–4, 11 (Jan. 1, 1934): 9–10, 20 (June 5, 1934): 23; Tarr, 217–30, 253–54.

38. *Acción Chilena* 2, no. 4 (May 16, 1934): 124.

39. *BIMR* 1, nos. 19 (May 21, 1934): 82, and 20 (June 5, 1934): 6; Sevier, Santiago, no. 209, Oct. 16, 1934, 825.00/867; Mitchell, Oct. 16, 1934, Desp. 275, FO 420/286, A8470/230/9; Bravo Ríos, 55.

40. Cuadra Poisson, *La verdad*, 3–19, 25–33; *BIMR* 3, no. 47 (Aug. 8, 1935): 1, 3; *Caupolicán* 3, nos. 52 (2d half Oct. 1935): 4–8, 16, and 53 (1st half Nov. 1935): 1, 3; *El Mercurio*, July 25, 1935, pp. 20, 32; *El Imparcial*, July 2, 1936, p. 4; *Hoy*, no. 206 (Nov. 1, 1935): 25–26.

41. Weeks, no. 2294, July 21, 1936, 825.1053/15; *El Mercurio*, July 4, 1936, p. 13, and July 6, 1936, p. 1; *El Imparcial*, July 1–2, 1936; *Hoy*, no. 263 (Dec. 3, 1936): 11–12; *Trabajo*, July 2, 1936, p. 3. *Trabajo* claimed that Milicianos hoped to duplicate the MNS behind a democratic facade; see Oct. 23, 1936, p. 2, and Oct. 26, 1936, p. 3.

42. On Republican Union, see *Unión Republicana*; *Cartilla de la Unión Republicana*; *Progreso* (Valparaíso). On National Action, see *La Aurora* (Santiago), Oct. 17, 1936. On AR's program, see Acción Republicana. See also *Caupolicán* 4, no. 79 (2d half Dec. 1936): 51; *Acción Republicana* (Santiago), Aug. 1938, pp. 3–4. AR member Jermán Spoerer C. opposed virtually all state interference in the economy, except for a government-sponsored corporatist entity, the Consejo Económico Nacional, which the entire party supported. The presence of feminist Amanda Labarca in the AR probably accounted for its stand on women, although one wonders how much

voice they would have had in a corporatist system with plural voting. On Labarca, see Lavrin, *Women*, esp. 286–88, 308–9, 361–62.

43. *Trabajo*, July 14, 1936, p. 1; Oct. 17, 1936, p. 1; Oct. 23, 1936, p. 3; Nov. 16, 1936, p. 1; Drake, "Corporatism," 102–3; *El Mercurio*, June 5, 1934, p. 9, and Nov. 15, 1936, p. 15; *El Diario Ilustrado*, Nov. 16, 1936, p. 11; Legión Cívica de Chile; *El Imparcial*, July 12, 1937, p. 16; Diputados (Sept. 8, 1937): 3134–36, 3140, 3143. Other small reformist vehicles of the right included the Partido Agrario and the Catholic parties alluded to in note 126.

44. *Plan de acción*, 13–14; Biblioteca Nacista No. 6 (1932): 4–5; *El Imparcial*, Aug. 13, 1932, p. 2, and Apr. 8, 1933, p. 7.

45. *Acción Chilena* 4, no. 2 (1935): 81.

46. Ibid., 81–82.

47. Biblioteca Nacista No. 6 (1932): 42; *El Imparcial*, Aug. 27, 1932, p. 2; González, *Nacismo o Comunismo*, 9; González von Marées, *La violencia nacista*, 2.

48. Weeks, Report 1740, Aug. 9, 1933, 825.00/811; Mena in *Acción Chilena* 4, no. 2 (1935): 83; *El Imparcial*, Mar. 27, 1933, p. 1; *Trabajo*, June 8, 1933, p. 2, and Oct. 12, 1933, p. 1; *El Mercurio*, Aug. 7, 1933, p. 13; *La Opinión*, Aug. 7, 1933, p. 1. Cullen noted that the British Union of Fascists also used violence to attract recruits, although it usually was not the main instigator.

49. Naval Intelligence Report, Aug. 28, 1933, 104–400, 825.00/813; *El Mercurio*, Aug. 28, 1933, p. 12; *La Opinión*, Aug. 28, 1933, p. 1, and Aug. 30, 1933, p. 1; *Trabajo*, Aug. 31, 1933, p. 1.

50. For the entire debate, see Diputados (Aug. 28, 1933): 2610–17, (Aug. 29, 1933): 2672–78, (Aug. 30, 1933): 2776, (Sept. 4, 1933): 2878–97, (Sept. 5, 1933): 2956–58. See also *La Nación* (Santiago), Sept. 3, 1933, p. 11; *La Opinión*, Aug. 29, 1933, p. 1, and Aug. 30, 1933, p. 1; *El Mercurio*, Aug. 30, 1933, p. 11.

51. Sáenz B., 252; *El Diario Ilustrado*, July 26–28, 1934.

52. Bombal, Valdivia, with attachments, June 5, 1934, no. 197, Ministerio del Interior, Providencias confidenciales 1934, 2, ANC; *Trabajo*, June 14, 1934, p. 2; *El Mercurio*, Sept. 13, 1933, p. 11; *La Opinión*, June 29, 1934, p. 3; Potashnik, 258. On government surveillance, see Nos. 190, 193, 195–97, Ministerio del Interior, Providencias confidenciales 1934, 2, ANC. Etchepare and Stewart, 587, however, claimed that throughout its tenure Alessandri's administration tangled with the MNS.

53. *La Opinión*, June 21–22; June 28, 1934, p. 2; *El Mercurio*, June 21–22, June 26–27, July 19–20, 1934; *Acción Chilena* 4, no. 2 (1935): 85. The Socialists began to form militias in May 1934; see Valdivia Ortiz de Zárate, "Las Milicias Socialistas," 161. On the Socialist and Communist militias, see also *Trabajo*, Feb. 7, 1935, p. 3; Senadores (Nov. 26, 1935): 861; Jobet, 120.

54. Salas Romo, June 22, 1934, no. 435, and July 8, 1934, no. 486, Ministerio del Interior, Oficios 1934, ANC; *Consigna* (Santiago), July 7, 1934, p. 1; *Trabajo*, July 26, 1934, p. 4, and Oct. 6, 1934, p. 1.

55. Guarello, interview; *Izquierda* (Santiago), Apr. 3, 1935, pp. 2, 4; Mayorga,

"Cuando el PS," 14; *El Mercurio,* June 14-16, 1935; communication from Carlos Maldonado Prieto.

56. A. Douglas, 696-97. For a gender analysis of the left that includes considerations of masculinity, see Rosemblatt.

57. Alliende González, 82; *Trabajo,* Sept. 25, 1935, p. 1, and Oct. 2, 1935, p. 3; *La Revista Católica* 35, no. 795 (Sept. 28, 1935): 271; *El Diario Ilustrado,* Sept. 24, 1935, p. 3.

58. Diputados (Nov. 6, 1935): 366-71, (Nov. 13, 1935): 608-9, 611-12; *La Opinión,* Oct. 14, 1935, pp. 1, 4, and Oct. 15, 1935, p. 1; *Trabajo,* Nov. 9, 1935, p. 3; *Consigna,* Oct. 19, 1935, p. 1; *El Mercurio,* Oct. 14, 1935, p. 22, and Oct. 15, 1935, p. 21; *La Protesta,* Oct. 19, 1935, p. 1.

59. Diputados (Nov. 6, 1935): 370, (Nov. 13, 1935): 608-9, 612; *El Mercurio,* Oct. 16, 1935, p. 15; *Hoy,* no. 204 (Oct. 18, 1935): 6, 12, and no. 209 (Nov. 22, 1935): 23; *La Opinión,* Oct. 16, 1935, p. 1; Oct. 17, 1935, p. 3; Oct. 20, 1935, p. 1; Nov. 7, 1935, p. 1; Nov. 8, 1935, p. 3; *Consigna,* Nov. 16, 1935, p. 3.

60. Senadores (Nov. 26, 1935): 506-10, (Dec. 11, 1935): 856-63; *Acción Chilena* 4, no. 3 (1935): iv-v; *Trabajo,* Nov. 23, 1935, 1.

61. *Trabajo,* June 15, 1936, p. 1; *South Pacific Mail,* June 18, 1936, p. 18; *El Mercurio,* June 14, 1936, p. 34; June 15, 1936, p. 15; June 20, 1936, p. 19; Mayorga, "El camino," 19; *Consigna,* June 20, 1936, pp. 1-2.

62. Diputados (June 15, 1936): 823; Senadores (June 15, 1936): 386-90; *Consigna,* July 25, 1936, p. 3; *La Revista Católica* 36, no. 811 (June 27, 1936): 474; *El Mercurio,* June 19, 1936, p. 16.

63. González in *Hoy,* no. 271 (Jan. 28, 1937): 13; Potashnik, 237-38; *Vida Nueva,* Nov. 24, 1935, p. 2; Vago, 291, 293, 302-4, 307-10. As Potashnik noted, the destruction of membership lists and the fact that many Nacistas hid their affiliation make it difficult to study their backgrounds.

64. *La senda; Veinte años,* 55-81.

65. Luco, 21-22; Guarello, interview; *Hoy,* no. 268 (Jan. 7, 1937): 13, and no. 270 (Jan. 21, 1937): 14; Vago, 295, 299, 302, 315.

66. *El jefe*'s claim in Armour, Santiago, no. 439, Dec. 28, 1938, 825.00 Revolutions/256; Diputados (Nov. 16, 1936): 318; *La senda,* 91; *Consigna,* July 25, 1936, p. 3; Potashnik, 280-81.

67. Armour, Santiago, no. 439, Dec. 28, 1938, 825.00 Revolutions/256; Young, 322; Potashnik, 216, 248.

68. Pamphlet, 4-5. Most selections in Muhlberger stress the multiclass and "shifting appeal" (152) of fascism.

69. Pamphlet, 6; Biblioteca Nacista No. 6 (1932): 6, 11-14; Núcleo Nacista de Temuco, 2; *El Imparcial,* July 16, 1932, p. 2; *Trabajo,* Aug. 17, 1933, p. 5; Jan. 25, 1934, p. 3; and Feb. 1, 1934, p. 1; *Plan de acción,* 2.

70. Mayorga, "Alessandri," 18; Geary, 459.

71. Biblioteca Nacista No. 2 (n.d.): 15-20, quotes on 19 and 20.

72. González von Marées, *Pueblo,* 6-7, 9.

73. Guarello, interview; *Acción Chilena* 4, no. 2 (1935): 133–37.

74. *Acción Chilena* 4, no. 1 (1935): 26–40; *Trabajo*, Aug. 3, 1935, p. 2.

75. Mayorga, "Alessandri," 18; Matta, esp. 130–38; R. G. Parker, 140.

76. Mayorga, "Jorge González," 42 ; *Acción Chilena* 2, no. 5 (May 23, 1934): supplement, 4.

77. *Hoy*, no. 160 (Dec. 14, 1934): 7. On the genesis of such rituals, see Mosse, *The Nationalization*; on marching and solidarity, see McNeill.

78. The Socialist and Communist militias, however, also sported uniforms, and the charisma of Socialist leaders like Grove, the populism of Socialist platforms, and the Socialists' youthful image made this party's appeal more than theoretical. See Drake, *Socialism*, esp. 93–96.

79. *Trabajo*, Aug. 10, 1933, p. 3; Robertson Rodríguez, 109–10. *Acción Chilena* 1, no. 12 (Apr. 12, 1934): 355; 2, no. 2 (Nov. 1934): 78; 4, no. 2 (1935): 78, 129.

80. Quote from Núcleo Nacista de Temuco, 16. See also *Trabajo*, Feb. 22, 1936, p. 3; and Apr. 29, 1936, p. 6; *Jota* 1, no. 1 (Sept. 18, 1937): 3.

81. Keller R., *La locura*; Young, 320 n. 32; Mosse, *Nationalism and Sexuality*, 153–80; Burleigh and Wippermann, 265, 273; De Grazia, 43, 69–71, 79–82, 112. Nazis sometimes undermined the bourgeois family; see Koonz, 153, 178, 180, 197, 398–400. Masculinity has also been important for the left. Significantly, one of its ways of criticizing Nacistas was to deny their manhood; for example, the leftist *Tribuna Juvenil* (Santiago), Mar. 21, 1935, p. 4, taunted Nacistas as homosexuals. On conflict among mineworkers over respectable versus rebellious forms of manliness, see Klubock.

82. Recabarren Valenzuela, 55; *Trabajo*, Mar. 8, 1934, p. 3, and Oct. 25, 1934, p. 1; González, *El problema*, 29–30, 52–54; Mayorga, "Jorge González," 42; *Acción Chilena* 1, no. 5 (Feb. 22, 1934): 131–32; 2, no. 8 (Sept. 1934): 319–20; 4, no. 1 (1935): 21; 4, no. 2 (1935): 142–44; 4, no. 3 (1935): 145–57; 6, no. 1 (1937): iv.

83. *La Nación*, Sept. 7–8, 10–11, 1933; González, *El problema*, 19.

84. *Acción Chilena* 6, no. 1 (1937): V; González, *El problema*, 54–56.

85. For population figures, see Cohen, 128; *American Jewish Yearbook 1936–37*, 38: 559; Nes-El, 73. See also Nes-El, 73–82; Cohen, 134–35; Senderey, 11–13, 122, 219–22.

86. For examples, see Diputados, (June 30, 1931): 524; Latcham, 51; Bicheno, 373; Drake, *Socialism*, 162, 184; *Consigna*, July 7, 1934, p. 6; *Acción Comunal* (Santiago), 4th week July 1936, 4. Latcham, however, later defended Jewish immigration and denounced antisemitism; see *Mundo Judío* (Santiago), Dec. 12, 1935, p. 3.

87. *Mundo Judío*, Feb. 21, 1935, p. 1, noted this discrepancy, although it did not explain it. See also *Mundo Judío*, Oct. 31, 1935, p. 3. *Acción Chilena* became officially Naci in December 1934, although Keller had edited this profascist journal since its inception in January 1934. For a fuller account of evolving Naci opinions on Jews, see Deutsch, "Anti-Semitism."

88. Núcleo Nacista de Temuco, 27; *Trabajo*, Oct. 1934. Sznajder, in "El movimiento," 61–70, assigns more importance to early Naci antisemitism than I.

89. *Trabajo*, Apr. 18, 1935, p. 1; *El Rayo* (Valdivia), Apr.–June 1935.

90. Gamboa in *Acción Chilena* 1, no. 5 (Feb. 22, 1934): 133; Cox in 4, no. 2 (1935): 140; *El Rayo*, June 26, 1936, p. 2.

91. *Acción Chilena* 6, no. 1 (1937): 1–14.

92. *Hoy*, no. 271 (Jan. 28, 1937): 11–12; *Trabajo*, May 23, 1936, 3; Young, 328, note 59.

93. *Trabajo*, June 17, 1936, p. 1, and June 22, 1936, p. 6; *Mundo Judío*, June 18, 1936, p. 3; *El Rayo*, June 26, 1936, p. 2.

94. *Trabajo*, June 18, 1936, p. 3, and June 23, 1936, p. 3.

95. *Trabajo*, Oct. 26, 1935, p. 3.

96. Ibid., June 6, p. 3, June 16, p. 3, June 22, p. 1, July 4, 1936, p. 10, and Mar. 21, 1937, p. 3; *Acción Chilena* 5, no. 1 (1936): 8. On this conspiracy theory as a mobilizing myth, see Sznajder, "El movimiento," 64–69.

97. *Mundo Judío*, Dec. 26, 1935, p. 3. A nonviolent antisemitism is not necessarily less radical, according to Bergman, 44–45.

98. *Trabajo*, June 9, 1936, p. 6; Biblioteca Nacista No. 2 (n.d.): 22; Núcleo Nacista de Temuco, 25; Sánchez in *Acción Chilena* 1, nos. 2 (Jan. 31, 1934): 34, 3 (Feb. 7, 1934): 65–69, 10 (Mar. 29, 1934): 296, and 2, no. 8 (Sept. 1934): 322–24. The MNS explicitly criticized the racism of German National Socialists in Chile; see *Trabajo*, July 5, 1935, p. 3, and July 20, 1935, p. 3. Despite the ideological overlap between them, Chilean Nacistas maintained some distance from the German Nazis, who for their part preferred to focus on the local German community. See Gaudig and Veit (1988); *Hoy*, no. 271 (Jan. 28, 1937): 14; Young, 317.

99. González in *Trabajo*, Dec. 11, 1934, p. 3. For information in this and the next paragraph, see *Acción Chilena* 5, no. 1 (1936): 51–53; Carrera in *El Rayo*, Apr. 3, 1935, p. 1; *Trabajo*, Apr. 27, 1933, p. 13; Jan. 11, 1934, p. 3; Feb. 8, 1934, p. 3; Mar. 14, 1935, p. 5; Apr. 25, 1936, p. 2; June 10, 1936, p. 6; July 16, 1936, p. 10.

100. On the Movimiento Pro Emancipación de Mujeres de Chile, see Rojas Mira, "Hacia la formación," 161–63; Gaviola et al., 40–45; Lavrin, *Women*, esp. 310–12; Antezana-Pernet.

101. While it approved of German policies cutting female enrollment in universities, it was unclear whether the MNS intended to go that far. On women's roles, see *Acción Chilena* 4, no. 2 (1935): 105, and 5, no. 1 (1936): 53–56; *Trabajo*, Jan. 11, 1934, p. 3; Mar. 14, 1935, p. 5; Aug. 3, 1935, p. 2; Aug. 4, 1935, p. 3; Apr. 25, 1936, p. 2; May 20, 1936, p. 6; June 10, 1936, p. 6. These notions greatly resembled those of European fascists. See De Grazia; Koonz; Durham.

102. *Trabajo*, Dec. 11, 1935, p. 3; Dec. 21, 1935, p. 2; Apr. 17, 1936, p. 6; Apr. 22, 1936, p. 2; Aug. 13, 1937, p. 3; *Acción Chilena* 4, no. 3 (1935): vi, and 5, no. 2 (1936): 119; González von Marées, *Pueblo*, 12.

103. *Trabajo*, Apr. 17, 1936, p. 6; *Consigna*, June 23, 1934, pp. 2, 5; *El Mercurio*, June 4, 1934, pp. 3, 9; Acción Nacional de Mujeres de Chile; figure in Lavrin, *Women*, 313; Gaviola et al., 61.

104. *Trabajo*, Nov. 16, 1935, p. 1; Dec. 21, 1935, p. 3; Mar. 21, 1936, p. 2; Potashnik,

244. The feminine brigades included married and unmarried women, unlike the LPA.

105. *Trabajo*, Nov. 27, 1935, p. 2; Apr. 17, 1936, p. 6; July 18, 1936, p. 5; Nov. 6, 1936, p. 6; Oct. 31, 1937, p. 3; Mar. 4, 1938, p. 3; *Acción Chilena* 5, no. 2 (1936): 119; *Veinte años*, 20; Potashnik, 244.

106. Guarello, interview; *Trabajo*, Nov. 16, 1935, p. 1; Mar. 21, 1936, p. 2; Mar. 28, 1936, p. 2; Apr. 6, 1936, p. 5; Apr. 22, 1936, p. 2; July 18, 1936, p. 5; Dec. 10, 1936, p. 7; Aug. 12, 1937, p. 6; Oct. 31, 1937, p. 3; Nov. 5, 1937, p. 2; Dec. 22, 1937, p. 1; Feb. 9, 1938, p. 2; Feb. 13, 1938, p. 2; July 18, 1939, p. 4.

107. *Trabajo*, Dec. 14, 1935, p. 3; Apr. 17, 1936, p. 6; May 6, 1936, p. 6; Nov. 6, 1936, p. 6; Dec. 9, 1936, p. 1; Dec. 10, 1936, p. 7; May 22, 1937, p. 1; Nov. 6, 1937, p. 4; Higonnet et al., 118–19; Cassin-Scott and McBride, 15, 18.

108. Diputados (Aug. 26, 1936): 2963–64; Senadores (Aug. 25, 1936): 1553; Mayorga, "El camino," 18; *La Opinión*, Aug. 24, 1936, p. 3; *Zig-Zag*, no. 1642 (Sept. 11, 1936); *Consigna*, Sept. 5, 1936, 1.

109. *Trabajo*, Aug. 26, 1936, p. 1; Senadores (Aug. 25, 1936): 1551, 1554–55; *La Nación*, Sept. 3, 1936, p. 3.

110. González von Marées, *La violencia*; Keller in *Zig-Zag*, no. 1642 (Sept. 11, 1936).

111. *Trabajo*, Sept. 2–3, Sept. 8, 1936, pp. 1, 7; *La Nación*, Sept. 3, 1936, p. 3; *El Diario Ilustrado*, Aug. 29, 1936, p. 9.

112. *El Mercurio*, Nov. 16–21, 1936; Senadores (Nov. 17, 1936): 166; Mitchell, Santiago, Nov. 25, 1936, Desp. 304, FO 420, no. 91, A9640/74/9.

113. Serruys Gana, Talca, Nov. 25, 1936, No. 517, Ministerio del Interior, Providencias confidenciales 1936, ANC; *El Diario Ilustrado*, Nov. 21–22, 1936; Diputados (Nov. 16, 1936): 271; *Trabajo*, Nov. 17, 1936, p. 1; Nov. 27, 1936, p. 1; *El Mercurio*, Nov. 17–18, 1936; Mayorga, "Alessandri," 19; Donoso, *Alessandri*, 209 n. 3.

114. *El Diario Ilustrado*, Nov. 17–18, 1936, and Nov. 27, 1936, p. 14; *Trabajo*, Nov. 28, 1936, p. 1; *Caupolicán* 4, no. 78 (1st half Dec. 1936): 7, 21; Senadores (Nov. 17, 1936): 163–70.

115. Diputados (Dec. 14, 1936): 750; *El Mercurio*, Nov. 24, 1936, p. 3; *Trabajo*, Dec. 4, 1936, p. 6, and Dec. 23, 1936, pp. 6–7.

116. *El Diario Ilustrado*, Nov. 23, 1936, p. 7, and Nov. 25–27, 1936.

117. *Trabajo*, Mar. 17, 1937, pp. 1, 5.

118. *Hoy*, no. 268 (Jan. 7, 1937): 11; *Trabajo*, June 15, 1936, pp. 3, 8; June 16, 1936, p. 11; Dec. 12, 1937, p. 5; Gentile.

119. *Trabajo*, Nov. 11, 1936, p. 3.

120. Ibid., Oct. 19, 1933, p. 3, June 12, 1936, p. 3, June 26, 1936, p. 3.

121. Boizard in *Trabajo*, May 10, 1934, p. 3; González in May 17, 1934, p. 3, see also Mar. 24, 1937, p. 3; Lira in *Acción Chilena* 4, no. 2 (1935): 120–24.

122. Baena in *Trabajo*, July 4, 1936, p. 10; Lira in *Acción Chilena* 4, no. 2 (1935): 123.

123. *Trabajo*, Sept. 22, 1935, p. 3; June 12–13, 1936; June 19, 1936, p. 3; *Hoy*, no. 274

(Feb. 18, 1937): 18; *¡Católicos!*, attached to Aránguiz Latorre, Valdivia, Mar. 29, 1938, no. 103, Ministerio del Interior, Providencias confidenciales 1938, 1, ANC.

124. Nacismo Chileno, esp. 13; *Trabajo*, June 26, 1936, p. 3; González, *Nacismo*, 10; *Reportaje*, attached to Drago Ramírez, Chiloe, Sept. 7, 1938, Ministerio del Interior, Providencias confidenciales 1938, 3, ANC; *La Nación*, Sept. 5, 1936, p. 8; Paul W. Drake, "Chile," in Falcoff and Pike, 245–90.

125. *Acción* (La Serena), Dec. 12, 1936, p. 2; *Trabajo*, Aug. 16, 1934, p. 4; May 15, 1935, p. 1; May 25, 1935, p. 4; Feb. 29, 1936, p. 3; Aug. 11, 1937, p. 3; Aug. 12, 1937, p. 8; Keller R., *Una revolución*, 9; *Acción Chilena* 2, no. 6 (July 1934): supplement, V, and 4, no. 2 (1935): 127; M. T. Covarrubias, 27 n. 13; *La Revista Católica* 35, no. 799 (Nov. 30, 1935): 455–60; *Hoy*, no. 211 (Dec. 4, 1935): 13–14; Pius XI, "On Reconstructing the Social Order," in McLaughlin, 218–78.

126. Mayorga, "El jesuita rebelde," and "Cuando Frei," 20; Gómez Ugarte, 51, 55, 60–63, 77, 79; Boizard, *La democracia*, 146–58. On the reformist Catholic groups and parties—some of which combined paternalist and radical ideas—see Grayson, 86–94; Salinas C., *Clotario Blest*, 33–37, 41; Partido Corporativo Popular; Partido Social Cristiano; *El Imparcial*, Apr. 24, 1935, p. 5; *Hoy*, no. 212 (Dec. 11, 1935): 12–13; Magnet, 149–50. On Eyzaguirre, see Gazmuri Riveros et al.

127. *Lircay* (Santiago), Nov. 8, 1935, p. 1. This group was the core of the future Falange and Christian Democratic Party.

128. Gómez Ugarte, 79; Fariña Vicuña; *Estudios* 6, no. 72 (Nov. 1938): 31–34; *Estudios* 3, no. 32 (July 1935): 66–71; *Lircay*, Oct. 3, 1936, p. 5; *Hoy*, no. 255 (Oct. 8, 1936): 2; Boizard, *La democracia*, 182; Magnet, 208–10; Góngora, "Libertad," 44. On Dollfuss, see Jill Lewis, "Conservatives and Fascists in Austria, 1918–34," in Blinkhorn, 98–117.

129. *Lircay*, June 27, 1936, p. 3, and Aug. 29, 1936, p. 1; *Falange*, no. 5 (Aug. 1934): 3. This statement against violence resembled the viewpoint of Jacques Maritain, whose influence on the young Conservatives grew over time; see Drake, "Chile," in Falcoff and Pike, 258–59; Grayson, 118; Araneda Bravo, *Historia*, 729.

130. *Trabajo*, June 20, 1936, pp. 3, 8; Feb. 27, 1937, p. 6; Aug. 12, 1937, p. 3; *Reportaje*; Recabarren Valenzuela, 38.

131. *Hoy*, no. 270 (Jan. 21, 1937): 14; Góngora, "Libertad," 43; Araneda Bravo, *El clero*, 33; Mayorga, "Cuando Frei," 20–21; Grayson, 144; Boizard, *La democracia*, 185–86, 189–90; *Trabajo*, Aug. 8, 1936, p. 1; Sept. 15, 1936, p. 3; Oct. 9, 1937, p. 3; Payne, *Falange*, 18.

132. *Hoy*, no. 268 (Jan. 7, 1937): 13; *La Revista Católica* 36, no. 817 (Sept. 26, 1936): 315–16; Camp, 18.

133. *Trabajo*, Oct. 27, 1936, p. 6; Nov. 9, 1936, pp. 1, 8; Feb. 28, 1937, p. 1; *Consigna*, Nov. 21, 1936, p. 2; Arriagada Valdivieso, Santiago, Feb. 27, 1937, no. 79, Ministerio del Interior, Providencias confidenciales 1937, 1, ANC.

134. Arriagada Valdivieso, Santiago, June 22, 1937, Ministerio del Interior, Providencias confidenciales 1937, 1, ANC; Merrill, no. 188, Sept. 24, 1937, C-10-N, 16174-F, U.S., RG 38; *El Mercurio*, Apr. 10, 1937, p. 15; *La Revista Católica* 37, no. 830 (May 29, 1937): 439; *Trabajo*, Apr. 18, 1937, pp. 1, 4, and May 22–23, 1937.

135. Diputados (May 25, 1937): 97–100; *El Mercurio*, May 25, 1937, p. 11, and May 26, 1937, p. 16; *Trabajo*, May 25, 1937, p. 8; Juan J. Linz, "Political Space and Fascism as a Late-Comer," in Larsen et al., 153–56, 167–69.

136. Diputados (July 12, 1937): 1036–45, (Aug. 25, 1937): 2539; *El Mercurio*, July 12, 1937, p. 13; *Trabajo*, Aug. 25, 1937, pp. 1, 7; *Consigna*, Aug. 28, 1937, p. 4. Barrenechea defined fascism as the antidemocratic and violent defense of capitalism.

137. Diputados (July 13, 1937): 1118–21; *El Mercurio*, July 13, 1937, p. 3.

138. Diputados (Jan. 4, 1938): 1318–20; *El Mercurio*, Jan. 5, 1938, p. 15.

139. For information in this and the next paragraph, see *El Mercurio*, May 22, 1938, pp. 36–37, and May 24, 1938, pp. 3, 17, 18; Diputados (May 23, 1938): 95–112, (May 24, 1938): 151–59, (May 25, 1938): 199–203; *Trabajo*, May 22, 1938, 1, 8; Alessandri Palma, 3: 167–77; Donoso, *Alessandri*, 241–45; Boizard, *Historia*, 13–26; Mayorga, "Alessandri," 19, and "González," 42; Young, 324.

140. Diputados (May 23, 1938): 108; *Trabajo*, May 25, 1938, p. 3; May 28, 1938, p. 3; May 31, 1938, p. 6. On German Chileans' disgust with the MNS, see Aránguiz Latorre, Mar. 29, 1938, no. 103, Ministerio del Interior, Providencias confidenciales, 1938, 2, ANC.

141. *El Diario Ilustrado*, May 25, 1938, p. 4, and May 29, 1938, p. 8; *Acción Republicana*, Mar. 1938, p. 3.

142. *Trabajo*, Jan. 26–27, 1938; *Mundo Judío*, Feb. 3, 1938, pp. 1, 5–6, and July 21, 1938, pp. 5–6. See also Deutsch, "Anti-Semitism."

143. *Trabajo*, Oct. 13, 1937, p. 1; *La Opinión*, June 2, 1938, p. 3; Orrego V., 90–91, 99; Alliende González, 147; Nunn, *Military*, 232.

144. Boizard, *Historia*, 41–43, 53; Moulián and Torres Dujisin, 70–71, 74, 131, 136.

145. On the putsch and political fallout, see *Hoy* (Nov. 29, 1938): supplement; RSR; *Ibáñez*; Donoso, *Alessandri*, 256–323; Potashnik, 301–30; Alliende González, 115–43; Young, 323–26; *La senda*, 9–22. Würth Rojas, 209, agreed with Naci sources that Ibáñez was involved in the coup except at the end.

146. *Ideología*; *El Imparcial*, Aug. 2, 1932, p. 2; Aug. 30, 1932, p. 2; Sept. 13, 1932, p. 2; *El Mercurio*, June 20, 1932, p. 7; June 26, 1932, p. 5; June 28, 1932, p. 7; July 1, 1932, p. 18; July 29, 1932, p. 3.

147. *El Imparcial*, Sept. 21, 1932, p. 2, and Nov. 2, 1932, p. 2; Gunther, no. 85, Sept. 11, 1933, C-10-N, 16174-E, U.S., RG 38; *Trabajo*, Mar. 28, 1935, p. 1; Feb. 2, 1938, p. 1; *Acción Chilena* 4, no. 2 (1935): 85; Alexander, 680; Mayorga, "La fugaz," 19; Maldonado Prieto, "Entre reacción," 49, 57, and "La Prusia."

148. Olavarría Bravo, 351; Orrego V., 94; Boizard, *Historia*, 87–88.

149. Leigh-Smith, Sept. 8, 1938, Desp. 190, FO 420/290, no. 37, A7177/571/9; *Trabajo*, Jan. 17, 1939, pp. 2–5, 9; Alessandri Palma, 3: 193–201. Arriagada was imprisoned for his role in the massacre.

150. The entire debate is found in Diputados (Sept. 6, 1938): 2904–29, (Sept. 7, 1938): 2986–3006, (Sept. 9, 1938): 3085–3128, (Sept. 10, 1938): 3141–76. See also Boizard, *Historia*, 92.

151. *Trabajo*, Jan. 17, 1939, pp. 1–2; Vanguardia Popular Socialista.

152. Recabarren Valenzuela, 71, 76–79; Diputados (Mar. 8, 1939): 730–39, 754–57; *Trabajo*, Nov. 30, 1939, pp. 1–2; Dec. 1, 1939, p. 1; Dec. 8, 1939, pp. 1, 3; Dec. 10, 1939, p. 1; Jan. 19, 1940, pp. 1, 4; May 7, 1940, p. 3; Feb. 11, 1941, p. 3. The carryover is especially clear in González von Marées, *El mal.*

153. *Trabajo*, Jan. 6, 1940, p. 3; *La Patria* (Santiago), June 16, 1939, p. 3, and July 1, 1939, p. 2; *La Crítica* (Santiago), Oct. 27, 1939, p. 5; Partido Nacional Fascista; *El Sol* (Santiago), Mar. 30, 1939, p. 3; *Ercilla*, Aug. 23, 1939, p. 6; Movimiento Nacional de Chile; Robertson Rodríguez and Banoviez, 44–51; Nunn, *Military*, 242–43, *El Imparcial*, Aug. 26, 1939, p. 3; RFW, Santiago, Sept. 8, 1939, 825.00/1172; Bowers, Santiago, no. 1864, Sept. 27, 1941, 825.00/1420; Valdivia Ortiz de Zárate, "Las nuevas voces." On the resurgence of radical rightist sentiment in the military in the late 1930s and 1940s, see Maldonado Prieto, "La Prusia."

154. *Ercilla*, July 17, 1940, p. 1; González von Marées, *Tres discursos*, 36–47; Olavarría Bravo, 1: 523–27; *El Mercurio*, Oct. 16–17, 1940; Oct. 20, 1940, pp. 29, 32; Oct. 23, 1940, p. 13; May 17, 1941, p. 13; May 25, 1941, pp. 5, 31; *Mundo Judío*, Aug. 1, 1941, 3–5; Etchepare and Stewart, 590.

155. Mundt, 206.

156. Payne, *Fascism*, 7–14.

157. Sznajder, "A Case," 288–90; on fascism and conservatism, see Blinkhorn.

158. Weiss, 139, 156.

Chapter 10   Argentina: For Fatherland, Labor, and Social Justice

1. On Yrigoyen's petroleum nationalism, see Solberg, *Oil.*

2. See Potter.

3. Liga, *Primer Congreso*, 41 (quote); Liga, *Discurso pronunciado por el presidente*; *El Pueblo*, Feb. 19, 1921; Liga, *Misión*, 1; Liga, *Sexto Congreso*, 39; *La Nueva República* (*LNR*) (Buenos Aires), no. 29 (Aug. 25, 1928): 2 (quote).

4. Liga, *Noveno Congreso*, 555; Liga, *Restauración*, 6; Bliss, Buenos Aires, Desp. 617, July 31, 1929, 835.00/436; "A," Buenos Aires, no. 184, Aug. 2, 1928, and no. 249, Oct. 19, 1928, C-10-K, 12921-D, and no. 209, Aug. 7, 1929, C-10-L, 14632-C, U.S., RG 38; Tamarin, 72–75; Horowitz, *Argentine Unions*, 59–67; Korzeniewicz, "Labor Politics."

5. Figures in David Rock, "Argentina, 1930–1946," in Bethell, *Argentina*, 188. See also Javier Villanueva, "Economic Development," trans. Mark Falcoff, in Falcoff and Dolkart, 60–63; Tulchin, June 19, 1970, 902.

6. Carulla, *Al filo*, 97–98, 138, 145–49, 158–60. See also C. Ibarguren (h.), *Roberto de Laferrère*, 25–27; C. Ibarguren, *La historia*, 323–25. On Sorel's influence on the right, see Roth; Sternhill. I capitalize and use the Spanish word *Nacionalismo* to distinguish this specific Argentine movement from other manifestations of nationalism.

7. Lugones, *La organización*, 11, 60–64; J. Irazusta, *Genio y figura de Lugones*, 111; *LNR*, no. 24 (July 21, 1928): 1; Palacio, "Lugones."

8. *Universitas* 9, no. 38 (July–Sept. 1975): 23–24, 51–52; *Número*, no. 1 (Jan. 1930): 5–6; Rapalo, 53. Changed in orientation, *Criterio* is still being published.

9. On foreign influences, see *Criterio*, no. 32 (Oct. 11, 1928): 43–44, and no. 58 (Apr. 11, 1929): 457–59; *LNR*, no. 7 (Mar. 1, 1928): 1; David Rock, "Antecedents of the Argentine Right," in Deutsch and Dolkart, *Argentine Right*, 1–34.

10. *Universitas* 9, no. 38 (July–Sept. 1975): 23; Irazusta to Pérez Mariluz, Dec. 3, 1925, vol. 1, and diary entry, Aug. 15, 1925, Irazusta archive, Papers, vol. 2; C. Ibarguren, *La historia*, 369; *LNR*, no. 1 (Dec. 1, 1927): 3. See the discussion above of Jackson de Figueiredo's views of Maurras.

11. Carulla had previously founded *La Voz Nacional*, which faded after a few months. See Carulla, *Al filo*, 228–31, 241–42; C. Ibarguren (h.), *Roberto de Laferrère*, 28–29; *LNR*, no. 1 (Dec. 1, 1927): 1–2; J. Irazusta, "Historia de La Nueva República," MS, Irazusta archive, Papers, vol. 2; J. Irazusta, *Memorias*, 176–78, 181.

12. Rodolfo Irazusta in *LNR*, no. 12 (Apr. 28, 1928): 1; see also no. 43 (Dec. 1, 1928): 4.

13. *LNR*, no. 29 (Aug. 25, 1928): 1.

14. *LNR*, nos. 1 (Dec. 1, 1927): 2, and 12 (Apr. 28, 1928): 1. See also nos. 38 (Oct. 27, 1928): 1, and 49 (June 14, 1930): 4; C. Ibarguren (h.), *Laferrère*, 12–13; F. Ibarguren, 17.

15. García Molina and Mayo, 1: 22, 69–70, 2: 157; García and Rodríguez Molas, 1: 111–12; Gontrán de Güemes, "El año 27 Uriburu se negó a intervenir en una revolución," *Hechos en el Mundo*, Feb. 4, 1957, n.p., clipping, Irazusta archive, Papers, vol. 2; Instituto Torcuato di Tella, Irazusta, 15–16; C. Ibarguren (h.), *Respuestas*, 9; Carulla, *Al filo*, 247–53; Gutiérrez de Miguel, 91–92.

16. Liga, *Restauración*, 10.

17. On the revolution, see *La revolución*, 11–74; Rouquié, *Poder militar*, 1: 184–98; Potash, 29–54; Goldwert, 12–29; Etchepareborda, "Aspectos"; Sarobe; Perón, 13–82; García Molina and Mayo, 1: 110–26, 2: 127–89; Navarro Gerassi, *Los nacionalistas*, 55–67; C. Ibarguren (h.), *Respuestas*, 5–11; *LNR*, nos. 52–60 (July–Aug. 1930); Quesada, 74–77, 80; Gutiérrez de Miguel, 112, 173; Liga, *La Liga*. Nor did the Liga Republicana and *LNR* always agree; see Zuleta Alvarez, *El nacionalismo*, 1: 238.

18. Argentina, Presidente, 40–52; A. Bunge, "La República," 3–4; Béjar, *Uriburu*, 18–23. Uriburu belonged to the elite of Salta province, which had opposed oil nationalization, and his close associates included figures tied to foreign oil interests. Nevertheless, his oil policies suggest that foreign oil companies did not cause the coup of 1930, although historians have not had access to company records. On this controversy, see Solberg, *Oil*, 121, 153–54, 158; and Mayo et al.

19. *Caras y Caretas*, no. 1669 (Sept. 27, 1930); C. Ibarguren, *La historia*, 383–84; Barbero and Devoto, 161–63; García and Rodríguez Molas, 1: 69; Carulla, *Al filo*, 295–96; Potash, 64–65. I derived the number of advisers from the press and biographical sources.

20. Newton, "Not for Export"; Boffi, 164, 190–91, 223, 226, 230, 234–42; numbers in Potash, 58; Rouquié, *El estado*, 225; Rodríguez Molas, 95–97; Unamuno.

21. Horowitz, "Ideologías," 282–83, and *Argentine Unions*, 68–71; Tamarin, 87–89; Rouquié, *El estado*, 230–32.

22. Martínez Zuviría, Paris, Apr. 25, 1931, and Videla Dorna, La Paz, Bolivia, June

22, 1931, to Uriburu, Private Letters, Notebook 4, José Félix Uriburu archive, Archivo General de la Nación (AGN), Argentina; Potash, 66–67.

23. Bliss, Buenos Aires, no. 1230, June 10, 1931, 835.00/543, in U.S., Department of State, Records . . . Argentina, 1930–1939, National Archives microfilm copy M1230; *La Vanguardia,* Feb. 16, 1931, p. 1, and May 17, 1931, p. 1; *La Fronda,* Mar. 26, 1931, p. 2; Apr. 25, 1931, p. 6; Apr. 27–28, 1931; and May 17, 1931, pp. 1, 3; *Diputados* (May 11, 1932): 253–55, 257; Uriburu, 115; *Caras y Caretas,* no. 1700 (May 2, 1931); Josephs, 266–67; García Molina and Mayo, 1: 95–96, 2: 220. On the LCA's ideology, see "Declaración."

24. Medina to Uriburu, June 8, 1931, in Private Letters, Notebook 4, Uriburu archive, AGN; *Diputados* (May 11, 1932): 254–55; *La Vanguardia,* May 20, 1931, p. 3, and June 24, 1931, p. 1; *Criterio,* no. 169 (May 28, 1931): 289; *La Fronda,* May 18, 1931, p. 3, and May 30, 1931, p. 1.

25. Carulla to Pena, Buenos Aires, Nov. 4, 1937, Plínio Salgado Collection, Arquivo Público e Histórico do Município de Rio Claro (APHMRC), Rio Claro, Brazil; *Il Mattino D'Italia,* n.d., file 37727, Archivo de *La Prensa;* Sarobe, 206; *La Fronda,* June 12, 1931, p. 3, and June 15, 1931, p. 3; C. Ibarguren (h.), *Laferrère,* 54. Estimates of LCA strength varied widely.

26. *La Vanguardia,* July 15, 1931, p. 1; *La Prensa,* May 19 and June 17, 1931; Boffi, 249; C. Ibarguren (h.), *Laferrère,* 54–55; *LNR,* no. 100 (Oct. 20, 1931): 1.

27. Sarobe, 208; García Molina and Mayo, 2: 222.

28. Boffi, 251–57; *La Prensa,* Oct. 26, 1946, n.p., and *El Mundo,* Oct. 26, 1946, n.p., clippings, file 20137, Archivo de *La Prensa;* Luna, *Alvear,* 132–33; Carlés, "Exégesis"; Caterina, 206.

29. *LNR,* nos. 90 (Oct. 8, 1931): 1, 91 (Oct. 9, 1931): 1, 92 (Oct. 10, 1931): 1.

30. Lugones, *La grande Argentina,* 134–37, and *El estado,* 53; *Acción Republicana. Preámbulo,* 9–12, 15; J. Irazusta, *Memorias,* 205–7, 219–20.

31. *LNR,* R. Irazusta in nos. 57 (Aug. 9, 1930): 1, and 69 (Nov. 8, 1930): 1, Tezanos Pinto in nos. 74 (Dec. 13, 1930): 2, and 75 (Dec. 20, 1930): 2, no. 85 (Mar. 7, 1931): 1, no. 105 (Oct. 26, 1931): 1; Julio Irazusta, "La oligarquía conservadora y los estancieros," in J. Irazusta, *El pensamiento,* 2: 166–68; *Acción Republicana. Preámbulo,* 7.

32. This information comes from a study of 134 members of the Liga Republicana; 154 members of the Legión de Mayo; 18 *LNR* contributors, some of whom also belonged to Acción Republicana; 34 members of the LCA; and 32 members of two or more of these groups. See Argentine biographical section of the bibliography. "Close relationships" are defined as those of siblings, first and second cousins, fathers and sons, grandfathers and grandsons, uncles and nephews, and brothers-in-law.

33. Uriburu, *La palabra,* 75. On politics in this period see, among other sources, Béjar, *Uriburu,* 36–52; Alberto Ciria, "Los partidos políticos durante el período de la restauración conservadora (1930–1943)," in *La década infame,* 65–75.

34. Ronald H. Dolkart, "The Right in the Década Infame, 1930–1943," in Deutsch and Dolkart, 69; on Conservative divisions and fraud, see Béjar, "Otra vez," 199–207.

35. On the Pact and its effects, see P. H. Lewis, *The Crisis*, 38–46; Norberto Galasso, "La economía bajo el signo de la entrega," in *La década infame*, 140–71; Rock, *Argentina*, 222–27; Villanueva, "Economic Development," in Falcoff and Dolkart, 64–74.

36. Repetto in *Diputados* (May 12, 1933): 140; Repetto, 50–52; Walter, *The Socialist Party*, 69–71, 229–30; Matsushita, 87, 186; Rock, *Argentina*, 229–30; Horowitz, *Argentine Unions*, 88, 128; Bergquist; Klubock. There is research under way on a Socialist faction that supported economic nationalism; I thank Raanan Rein for this observation.

37. Ortiz Pereyra, esp. 53–54, 82–86, 137; Dorn; Barbero and Devoto, 125–42; Brown, 144; Brauner Rodgers. Caterina, 44, 236, 274 n. 196, suggests that the LPA's incipient economic nationalism might have affected Torre, who joined the LPA in 1919. Whether he was an active member, however, is unclear.

38. R. and J. Irazusta; on the Nacionalistas' appropriation of Argentine nationalism, see Cane, 457.

39. Letters from and clippings of articles by the individuals and periodical mentioned, and Pedro Juan Vignale, "Sentido de los libros," *La Gaceta de Buenos Aires* (July 21, 1934), n.p., Irazusta archive, Papers, vol. 4; *Crisol* (Buenos Aires), Apr. 7, 1935, n.p., and *El Censor* (Buenos Aires), Aug. 6, 1935, n.p., Irazusta archive, Papers, vol. 5.

40. Instituto di Tella, Irazusta, 22–24; *LNR*, nos. 107 (Oct. 28, 1931): 1, and 108 (Oct. 29, 1931): 1; Quijada, 74–75; Gálvez, *Este pueblo*, 28, 95, and *Vida*; *La Fronda*, May 11, 1932, p. 1. The Irazustas left the UCR behind when they formed the Liberating Party in 1941, followed by the Republican Union in 1955.

41. See the useful chart of these and other groups in Buchrucker, 116–17. On the divisions in Nacionalismo in Argentina as a whole and in Santa Fe province, see Macor and Iglesias, 158–60, 197.

42. On the Silveyra incident, see *La Fronda*, Sept. 2, 1934, p. 3, and *La Vanguardia*, Sept. 2–3, 1934. For other examples of disagreement among Nacionalistas, see *La Fronda*, Feb. 13, 1932, p. 1; Feb. 16, 1932, p. 1; Jan. 20, 1934, p. 3; Jan. 24, 1934, p. 3; *La Vanguardia*, Mar. 12, 1934, p. 1.

43. Comisión de Estudios separates Catholic from political Nacionalismo. Nascimbene and Neuman divide Nacionalistas into the "explicit authoritarian right" of the older generation of Ibarguren, Gálvez, Lugones, and Uriburu and the younger, more radical Catholic generation. Zuleta Alvarez, in *El nacionalismo*, distinguishes the pragmatic Irazusta group, or *"nacionalistas republicanos,"* to which he belonged, from all the rest, whom he considers the more Catholic, rigid, and militaristic *"nacionalistas doctrinarios."* These categories becloud more than they illuminate. The Catholic groups did not abjure political activity, and Catholicism influenced the political ones. Members of the older and younger generations often belonged to the same groups. To designate the youth as Catholic ignores the importance of Catholic doctrine for their elders and, in the case of the Irazustas and

other figures (whom Zuleta Alvarez and Comisión de Estudios pointedly did not consider Catholic), exaggerates it. It makes little sense to set up a dichotomy between the tiny Irazusta circle and the bulk of Nacionalismo, particularly since the latter respected and learned from the former.

44. The Mussolini, Franco, Dollfuss, and Pétain regimes also represented this kind of coalition; see the respective chapters in Blinkhorn.

45. C. Ibarguren (h.), *Laferrère*, 56–64; *La Fronda*, Feb. 28–29, 1932; *La Vanguardia*, Feb. 29, 1932, p. 1.

46. Argentina, Consejo Deliberante (Mar. 18, 1932): 264–67; *Diputados* (May 11, 1932): 253; *La Vanguardia*, Feb. 7, 1932, p. 1; Potash, 90; Zuleta Alvarez, *El nacionalismo*, 1: 278; Horowitz, *Argentine Unions*, 16, 133.

47. Bliss, Desp. no. 1673, June 17, 1932, 835.00/632; Acción Nacionalista Argentina, *La Iuyamtorg*, Tamarin, 96; Matsushita, 102–3; Horowitz, "Ideologías," 284–87; Gaudio and Pilone, "El desarrollo," and "Estado."

48. Comisión Popular Argentina Contra el Comunismo, flier of Aug. 2, 1932 (Buenos Aires: n.p., 1932); *Diputados*, (Aug. 19, 1932): 266–69; *La Fronda*, July 19, 1932, p. 5; Aug. 7, 1932, p. 3; Aug. 20, 1932, p. 1; *Crisol* (Buenos Aires), Aug. 21, 1932, p. 1, and Sept. 1, 1932, p. 1; *Represión*, 5–6; Macleay, Buenos Aires, Aug. 29, 1932, no. 35, A6184/6184/51, FO 420/284; *La Nación*, Aug. 21, 1932, p. 7; *Caras y Caretas*, no. 1769 (Aug. 27, 1932).

49. Consejo Deliberante (Dec. 6, 1932): 4423–35, 4462; *La Vanguardia*, Dec. 4–7, 1932; Walter, *Politics*, 158–59. On ANA/ADUNA, see Acción Nacionalista Argentina, *Doctrina* and *Acusación*.

50. *Diputados* (Dec. 7, 1932): 206–27 (Uriburu on 216), 240; *La Vanguardia*, Dec. 10, 1932, p. 1.

51. On the May 25, 1933 incident, see Consejo Deliberante (May 19, 1933): 816; *La Vanguardia*, May 26, 1933, p. 10; *El Mercurio*, May 26, 1933, p. 1; *Crisol*, May 26, 1933, p. 1; *La Nación*, May 26, 1933, pp. 8, 10, and May 28, 1933, p. 8. See also Consejo Deliberante (May 19, 1933): 714–30, (May 26, 1933): 807, 814–38, (June 16, 1933): 1042–62.

52. *Diputados* (Sept. 12, 1933): 142–49.

53. Anquín, inside cover; *LNR*, nos. 68 (Nov. 1, 1930): 2, and 72 (Nov. 29, 1930): 2; Zuleta Alvarez, *El nacionalismo*, 1: 182, 248, 291–92; Navarro Gerassi, *Los nacionalistas*, 95–96; F. Ibarguren, 114–16. See also Newton, "Ducini." On Catholicism in Córdoba, see Liebscher, "Toward a Pious Republic."

54. *El País* (Córdoba), Sept. 7, 1933, p. 6, and Sept. 11, 1933, p. 6; *La Nación*, June 20, 1931; *La Voz del Interior*, Oct. 4–5, 1933. Note the distinction between Democrats (members of the Democratic Party) and democrats (advocates of democracy).

55. *La Fronda*, Aug. 8, 1933, p. 5; *La Vanguardia*, Mar. 24, 1933, pp. 1–2; May 7, 1933, p. 9; June 14, 1933, p. 1; June 30, 1933, p. 2; July 12, 1933, p. 1; July 22, 1933, p. 7; *Camisa Negra* (Buenos Aires), no. 7 (1st half Oct. 1933): 1, box 18, YIVO archive, Buenos Aires.

56. *La Fronda*, Oct. 1, 1933, p. 1; *Los Principios*, Sept. 7, 1933, pp. 1, 6; Sept. 29, 1933, pp. 5, 8; Oct. 6, 1933, p. 8; *La Vanguardia*, Sept. 10, 1933, p. 2; Sept. 13–14, 1933; Sept. 30, 1933, p. 1; *La Voz del Interior*, Sept. 28–29, 1933.

57. *Crisol*, Oct. 6, 1933, p. 1; *El País*, Sept. 29–30, 1933; *Los Prinicipios*, Sept. 30, 1933, pp. 1, 5; *La Vanguardia*, Sept. 29–30, 1933; *La Voz del Interior*, Sept. 29, 1933, p. 7; Oct. 12, 1933, p. 4.

58. Argentina, Legislatura de Córdoba, Diputados (Nov. 18, 1936): 1304; *El País*, Oct. 1, 1933, p. 3; *Los Principios*, Oct. 25, 1933, pp. 1, 2; *La Vanguardia*, Oct. 4, 1933, p. 1; Oct. 25, 1933, p. 1; Nov. 13, 1933, p. 3; June 9, 1934, p. 1, Aug. 9, 1934, p. 1; *La Voz del Interior*, Oct. 1, 1933, p. 5.

59. Córdoba, Diputados (Sept. 29 and 30, 1933): 25–26; *El País*, Oct. 4, 1933, p. 5; *Los Principios*, Oct. 6, 1933, pp. 3, 8; Oct. 22, 1933, p. 2; Oct. 25, 1933, p. 2; *La Vanguardia*, Oct. 7, 1933, p. 1, and Oct. 10, 1933, p. 1; *La Voz del Interior*, Oct. 5, 1933, p. 5; Oct. 12, 1933, p. 7; Nov. 2, 1933, pp. 5, 11, 15; Nov. 10–11, 1933. Torres was the widow of Rafael Núñez.

60. *Diputados* (Sept. 29 and 30, 1933): 166–82. Lima would serve as Peronist Héctor Cámpora's (1973) vice-president. After Nacionalistas attacked leftist centers in Tucumán and Salta in April and June 1935, respectively, Socialists again demanded an explanation for the LCA's *personería jurídica*. Minister of Justice and Education Manuel de Iriondo, a former LPA leader, cited the LCA's "laudable ends" as justification. On the incidents, see *La Gaceta* (Tucumán), Apr. 25, 1935, pp. 1, 10; *La Fronda*, Apr. 28, 1935, p. 3; *La Vanguardia*, June 12–14, 1935. For the Socialist-Iriondo exchange, see *Diputados* (June 12, 1935): 354–71, and (June 26, 1935): 510–37, 558–64.

61. *Camisa Negra*, no. 7 (1st half Oct. 1933): 1. On Nacionalista violence in Entre Ríos and Santa Fe provinces, for example, see Macor and Iglesias, 158, 163, 169–70, 176–77.

62. *La Fronda*, July 30, 1934, pp. 1, 6; *La Vanguardia*, June 6, 1934, p. 1; July 16, 1934, p. 1; July 18, 1934, p. 1; July 29, 1934, pp. 1, 14; July 31, 1934, p. 3; Aug. 2, 1934, p. 4; Aug. 6, 1934, p. 1.

63. *Diputados* (Aug. 1, 1934): 784; *La Vanguardia*, July 30, 1934, p. 10; Aug. 16, 1934, p. 1; Aug. 22, 1934, p. 1; *La Protesta*, Aug. 1934, p. 3.

64. *Diputados* (Aug. 1, 1934): 779–802.

65. *Los Principios*, Sept. 18, 1933, p. 1; *La Vanguardia*, Sept. 18–19, 1933; *Diputados* (Sept. 29–30, 1933): 167; Walter, *Province*, 132. On the divisions, see Béjar, "Otra vez."

66. Cox, no. 635, Mar. 15, 1935, 835.00/693, and Walter, *The Province*, 133–41, described the crisis. See also *La Fronda*, Mar. 8, 1935, p. 3, and Mar. 12, 1935, p. 5; *La Vanguardia*, June 7, 1933, p. 1; Mar. 7–9, 1935; F. Ibarguren, 266–68.

67. *La Vanguardia*, Mar. 13, 1935, p. 3.

68. Ibid., Mar. 10, p. 2, Mar. 14–15, 1935; *La Fronda*, Mar. 13, 1935, p. 3; Mar. 14, 1935, p. 3; Mar. 22, 1935, p. 5; F. Ibarguren, 273.

69. *La Fronda*, Mar. 16–17, 1935; *La Vanguardia*, Mar. 17, 1935, p. 12.

70. Statistics in Vásquez-Presedo, 2: 47; Weddell, Buenos Aires, No. 1209, June 4, 1936, 835.00/747; Ferrero, 1: 92–95; Bou, 8–13, 16; Horowitz, *Argentine Unions*, 72, 97–98; F. Ibarguren, 324.

71. Navarro Gerassi, 96; Bou, 16, 22; Mark Falcoff, "Argentina," in Falcoff and Pike, 305; *La Vanguardia*, Sept. 6, 1936, p. 1.

72. *La Voz del Interior*, Aug. 17–18 and 24–26, 1936.

73. Ibid., Aug. 25–26, 1936; *La Vanguardia*, Aug. 25, 1936, p. 7; Aug. 27, 1936, p. 1; Aug. 31, 1936, p. 1; *Crisol*, Aug. 27, 1936, pp. 1, 3. On the ramifications of the incident, see *Los Principios*, Nov. 1, 1936, p. 7; Nov. 6–7, 1936; Nov. 9, 1936, p. 5; *El País*, Oct. 19, 1936, p. 5, and Nov. 7–8, 1936.

74. Córdoba, Diputados (Nov. 18, 1936): 1232–1309; Provincia de Córdoba, 21–28; *La Voz del Interior*, Nov. 11, 1936, p. 7; *La Vanguardia*, Nov. 11, 1936, p. 7; Nov. 13, 1936, p. 7; Nov. 23, 1936, p. 7.

75. *La Vanguardia*, Aug. 12–13, Aug. 17–19, Aug. 21, 1938, p. 7; *Los Principios*, Aug. 11–13, 1938.

76. *Bandera Argentina* (Buenos Aires), Aug. 18, 1938, p. 3; *La Fronda*, Aug. 13, 1938, p. 6; *Los Principios*, Aug. 13, 1938, p. 6; *La Voz del Interior*, Aug. 13, 1938, p. 7; Aug. 16, 1938, p. 7; *Crisol*, Aug. 27, 1938, p. 3.

77. *Clarinada* 2, no. 17 (Sept. 1938): 3–4; *Los Principios*, Aug. 13–14, 1938; Aug. 17, 1938, p. 4; *La Vanguardia*, Aug. 14, 1938, p. 7; *La Fronda*, Aug. 14, 1938, p. 3; *Noticias Gráficas* (Buenos Aires), Apr. 5, 1939, p. 5.

78. L. Gallardo, *A.D.U.N.A.*; Fascismo Argentino in *Los Principios*, Oct. 8, 1933, p. 3; Kinkelín quoted in *La Vanguardia*, Aug. 3, 1933, p. 1; *Crisol*, Sept. 30, 1933, p. 1.

79. *Basta* 1, no. 7 (July 1935): n.p.; see also Dolkart, "The Right," in Deutsch and Dolkart, 71.

80. Osés in *Clarinada* 2, no. 13 (May 1938): 34; *Crisol*, Sept. 1, 1932, p. 1. On Silveyra's legal difficulties, see Clippings File, envelope 222, Delegación de Asociaciones Israelitas Argentinas (DAIA) archive, Buenos Aires.

81. *Clarinada* 1, no. 2 (June 1937): 2; Silveyra, *El comunismo*, esp. 19–34, 37–45, 227, and *Imperialismo*, esp. 24.

82. Examples of these activities are found in Silveyra, "Historia"; *Clarinada* 1, no. 1 (May 1937): 24; *Demanda contra 'Clarinada'*. See ads in *Clarinada* 2, no. 23 (Mar. 31, 1939): 67, 81, 92, 94, 96, and back cover.

83. *Clarinada* 1, no. 1 (May 1937): 5; *Represión*; Argentina, Senado de la Nación, and Provincia de Buenos Aires, 1: 177–80; Henderson, Buenos Aires, disp. no. 278, Aug. 11, 1936, no. 39, A7271/77/2; Balesta, 65, 73–74, 89; Korzeniewicz, "Labor Unrest," 23. According to Cane, 454, Sánchez Sorondo's bill showed the right's unwillingness to accept an alliance of democratic and Communist forces.

84. Silveyra, *El comunismo*, 524–28.

85. Ibid., 522–23; Weddell, no. 1476, Jan. 30, 1937, 835.00/772. For suspicions of state involvement in the economy and on the side of the poor, see Lugones, *La grande argentina*, 88–89; *LNR*, nos. 20 (June 23, 1928): 1, and 31 (Sept. 8, 1928): 2; *Camisa Negra* no. 7 (1st half Oct. 1933): 3; *Combate*, n.d., box 18, YIVO archive; Guardia Argentina, *Propósitos*, 14.

86. Gálvez, *Este pueblo*, 102–3, 119–20, 123–24, 128; *Crisol*, Aug. 30, 1934, p. 3. Gálvez later attempted unconvincingly to obscure his fascist sympathies in *Recuerdos de la vida literaria: Entre la novela*, 164.

87. *Clarinada* 2, no. 23 (Mar. 31, 1939): 23.

88. C. Ibarguren, *La inquietud,* 95–105; Otero Oliva, 32, 36, 47–48, 50, 57; L. Gallardo, *A.D.U.N.A.,* 13–15; Guardia Argentina, *Propósitos,* 4; Partido de la Juventud, 7–11; Nacionalismo Laborista in El Nacionalismo Argentino, *Voz,* 15–16, 34–36; El Nacionalismo Argentino, *Estatutos,* 5–6; Glave, 42–82. Nacionalista Alberto Ottalagano asserted that the entire movement favored social justice; see Macor and Iglesias, 165.

89. Statistics in Walter, *The Province,* 2; Dolkart, "Buenos Aires Province," 8–17, 19–20, and "Manuel A. Fresco"; Provincia de Buenos Aires, 1: 225–94, 306–7, 2: 55–72; Balesta, 41; Horowitz, *Argentine Unions,* 19, 118, 120; Korzeniewicz, "Labor Unrest," 18–22.

90. Provincia de Buenos Aires, 2: 84–98; Balesta, 63–64.

91. L. Gallardo, *A.D.U.N.A.,* 14; Guardia Argentina, *Propositos,* 3, 4, 9.

92. El Nacionalismo Argentino, *Estatutos,* 4–5; Guardia Argentina, *Concentración,* 9, 23, and *Propósitos,* 4, 13, 16.

93. *Bandera Argentina,* Jan. 18, 1938, p. 2.

94. Doll, 227, 357–67 (from 1939); Palacio, *La historia,* 53–55, 69–71; Payne, *Fascism,* 10.

95. J. Irazusta, *Estudios,* 265–67 (original date of publication not given, but it was probably in the 1930s); Doll, 91; Zuleta Alvarez, *El nacionalismo,* 1: 50, 356; Hernández Arregui, 271, 279.

96. Rock, *Authoritarian Argentina,* 119; *La Vanguardia,* July 28, 1934, p. 1; *La Fronda,* July 15, 1935, p. 1; *Revista del Instituto Juan Manuel de Rosas de Investigaciones Históricas* 1, no. 4 (1939); Kroeber, 13–15, 21; Hernández, 66 (which refers to the Instituto in Santa Fe as the Centro de Estudios Argentinistas); Macor and Iglesias, 164, 179.

97. Font Ezcurra in *Revista del Instituto Juan Manuel de Rosas de Investigaciones Históricas* 1, no. 4 (1939): 134; *Sarmiento el indeseable;* Osés, *El nacionalismo,* 28; Nascimbene and Neuman, 132. Not all Nacionalistas embraced Rosas; see LCA member Valenti Ferro, 129.

98. Falcoff, "Argentine Nationalism," and "Raúl Scalabrini Ortiz"; Spektorowski, "Ideological Origins," 167–68; Hernández, 74–75; C. Ibarguren (h.), *Respuestas,* 19; Zuleta Alvarez, *El nacionalismo,* 1: 336–37; Hernández Arregui, 359.

99. Meinvielle, *Concepción,* esp. 16, 20, 22–23, 29, 34, 81, 84–85. See also Lastra, 44–46; Torre's critique of Catholic views of capitalism in *Escritos,* 3: 43–74.

100. Meinvielle, *Concepción,* 110–12, 115, 118, 126, 128–31.

101. Meinvielle, *El judío,* esp. 10–13, 25–27, 37, 40–43. To those who pointed out that Communists and other Nacionalista targets were not Jewish, Nacionalista Walter Degreff (pp. 6, 7, 30–31) noted that the cowardly Jews were secretive. He added that Jews had conscious and unconscious followers; even if the second group did not intentionally serve Jewish interests, they were no less "Jewish." Compare Meinvielle's views with Alvaro Bomilcar's division of the world into the Jewish and military orders and with the Nacistas' designation of all modernist forces as Jewish.

102. Meinvielle, esp. 59, 64–67, 82–84, 94, 97, 99–104, 107, 109, 112–15, 121–25, 131. The famous Catholic thinker Jacques Maritain expressly warned against making "the Jew" the cause of all evil, although he did not completely avoid antisemitism; see "Nota."

103. Meinvielle, *Concepción*, 140–41; Kleiner, 1: 27; *Encyclopedia Judaica*, 6: 582.

104. Meinvielle, *Concepción*, 154–55, 214–15, 228, 253–54, and *El judío*, 141, 144–45.

105. Deutsch, "Argentine Right," 115. On radical antisemitism among Nacionalistas in Santa Fe province, see Martín.

106. *Criterio*, nos. 194 (Nov. 19, 1931): 241, and 239 (Sept. 29, 1932): 300–302. On the radical antisemitism sometimes found in *Criterio*, see Deutsch, "Argentine Right." Ivereigh, 90, 230 n. 42, attributed Catholic antisemitism in the 1930s to Meinvielle and noted that *Criterio* criticized his views, without discussing the many examples of antisemitism in that journal.

107. Figures in DellaPergola, 92; *American Jewish Yearbook*, 45 (1943–44): 580; Newton, "Indifferent Sanctuary," 395. See Sofer, 91–119, on economic mobility; and Avni, *Argentina*, 128–74, on immigration.

108. *Criterio*, nos. 289 (Sept. 14, 1933): 30–31, 306 (Jan. 11, 1934): 33–34, 382 (June 27, 1935): 204, and 559 (Nov. 17, 1938): 288.

109. Ibid., no. 593 (July 13, 1939): 245–50.

110. Filippo, *Conferencias*, 202–26; and *La palabra*. On his role under Perón, see Caimari, *Perón*, 76, 122–23. C. Ibarguren agreed that Marxism was Jewish in *La crisis*, 35, 38.

111. Wast (Martínez Zuviría), esp. 14, 24, 30, 40, 147; Agresti, 34–41. Even Lugones, who in the 1930s made some antisemitic statements (see *El estado*, 31), regarded the Protocols as fake; see *Mundo Israelita*, Mar. 28, 1936, p. 6.

112. Tiempo, esp. 8–10, 42, 45, 51; Doll, 61–62; *La Fronda*, Sept. 8, 1935, p. 1; Feb. 16, 1936, p. 1; *Criterio*, nos. 385 (July 18, 1935): 282, and 390 (Aug. 22, 1935): 400.

113. *Clarinada* 1, nos. 1 (May 1937): cover, and 3 (June 12, 1937): 19; *Crisol*, Oct. 27, 1937, p. 3; *Crítica*, Oct 16, 1937, p. 6. See also *Combate*, no. 31 (Dec. 1936): 1; "Nacionalista: Boicot a Rusos o Judíos," flier (General Sarmiento, Apr. 12, 1937); *Contra* (Buenos Aires) 1, no. 1 (Sept. 1937): 4, all in box 18, YIVO archive. In addition, see *Bandera Argentina*, Jan. 26, 1938, p. 1.

114. On this and a similar incident in July 1933, see *La Vanguardia*, Aug. 19, 1932, p. 1; Aug. 10, 1934, p. 1; Aug. 17, 1934, p. 1; *La Fronda*, July 15, 1933, p. 6; *Diputados* (Aug. 19, 1932): 267–68.

115. *Crisol*, Mar. 29, 1934, p. 1, Apr. 1, 1934, p. 1, Apr. 3, 1934, p. 1; *La Vanguardia*, Mar. 31, 1934, pp. 1, 10; Sept. 9–10, 1934; *Judaica* (Buenos Aires) 16 (Oct. 1934): 172–76.

116. *La Vanguardia*, Dec. 17–18, 1934; *La Nación*, Dec. 17, 1934, p. 6, and Dec. 21, 1934, p. 12; *La Prensa*, Dec. 17, 1934, p. 10; *La Fronda*, Jan. 17, 1935, p. 5; *Noticias Gráficas* (Buenos Aires), Sept. 16, 1937, p. 7.

117. *Contra* 1, no. 1 (Sept. 1937): 6; *Noticias Gráficas*, Sept. 16, 1937, p. 7; *La Van-*

guardia, Jan. 23, 1935, p. 1; *Mundo Israelita*, Feb. 2, 1935, p. 1; Newton, *The "Nazi Menace,"* 49–50, 394 n. 49. Newton (p. 245) suggests the Gestapo recruited Wilke and his cohorts.

118. Metz; Hernández Arregui, 360–61; Córdoba, Diputados (Nov. 18, 1936): 1291; Newton, "Indifferent Sanctuary," 395, and *The "Nazi Menace,"* 134–35, 191; Asociación de Escuelas Populares; *American Jewish Yearbook*, 36 (1937–38): 488–89.

119. *Criterio*, no. 443 (Aug. 27, 1936): 393; Partido de la Juventud, 9; Clementi, "El miedo," 211–12; G. Gallardo; Palacio, *La historia*, 62.

120. *Mundo Israelita*, Dec. 21, 1935, p. 1.

121. Falcoff, "Argentina," in Falcoff and Pike, 297–301; Gibson, *Class*, 59–61; A. Bunge, *Una nueva argentina*, 51–60. As Gibson notes, there were differences among conservatives at the provincial level. Conservatives were flexible enough to welcome union members to their list of candidates; see Ferrari Etcheberry.

122. *FONA*; *Crisol*, Aug. 13, 1933, p. 2; *Camisa Negra*, no. 7 (1st half of Oct. 1933): 4; Passalacqua Eliçabe. *El Pueblo*, May 1, 1937, p. 3, named some Nacionalista labor groups.

123. *La Fronda*, Oct. 7, 1937, p. 5; Lezica, 99; Armour, Buenos Aires, no. 3078, Jan. 16, 1942, 835.00/1130, U.S. Department of State, Records . . . Argentina, 1940–1944, National Archives microfilm copy M1322; C. Ibarguren (h.), *Respuestas*, 28–29; Josephs, 265.

124. See Alianza. *Bandera Argentina*, Aug. 9, 1938, p. 4, and Imaz, 29, described the symbol. On the AJN's social views, see also Spektorowski, "Argentina," 74–76.

125. Baker, Buenos Aires, no. 5906, Dec. 6, 1938, 2657-L-127/3, U.S., RG 165; *La Fronda*, Nov. 29, 1938, pp. 3, 5, and Dec. 2, 1938, p. 2; *La Razón*, Aug. 25, 1940, p. 7; *Crisol*, May 25, 1938, p. 5.

126. *Clarinada* 1, no. 12 (Apr. 1938): 5; *Bandera Argentina*, May 1, 1938, p. 1; *Crisol*, May 3, 1938, pp. 1, 3; *La Fronda*, May 3, 1939, p. 11; *La Prensa*, May 1–2, 1938.

127. *Crisol*, July 9, 1938, p. 3; *La Fronda*, July 8–9, 1938; *Bandera Argentina*, July 9, 1938, p. 7.

128. *La Fronda*, Oct. 4, 1938, p. 1; *Crítica*, Aug. 26–27, 1940; *La Vanguardia*, Aug. 27, 1940, p. 3; C. Ibarguren (h.), *Respuestas*, 29.

129. For these and other examples, see Alianza; *La Fronda*, Oct. 7, 1937, p. 5; *El Pampero* (Buenos Aires), Nov. 4, 1939, p. 7; Passalacqua Eliçabe, 68; Fascismo Argentino; Gálvez, *Este pueblo*, 7–10, 31–32, 35, 41; L. Gallardo, *A.D.U.N.A.*.

130. Osés, *Medios*, 27 (from 1941); *Bandera Argentina*, Jan. 18, 1938, p. 2, and Sept. 2, 1938, p. 1; Ferla, 49–50; *Clarinada* 2, no. 14 (June 1938): 54; Passalacqua Eliçabe, 50; *Crisol*, May 8, 1942, p. 2; *Bandera Argentina*, Aug. 23, 1932.

131. *LNR* 1, no. 12 (Apr. 28, 1928): 1.

132. *Bandera Argentina*, July 7, 1938, p. 1; *La Fronda*, Aug. 19, 1932, p. 1; Ramos in Cuadernos Adunistas no. 1, 3–4; Bianchi and Sanchis, 32–35; Carlson, 169–80; Lavrin, *Women*, 275–85.

133. *La Fronda*, June 12, 1931, p. 3, and June 17, 1931, p. 6; *La Prensa*, June 17, 1931.

134. *La Fronda*, July 15, 1931, p. 3, July 24, 1931, p. 3, Aug. 14, 1931, p. 3, Aug. 19, 1931, p. 3, May 11, 1932, p. 6, July 20, 1932, p. 1, Aug. 22, 1932, p. 1, Aug. 21, 1933, p. 3, Apr. 29, 1934, pp. 1–2; *La Nación*, Dec. 8, 1934, p. 9; *Bandera Argentina*, Sept. 17, 1936, p. 1.

135. Passalacqua Eliçabe, 153; *Crisol*, June 4, 1933, p. 1, June 6, 1933, p. 1, Aug. 20, 1933, p. 5; *La Prensa*, May 17, 1933, p. 15; *La Fronda*, June 21, 1932, p. 1; July 21, 1933, p. 6, Aug. 17, 1933, p. 6, Sept. 5, 1935, p. 1, Sept. 13, 1937, p. 1.

136. Giménez in *La Fronda*, Aug. 5, 1932, p. 6; see also Aug. 29, 1933, p. 6, and *La Nación*, Sept. 1, 1934, pp. 3, 7.

137. *Crisol*, Aug. 2, 1940, p. 3, and Dec. 28, 1940, p. 3; Navarro Gerassi, 148.

138. *Crisol*, Dec. 16, 1941, p. 3. The extremist aspects of the speech resemble those of the pro-Nazi Mothers' Movement in the U.S.; see Jeansonne.

139. *Crisol*, Dec. 21, 1941, p. 3; McClintock, 273. I thank Ana María Kapelucz-Poppi for the observation on school uniforms.

140. Baker, no. 5745, Mar. 3, 1938, 835.00F/3; C. Ibarguren (h.), *Laferrère*, 79; names taken from Lezica, 105–14. The Nacionalistas of 1941 seemed older than those of earlier years—40 versus 33 years old—but I found the ages of only fourteen individuals. See Argentine biographical section of the bibliography. Journalist Sax Bradford, 138, noted the presence of a few aristocrats and intellectuals alongside large numbers of considerably less privileged youth in the AJN.

141. Newton, *The "Nazi Menace,"* 131; Davis, no. 717, May 20, 1940, 835.00/N57. In 1943 Bradford, 140, estimated 300,000 to 500,000. Juan Carulla, however, claimed that *Bandera Argentina* and *La Fronda* had only 20,000 readers apiece; see Carulla to Penna, Nov. 4, 1937, Salgado Collection, APHMRC.

142. Rouquié, *Poder militar*, 1: 279, 281; García and Rodríguez Molas, 2: 147–55, 162–63, 179; Potash, 101–2.

143. L. Gallardo, *Las fuerzas armadas*; Genta, *La formación*; Clementi, "Una guía," 42–44; Zanatta, *Del estado*, 350–51; Zuleta Alvarez, *El nacionalismo*, 2: 764–67; F. Ibarguren, 357–60. On the penetration of Catholic Nacionalismo in the armed forces, see Zanatta, *Del estado*, esp. 139–55, 218–36, 345–65.

144. Circular, June 5, 1936, in Legajo 61, Agustín Justo archive, AGN.

145. On Defensa Social Argentina, see *La Vanguardia*, July 14, 1937, p. 8, and *La Fronda*, Dec. 8, 1938, p. 4. On ANA, see "A," Buenos Aires, no. 56, May 15, 1933, C-10-L, 14632-D, U.S., RG 38. On Fasola Castaño, see Rouquié, *Poder militar*, 1: 283; Weddell, no. 1096, Mar. 20, 1936, 835.00/738; *La Voz del Interior*, Mar. 14, 1936, pp. 3, 5; *Bandera Argentina*, Mar. 24, 1936, p. 1, and May 1, 1937, p. 3; Osés, *¡Y ésta es la verdad!*; Caterina, 156–57, note 203 on 180. See also C. Ibarguren (h.), *Laferrère*, 67–68; F. Ibarguren, 226, 228–30.

146. Baker, no. 5907, Dec. 7, 1938, 2657-L-127/4, U.S., RG 165; Dodd, Desp. 286, no. 12, A6967/307/2, FO 420/290; Potash, 95–98; Rouquié, *Poder militar*, 1: 283. Molina, unlike Fasola Castaño, hardly operated alone.

147. Goldwert, 44; Potash, 111; Rouquié, *Poder militar*, 1: 283; García Molina and Mayo, 1: 14.

148. Rivero de Olazábal; F. Ibarguren, 213–15, 391–95; Castellani, *Sentir la Argentina*, 11, 15, 22; Mallimaci, esp. 21; Nascimbene and Neuman, esp. 128–30. The best analysis of the church and Nacionalismo is Zanatta, *Del estado.*

149. *Restauración; El Pueblo*, June 13, 1937, p. 3; Lezica, 100–104; Armour, no. 3078, Jan. 16, 1942, 835.00/1130.

150. *La Fronda*, Oct. 11–13, 1934; *La Nación*, Dec. 8, 1934, p. 9; Carulla, *Al filo*, 311–13; Ciria, 169–70; Comisión de Estudios, 54; Burdick, 33–34; Ivereigh, 76–77.

151. Figures in Rock, *Authoritarian*, 101, and Ciria, 173; see also Ciria, 162–66; Mallimaci, 23, 26; Castellani, *Reforma*, 26–27. A greater victory would be the military government's (1943–46) decree reinserting religion into public education.

152. *La Fronda*, July 1, 1940, p. 2; Romero Carranza, 275, 286; de Andrea, *La Encíclica*, 22, 27, 29, 31–32; Forni, 218; Burdick, 33; Caimari, *Perón*, 87.

153. *Criterio*, no. 298 (Nov. 16, 1933): 245–48; on integral Catholicism, see Mallimaci, esp. 15. Newton claimed Franceschi was a fascist in "Ducini," 49 n. 38.

154. *Criterio*, nos. 140 (Nov. 6, 1930): 593–95, 141 (Nov. 13, 1930): 625–26, and 290 (Sept. 21, 1933): 53–56; Ivereigh, 115–17; Zanatta, *Del estado*, 192–94; Floria and Montserrat.

155. Ezcurra Medrano, 5–6, 30–31, 33–34, 36–37, 40–41, 49.

156. *Baluarte*, nos. 15–16 (Sept. 1933): 41; Llambías, 75–76. Although he claimed to oppose totalitarianism, Franceschi told Catholics to serve their country even if it were under this type of regime, conceding that they could choose to resist unjust laws in extreme cases; see *Totalitarismo*, 23–25, 86–87.

157. *Criterio*, no. 148 (Jan. 1, 1931): 13; Meinvielle, *Un juicio católico*, 38–45, 52, 57. For his views on Germany, see Meinvielle, *Entre la iglesia* and *Hacia la cristiandad.* While he did not go as far as Meinvielle, Franceschi nevertheless praised the Spanish Nationalists. On the church and Spain, see Falcoff, "Argentina," in Falcoff and Pike, 323–27.

158. Maritain, "Con el pueblo"; Floria and Montserrat, 772–78.

159. See Pico.

160. Silveyra in *Clarinada* 2, no. 23 (Mar. 31, 1939): 3. For similar statements, see Osés, *Medios*, 95 (from 1941); Doll, 188–89, 192; Palacio, *La historia*, 150–51. Rock cites various Nacionalistas who denied fascist ties or influences in *Authoritarian Argentina*, 109. According to Nacionalista Alberto Ottalagano, hidden and open fascists made up the movement; see Macor and Iglesias, 161.

161. On these and other examples of such links, see Newton, *The "Nazi Menace,"* 124, 134–36, 138, 186; Falcoff, "Argentina," in Falcoff and Pike, 322; Carulla, *Al filo*, 316–19; Lezica, 101; Jackisch; Sutin. On the commission, see Diputados (May 18, 1938): 210–30, (May 17, 1939): 133–36, (June 7, 1939): 396–423, (June 9, 1939): 473–509, (June 15, 1939): 597–654, (June 16, 1939): 686–708, (June 23, 1939): 909–66.

162. F. Ibarguren, 14; Amadeo, 113–15.

163. May 11, 1937, p. 1.

164. Navarro Gerassi, 105; Rock, *Authoritarian Argentina*, 108; Newton, *The "Nazi*

Menace," 137; Buchrucker, 230–34; Nascimbene and Neuman, 128, 134–36, 140 n. 43; Spektorowski, "Ideological Origins," 177.

165. Payne, in *Fascism*, 116, 134, accepted the Iron Guard as a fascist movement but not Rex; Weber, 96–105, 122–29, accepted both. See also Yeshayahu Jelinek, "Clergy and Fascism: The Hlinka Party in Slovakia and the Croatian Ustasha Movement," in Larsen et al., 369–75.

166. Payne, *Fascism*, 7.

167. "Conclusion," in Deutsch and Dolkart, 182.

168. Instituto Torcuato di Tella, Irazusta, 16 (quote), 22, 40; Carulla, *Al filo*, 314. The 20,000 Nacistas represented about 0.4 percent of the Chilean population in 1938. If one employs the figure given above of 300,000, Nacionalistas represented about 2 percent of the Argentine population in 1940. I used the population estimates in Wilkie et al., 106–7.

Chapter 11 Brazil: A Revolution of the Heart and Soul

1. Marcelo de Paiva Abreu, "O Brasil e a economia mundial (1929–1945)," in Fausto, *O Brasil republicano*, 4: 17.

2. Oliveira, "Elite," 91; Carone, "Coleção Azul"; Holloway.

3. Bak; Flynn, *Brazil*, 99–100.

4. Centro de Pesquisa, interview with Batista, 32; Forjaz, 69–94; Conniff, "Tenentes"; Flynn, "Revolutionary Legion," 63–105; (in biographical section) Beloch and Abreu, 1: 811–14. On Campos, see Medeiros, 9–51.

5. *Pátria Nova* (São Paulo) 1, nos. 1 (n.d.): 25, 2 (Dec. 1929): 27–28, 65, and 3 (Mar. 1930): 70. On the ASB, see Carone, *A segunda república*, 290–95; Borba, 18. The fact that these groups intended to create colorful uniformed militias—white shirts for Pátria Nova and blue shirts for the ASB—may have prompted Borba's use of the term *butterfly*.

6. *Brazílea*, no. 9 (Apr. 1932): 16; Lima Sobrinho, 509–12; Paula to Teixeira de Freitas, Rio de Janeiro, Aug. 19, 1936, Mário Augusto Teixeira de Freitas archive, Arquivo Nacional (AN), Rio de Janeiro; *Fon-Fon* (Rio de Janeiro), Dec. 9, 1933, p. 34; Brazil, *Diário do Poder Legislativo* (June 9, 1936): 301; Lesser, *Welcoming*, 57–58.

7. Melo, *A marcha*, 7, 23–24, 60–61; Melo, *Comunismo*; Melo, *República*; Trindade, "Plínio Salgado," 30–31.

8. *A Razão* (São Paulo), Oct. 29, 1931, p. 1; Trindade, "Plínio Salgado," 20–23; Beloch and Abreu, 1: 551; Sombra, 45–57.

9. San Tiago Dantas, for example, indicated his views of Fascism in Caju's magazine, *Revista de Estudos Jurídicos e Sociais*, no. 4 (Aug. 1931): 136–41.

10. Salgado, *Despertemos*, 10–14, 39–40, 50–51, 68 (from 1926–27).

11. Flynn, "Revolutionary Legion," 76–77, 85–87; Reale, *Memórias*, 1: 59; M. Vieira, 73; Trindade, "O fascismo," 7; *Brazílea*, 2d phase, 1 (Aug. 1931): 26.

12. Ruy de Arruda, "Apontamentos sobre a ação política de Plínio Salgado," MS, 16–17, box RA/PI, *Oriente* File, Ruy de Arruda collection, APHMRC; Trin-

dade, "Plínio Salgado," 37; *A Razão*, Oct. 21, 1931, p. 3, and May 1, 1932, p. 1. For anti-bourgeois statements, see Salgado, *Despertemos*, 167; and *O soffrimento*, 18–19, 43, 49, 80, 84, 94, 99–101, 110, 116, 165, 198 (from *A Razão*).

13. *A Razão*, May 15, 1932, p. 3; Melo, *A marcha*, 61–64; Broxson, 41–43.

14. Melo, *A marcha*, 64–66; M. Vieira, 77; Skidmore, *Politics in Brazil*, 15–18.

15. The text of the manifesto is found in Carone, *A segunda república*, 309–15.

16. Broxson, 60.

17. Levine, *Vargas Regime*, 32–33, 59–60.

18. On one *bandeira*, that of Barroso and Reale in late 1933, see newspaper articles and fliers, Nov. 1933–Jan. 1934, Clippings File, Gustavo Barroso archive, Museu Histórico Nacional (MHN), Rio de Janeiro. See also *Anauê!* (Mogy-Mirim, São Paulo), Aug. 18, 1935, p. 1; Reale, *Memórias*, 1: 95–96, 99; Lacerda, 27; Corrêa, "Integralismo," 64–65. On the beginnings of one nucleus, see Corrêa, "Ação," 68–71, and appendix 4.

19. *Monitor Integralista* (São Paulo), 2, no. 1 (1st half Dec. 1933): 4, no. 3 (1st half Jan. 1934): 3, no. 4 (2d half Jan. 1934): 1, no. 5 (2d half Feb. 1934): 3; Broxson, 77–78.

20. *Monitor Integralista*, 3, nos. 3 (1st half Jan. 1934): 1 and 3, 5 (2d half Feb. 1934): 3, 7 (2d half Aug. 1934): 3–4, 10; Salgado, *Cartas*, 13, 15, 20; Araújo, 73–74, 87.

21. *Monitor Integralista*, 3, no. 5 (2d half Feb. 1934): 6.

22. Ibid., 3, no. 8 (1st half Dec. 1934): 2; Barroso, *O que o integralista*, 57–70. The title of this book may refer back to Dória's handbook for the Liga Nacionalista.

23. This information reflects the organizational structure as it evolved into the late 1930s. See Trindade, *Integralismo*, 180–95; Levine, *The Vargas Regime*, 84–85; Broxson, 81–83, 190–93; Reale, *Memórias*, 1: 81.

24. Corrêa, "Ação," 65–66; Broxson, 84; insignia in Integralismo File, Arquivo Leuenroth, IFCH/UNICAMP, Campinas.

25. Barroso, *O que o integralista*, 35–39, 43, 147; Salgado, *O que é o integralismo*, 27–29, 47, 66–67.

26. *Fon-Fon*, Nov. 4, 1933, p. 62, Dec. 28, 1935, p. 36; *Anauê!* (Rio de Janeiro), no. 20 (Oct. 1937): 9; *Ação* (São Paulo), Dec. 4, 1936, p. 3; *A Offensiva* (Rio de Janeiro, AO), July 16, 1937, p. 7; round picture in Integralismo File, Arquivo Leuenroth; number of periodicals in Salgado to Vargas, AAP 38.01.28, Serie ANL/AIB, in Augusto do Amaral Peixoto archive, Centro de Pesquisa e Documentação de História Contemporânea do Brasil da Fundação Getúlio Vargas (CPDOC/FGV), Rio de Janeiro.

27. The anti-AIB socialist newspaper *A Platéia* acknowledged the beauty and power of such practices; see Oct. 9, 1934, p. 3.

28. Trindade, *Integralismo*, 188; Barroso in *Fon-Fon*, Nov. 4, 1933, p. 62; *Anauê!*, no. 3 (Aug. 1935): 51; Reale in *OESP*, May 14, 1978, p. 14, and *Memórias*, 1: 78; *Correio da Manhã* (Rio de Janeiro, CM), June 24, 1934, p. 2.

29. Trindade, *Integralismo*, 186–88; Barroso, *O que o integralista*, 161–203, and chart on militia structure in appendix; Beloch and Abreu, 3: 2314–18; percentage in Broxson, 87 n. 1.

30. Dantas in *Ação*, Jan. 12, 1937, p. 4; Salgado, *A doutrina*, 180, 182; *CM*, Sept. 8, 1934, p. 5; box 59, case 606, Belmiro de Lima Valverde and others, Tribunal de Segurança Nacional, AN; Levine, *Vargas Regime*, 84, 86; Trindade, *Integralismo*, 187.

31. On these and other incidents, see *O Homem Livre* (Recife), July 5, 1934, p. 1, July 19, 1934, p. 1, July 27, 1934, pp. 1, 5, Aug. 2, 1934, p. 1; *A Plebe*, Nov. 4, 1933, p. 1, Nov. 18, 1933, p. 1, July 21, 1934, p. 4; *Vanguarda Estudantil* (São Paulo), n.d. [probably late 1933], p. 3; *AO*, July 12, 1934, p. 8, Aug. 23, 1934, pp. 2, 8.

32. Carone, *O P.C.B.*, 1: 172–81; Levine, *Vargas Regime*, 32–33, 60–65, 79 (figure on ANL members); Wolfe, *Working Women*, 51–52, 54; Spalding, *Organized Labor*, 180 (figure on unions); Pinheiro, 272.

33. Centro de Pesquisa, interview with Melo, 61; *AO*, Oct. 11, 1934, p. 3; *CM*, Oct. 4, 1934, p. 8; *OESP*, Oct. 4, 1934, 8.

34. On the incident, see Maffei; *CM*, Oct. 7, p. 5, Oct. 9, 1934, pp. 1, 3; *OESP*, Oct. 9, 1934, p. 8; *AO*, Oct. 11, 1934, pp. 1, 5, 7, 8, Nov. 22, 1934, p. 1; *A Platéia* (São Paulo), Oct. 5–6, 8–9, 1934; *A Plebe*, Sept. 29, 1934, p. 1, Oct. 13, 1934, pp. 1, 4; Brown, Rio de Janeiro, no. 1333, Oct. 9, 1934, 2657-K-70/11, U.S., RG 165.

35. *CM*, Oct. 10, 1934, p. 5.

36. *A Platéia*, Nov. 12, 1934, p. 1; Vargas to Aranha, Rio de Janeiro, OA 34.10.16/1, Oswaldo Aranha archive, CPDOC/FGV; Salgado in *AO*, Feb. 21, 1935, p. 1.

37. Partial text of the law in Carone, *A segunda república*, 58–64; Seeds, Petrópolis, no. 112, Apr. 7, 1935, A3834/120/6, Desp. no. 90E, FO 420/287; *AO*, Mar. 30, 1935, p. 1; Hilton, "Ação," 5; Broxson, 120.

38. Gertz, *O fascismo*, 112–13; Seeds, Petrópolis, Desp. no. 68, Mar. 10, 1935, no. 98, A 2993/120/6, FO 420/287; *CM*, Feb. 26–28 and Mar. 5, 1935, 2; *AO*, Feb. 28, 1935, pp. 1, 8, and Mar. 7, 1935, pp. 1, 3.

39. *CM*, Mar. 7–9, 1935; *Monitor Integralista* 3, no. 10 (May 7, 1935): 2.

40. *A Platéia*, Apr. 24, 1935, p. 1.

41. Gordon, Rio de Janeiro, no. 691, June 12, 1935, 832.00/953, and no. 704, June 20, 1935, 832.00/954, in U.S., Department of State, Records . . . Brazil, 1930–1939, National Archives microfilm copy 1472; Brown, Rio de Janeiro, Report 1466, June 12, 1935, 2657-K-70-15, U.S., RG 165; *CM*, June 10, 1935, pp. 1, 3, June 12–13, 1935; *AO*, June 12, 1935, p. 12.

42. Corrêa, "Ação," 55–59; *CM*, July 7, 1935, p. 3; Sackville, Rio de Janeiro, no. 1469, June 20, 1935, 2657-K-16, U.S., RG 165; Levine, *Vargas Regime*, 101–2.

43. Scotten, Rio de Janeiro, no. 750, Aug. 8, 1935, 832.00/960; Sackville, July 17, 1935, no. 1485, 2657-K-18, U.S., RG 165; *CM*, July 9, 1935, p. 6, and July 16, 1935, p. 4.

44. *AO*, Nov. 9, 1935, p. 1.

45. *Diário* (Nov. 1, 1935): 7223–26. Under Vargas's plan, occupational groupings chose some of the deputies to the constituent assembly and later the Congress—an indication of his corporatist leanings. These were known as class deputies.

46. The entire debate is in *Diário* (Nov. 20, 1935): 8008–16.

47. Sackville, no. 1568, Nov. 22, 1935, 2657-K-70/19, U.S., RG 165; *CM*, Nov. 17, 1935, p. 4, Nov. 19, 1935, p. 6, Nov. 21, 1935, p. 5.

48. *CM*, Nov. 22, 1935, p. 5; Hilton, *A rebelião*, 67, 70–73; José Nilo Tavares, "1935: Reavaliação de análise," in Tavares, 72–74.

49. Centro de Pesquisa, interview with Figueiredo, 20; Tavares, "1935," in Tavares, 84–91; Hilton, *A rebelião*, 97, 119; Levine, *Vargas Regime*, 122–33 (figures on 130).

50. On the corporatist thinkers, see E. Vieira; Medeiros; Needell, "History"; Schwartzman et al. See also Spalding, *Organized Labor*, 179–80; M. Pena, 155.

51. *AO*, Nov. 30, 1935, p. 1; Hilton, *A rebelião*, 119; Broxson, 147.

52. Sobrinho to Aranha, São Paulo, OA 35.08.20/2, Aranha archive, CPDOC/ FGV; Hilton, "Ação," 4–5, on the numbers of winning candidates. See also Mota to Dantas, Fortaleza, Aug. 21, 1935, box 24, packet 1, San Tiago Dantas archive, AN; *Monitor Integralista* 5, no. 22 (Oct. 7, 1937): 8.

53. Reale in *OESP*, May 14, 1978, p. 14; Reale, *Memórias*, 1: 82, 86; Reale, *Obras*, 1: 9; Melo, *A marcha*, 108–9. Rômulo Almeida, 37, divided AIB intellectuals differently.

54. Reale, *Obras*, 1: 9, and *Memórias*, 1: 63, 99; Melo, *A marcha*, 108–9.

55. On the family, see Barroso in *Panorama* 1, no. 1 (Jan. 1936): 10; Salgado, *A doutrina*, 34–36, and *O soffrimento*, 43; *Doutrina* 1, no. 2 (July 1937): 2; *Monitor Integralista* 5, no. 18 (Apr. 10, 1937): 4.

56. Cortines in *AO*, July 18, 1937, p. 12; use of word *endireitar* on AIB "currency" in Integralismo File, Arquivo Leuenroth.

57. *Ação*, Jan. 18, 1937, p. 4. This article referred to an account in *Acción Chilena*, noting that initially Nacismo attracted members of the bourgeoisie frightened by the Socialist Republic, but when the danger of communism receded they moved back into the liberal capitalist parties. For other statements distinguishing the AIB from reaction, see *O Integralista* (São Paulo) 4, no. 18 (Sept. 1936): 1; Barroso in *Fon-Fon*, Nov. 4, 1933, p. 60; Reale in *Ação*, Mar. 13, 1937, p. 4.

58. *AO*, May 31, 1934, p. 1, and Dec. 20, 1934, p. 1; Salgado, *O soffrimento*, 94.

59. Salgado, *A doutrina*, 21, and *O que é o integralismo*, 77; *Ação*, Jan. 8, 1937, p. 4.

60. Salgado, *O que é o integralismo*, 82–108.

61. Salgado in *A Idéia* (Aracati, Ceará), Dec. 15, 1935, p. 2; Viveiros, 29, 32; *A Platéia*, Sept. 29, 1934, p. 1.

62. *Panorama* 1, no. 3 (Mar. 1936): 26–30.

63. Salgado, *Cartas*, 92; Reale in *Obras*, 2: 264, and *Ação*, Nov. 7, 1936, p. 1; Almeida, 25–26, 35–36.

64. J. Venceslau Júnior, "O que significa 'Revolução Integralista,'" in *Enciclopédia do Integralismo*, 4: 67–69; Salgado, *Cartas*, 18, and *A doutrina*, 13–19, 24–25. See also Barroso in *O Sigma* (n.p.), July 6, 1935, Clippings File, Barroso archive, MHN; Araújo, esp. 63; Chasin, 494–515; Maio, "'Nem Rotschild,'" 117–21, 126. This thesis was published under the same title.

65. Fleming in *Província de Guanabara* (Rio de Janeiro) 1, no. 5 (June 13, 1937): 2, 8; Barroso, *O que o integralista*, 135–37. As Vasconcellos noted (p. 25), European fascists similarly opposed capitalism. See also Corbisier, 19.

66. Reale, *Obras*, 2: 83, 85–86.

67. Ibid., 2: 87, 115; Salgado in *AO*, Jan. 28, 1936, p. 12. This goal of freeing one's

nation from imperialism also characterized European fascism; see Zeev Sternhill, "Fascist Ideology," in Laqueur, 335.

68. Reale, *Obras*, 2: 236–38, 241–42, 248.

69. Ibid., 2: 239, 249–52, 273.

70. *Doutrina* 1, no. 2 (July 1937): 2–4; Victor Pujol, "O estado integralista," in *Enciclopédia do Integralismo*, 2: 134–35, 138 (quote); Villar in *AO*, July 3, 1937, p. 1. Compare this party program with the list of "what the Integralista wants" of 1934, described above.

71. *Ação*, Nov. 23, 1936, p. 3, Nov. 30, 1936, p. 4, Jan. 22, 1937, p. 4. Chasin, 607, noted that Salgado envisioned a nation of small rural holdings.

72. Barroso, *O que o integralista*, 71.

73. *AO*, Jan. 3, 1935, pp. 6, 8; *Ação*, Oct. 1, 1937, p. 11; *Anauê!*, no. 13 (Mar. 1937): 7, 56. Grant, 38, cites Pujol's story to show the Integralistas' regard for female intelligence and morality.

74. Reale, *Obras*, 2: 284–87; *AO*, Feb. 9, 1936, p. 16, July 4, 1937, p. 16; *Doutrina* 1, no. 2 (July 1937): 5; *Anauê* (Jaú, São Paulo), Aug. 22, 1935, p. 2; Barroso, *O que o integralista*, 26–28, 48–50, and *Integralismo*. On corporatist structures, see Reale, *Obras*, 3: 22–23, and *ABC*, 85–95. Despite the similarities between some of these reforms and those passed at the national level in the early 1930s, Integralistas criticized Vargas's measures, including the eight-hour day, for ignoring workers' needs, promoting individualism and class struggle, and favoring employers. See *AO*, July 5, 1934, p. 7; Reale, *Obras*, 3: 51; *Ação*, Oct. 12, 1936, pp. 1–2; Barroso, *O que o integralista*, 55. For industrialists' views of Vargas's labor legislation, see Weinstein, 60–63.

75. *Século XX* (Rio de Janeiro), Dec. 17, 1935, p. 3; *AO*, Jan. 24, 1935, p. 6, and Feb. 7, 1935, p. 8.

76. *Anauê!*, no. 15 (May 1937): 9; Mota in *Ação*, Apr. 14, 1937, p. 4; *AO*, Feb. 7, 1935, p. 8; Reale in *Anauê* (Jaú), Aug. 22, 1935, 2. See also *A Tribuna* (Mococa, São Paulo), Nov. 22, 1934, p. 2.

77. Broxson, 218–21, 225 n. 1; *AO*, Jan. 28, 1936, p. 12.

78. *AO*, Aug. 25, 1936, p. 6, Dec. 6, 1936, pp. 1, 9, Dec. 8–9, 1936, Dec. 11, 1936, p. 9; *Ação*, Dec. 7, 1936, p. 1; Carone, *A segunda república*, 320–22.

79. *CM*, June 8, 1937, pp. 3–4; *AO*, June 8, 1937, p. 2; *Ação*, June 17, 1937, p. 1; Moreira to Dantas, Fortaleza, Sept. 9, 1937, box 25, packet 1, Dantas archive, AN. On those who left the AIB, and the attacks, see Clippings, Integralismo File, Arquivo Leuenroth; *Diário de São Paulo*, June 15, 1937, and June 18–20, 1937; *Ação*, June 21, 1937, pp. 4, 6. I found no evidence that Mota joined the Communists; he did, however, return to the army and become a general.

80. For example, see Oliveira in *A Ordem*, nos. 11 (Jan. 1931): 44–52, and 41–42 (July–Aug. 1933): 555–56; Santos in *A Ordem*, no. 10 (Dec. 1930): 250. See also Lima in *Diário de São Paulo*, Oct. 27, 1936, p. 6; A. Franco, 28. Franco's book was part of the nationalist, petit-bourgeois Coleção Azul. After 1945 he became a prominent member of the conservative anti-Vargas National Democratic Union (UDN) party.

Oliveira founded the reactionary Tradição, Família, e Propiedad in 1960; see *La Nación* (Buenos Aires), Dec. 9, 1995, p. 10.

81. Foster, Dec. 13, 1937, São Paulo, Report 106, 832.00 Nazi/9; Lesser, *Welcoming*, 179–80; Levine, "Brazil's Jews," 47–48; Henrique Rattner, "Economic and Social Mobility of Jews in Brazil," in Elkin and Merkx, 190–91.

82. *Civilização* (São Paulo), June 23, 1934, n.p., and *Diário de Minas*, Oct. 23, 1937, n.p., Clippings File, Barroso archive, MHN; on Barroso's life, see Maio, "Nem Rotschild," 47–82.

83. Among Barroso's many works, see *O que o integralista*, 127–29; *Integralismo*, 24, 114; *Judaísmo*, 10–12, 21, 24–25, 59, 61–63, 65, 67, 101, 105, 129, 154; *Roosevelt*, esp. 27–35; Barroso in *AO*, Aug. 3, 1935, p. 2. See also Maio, "'Nem Rotschild,'" 83–121; Carneiro, 354–74. Gilberto Freyre's resistance to modernity also accounted for his antisemitism, according to Needell, "Identity," 73–75.

84. Barroso, *Brasil*, 48, 132; Barroso, *O que o integralista*, 133; *Protocolos dos Sabios de Sião*. See also Schulman, 36–42; Levisky, 7–20; *Diário da Noite* (Belo Horizonte), Aug. 16, 1935, n.p., and *AO*, Aug. 11, 1935, n.p., both in Clippings File, Barroso archive, MHN.

85. *AO*, Dec. 13, 1934, pp. 1, 4; see also Reale, *Obras*, 2: 281. On Jews in the AIB, see Gertz, *O fascismo*, 191.

86. Reale, *Obras*, 1: 177–82, 2: 236 n. 1, 251; *Panorama* 1, no. 6 (June 1936): 18.

87. Reale, *ABC*, 44, 98, 102, 118.

88. Glickman, "The Image," 94; *Aço Verde* (São Paulo), July 6, 1935, pp. 1–2; Salgado, *Cartas*, 113, 120, and *A doutrina*, 44, 119, 120, 124, 127.

89. Lipiner, 142–43; Lesser, *Welcoming*, 61; *AO*, Dec. 13, 1934, p. 4; *Diário de São Paulo*, Dec. 2, 1934, p. 12.

90. *Panorama* 1, nos. 4–5 (Apr.–May 1936): 3–5. This clause on a Jewish homeland helps explain why many rightists would support the state of Israel.

91. Barroso to Salgado, Rio de Janeiro, Pi 36.10.10/1, Correspondence, Salgado collection, APHMRC; *Diário de São Paulo*, May 1, 1936, p. 3; May 14, 1936, p. 3; June 14, 1936, p. 11; June 16, 1936, p. 4; June 18, 1936, p. 3; Levine, *Vargas Regime*, 89. See also unpaginated clippings from *Diário da Noite* (Rio de Janeiro), Apr. 13, 1936, Apr. 16, 1936, May 16, 1936, June 10, 1936, Mar. 27, 1937; *Século XX*, Mar. 19, 1936, Mar. 24, 1936, Apr. 21, 1936; *Estado de Minas*, Mar. 24, 1937, in Clippings File, Barroso archive, MHN. Like Freitas, Salgado also had good relations with some Jews, such as Horácio Lafer, a Paulista industrialist. See Maio, "'Nem Rotschild,'" 76.

92. Trindade, *Integralismo*, 161–62, and interview with Wagner, 5. See also Trindade, interview with Corbisier, 19.

93. I found full runs of major periodicals of Rio de Janeiro and São Paulo, like *AO*, *Ação*, *Panorama*, and *Anauê!*, but only isolated issues of papers from smaller cities and towns. Full runs of the minor publications might have provided even more evidence of antisemitism. Integralista periodicals are housed in the Biblioteca Nacional and Casa Rui Barbosa (Rio de Janeiro), Arquivo do Estado (São Paulo),

Arquivo Leuenroth (IFCH/UNICAMP), and APHMRC. Antisemitic works include Maciel; Venceslau Júnior, 139–46; Pompeo; d'Albuquerque; Gouvêa.

94. Coote, Rio de Janeiro, Desp. no. 323, Oct. 3, 1936, FO 420/288, no. 64, A 8431/68/6; *AO*, July 19, 1934, p. 3; *Jewish Daily* (New York), Apr. 3, 1934, n.p., Clippings File, Barroso archive, MHN; Lesser, "Immigration," and *Welcoming*. See also Pena to Carulla, Rio de Janeiro, Pi 37.09.16/1; Pena to Carulla, Pi 37.09.23/1; Pena to Silveyra, Pi 37.11.03/1, Correspondence, Salgado collection, APHMRC.

95. Maciel, 146; *Ação*, Jan. 15, 1937, p. 4. Andrews, in "Brazilian Racial Democracy," 486, concludes that the AIB was born in São Paulo, the state most affected by immigration, because of xenophobia. As noted below, however, the AIB recruited heavily among certain immigrant groups, including Italians.

96. *Ação*, Dec. 23, 1936, p. 4; Reale, *Obras*, 3: 33–34; Salgado, *Despertemos*, 40, 46, 51; Borba, 18; *Anauê!*, nos. 2 (May 1935): 15, and 10 (May 1936): 14–19; Lesser, "Immigration," 29–30, and *Welcoming*, 86; Borges, "Puffy," 255; Needell, "History."

97. *Aço Verde*, June 6, 1935, p. 3; Barroso in *AO*, Aug. 3, 1935, p. 3; *Ação*, May 14, 1937, p. 1; Andrews, *Blacks*, 147–55; Levine, "First Afro-Brazilian Congress," 186; Butler, 198, 200.

98. Viana to Aranha, OA 35.11.09/2, Aranha archive, CPDOC/FGV; Seitenfus, 56; Lauerhass, 207. National population estimates are found in Wilkie et al., 106–7; membership estimates for Nacistas and Nacionalistas are from note 168 of the previous chapter. The Sinarquista movement of Mexico may have been larger than Integralismo, but it is unclear whether it was fascist; see Meyer, 44, 130–33, 148–49.

99. Trindade, *Integralismo*, 144–46, 150–51; Gertz, *O fascismo*, 168–69; Muhlberger.

100. Gertz, *O fascismo*, 197–98; Trindade, *Integralismo*, 152–53; *Anauê!*, no. 2 (May 1935): cover; *O Integralista* 3, no. 5 (June 1935): 2, 3. See also *Monitor Integralista* 5, no. 18 (Apr. 10, 1937): 4.

101. *AO*, May 17, 1934, p. 2; *Quarta Humanidade* (Itajuba, Minas Gerais), Sept. 7, 1935, p. 4; *O Homem Livre*, Sept. 8, 1934, p. 3. On Barroso, see *O Globo*, Oct. 9, 1934, n.p.; *Jornal do Povo*, Oct. 11, 1934, n.p.; *AO*, Oct. 11, 1934, n.p., all in Clippings File, Barroso archive, MHN. I thank Barbara Weinstein for helping me decipher this phrase.

102. Reale, *Obras*, 2: 100–101; Salgado cited in *O Homem Livre*, July 5, 1934, p. 1; *A Voz d'Oeste* (Riberão Preto, São Paulo), July 5, 1934, p. 1. See also *O Integralista* 3, no. 5 (June 1935): 2; Dantas, *AO*, Oct. 25, 1934, p. 2.

103. *Fon-Fon*, Dec. 30, 1933, p. 36; *AO*, May 24, 1934, p. 8, and June 28, 1934, p. 1; Trindade, interview with Corbisier, 3; figure in Broxson, 197.

104. Trindade, interviews with Corbisier, 3, and with Wagner, 1; *AO*, July 4, 1937, p. 15; *Anauê!*, nos. 15 (May 1937): 58–59, 16 (June 1937): 10, 59, and 18 (Aug. 1937): 62.

105. Trindade, *Integralismo*, 160; *Anauê!*, no. 11 (July 1936): 26, Perez in no. 21 (Nov. 1937): 49; *Panorama* 1, no. 1 (Jan. 1936): 10–11; *AO*, June 16, 1935, p. 5.

106. Margarida Corbisier praised the "virgin potentiality" of young men in *Enciclopédia do Integralismo*, 5: 55–60; see also Vasconcellos, 29–30.

107. *Anauê!*, no. 21 (Nov. 1937): 49; Barroso, *Integralismo*, 284; Salgado in *AO*, Jan. 17, 1935, p. 1.

108. C. Salgado in *Província de Guanabara*, Apr. 19, 1937, p. 2; Henriques in *AO*, Oct. 11, 1936, p. 15.

109. Trindade, interviews with Wagner, 1, and with Corbisier, 1–2, 14; *AO*, Jan. 1, 1937, p. 4; *Anauê!*, nos. 15 (May 1937): 58–59, 16 (June 1937): 10, 18 (Aug. 1937): 62; *Brasil Feminino* (Rio de Janeiro), no. 36 (June 1937): 32–33.

110. *Monitor Integralista* 5, no. 19 (May 12, 1937): 4.

111. Hahner, *Emancipating*, 175. Founded by Ribeiro in 1932, *Brasil Feminino* had favored the vote and greater freedoms for women without removing them from the home; its official adoption of Integralismo did not entail a change in views. On its orientation, see 1, no. 2 (Mar. 1932): 5. *AO* started its weekly Blusa Verde page in September 1936; *Anauê!* had significant female-oriented content from its inception.

112. Perez in *Anauê!*, nos. 11 (July 1936): 8, and 12 (Sept. 1936): 31; Esteves in 1 (Jan. 1935): n.p. See also *AO*, Sept. 8, 1936, p. 1.

113. These views were not terribly different from those of most Brazilian writers; see Besse. Moreover, ads for higher education appeared in the women's sections of AIB periodicals; see Grant, 40. See also Perez in *Anauê!*, no. 11 (July 1936): 8; Albuquerque in *Brasil Feminino*, no. 38 (Nov. 1937): 22–23; and *Monitor Integralista* 4, no. 16 (Dec. 5, 1936): 6; *AO*, Sept. 8, 1936, p. 1. In the 1940s Salgado added that one need not have children in order to be a mother; the important thing was that a woman use her maternal feelings. His view of women working outside the home as biologically abnormal, however, was much more conservative than those expressed in this paragraph. See Salgado, *A mulher*, 73–75, 94.

114. *Monitor Integralista* 4, no. 16 (Dec. 5, 1936): 5–6; *AO*, Jan. 17, 1937, p. 13; *Anauê!*, nos. 2 (May 1935): 26, 15 (May 1937): 41, 19 (Sept. 1937): 49, 22 (Dec. 1937): 32–33; *Brasil Feminino*, no. 38 (Nov. 1937): 15, (Salgado) 21, 33. Despite its view of Hollywood films, ads for them appeared in *AO*, as Grant points out, 18, 45.

115. The AIB press regularly reported on female activities. See, especially, *AO*, Jan. 3, 1937, p. 15, July 18, 1937, p. 12; *Brasil Feminino*, no. 38 (Nov. 1937): 24; *Monitor Integralista* 2, no. 8 (1st half Dec. 1934): 8. The AIB's national secretariat of social assistance was, however, separate from the women's secretariat.

116. *Brasil Feminino*, no. 38 (Nov. 1937): 31; *Monitor Integralista* 2, no. 8 (1st half Dec. 1934): 9; *Anauê!*, no. 10 (May 1936): 12; *AO*, Aug. 23, 1934, Nov. 29, 1934, p. 4, p. 8, Dec. 6, 1934, p. 4, Jan. 24, 1935, p. 4, Mar. 23, 1935, p. 5, June 15, 1935, p. 8, June 10, 1937, p. 3.

117. *AO*, Oct. 3, 1936, p. 1, Oct. 16–18, 1936; June 25, 1937, p. 1.

118. Hahner, *Emancipating*, 144–61; Besse, 164–78.

119. *AO*, Oct. 17, 1936, p. 5, May 1, 1937, pp. 1, 2, Jan. 17, 1937, p. 13, June 12, 1937, p. 1; *Ação*, Oct. 7, 1937, p. 13; *Brasil Feminino*, no. 36 (June 1937): 25.

120. *Enciclopédia do Integralismo*, 9: 56, 67–68; *AO*, Oct. 11, 1936, p. 15, Oct. 17, 1936, p. 4; Perez in *Anauê!*, no. 19 (Sept. 1937): 58.

121. Bittencourt in *AO*, Jan. 17, 1937, p. 13; *Anauê!*, no. 4 (Oct. 1935): 29; *Brasil Fem-*

inino, nos. 36 (June 1937): 22, 46, and 38 (Nov. 1937): 1, 8. See also Salgado in *AO,* Oct. 17, 1936, p. 2; Viveiros, 79–80. These notions resembled the Catholic feminism described in Besse, 183–90.

122. Martins, 20; Reale, *Memórias,* 1: 88; *Ação,* Dec. 23, 1936, p. 4, and Oct. 17, 1937, p. 18; Pagano in *Panorama* 1, no. 11 (1936): 12–17; *Diário de São Paulo,* June 18, 1936, p. 7; Whitehead, Rio de Janeiro, no. 90, Apr. 2, 1936, C-10-N, 15991-G, U.S., RG 38; Broxson, 94.

123. Pessôa, 248–49, 255–56; Viveiros, 78–79; *AO,* Sept. 1, 1936, p. 2, Sept. 8, 1936, pp. 1, 4, Oct. 16, 1936, p. 2; *Ação,* Dec. 1, 1936, p. 1; *Diário de São Paulo,* Sept. 10, 1936, p. 5; box 38, folder 76 (b) Ligas: Liga da Defesa Nacional, Freitas archive, AN. During the Estado Novo, the LDN tilted toward democracy; see Centro de Pesquisa, interview with Leal, 114–18.

124. *A Província* (Bahia), June 8, 1935, p. 8; *AO,* Mar. 8, 1936, p. 3, Oct. 15, 1936, p. 5; *Ação,* Jan. 19, 1937, p. 4; box 5, folder 105 (c) Sociedades: Sociedade dos Amigos de Alberto Torres, Freitas archive, AN; Lima Sobrinho, 510, 513–15; Centro de Pesquisa, interview with Lima Sobrinho, 124–26, 130–31.

125. Reale in *Panorama* 1, no. 6 (June 1936): 11–18, and *Ação,* Jan. 9, 1937, p. 1; *Anauê!,* no. 3 (Aug. 1935): 20, 27; Maciel, 146–47; Vasconcellos, 47–48, 50. Barroso was more approving of German racial views than other Integralistas; see Borba, 18.

126. Brazil, Santa Catarina, 147–48, photos between 154 and 155, 163; Letter Pi 36.07.05/1, Correspondence, Salgado collection, AHPMRC; União Nacional dos Estudantes in ACF 006f, Aidano do Couto Ferraz archive, CPDOC/FGV; *CM,* Aug. 26, 1937, p. 4; *Diário* (Aug. 24, 1937): 39976–78; *AO,* Oct. 12, 1935, p. 3, Feb. 9, 1936, p. 9; *Panorama* 1, no. 7 (July 1936): 58; Gertz, *O fascismo,* 112, 187, 194, 197. On AIB relations with the Italian government, see Ciano, 30; Seitenfus, 116–22; Trento, 1601–11. On AIB relations with Nazis, see Hilton, "Ação," 12–13; Gertz, *O fascismo,* 156–58, 188, 193; Gertz, "Influéncia." The AIB maintained friendly ties with Nacistas and Nacionalistas through its national secretariat of external relations; see Correspondence, Salgado collection, APHMRC.

127. *CM,* Sept. 11, 1936, p. 7; *Diário* (Sept. 9, 1936): 16835–36, (Sept. 16, 1936): 17152–57; *AO,* May 27, 1936, pp. 1, 2, Sept. 1, 1936, p. 4, Oct. 21, 1936, p. 1, Feb. 17, 1937, p. 1, May 4, 1937, p. 1; Ray, Porto Alegre, no. 27, Sept. 8, 1937, 832.00/1051; and especially Gertz, "Nazismo," and *O fascismo,* 112, 166–67, 183.

128. *Diário* (Sept. 16, 1936): 17152; *AO,* Jan. 31, 1936, p. 3, July 3, 1936, p. 1; *CM,* Feb. 11, 1936, p. 3, and Feb. 12, 1936, pp. 3, 5.

129. Lacerda; *CM,* Sept. 6, 1936, p. 2, and Sept. 8, 1936, p. 9; *AO,* Feb. 9, 1936, p. 9; Coote, Rio de Janeiro, Desp. no. 323, Oct. 3, 1936, no. 64 A 8431/68/6, FO 420/288; *Diário* (Sept. 9, 1936): 16848, (Sept. 12, 1936): 16970–71, (Sept. 15, 1936): 17095–98, 17107–10, (Sept. 23, 1936): 17619–20; Centro de Pesquisa, interview with Magalhães, 149–50; Pang, 195–201. I thank Eul-Soo Pang for his insight on Bahia as a model.

130. Centro de Pesquisa, interview with Magalhães, 150.

131. *AO,* June 25, 1937, p. 1; *CM,* Mar. 19, 1937, p. 3; *Jornal do Commércio,* Feb. 3, 1937, p. 3; *Diário* (Mar. 20, 1937): 28161, 28196–97.

132. The entire debate is found in *Diário* (Sept. 4, 1936): 16483–88, (Sept. 5, 1936): 16523–26, (Sept. 9, 1936): 16834–37, 16848–50, (Sept. 12, 1936): 16970–75, (Sept. 15, 1936): 17095–98, 17107–19, (Sept. 16, 1936): 17152–62, (Sept. 21, 1936): 17518, (Sept. 23, 1936): 17618–22.

133. Aside from ibid., see *CM*, Sept. 9, 1936, p. 4; D'Araújo, 35.

134. *Diário de São Paulo*, Oct. 20, 1936, pp. 1, 6; *Diário* (Apr. 27, 1937): 29735–37.

135. *A União*, Dec. 30, 1934, n.p., Clippings File, Barroso archive, MHN; Reale, *Obras*, 3: 34–35; Barroso, *Integralismo*. Araújo, 82–83, found the Catholic spiritual "revolution" far more elitist than the AIB's version.

136. Salgado in *Anauê!*, no. 18 (Aug. 1937): 11. For claims similar to Salgado's, see Barroso, *Integralismo*; Ação Integralista Brasileira.

137. Sackville, Rio de Janeiro, no. 1485, July 17, 1935, 2657-K-70-18, U.S., RG 165; Salgado, *O integralismo perante a nação*, 104–7; *Ação*, Nov. 10, 1936, p. 1; July 29, 1937, p. 1; Nov. 11, 1937, p. 5; *AO*, Apr. 21, 1936, p. 4; *A Idéia* (Aracati, Ceará), Dec. 15, 1935, p. 1; Williams, "Integralism," 443–45; Lustosa, "A igreja e o integralismo," 518–20; Broxson, 214.

138. *Anauê!*, no. 6 (Jan. 1936): 15; *Ação*, Oct. 28, 1936, p. 1, and Aug. 9, 1937, pp. 1, 3; *AO*, Aug. 21, p. 3, and Oct. 6, 1937, p. 3; *Enciclopédia do Integralismo*, 5: 73–75; Trindade, interview with Corbisier, 4–5, 8; Williams, "Integralism," 442.

139. *Monitor Integralista* 5, no. 18 (Apr. 10, 1937): 12; *Ação*, Oct. 8, 1936, pp. 1–2, Oct. 9, 1936, p. 3, Oct. 7, 1937, p. 12; *AO*, Sept. 20, 1936, pp. 9–10. This ritual became part of the celebration of the founding of the AIB with its fourth anniversary. For an observer's opinion of it, see Centro de Pesquisa, interview with Chagas, 61.

140. *Monitor Integralista* 5, no. 18 (Apr. 10, 1937): 6–14; *Diário* (Sept. 12, 1936): 16974; *Anauê!*, nos. 6 (1st half Jan. 1936): 3–5, 13, 20 (Oct. 1937): cover, no. 22 (Dec. 1937): 26; Trindade, interview with Corbisier, 14; Araújo, 63.

141. *A Ordem*, nos. 58 (Dec. 1934): 405–13, 59 (Jan. 1935): 5–15, 60 (Feb. 1935): 81–86, 65 (July 1935): 5–14. The AIB press testified to the presence of at least three Integralista Protestant ministers.

142. *Diário de São Paulo*, Oct. 23, 1936, pp. 1, 6, and Oct. 27, 1936, p. 6; *A Ordem* 59, no. 5 (May 1958): 59–61.

143. Lima, 133–53; Williams, "Politicization"; A. Gomes, 96–97 (statistic), 103–8; Santo Rosário, 302–34; José Oscar Beozzo, "A igreja entre a revolução de 1930, o Estado Novo e a redemocratização," in Fausto, *O Brasil republicano*, 4: 301–15, 321–24.

144. *Unitas* (Porto Alegre) 18, nos. 3–4 (Mar.–Apr. 1931): 229; *O Século* (São Paulo), Nov. 12, 1933, p. 1, and Nov. 26, 1933, p. 1; *O Legionário* (São Paulo), Feb. 2, 1936, p. 3; *Diário* (Nov. 20, 1935): 8010; *CM*, Feb. 7, 1936, p. 3; Carone, *A segunda república*, 306–8; *Semana Religiosa* (Porto Alegre), May 18, 1935, p. 1–2; *Ação*, Feb. 8, 1937, p. 3; *AO*, May 27, 1936, p. 2.

145. Williams, "Integralism," 448–49.

146. *AO*, Feb. 14, 1935, p. 8, July 24, 1937, p. 2, July 25, 1937, p. 9; *Aço Verde*, May 30, 1935, p. 3; Pompeo, 26; *Jornal do Povo* (Ponte Nova, Minas Gerais), Oct. 27, 1935, n.p., Clippings File, Barroso archive, MHN; *O Legionário*, June 23, 1935, p. 1.

147. Trindade, interview with Corbisier, 24; *O A.U.C.* (São Paulo), no. 16 (July 1935): 3; *O Legionário*, Sept. 2, 1934, p. 1, Oct. 10, 1937, pp. 1–2; Linhares, 49; container 486, document 9, José Carlos de Macedo Soares collection, IHGB; *A Ordem* 59, no. 2 (Feb. 1958): 99; *AO*, Sept. 13, 1934, p. 2.

148. *AO*, Sept. 13, 1934, p. 2; Montenegro, 26, 29, 32; Williams, "Integralism," 445. The sources differ on Câmara's degree of success in resisting Leme.

149. *Variedades* (São Paulo), Oct. 1933, p. 2; Salgado in *AO*, Dec. 20, 1934, p. 4; Santos in *Panorama* 1, no. 12 (1937): 27; *Anauê!*, nos. 3 (Aug. 1935): 7, and 4 (Oct. 1935): 8; *A Ordem* 59, no. 5 (May 1958): 61.

150. Beozzo, "A igreja," in Fausto, *O Brasil republicano*, 4: 320–21, emphasized the ties to the state; Williams, "Integralism," 447, 449–50, the friendship with the AIB; and Lustosa, "A igreja e o integralismo," 512–13, 528, disagreement within the hierarchy leading to paralysis.

151. The Workers' Party of Brazil, of leftist orientation, it seems, asked the Superior Electoral Tribunal to cancel its political party registration on the grounds that the AIB was a denationalizing and extremist force, but the court rejected the petition in June 1936. See *AO*, Apr. 12, 1936, p. 11, and June 2, 1936, pp. 1, 4.

152. Foster, São Paulo, no. 78, July 19, 1937, 832.00/1041; *AO*, July 20–21, 1937; *CM*, July 20–22, 1937.

153. *AO*, Aug. 17, 1937, p. 1, and Aug. 21, 1937, pp. 1, 3; *CM*, Aug. 17–20, 1937; Ray, Porto Alegre, no. 19, Aug. 13, 1937, 832.00/1050; Scotten, Rio de Janeiro, no. 5, Aug. 25, 1937, 832.00/1046; D'Araújo, 86.

154. Scotten, no. 5, Aug. 25, 1937, 832.00/1046; *CM*, Aug. 21–22, 1937, and Aug. 25, 1937, p. 4; *Diário* (Aug. 21, 1937): 39655–56, (Aug. 24, 1937): 39973–76, (Aug. 26, 1937): 40251–52. The Chefe claimed that Soares's statements contradicted his previously expressed sympathies for the Sigma, which the minister denied. See *CM*, Aug. 24, 1937, p. 5.

155. Centro de Pesquisa, interview with Peixoto, 282; Reale, *Memórias*, 1: 79; *Doutrina* 1, no. 2 (July 1937): 3; *Ação*, Jan. 12, 1937, p. 4, and Aug. 6, 1937, p. 1; *Anauê*, no. 20 (Oct. 1937): 52; *AO*, Oct. 25, 1934, p. 3, and Nov. 1, 1934, p. 1; Broxson, 58; V. Costa, 23.

156. Mota to Dantas, Rio de Janeiro, Apr. 16, 1935, box 24, packet 1, Dantas archive, AN; V. Costa, 22; Broxson, 200, 214; Hilton, "Ação," 14; Trento, 1610; *AO*, Jan. 3, 1936, p. 1; Processo no. 606, box 59, vol. 2, cases 266–67, Tribunal de Segurança Nacional, AN; Centro de Pesquisa, interview with Peixoto, 282; Scotten, no. 126, Nov. 6, 1937, 832.00/1083.

157. *AO*, Feb. 14, 1935, p. 8, and Feb. 2, 1936, p. 1; Centro de Pesquisa, interview with Peixoto, 259, 284, 295; *Diário da Noite*, July 4, 1935, n.p., Clippings File, Barroso archive, MHN; Reale, *Memórias*, 1: 119; *Monitor Integralista*, no. 1 (1st half Dec. 1933): 1; *Anauê!*, no. 13 (Mar. 1937): 50; *CM*, Sept. 8, 1934, p. 5.

158. Mitchell, Rio de Janeiro, No. 1722, Oct. 20, 1936, 2657-K-70/43, U.S., RG 165; *Diário* (Sept. 16, 1936): 17155; Silvado in *CM*, Apr. 8, 1936, n.p., Livro de Recortes,

US-20-5, 35–36; *Ação* (Riberão Preto, São Paulo), Jan. 8, 1935, p. 3; Carvalho, "Armed Forces," 208, 217; Góes Monteiro to Vargas, 34.01.04, 0747/1–0757/2, Getúlio Vargas archive, CPDOC/FGV; Reale, *Memórias*, 1: 123.

159. Centro de Pesquisa, interview with Trigueiro, 106; Carvalho, "Armed Forces," 210–11, 218; Hilton, "Ação," 20.

160. See the Centro de Pesquisa interviews with Almeida, 167, Lima Sobrinho, 131, and Peixoto, 298. See also Scotten, no. 1382, May 15, 1937, 832.00/1027.

161. Fliers, container 695, folder 7, and container 697, folder 5, Instituto Histórico collection, IHGB; Lenharo, 190–91; *CM*, Nov. 12, 1937, p. 2, and Nov. 13, 1937, p. 10; Beloch and Abreu, 2: 1059.

162. Scotten, no. 1420, June 19, 1937, 832.00/1038; Salgado to Vargas, AAP 38.01.28, ANL/AIB, Augusto do Amaral Peixoto archive, CPDOC/FGV.

163. *AO*, Oct. 1–2, 1937; Camargo et al., 214–20.

164. *AO*, Nov. 2, 1937, p. 1; Scotten, no. 126, Nov. 6, 1937, 832.00/1083; Caffery, Rio de Janeiro, no. 455, Mar. 28, 1938, 832.00/1183; Broxson, 278, 280.

165. Viana to Aranha, Rio de Janeiro, OA 37.10.30/3, Aranha archive, CPDOC/FGV; Salgado to Vargas, AAP 38.01.28, ANL/AIB, Peixoto archive, CPDOC/FGV; *CM*, Dec. 4, 1937, p. 14, Dec. 7, 1937, p. 2, Jan. 19, 1938, pp. 4, 14; *OESP*, May 14, 1978, p. 14; Camargo et al., 199; vol. 2, case 146, Gustavo Barroso, Tribunal de Segurança Nacional, AN.

166. See Letters to Aranha from Leães Sobrinho, São Paulo, OA 34.11.12, Viana, Rio de Janeiro, OA 35.11.09/2, and Silveira, Rio de Janeiro, OA 35.11.26/2, Aranha archive, CPDOC/FGV; Centro de Pesquisa, interview with Lima Sobrinho, 131–32. See also *OESP*, May 14, 1978, p. 15; Reale, *Memórias*, 1: 121–24; Letters Pi 38.01.30/1 and 38.01.31/1, Correspondence, Salgado collection, APHMRC.

167. Cavalcanti to Dutra, GV 37.12.02, 0843/1–0844/2, and "Convem Saber," GV 37.12.35, 0869/1, Vargas archive, CPDOC/FGV; Carvalho, "Armed Forces," 209; Levine, *Vargas Regime*, 178.

168. Dulles, *Vargas*, 181–94; Reale, *Memórias*, 1: 127, 129; Trento, 1610, 1612; Centro de Pesquisa, interview with Magalhães, 152; vol. 1, case 15, Tribunal de Segurança Nacional, AN; Mitchell, no. 2093, May 12, 1938, 2657-K-70/65, U.S., RG 165; Scotten, no. 415, Mar. 14, 1938, 832.00/1179; Ray, Porto Alegre, no. 80, May 27, 1938, 835.00 Nazi/43; Caffery, Rio de Janeiro, no. 581, May 12, 1938, and no. 591, May 16, 1938, 832.00 Revolutions/604 and 607. No evidence surfaced of Italian or German involvement in the coups, although some plotters sought refuge in the Italian embassy.

Chapter 12 Conclusion

1. R. Griffin, 44–45.

2. As Manuel Seoane wrote, fascists in South America "fall in the hands of the right which winds up controlling them." See *Hoy*, no. 272 (Feb. 4, 1937): 12–13 (quote on 12).

The Legacy

1. Channel 13, Santiago, Chile, Oct. 9, 1989. One could argue, however, that the diehard pro-Pinochet Independent Democratic Union (UDI) is proud of its right-wing identity.

2. For tracking the careers of Integralistas and Nacistas after 1938, I have relied heavily on the indispensable Beloch and Abreu, in the Brazilian biographical section, and works in the Chilean biographical section of the bibliography, respectively. While concentrating on extreme right-wing women during the Allende years, Power describes prior female involvement in such movements. For other sources on rightist women, see below, notes 5 and 16.

3. Although not the focus of this chapter, changes in the moderate right since 1939 are worthy of study. I thank Charles Bergquist for his observations on the cold war and the right.

4. On the evolution of extreme rightist groups, see Maldonado Prieto, "AChA," and "Grupos"; Fariña Vicuña, "El pensamiento"; Ramírez Necochea, "El fascismo"; Bicheno; *Estanquero*, esp. no. 1 (Nov. 16, 1946); Fernández; Valdivia Ortiz de Zárate, "Nacionalismo e ibañismo," "El nacionalismo chileno," and "Camino," 9–26; Arnello Romo; Etchepare and Stewart, 594.

5. Correa S., 15–19; Burnett, 180, 263, 274–75; Scully, 107–8; Drake, "Corporatism," 110–14. On the women, see Power; Crummett; Mattelart; Rojas Mira, "Construyendo un lugar," 206–12.

6. Guarello; Lux; Mayorga, "Alessandri," 18–19; Recabarren Valenzuela, 15; Alliende González, 180–81; Etchepare and Stewart, 592–94, 598.

7. Ramírez Necochea, "El fascismo," 27–29, 32–33; Cristi and Ruiz, esp. 105, 109, 119–20, 125–28; Sigmund, 30–31, 93; Valdés; Margaret E. Crahan, "National Security Ideology and Human Rights," in Crahan, 106–7.

8. Cristi and Ruiz, 136–39.

9. Ibid., 140–57, offer Mario Góngora as an example of a recalcitrant rightist statist. On criticism by former Nacis, see Etchepare and Stewart, 594–95.

10. Constable and Valenzuela, 287–89, 297, 299, 315–16; Alan Angell, "Chile since 1958," in Bethell, *Chile*, 197–98; *Cosas: Una Revista Internacional*, no. 227 (June 13, 1985): 11–13; Scully, 194–95.

11. *Miami Herald*, Dec. 30, 1993; *Latin American Weekly Report* (London) Mar. 24, 1994, p. 124, and Apr. 28, 1994, p. 180; Timothy R. Scully, "Reconstituting Party Politics in Chile," in Mainwaring and Scully, 128–31.

12. Campos Menéndez, esp. 244–45; *La Época* (Santiago), Aug. 18, 1987, p. 24.

13. Reale, *Memorias*, 1: 165; Levine, *Vargas Regime*, 166–75. On the Estado Novo, see also Lenharo; Loewenstein; Oliveira, Velloso, and Gomes; Schwartzman, Bomeny, and Costa; Wolfe, "'Father,'" 84–87, and "Faustian Bargain"; Salgado, *O integralismo na vida*, 64–85; Marilena Chaui, "Notas sobre o pensamento conservador nos anos 30: Plínio Salgado," in Morães, Antunes, and Ferrante, 35.

14. Lesser, *Welcoming*, 96–171.

15. Carone, *A terceira república*, 462; Corbisier, 19; Almeida, 37–39; *Diário de Notícias* (Rio de Janeiro), Sept. 27, 1942, section 1, 5, Oct. 1, 1942, section 1, 5, Oct. 4, 1942, section 1, 5, Oct. 8, 1942, section 1, 5, Oct. 11, 1942, section 1, 5, 8, Oct. 18, 1942, section 1, 5; *OESP*, Feb. 1, 1942, 8; Dantas, "Rompimento com o Integralismo" file, Oct. 6, 1942, in Dantas archive, box 30, packet 2, "Papéis Políticos," AN.

16. Dreifus; Skidmore, *Politics*; on women, see Simões.

17. On Brazilian parties, see Maria do Carmo Campello de Souza, "El sistema," in Jaguaribe, 171–215. On PRONA, see *Financial Times of London*, Sept. 14, 1994; *Latin American Weekly Report*, Oct. 27, 1994, p. 490.

18. Antoine, 23–24; Reale, *Memórias*, 1: 194–98, 203, 231; Flynn, *Brazil*, 177; Almeida; *La Nación* (Buenos Aires), Dec. 9, 1995, p. 10.

19. Antoine, 41, 59, 61; Flynn, *Brazil*, 92 n. 28, and 372.

20. "In sixty years, the Nationalist movement had barely changed," Rock noted in *Authoritarian Argentina*, 236, referring to 1990. The continuing Nacionalista-Catholic connection is clear in Marsal and Arent, 39.

21. For surveys of Nacionalismo after 1939, see Rock, *Authoritarian Argentina*, 125–244; Deutsch and Dolkart, 88–188; Navarro Gerassi, 175–234; González Janzen; Bra; Comisión de Estudios. On Nacionalistas in the Peronist parties, including ones of the interior, see Arias and García Heras; Macor and Iglesias.

22. Gibson, *Class*, and "Democracy"; Espinal. I thank Paul Lewis for his observations on recent electoral politics.

23. Nicaragua Solidarity Network, May 21, 1995, p. 1, and July 9, 1995, p. 4. On contemporary Nacionalista groups and their international ties, see Díaz and Zucco, 137–63. As of November 1998, the bombing remains an unsolved crime, and many have speculated over the possibility of Middle Eastern involvement. Nevertheless, it appears that extreme right-wing elements participated in it and have obstructed the investigation. See Kiernan; Klich, 230–32.

24. Zuleta Alvarez, *El nacionalismo*, 2: 549–64; Rock, *Authoritarian Argentina*, 186.

25. Rock, *Authoritarian Argentina*, 189, 240.

26. Nicaragua Solidarity Network, June 30, 1996, p. 6, and July 14, 1996, p. 1.

27. Navarro Gerassi, 145; Irazusta, conversation with the author, Buenos Aires, 1977; *New York Times*, July 30, 1995.

28. For a discussion of Viana and Barroso, see Rodrigues, 193–200. See also Barbosa Lima Sobrinho, "Brasil—colônia de banqueiros," *Jornal do Brasil*, May 21, 1989, n.p., and Marcos Chor Maio's response in "Face polêmica: O tempo obscureceu a ligação de Gustavo Barroso com o integralismo," *Jornal do Brasil*, May 28, 1989, n.p. I thank Maio for these clippings.

29. Bejares González.

30. Horowitz, "Industrialists," quote on 212, see also 212–13; Drake, *Socialism*, 2, 6–9; Michael L. Conniff, "Introduction: Toward A Comparative Definition of Populism," in Conniff, *Latin American Populism*, 3–30.

31. Garay Vera, esp. 54–58, quote on 231; Bicheno, 381–85; Ramírez Necochea, "El fascismo," 22–23; Recabarren Valenzuela, 67–68; Etchepare and Stewart, 593.

32. Bray, 38; Paul Drake, "Chile, 1930–1958," in Bethell, ed., *Chile*, 123–26.

33. Marilena Chaui, "Apontamentos para uma crítica da Ação Integralista Brasileira," in Chaui and Franco, 111–12; Toledo, 184, 186–90, and "Teoria e ideologia na perspectiva do ISEB," in Morães, Antunes, and Ferrante, 228; Sodré, 20, 22–23; Pécaut, 107–11; *OESP*, May 14, 1978, p. 15. On the well-known sociologist Guerreiro Ramos's membership in the AIB, see Almeida, 37; Centro de Pesquisa, interview with Melo, 62. I found an admiring letter from Guerreiro Ramos to extreme rightist Alvaro Bomilcar, dated Feb. 27, 1954, in a library book in Brazil.

34. Toledo, 69, 71, 75, 78, 117–18, 122–23; Pécaut, 108; Vasconcellos, 19. One might conclude that this analysis presaged recent thinking among leftists, who now examine social groups as well as classes. But leftists today also deconstruct and demystify the "nation."

35. Chaui, esp. 48, 82–84; Maria Sylvia Carvalho Franco, "O tempo das ilusões," in Chaui and Franco, 163; Pécaut, 121, 136–37, 158.

36. My discussion of Peronism draws upon points in Deutsch, *Counterrevolution*, 236–39, and Deutsch and Dolkart, 183–84. See also Falcoff and Dolkart, 197; Lewis, "Was Perón a Fascist?"; James, 7–40; and Martínez, esp. 124–25, 138, 206, 214, 257, 294, 352. The last, a novel, is based on historical documentation.

37. Amadeo, 119. On Peronism and the Jews, see Corbière; and Caimari, "Peronist Christianity," 111–14.

38. Rock, in *Authoritarian Argentina*, esp. 148–49, judged the Nacionalista and fascist impact on Peronism as substantial, while Buchrucker emphasized the influence of FORJA and what he called populist nationalism. McLynn stressed the traditional elements of Peronist ideology without linking them to Nacionalismo.

39. Comisión de Estudios, 88–91.

40. There are a few exceptions to the scholarly trend, although of these only Paul Lewis explored the issue in depth, in "The Right and Military Rule, 1955–1983," in Deutsch and Dolkart, 147–80. Crahan, 105–7, noted right-wing Catholic and military antecedents. McCann, "Formative," described army thinking in earlier years as a precursor of national security doctrine. Arriagada Herrera, 71, traced antileftism in the Chilean military back to the early 1900s. Skidmore, in "Workers," showed that rightist responses to workers in the post–World War I era resembled bureaucratic-authoritarian policies. See also Pinkney, esp. 14, 17, 57–58. Classic works on bureaucratic authoritarianism include O'Donnell and Collier.

41. I focus on domestic rightist influences on military economic policy, rather than outside forces such as the International Monetary Fund.

42. On the extreme right and the "Tacnazo," see Valdivia Ortiz de Zárate, "Camino," 27–63.

43. Manuel Antonio Garretón, "Political Processes in an Authoritarian Regime: The Dynamics of Institutionalization and Opposition in Chile, 1973–1980," in Valen-

zuela and Valenzuela, 161–62; Constable and Valenzuela, 169, 288; communication from Carlos Maldonado. On the differences between Chilean (and, to a lesser extent, Argentine) and Brazilian economic policies under the military, see Schamis.

44. On the Brazilian military, see Stepan, esp. 179, 250–52; Skidmore, *Politics of Military Rule*; Flynn, *Brazil.*

45. Navarro Gerassi, 175–94; Walter, "The Right and the Peronists, 1943–1955," in Deutsch and Dolkart, 101–6; Comisión de Estudios, 65–67. The Grupo Organizador y Unificador changed its name to Grupo Obra de Unificación after the coup.

46. On the Argentine military, see Lewis, "The Right," in Deutsch and Dolkart; Rock, *Authoritarian Argentina*; Rouquié, *Poder militar*, 2. See also Senkman, *El antisemitismo.*

47. Clementi, "Una guía"; García and Rodríguez Molas, 5: 482–89; Zuleta Alvarez, *El nacionalismo*, 2: 764–67; Navarro Gerassi, 230.

48. Arnold Spitta, "El 'Proceso de Reorganización Nacional' de 1976 a 1981: Los objetivos básicos y su realización práctica," in Waldmann and Garzón Valdés, 84.

49. Smith, 283–355; *La Iglesia del silencio*; Constable and Valenzuela, 92–93, 100; Skidmore, *Politics of Military Rule*, 136–38, 182–85; Bruneau, *The Political Transformation*, 177–216; Weschler, 7–79.

50. Mignone, *Iglesia*. Liebscher offered a less condemnatory view in "The Church." See also Warszawski, esp. 218, 226–28, 236; Laguna; and Conferencia Episcopal Argentina. Critics dismissed the church's 1996 statement as too little, too late; see *Information Services on Latin America* 51 (May 1996): 220. On Scilingo, see Verbitsky, 29–30. Whether priests similarly absolved Brazilian and Chilean officers is unclear. One might add that the papal nuncio, Cardinal Pio Laghi, had a cordial relationship with the junta. See *Latin American News Update*, June 1995, p. 25.

51. Mignone, *Iglesia*; Zanatta, "Religión." Warszawski, 223, observed that the church under the Proceso again pushed for access to public education and achieved some of its demands.

52. Ghio, 302–4.

53. Valdivia Ortiz de Zárate saw extreme rightist forces in Chile as marginal, in "Las nuevas voces," 137.

54. I thank Margaret Power and especially Steve Volk for their valuable observations.

BIBLIOGRAPHY

Archives

ARGENTINA

Archivo de *La Prensa*. Buenos Aires.
Archivo General de la Nación. Buenos Aires.
  Agustín Justo archive.
  José Félix Uriburu archive.
Archivo Gráfico de la Nación. Buenos Aires.
Delegación de Asociaciones Israelitas Argentinas Archivo de Prensa.
  Buenos Aires.
  Clippings.
Julio Irazusta archive. Papers. Las Casuarinas, Entre Ríos.
Liga Patriótica Argentina archive. Brigada 19 de la Capital Federal. Buenos Aires.
  Libro de Actas.
YIVO archive. Buenos Aires.
  Newspapers and clippings.

BRAZIL

Arquivo do Estado de São Paulo. São Paulo.
  Newspapers.
Arquivo Leuenroth. Instituto de Filosofia e Ciências Humanas, Universidade
  Estadual de Campinas. Campinas.
  Integralismo file.
  Newspapers.

Arquivo Nacional. Rio de Janeiro.
　　Mário Augusto Teixeira de Freitas archive.
　　San Tiago Dantas archive
　　Tribunal de Segurança Nacional.
Arquivo Público e Histórico do Município de Rio Claro. Rio Claro.
　　Plínio Salgado collection.
　　Ruy de Arruda collection.
　　Newspapers.
　　Photographs.
Centro de Pesquisa e Documentação de História Contemporânea do Brasil
　　da Fundação Getúlio Vargas. Rio de Janeiro.
　　Aidano do Couto Ferraz archive.
　　Augusto do Amaral Peixoto archive.
　　Getúlio Vargas archive.
　　Oswaldo Aranha archive.
Instituto Histórico e Geográfico Brasileiro. Rio de Janeiro.
　　Araújo Goés collection.
　　Epitácio Pessôa archive.
　　Instituto Histórico collection.
　　José Carlos de Macedo Soares collection.
Instituto Histórico e Geográfico de São Paulo.
　　Liga Nacionalista papers.
Museu Histórico Nacional. Rio de Janeiro.
　　Gustavo Barroso archive.

CHILE

Archivo Nacional. Santiago.
　　Ministerio del Interior.
Museo Histórico Nacional. Santiago.
　　Departamento de Fotografía.

GREAT BRITAIN

Public Record Office. London.
　　Foreign Office.

UNITED STATES

National Archives. Washington, D.C.
　　Record Group 38. Chief of Naval Operations. Intelligence Division.
　　　　Naval Attaché Reports, 1886–1939.
　　Record Group 59. General Records of the Department of State.
　　Record Group 165. Military Intelligence Division.

Periodicals

ARGENTINA (OF BUENOS AIRES, UNLESS OTHERWISE STATED)

Baluarte, 1933.

Bandera Argentina, 1936–38.

Basta, 1935.

Boletín de Servicios de la Asociación del Trabajo, 1920.

Camisa Negra, 1933.

La Capital (Rosario), 1919, 1921.

Caras y Caretas, 1901, 1919, 1930–32.

El Censor, 1935.

Clarinada, 1937–39.

Combate, 1936 and n.d.

Contra, 1937.

Crisol, 1932–34, 1936–38, 1940–42.

Criterio, 1928–39.

Crítica, 1937, 1940.

La Época, 1919.

La Fronda, 1919–21, 1931–40.

La Gaceta (Tucumán), 1935.

La Gaceta de Buenos Aires, 1934.

Hechos en el Mundo, 1957.

La Internacional, 1924.

Judaica, 1934.

La Mañana, 1915.

Il Mattino D'Italia, n.d.

El Mundo, 1946.

Mundo Israelita, 1935–36.

La Nación, 1909, 1918–21, 1931–32, 1934, 1969, 1995.

Nosotros, 1918.

Noticias Gráficas, 1937, 1939.

La Nueva República, 1927–28, 1930–31.

Número, 1930.

El País (Córdoba), 1933, 1936, 1938.

El Pampero

La Prensa, 1901–2, 1918–21, 1931, 1933–34, 1938, 1946.

Los Principios (Córdoba), 1920, 1933–34, 1936, 1938.

La Protesta, 1919, 1922–23, 1934.

El Pueblo, 1919, 1921, 1937.

La Razón, 1919, 1940.

Review of the River Plate, 1919, 1970.

Revista del Instituto Juan Manuel de Rosas de Investigaciones Históricas, 1939.

Revista Militar, 1919.

Sur, 1937.

Universitas, 1975.

La Vanguardia, 1919–21, 1931–40.

Vida Nuestra, 1919, 1921.

Vida Nuestra (Córdoba), 1934.

La Voz del Interior (Córdoba), 1919, 1933–34, 1936.

BRAZIL (OF RIO DE JANEIRO, UNLESS OTHERWISE STATED)

Ação (Riberão Preto, São Paulo), 1935.

Ação (São Paulo), 1936–37.

Aço Verde (São Paulo), 1935.

Anauê! 1935–37.

Anauê! (Jaú, São Paulo), 1935.

Anauê! (Mogy-Mirim, São Paulo), 1935.

O A.U.C. (São Paulo), 1935.

Brasil Feminino, 1937.

Brazílea, 1917, 1931–32.

Civilização (São Paulo), 1934.

Correio da Manhã, 1920, 1934–38.

Diário da Noite, 1935–36.

Diário da Noite (Belo Horizonte), 1935.

Diário de Minas (Belo Horizonte), 1937.

Diário de Notícias, 1942.

Diário de São Paulo, 1933–34, 1936.

Doutrina, 1937.

Estado de Minas (Belo Horizonte), 1937.

O Estado de São Paulo (*OESP*), 1915, 1916, 1919, 1920, 1934, 1942, 1965, 1978.

Fon-Fon, 1933, 1935.

Gil Blas, 1919–23.

O Globo (place unknown), 1934.

Hierarchia, 1931–32.

O Homem Livre (Recife), 1934.

A Idéia (Aracati, Ceará), 1935.

O Integralista (São Paulo), 1936.

Jornal do Brasil, 1989.

Jornal do Commércio, 1919, 1924.

Jornal do Povo (place unknown), 1934.

Jornal do Povo (Ponte Nova, Minas Gerais), 1935.

O Legionário (São Paulo), 1934–36.

Monitor Integralista (São Paulo), 1933–37.

O Nacionalista (Araraquara, São Paulo), 1935.

O Nacionalista (Porto Alegre), 1922.

A Offensiva, 1934–37.

A Ordem, 1926, 1930–31, 1933–35, 1958.
Panorama, 1936–37.
Pátria Nova (São Paulo), 1929–30.
A Platéia (São Paulo), 1934–35.
A Plebe (São Paulo), 1933–34.
Política (São Paulo), 1932.
A Província (Bahia), 1935.
Província de Guanabara, 1937.
Quarta Humanidade (Itajuba, Minas Gerais), 1935
A Razão (São Paulo), 1931–32.
Revista de Estudos Jurídicos e Sociais, 1931.
Revista do Brasil (São Paulo), 1916.
O Século (São Paulo), 1933.
Século XX, 1935–36.
Semana Religiosa (Porto Alegre), 1935.
O Sigma (place unknown), 1935.
A Tribuna (Mococa, São Paulo), 1934.
A União, 1934.
Unitas (Porto Alegre), 1931.
Vanguarda Estudantil (São Paulo), 1933.
Variedades (São Paulo), 1933.
Voz d'Oeste (Riberão Preto, São Paulo), 1934.

CHILE (OF SANTIAGO, UNLESS OTHERWISE STATED)

Acción Chilena, 1934–37.
Acción Comunal, 1936.
Acción Republicana, 1938.
La Aurora, 1936.
Babel, 1945.
Boletín Informativo de la Milicia Republicana, 1932–35.
Caupolicán, 1935–37.
El Comercio (Pisagua), 1911.
Consigna, 1934–37.
Cosas: Una Revista Internacional, 1985.
La Crítica, 1939.
El Despertar de los Trabajadores (Iquique), 1912.
El Diario Ilustrado, 1918, 1920, 1933–36, 1938.
La Época, 1987, 1989.
Ercilla, 1939–40, 1966–68.
Estanquero, 1946.
Estudios, 1935, 1938.
Falange, 1934.
Frente
El Grito Popular (Iquique), 1911.

Hoy, 1933–38.
El Imparcial, 1932–37, 1939.
Izquierda, 1934–35.
Jota, 1937.
Julio Barrenechea (Temuco), 1937.
Justicia, 1911, 1925.
La Liga Patriótica (Iquique), 1919.
Lircay, 1935–36.
El Magallanes (Punta Arenas), 1920.
El Mercurio, 1918–22, 1932–41, 1983.
Mundo Judío, 1935–36, 1938, 1941.
La Nación, 1933, 1936.
La Opinión, 1933–36, 1938.
El Pacífico (Tacna), 1911.
El Pacífico (Tacna-Arica), 1911.
El Paladín (Antofagasta), 1919.
La Patria, 1939.
Progreso (Valparaíso), 1934.
La Protesta, 1935.
El Rayo (Valdivia), 1935–36.
La Revista Católica, 1933, 1935–37.
El Socialista (Antofagasta), 1918–20.
El Sol, 1939.
South Pacific Mail, 1936.
Trabajo, 1933–40.
Tribuna Juvenil, 1935.
Vida Nueva (Osorno), 1934–35.
La Voz del Sur (Tacna), 1911.
Zig-Zag, 1911, 1934, 1936.

GREAT BRITAIN

Financial Times of London, 1994.
Latin American Weekly Report (London), 1993–95.

UNITED STATES

Information Services on Latin America, 1996.
The Jewish Daily (New York), 1934.
Latin American News Update, 1995.
Miami Herald, 1993.
New York Times, 1995.
Nicaragua Solidarity Network of Greater New York. *Weekly News Update on the Americas*, 1995, 1996.

Biographical Sources

ARGENTINA

Abad de Santillán, Diego, ed. *Gran enciclopedia argentina.* 9 vols. Buenos Aires: Ediar, 1956–63.

Archivo de *La Prensa.* Buenos Aires.

Calvo, Carlos. *Nobiliario del Antiguo Virreynato del Río de la Plata.* 6 vols. Buenos Aires: La Facultad, 1936–43.

Corbella Figini, Roberto. *Guía del ganadero: Tomo bovinos.* Buenos Aires: Corfi, 1946.

Cutolo, Vicente Osvaldo. *Nuevo diccionario biográfico argentino (1750–1930).* 6 vols. Buenos Aires: Elche, 1968–83.

Diccionario biográfico de hombres de negocios: Biografías contemporáneas. Buenos Aires: Veritas, 1945.

Guía de sociedades anónimas. Buenos Aires: A. Dorr Mansilla, 1923, 1932, 1950.

Guía de sociedades anónimas. Buenos Aires: Roetzler, 1936, 1940, 1950.

Guía social argentina "Régar." Buenos Aires: Régar, 1928.

Guía social Palma. Buenos Aires: Palma, 1929, 1945.

Jockey Club. *Nómina de los socios.* Buenos Aires: Jockey Club, 1926, 1943.

Libro de Oro. *Guía de familias.* Buenos Aires: La Aurora de V. Guerra, 1911, 1923; Peuser, 1932, 1936; Kraft, 1942, 1943.

"Nómina de socios." *Anales de la Sociedad Rural Argentina* 52 (Feb. 1918): 116–34.

Parker, William Belmont, ed. *Argentines of Today.* 2 vols. Buenos Aires: n.p., 1920.

Quién es Quién. Buenos Aires: Guillermo Kraft, 1939, 1943, 1950.

Sciurano Casteñeda, Adolfo, ed. *Album de oro de la mujer argentina.* Buenos Aires: n.p., 1930.

Sociedad Inteligencia Sudamericana. *Hombres del dia 1917, el diccionario biográfico argentino.* Buenos Aires: n.p., 1917.

Sociedad Rural Argentina. *Nómina de socios.* Buenos Aires: Gadola, 1938, 1948; Americana, 1956; n.p., 1962.

Sosa de Newton, Lily. *Diccionario biográfico de mujeres argentinas.* Buenos Aires: Plus Ultra, 1972, 1980.

Udaondo, Enrique. *Diccionario biográfico argentino.* Buenos Aires: n.p., 1938.

BRAZIL

Abranches, Dunshee de. *Governos e congressos dos Estados Unidos do Brazil.* 2 vols. São Paulo: M. Abranches, 1918.

Beloch, Israel, and Alzira A. Abreu, eds. *Diccionário histórico-bibliográfico brasileiro, 1930–1983.* 4 vols. Rio de Janeiro: Ed. Forense-Universitária, CPDOC/FINEP, 1984.

Bittencourt, Adalzira. *Diccionário bio-bibliográfico de mulheres ilustres, notáveis, e intelectuais do Brasil.* 3 vols. Rio de Janeiro: Pongetti, 1969–72.

Grande Enciclopédia Delta Larousse. Rio de Janeiro: Delta, 1974.

Menezes, Raimundo de. *Diccionário literário brasileiro ilustrado.* 5 vols. São Paulo: Edição Saraiva, 1969.

Mulheres do Brasil (Pensamento e ação). 2 vols. Fortaleza: Editôra Henriqueta Galeno, 1971.

Quem é quem no Brasil. Biografias contemporâneas. 3d ed. São Paulo: Sociedade Brasileira de Expansão Comercial, n.d.

CHILE

Céspedes, Mario and Lelia Garreaud. *Gran diccionario de Chile.* 2 vols. Santiago: Importadora Alfa, 1988.

Diccionario biográfico de Chile. Santiago: Editores Empresa Periodística "Chile," 1936, 1938.

Durand, Georgina. *Mis entrevistas. Escritores, artistas y hombres de ciencia de Chile.* 2 vols. Santiago: Editorial Nascimento, 1943, 1945.

Espinosa, Januario. *Figuras de la política chilena: Primera serie.* Santiago: Imprenta Universitaria, 1945.

Figueroa, Virgilio. *Diccionario histórico, biográfico y bibliográfico de Chile.* 5 vols. Santiago: Balcells, 1925–31.

Fuentes, Jordi, and Lía Cortés. *Diccionario político de Chile (1810–1966).* Santiago: Editorial Orbe, 1967.

Fuentes, Jordi, Lía Cortés, Fernando Castillo Infante, and Arturo Valdés Phillips. *Diccionario histórico de Chile.* 8th ed. Santiago: Zig-Zag, 1984.

Parker, William Belmont, ed. *Chileans of Today.* Santiago: Imprenta Universitaria, 1920.

OTHER SOURCES

Abad de Santillán, Diego. *La F.O.R.A.: ideología y trayectoria del movimiento obrero revolucionario en la Argentina.* Buenos Aires: Nervio, 1933.

Ação Imperial Patrianovista Brasileira (Pátria-Nova). *Orgânica patrianovista.* São Paulo: n.p., 1950.

Ação Integralista Brasileira. *Os católicos e o integralismo.* Rio de Janeiro: Secretaria Nacional de Propaganda, n.d.

A accão da Liga Nacionalista. São Paulo: Olegário Ribeiro, Lobato, 1919.

Acción Nacional de Mujeres de Chile. *Reportaje a la Señora Presidenta de la Acción Nacional de Mujeres de Chile, Doña Adela Edwards de Salas.* Santiago: n.p., n.d.

Acción Nacionalista Argentina. *Acusación al socialismo.* Buenos Aires: n.p., 1932.

———. *Doctrina del "Adunismo" Nacional.* Buenos Aires: n.p., 1933.

———. (ANA) *La Iuyamtorg y el Comunismo.* Buenos Aires: n.p., 1932.

Acción Republicana. *Preámbulo y programa.* Buenos Aires: n.p., 1931.

———. *Programa y estatutos.* Santiago: Talleres Tipográficos de La Aurora, 1937.

Actividades femeninas en Chile. Santiago: Imprenta La Ilustración, 1928.

Adelman, Jeremy, ed. *Essays in Argentine Labour History, 1870–1930.* London: Macmillan, 1992.

———. "State and Labour in Argentina: The Port Workers of Buenos Aires, 1910–21." *Journal of Latin American Studies* 25 (Feb. 1993): 73–102.

Agresti, Mabel Susana. "Hugo Wast: el escritor y su contexto." *Todo Es Historia*, no. 208 (Aug. 1984): 34–41.

Albert, Bill. *South America and the First World War: The Impact of the War on Brazil, Argentina, Peru, and Chile.* Cambridge: Cambridge University Press, 1988.

Alessandri Palma, Arturo. *Recuerdos de gobierno.* 3 vols. Santiago: Editorial Nascimento, 1967.

Alexander, Robert. *Arturo Alessandri: A Political Biography.* 2 vols. Ann Arbor: University Microfilms International, 1977.

Aliaga Roja, Fernando. *Itinerario histórico: De los círculos de estudios a las comunidades juveniles de base.* Santiago: Equipo de Servicios de la Juventud, 1977.

Alianza de la Juventud Nacionalista. *Postulados de nuestra lucha.* Buenos Aires: n.p., n.d.

Alliende González, Rodrigo. *El jefe: La vida de Jorge González von Marées.* Santiago: Los Castaños, 1990.

Almeida, Rômulo. *Rômulo: Voltado para o futuro.* Fortaleza, Brazil: Associação dos Sociólogos do Estado da Bahia, 1986.

Alonso, Paula. "Politics and Elections in Buenos Aires, 1890–1898: The Performance of the Radical Party." *Journal of Latin American Studies* 25 (Oct. 1993): 465–87.

Alves, Branca Moreira. *Ideologia e feminismo: A luta da mulher pelo voto no Brasil.* Petrópolis, Brazil: Vozes, 1980.

Amadeo, Mario. *Ayer, hoy, mañana.* 5th ed. Buenos Aires: Gure, 1956.

American Jewish Yearbook. Philadelphia: Jewish Publication Society of America, 1922, 1937, 1938.

Anderson, Benedict. *Imagined Communities: Reflections on the Origin and Spread of Nationalism.* 2d ed. New York: Verso, 1991.

Andrea, Miguel de. *La Encíclica "Rerum Novarum" y la actualidad argentina.* Buenos Aires: Universidad de Buenos Aires, Facultad de Derecho y Ciencias Sociales, 1941.

———. *Obras completas.* Vol. 2, *La perturbación social contemporánea.* Buenos Aires: Difusión, 1944.

———. *Oración patriótica de acción de gracias por el éxito de las fiestas del Centenario pronunciada por el Mons. Dr. Miguel de Andrea el día 2 de junio de 1910.* Buenos Aires: Alfa y Omega, 1910.

———. *Pensamiento cristiano y democrático de monseñor de Andrea: Homenaje del Congreso Nacional.* Buenos Aires: Congreso de la Nación, 1963.

Andrews, George Reid. "Black and White Workers: São Paulo, Brazil, 1888–1928," *Hispanic American Historical Review* 68 (Aug. 1988): 491–524.

———. *Blacks and Whites in São Paulo, Brazil, 1888–1988.* Madison: University of Wisconsin Press, 1991.

———. "Brazilian Racial Democracy, 1900–1990: An American Counterpoint." *Journal of Contemporary History* 31 (July 1996): 483–507.

Anquín, Nimio de. *Escritos políticos*. Rosario, Argentina: Instituto Leopoldo Lugones, 1972.

Antezana-Pernet, Corinne. "Fighting for Their Welfare: Grassroots Activism in the Movimiento Pro-Emancipación de la Mujer Chilena (MEMCH), 1937–1949." Paper presented at the American Historical Association meeting, New York, Jan. 1997.

Antoine, Pe. Charles. *O integrismo brasileiro*. Trans. João Guilherme Linke. Rio de Janeiro: Civilização Brasileira, 1980.

Araneda Bravo, Fidel. *El Arzobispo Errázuriz y la evolución política y social de Chile*. Santiago: Editorial Jurídica de Chile, 1956.

———. *El clero en el acontecer político chileno, 1935–1960*. Santiago: Editorial Emisión, 1988.

———. *Historia de la iglesia en Chile*. Santiago: Paulinas, 1986.

Araújo, Ricardo Benzaquen de. *Totalitarismo e revolução: O integralismo de Plínio Salgado*. Rio de Janeiro: Jorge Zahar, 1988.

Araújo Salvadores, Clodomiro. Interview with author. Buenos Aires, Nov. 3, 1977.

Argentina. Congreso Nacional. *Diario de sesiones de la Cámara de Diputados*, 1920–22, 1932–39.

———. Consejo Deliberante de la Ciudad de Buenos Aires. *Versión taquigráfica*, 1932–33.

———. Dirección Nacional del Servicio Estadístico. *Cuarto censo general de la Nación*. 3 vols. Buenos Aires: Dirección General del Servicio Estadístico Nacional, 1947–52.

———. Legislatura de Córdoba. Cámara de Diputados. *Diario de sesiones*. 1936.

———. Policía de la Capital Federal. *Orden del día* 34 (1920): 832–34.

———. Policía de la Capital Federal. *Memoria: Antecedentes y datos estadísticos correspondientes al año 1921*. Buenos Aires: n.p., 1922.

———. Presidente. *Mensaje del Presidente Provisional de la Nación: Teniente General José F. Uriburu al Pueblo de la República. La obra de gobierno y de administración del 6 de septiembre de 1930 al 6 de septiembre de 1931*. Buenos Aires: Cámara de Diputados, 1931.

———. Provincia de Buenos Aires. *Memoria del Ministro de Gobierno: 18 de febrero de 1936 al 30 de abril de 1937*. Vol. 1. La Plata: Taller de Impresiones Oficiales, 1937.

———. Provincia de Córdoba. *Memoria del Ministerio de Gobierno correspondiente al ejercicio de 1937*. Córdoba: n.p., 1938.

———. Provincia de Entre Ríos. *Memoria de los Ministerios de Gobierno, Hacienda, Justicia e Instrucción Pública, 1918–1922*. 3 vols. Paraná: n.p., 1922.

———. Senado de la Nación. *Represión del Comunismo: Proyecto de ley, informe y antecedentes por el senador Matías G. Sánchez Sorondo*. 2 vols. Buenos Aires: Congreso Nacional, 1938, 1940.

Arias, María F., and Raúl García Heras. "Carisma disperso y rebelión: Los partidos neoperonistas." In *Perón del exilio al poder,* ed. Samuel Amaral and Mariano Ben Plotkin, 95–125. Buenos Aires: Cántaro, 1993.

Arnello Romo, Mario. *Proceso a una democracia (El pensamiento político de Jorge Prat).* Santiago: El Imparcial, 1965.

Arriagada Herrera, Genaro. *El pensamiento político de los militares.* 2d ed. Santiago: Aconcagua, 1986.

Ascher, Abraham, and Guenter Lewy. "National Bolshevism in Weimar Germany: Alliance of Political Extremes Against Democracy." *Social Research* 23, no. 4 (1956): 450–80.

Asociación de Escuelas Populares Israelitas de la República Argentina. *La verdad sobre el allanamiento de nuestras escuelas.* Buenos Aires: n.p., 1937.

Asociación del Trabajo. *Normas de acción.* Buenos Aires: n.p., 1921.

———. *¿Qué es la Asociación del Trabajo?* Buenos Aires: n.p., 1921.

Astorga, Luz María. "La Milicia Republicana, 1932–1935, recuerdan ex-oficiales y tropas." *El Mercurio, Revista del Domingo,* Mar. 6, 1983, pp. 10–12.

Auza, Néstor T. *Aciertos y fracasos sociales del catolicismo argentino.* 3 vols. Buenos Aires: Docencia, Don Bosco, Guadalupe, 1987.

———. *Los católicos argentinos: su experiencia política y social.* Buenos Aires: Diagrama, 1962.

———. *Periodismo y feminismo en la Argentina, 1830–1930.* Buenos Aires: Emecé, 1988.

Avni, Haim. "¿Antisemitismo estatal en la Argentina?" *Coloquio* 4, no. 8 (winter 1982): 49–67.

———. *Argentina and the Jews: A History of Jewish Immigration.* Trans. Gila Brand. Tuscaloosa: University of Alabama Press, 1991.

Azaretto, Roberto. *Historia de las fuerzas conservadoras.* Buenos Aires: Centro Editor de América Latina, 1983.

Azzi, Riolando. *Presença da igreja católica na sociedade brasileira.* Rio de Janeiro: Cadernos do ISER, no. 13, n.d.

Babini, Nicolás. "La Semana Trágica: Pesadilla de una siesta de verano." *Todo Es Historia,* no. 5 (Sept. 1967): 8–20.

Bader, Thomas. "Early Positivistic Thought and Ideological Conflict in Chile." *The Americas* 27 (Apr. 1976): 376–93.

Bagú, Sergio. "Tres oligarquías, tres nacionalismos: Chile, Argentina, Uruguay." *Cuadernos Políticos* (Jan.–Mar. 1975): 6–17.

Bak, Joan L. "Cartels, Cooperatives, and Corporatism: Getúlio Vargas in Rio Grande do Sul on the Eve of Brazil's 1930 Revolution." *Hispanic American Historical Review* 63 (May 1983): 255–75.

Bakota, Carlos Steven. "Crisis and the Middle Classes: The Ascendancy of Brazilian Nationalism, 1914–1922." Ph.D. diss., UCLA, 1973.

Balesta, Luis M., comp. *Conversando con el pueblo (Discursos del Dr. Manuel A. Fresco).* Buenos Aires: Damiano, 1938.

Bandecchi, Pedro Brasil. *Liga Nacionalista.* São Paulo: Parma, 1980.

Barbero, María Inés, and Fernando Devoto. *Los nacionalistas.* Buenos Aires: Centro Editor de América Latina, 1983.

Barbosa, Rui. *Discursos, orações, e conferências.* 3 vols. São Paulo: Livraria Editora Iracema, 1966.

Baron, Ava, ed. *Work Engendered: Toward a New History of American Labor.* Ithaca, N.Y.: Cornell University Press, 1991.

Barría Serón, Jorge I. *Los movimientos sociales de Chile desde 1910 hasta 1926 (Aspecto político y social).* Santiago: Editorial Universitaria, 1960.

Barros, Roque Spencer Maciel de Barros. *A ilustração brasileira e a idéia de universidade.* São Paulo: Universidade de São Paulo, Faculdade de Filosofia, Ciências e Letras, 1959.

Barroso, Gustavo. *Brasil—Colônia de banqueiros (História dos empréstimos de 1824 a 1934).* 2d ed. Rio de Janeiro: Civilização Brasileira, 1934.

———. *Integralismo e catolicismo.* Rio de Janeiro: Empresa Editora ABC Limitada, 1937.

———. *Judaísmo, maçonaria, e comunismo.* Rio de Janeiro: Civilização Brasileira, 1937.

———. *Roosevelt es judío.* Trans. Mario Busatto. Buenos Aires: La Mazorca, 1938.

———, ed. *O que o integralista deve saber.* Rio de Janeiro: Civilização Brasileira, 1935.

Bayer, Osvaldo. *Los vengadores de la Patagonia trágica.* 4 vols. Buenos Aires: Galerna, 1972–74; Bruguera Argentina, 1984.

Baylac de Eizaguirre, María Luján. Interview with author. Buenos Aires, July 6, 1981.

Beattie, Peter M. "The House, the Street, and the Barracks: Reform and Honorable Masculine Social Space in Brazil, 1864–1945." *Hispanic American Historical Review* 76 (Aug. 1996): 439–74.

Beauchemin, Ernesto Moreno. *Historia del movimiento sindical chileno. Una visión critiana.* Santiago: Instituto Chileno de Estudios Humanísticos, 1986.

Beiguelman, Paula. *Os companheiros de São Paulo.* São Paulo: Símbolo, 1977.

Béjar, María Dolores. "Otra vez la historia política: El conservadorismo bonaerense en los años treinta." *Anuario del IEHS* 1 (1986): 199–227.

———. *Uriburu y Justo: el auge conservador (1930–1935).* Buenos Aires: Centro Editor de América Latina, 1983.

Bejares González, Hernán, General de Brigada. *Portales y su proyección histórica.* Santiago: Encina, 1976.

Beozzo, José Oscar. "Padre Júlio Maria—Uma teología liberal-republicana numa igreja monarquista e conservadora." In *História da teologia na América Latina,* 107–26. São Paulo: Paulinas, 1981.

Bergman, Shlomo. "Some Methodological Errors in the Study of Antisemitism." *Jewish Social Studies* 5 (1943): 43–60.

Bergquist, Charles. *Labor in Latin America: Comparative Essays on Chile, Argentina, Venezuela, and Colombia.* Stanford, Calif.: Stanford University Press, 1986.

Bertoni, Lilia Ana. "La hora de la confraternidad: Los inmigrantes y la Argentina en conflicto, 1895–1901." *Estudios Migratorios Latinoamericanos*, no. 32 (Apr. 1996): 61–84.

Besse, Susan K. *Restructuring Patriarchy: The Modernization of Gender Inequality in Brazil, 1914–1940*. Chapel Hill: University of North Carolina Press, 1996.

Bethell, Leslie, ed. *Argentina Since Independence*. Cambridge: Cambridge University Press, 1993.

———. *Brazil: Empire and Republic, 1822–1930*. Cambridge: Cambridge University Press, 1989.

———. *Cambridge History of Latin America*. Vol. 4, *c. 1870–1930*. Cambridge: Cambridge University Press, 1986.

———. *Chile Since Independence*. Cambridge: Cambridge University Press, 1993.

Bianchi, Susana, and Norma Sanchis. *El partido peronista femenino: Primera parte (1949/1955)*. Buenos Aires: Centro Editor de América Latina, 1988.

Biblioteca Nacista No. 1. *El movimiento nacional-socialista de Chile (M.N.S.): Declaraciones fundamentales. Plan de acción—Organización—Programa*. Santiago: Imprenta La Tracción, 1932.

———. No. 1 [*sic*]. *El movimiento nacional-socialista de Chile (M.N.S.)*. Santiago: Imprenta La República, 1934.

———. No. 1 [*sic*]. *El movimiento nacional-socialista de Chile (M.N.S.)*. Valparaíso: M.N.S., n.d.

———. No. 2. *El movimiento nacional-socialista de Chile: Como única solución a la crisis política y social de la república*. Santiago: La Tracción, n.d.

———. No. 6. *Ideario nacista: Colección de artículos publicados en la página nacional-socialista del diario El Imparcial*. Santiago: Cóndor, 1932.

———. No. 7. *Movimiento nacional-socialista de Chile: Carta Orgánica del Departamento de la Juventud Nacional Socialista (J.N.S.)*. Santiago: Corrial, 1933.

Bibliotheca da Liga da Defesa Nacional. *Discursos proferidos na sessão pública solemne de 12 de outubro de 1923*. Rio de Janeiro: Brasileira "Lux," 1924.

Bicheno, H. E. "Anti-Parliamentary Themes in Chilean History, 1920–70." *Government and Opposition* 7 (summer 1972): 351–88.

Bilac, Olavo. *A defesa nacional (discursos)*. Rio de Janeiro: Edições da Liga da Defesa Nacional, 1917.

———. *Ultimas conferências e discursos*. Rio de Janeiro: Livraria Francisco Alves, 1924.

Bilsky, Edgardo J. *La Semana Trágica*. Buenos Aires: Centro Editor de América Latina, 1984.

Blee, Kathleen M. *Women of the Klan: Racism and Gender in the 1920s*. Berkeley: University of California Press, 1991.

Blinkhorn, Martin, ed. *Fascists and Conservatives: The Radical Right and the Establishment in Twentieth-Century Europe*. London: Unwin Hyman, 1990.

Boffi, Luis L. *Juventud, universidad, y patria: Bajo la tiranía del sable*. Buenos Aires: Claridad, 1933.

Boizard, Ricardo. *La democracia cristiana en Chile (Un mundo que nace entre dos guerras)*. Santiago: Orbe, 1963.

―――. *Historia de una derrota (25 de octubre de 1938)*. Santiago: Orbe, 1941.

Bomilcar, Alvaro. *A política no Brazil ou o nacionalismo radical*. Rio de Janeiro: Leite, Ribeiro, and Maurillo, 1920.

―――. *O preconceito da raça no Brasil*. Rio de Janeiro: Aurora, 1916.

Bonilla, Frank, and Myron Glazer. *Student Politics in Chile*. New York: Basic Books, 1970.

Borba, Osorio. "História de camisas." *Diretrizes* 1 (June 1938): 17–19.

Borges, Dain. *The Family in Bahia, 1870–1945*. Stanford, Calif.: Stanford University Press, 1992.

―――. "'Puffy, Ugly, Slothful and Inert': Degeneration in Brazilian Social Thought, 1880–1940." *Journal of Latin American Studies* 25 (May 1993): 235–56.

Borrero, José María. *La patagonia trágica*. 2d ed. Buenos Aires: Americana, 1957.

Bou, Marilú. "1936: El fraude, el frente, el fascismo." *Todo Es Historia*, no. 237 (Feb. 1987): 8–25.

Bra, Gerardo. "¿Nacionalismo, nazionalismo, o nacionalismo frontal?" *Todo Es Historia*, no. 308 (Mar. 1993), 82–91.

Bradford, Sax. *The Battle for Buenos Aires*. New York: Harcourt, Brace, 1943.

Brasil, J. F. de Assis. *Idéia de pátria*. São Paulo: Piratininga, 1918.

Brauner Rodgers, Susana. "El nacionalismo yrigoyenista, 1930–1943." *Estudios Interdisciplinarios de América Latina y el Caribe* 1 (July–Dec. 1990): 79–98.

Bravo Hayley, Julio P. *Republicanismo*. Santiago: Imprenta Nascimento, 1933.

Bravo Ríos, Leonidas. *Lo que supo un auditor de guerra*. Santiago: Editorial del Pacifico, 1955.

Bray, Donald W. "Peronism in Chile." *Hispanic American Historical Review* 47 (Feb. 1967): 38–49.

Brazil. Congresso Nacional. *Annães da Câmara dos Deputados*, 1920–22, 1936.

―――. *Diário do Poder Legislativo: Câmara dos Deputados*, 1935–37.

―――. Estado de São Paulo. Secretaria da Justiça e da Segurança Publica. *Relatorio apresentado ao Exm. Sr. Dr. Washington Luis Pereira de Sousa*. São Paulo: Garraux, 1921.

―――. Ministério da Agricultura, Indústria, e Commércio. Directoria Geral de Estadística. *Recenseamento do Brazil realizado em 1 de septembro de 1920*. 5 vols. Rio de Janeiro: Estadística, 1927.

―――. Santa Catarina. Delegacia da Ordem Política e Social. *O punhal nazista no coração do Brasil*. 2d ed. Florianópolis: Imprensa Oficial do Estado, 1944.

Brinkley, Alan. "The Problem of American Conservatism." *American Historical Review* 99 (Apr. 1994): 409–29.

Brookshaw, David. *Race and Color in Brazilian Literature*. Metuchen, N.J.: Scarecrow Press, 1986.

Brown, Paul Everett. "Ideological Origins of Modern Argentine Nationalism." Ph.D. diss., Claremont Graduate School, 1965.

Broxson, Elmer R. "Plínio Salgado and Brazilian Integralism, 1932–1938." Ph.D. diss., Catholic University, 1972.

Bruneau, Thomas C. *The Political Transformation of the Brazilian Catholic Church.* Cambridge: Cambridge University Press, 1974.

————. "Power and Influence: Analysis of the Church in Latin America and the Case of Brazil." *Latin American Research Review* 8 (summer 1973): 25–51.

Buchrucker, Cristián. *Nacionalismo y peronismo: La Argentina en la crisis ideológica mundial (1927–1955).* Buenos Aires: Sudamericana, 1987.

Bunge, Alejandro E. *Una nueva argentina.* Buenos Aires: Guillermo Kraft, 1940.

————. "La República Argentina define su política económica nacional." *Revista de Economía Argentina* 18, no. 163 (1932): 3–4.

Bunge, Carlos Octavio. *Nuestra America (ensayo de psicología social).* 6th ed. Buenos Aires: L. J. Rosso, 1918.

Burdick, Michael A. *For God and the Fatherland: Religion and Politics in Argentina.* Albany: State University of New York Press, 1995.

Burleigh, Michael, and Wolfgang Wippermann. *The Racial State: Germany, 1933–1945.* Cambridge: Cambridge University Press, 1991.

Burnett, Ben G. *Political Groups in Chile: The Dialogue Between Order and Change.* Austin: University of Texas Press, 1970.

Burns, E. Bradford. *A History of Brazil.* New York: Columbia University Press, 1970.

Bushnell, David. *Reform and Reaction in the Platine Provinces, 1810–1852.* Gainesville: University Presses of Florida, 1983.

Butler, Kim D. "Up from Slavery: Afro-Brazilian Activism in São Paulo, 1888–1938." *The Americas* 49 (Oct. 1992): 179–206.

Byrnes, Robert F. *Antisemitism in Modern France.* New Brunswick, N.J.: Rutgers University Press, 1950.

Caballero C., Enrique. *Balance de una obra social.* Santiago: Selecta, 1923.

————. *El capital ante los problemas del trabajo.* Santiago: Biblioteca de Ciencias Sociales, 1922.

Caimari, Lila M. "Peronist Christianity and Non-Catholic Religions: Politics and Ecumenism (1943–55)." *Canadian Journal of Latin American and Caribbean Studies* 20, nos. 39–40 (1995): 105–24.

————. *Perón y la iglesia católica: religión, estado, y sociedad en la Argentina (1943–1955).* Buenos Aires: Ariel Historia, 1994.

Camargo, Aspásia, Dulce Chaves Pandolfi, Eduardo Rodrigues Gomes, Maria Celina Soares D'Araújo, and Mario Grynszpan. *O golpe silencioso: As origens da república corporativa.* Rio de Janeiro: Rio Fundo, 1989.

Cameron, W. H. Morton, ed. *Enciclopedia comercial (Encyclopedia Commercial): Unico órgano oficial, anual o bienal, de la British and Latin American Chamber of Commerce. Argentina, Brasil, Chile, Perú, Uruguay. Suplemento Británico.* London: Globe Encyclopedia, 1922.

Camp, Richard L. *The Papal Ideology of Social Reform: A Study in Historical Development, 1878–1967.* Leiden, The Netherlands: E. J. Brill, 1967.

Campos Menéndez, Enrique, ed. *Pensamiento nacionalista*. Santiago: Editora Nacional Gabriela Mistral, 1974.

Cane, James. "'Unity for the Defense of Culture': The AIAPE and the Cultural Politics of Argentine Anti-Fascism, 1935–1943." *Hispanic American Historical Review* 77 (Aug. 1997): 443–82.

Canedo, Alfredo. *Aspectos del pensamiento político de Leopoldo Lugones*. Buenos Aires: Marcos, 1974.

Cantón, Darío. *La política de los militares argentinos, 1900–1971*. Buenos Aires: Siglo XXI, 1971.

Carlés, Manuel. "Diplomacia y estrategia: Conferencia dada en el Colegio Militar de la Nación por el Dr. Manuel Carlés. Junio de 1915." Supplement of *Revista Militar* (1915).

———. "Exégesis sobre la personalidad y la política del Dr. Marcelo T. de Alvear." Introduction to *Democracia*, by Marcelo T. de Alvear, 9–25. Buenos Aires: M. Gleizer, 1936.

Carlson, Marifran. *¡Feminismo! The Women's Movement in Argentina from Its Beginnings to Evita Perón*. Chicago: Academy Chicago, 1986.

Carneiro, Maria Luiza Tucci. *O antisemitismo na era Vargas: Fantasmas de uma geração (1930–1945)*. São Paulo: Brasiliense, 1988.

Carone, Edgard. "Coleção Azul: Crítica pequeno-burguesa da crise brasileira depois de 1930." *Revista Brasileira de Estudos Políticos*, nos. 25–26 (July 1968/Jan. 1969): 249–95.

———. *Movimento operário no Brasil (1877–1944)*. 2d ed. São Paulo: Difel, 1984.

———. *O P.C.B. (1922–1943)*. 3 vols. São Paulo: Difel, 1982.

———. *A primeira república (1889–1930): Texto e contexto*. 2d ed. São Paulo: Corpo e Alma, 1970.

———. *A segunda república (1930–1937)*. 3d ed. São Paulo: Difel, 1978.

———. *O tenentismo: Acontecimentos—personagens—programas*. São Paulo: Difel, 1975.

———. *A terceira república (1937–1945)*. 2d ed. São Paulo: Difel, 1982.

Cartilla de la Unión Republicana. Santiago: n.p., 1933.

Carulla, Juan E. *Al filo del medio siglo*. Paraná, Argentina: Llanura, 1951.

———. *Valor ético de la revolución del 6 de septiembre de 1930*. Buenos Aires: n.p., 1931.

Carvalho, José Murilo de. "Armed Forces and Politics in Brazil, 1930–1945." *Hispanic American Historical Review* 62 (May 1982): 193–223.

———. *Os bestializados: O Rio de Janeiro e a República que não foi*. São Paulo: Companhia das Letras, 1987.

———. *A construção da ordem: A elite política imperial*. Rio de Janeiro: Campus, 1980.

———. *A formação das almas: O imaginário da república no Brasil*. São Paulo: Companhia das Letras, 1990.

Cassin-Scott, Jack, and Angus McBride. *Women at War, 1939–45*. London: Osprey, 1980.

Castellani, Leonardo. *Reforma de la ensenanza*. Buenos Aires: Difusión, 1939.

———. *Sentir la Argentina. Leopoldo Lugones*. Buenos Aires: Adsum, 1938.

Caterina, Luis María. *La Liga Patriótica Argentina: Un grupo de presión frente a las convulsiones sociales de la década del '20*. Buenos Aires: Corregidor, 1995.

Cavalcanti, Themistocles Brandão, ed. *Las constituciones de los Estados Unidos del Brasil*. Madrid: Instituto de Estudios Políticos, 1958.

Celso, Afonso. *Porque me ufano do meu paiz*. 9th ed. Rio de Janeiro: Livraria Garnier, n.d. [1901].

Centro de Documentación e Informacíon sobre Judaísmo Argentino "Marc Turkow." *Bibliografía temática sobre judaísmo argentino*. No. 3, *Antisemitismo en la Argentina - 1909-1929*. Buenos Aires: AMIA, 1985.

Centro de Pesquisa e Documentação de História Contemporânea do Brasil da Fundação Getúlio Vargas. Rio de Janeiro. Oral History Project.

———. Interview with Alexandre José de Barbosa Lima Sobrinho, 1981.

———. Interview with Aristides Leal, 1979.

———. Interview with Augusto do Amaral Peixoto, 1982.

———. Interview with Guilherme Figueiredo, 1979.

———. Interview with José Américo de Almeida, 1979.

———. Interview with José Joffily Bezerra de Melo, 1982.

———. Interview with Juraci Magalhães, 1981.

———. Interview with Odilon Batista, 1980.

———. Interview with Oswaldo Trigueiro, 1981.

———. Interview with Paulo Pinheiro Chagas, 1985.

Chacon, Vamireh. "A social democracia brasileira." *Revista Brasileira de Estudos Políticos* 51 (1980): 123-54.

Chalmers, Douglas A., Maria do Carmo Campello de Souza, and Atilio A. Borón, eds. *The Right and Democracy in Latin America*. New York: Praeger, 1992.

Chasin, J. *O integralismo de Plínio Salgado: Forma de regressividade no capitalismo híper-tardio*. São Paulo: Livraria Editora Ciências Humanas, 1978.

Chaui, Marilena. *Seminários*. 2d ed. São Paulo: Brasiliense, 1984.

Chaui, Marilena, and Maria Sylvia Carvalho Franco. *Ideologia e mobilização popular*. Rio de Janeiro: Paz e Terra, Centro de Estudos de Cultura Contemporânea, 1978.

Chiaramonte, José Carlos. *Nacionalismo y liberalismo económicos en Argentina, 1860-1880*. Buenos Aires: Solar/Hachette, 1971.

Chile. *Censo de población de la República levantada el 15 de diciembre de 1920*. Santiago: Soc. Imp. y Litografía Universo, 1925.

———. Comisión Central del Censo. *Censo de la República de Chile levantado el 28 de noviembre de 1907*. Santiago: Sociedad Imprenta y Litografía Universo, 1908.

———. Congreso. Cámara de Diputados. *Boletín de sesiones*, 1911, 1918, 1920, 1931-39.

———. Congreso. Cámara de Senadores. *Boletín de sesiones*, 1920, 1934-36.

Ciafardo, Eduardo A. "Las Damas de Beneficencia y la participación social de la mujer en la ciudad de Buenos Aires, 1880-1920." *Anuario del IEHS* 5 (1990): 161-70.

Ciano, Galeazzo. *Ciano's Hidden Diary, 1937–1938.* Trans. Andreas Mayor. New York: E. P. Dutton, 1953.

Cifuentes, Abdón. *Memorias.* 2 vols. Santiago: Nascimento, 1936.

Cifuentes, José María. *La cuestión social y el partido conservador.* Santiago: Imprenta Chile, 1921.

Ciria, Alberto. *Parties and Power in Modern Argentina.* Trans. Carlos A. Astiz and Mary F. McCarthy. Albany: State University of New York Press, 1974.

Clementi, Hebe. "Una guía del último nacionalismo argentino: El pensamiento de Jordán Bruno Genta." *Todo Es Historia,* no. 253 (July 1988): 38–49.

———. "El miedo a la inmigración." *Primeras Jornadas Nacionales de Estudios sobre Inmigración en la Argentina—5, 6, 7 de noviembre de 1981.* Buenos Aires: Ministerio de Educación y Justicia, Sección de Cultura, 1985. Pp. 173–213.

Coelho Neto, Henrique. *Brevário cívico.* Rio de Janeiro: Empreza Industrial Editora "O Norte," 1921.

Cohen, Jacob Xenob. *Jewish Life in South America: A Survey for the American Jewish Congress.* New York: Bloch, 1941.

Collier, David, ed. *The New Authoritarianism in Latin America.* Princeton, N.J.: Princeton University Press, 1979.

Collier, Ruth Berins, and David Collier. *Shaping the Political Arena.* Princeton, N.J.: Princeton University Press, 1991.

Collier, Simon. "Conservatismo chileno, 1830–1860: Temas e imágenes." *Nueva Historia* 2 (Jan.–Mar. 1983): 143–63.

Comisión de Estudios de la Sociedad Argentina de Defensa de la Tradición, Familia, y Propiedad. *El nacionalismo: una incógnita en constante evolución.* Buenos Aires: Tradición, Familia, y Propiedad, 1970.

Comisión Popular Argentina Contra el Comunismo. Flier. Buenos Aires: n.p., 1932.

Comité Ejecutivo de la Gran Colecta Nacional. *La paz social.* Buenos Aires: n.p., 1919.

Conferencia Episcopal Argentina. *La iglesia y los derechos humanos.* Buenos Aires: Conferencia Episcopal Argentina, 1984.

Conniff, Michael. "The Tenentes in Power: A New Perspective on the Brazilian Revolution of 1930." *Journal of Latin American Studies* 10 (May 1978): 61–82.

———. "Voluntary Associations in Rio de Janeiro, 1870–1945: A New Approach to Urban Social Dynamics." *Journal of Inter-American Studies and World Affairs* 17 (Feb. 1975): 64–81.

———, ed. *Latin American Populism in Comparative Perspective.* Albuquerque: University of New Mexico Press, 1982.

Conniff, Michael L., and Frank D. McCann, eds. *Modern Brazil: Elites and Masses in Historical Perspective.* Lincoln: University of Nebraska Press, 1989.

Constable, Pamela, and Arturo Valenzuela. *A Nation of Enemies: Chile Under Pinochet.* New York: Norton, 1991.

Converse, Christel. "Culture and Nationalism Among the German Chileans in the 1930s." *MACLAS Latin American Essays* 4 (1990): 117–24.

Corbière, Emilio J. "Perón y los judíos." *Todo Es Historia*, no. 252 (June 1988): 6–35.

Corbisier, Roland. "Plínio Salgado: Quem te viu e quem te ve." *Politika*, no. 63 (Jan. 1–6, 1973): 18–19.

Cornblit, Oscar. "La opción conservadora en la política argentina." *Desarrollo Económico* 14 (Jan.–Mar. 1975): 599–639.

Corrêa, Maurício de Castro. "Ação Integralista Brasileira e seus reflexos em Juiz de Fora." MS, 1973.

———. "Integralismo: O malogro do fascismo no Brasil." *História* 11 (Mar. 1974): 60–71.

Correa S., Sofía. "La derecha en Chile contemporáneo: la pérdida del control estatal." *Revista de Ciencia Política* 11, no. 1 (1989): 5–19.

Costa, Emília Viotti da. *The Brazilian Empire: Myths and Histories.* 2d ed. Chicago: Dorsey Press, 1988.

Costa, João Cruz. *A History of Ideas in Brazil.* Trans. Suzette Macedo. Berkeley: University of California Press, 1964.

Costa, Vanda Maria Ribeiro. "Com rancor e com afeto: rebeliões militares na década de trinta." Research report. Rio de Janeiro: CPDOC/FGV, 1984.

Covarrubias, María Teresa. *1938: La rebelión de los jóvenes. Partido Conservador y Falange Nacional.* Santiago: Aconcagua, 1987.

Covarrubias, Paz, and Rolando Franco, eds. *Chile: mujer y sociedad.* Santiago: Alfabeta Impresores, 1978.

Crahan, Margaret E., ed. *Human Rights and Basic Needs in the Americas.* Washington, D.C.: Georgetown University Press, 1982.

Cristi, Renato, and Carlos Ruiz. *El pensamiento conservador en Chile.* Santiago: Editorial Universitaria, 1992.

———. "Pensamiento conservador en Chile (1903–1974)." *Opciones* 9 (May–Sept. 1986): 121–46.

Crummett, María de los Angeles. "El Poder Femenino: The Mobilization of Women Against Socialism in Chile." *Latin American Perspectives* 4 (fall 1977): 103–13.

Cuadernos Adunistas no. 1. *Democracia nueva.* Buenos Aires: n.p., 1932.

Cuadra Poisson, Jorge de la. *La revolución que viene.* Santiago: Nascimento, 1931.

———. *La verdad de las incidencias milicianas.* Santiago: La Nación, 1935.

Cullen, Stephen M. "Political Violence: The Case of the British Union of Fascists." *Journal of Contemporary History* 28 (Apr. 1993): 245–67.

Cunha, Euclides da. *Rebellion in the Backlands.* Trans. from *Os sertões.* Chicago: University of Chicago Press, 1944.

d'Albuquerque, Tenório. *Integralismo, Nazismo, e Fascismo: estudos comparativos dos tres regimes.* Rio de Janeiro: Minerva, 1937.

D'Araújo, Maria Celina Soares. "Militares, repressão e o discurso anticomunista no golpe de 1937." Rio de Janeiro: CPDOC/FGV research report, 1984.

Davies, Alan T. "Religion and Racism: The Case of French Anti-Semitism." *Journal of Church and State* 20, no. 2 (1978): 273–86.

Dean, Warren. *The Industrialization of São Paulo, 1880–1945*. Austin: University of Texas Press, 1969.

Debané, Nicolau José. *Economia nacional e nacionalismo econômico*. São Paulo: Brazil, 1917.

———. *Subsídios para o estudo da economia nacional brasileira: A pesca e os pescadores no Brasil, no ponto de vista econômico e social*. Rio de Janeiro: Nacional, 1924.

La década infame. Buenos Aires: Carlos Pérez, 1969.

"Declaración de principios de la Legión." MS, photocopy, n.d.

De Grand, Alexander. *Italian Fascism: Its Origins and Development*. Lincoln: University of Nebraska Press, 1982.

———. "Women Under Italian Fascism." *Historical Journal* 19, no. 4 (1976): 947–68.

De Grazia, Victoria. *How Fascism Ruled Women: Italy, 1922–1945*. Berkeley: University of California Press, 1992.

Degreff, Walter. *Judiadas, judiones, judíos, y judihuelos: Acción usurpadora de los judíos en el mundo moderno*. Buenos Aires: Francisco A. Colombo, 1936.

Delamare, Alcibiades. *As duas bandeiras: Catholicismo e Brazilidade (Discursos e conferências)*. Rio de Janeiro: Centro D. Vital, Annuario do Brazil, 1924.

———. *Línguas de fogo: Discursos e conferências*. Rio de Janeiro: Annuario do Brasil, 1926.

Della Cava, Ralph. "Catholicism and Society in Twentieth-Century Brazil." *Latin American Research Review* 11, no. 2 (1976): 7–49.

DellaPergola, Sergio. "Demographic Trends of Latin American Jewry." In *The Jewish Presence in Latin America*, ed. Judith Laikin Elkin and Gilbert W. Merkx, 85–134. Boston: Allen and Unwin, 1987.

Demanda contra 'Clarinada'. Buenos Aires: n.p., 1939.

DeShazo, Peter. *Urban Workers and Labor Unions in Chile, 1902–1927*. Madison: University of Wisconsin Press, 1983.

Deutsch, Sandra McGee. "Anti-Semitism and the Chilean Movimiento Nacional Socialista, 1932–1941." In *The Jewish Diaspora in Latin America*, ed. David Sheinin and Lois Baer Barr, 161–81. New York: Garland, 1996.

———. "The Argentine Right and the Jews, 1900–1932." *Journal of Latin American Studies* 18 (May 1986): 113–34.

———. "The Catholic Church, Work, and Womanhood in Argentina, 1890–1930." *Gender and History* 3 (autumn 1991): 304–25.

———. *Counterrevolution in Argentina, 1900–1932: The Argentine Patriotic League*. Lincoln: University of Nebraska Press, 1986.

Deutsch, Sandra McGee, and Ronald H. Dolkart, eds. *The Argentine Right: Its History and Intellectual Origins, 1910 to the Present*. Wilmington, Del.: Scholarly Resources Press, 1993.

Díaz, Claudio, and Antonio Zucco. *La ultraderecha argentina y su conexión internacional*. Buenos Aires: Contrapunto, 1987.

Diehl, James M. *Paramilitary Politics in Weimar Germany.* Bloomington: Indiana University Press, 1977.

Dolkart, Ronald H. "Buenos Aires Province Under Manuel Fresco, 1936–1940: A Nacionalista Policy of Labor Legislation and Social Control." Paper presented at the American Historical Association meeting, New York, Dec. 1985.

———. "Manuel A. Fresco, Governor of the Province of Buenos Aires, 1936–1940: A Study of the Argentine Right and Its Response to Economic and Social Change." Ph.D. diss., UCLA, 1969.

Doll, Ramón. *Acerca de una política nacional.* Buenos Aires: Dictio, 1975.

Domínguez, Crisanto. *Rebelión en la selva.* Buenos Aires: Ayacucho, 1948.

Donoso, Ricardo. *Alessandri, agitador y demoledor: Cincuenta años de historia política de Chile.* Vol. 1. Mexico: Fondo de Cultura Económica, 1953.

———. *Las ideas políticas en Chile.* Mexico: Fondo de Cultura Económica, 1946.

Dória, Antônio de Sampaio. *O que o cidadão deve saber (Manual de instrucção cívica).* São Paulo: Olegário Ribeiro, 1919.

Dorn, Georgette Magassy. "Idealism Versus Reality: The Failure of an Argentine Political Leader, Lisandro de la Torre." Ph.D. diss., Georgetown University, 1981.

Douglas, Allen. "Violence and Fascism: The Case of the Faisceau." *Journal of Contemporary History* 19 (Oct. 1984): 689–712.

Douglas, Mary. *Natural Symbols: Explorations in Cosmology.* New York: Random House Vintage Books, 1973.

Drake, Paul W. "Corporatism and Functionalism in Modern Chilean Politics." *Journal of Latin American Studies* 10, no. 1 (1978): 83–116.

———. *Socialism and Populism in Chile, 1932–52.* Urbana: University of Illinois Press, 1978.

Dreifus, René Armand. *1964: A conquista do estado. Ação política, poder e golpe de classe.* Trans. Ayeska Branca de Oliveira Farias, Ceres Ribeiro Pires de Freitas, Else Ribeiro Pires Vieira, Glória Maia de Mello Carvalho. 5th ed. Petrópolis, Brazil: Vozes, 1987.

Dulles, John W. F. *Anarchists and Communists in Brazil, 1900–1935.* Austin: University of Texas Press, 1973.

———. *Vargas of Brazil: A Political Biography.* Austin: University of Texas Press, 1967.

Durham, Martin. "Gender and the British Union of Fascists." *Journal of Contemporary History* 27 (July 1992): 513–29.

Dutra, Eliana Regina de Freitas Dutra. "A Igreja e as classes populares em Minas na década de vinte." *Revista Brasileira de Estudos Políticos* 49 (July 1979): 71–98.

Eakin, Marshall C. "Race and Identity: Sílvio Romero, Science, and Social Thought in Late-Nineteenth-Century Brazil." *Luso-Brazilian Review* 22 (winter 1985): 151–74.

Eatwell, Roger, and Noel O'Sullivan, eds. *The Nature of the Right: American and European Politics and Political Thought Since 1789.* Boston: Twayne, 1990.

Eça de Queiroz. Introduction to *Collectáneas,* by Eduardo Prado. Vol. 1. São Paulo: Escola Typográphica Salesiana, 1904–5.

Edwards, Alberto. *La fronda aristocrática: Historia política de Chile.* 6th ed. Santiago: Pacífico, 1966.

Elkin, Judith Laikin. *Jews of the Latin American Republics.* Chapel Hill: University of North Carolina Press, 1980.

Elkin, Judith Laikin, and Gilbert W. Merkx, eds. *The Jewish Presence in Latin America.* Boston: Allen and Unwin, 1987.

Enciclopédia do Integralismo: Estudos e depoimentos. 9 vols. Rio de Janeiro: Livraria Clássica Brasileira, 1958–59.

Encina, Francisco A. *Nuestra inferioridad económica: Sus causas, sus consequencias.* Santiago: Imprenta Universitaria, 1912.

Encyclopedia Judaica. 16 vols. Jerusalem: Keter, 1972.

Errázuriz, Crescente. *Algo de lo que he visto: Memorias de don Crescente Errázuriz.* Santiago: Nascimento, 1934.

————. *Obras de Crescente Errázuriz.* Ed. by Raúl Silva Castro. Vol. 3, *Obras pastorales escogidas.* Santiago: Imprenta Zig-Zag, 1936.

Espinal, Rosario. "The Right and the New Right in Latin America." In *The United States and Latin America in the 1990s: Beyond the Cold War,* ed. Jonathan Hartlyn, Lars Shoultz, and Augusto Varas, 86–99. Chapel Hill: University of North Carolina Press, 1993.

Esposito, Elisa. "La Federación de Asociaciones Católicas de Empleadas." *Boletín de la Acción Católica Argentina* (Apr. 1951): 109–12.

Estatutos da Liga da Defesa Nacional. Rio de Janeiro: Jornal do Commércio, 1916.

Estrada, José Manuel. "Discursos sobre el liberalismo." In *Pensamiento conservador (1815–1898),* ed. José Luis Romero and Luis Alberto Romero, 254–72. Caracas: Biblioteca Ayacucho, 1978.

Etchepare, Jaime Antonio, and Hamish I. Stewart. "Nazism in Chile: A Particular Type of Fascism in South America." *Journal of Contemporary History* 30, no. 4 (1995): 577–605.

Etchepareborda, Roberto. "Aspectos políticos de la crisis de 1930." *Revista de Historia* 3 (1958): 7–40.

————. *Zeballos y la política exterior argentina.* Buenos Aires: Pleamar, 1982.

Ezcurra, Marta. Interview with author. Buenos Aires, July 6, 1981.

Ezcurra Medrano, Alberto. *Catolicismo y nacionalismo.* 2d ed. Buenos Aires: Adsum, 1939.

Falcoff, Mark. "Argentine Nationalism on the Eve of Perón: The Force of Radical Orientation of Young Argentina and Its Rivals, 1935-1945." Ph.D. diss., Princeton University, 1970.

————. "Economic Dependency in a Conservative Mirror: Alejandro Bunge and the Argentine Frustration, 1919-1943." *Inter-American Economic Affairs* 35 (spring 1982): 57–75.

————. "Raúl Scalabrini Ortiz: The Making of an Argentine Nationalist." *Hispanic American Historical Review* 52 (Feb. 1972): 74–101.

Falcoff, Mark, and Frederick B. Pike, eds. *The Spanish Civil War, 1936–39: American Hemispheric Perspectives.* Lincoln: University of Nebraska Press, 1982.

Falcoff, Mark, and Ronald H. Dolkart, eds. *Prologue to Perón: Argentina in Depression and War, 1930–1945.* Berkeley: University of California Press, 1975.

Fariña Vicuña, Carmen. "Notas sobre el pensamiento corporativo de la Juventud Conservadora a través del periódico 'Lircay' (1934–40)." *Revista de Ciencias Políticas* 9, no. 1 (1987): 27–45.

———. "El pensamiento corporativo en las revistas 'Estanquero' (1946–1955) y 'Política y Espíritu' (1945–1975)." *Revista de Ciencia Política* 12, no. 1–2 (1990): 119–42.

Fascismo Argentino. *Chivo expiatorio.* Buenos Aires: n.p., 1932.

Fausto, Boris, ed. *História geral da civilização brasileira.* Part 3, *O Brasil republicano.* 4 vols. 3d ed. São Paulo: Difel, 1985.

———. *Trabalho urbano e conflito social (1890–1920).* São Paulo: Difel, 1976.

Feijoó, María del Carmen. "Las luchas feministas." *Todo Es Historia,* no. 28 (Jan. 1978): 7–23.

Ferla, Salvador. *Doctrina del nacionalismo.* Buenos Aires: Rafael, 1947.

Fernández, M. Elisa. "Beyond Partisan Politics in Chile: The Carlos Ibáñez Period and the Politics of Ultranationalism between 1952 and 1958." Ph.D. diss., University of Miami, 1996.

Ferrari Etcheberry, Alberto. "Sindicalistas en la bancada conservadora." *Todo Es Historia,* no. 314 (Sept. 1993): 74–83.

Ferrero, Roberto A. *Sabattini y la decadencia del yrigoyenismo.* 2 vols. Buenos Aires: Centro Editor de América Latina, 1984.

Figueiredo, Jackson de. *Affirmações.* Rio de Janeiro: Annuario do Brasil, 1924.

———. *A columna de fogo (7-24—7-25).* Rio de Janeiro: Annuario do Brasil, 1925.

———. "Epitácio Pessôa e a mocidade reaccionária do Brazil contemporâneo." In *Epitácio Pessôa e o juizo de seus contemporâneos,* 274–82. Rio de Janeiro: Livraria Francisco Alves, 1925.

———. *Do nacionalismo na hora presente.* Rio de Janeiro: Livraria Cathólica, 1921.

———. *A questão social na philosophia de Farias Brito.* Rio de Janeiro: Revista dos Tribunaes, 1919.

———. *A reaccaõ do bom senso: Contra o demagogismo e a anarchia militar.* Rio de Janeiro: Annuario do Brasil, 1922.

Filippo, Virgilio. *Conferencias radiotelefónicas.* Buenos Aires: Tor, 1936.

———. *La palabra de un sacerdote: Por qué es un peligro el judaísmo.* Buenos Aires: n.p., 1940.

Fiorito, Susana. "Un drama olvidado: Las huelgas patagónicas de 1920–1921." *Polémica,* no. 54 (1971): 92–96.

Fischer, Conan. "Class Enemies or Class Brothers? Communist-Nazi Relations in Germany, 1929–33." *European History Quarterly* 15 (July 1985): 259–79.

———. "The KPD and Nazism: A Reply to Dick Geary." *European History Quarterly* 15 (Oct. 1985): 465–71.

Floria, Carlos Alberto, and Marcelo Montserrat. "La política desde *Criterio* (1928–1977)." *Criterio*, nos. 1777–78 (Dec. 24, 1977): 762–89.

Flynn, Peter. *Brazil: A Political Analysis.* London: Benn; Boulder, Colo.: Westview, 1978.

————. "The Revolutionary Legion and the Brazilian Revolution of 1930." *St. Antony's Papers,* no. 22 (1970).

Fogarty, Michael P. *Christian Democracy in Western Europe, 1820–1953.* London: Routledge and Kegan Paul, 1957.

Font, Mauricio A. *Coffee, Contention, and Change in the Making of Modern Brasil.* Cambridge, Eng.: Basil Blackwell, 1990.

Font, Miguel J., ed. *La mujer: Encuesta feminista argentina. Hacia la formación de una Liga Feminista Sudamericana.* Buenos Aires: Costa Hnos., 1921.

Forjaz, Maria Cecília Spina. *Tenentismo e forças armadas na revolução de 30.* Rio de Janeiro: Forense Universitária, 1988.

Forni, Floreal. "Catolicismo y peronismo (1)." *Unidos* 4, no. 14 (Apr. 1987): 211–26.

Fragoso, Hugo. "A igreja na formação do estado liberal (1840–1875)." In *História da igreja no Brasil: Ensaio de interpretação a partir do povo.* Vol. 2, *A igreja no Brasil no século XIX,* ed. João Fagundes Hauck, Hugo Fragoso, José Oscar Beozzo, Klaus Van Der Grijp, and Benno Brod, 143–253. Petrópolis, Brazil: Editora Vozes, 1980.

Franceschi, Gustavo J. *La democracia y la iglesia.* Buenos Aires: Agencia General de Librería y Publicaciones, 1918.

————. *Totalitarismo, liberalismo, catolicismo . . .* Buenos Aires: Asociación de los Jóvenes de la Acción Católica Argentina, 1940.

————. *Tres estudios sobre la familia: Origen de la familia, su constitución interna, su función social.* Buenos Aires: Agencia General de Librería y Publicaciones, 1923.

Franco, Afonso Arinos de Melo. *Preparação ao nacionalismo (carta aos que tem vinte annos).* Rio de Janeiro: Civilização Brasileira, 1934.

Franco, Celina do Amaral Peixoto Moreira, Lúcia Lippi Oliveira, and Maria Aparecida Alves Hime. "O contexto político na revolução de trinta." *Dados,* no. 7 (1970): 118–33.

Freire, Laudelino. *Conferência sobre o thema da defesa da língua nacional.* Rio de Janeiro: Rohe, 1920.

French, John D. "Industrial Workers and the Origin of Populist Politics in the ABC Region of Greater São Paulo, Brazil, 1900–1950." Ph.D. diss., Yale University, 1985.

El Frente Nacional y su plan de acción política. Santiago: n.p., n.d.

Friedländer, Saul. *Nazi Germany and the Jews.* Vol. 1, *The Years of Persecution, 1933–1939.* New York: HarperCollins, 1997.

Furlong, Guillermo S. J. "El catolicismo argentino entre 1860 y 1930." In *Historia argentina contemporánea, 1862–1930,* vol. 2, *Historia de las instituciones y la cultura,* ed. Academia Nacional de la Historia, 251–92. Buenos Aires: Ateneo, 1964.

Gallardo, Guillermo. "Programa de la L.C.A.: II, Reglamentar en forma severa la admisión y residencia de los extranjeros." MS, photocopy, n.d.

Gallardo, Luis F. *A.D.U.N.A.: El por qué de la violencia. Nuestros enemigos. Nuestro programa*. Buenos Aires: n.p., 1933.

————. *Las fuerzas armadas y la defensa nacional*. Buenos Aires: n.p., 1936.

Gálvez, Manuel. *El diario de Gabriel Quiroga: opiniones sobre la vida argentina*. Buenos Aires: A. Moen, 1910.

————. *Este pueblo necesita*. Buenos Aires: A. García Santos, 1934.

————. *La inseguridad de la vida obrera: Informe sobre el paro forzoso*. Buenos Aires: Alsina, 1913.

————. *Recuerdos de la vida literaria: Amigos y maestros de mi juventud*. Buenos Aires: Guillermo Kraft, 1944.

————. *Recuerdos de la vida literaria: Entre la novela y la historia*. Buenos Aires: Libreria Hachette, 1962.

————. *El solar de la raza*. 7th ed. Buenos Aires: Poblet, 1943.

————. *Vida de Hipolito Yrigoyen—el hombre del misterio*. Buenos Aires: G. Kraft, 1939.

Gálvez de Tiscornia, Lucía. "La Iglesia en la Argentina." *Todo Es Historia*, no. 238 (Mar. 1987): 8–43.

Garay Vera, Cristián. *El Partido Agrario-Laborista, 1945–1958*. Santiago: Andrés Bello, 1990.

García, Alicia S., and Ricardo Rodríguez Molas. *Textos y documentos. El autoritarismo y los argentinos: La hora de la espada (1924–1946)*. 3 vols. Buenos Aires: Centro Editor de América Latina, 1988.

García Molina, Fernando, and Carlos A. Mayo. *Archivo del general Uriburu: autoritarismo y ejército*. 2 vols. Buenos Aires: Centro Editor de América Latina, 1986.

Gaudig, Olaf, and Peter Veit. " . . . Y mañana el mundo entero! Antecedentes para la historia del nacionalsocialismo en Chile." MS, n.d.

————. "¡ . . . Y mañana el mundo entero! Antecedentes para la historia del nacionalsocialismo en Chile." *Araucaria de Chile*, no. 41 (1988): 99–117.

Gaudio, Ricardo, and Jorge Pilone. "El desarrollo de la negociación colectiva durante la etapa de modernización industrial en la Argentina, 1935–1943." *Desarrollo Económico* 23, no. 90 (July–Sept. 1983): 255–86.

————. "Estado y relaciones laborales en el período previo al surgimiento del peronismo, 1935–1943." *Desarrollo Económico* 24, no. 94 (July–Sept. 1984): 235–73.

Gaviola A., Edda, Ximena Jiles M., Lorella Lopresti M., and Claudia Rojas Mira. *Queremos votar en las próximas elecciones: historia del movimiento femenino chileno, 1913–1952*. Santiago: La Morada, Fempress/ILET, ISIS, Librería Lila, Pemci, 1986.

Gazmuri Riveros, Cristián. "Notas sobre la influencia del racismo en la obra de Nicolás Palacios, Francisco A. Encina, y Alberto Cabero." *Historia* 16 (1981): 225–47.

————. *Testimonios de una crisis: Chile, 1900–1925*. Santiago: Editorial Universitaria, 1979.

Gazmuri Riveros, Cristián, Mariana Aylwin Oyarzún, and Juan Carlos González Ransanz. *Perspectiva de Jaime Eyzaguirre*. Santiago: Aconcagua, 1977.

Geary, Dick. "Nazis and Workers: A Response to Conan Fischer's 'Class Enemies or Class Brothers?'" *European History Quarterly* 15 (Oct. 1985): 453–64.

Genta, Dr. Jordán B. *La formación de la inteligencia ético-política del militar argentino.* Buenos Aires: Talleres Graf. D. Cersosimo, 1941.

Gentile, Emilio. "Fascism as Political Religion." *Journal of Contemporary History* 25 (May–June 1990): 229–51.

Germani, Gino. "Antisemitismo ideológico y antisemitismo tradicional." *Comentario* 34 (1962): 55–63.

———. *Authoritarianism, Fascism, and National Populism.* New Brunswick, N.J.: Transaction Books, 1978.

Gertz, René. *O fascismo no sul do Brasil: Germanismo, Nazismo, Integralismo.* Porto Alegre, Brazil: Mercado Aberto, 1987.

———. "Influéncia política alemã no Brasil na década de 1930." *Estudios Interdisciplinarios de América Latina y el Caribe* 7 (Jan.–June 1996): 85–106.

———. "Nazismo, Fascismo, Integralismo e o apoio das oligarquias do Rio Grande do Sul e de Santa Catarina ao Estado Novo." *Revista Estudos Ibero-Americanos* 14 (July 1988): 21–30.

Ghio, José María. "Relgion and Politics in Argentina: From Integralist to Populist Nationalism." In *Es igual pero distinto: Essays in the Histories of Canada and Argentina,* ed. David Sheinin and Carlos A. Mayo, 295–304. Peterborough, Canada, and Mar del Plata, Argentina: Frost Centre for Canadian Heritage and Development Studies, Trent University, and Grupo Sociedad y Estado, Universidad Nacional de Mar del Plata, 1997.

Gibson, Edward L. *Class and Conservative Parties: Argentina in Comparative Perspective.* Baltimore: Johns Hopkins University Press, 1996.

———. "Democracy and the New Electoral Right in Argentina." *Journal of Inter-American Studies and World Affairs* 32 (fall 1990): 177–228.

Gilman, Sander. *The Jew's Body.* New York: Routledge, Chapman, and Hall, 1991.

Giménez, Antonio A. Interview with author. Buenos Aires, June 1977.

Glauert, Earl T. "Ricardo Rojas and the Emergence of Argentine Cultural Nationalism." *Hispanic American Historical Review* 43 (Feb. 1963): 1–13.

Glave, Guido. *Economía dirigida de la democracia corporativa argentina.* Buenos Aires: Luis L. Gotelli, 1936.

Glickman, Nora. "The Image of the Jew in Brazilian and Argentinian Literature." Ph.D. diss., New York University, 1978.

———. "The Jewish White Slave Trade in Latin American Writings." *American Jewish Archives* 34 (Nov. 1982): 178–89.

Godio, Julio. *La Semana Trágica de enero de 1919.* Buenos Aires: Granica, 1972.

Godoy, Hernán. "El pensamiento nacionalista en Chile a comienzos del siglo XX." *Dilemas,* no. 9 (Dec. 1973): 32–39.

Goldwert, Marvin. *Democracy, Militarism, and Nationalism in Argentina, 1930–1966: An Interpretation.* Austin: University of Texas Press, 1972.

Gomes, Angela de Castro. "Silêncio e orações: as relações estado, igreja e classe tra-balhadoral no pós-34." *Religião e Sociedade* 14 (Mar. 1987): 88–110.

Gomes, Eduardo Rodrigues. "Campo contra cidade: O ruralismo e a crise oligár-quica no pensamento político brasileiro, 1910/1935." *Revista Brasileira de Estudos Políticos*, no. 56 (1983): 49–96.

Gomes, Perillo. *Ensaios de crítica doutrinária*. Rio de Janeiro: Editores Centro D. Vi-tal, Alvaro Pinto, Annuario do Brasil, 1923.

Gómez Ugarte, Jorge. *Ese cuarto de siglo . . . Veinticinco años de vida universitaria en la A.N.E.C.: 1915–1941*. Santiago: Andrés Bello, 1985.

Góngora, Mario. *Ensayo histórico sobre la noción de estado en Chile en los siglos XIX y XX*. Santiago: Editorial Universitaria, 1986.

———. "Libertad política y concepto económico de gobierno en Chile hacia 1915–1935." *Historia* 20 (1985): 11–46.

González, Jorge. *La concepción nacista del estado*. Santiago: Juan Yunis S., 1934.

———. *Nacismo o comunismo*. Santiago: El Esfuerzo, 1936.

———. *El problema del hambre (Sus causas y su solución)*. Santiago: Ercilla, 1937.

González Janzen, Ignacio. *La Triple-A*. Buenos Aires: Contrapunto, 1986.

González Miranda, Sergio, Carlos Maldonado Prieto, and Sandra McGee Deutsch. "Las Ligas Patrióticas: Un caso de nacionalismo, xenofobia, y lucha social en Chile." *Canadian Review of Studies in Nationalism* 21, nos. 1–2 (1994): 57–69.

González von Marées, Jorge. *El mal de Chile (sus causas y sus remedios)*. Santiago: Portales, 1940.

———. *Pueblo y estado*. Santiago: Antares, 1936.

———. *Tres discursos parlamentarios*. Santiago: n.p., n.d.

———. *La verdadera revolución*. Santiago: Talleres Gráficos Unión Literaria, 1936.

———. *La violencia nacista y los partidos políticos*. Santiago: El Esfuerzo, 1936.

Gori, Gaston. *La Forestal (La tragedia del quebracho colorado)*. 2d ed. Buenos Aires: Proyección, 1974.

Gouvêa, Oswaldo. *Os judeus do cinema*. Rio de Janeiro: Gráphica São Jorge, 1935.

Grant, Emma. "Feminism in Fascism: A Study of Brazil's Integralist Movement." Se-nior honors thesis, Connecticut College, 1996.

Grayson, George. *El Partido Demócrata Cristiano*. Trans. Adolfo Murguía Zuriar-raín. Santiago: Francisco de Aguirre, 1968.

Great Britain. Parliament. House of Commons. *Sessional Papers*. Accounts and Pa-pers. Session Feb. 10, 1920–Dec. 23, 1920. Vol. 17 of 26 vols.

———. Public Record Office. Foreign Office. Confidential file on Latin America. Microfilm.

Grierson, Cecilia. *Decadencia del Consejo Nacional de Mujeres de la República Ar-gentina*. Buenos Aires: n.p., 1910.

Griffin, Charles C. "Francisco Encina and Revisionism in Chilean History." *Hispanic American Historical Review* 37 (Feb. 1957): 1–28.

Griffin, Roger. *The Nature of Fascism*. New York: Routledge, 1993.

Griffiths, Richard. "Anticapitalism and the French Extra-Parliamentary Right, 1870–1940." *Journal of Contemporary History* 13 (Oct. 1978): 721–40.

Guardia Argentina. *Concentración de fuerzas nacionalistas: Expresión de propósitos.* Buenos Aires: Talleres Gráficos de la Guardia Argentina, 1934.

———. *Propósitos.* Buenos Aires: n.p., 1933.

Guarello, Jorge. Interview with author. Valparaíso, Chile, Nov. 21, 1989.

Gutiérrez de Miguel, V. *La revolución argentina: Relato de un testigo presencial.* Madrid: Compañía Ibero Americana de Publicaciones, 1930.

Guy, Donna. *Sex and Danger in Buenos Aires: Prostitution, Family, and Nation in Argentina.* Lincoln: University of Nebraska Press, 1991.

Hahner, June Edith. *Civilian-Military Relations in Brazil, 1889–1898.* Columbia: University of South Carolina Press, 1969.

———. *Emancipating the Female Sex: The Struggle for Women's Rights in Brazil, 1850–1940.* Durham, N.C.: Duke University Press, 1990.

———. "Jacobinos Versus Gallegos: Urban Radicals Versus Portuguese Immigrants in Rio de Janeiro in the 1890s." *Journal of Inter-American Studies and World Affairs* 18 (May 1976): 125–54.

———. *Poverty and Politics: The Urban Poor in Brazil, 1870–1920.* Albuquerque: University of New Mexico Press, 1986.

Hale, Charles A. "The Reconstruction of Nineteenth-Century Politics in Spanish America: A Case for the History of Ideas." *Latin American Research Review* 8 (summer 1973): 53–74.

Hall, Michael M. "Immigration and the Early São Paulo Working Class." *Jahrbuch für Geschichte von Staat, Wirtschaft, und Gesellschaft Lateinamerikas* 12 (1975): 393–407.

Hauck, João Fagundes. Introduction to *A igreja e o povo,* by Padre Júlio Maria. São Paulo: Edições Loyola/CEPEHIB, 1983 [1900].

Heise González, Julio. *Historia de Chile: El período parlamentario 1861–1925.* Santiago: Andrés Bello, 1974.

Hennessy, Alistair. "Fascism and Populism in Latin America." In *Fascism, a Reader's Guide: Analyses, Interpretations, Bibliography,* ed. Walter Laqueur, 255–94. Berkeley: University of California Press, 1976.

Hernández, G. Cuadrado. "La rebelión de los braceros." *Todo Es Historia,* no. 185 (Oct. 1982): 78–96.

Hernández, Pablo J. *Conversaciones con José M. Rosa.* Buenos Aires: Colihue/Hachette, 1978.

Hernández Arregui, Juan José. *La formación de la consciencia nacional (1930–1960).* Buenos Aires: Hachea, 1960.

Herrera, Emilio. *Los prejuicios raciales en la argentina del 80: Julián Martel y su novela "La Bolsa."* Buenos Aires: Ediciones del Taller Literario Abraxas, 1985.

Higonnet, Margaret Randolph, Jane Jenson, Sonya Michel, and Margaret Collins Weitz, eds. *Behind the Lines: Gender and the Two World Wars.* New Haven, Conn.: Yale University Press, 1987.

Hilton, Stanley E. "Ação Integralista Brasileira: Fascism in Brazil, 1932–1938." *Luso-Brazilian Review* 9 (winter 1972): 3–29.

———. *A rebeliaõ vermelha.* Rio de Janeiro: Record, 1986.

Hirschman, Albert O. *The Rhetoric of Reaction: Perversity, Futility, Jeopardy.* Cambridge: Belknap Press of Harvard University Press, 1991.

Hobsbawm, Eric, and Terence Ranger, eds. *The Invention of Tradition.* Cambridge: Cambridge University Press, 1983.

Hollander, Nancy Caro. "Women in the Political Economy of Argentina." Ph.D. diss., UCLA, 1974.

Holloway, Thomas H. *Immigrants on the Land: Coffee and Society in São Paulo, 1886–1934.* Chapel Hill: University of North Carolina Press, 1980.

Horowitz, Joel. "Argentina's Failed General Strike of 1921: A Critical Moment in the Radicals' Relations with Unions." *Hispanic American Historical Review* 75 (Feb. 1995): 57–79.

———. *Argentine Unions, the State, and the Rise of Perón, 1930–1945.* Berkeley: Institute of International Studies, University of California, no. 76, 1990.

———. "Ideologías sindicales y políticas estatales en la Argentina, 1930–1943." *Desarrollo Económico* 24, no. 94 (July–Sept. 1984): 275–95.

———. "Industrialists and the Rise of Perón, 1943–1946: Some Implications for the Conceptualization of Populism." *The Americas* 47 (Oct. 1990): 199–218.

———. "When Argentine Employers and Workers Agreed: Opposition to a Government Pension Plan in 1923 and 1924." Paper presented at the Latin American Studies Association meeting, Washington, D.C., September 1995.

Houseman, Philip Joseph. "Chilean Nationalism, 1920–1952." Ph.D. diss., Stanford University, 1961.

Hunt, Lynn, ed. *The New Cultural History.* Berkeley: University of California Press, 1989.

Hutchison, Elizabeth. "El feminismo en el movimiento obrero chileno: La emancipación de la mujer en la prensa obrera feminista, 1905–1908." Documento de Trabajo, Serie Contribuciones no. 80. Santiago: FLACSO-Chile, 1992.

———. "Working Women of Santiago: Gender and Social Transformation in Urban Chile, 1887–1927." Ph.D. diss., University of California–Berkeley, 1995.

Ibáñez y el 5 de septiembre: Aquí yacen los que cumplieron. Santiago: La Nación, 1939.

Ibarguren, Carlos. *La crisis política del mundo.* Buenos Aires: López, 1933.

———. *La historia que he vivido.* 2d ed. Buenos Aires: Editorial Universitaria de Buenos Aires, 1969.

———. *La inquietud de esta hora: liberalismo, corporativismo, nacionalismo.* Buenos Aires: Roldán, 1934.

Ibarguren, Carlos Jr. *Respuestas a un cuestionario acerca del nacionalismo, 1930–1945.* Buenos Aires: Dorrego, 1971.

———. *Roberto de Laferrère: Periodismo-política-historia.* Buenos Aires: Editorial Universitaria de Buenos Aires, 1970.

Ibarguren, Federico. *Orígenes del nacionalismo argentino.* Buenos Aires: Calcius, 1969.

Ideología de la Acción Nacionalista de Chile. Santiago: La Cruz Svástica, 1932.

La Iglesia del silencio en Chile: Un tema de meditación para los católicos latinoamericanos. Bogotá: Sociedad Colombiana de Defensa de la Tradición, Familia, y Propiedad, 1976.

Iglesias, Francisco. "Capítulo de história das idéias no Brasil: Estudo sobre o pensamento reacionário: Jackson de Figueiredo." *Revista Brasileira de Ciências Sociais* 2 (July 1962): 3–52.

Imaz, José Luis de. "Alejandro E. Bunge, economista y sociólogo (1880–1943)." *Desarrollo Económico* 14 (Oct.–Dec. 1974): 545–67.

———. *Promediados los cuarenta (no pesa la mochila).* Buenos Aires: Sudamericana, 1977.

Iñíquez Irarrázaval, Pedro Felipe. *Notas sobre el desarrollo del pensamiento social en Chile (1901–1906).* Santiago: Jurídica de Chile, 1968.

Instituto Torcuato di Tella. Oral history project. Interview with Arturo Jauretche, 1971.

———. Interview with Julio Irazusta, 1971.

Irazusta, Julio. *Balance de siglo y medio.* Buenos Aires: La Balandra, 1972.

———. *Estudios histórico-políticos: El liberalismo y el socialismo y otros ensayos económicos.* Buenos Aires: Dictio, 1973.

———. *Genio y figura de Leopoldo Lugones.* Buenos Aires: Editorial Universitaria de Buenos Aires, 1968.

———. *Memorias: Historia de un historiador a la fuerza.* Buenos Aires: Culturales Argentinas, 1975.

———, ed. *El pensamiento político nacionalista.* Vol. 2, *La revolución de 1930.* Buenos Aires: Obligado Editora, 1975.

Irazusta, Rodolfo, and Julio Irazusta. *La Argentina y el imperialismo británico: Los eslabones de una cadena, 1806–1933.* Buenos Aires: Argentinas Condor, 1934.

Irvine, William D. "Fascism in France and the Strange Case of the Croix de Feu." *Journal of Modern History* 63 (June 1991): 271–95.

———. "French Conservatives and the 'New Right' During the 1930s." *French Historical Studies* 8 (fall 1974): 534–62.

Iscaro, Rubén. *Historia del movimiento sindical.* 2 vols. Buenos Aires: Fundamentos, 1973.

Ivereigh, Austen. *Catholicism and Politics in Argentina, 1810–1960.* New York: St. Martin's Press, 1995.

Izquierdo Fernández, Gonzalo. "Octubre de 1905: Un episodio en la historia social chilena." *Historia* 13 (1976): 55–96.

Jackisch, Carlota. *El nazismo y los refugiados alemanes en la Argentina, 1933–1945.* Buenos Aires: Editorial del Belgrano, 1989.

Jaguaribe, Hélio, comp. *La sociedad, el estado y los partidos en la actualidad brasileña.* Trans. Eduardo L. Suárez. 2 vols. Mexico: Fondo de Cultura Económica, 1992.

James, Daniel. *Resistance and Integration: Peronism and the Argentine Working Class, 1946–1976.* Cambridge: Cambridge University Press, 1988.

Janotti, Maria de Lourdes Monaco. "The Monarchist Response to the Beginnings of the Brazilian Republic." *The Americas* 48 (Oct. 1991): 223–43.

Jeansonne, Glen. *Women of the Far Right: The Mothers' Movement and World War II.* Chicago: University of Chicago Press, 1997.

Jefferson, Mark. *Peopling the Argentine Pampa.* New York: American Geographical Society, 1926.

Jobet, Julio César. *El partido socialista de Chile.* Vol. 1. Santiago: Prensa Latinoamericana, 1971.

Josephs, Ray. *Argentine Diary: The Inside Story of the Coming of Fascism.* New York: Random House, 1944.

Júlio Maria, Padre. *O catolicismo no Brasil (memória histórica).* Rio de Janeiro: Livraria Agir Editora, 1950 [1900].

———. *A igreja e o povo.* São Paulo: Loyola/CEPEHIB, 1983 [1900].

Kaempffer Villagrán, Guillermo. *Así sucedió, 1850–1925: Sangrientos episodios de la lucha obrera en Chile.* Santiago: n.p., 1962.

Keith, Henry Hunt. "The Symbiosis of Love and Hate in Luso-Brazilian Relations, 1822–1922." *Stvdia*, nos. 43–44 (Jan.–Dec. 1980): 325–42.

Kele, Max H. *Nazis and Workers: National Socialist Appeals to German Labor, 1919–1933.* Chapel Hill: University of North Carolina Press, 1972.

Keller R., Carlos. *La eterna crisis chilena.* Santiago: Nascimento, 1931.

———. *La locura de Juan Bernales.* Santiago: Sociedad Amigos del Libro, 1949.

———. *Una revolución en marcha: El movimiento nacional-socialista ante la política del país.* Santiago: Nacista, 1938.

Keogh, Dermot, ed. *Church and Politics in Latin America.* New York: St. Martin's Press, 1990.

Kiernan, Sergio. "Waiting for Justice: Two Years After the AMIA Bombing." International Perspectives no. 34. New York: American Jewish Committee, 1996.

Klein, Herbert S. "The Social and Economic Integration of Portuguese Immigrants in Brazil in the Late Nineteenth and Twentieth Centuries." *Journal of Latin American Studies* 23 (May 1991): 309–37.

Kleiner, Alberto, comp. *Los políticos argentinos y el anti-semitismo.* 3 vols. Buenos Aires: Libreros y Editores del Polígono, 1984.

Klich, Ignacio. "Argentina." In *American Jewish Yearbook 1996*, 227–37. New York: American Jewish Committee, 1996.

Klimpel, Felicitas. *La mujer chilena (El aporte femenino al Progreso de Chile), 1910–1960.* Santiago: Andrés Bello, 1962.

Klubock, Thomas Miller. "Working-Class Masculinity, Middle-Class Morality, and Labor Politics in the Chilean Copper Mines." *Journal of Social History* 30 (winter 1996): 435–64.

Koonz, Claudia. *Mothers in the Fatherland: Women, the Family, and Nazi Politics.* New York: St. Martin's Press, 1987.

Korzeniewicz, Roberto P. "The Labor Politics of Radicalism: The Santa Fe Crisis of 1928." *Hispanic American Historical Review* 73 (Feb. 1993): 1–32.

―――. "Labor Unrest in Argentina, 1930-1943." *Latin American Research Review* 28, no. 1 (1993): 7-40.

―――. "The Labour Movement and the State in Argentina, 1887-1907." *Bulletin of Latin American Research* 8, no. 1 (1989): 25-45.

Krebs, Ricardo, ed. *Catolicismo y laicismo: Seis estudios.* Santiago: Ediciones Nueva Universidad, 1981.

Kroeber, Clifton B. "Rosas and the Revision of Argentine History, 1880-1955." *Revista Inter-Americana de Bibliografía* 10, no. 9 (Jan.-Mar. 1960): 3-25.

Lacerda, Carlos. "O São Francisco e o integralismo." *Diretrizes* 1 (July 1938): 37-39; 1 (Aug. 1938): 27-30.

Laguna, Justo. "La iglesia y diez años de democracia." *Todo Es Historia*, no. 317 (Dec. 1993): 8.

Landsberger, Henry A. "Time, Persons, Doctrine: The Modernization of the Church in Chile." In *The Church and Social Change in Latin America*, ed. Henry A. Landsberger, 77-94. Notre Dame, Ind.: University of Notre Dame Press, 1970.

La Palma de Emery, Celia. *Discursos y conferencias: Acción pública y privada en favor de la mujer y del niño en la República Argentina.* Buenos Aires: Alfa y Omega, 1910.

Laqueur, Walter, ed. *Fascism, a Reader's Guide: Analyses, Interpretations, Bibliography.* Berkeley: University of California Press, 1976.

Large, David. "The Politics of Law and Order: Counterrevolutionary Self-Defense Organizations in Central Europe, 1918-1923." Ph.D. diss., University of California-Berkeley, 1974.

Larsen, Stein Ugelvik, Bernt Hagtvet, and Jan Petter Myklebust, eds. *Who Were the Fascists? Social Roots of European Fascism.* Bergen, Norway: Universitetsforlaget, 1980.

Lastra, Bonifacio. *Bajo el signo nacionalista: Escritos y discursos.* Buenos Aires: Alianza, 1944.

Latcham, Ricardo A. *Chuquicamata estado yankee (visión de la montaña roja).* Santiago: Nascimento, 1926.

Latourette, Kenneth S. *Christianity in a Revolutionary Age.* Vol. 1, *The Nineteenth Century in Europe: Background and Roman Catholic Phase.* New York: Harper, 1958.

Lauerhass, Ludwig Jr. "Getúlio Vargas and the Triumph of Brazilian Nationalism: A Study on the Rise of the Nationalist Generation of 1930." Ph.D. diss., UCLA, 1972.

Lavrin, Asunción. *Women, Feminism, and Social Change in Argentina, Chile, and Uruguay, 1890-1940.* Lincoln: University of Nebraska Press, 1995.

―――. "Women, Labor, and the Left: Argentina and Chile, 1890-1925." *Journal of Women's History* 1 (fall 1989): 88-116.

Leão, A. Carneiro. *São Paulo em 1920.* Rio de Janeiro: Annuario Americano, 1920.

Legión Cívica de Chile. *Estatuto Orgánico.* Santiago: La Nación, n.d.

Leme, Marisa Sáenz. *A ideologia dos industriais brasileiros (1919-1945).* Petrópolis, Brazil: Vozes, 1978.

Lenharo, Alcir. *A sacralização da política*. Campinas, Brazil: Papirus, 1986.

Lesser, Jeffrey. "From Pedlars to Proprietors: Lebanese, Syrian, and Jewish Immigrants in Brazil." In *The Lebanese in the World: A Century of Emigration*, ed. Albert Hourani and Nadim Shehadi, 393-410. London: I. B. Tauris, 1991.

———. "Immigration and Shifting Concepts of National Identity in Brazil During the Vargas Era." *Luso-Brazilian Review* 31 (winter 1994): 27-48.

———. "Pawns of the Powerful: Jewish Immigration to Brazil, 1904-1945." Ph.D. diss., New York University, 1989.

———. *Welcoming the Undesirables: Brazil and the Jewish Question*. Berkeley: University of California Press, 1995.

Levi, Darrell. *The Prados of São Paulo, Brazil: An Elite Family and Social Change, 1840-1930*. Athens: University of Georgia Press, 1987.

Levine, Robert M. "Brazil's Jews During the Vargas Era and After." *Luso-Brazilian Review* 5 (June 1968): 45-58.

———. "The First Afro-Brazilian Congress: Opportunities for the Study of Race in the Brazilian Northeast." *Race* 15 (Oct. 1973): 185-93.

———. *The Vargas Regime: The Critical Years, 1934-1938*. New York: Columbia University Press, 1970.

Levisky, Fernando. *Israel no Brasil*. São Paulo: Edições e Publicações Brasil, 1936.

Lewis, Paul H. *The Crisis of Argentine Capitalism*. Chapel Hill: University of North Carolina Press, 1990.

———. "Was Perón a Fascist? An Inquiry into the Nature of Fascism." *Journal of Politics* 42 (1980): 242-56.

Lewis, Stephen E. "Myth and the History of Chile's Araucanians." *Radical History Review* 58 (winter 1994): 112-41.

Lezica, Manuel de. *Recuerdos de un nacionalista*. Buenos Aires: Astral, 1968.

Liebscher, Arthur F. "The Church and Argentina's Crisis of Conscience." *America* 155, no. 16 (Nov. 29, 1986): 342-45.

———. "Toward a Pious Republic: Argentine Social Catholicism in Córdoba, 1895-1930." *Journal of Church and State* 30 (autumn 1988): 549-67.

Liga de Damas Chilenas. *Memoria correspondiente al año 1929*. Santiago: Arturo Prat, 1929.

Liga Patriótica Argentina. *Acción civilizadora de las escuelas de la Liga Patriótica Argentina*. Buenos Aires: n.p., 1921.

———. *Acción civilizadora de las escuelas de la Liga Patriótica Argentina, 23 abril 1922*. Buenos Aires: n.p., 1922.

———. *Campaña de Santa Cruz: Homenaje al Ejército y Armada*. Buenos Aires: n.p., 1922.

———. *Catecismo de la doctrina patria*. Buenos Aires: n.p., 1921.

———. *Congreso General de Territorios Nacionales*. Buenos Aires: L. J. Rosso, 1927.

———. *Cuarto Congreso Nacionalista de la Liga Patriótica Argentina*. Buenos Aires: A. Baiocco, 1923.

———. *El culto de la Patagonia: Sucesos de Santa Cruz.* Buenos Aires: n.p., 1922.

———. *Definição de Liga Patriótica Argentina (Guia do bom senso social).* Buenos Aires: n.p., 1922.

———. *Definición de la Liga Patriótica Argentina (Guía del buen sentido social).* Buenos Aires: n.p., 1921.

———. *Discurso pronunciado por el Dr. Manuel Carlés ante la honorable Sociedad de Beneficencia el 26 de mayo de 1919 en el acto de la distribución de los Premios a la Virtud.* Buenos Aires: n.p., 1919.

———. *Discurso pronunciado por el presidente de la Liga Patriótica Argentina, Dr. Manuel Carlés en la reunión celebrada por la honorable Junta de Gobierno en honor de los delegados de la Asociación de Empleados de Comercio de Rio de Janeiro.* Buenos Aires: n.p., 1924.

———. *Discursos pronunciados en el acto inaugural y veredicto del Jurado de la Cuarta Exposición Nacional de Tejidos y Bordados, 4–20 agosto 1923.* Buenos Aires: n.p., 1923.

———. *Estatutos.* Buenos Aires: Rinaldi, 1919.

———. *Humanitarismo práctico. La Liga Patriótica Argentina en Gualeguaychú.* Buenos Aires: n.p., 1921.

———. *La Liga Patriótica y la revolución del 6 de septiembre de 1930.* Buenos Aires: Biblioteca de la Liga Patriótica Argentina, 1930.

———. *Misión y doctrina de la Liga Patriótica Argentina.* Buenos Aires: n.p., 1956.

———. *Noveno Congreso Nacionalista organizado por la Liga Patriótica Argentina.* Buenos Aires: P. Ventriglia, 1928.

———. *Octavo Congreso Nacionalista organizado por la Liga Patriótica Argentina.* Buenos Aires: Caporaletti, 1927.

———. *Primer Congreso de Trabajadores de la Liga Patriótica Argentina.* Buenos Aires: L. J. Rosso, 1922.

———. *Primero de Mayo Argentino: Conmemoración del pronunciamiento de Urquiza en Entre Ríos.* Buenos Aires: n.p., 1921.

———. *El programa de la Liga Patriótica Argentina y la educación por el ejemplo (Como una consagración del concepto Patria).* Buenos Aires: n.p., 1923.

———. *Quinto Congreso Nacionalista de Trabajadores, organizado por la Liga Patriótica Argentina.* Buenos Aires: A. Baiocco y Rivadavia, 1924.

———. *Restauración de la Moral Argentina.* Buenos Aires: n.p., 1930.

———. *Séptimo Congreso Nacionalista de la Liga Patriótica Argentina.* Buenos Aires: n.p., 1926.

———. *Sexto Congreso Nacionalista de Trabajadores organizado por la Liga Patriótica Argentina.* Buenos Aires: P. Ventriglia, 1925.

———. *Solemne homenaje de la Liga Patriótica Militar de Chile a la Liga Patriótica Argentina.* Santiago: n.p., 1922.

———. *Tercer Congreso de Trabajadores de la Liga Patriótica Argentina.* Buenos Aires: n.p., 1922.

———. Brigada 19 y 20. *La verdad de la Liga Patriótica Argentina.* Buenos Aires: n.p., 1950.
———. Comisión Central de Señoritas de la Liga Patriótica Argentina. *Memoria de diez escuelas obreras, 1924-mayo-1925.* Buenos Aires: n.p., 1925.
———. Comisión Central de Señoritas de la Liga Patriótica Argentina. *Memoria 1927 mayo 1928.* Buenos Aires: n.p., 1928.
———. Comisión de Bellas Artes. Brigadas de Señoras de la Liga Patriótica Argentina. *Discursos pronunciados en el acto inaugural y veredicto del Jurado de la Tercera Exposición Nacional de Tejidos y Bordados 1–15 julio 1922.* Buenos Aires: n.p., 1922.
———. Comisión de Señoritas de la Liga Patriótica Argentina. *Sus escuelas de obreras en las fábricas.* Buenos Aires: Biblioteca de la Liga Patriótica Argentina, 1922.
Lima, Alceu Amoroso. *Indicações políticas: Da revolução a constituição.* Rio de Janeiro: Civilização Brasileira, 1936.
Lima Sobrinho, Alejandre José Barbosa. *Presença de Alberto Torres (sua vida e pensamento).* Rio de Janeiro: Civilização Brasileira, 1968.
Linhares, Josephat. *O integralismo à luz da doutrina social cathólica.* N.p.: Gadelha, 1933.
Lipiner, Elias. *Breve historia dos judeus no Brasil.* Rio de Janeiro: Edições Biblos, 1962.
Livro de Recortes de Jornais e Revistas. Faculdade de Direito de São Paulo.
La llamada movilización de 1920 (Antecedentes y documentos). Santiago: Escuela Tip. "La Gratitud Nacional," 1923.
Llambías, Héctor. *La dialéctica comunista y el concepto de la libertad.* Buenos Aires: Gladium, 1938.
Lobato, Mirta Zaida. "Mujeres en la fábrica, el caso de las obreras del frigorífico Armour, 1915–1969." *Anuario del IEHS* 5 (1990): 171–205.
Loewenstein, Karl. *Brazil Under Vargas.* New York: Macmillan, 1942.
Love, Joseph L. *Rio Grande do Sul and Brazilian Regionalism 1882–1930.* Stanford, Calif.: Stanford University Press, 1971.
———. *São Paulo in the Brazilian Federation, 1889–1937.* Stanford, Calif.: Stanford University Press, 1980.
Loveman, Brian. *Chile: The Legacy of Hispanic Capitalism.* 2d ed. New York: Oxford University Press, 1988.
———. *Struggle in the Countryside: Politics and Rural Labor in Chile, 1919–1973.* Bloomington: Indiana University Press, 1976.
Luco, Germán. "¿Fué Ibáñez el precursor del nacismo?" *Revista del Pacífico* 1 (Sept. 1935): 19–22, 84.
Luebke, Frederick C. *Germans in Brazil: A Comparative History of Cultural Conflict During World War I.* Baton Rouge: Louisiana State University Press, 1987.
Lugones, Leopoldo. *El estado equitativo (ensayo sobre la realidad argentina).* Buenos Aires: La Editora Argentina, 1932.

———. *La grande Argentina.* 2d ed. Buenos Aires: Huemul, 1962.

———. *La organización de la paz.* Buenos Aires: La Editora Argentina, 1925.

Luna, Félix. *Alvear.* Buenos Aires: Libros Argentinos, 1958.

———. *Yrigoyen.* Buenos Aires: Desarrollo, 1964.

Lustosa, Oscar de Figueiredo. *A igreja católica no Brasil e o regime republicano: Um aprendizado de liberdade.* São Paulo: Loyola/CEPEHIB, 1990.

———. "A igreja e o integralismo no Brasil—1932-1939 (notas e indicações)." *Revista de História* 54, no. 108 (Oct.–Dec. 1976): 503-32.

———. *Igreja e política no Brasil: Do Partido Católico à L.E.C. (1874-1945).* São Paulo: Loyola, 1983.

Lux, Dr. "De Nazi a Liberal." *Nuevo Zig-Zag,* July 15, 1950, p. 29.

Luz, Nícia Vilela. *A luta pela industrialização do Brasil.* 2d ed. São Paulo: Alfa y Omega, 1975.

McCann, Frank D. "The Formative Period of Twentieth-Century Brazilian Army Thought, 1900-1922." *Hispanic American Historical Review* 64 (Nov. 1984): 737-65.

———. "The Nation in Arms: Obligatory Military Service During the Old Republic." In *Essays Concerning the Socioeconomic History of Brazil and Portuguese India,* ed. Dauril Alden and Warren Dean, 211-43. Gainesville: University Presses of Florida, 1977.

———. "Origins of the 'New Professional' of the Brazilian Military." *Journal of Inter-American Studies and World Affairs* 21 (Nov. 1979): 505-22.

———. "Vargas and the Destruction of the Brazilian Integralista and Nazi Parties." *The Americas* 26 (July 1969): 15-34.

Macciocchi, Maria-Antonietta. "Female Sexuality in Fascist Ideology." *Feminist Review,* no. 1 (1979): 67-82.

McClelland, J. S., ed. *The French Right: From De Maistre to Maurras.* Trans. John Frears. London: Jonathan Cape, 1970.

McClintock, Anne. "No Longer in a Future Heaven: Nationalism, Gender, and Race." In *Becoming National: A Reader,* ed. Geoff Eley and Ronald Grigor Suny, 259-84. New York: Oxford University Press, 1996.

McGee, Sandra F. "Female Right-Wing Activists in Buenos Aires, 1900-1932." In *Women and the Structure of Society,* ed. Barbara J. Harris and Jo Ann K. McNamara, 85-97. Durham, N.C.: Duke University Press, 1984.

———. "The Visible and Invisible Liga Patriótica Argentina, 1919-1928: Gender Roles and the Right Wing." *Hispanic American Historical Review* 64 (May 1984): 233-58.

Maciel, Anor Butler. *Nacionalismo, o problema judaico no mundo e no Brasil—O nacional socialismo.* Porto Alegre, Brazil: Edição da Livraria do Globo, 1937.

McLain, W. Douglas Jr. "Alberto Torres, *Ad Hoc* Nationalist." *Luso-Brazilian Review* 4 (Dec. 1967): 17-34.

McLaughlin, Terence P., ed. *The Church and the Reconstruction of the Modern World: The Social Encyclicals of Pius XI.* Garden City, N.J.: Doubleday, 1957.

McLynn, F. J. "The Political Thought of Juan Domingo Perón." *Boletín de Estudios Latinoamericanos y del Caribe*, no. 22 (June 1982): 15–23.

McNeill, William H. *Dance and Drill in Human History*. Cambridge: Harvard University Press, 1997.

Macor, Darío, and Eduardo Iglesias. *El peronismo antes del peronismo: Memoria e historia en los orígenes del peronismo santafesino*. Santa Fe, Argentina: Centro de Publicaciones, Universidad Nacional del Litoral, 1997.

Maffei, Eduardo. *A batalha da Praça da Sé*. Rio de Janeiro: Philobiblion, 1984.

Magalhães Júnior, Raymundo. *Olavo Bilac e sua época*. Rio de Janeiro: Americana, 1974.

Magnet, Alejandro. *El padre Hurtado*. Santiago: Pacífico, 1954.

Mainwaring, Scott, and Timothy R. Scully, eds. *Building Democratic Institutions: Party Systems in Latin America*. Stanford, Calif.: Stanford University Press, 1995.

Maio, Marcos Chor. "'Nem Rotschild nem Trotsky': O pensamento anti-semita de Gustavo Barroso." M.A. thesis, IUPERJ, 1991.

———. *Nem Rotschild nem Trotsky: O pensamento anti-semita de Gustavo Barroso*. Rio de Janeiro: Imago, 1992.

Malamud, Carlos. "El Partido Demócrata Progresista: Un intento fallido de construir un partido nacional liberal-conservador." *Desarrollo Económico* 35, no. 138 (July–Sept. 1995): 289–308.

Maldonado Prieto, Carlos. "AChA y la proscripción del Partido Comunista en Chile, 1946–1948." Santiago: Contribuciones Programa FLACSO-Chile, no. 60, 1989.

———. "Los Carabineros de Chile: Historia de una policía militarizada." *Ibero Americana* 20, no. 3 (1990): 3–31.

———. "Entre reacción civilista y constitucionalismo formal: Las fuerzas armadas chilenas en el período 1931–1938." Santiago: Contribuciones FLACSO-Chile, no. 55, 1988.

———. "Grupos paramilitares de derecha en Chile, 1900–1950." MS, 1993.

———. *La Milicia Republicana: Historia de un exército civil en Chile*. Santiago: Servicio Universitario Mundial, 1988.

———. "La 'Prusia de América del Sur': Acerca de las relaciones militares chileno-germanas, 1927–1945." *Estudios Sociales*, no. 73 (3d trimester 1992): 75–102.

Mallimaci, Fortunato. *El catolicismo integral en la Argentina (1930–1946)*. Buenos Aires: Biblos—Fundación Simón Rodríguez, 1988.

Manns, Patricio. *Las grandes masacres*. Santiago: Empresa Editora Nacional Quimantú, 1972.

Manor, Paul. "The Liga Nacionalista de São Paulo: A Political Reformist Group in Paulista Academic of Yore: 1917–1924." *Jahrbuch für Geschichte von Staat, Wirtschaft, und Gesellschaft Lateinamerikas* 17 (1980): 317–53.

Maram, Sheldon Leslie. *Anarquistas, imigrantes, e o movimento operário brasileiro, 1890–1920*. Trans. José Eduardo Ribeiro Moretzsohn. Rio de Janeiro: Paz e Terra, 1979.

————. "Labor and the Left in Brazil, 1890–1921: A Movement Aborted." *Hispanic American Historical Review* 57 (May 1977): 254–72.

Marcondes, J. V. Freitas. "Social Legislation in Brazil." In *Brazil: Portrait of Half a Continent*, ed. T. Lynn Smith and Alexander Marchant, 382–401. Westport, Conn.: Greenwood Press, 1972 [1951].

A margem da história da república: ideais, crenças e affirmações: Inquérito por escriptores da geração nascida com a república. Rio de Janeiro: Annuario do Brasil, 1924.

Margulies, Marcos. "Ayer y mañana: Demografía de las comunidades judías en el Brasil." In *Comunidades Judías de Latinoamérica (1971–72)*, ed. Oficina Sudamericana del Comité Judío Americano, 323–29. Buenos Aires: Américalee S.R.L., 1974.

Maritain, Jacques. "Con el pueblo." *Sur* (Buenos Aires) 7, no. 31 (Apr. 1937): 7–49.

————. "Nota sobre la cuestión judía." *Estudios* 2, no. 22 (Sept. 1934): 34–36.

Marotta, Sebastián. *El movimiento sindical argentino: Su génesis y desarrollo*. 3 vols. Buenos Aires: Lacio, 1960–61, 1970.

Marsal, Juan F. and Margery J. Arent. "La derecha intelectual argentina: Análisis de la ideología y la acción política de un grupo de intelectuales." Buenos Aires: Instituto Torcuato di Tella, Centro de Investigaciones Sociales, Documento de Trabajo no. 73, 1970.

Marson, Adalberto. *A ideologia nacionalista em Alberto Torres*. São Paulo: Duas Cidades, 1979.

Martel, Julián (José María Miró). *La bolsa*. Buenos Aires: La Nación, 1909 [1891].

Martín, María Pía. "Anti-imperialismo y cuestión judía en el nacionalismo católico rosarino (1920–1930)." *Anuario* (Rosario) 17 (1995–96): 355–67.

Martínez, Tomás Eloy. *La novela de Perón*. Buenos Aires: Legasa Literaria, 1985.

Martins, Justino. "Como era verde o meu Brasil." *Diretrizes*, no. 90 (Mar. 19, 1942): cover, 5–6, 18–20, 32.

Masiello, Francine. *Between Civilization and Barbarism: Women, Nation, and Literary Culture in Modern Argentina*. Lincoln: University of Nebraska Press, 1992.

Matsushita, Hiroshi. *Movimiento obrero argentino 1930–1945: Sus proyecciones en los orígenes del peronismo*. Buenos Aires: Siglo Veinte, 1983.

Matta, Robert da. *Carnavais, malandros e heróis: Para uma sociologia do dilema brasileiro*. 4th ed. Rio de Janeiro: Zahar, 1983.

Mattelart, Michele. "Chile: The Feminine Side of the Coup, or When Bourgeois Women Take to the Streets." *NACLA's Latin America and Empire Report* 9 (Sept. 1975): 14–25.

Mayer, Arno J. *Dynamics of Counterrevolution in Europe, 1870–1956: An Analytic Framework*. New York: Harper and Row, 1971.

————. "Postwar Nationalisms, 1918–1919." *Past and Present* (July 1966): 114–26.

Mayo, Carlos A., Osvaldo Andino, and Fernando García Molina. *Diplomacia, política y petróleo en la Argentina*. Buenos Aires: Rincón, 1976.

Mayorga, Wilfredo. "Alessandri y el Nacismo frente a frente." *Ercilla*, Apr. 27, 1966, 18–19.

——. "El camino de la violencia." *Ercilla*, May 11, 1966, 18–19.

——. "Cuando el PS gritaba viva el Ejército." *Ercilla*, May 4, 1966, 14–15.

——. "Cuando Frei recuerda." *Ercilla*, July 27, 1966, 20–21, 25.

——. "La difícil generación del 20." *Ercilla*, June 5–11, 1968, 43–44.

——. "Los estudiantes del año 20." *Ercilla*, June 12–18, 1968, 43–44.

——. "Fuego contra la Milicia." *Ercilla*, Apr. 13, 1966, 18–19.

——. "La fugaz violencia del nacismo." *Ercilla*, Apr. 20, 1966, 18–19.

——. "Gustavo Ross Santa María." *Ercilla*, May 25, 1966, 18–19.

——. "El jesuita rebelde." *Ercilla*, Apr. 17, 1968, 15.

——. "Jorge González von Marées, el jefe." *Ercilla*, Oct. 23–29, 1968, 41–42.

——. "La Milicia Republicana." *Ercilla*, Apr. 6, 1966, 18–19.

——. "Punta Arenas: Asalto a la Federación Obrera." *Ercilla*, Aug. 16, 1967, 15.

Mayorga Santana, Ramiro. "Las milicias republicanas." *Revista Chilena de Historia y Geografía* 154 (1986): 108–30.

Mecham, J. Lloyd. *Church and State in Latin America*. Rev. ed. Chapel Hill: University of North Carolina Press, 1934.

Medeiros, Jarbas. *Ideologia autoritária no Brasil, 1930–1945*. Rio de Janeiro: Fundação Getúlio Vargas, 1978.

Meinvielle, Julio. *Concepción católica de la economía*. Buenos Aires: Cursos de Cultura Católica, 1936.

——. *Entre la iglesia y el reich*. Buenos Aires: Adsum, 1937.

——. *Hacia la cristiandad: Apuntes para una filosofía de la historia*. Buenos Aires: Adsum, 1940.

——. *El judío*. Buenos Aires: Antidoto, 1936.

——. *Un juicio católico sobre los problemas nuevos de la política*. Buenos Aires: Gladium, 1937.

Melo, Olbiano de. *Comunismo ou Fascismo?* Rio de Janeiro: Terra de Sol, 1931.

——. *A marcha da revolução social no Brasil (Ensaio histórico-sociológico do período 1922 a 1954)*. Rio de Janeiro: O Cruzeiro, 1957.

——. *República syndicalista dos Estados Unidos do Brazil (Bases para organização do estado syndical corporativo brasileiro)*. 2d ed. Rio de Janeiro: Terra de Sol, 1931.

Memoria y balance de la Asociación del Trabajo de Chile, Año 1921–1922. Santiago: n.p., 1923.

Merrick, Thomas W., and Douglas H. Graham. *Population and Economic Development in Brazil: 1800 to the Present*. Baltimore: Johns Hopkins University Press, 1979.

Mesquita Filho, Júlio de. *A crise nacional: reflexões em torno de uma data*. São Paulo: Seccão de Obras d' "O Estado de São Paulo," 1925.

Metz, Allan. "La encuesta de la revista "Claridad" de marzo de 1939." *Coloquio*, no. 23 (Apr. 1990): 27–44.

Meyer, Jean. *El sinarquismo: ¿un fascismo mexicano? 1937–1947*. Trans. Aurelio Garzón del Camino. Mexico City: Joaquín Mortiz, 1979.

Miceli, Sérgio. "A gestão diocesana na República Velha," *Religião e Sociedade* 12, no. 1 (Aug. 1985): 92–111.

Mignone, Emilio F. *Iglesia y dictadura: el papel de la iglesia a la luz de sus relaciones con el régimen militar.* Buenos Aires: Pensamiento Nacional, 1986.

Millar Carvacho, René. "Significado y antecedentes del movimiento militar de 1924." *Historia* 11 (1972–73): 7–102.

Mirelman, Victor A. *Jewish Buenos Aires, 1890–1930: In Search of an Identity.* Detroit: Wayne State University Press, 1990.

——. "The Jewish Community Versus Crime: The Case of White Slavery in Buenos Aires." *Jewish Social Studies* 46, no. 2 (spring 1984): 145–68.

——. "The Semana Trágica of 1919 and the Jews in Argentina." *Jewish Social Studies* 37 (Jan. 1975): 61–73.

Montenegro, João Alfredo de Sousa. *O integralismo no Ceará. Variações ideológicas.* Fortaleza: Imprensa Oficial do Ceará, 1986.

Monteón, Michael. "The *enganche* in the Chilean Nitrate Sector, 1880–1930." *Latin American Perspectives* 6 (summer 1979): 66–79.

Moody, Joseph N., ed. *Church and Society: Catholic Social and Political Thought and Movements, 1789–1950.* New York: Arts, 1953.

Moore, Leonard J. *Citizen Klansmen: The Ku Klux Klan in Indiana, 1921–1928.* Chapel Hill: University of North Carolina Press, 1991.

Morães, Reginaldo, Ricardo Antunes, Vera B. Ferrante, eds. *Inteligência brasileira.* São Paulo: Brasiliense, 1986.

Mörner, Magnus, Julia Fawaz de Viñuela, and John D. French. "Comparative Approaches to Latin American History." *Latin American Research Review* 27, no. 3 (1982): 55–90.

Morris, James O. *Elites, Intellectuals, and Consensus: A Study of the Social Question and the Industrial Relations System in Chile.* Ithaca: New York State School of Industrial and Labor Relations, Cornell University, 1966.

Mosse, George L. "The French Right and the Working Classes: Les Jaunes." *Journal of Contemporary History* 7 (July–Oct. 1972): 185–208.

——. *Nationalism and Sexuality: Middle-Class Morality and Sexual Norms in Modern Europe.* Madison: University of Wisconsin Press, 1985.

——. *The Nationalization of the Masses: Political Symbolism and Mass Movements in Germany from the Napoleonic Wars Through the Third Reich.* Ithaca, N.Y.: Cornell University Press, 1975.

Moulián, Tomás, and Isabel Torres Dujisin. *Discusiones entre honorables: Las candidaturas presidenciales de la derecha 1938–1946.* Santiago: FLACSO, 1989.

Moura, D. Odilão. *As idéias católicas no Brasil. Direções do pensamento católico do Brasil no século XX.* São Paulo: Convívio, 1978.

Movimiento Nacional de Chile. *Chileno: El Movimiento Nacional de Chile pide tu concurso.* Santiago: La Ilustración, 1940.

El movimiento nacional-socialista (M.N.S.). Santiago: Pacífico, 1933.

Muhlberger, Detlef, ed. *The Social Basis of European Fascist Movements*. New York: Croom Helm, 1987.

Mundt, Tito. *Yo lo conocí: 204 personajes en busca del autor*. Santiago: Empresa Editora Zig-Zag, 1965.

Murmis, Miguel, and Juan Carlos Portantiero. *Estudios sobre los orígenes del peronismo*. 2 vols. Buenos Aires: Siglo XXI, 1971–73.

Murray, Robert K. *Red Scare: A Study in National Hysteria, 1919–1920*. 2d ed. New York: McGraw-Hill, 1964.

Nachman, Robert G. "Positivism, Modernization, and the Middle Class in Brazil." *Hispanic American Historical Review* 57 (Feb. 1977): 1–23.

Nacionalismo Argentino, El. *Estatutos del Consejo Superior del Nacionalismo Argentino*. Buenos Aires: n.p., 1941.

———. *Voz nacionalista*. Buenos Aires: n.p., 1935.

"Nacionalista: Boicot a rusos o judíos." Flier. General Sarmiento, Buenos Aires, Apr. 12, 1937.

Nacismo Chileno. *Visión de un simpatizante*. Curicó: Librería Imprenta Chile, 1936.

Nagle, Jorge. *Educação e sociedade na primeira república*. São Paulo: Editora Pedagógica e Universitária, Editora da Universidade de São Paulo, 1974.

Nascimbene, Mario C., and Mauricio Isaac Neuman. "El nacionalismo católico, el fascismo y la inmigración en la Argentina (1927–1943): una aproximación teórica." *Estudios Interdisciplinarios de América Latina y el Caribe* 4 (Jan.–June 1993): 115–40.

Navarro, Marysa. "Hidden, Silent, and Anonymous: Women Workers in the Argentine Trade Union Movement." In *The World of Women's Trade Unionism: Comparative Historical Essays*, ed. Norbert C. Soldon, 167–86. Westport, Conn.: Greenwood Press, 1985.

Navarro Gerassi, Marysa. *Los nacionalistas*. Trans. Alberto Ciria. Buenos Aires: Jorge Alvarez, 1968.

Nes-El, Moshe. "La inmigración judía a Chile durante 1929–1939." *Coloquio* 4 (autumn 1982): 73–88.

Needell, Jeffrey D. "Brasilien 1830–1889." In *Handbuch der Geschichte Lateinamerikas*, vol. 2, ed. Raymond Buve and John Fisher, 441–98. Stuttgart: Klett-Cotta, 1992.

———. "History, Race, and the State in the Thought of Oliveira Viana." *Hispanic American Historical Review* 75 (Feb. 1995): 1–30.

———. "Identity, Race, Gender, and Modernity in the Origins of Gilberto Freyre's *Oeuvre*." *American Historical Review* 100 (Feb. 1995): 51–77.

———. "A Liberal Embraces Monarchy: Joaquim Nabuco and Conservative Historiography." *The Americas* 48 (Oct. 1991): 159–79.

———. "The *Revolta Contra Vacina* of 1904: The Revolt Against 'Modernization' in *Belle-Époque* Rio de Janeiro." *Hispanic American Historical Review* 67 (May 1987): 233–69.

————. *A Tropical Belle Epoque: Elite Culture and Society in Turn-of-the-Century Rio de Janeiro.* Cambridge: Cambridge University Press, 1987.

Newton, Ronald C. "Ducini, Prominenti, Antifascisti: Italian Fascism and the Italo-Argentine Collectivity, 1922–1945." *The Americas* 51 (July 1994): 41–66.

————. "Indifferent Sanctuary: German-Speaking Refugees and Exiles in Argentina, 1933–1945." *Journal of Interamerican Studies and World Affairs* 24 (Nov. 1982): 395–417.

————. *The 'Nazi Menace' in Argentina, 1931–1947.* Stanford, Calif.: Stanford University Press, 1992.

————. "Not for Export (?): Italian Fascism and the Argentine Right." In *Rocky Mountain Council for Latin American Studies: Proceedings from the 41st and 42d Annual Meetings,* ed. Theo R. Crevenna, 127–42. Albuquerque: Latin American Institute, University of New Mexico, 1995.

Niklison, José Elías. "Acción social católica obrera." *Boletín del Departamento Nacional del Trabajo,* no. 46 (Mar. 1920).

Nogueira, Hamilton. *A doutrina da ordem.* Rio de Janeiro: Editores Centro D. Vital, Annuario do Brasil, 1925.

————. *Jackson de Figueiredo: O doutrinário católico.* Rio de Janeiro: Terra de Sol, 1927.

————. "Reflexões contra-revolucionárias." *A Ordem* 5, no. 51 (July 1926): 218-19.

Nogueira Filho, Paulo. *Ideais e lutas de um burguês progressista: O Partido Democrático e a revolução de 1930.* 2 vols. São Paulo: Anhambi, 1958.

Nolte, Ernst. *Three Faces of Fascism: Action Francaise, Italian Fascism, National Socialism.* Trans. Leila Vennewitz. New York: New American Library, 1964.

Núcleo Nacista de Temuco. *Nacismo chileno.* Temuco: Aldea, 1933.

Nunn, Frederick. *Chilean Politics, 1920–1931: The Honorable Mission of the Armed Forces.* Albuquerque: University of New Mexico Press, 1970.

————. "Emil Korner and the Prussianization of the Chilean Army: Origins, Process, and Consequences, 1885–1920." *Hispanic American Historical Review* 50 (May 1970): 300–322.

————. *The Military in Chilean History: Essays on Civil-Military Relations, 1810–1973.* Albuquerque: University of New Mexico Press, 1976.

————. *Yesterday's Soldiers: European Military Professionalism in South America, 1890–1940.* Lincoln: University of Nebraska Press, 1983.

O'Donnell, Guillermo. *Modernization and Bureaucratic-Authoritarianism: Studies in South American Politics.* Berkeley: Institute of International Studies, University of California, 1973.

Olavarría Bravo, Arturo. *Chile entre dos Alessandri. Memorias políticas.* Vol. 1. Santiago: Nascimento, 1962.

Oliveira, Lúcia Lippi. "Elite intelectual e debate político nos anos 30." *Dados,* no. 22 (1979): 75–97.

————. "Ilha de Vera Cruz, Terra de Santa Cruz, Brasil: um estudo sobre o nacionalismo." Ph.D. diss., Universidade de São Paulo, 1986.

————. *A questão nacional na primeira república.* São Paulo: Brasiliense, 1990.

Oliveira, Lúcia Lippi, Mônica Pimenta Velloso, and Angela Maria Castro Gomes. *Estado Novo: Ideologia e poder.* Rio de Janeiro: Zahar, 1982.

Onega, Gladys S. *La inmigración en la literatura argentina.* Buenos Aires: Galerna, 1969.

O'Neil, Charles Francis. "The Search for Order and Progress: Brazilian Mass Education, 1915–1935." Ph.D. diss., University of Texas at Austin, 1975.

O'Neill, Sister M. Ancilla. *Tristão de Athayde and the Catholic Social Movement in Brazil.* Washington, D.C.: Catholic University of America Press, 1939.

Orrego V., Claudio. *Testigos del siglo XX: Tobías Barros Ortiz.* Santiago: Aconcagua, 1979.

Ortiz, Eduardo. "Un caso de retorno a los cuarteles: Chile en 1932." *Opciones* 15 (Jan.–Apr. 1989): 141–53.

Ortiz Pereyra, Manuel. *Por nuestra redención cultural y económica (apuntes de crítica social argentina).* Buenos Aires: Peuser, 1928.

Osés, Enrique P. *¡Y esta es la verdad! Los beneficiarios de una Revolución.* Buenos Aires: Crisol, 1936.

————. *Medios y fines del nacionalismo.* 2d ed. Buenos Aires: Sudestada, 1968.

————. *El nacionalismo ante la elección presidencial: Contra todos los partidos políticos.* Buenos Aires: Crisol, 1937.

Otero Oliva, Teótimo. *Esquema de un plan de política y economía nacionalista.* Buenos Aires: Librería Nacional Lajouane, 1936.

Pagano, Sebastião. *Eduardo Prado e sua época.* São Paulo: O Cetro, n.d.

Palacio, Ernesto. *La historia falsificada.* Buenos Aires: Difusión, 1939.

————. "Lugones vivo." *Sexto Continente* (Sept. 1949): 16–21.

Palacios, Nicolás. *Raza chilena: Libro escrito por un chileno i para los chilenos.* Valparaíso: Alemana de Gustavo Schafer, 1904.

Pamphlet with cover torn off (Biblioteca del Congreso Y-5, 93-H). Santiago: Cóndor, 1932.

Pang, Eul-Soo. *Bahia in the First Brazilian Republic: Coronelismo and Oligarchies, 1889–1934.* Gainesville: University of Florida Press, 1979.

Parker, Andrew, ed. *Nationalisms and Sexualities.* New York: Routledge, 1992.

Parker, Richard G. *Bodies, Pleasures, and Passions: Sexual Culture in Brazil.* Boston: Beacon, 1991.

Partido Corporativo Popular. *Declaración de principios.* Santiago: La Fama, 1934.

Partido de la Juventud Social Nacionalista Argentina. *Su contenido—sus fines.* Buenos Aires: n.p., 1933.

Partido Nacional Fascista. *Plan de acción.* Santiago: Tartuffo, 1939.

Partido Social Cristiano. Untitled pamphlet (cover torn off). Santiago: América, n.d.

Passalacqua Eliçabe, H. V. *El movimiento fascista argentino.* Buenos Aires: La Argentina, 1935.

Payá, Carlos Manuel, and Eduardo José Cárdenas. "Manuel Gálvez y Ricardo Rojas, protonacionalistas." *Todo Es Historia*, no. 107 (April 1976): 32–48.

————. *El primer nacionalismo argentino en Manuel Gálvez y Ricardo Rojas.* Buenos Aires: A. Peña Lillo, 1978.

Payne, Stanley G. *Falange.* Stanford, Calif.: Stanford University Press, 1961.

————. *Fascism: Comparison and Definition.* Madison: University of Wisconsin Press, 1980.

————. "Political Violence During the Spanish Second Republic." *Journal of Contemporary History* 25 (May–June 1990): 269–88.

Peard, Julyan G. "Tropical Disorder and the Forging of a Brazilian Medical Identity, 1860–1890." *Hispanic American Historical Review* 77 (Feb. 1997): 1–44.

Pécaut, Daniel. *Os intelectuais e a política no Brasil: Entre o povo e a nação.* Trans. Maria Júlia Goldwasser. São Paulo: Atica, 1990.

Pena, Maria Valéria Junho. *Mulheres e trabalhadoras: Presença feminina na constituição do sistema fabril.* Rio de Janeiro: Paz e Terra, 1981.

Pena, Maria Valéria Junho, and Elça Mendonça Lima. "Lutas ilusórias: A mulher na política operária da primeira república." In *Mulher, mulheres,* ed. Carmen Barroso and Albertina Oliveira Costa, 17–32. São Paulo: Cortez Editora, Fundação Carlos Chagas, 1983.

Penna, Belisário. *Saneamento do Brasil.* Rio de Janeiro: Revista dos Tribunaes, 1918.

Pereira, Nilo. *Conflitos entre a igreja e o estado no Brasil.* 2d ed. Recife, Brazil: Massangana, 1982.

Perón, Juan. *Tres revoluciones militares.* Buenos Aires: Escorpión, 1963.

Pessôa, Pantaleão. *Reminiscências e imposições de uma vida (1885–1965).* Rio de Janeiro: n.p., 1972.

Pico, César E. *Carta a Jacques Maritain sobre la colaboración de los católicos con los movimientos de tipo fascista.* Buenos Aires: Adsum, 1937.

Pike, Frederick B. *Chile and the United States, 1880–1962: The Emergence of Chile's Social Crisis and the Challenge to United States Diplomacy.* Notre Dame, Ind.: University of Notre Dame Press, 1963.

Piñero, Octavio A. *Los orígenes y la trágica semana de enero de 1919.* Buenos Aires: n.p., 1956.

Pinheiro, Paulo Sérgio. *Estratégias da ilusão: A revolução mundial e o Brasil, 1922–1935.* São Paulo: Companhia das Letras, 1991.

Pinheiro, Paulo Sérgio, and Michael M. Hall, eds. *A classe operária no Brasil, 1889–1930: Documentos.* 2 vols. São Paulo: Brasiliense, 1981.

Pinkney, Robert. *Right-Wing Military Government.* Boston: Twayne, 1990.

Pinochet Le-Brun, Tancredo. *La conquista de Chile en el siglo XX.* Santiago: La Ilustración, 1909.

Pinto Lagarrigue, Fernando. *Crónica política del siglo xx: Desde Errázuriz Echaurren hasta Alessandri Palma.* Santiago: Orbe, 1972.

Piragibe, José. *Deus e o trabalho (questões da actualidade).* Rio de Janeiro: Jornal do Commércio, 1919.

Plan de acción del Movimiento Nacional-Socialista de Chile (M.N.S.). Santiago: La Cruz Svástica, 1932.

Pomer, León. "Pueblo, barbarie, racismo." *Todo Es Historia*, no. 247 (Jan. 1988): 62–81.

Pompeo, A. (Antônio). *Porque é que sou integralista*. São Paulo: Empreza Gráphica Revista dos Tribunais, 1935.

Potash, Robert A. *The Army and Politics in Argentina, 1928–1945: Yrigoyen to Perón*. Stanford, Calif.: Stanford University Press, 1969.

Potashnik, Michael. "Nacismo: National Socialism in Chile, 1932–1938." Ph.D. diss., UCLA, 1974.

Potter, Anne L. "The Failure of Democracy in Argentina, 1916–1930: An Institutional Perspective." *Journal of Latin American Studies* 13 (May 1981): 83–109.

Power, Margaret MacDonald. "Gender, the Right, and Anti-Democratic Politics in Chile, 1964–1973." Ph.D. diss., University of Illinois at Chicago, 1996.

Prado, Antônio Antoni. *1922—Itinerário de uma falsa vanguarda: Os dissidentes, a Semana, e o Integralismo*. São Paulo: Brasiliense, 1983.

Prado, Eduardo. *Fastos da dictadura militar no Brasil*. São Paulo: Escola Typográphica Salesiana, 1902 [1890].

———. *La ilusión yanqui (A ilusão americana, 1893)*. Trans. Carlos Pereya. Madrid: Ed. America, n.d.

"Programa del Partido Social Demócrata." Valparaíso: n.p., 1901.

Protocolos dos Sabios de Sião. Trans. Gustavo Barroso. Rio de Janeiro: Minerva, 1936.

Pulzer, Peter G. J. *The Rise of Political Anti-Semitism in Germany and Austria*. New York: Wiley, 1964.

Queiroz, Suely Robles Reis. *Os radicais da república. Jacobinismo: ideologia e ação, 1893–1897*. São Paulo: Brasiliense, 1986.

———. "Reflections on Brazilian Jacobinism of the First Decade of the Republic (1893–1897)." *The Americas* 48 (Oct. 1991): 181–205.

Quesada, Julio A. *Orígenes de la revolución del 6 de septiembre de 1930 (Rosas e Yrigoyen)*. Buenos Aires: Porter, 1930.

Quijada, Mónica. *Manuel Gálvez: 60 años de pensamiento nacionalista*. Buenos Aires: Centro Editor de América Latina, 1985.

Quiroga, Patricio, and Carlos Maldonado. *El prusianismo en las fuerzas armadas chilenas*. Santiago: Documentas, 1988.

Rachum, Ilan. "Nationalism and Revolution in Brazil, 1922–1930: A Study of Intellectual, Military, and Political Protestors and of the Assault on the Old Republic." Ph.D. diss., Columbia University, 1970.

Rago, Margareth. *Do cabaré ao lar: a utopia da cidade disciplinar. Brasil, 1890–1930*. Rio de Janeiro: Paz e Terra, 1985.

Ramírez Necochea, Hernán. "El fascismo en la evolución política de Chile hasta 1970." *Araucaria de Chile* (Madrid), no. 1 (1978): 9–33.

———. *Origen y formación del Partido Comunista de Chile (Ensayo de historia del Partido)*. Santiago: Austral, 1965.

Ramos, Alberto Guerreiro. *A crise do poder no Brasil (Problemas da Revolução Nacional Brasileiro)*. Rio de Janeiro: Zahar, 1961.

————. *Introdução crítica a sociologia brasileira.* Rio de Janeiro: Andes, 1957.

Rapalo, María Ester. "La Iglesia Católica Argentina y el autoritarismo político: la revista *Criterio,* 1928–1931." *Anuario del IEHS* 5 (1990): 51–69.

Reale, Miguel. *ABC do Integralismo.* Rio de Janeiro: Livraria José Olympio Editora, 1935.

————. *Memórias.* Vol. 1, *Destinos cruzados.* São Paulo: Saraiva, 1987.

————. *Obras políticas (primera fase—1931/1937).* 3 vols. Brasília: Editora Universidade de Brasília, 1983.

Recabarren Valenzuela, Sergio. *Mensaje vigente.* Santiago: n.p., 1964.

Recalde, Héctor. *La iglesia y la cuestión social (1874–1910).* Buenos Aires: Centro Editor de América Latina, 1985.

Remmer, Karen L. *Party Competition in Argentina and Chile: Political Recruitment and Public Policy, 1890–1930.* Lincoln: University of Nebraska Press, 1984.

Rennie, Ysabel F. *The Argentine Republic.* New York: Macmillan, 1945.

Repetto, Nicolás. *Mi paso por la política: De Uriburu a Perón.* Buenos Aires: Santiago Rueda, 1957.

Reportaje conservador al Jefe del Nacismo. Santiago: La Ilustración, 1936.

Represión de actividades comunistas. Buenos Aires: n.p., n.d.

Restauración. *Declaración de principios.* 2d ed. Buenos Aires: n.p., 1937.

A Revolução de 30: Seminário Internacional. Brasília: Editora Universidade de Brasília, 1983.

La revolución del 6 de septiembre de 1930: Su motivo, sus hombres, su gobierno. Apuntes para un capítulo de la Historia Nacional. Buenos Aires: n.p., 1931.

Ribuffo, Leo P. "Why Is There So Much Conservatism in the United States and Why Do So Few Historians Know Anything About It?" *American Historical Review* 99 (April 1994): 438–49.

Ridings, Eugene W. "Business, Nationality, and Dependency in Late-Nineteenth-Century Brazil." *Journal of Latin American Studies* 14 (May 1982): 55–96.

Rivanera Carlés, Federico. *El judaísmo y la Semana Trágica: La verdadera historia de los sucesos de enero de 1919.* Buenos Aires: Artes Gráficas, 1986.

Rivas Vicuña, Manuel. *Historia política y parlamentaria de Chile.* Vol. 2. Santiago: Biblioteca Nacional, 1964.

Rivero de Olazábal, Raúl. *Por una cultura católica: El compromiso de una generación argentina.* Buenos Aires: Claretiana, 1986.

Robertson Rodríguez, Erwin. "Las ideas nacional-socialistas en Chile, 1932–1938." *Dimensión Histórica de Chile* 1 (1984): 92–129.

Robertson Rodríguez, Erwin, and Pedro Banoviez. "Testimonio histórico, Guillermo Izquierdo Araya." *Dimensión Histórica de Chile* 1 (1984): 23–91.

Robin, Martin. *Shades of Right: Nativist and Fascist Politics in Canada, 1920–1940.* Toronto: University of Toronto Press, 1992.

Rock, David. *Argentina, 1516–1987: From Spanish Colonization to Alfonsín.* 2d ed. Berkeley: University of California Press, 1987.

———. *Authoritarian Argentina: The Nationalist Movement, Its History and Its Impact.* Berkeley: University of California Press, 1993.

———. "Intellectual Precursors of Conservative Nationalism in Argentina, 1900–27." *Hispanic American Historical Review* 67 (May 1987): 271–300.

———. "Lucha civil en la Argentina: La Semana Trágica de enero de 1919." *Desarrollo Económico* 11 (Mar. 1972): 165–215.

———. *Politics in Argentina, 1890–1930: The Rise and Fall of Radicalism.* Cambridge: Cambridge University Press, 1975.

Roddick, Jackie. "The Failure of Populism in Chile: Labour Movement and Politics Before World War II." *Boletín de Estudios Latinoamericanos y del Caribe* 31 (Dec. 1981): 61–90.

Rodó, José Enrique. *Ariel.* Chicago: Benj. H. Sanborn, 1928 [1900].

Rodrigues, José Honório. *História da história do Brasil.* Part 2, vol. 1. São Paulo: Nacional, 1988.

Rodríguez Molas, Ricardo. *Historia de la tortura y el orden represivo en la Argentina.* Buenos Aires: Eudeba, 1985.

Rogger, Hans, and Eugen Weber, eds. *The European Right: A Historical Profile.* Berkeley: University of California Press, 1965.

Rojas, Ricardo. *Obras de Ricardo Rojas.* Vol. 4, *La restauración nacionalista: Crítica de la educación argentina y bases para una reforma en el estudio de las humanidades modernas.* 2d ed. Buenos Aires: Juan Roldán, 1922.

Rojas Mira, Claudia. "Construyendo un lugar: mujeres en movimiento (1964–1973)." MS, 1997.

———. "Hacia la formación de una conciencia feminista en Chile: antecedentes históricos, 1913–1952." *Secuencia,* no. 36 (Sept.–Dec. 1996): 151–73.

Romano, Roberto. *Igreja contra estado (crítica ao populismo católico).* São Paulo: Kairós Livraria e Editora, 1979.

Romariz, José R. *La semana trágica: Relato de los hechos sangrientos del año 1919.* Buenos Aires: Hemispherio, 1952.

Romero, José Luis. *A History of Argentine Political Thought.* Trans. Thomas F. McGann. Stanford, Calif.: Stanford University Press, 1963.

———. *El pensamiento de la derecha latinoamericana.* Buenos Aires: Paidós, 1970.

Romero, Sílvio. *História da literatura brasileira.* 5 vols. Rio de Janeiro: José Olympio, 1949 [1888].

Romero Carranza, Ambrosio. *Itinerario de Monseñor de Andrea.* Buenos Aires: Impresora Argentina, 1957.

Romero Carranza, Ambrosio, Alberto Rodríguez Varela, and Eduardo Ventura Flores Pirán. *Historia política de la Argentina.* Vol. 3, *Desde 1862 hasta 1928.* Buenos Aires: Pannedille, 1975.

Rosemblatt, Karin A. "Gendered Compromises: Political Cultures, Socialist Politics, and the State in Chile, 1920–1950." Ph.D. diss., University of Wisconsin–Madison, 1996.

Rosenhaft, Eve. "The KPD in the Weimar Republic and the Problem of Terror During the 'Third Period,' 1919–33." In *Social Protest, Violence, and Terror in Nineteenth- and Twentieth-Century Europe*, ed. Wolfgang J. Mommsen and Gerhard Hirschfeld, 342–66. New York: St. Martin's Press, 1982.

Roth, Jack J. "The Roots of Italian Fascism: Sorel and Sorelismo." *Journal of Modern History* 39 (Mar. 1967): 30–45.

Rouquié, Alain. *El estado militar en América Latina.* Trans. Daniel Zadunaisky. Buenos Aires: Emecé, 1984.

———. *Poder militar y sociedad política en la Argentina.* 2 vols. Trans. Arturo Iglesias Echegaray. Buenos Aires: Emecé, 1981.

RSR. *La verdad sobre los sucesos del 5 de septiembre de 1938.* Santiago: Libertad, 1939.

Ruibal, Juan. "Anticlericalismo y religiosidad." *Todo Es Historia*, no. 238 (Mar. 1987): 58–67.

Ruiz, Carlos. "Tendencias ideológicas de la historiografía chilena del siglo XX." *Escritos de Teoría* 2 (Sept. 1977): 121–34.

Ruschi, María Isabel de. *El diario "El Pueblo" y la realidad socio-cultural de la Argentina a principios del siglo XX.* Buenos Aires: Guadalupe, 1988.

Sábato, Hilda. "Citizenship, Political Participation, and the Formation of the Public Sphere in Buenos Aires, 1850s–1880s." *Past and Present*, no. 136 (Aug. 1992): 139–63.

Saénz B., Sonia. "El pensamiento liberal chileno en un medio de comunicación de masas: Chile, 1931–1938." *Escritos de Teoría* 3–4 (Dec. 1978–Jan. 1979): 243–66.

Sáez Morales, Carlos. *Recuerdos de un soldado: El ejército y la política.* 3 vols. Santiago: Biblioteca Ercilla, 1933.

Sahni, Varun. "Not Quite British: A Study of External Influences on the Argentine Navy." *Journal of Latin American Studies* 25 (Oct. 1993): 489–513.

Salgado, Plínio. *Cartas aos "Camisas-Verdes."* Rio de Janeiro: Livraria José Olympio, 1935.

———. *Despertemos a nação!* Rio de Janeiro: Livraria José Olympio, 1935.

———. *A doutrina do sigma.* 2d ed. Rio de Janeiro: Schmidt, 1937.

———. *O integralismo na vida brasileira.* Rio de Janeiro: Livraria Clássica Brasileira, 1958.

———. *O integralismo perante a nação.* 2d ed. Rio de Janeiro: n.p., 1950.

———. *A mulher no século XX.* 2d ed. São Paulo: Guanumby, 1949.

———. *O que é o integralismo.* Rio de Janeiro: Schmidt, 1933.

———. *O soffrimento universal.* 3d ed. Rio de Janeiro: Livraria José Olympio, 1936.

Salinas C., Maximiliano. *Clotario Blest.* Santiago: Arzobispado de Santiago, Vicarial de Pastoral Obrera, 1980.

———. "Cristianismo popular en Chile, 1880–1920: Un esquema sobre el factor religioso en las clases subalternas durante el capitalismo oligárquico." *Nueva Historia* 3 (Oct.–Dec. 1984): 275–302.

———. "Teología católica y pensamiento burgués en Chile, 1880–1920." In *Raíces de la teología latinoamericana: Nuevos materiales para la historia de la teología*, ed. Pablo Richard, 173–90. San José, Costa Rica: Cehila, 1985.

Sánchez Gamarra, Alfredo. *Vida del padre Grote. Redentorista. Apóstol social cristiano en hispanoamérica.* Madrid: Stvdivm de Cultura, 1949.

Sandberg, Harry O. "The Jews of Latin America." In *American Jewish Yearbook, 1917-1918,* 35-105. Philadelphia: Jewish Publication Society of America, 1917.

Santa Rosa, Virgínio. *O sentido de tenentismo.* 3d ed. São Paulo: Alfa y Omega, 1976.

Santo Rosário, Irmã Maria Regina do (Laurita Pessôa Raja Gabaglia). *O Cardeal Leme (1882-1942).* Rio de Janeiro: Livraria José Olympio, 1962.

Sarmiento el indeseable. Buenos Aires: La Mazorca, n.d.

Sarobe, José María. *Memorias sobre la revolución del 6 de septiembre de 1930.* Buenos Aires: Gure, 1957.

Sater, William F. "The Abortive Kronstadt: The Chilean Naval Mutiny of 1931." *Hispanic American Historical Review* 60 (May 1980): 239-68.

———. "Race and Immigration During the War of the Pacific." *Historia* 22 (1987): 313-23.

Schamis, Hector E. "Reconceptualizing Latin American Authoritarianism in the 1970s: From Bureaucratic-Authoritarianism to Neoconservatism." *Comparative Politics* 23 (Jan. 1991): 201-20.

Schiff, Warren. "The Influence of the German Armed Forces and War Industry on Argentina, 1880-1914." *Hispanic American Historical Review* 52 (Nov. 1972): 436-55.

Schmidt, Afonso. *Palavras de um comunista brasileiro à Liga Nacionalista e à mocidade das escolas.* Rio de Janeiro: n.p., 1920.

Schulman, Bernardo. *Em legítima defeza: a voz de um judeu brasileiro.* 4th ed. Curitiba: Copygraf, 1987.

Schwartzman, Simon, Helena Maria Bousquet Bomeny, and Vanda Maria Ribeiro Costa. *Tempos de Capanema.* Rio de Janeiro: Paz e Terra; São Paulo: EDUSP, 1984.

Scobie, James R. *Buenos Aires: Plaza to Suburb, 1870-1910.* New York: Oxford University Press, 1974.

Scott, Joan W. "Gender: A Useful Category of Historical Analysis." *American Historical Review* 91 (Dec. 1986): 1053-75.

Scully, Timothy. *Party Politics in Nineteenth- and Twentieth-Century Chile.* Stanford, Calif.: Stanford University Press, 1992.

Sebreli, Juan José. *La cuestión judía en la Argentina.* Buenos Aires: Tiempo Contemporáneo, 1968.

Seitenfus, Ricardo Antônio Silva. *O Brasil de Getúlio Vargas e a formação dos blocos, 1930-1942: O processo do envolvimento brasileiro na II Guerra Mundial.* São Paulo: Nacional, 1985.

La senda del sacrificio: 5 de septiembre de 1938. Santiago: Nascimento, 1940.

Senderey, Moisés. *Historia de la colectividad israelita de Chile.* Santiago: Dos Ydische Wort, 1956.

Senkman, Leonardo, ed. *El antisemitismo en la Argentina.* 3 vols. 2d ed. Buenos Aires: Centro Editor de América Latina, 1989.

Serrano, Jonathas. *Júlio Maria.* Rio de Janeiro: Livraria Boa, n.d.

Shipley, Robert Edward. "On the Outside Looking In: A Social History of the 'Por-

teño' Worker During the 'Golden Age' of Argentine Development, 1914–1930."
Ph.D. diss., Rutgers University, 1977.

Siete ensayos sobre Arturo Alessandri Palma. Santiago: Instituto Chileno de Estudios
Humanísticos, 1979.

Sigmund, Paul E. *The United States and Democracy in Chile.* Baltimore: Johns Hopkins University Press, 1993.

Silva Vargas, Fernando. "Notas sobre el pensamiento social católico a fines del siglo
XIX." *Historia* 4 (1965): 237–62.

Silveyra, Carlos M. *El comunismo en la Argentina: Origen—desarrollo—organización actual.* Buenos Aires: López, 1936.

———. "Historia y desarrollo del comunismo en nuestro país." *Revista Militar,* no.
385, Anexo A (1933).

———. *Imperialismo y comunismo.* Buenos Aires: Patria, n.d.

Simão, Azis. *Sindicato e estado: Suas relações na formação do proletariado de São
Paulo.* São Paulo: Dominus, 1966.

Simões, Solange de Deus. *Deus, pátria, e familia: as mulheres no golpe de 1964.* Petrópolis, Brazil: Vozes, 1985.

Skidmore, Thomas E. *Black into White: Race and Nationality in Brazilian Thought.*
New York: Oxford University Press, 1974.

———. "Eduardo Prado: A Conservative Nationalist Critic of the Early Brazilian
Republic, 1889–1901." *Luso-Brazilian Review* 12 (winter 1975): 149–61.

———. *Politics in Brazil: An Experiment in Democracy.* New York: Oxford University Press, 1967.

———. *The Politics of Military Rule in Brazil, 1964–85.* New York: Oxford University
Press, 1988.

———. "Racial Ideas and Social Policy in Brazil, 1870–1940." In *The Idea of Race in
Latin America, 1870–1940,* ed. Richard Graham, 7-36. Austin: University of Texas
Press, 1990.

———. "Workers and Soldiers: Urban Labor Movements and Elite Responses in
Twentieth-Century Latin America." In *Elites, Masses, and Modernization in Latin
America, 1850–1930,* ed. Virginia Bernhard, 79-126. Austin: University of Texas
Press, 1979.

Slatta, Richard. "The Gaucho in Argentina's Quest for National Identity." *Canadian
Review of Studies in Nationalism* 12, no. 1 (1985): 99–122.

Smith, Brian H. *The Church and Politics in Chile: Challenges to Modern Catholicism.*
Princeton, N.J.: Princeton University Press, 1982.

Socialismo nacional. Santiago: La Cruz Svástica, 1932.

Sodré, Nelson Werneck. *A verdade sobre o ISEB.* Rio de Janeiro: Avenir, 1978.

Sofer, Eugene F. *From Pale to Pampa: A Social History of the Jews of Buenos Aires.*
New York: Holmes and Meier, 1982.

Solberg, Carl. *Immigration and Nationalism: Argentina and Chile, 1890–1914.* Austin:
University of Texas Press, 1970.

————. *Oil and Nationalism in Argentina: A History*. Stanford, Calif.: Stanford University Press, 1979.

Solominsky, Nahum. *La semana trágica en la Argentina*. Buenos Aires: Ejecutivo Sudamericano del Congreso Judío Mundial, 1971.

Sombra, Severino. *O ideal legionário*. Ceará, Brazil: Gadelha, 1931.

Somervell, Philip. "Naval Affairs in Chilean Politics, 1910–1932." *Journal of Latin American Studies* 16 (Nov. 1984): 381–402.

Soucy, Robert. *French Fascism: The First Wave, 1924–1933*. New Haven, Conn.: Yale University Press, 1986.

Spalding, Hobart A. Jr. *La clase trabajadora argentina (documentos para su historia 1890/1912)*. Buenos Aires: Galerna, 1970.

————. "Education in Argentina, 1890–1914: The Limits of Oligarchical Reform." *Journal of Interdisciplinary History* 3 (summer 1972): 31–61.

————. *Organized Labor in Latin America: Historical Case Studies of Urban Workers in Dependent Societies*. New York: Harper and Row, 1977.

————. "Sociology in Argentina." In *Positivism in Latin America, 1850–1900: Are Order and Progress Reconcilable?* ed. Ralph Lee Woodward Jr., 50–59. Lexington, Mass.: D. C. Heath, 1971.

Spektorowski, Alberto. "Argentina, 1930–1940: nacionalismo integral, justicia social y clase obrera." *Estudios Interdisciplinarios de América Latina y el Caribe* 2, no. 1 (1990): 61–79.

————. "The Ideological Origins of Right and Left Nationalism in Argentina, 1930–43." *Journal of Contemporary History* 29 (Jan. 1994): 155–84.

Sperber, Jonathan. "Festivals of National Unity in the German Revolution of 1848–1849." *Past and Present*, no. 136 (Aug. 1992): 114–38.

Spoerer C., Jermán. *Simbiosis del capital y el trabajo: La función armónica del Capital y Trabajo como solución del Problema Social*. Santiago: Chile, 1938.

Stepan, Alfred. *The Military in Politics: Changing Patterns in Brazil*. Princeton, N.J.: Princeton University Press, 1988.

Stepan, Nancy Leys. *"The Hour of Eugenics": Race, Gender, and Nation in Latin America*. Ithaca, N.Y.: Cornell University Press, 1991.

Sternhill, Zeev. *Neither Right nor Left: Fascist Ideology in France*. Trans. David Maisel. Berkeley: University of California Press, 1986.

Stickell, Arthur Lawrence Jr. "Migration and Mining: Labor in Northern Chile in the Nitrate Era, 1880–1940." Ph.D. diss., Indiana University, 1979.

Strawbridge, George Jr. "Militarism and Nationalism in Chile, 1920–1932." Ph.D. diss., University of Pennsylvania, 1968.

Subercaseaux, Bernardo. *Fin de siglo: la época de Balmaceda. Modernización y cultura en Chile*. Santiago: Aconcagua, 1988.

Subercaseaux, Guillermo. *Los ideales nacionalistas ante el doctrinarismo de nuestros partidos políticos históricos*. Santiago: Imprenta Universitaria, 1918.

————. *La política social nacionalista moderna*. Santiago: La Cruz Svástica, 1932.

————. *El régimen socialista: estudio crítico.* Santiago: Biblioteca de Ciencias Sociales, 1922.

Sutin, Stewart Edward. "The Impact of Nazism on the Germans of Argentina." Ph.D. diss., University of Texas at Austin, 1975.

Sznajder, Mario. "A Case of Non-European Fascism: Chilean National Socialism in the 1930s." *Journal of Contemporary History* 28 (Apr. 1993): 269–96.

————. "El movimiento nacional-socialista: Antisemitismo y movilización política en Chile en la década del treinta." *Coloquio,* no. 21 (1989): 61–70.

Tamarin, David. *The Argentine Labor Movement, 1930–1945: A Study in the Origins of Peronism.* Albuquerque: University of New Mexico Press, 1985.

Tarr, Terence Stephen. "Military Intervention and Civilian Reaction in Chile, 1924–1936." Ph.D. diss., University of Florida, 1960.

Tavares, José Nilo, ed. *Novembro de 1935: Meio século depois.* Petrópolis, Brazil: Vozes, 1985.

Teixeira, Palmira Petratti. *A fábrica do sonho: Trajetoria do industrial Jorge Street.* Rio de Janeiro: Paz e Terra, 1990.

Tiempo, César (Israel Zeitlin). *La campaña antisemita y el director de la Biblioteca Nacional.* Buenos Aires: Mundo Israelita, 1935.

Tissera, Ramón. "Revolución social en la selva." *Todo Es Historia,* no. 12 (Apr. 1968): 64–75.

Todaro, Margaret Patrice. "Pastors, Prophets, and Politicians: A Study of the Brazilian Catholic Church, 1916–1945." Ph.D. diss., Columbia University, 1971.

Toledo, Caio Navarro de. *ISEB: Fábrica de ideologias.* São Paulo: Atica, 1977.

Topik, Steven Curtis. "Economic Nationalism and the State in an Underdeveloped Country: Brazil, 1889–1930." Ph.D. diss., University of Texas at Austin, 1978.

————. "The Economic Role of the State in Liberal Regimes: Brazil and Mexico Compared, 1888–1910." In *Guiding the Invisible Hand: Economic Liberalism and the State in Latin American History,* ed. Joseph L. Love and Nils Jacobsen, 117–44. New York: Praeger, 1988.

————. "Middle-Class Brazilian Nationalism, 1889–1930: From Radicalism to Reaction." *Social Science Quarterly* 59 (June 1978): 93–104.

Torre, Lisandro de la. *Escritos y discursos.* 4th ed. Buenos Aires: Colegio Libre de Estudios Superiores, 1953.

————. *Obras.* Vol. 5, *Campañas presidenciales.* Ed. Raúl Larra. 2d ed. Buenos Aires: Hemispherio, 1952.

Torres, Alberto. *As fontes da vida no Brasil.* Rio de Janeiro: Papelaria Brazil, 1915.

————. *A organização nacional. Primeira parte: A constituição.* Rio de Janeiro: Nacional, 1914.

————. *O problema nacional brasileiro: Introdução a um programma de organização nacional.* Rio de Janeiro: Nacional, 1914.

Trento, Angelo. "Relações entre fascismo e integralismo: o ponto-de-vista do Ministério dos Negócios Estrangeiros Italiano." *Ciência e Cultura* 34 (Dec. 1982): 1601–13.

Trindade, Hélgio Henrique. "O fascismo brasileiro." *Polítika*, no. 57 (Nov. 20-26, 1972): 3-11.

———. *Integralismo (O fascismo brasileiro na década de 30)*. São Paulo: Difel, 1974.

———. Interview with Aurora Nunes Wagner, 1969-70.

———. Interview with Margarida Corbisier, 1969-70.

———. "Plínio Salgado e a revolução de 30: antecedentes." *Revista Brasileira de Estudos Políticos*, no. 38 (Jan. 1974): 9-56.

Tulchin, Joseph S. "The Argentine Economy During the First World War." *Review of the River Plate*, June 19, 1970, pp. 900-903; June 30, 1970, pp. 965-67; July 10, 1970, pp. 44-46.

Unamuno, Miguel. "La primera gran represión." *Todo Es Historia*, no. 248 (Feb. 1988): 6-33.

União Nacional dos Estudantes. *Quinta Coluna e Integralismo*. N.p.: n.p., 1943.

Unión Republicana. *Declaraciones de sus Juntas Generales de Directorios (1934-1935-1936)*. Santiago: Zig-Zag, 1936.

Unión Republicana. Santiago: Cervantes, 1932.

United States. Department of State. Records of the Department of State Relating to the Internal Affairs of Argentina, 1910-1929. National Archives microfilm copy M514.

———. Records of the Department of State Relating to the Internal Affairs of Argentina, 1930-1939. National Archives microfilm copy M1230.

———. Records of the Department of State Relating to the Internal Affairs of Argentina, 1940-1944. National Archives microfilm copy M1322.

———. Records of the Department of State Relating to the Internal Affairs of Brazil, 1910-1929. National Archives microfilm copy M519.

———. Records of the Department of State Relating to the Internal Affairs of Brazil, 1930-1939. National Archives microfilm copy 1472.

———. Records of the Department of State Relating to the Internal Affairs of Chile, 1910-1929. National Archives microfilm copy M487.

Uriburu, José Félix. *La palabra del General Uriburu: Discursos, manifiestos, declaraciones, y cartas publicadas durante su gobierno*. 2d ed. Buenos Aires: Roldán, 1933.

Vago, Raphael. "Eastern Europe." In *The Social Basis of European Fascist Movements*, ed. Detlef Muhlberger, 281-319. New York: Croom Helm, 1987.

Valdés, Juan Gabriel. *La escuela de Chicago*. Buenos Aires: Zeta, 1989.

Valdés Cange, Julio (Alejandro Venegas). *Sinceridad: Chile íntimo en 1910*. 2d ed. Santiago: Universitaria, 1910.

Valdivia Ortiz de Zárate, Verónica. "Camino al golpe: El nacionalismo chileno a la caza de las fuerzas armadas." Dirección de Investigación, Serie de Investigaciones no. 11. Santiago: Universidad Católica Blas Cañas, 1995.

———. "Los civiles en armas: La Milicia Republicana, 1932-1936." M.A. thesis, Universidad de Santiago, 1989.

———. *La Milicia Republicana: Los civiles en armas, 1932-1936*. Santiago: Dirección de Bibliotecas, Archivos y Museos, 1992.

———. "Las Milicias Socialistas (1934–1941)." *Mapocho*, no. 33 (1st semester 1993): 157–80.

———. "El nacionalismo chileno en los años del frente popular (1938–1952)." Dirección de Investigación, Serie de Investigaciones no. 3. Santiago: Universidad Católica Blas Cañas, 1995.

———. "Nacionalismo e ibañismo." Dirección de Investigación, Serie de Investigaciones no. 8. Santiago: Universidad Católica Blas Cañas, 1995.

———. "Las nuevas voces del nacionalismo chileno: 1938–1942." *Boletín de Historia y Geografía*, no. 10 (1993): 119–39.

Valenti Ferro, Enzo. *La crisis social y política argentina*. Buenos Aires: Librería y Editorial La Facultad, 1937.

Valenzuela, J. Samuel, and Arturo Valenzuela, eds. *Military Rule in Chile: Dictatorship and Oppositions*. Baltimore: Johns Hopkins University Press, 1986.

Valle, Carmen (Blanca Subercaseaux de Valdés). *Amalia Errázuriz de Subercaseaux*. Buenos Aires: Emecé, 1946.

Vanguardia Popular Socialista. Departamento de Propaganda. *Declaración doctrinaria y plan de acción inmediata de la Vanguardia Popular Socialista*. Santiago: Vanguardia, 1939.

Vargas Cariola, Juan Eduardo. "Dos mentalidades políticas a comienzos de siglo XX: Los partidos tradicionales y la tendencia nacionalista." *Revista de Ciencias Sociales*, no. 8 (1975): 193–214.

Vasconcellos, Gilberto. *A ideologia curupira: análise do discurso integralista*. São Paulo: Brasiliense, 1979.

Vásquez-Presedo, Vicente. *Estadísticas históricas argentinas (comparadas)*. 2 vols. Buenos Aires: Macchi, 1971, 1976.

Veinte años: 5 de Septiembre 1938. 5 de Septiembre 1958. Santiago: Periodística Colectiva, 1958.

Vélez Rodríguez, Ricardo. *Castilhismo: Uma filosofia da República*. Porto Alegre, Brazil: Escola Superior de Teologia São Lourenço de Brindes; Caxias do Sul: Universidade de Caxias do Sul, 1980.

Velloso, Mônica Pimenta. "A brasilidade verde-amarela: nacionalismo e regionalismo paulista." Research report. Rio de Janeiro: CPDOC/FGV, 1987.

———. "A Ordem: Uma revista de doutrina, política e cultura católica." *Revista de Ciência Política* 21, no. 3 (1978): 117–59.

Venceslau Júnior, J. *O integralismo ao alcance de todos*. 2d ed. São Paulo: Soc. Impressora Brasileira, 1936.

Verba, Ericka Kim. "The *Círculo de Lectura de Señoras* [Ladies' Reading Circle] and the *Club de Señoras* [Ladies' Club] of Santiago, Chile: Middle- and Upper-Class Feminist Conversations (1915–1920)." *Journal of Women's History* 7 (fall 1995): 6–33.

———. "The *Liga de Damas Chilenas* [League of Chilean Ladies]: Angels of Peace and Harmony of the Social Question." Paper presented at the Latin American Studies Association meeting, Guadalajara, April 1997.

Verbitsky, Horacio. *The Flight: Confessions of an Argentine Dirty Warrior*. Trans. Esther Allen. New York: New Press, 1996.

Viana, Francisco José de Oliveira. *Pequenos estudos de psycologia social*. São Paulo: Monteiro Lobato, 1921.

Vicuña Fuentes, Carlos. *La libertad de opinar y el problema de Tacna y Arica*. Santiago: n.p., 1922.

Vieira, Evaldo Amaro. *Autoritarismo e corporativismo no Brasil (Oliveira Vianna & Companhia)*. 2d. ed. São Paulo: Cortez, 1981.

Vieira, Maria do Pilar de Araújo. "Em busca do Sigma: Estudo sobre as vísperas da fundação da A.I.B." M.A. thesis, Pontificia Universidade Católica, São Paulo, 1978.

Villaca, Antônio Carlos. *O pensamento católico no Brasil*. Rio de Janeiro: Zahar, 1975.

Villagrán Kramer, Francisco. "Conflictos entre la derecha." In *Izquierdas y derechas en Latinoamérica: Sus conflictos internos*, ed. Francisco Villagrán Kramer and Mario Monteforte Toledo, 69–127. Buenos Aires: Pleamar, 1968.

Viñas, David. *Literatura argentina y realidad política*. Buenos Aires: Jorge Alvarez, 1964.

Viveiros, Custodio de. *Os inimigos do Sigma*. Rio de Janeiro: Livraria H. Antunes, 1936.

Viviani Contreras, Guillermo. *Doctrinas sociales: Libro I de la parte doctrinal de sociología chilena. Capitalismo, anarquismo, socialismo, bolchevismo, y fascismo*. Santiago: Nascimento, 1927.

———. *Sociología chilena. Estudio de sociología general aplicada a nuestro país. Libro I Expositivo: Nuestro problema social*. Santiago: Nascimento, 1926.

Waisman, Carlos H. *Reversal of Development in Argentina: Postwar Counterrevolutionary Policies and Their Structural Consequences*. Princeton, N.J.: Princeton University Press, 1987.

Waldmann, Peter, and Ernesto Garzón Valdés, comps. *El poder militar en la Argentina (1976–1981): Aspectos históricos y sociopolíticos*. Frankfurt: Klaus Dieter Vervuert, 1982.

Walter, Richard J. *Politics and Urban Growth in Buenos Aires, 1910–1942*. Cambridge: Cambridge University Press, 1993.

———. *The Province of Buenos Aires and Argentine Politics*. Cambridge: Cambridge University Press, 1985.

———. *The Socialist Party of Argentina, 1890–1930*. Austin: University of Texas Press, 1977.

Warszawski, Paul. "Régimen militar, iglesia católica y comunidad judía en la República Argentina: Algunas ideas para un análisis comparativo." In *El legado del autoritarismo: Derechos humanos y antisemitismo en la Argentina contemporánea*, ed. Leonardo Senkman and Mario Sznajder, 217–38. Jerusalem and Buenos Aires: Instituto Harry S. Truman, Univ. Hebrea de Jerusalem; Nuevo Hacer and Grupo Editor Latinoamericano, 1995.

Wast, Hugo (Gustavo Martínez Zuviría). *El Kahal-Oro*. 22d ed. Buenos Aires: AOCRA, 1975.

Weber, Eugen. *Varieties of Fascism*. Princeton, N.J.: D. Van Nostrand, 1964.

Weinstein, Barbara. *For Social Peace in Brazil: Industrialists and the Remaking of the Working Class in São Paulo, 1920–1964*. Chapel Hill: University of North Carolina Press, 1996.

Weisbrot, Robert. *The Jews of Argentina*. Philadelphia: Jewish Publication Society, 1979.

Weiss, John. *Conservatism in Europe, 1770–1945: Traditionalism, Reaction, and Counter-revolution*. New York: Harcourt, Brace, Jovanovich, 1977.

Weschler, Lawrence. *A Miracle, a Universe: Settling Accounts with Torturers*. 2d ed. New York: Viking Penguin, 1991.

Whitaker, Arthur P., and David C. Jordan. *Nationalism in Contemporary Latin America*. New York: Free Press, 1966.

Wilkie, James W., Carlos Alberto Contreras, and Catherine Komisaruk, eds. *Statistical Abstract of Latin America*. Vol. 31, pt. 1. Los Angeles: UCLA Latin American Center Publications, 1995.

Williams, Margaret Todaro. "Integralism and the Brazilian Catholic Church." *Hispanic American Historical Review* 54 (Aug. 1974): 431–52.

———. "The Politicization of the Brazilian Catholic Church: The Catholic Electoral League." *Journal of Inter-American Studies and World Affairs* 16 (Aug. 1974): 301–25.

Wirth, John D. *Minas Gerais in the Brazilian Federation, 1889–1937*. Stanford, Calif.: Stanford University Press, 1977.

———. "Tenentismo in the Brazilian Revolution of 1930." *Hispanic American Historical Review* 44 (May 1964): 161–79.

Wolfe, Joel. "'Father of the Poor' or 'Mother of the Rich'?: Getúlio Vargas, Industrial Workers, and Constructions of Class, Gender, and Populism in São Paulo, 1930–1954." *Radical History Review* 58 (winter 1994): 81–111.

———. "The Faustian Bargain Not Made: Getúlio Vargas and Brazil's Industrial Workers, 1930–1945." *Luso-Brazilian Review* 31 (winter 1994): 77–95.

———. *Working Women, Working Men: São Paulo and the Rise of Brazil's Industrial Working Class, 1900–1955*. Durham, N.C.: Duke University Press, 1993.

Woll, Allen L. "The Catholic Historian in Nineteenth-Century Chile." *The Americas* 33, no. 3 (Jan. 1977): 470–89.

———. "Positivism and History in Nineteenth-Century Chile: José Victorino Lastarria and Valentín Letelier." *Journal of the History of Ideas* 37 (July–Sept. 1976): 493–506.

Woodward, C. Vann. "The Lash and the Knout." *New York Review of Books* 34, no. 18 (Nov. 19, 1989): 38–43.

World Almanac and Book of Facts for 1934. New York: New York World Telegram, 1934.

Wright, Thomas C. *Landowners and Reform in Chile: The Sociedad Nacional de Agricultura, 1919–1945*. Urbana: University of Illinois Press, 1982.

Würth Rojas, Ernesto. *Ibáñez: Caudillo enigmático*. 2d ed. Santiago: Pacífico, 1958.

Yeager, Gertrude M. "The Club de la Unión and Kinship: Social Aspects of Political Obstructionism in the Chilean Senate, 1920–1924." *The Americas* 35 (Apr. 1979): 539–72.

———. "Elite Education in Nineteenth-Century Chile." *Hispanic American Historical Review* 71 (Feb. 1991): 73–105.

Yohn, Susan M. "Will the Real Conservative Please Stand Up? or, The Pitfalls Involved in Examining Ideological Sympathies: A Comment on Alan Brinkley's 'Problem of American Conservatism.'" *American Historical Review* 99 (April 1994): 430–37.

Young, George F. W. "Jorge González von Marées: Chief of Chilean Nacismo." *Jahrbuch für Geschichte von Staat, Wirtschaft, und Gesellschaft Lateinamerikas* 11 (1974): 309–33.

Zanatta, Loris. *Del estado liberal a la nación católica: iglesia y ejército en los orígenes del peronismo, 1930–1943*. Quilmes, Argentina: Universidad Nacional de Quilmes, 1996.

———. "Religión, nación, y derechos humanos: El caso argentino en perspectiva histórica." MS, 1997.

Zeballos, Estanislao S. "Conferencia inaugural de la Liga Patriótica Nacional." *Revista de Derecho, Historia y Letras* 11 (Nov. 1901- Feb. 1902): 413–54.

———. "Gobierno Radical: Los sucesos de enero." *Revista de Derecho, Historia y Letras* 62 (Jan.–Apr. 1919): 273–83.

Zimmerman, Eduardo A. "Racial Ideas and Social Reform: Argentina, 1890–1916." *Hispanic American Historical Review* 72 (Feb. 1992): 23–46.

Zuleta Alvarez, Enrique. *Introducción a Maurras*. Buenos Aires: Nuevo Orden, 1965.

———. *El nacionalismo argentino*. 2 vols. Buenos Aires: La Bastilla, 1975.

Zurretti, Juan Carlos. *Nueva historia eclesiástica argentina: Del Concilio de Trento al Vaticano Segundo*. Buenos Aires: Itinerarium, 1972.

INDEX

In this index an "f" after a number indicates a separate reference on the next page, and an "ff" indicates separate references on the next two pages. A continuous discussion over two or more pages is indicated by a span of page numbers, e.g., "57-59."

Library of Congress Cataloging-in-Publication Data

Deutsch, Sandra McGee
  Las Derechas : the extreme right in Argentina, Brazil, and Chile,
1890–1939 / Sandra McGee Deutsch.
    p. cm.
  Includes bibliographical references and index.
  ISBN 0-8047-3208-6 (cloth : alk. paper)
  ISBN 0-8047-4599-4 (pbk. alk. paper)
  1. Argentina—Politics and government—1860–1910.
2. Argentina—Politics and government—1910–1943.
3. Brazil—Politics and government. 4. Chile—Politics and
govenment. 5. Radicalism—South America—History—
20th century. 6. Nationalism—South America—History—
20th century. 7. Fascism—South America—History—
20th century. I. Title. II. Title: Extreme right in Argentina,
Brazil, and Chile, 1890–1939
  F2847.D483   1999
  320.98'09'0413—dc21   99-19783

♾ This book is printed on acid-free, archival quality paper.

Original printing 1999
Last figure below indicates year of this printing:
08   07   06   05   04   03   02

Typeset by James P. Brommer in 10.5/12.5 Minion
and Minion display

CPSIA information can be obtained
at www.ICGtesting.com
Printed in the USA
JSHW011644101219
2908JS00001B/25